Star Lennon Designs

Fashion Design
Styling and Consultation

DAWN L. WILLIAMS
(818) 752-1739

www.wadsworth.com

wadsworth.com is the World Wide Web site for
Wadsworth Publishing Company and is your direct
source to dozens of online resources.

At *wadsworth.com* you can find out about
supplements, demonstration software, and
student resources. You can also send e-mail to
many of our authors and preview new publications
and exciting new technologies.

wadsworth.com
Changing the way the world learns®

ON THE EDGE

The U.S. in the 20th Century

ON THE EDGE

THE U.S. IN THE 20TH CENTURY

S E C O N D E D I T I O N

David A. Horowitz
Portland State University

Peter N. Carroll
Stanford University

West / Wadsworth
I(T)P® An International Thomson Publishing Company

Belmont, CA • Albany, NY • Bonn • Boston • Cincinnati • Detroit •
Johannesburg • London • Madrid • Melbourne • Mexico City •
New York • Paris • Singapore • Tokyo • Toronto • Washington

History Editor: Clark Baxter

Development Editor: Sharon Adams-Poore

Editorial Assistant: Amy Guastello

Print Buyer: Barbara Britton

Marketing Manager: Jay Hu

Composition: Thompson Type

Production: Hal Lockwood, Penmarin Books

Copy Editor: Ellen Kurek

Cover Design: Dare Porter/Real Time Design

Cover Photo Research: Roberta Spieckerman Associates

Cover Photographs: *Left:* Anna Shaw and Carrie Chapman Catt lead 1918 march for suffrage on Fifth Avenue, New York (Wide World Photos); *background:* Knights of Labor delegates (Corbis-Bettmann). *Right:* Elvis Presley, 1956, Tupelo, Mississippi (AP/Wide World Photo).

Printer: Courier/Kendallville

Printed in the United States of America
 3 4 5 6 7 8 9 10

For more information, contact Wadsworth Publishing Company, 10 Davis Drive, Belmont, CA 94002, or electronically at http://www.wadsworth.com

International Thomson Publishing Europe
Berkshire House 168-173
High Holborn
London, WC1V 7AA, England

International Thomson Editores
Campos Eliseos 385, Piso 7
Col. Polanco
11560 México D.F. México

Thomas Nelson Australia
102 Dodds Street
South Melbourne 3205
Victoria, Australia

International Thomson Publishing Asia
221 Henderson Road
#05-10 Henderson Building
Singapore 0315

Nelson Canada
1120 Birchmount Road
Scarborough, Ontario
Canada M1K 5G4

International Thomson Publishing Japan
Hirakawacho Kyowa Building, 3F
2-2-1 Hirakawacho
Chiyoda-ku, Tokyo 102, Japan

International Thomson Publishing GmbH
Königswinterer Strasse 418
53227 Bonn, Germany

International Thomson Publishing Southern Africa
Building 18, Constantia Park
240 Old Pretoria Road
Halfway House, 1685 South Africa

 This book is printed on acid-free recycled paper.

Library of Congress Cataloging-in-Publication Data

Horowitz, David A.
    On the edge : the U.S. in the 20th century / David A.
Horowitz, Peter N. Carroll. — 2nd ed.
        p.   cm.
    Includes bibliographical references and index.
    ISBN 0-314-12882-4
    1. United States—History—20th century.   I. Carroll, Peter N.
II. Title.
E741.H69   1997   97-47266
973.9—dc21

For

DAVID W. NOBLE

and to the memory of

LOIS NOBLE

CONTENTS

PREFACE

On the Edge: The U.S. in the 20th Century is an interpretive history that chronicles the challenges and dilemmas confronting modern society since the 1890s. The book follows two major themes. First, it traces the growth of corporate economic power and government consolidation at home and abroad. Second, it provides an account of the diverse peoples and social movements that have figured in the nation's development.

Seeking a balanced perspective, *On the Edge* provides equitable coverage to elites and out-groups, liberals and conservatives, modernists and traditionalists, and politicians and cultural figures. The text goes beyond the narration of conflict among powerful institutional leaders to portray the significant historical roles played by nominally powerless people—ranging from the working class and poor to the beleaguered middle class to women and the nation's racial, ethnic, and cultural minorities. But it also explains how technology, popular culture, and social innovation have vitalized mainstream life and institutions.

Our intention is to stimulate the critical perspective of instructors and students by combining narrative and analytic history in jargon-free prose. Although chapters follow a general chronological outline, they are divided into thematic sections to encourage conceptualization and provocative discussion. Four chapters focus primarily on cultural and social developments. Each chapter also includes three or four biographical sketches that use the lives of individuals to illuminate important themes of the period. Chapter reading lists concentrate on recent hardcover editions found in most college libraries. We have simplified graphs, charts, and tables for quick reference and easy comprehension. Monetary figures are conveyed in current dollars—the actual value for the period under discussion. Chapters 7–14 also appear in a separate volume, *On the Edge: The U.S. Since 1941,* available from this publisher.

David Horowitz extends appreciation of the aid, comfort, and sustenance of Gloria Myers Horowitz. Peter Carroll acknowledges the counsel and support of Jeannette Ferrary. The authors offer special thanks to Acquiring Editor Clark G. Baxter and Production Editor Hal Lockwood. Finally, we would like to thank our reviewers: Clarence Bolt, Camosun College; Rodney P. Carlisle, Rutgers University; James A. Jolly, Millersville University; Clay McShane, Northeastern University; Fraser Ottanelli, University of South Florida; Leo P. Ribuffo, George Washington University; and David L. Wilson, Southern Illinois University.

DAVID A. HOROWITZ and PETER N. CARROLL

ON THE EDGE

THE U.S. IN THE 20TH CENTURY

PROLOGUE

The last quarter of the nineteenth century brought an explosion of market activity in the United States that established new patterns of life during the next century. Although the corporate economy increased real wages, the nation's economic development was uneven and came at a horrific price. As the first generation to confront the full consequences of the industrial, technological, and financial revolutions, late-nineteenth-century workers, farmers, and small property-holders were awed and repelled by the consequences of dramatic social and economic change.

CORPORATE REVOLUTION

"An almost total revolution" was taking place "in every relation of the world's industrial and commercial system," observed economist David Wells in 1889. As the nation's gross national product tripled in the last thirty years of the century, a corporate restructuring of the U.S. economy took place. Business enterprises organized on a national scale required enormous amounts of capital and tightly managed organization. To establish corporations, entrepreneurs raised capital through sales of stock to investors, who then shared in profits generated by professional managers. Under the *Santa Clara* decision of 1886, the Supreme Court provided corporations with the legal status of individuals under the Fifth and Fourteenth Amendments, thereby protecting them against government deprivation of assets or earnings without due process.

New corporations like John D. Rockefeller's Standard Oil Company, which consolidated petroleum refining, increased the scale and efficiency of raw-materials processing. In another example, Scottish immigrant Andrew Carnegie combined new methods of ore refining and administration to build a steel empire that became the nation's first billion-dollar corporation. Meanwhile, engineer Frederick Winslow Taylor developed efficient tools like high-speed metal cutters that achieved industrial "economies of scale." Inventions such as the electric light, telephone, cash register, and elevator further accelerated the market revolution. Materials and finished products were distributed by a nationwide system of railroads whose coordination was facilitated when Congress created four standard time zones in 1883.

Although not heavily industrialized, the South played a role in the incorporation of the national economy. Once northern troops withdrew in 1877, political leaders sought to "redeem" the region by opening it to northern investment. Southerners had "fallen in love with work," *Atlanta Constitution* editor Henry W. Grady exulted in 1886. "Redeemer" regimes in such states as South Carolina, Mississippi, and Georgia lowered taxes, reduced government regulation, cut

1

public services, leased convict labor to industrialists, and sold or granted millions of acres of land to northern timber and mining interests. Corporate capitalism made its most dramatic gains in the burgeoning textile mills of the Piedmont in the Carolinas, Georgia, and Alabama, where poor white farmers offered the perfect nonmobile labor force for the manufacture of commodities of little added value.

Like the South, the West joined a national market economy with a desire to exploit land, minerals, and timber. Six western states from North Dakota to Washington were admitted to the Union between 1889 and 1890. Late-nineteenth-century citizens viewed the region as a frontier whose proximity to "Nature" fulfilled expectations of individual success and personal regeneration. Before its riches could be freed for development, however, investors required the federal government to replace the subsistence economy and communal land-holding practices of the native inhabitants. Forcing Native Americans to surrender their lands provoked warfare from Northern Plains Sioux, the Apache of the Southwest, and other tribes. Yet U.S. military attacks, the slaughter of the bison, western settlement, and railroad expansion ended resistance to white land tenure. The Dawes Act of 1887, which abolished communal ownership of land and divided individual allotments into 160-acre parcels, struck an additional blow against native sovereignty.

The conquest of Native Americans was the first stage of the incorporation of the West. Rich in minerals, lumber, and fishing grounds and tied by railroads to eastern markets, the region became a magnet for international capital. Mining made it one of the most urbanized and ethnically diverse sectors of the nation. By 1880 two-thirds of the population of the Colorado, Wyoming, and Montana territories lived in urban settings or on the outskirts of mining towns. Yet economic conditions rarely favored miners in a labor-intensive industry characterized by low wages and speed-ups. By the end of the century western miners averaged an annual income of $500.

U.S. cities, which housed one-third of the national population by 1890, were the breeding grounds of the corporate revolution. In steel-framed skyscrapers, first erected in Chicago, office and administrative functions were consolidated in the downtown core. Electric streetcars or trolleys, which appeared around 1890, increased available labor pools by widening commute distances. Mass transit also attracted middle-class shoppers to department stores. Cities such as New York, the home of nearly 2,000 millionaires by 1892, became showplaces for the new rich. Besides its fabulous mansions, grand hotels, and plush cafes, New York featured museums, lecture and concert halls, schools, and municipal parks constructed with the help of private benefactors. As a symbol of progress, the future of the U.S. metropolis was best expressed in the industrial and technological exhibits of the Chicago World's Fair, or Columbian Exposition of 1893, which conveyed the hope that material progress would produce a harmonious society.

Although corporate capitalism offered cheaper consumer prices, investor flexibility, and opportunities for white-collar employees, its successes often came at the cost of free competition. In 1879 Rockefeller's Standard Oil Company organized the nation's first trust, an arrangement by which stockholders from competing companies ceded industrial decision-making power in return for increased dividends. By the 1880s powerful trusts also dominated steel, copper, and sugar refining, leather processing, meat packing, and linseed oil production. Investment banking promoted further consolidation, particularly of rail lines, organized by Jay Gould, James Hill, Cornelius Vanderbilt, and other titans of industry. Business leaders insisted that natural laws of supply, demand, and competition governed the economy and should not be artificially disrupted by state intervention. Claiming to possess superior energy and initiative, Carnegie and Rockefeller embraced Herbert Spencer's Social Darwinism by portraying the market as the embodiment of a struggle for survival in which the most "fit" excelled. Capitalists also pursued commercial supremacy through the domination of overseas trade (see Chapter 2).

The high stakes of corporate competition prompted Samuel Clemens and Charles Dudley Warner to name their 1873 novel *The Gilded Age*. By the 1880s 10 percent of the population owned 70 percent of the national wealth. Figures for 1890 showed that the richest 2 percent of the people earned more than half the nation's aggregate income. Carnegie, who received more than $20 million a year by the end of the nineteenth century, sought to overcome a "robber baron" reputation by espousing the Gospel of Wealth, a doctrine that portrayed the elite as "trustees" of God's abundance who were obligated to improve the lives of others. The steel magnate donated $350 million of an estimated $400 million personal fortune to "self-help" philanthropies such as public libraries, and later created foundations to promote education and world peace.

IMMIGRANTS, WORKERS, AND LABOR PROTEST

As the Anglo-Protestant elite of major northern cities moved into corporations and national politics, a large segment of the nation's industrial and agricultural work force consisted of the more than 25 million immigrants from Europe, Asia, and Mexico who migrated to the United States between the Civil War and World War I. Irish and German newcomers were the most numerous of the nineteenth-century immigrants. Displaced by the enclosure of peasant holdings and widespread potato famine, 5.5 million Irish immigrants arrived on U.S. soil in the century before 1920. Half were women who found jobs in domestic service, factories, and mills. By 1880 one-third of New York City's population was Irish American; Irish Catholic children soon outnumbered Anglo-Protestants in Boston public schools. Irish and German Americans sought protection from nativist hostility through ethnic fraternal and burial societies, community newspapers, parochial schools, neighborhood commercial associations, and politics.

Irish and German political "bosses" used a highly personal style of leadership to win the loyalty of ethnic and working-class voters. Operating on the precinct and the ward levels, they regularly provided social services, jobs, and municipal contracts to constituents. Machine patrons such as New York's George Washington Plunkitt offered emergency food baskets and other aid to victims of fires and other disasters and sponsored recreational activities such as holiday picnics and music and sports clubs for children. Leaders like Plunkitt prided themselves on "knowing" their districts and treating constituents with respect. The ward-boss system thrived among Catholic and Jewish immigrants who came from cultures that emphasized collective charity and group support instead of Protestant individualism.

The highest proportion of foreign-born residents lived in the West. Although the superintendent of the census did not declare the continental frontier closed until 1890, the "wild West" long had been integrated into the urban-industrial frontier. Western agriculture, mining, logging, and processing plants required a huge labor force. German farmers dotted the Great Plains. Scandinavian loggers worked the fir forests of the northern Midwest and Pacific Northwest. Mountain-state mining operations sought Welsh, Polish, German, and Chinese workers. In southern Texas and California, where large-scale agriculture displaced the Mexican population and disrupted land-holding patterns, Hispanic men often worked for subsistence wages in construction while women toiled on a seasonal basis as poorly paid field hands or in food-processing plants.

Asian immigrants played a major role in the western economy. Between 1868 and 1924 nearly 275,000 Japanese came to Hawaii and California as contract workers, although many eventually succeeded as farmers, orchardists, and gardeners. By 1882 more than 100,000 foreign-born Chinese labored as migrant field hands, domestic servants, industrial wage earners, or restaurant and laundry proprietors. Anxieties over Asian labor competition provoked a wave of nativism in the western states. After Los Angeles mobs lynched eighteen Chinese laborers during the depression of the 1870s, California Workingmen Party leader Denis Kearny declared that "the Chinese must go! They are stealing our jobs." Similar violence in Wyoming led to the murder of twenty-eight Chinese in 1885. Under the Chinese Exclusion Act of 1882, the first immigration restriction law in U.S. history, the entry of Chinese laborers was prohibited, and Chinese Americans were denied naturalized citizenship.

The U.S. countryside also provided a labor force for urban factories, mills, processing plants, mines, construction sites, and railroad yards. Such work often was dangerous, debilitating, and a radical departure from traditional routines. Factory jobs required that repetitious tasks be performed on a strict schedule, a regimen that workers found monotonous, impersonal, and demeaning. Many laborers came from rural cultures whose seasonal work rhythms had not prepared them for industrial discipline and efficiency. "The tick of the clock is the boss in his anger," wrote Yiddish poet Morris Rosenfeld. Moreover, society offered employees virtually no protection from the vicissitudes of industrial life. Vulnerable to wage cuts and lay-offs in an economic system that killed one hundred employees a day, workers toiled an average of fifty-nine hours a week for less than $10 in earnings.

The first successful nationwide labor organization was the Knights of Labor. Although the union did not initially support strikes, local affiliates participated in a massive railroad walkout in 1877 and grew to 700,000 members after prevailing against Jay Gould's lines eight years later. Yet the reputation of the Knights failed to survive the Haymarket Square riot of 1886, when a dynamite bomb killed eight policemen and wounded seventy at a rally to protest police brutality against striking workers in Chicago. After the arrest and conviction of eight anarchist pamphleteers with no connection to the bombing and the execution of four defendants, a wave of public hysteria focused on the perceived threat of "European" class struggle. The American Federation of Labor (AFL), an organization of craft unions founded in 1886 by Samuel Gompers, soon began to replace the Knights as the dominant force in the labor movement. Espousing a pragmatic philosophy of "business unionism," the AFL concentrated on higher wages, job security, and improved working conditions for skilled laborers.

Despite the AFL's acceptance of capitalism, bitter labor disputes disrupted industrial life. After a 20 percent pay cut in 1892, workers at the Carnegie mill in Homestead, Pennsylvania, sought to affiliate with the AFL and confronted security forces in a shoot-out that resulted in sixteen deaths. When state militia ended the strike, Alexander Berkman, a Russian-born anarchist, wounded Carnegie general manager Henry Clay Frick in an assassination attempt. Meanwhile, the governor of Idaho declared martial law and requested federal troops to overpower striking silver miners. Two years later, pay cuts at the Illinois plant producing Pullman railroad cars led to a strike by the American Railway Union that spread to the entire midwestern rail system. After dispatching 14,000 troops to maintain order, the federal government issued a court injunction to prevent interference with rail transport of the mails. Arrested for contempt as the strike collapsed, union leader Eugene V. Debs spent six months in prison and declared himself a socialist upon his release.

SHARECROPPERS, FARMERS, AND POPULISTS

Once northern troops left the last states of the old Confederacy in 1877, southern planters stepped up their campaign to resume control of the plantation economy. Having lost half their capital in the form of slaves, cotton growers could not absorb the employment costs of field hands, overseers, and drivers. Because black laborers often were unwilling to sacrifice autonomy by working for wages, and landlords refused to sell or rent property to former charges, black families began to work for a share of the landlord's crop. In a capital-starved economy in which cotton was the only cash commodity, the crop itself became collateral. Southern landlords provided black sharecroppers with housing, stock, implements, and seed in return for half the proceeds. Crossroads mercantile stores intensified black dependency and debt by extending crop liens in exchange for credits for food, clothing, and supplies.

As Redeemer governments enforced the economic privileges of southern planters and colluded with northern railroad and banking interests, poor white and black farmers turned to populist protest. Vulnerable to the market forces of a growing international economy, cotton prices declined from thirty cents a pound in 1881 to less than six cents in 1890. Meanwhile, farmers were forced to repay increasing debt with the deflated dollars of a contracting currency. The Southern Farmers Alliance, formed in the 1880s by Texan Charles Macune, sought to offset the credit monopoly of banking and mercantile elites by mobilizing small cotton growers in marketing cooperatives and a farm-movement culture. Alliance leaders proposed a subtreasury plan to store crops in government warehouses until market prices rose. In 1890 Alliance candidates were elected across the South, and the Alliance sent Georgia's Tom Watson to Congress. Attacking "race antagonism" as a cause of poverty among blacks and whites, Watson told biracial audiences that "you are kept apart that you may be separately fleeced of your earnings."

Like southern cotton producers, western wheat growers were tied to prices, interest rates, and monetary policies set outside the region. In response, the National Farmers Alliance of the Northwest, organized in the 1880s, proposed an antimonopoly program of railroad regulation and monetary reform. Such agitation stimulated passage of the Interstate Commerce Act of 1887, which imposed "reasonable" and nondiscriminatory freight rates on the railroads and created the Interstate Commerce Commission (ICC), the first regulatory agency in U.S. history. Agrarian activity also helped to enact the Sherman Antitrust Act of 1890, which sought to prohibit restraints of trade and commerce against the public interest.

Alliance leaders hoped to offset the impact of falling prices on farmers and debtors by expanding the money supply. Accordingly, a coalition of northern and southern activists organized a convention of the People's or Populist Party in Omaha, Nebraska, in 1892. The party platform called for the unlimited coinage of silver at one-sixteenth the value of gold. The Populists also advocated government ownership of railroads and utilities, postal savings banks, a federal income tax, and direct election of U.S. senators by voters instead of state legislatures.

People's Party candidates won five Senate seats in the 1892 election while the party's presidential nominee, General James B. Weaver, received more than a million votes (8.5 percent of ballots cast). The movement's appeal intensified when a major economic depression set in during 1893. In the next four years nearly 500 banks and 15,000 businesses went bankrupt, and unemployment leaped to 20 percent. As farm prices sank, profits disappeared, and wages plummeted, unemployed followers of monetary reformer Jacob S. Coxey and sixteen other "industrial armies" mounted the first capitol demonstrations in history to demand government creation of public works programs.

THE NEW POLITICS OF THE 1890s

The activism of the 1890s built upon and encouraged an extensive body of work reflecting social and political dissent. In 1879 land reformer Henry George published *Progress and Poverty*, a widely read plea to prevent permanent division of social classes through adoption of a single tax on speculative income. Edward Bellamy's popular *Looking Backward: 2000–1887* (1888) criticized heartless economic competition and envisioned the creation of a cooperative commonwealth. In *A Hazard of New Fortunes* (1890), novelist William Dean Howells reached large audiences with a portrait of urban despair and class conflict. Meanwhile, the Christian perspective of reformer Henry D. Lloyd's *Wealth vs. Commonwealth* (1894) showed how the trusts victimized ordinary people. Populist monetary demands found their way into best-selling treatises such as William Harvey's *Coin's Financial School* (1894) and *The American People's Money* (1895) by Minnesota activist Ignatius Donnelly.

Depression social unrest sharpened deep social divisions and pushed voters into ideological camps. Until the 1890s Republicans and Democrats ran disciplined but nonsubstantive campaigns to mobilize evenly divided supporters for patronage and other "spoils." In the Midwest voters tended to split along ethnocultural lines; evangelical Protestants supported Republican Prohibition campaigns, and Roman Catholics and German Lutherans backed the Democrats. This political system was unable to survive Democratic President Grover

Exhibit P-1. Chronology of Major Events, 1876–1896

1876	Disputed presidential election between Democrat Samuel J. Tilden and Republican Rutherford B. Hayes
1877	Compromise provides for election of Hayes and withdrawal of federal troops from former Confederacy
1878	Bland-Allison Act requires U.S. Treasury to coin silver currency
1880	Election of Republican President James A. Garfield
1881	Assassination of Garfield
1882	Chinese Exclusion Act
1883	Pendleton Civil Service Act creates Civil Service Commission
	Supreme Court invalidates civil rights legislation
1884	Election of Democratic President Grover Cleveland
1886	Haymarket Square Riot, Chicago, Illinois
1887	Interstate Commerce Act creates Interstate Commerce Commission (ICC)
	Dawes Act abolishes Native American tribal sovereignty
1888	Election of Republican President Benjamin Harrison
1890	Sherman Antitrust Act
	Sherman Silver Purchase Act
	McKinley Tariff
1892	Creation of People's (Populist) Party
	Election of Democratic President Grover Cleveland
	Homestead Steel Strike
1893	Financial panic and the onset of the Depression of 1893–1897
	Repeal of the Sherman Silver Purchase Act
1894	Wilson-Gorman Tariff
	Pullman Strike
1896	Election of Republican President William McKinley

Cleveland's continued endorsement of the gold standard. As southern and western party loyalists defected to the Populists or Republicans in the 1894 congressional elections, currency reformers organized to take over the Democratic Party. The turning point came in 1896 when thirty-six-year-old William Jennings Bryan of Nebraska galvanized the Democratic National Convention with a passionate plea for free silver. "You shall not press down upon the brow of labor this crown of thorns," thundered Bryan. "You shall not crucify mankind upon a cross of gold."

The youngest man in history to be nominated for the presidency by a major party, Bryan embodied the heartland's producer democracy. Such values stressed the government's importance in ensuring autonomy and equality of opportunity in an economy characterized by individual property and freedom of contract. After a long and bitter debate, the People's Party agreed to "fusion" with the Democrats by endorsing Bryan's candidacy but selected Georgia's Tom Watson as its vice-presidential nominee. Meanwhile, united Republicans chose veteran Ohio politician William McKinley, a strong advocate of high tariffs and the gold standard, to lead their ticket. As the nineteenth century reached its final years, the nation's people looked to the future with a mixture of confidence and apprehension.

SUGGESTED READINGS

The rise of corporate capitalism is described in Alfred D. Chandler, Jr., *The Visible Hand: The Managerial Revolution in American Business* (1977). For social consequences, see Olivier Zunz, *Making America Corporate, 1870–1920* (1990), and Alan Trachtenberg, *The Incorporation of America: Culture and Society in the Gilded Age* (1982). For city department stores, see Susan Porter Benson, *Counter Cultures: Saleswomen, Managers, and Customers in American Department Stores, 1890–1940* (1986).

The definitive synthesis on the New South is Edward L. Ayers, *The Promise of the New South: Life After Reconstruction* (1992). See also Harold D. Woodman, *New South, New Law* (1995), and Dwight B. Billings, *Planters and the Making of a "New South"* (1979). For Native American policy in the West, see Robert Wooster, *The Military and United States Indian Policy, 1865–1903* (1988), which can be supplemented by Blue Clark, *Lone Wolf v. Hitcock: Treaty Rights and Indian Law at the End of the Nineteenth Century* (1995), and Sidney J. Harring, *Crow Dog's Case: American Indian Sovereignty, Tribal Law, and United States Law in the Nineteenth Century* (1994). Western economic development is surveyed in Rodman W. Paul, *The Far West and the Great Plains in Transition, 1859–1900* (1988).

The international dimension to U.S. immigration is addressed in Walter Nugent, *Crossings: The Great Transatlantic Migrations, 1870–1914* (1992). See also Alan M. Kraut, *The Huddled Masses: The Immigrant in American Society, 1880–1921* (1982). For a positive view of urban development, see the relevant sections of Stanley K. Schultz, *Constructing Urban Culture: American Cities and City Planning, 1800–1920* (1989). Industrial work culture is described in Bruce Laurie, *Artisans into Workers: Labor in Nineteenth-Century America* (1989), and David Montgomery, *Citizen Worker: The Experience of Workers in the United States with Democracy and the Free Market During the Nineteenth Century* (1993). For labor protest, see Kim Voss, *The Making of Exceptionalism: The Knights of Labor and Class Formation in the Nineteenth Century* (1994); Paul Avrich, *The Haymarket Tragedy* (1984); and Paul Krause, *The Battle for Homestead, 1880–1892: Politics, Culture, and Steel* (1992). See also Carl Smith, *Urban Disorder and the Shape of Belief: The Great Chicago Fire, the Haymarket Bomb, and the Model Town of Pullman* (1994).

Southern agriculture is analyzed in Edward Royce, *The Origins of Southern Sharecropping* (1993), and in Gerald David Jaynes, *Branches without Roots: Genesis of the Black Working Class in the American South, 1862–1882* (1986). Syntheses on the Populist movement include William A. Peffer, *Populism, Its Rise and Fall* (1992); Robert C. McMath, *American Populism: A Social History, 1877–1898* (1993); and Lawrence F. Goodwyn, *The Populist Moment: A Short History of the Agrarian Revolt in America* (1978). For regional studies, see Steve Hahn, *The Roots of Southern Populism: Yeoman Farmers and the Transformation of the Georgia Upcountry, 1850–1890* (1983), and Jeffrey Ostler, *Prairie Populism: The Fate of Agrarian Radicalism in Kansas, Nebraska, and Iowa, 1880–1892* (1993).

Midwestern antimonopoly sentiment is explored in David Thelen, *Paths of Resistance: Tradition and Democracy in Industrializing Missouri* (1991); in Steven L. Piott, *The Anti-Monopoly Persuasion: Popular Resistance to the Rise of Big Business in the Midwest* (1985); and in relevant segments of Andrew R.L. Cayton and Peter S. Onuf, *The Midwest and the Nation: Rethinking the History of an American Region* (1990). For ethnocultural politics, see Paul Kleppner, *The Cross of Culture: A Social Analysis* (1978), and *The Third Electoral System, 1853–1892* (1979). Useful analyses of politics appear in the relevant portions of Robert Kelley, *The Cultural Pattern in American Politics: The First Century* (1979), and Walter Dean Burnham, *Presidential Ballots, 1836–1892* (rev. ed., 1976). The definitive work on Bryan is LeRoy Ashby, *William Jennings Bryan: Champion of Democracy* (1987).

1

The first skyscraper, Chicago's ten-story Home Insurance Building, used a wrought- and cast-iron internal skeleton for the first six stories and steel beams for the next four. Its architect, Jenney, purposely disguised the innovative frame to make the structure resemble a conventional building.

Barnes-Crosby/Chicago Historical Society, no. ICHi – 19291

LIFE AT THE START OF AN AMERICAN CENTURY

"The twentieth century will be American," declared Indiana Senator Albert Beveridge. As the new century dawned, the city and the corporation began to shape a burgeoning industrial society. The central values of agrarian culture—individualism, free competition, and localism—faced challenges by the forces of technology, bureaucratic consolidation, and national market development. As organizations replaced individuals as the building blocks of modern life, people and institutions adjusted uneasily to a new era. Ethnic, racial, and gender diversity in the expanding labor force also challenged traditional norms, as did novel cultural styles and new forms of artistic and intellectual expression.

THE CONSOLIDATION OF CORPORATE CULTURE

Traumatized by the severe depression of 1893–1897, corporate leaders attempted to take control of market forces and to minimize competition by implementing mergers and consolidation. Between 1897 and 1904 managers engineered the merger of some 3,000 firms into 300 supercorporations. These giant units assumed control of 40 percent of national wealth. U.S. Steel produced more than 60 percent of the nation's steel in 1901, which provided the huge corporation with more income than the federal government. Eastern investment bankers such as J.P. Morgan amassed enormous amounts of money to capitalize corporate mergers. "I like a little competition," Morgan told congressional investigators. "I would rather have combination." In 1913 the Pujo Investigating Committee found that a multibillion dollar money trust underwritten by the Morgan and Rockefeller interests held 341 interlocking directorates in 112 separate enterprises. By 1910 seventy Americans had accumulated fortunes of at least $35 million each and held one-sixteenth of the nation's wealth.

Although economic consolidation lagged in retail trades, food processing, and specialized manufacturing, an important transition from proprietary to corporate capitalism took hold in railroading, oil, steel, copper, and other industries. By pioneering bureaucratic business methods, these integrated enterprises dispersed responsibility by retaining professional managers and administrators. By 1917 modern corporations dominated raw materials processing, large-scale manufacturing, distribution, and marketing. "The chief work of civilization *is to eliminate chance*, and that can only be done by foreseeing and planning," declared the manual for the J. Walter Thompson advertising agency in 1909. Corporate culture promoted the rapid growth of a "new" middle class

Exhibit 1-1. Recorded Mergers in Manufacturing and Mining, 1897–1905

1897	69
1899	1208
1901	423
1903	142
1905	226

Source: *Historical Statistics of the United States, Colonial Times to 1970* (1975).

Brown Brothers

The assembly line at the Ford Motor Company.

of nonproduction workers that encompassed executives, managers, and engineers as well as white-collar sales and clerical employees.

Technological innovation continued to energize economic development in the early twentieth century. New canning techniques and refrigerated rail cars allowed consumers nationwide to sample a wide variety of meats, fruits, and vegetables from California, Texas, and Florida. Meanwhile, the new century brought the development of electrical appliances such as fans, flatirons, stoves, sewing machines, and clothes washers, as well as the early use of synthetic rayon. Even more important were new applications of the internal combustion engine. In January 1901 the eruption of a gusher near Beaumont, Texas, stimulated the modern era of petroleum refining. Two years later Ohio brothers Orville and Wilbur Wright were the first to successfully fly a power-driven airplane at Kitty Hawk, North Carolina. Such efforts soon were dwarfed by another dramatic development—the automobile.

Although the first automobiles appeared to be literal "horseless carriages," the replacement of the tiller by the steering wheel and innovations such as the sliding-gear transmission, pneumatic tires, front bumpers, self-starters, headlights, and the four-cylinder engine revolutionized the industry. In 1908 Henry Ford, a Michigan farm boy who had moved to Detroit, unveiled his famous

FREDERICK WINSLOW TAYLOR
1856–1915

Stock Montage

Folk myth held that Frederick Winslow Taylor, the creator of "scientific management," died with a stopwatch in his hand. Taylor saw himself as a reformer striving to use professional skills to improve the lot of labor and the consumer. The son of an established eastern family from Germantown, Pennsylvania, Taylor turned to factory work when weak eyesight curbed his formal schooling. He rose quickly from common laborer to enter the new profession of engineering by taking night classes at the Stevens Institute of Technology. Taylor received about a hundred patents during his career, and his work led to a heat treatment for tools that increased the cutting capacity of steel by 200 to 300 percent.

As machines became more rational and efficient, Taylor grew interested in improving the efficiency of workers as well. Armed with a stopwatch, he kept precise records of the time workers needed to accomplish each task and kept track of every motion made during the process. Using such data to identify the elementary operations and to design the most efficient procedures for specific jobs, Taylor sought the "substitution of science for the rule of thumb." In a famous demonstration of his methods, the engineer quadrupled the amount of pig iron a worker could carry in a day.

These "time-and-motion" studies formed the basis of Taylor's theory of scientific management. In the 1890s Taylor started a management consulting business in Philadelphia by distributing a card that read, "Systematizing Shop Management and Manufacturing Costs a Speciality." Bethlehem Steel became his first major client. The first scientific management consultant in the world, Taylor even-

---

Model-T, an inexpensive automobile that the owner could easily drive and repair. Influenced by Frederick Winslow Taylor's principles of scientific management, Ford introduced the moving assembly line in 1914. By cutting the production time for an automobile from twelve and a half hours to ninety minutes, Ford reduced the average price of a Model-T from about $950 to $265. He was soon selling 500,000 cars a year.

By organizing time and motion in the most efficient manner, Taylor's scientific management increased industrial productivity. Nationwide manufacturing output per worker rose 76 percent between 1899 and 1914, although the work force grew only 36 percent and physical plants only 13 percent. Critics warned that Taylorism dispensed with skilled workers and bypassed craft unions. Yet "efficiency experts" insisted that the increasing surplus generated by the system could be shared by workers if they were willing to let management set output norms and wage rates. In Ford's case the use of the assembly line allowed the auto manufacturer to pay skilled workers $5 a day, double the prevailing wage in U.S. industry. Seeking to reduce turnover, Ford instituted the eight-hour day and the forty-hour week, which made him the virtual creator of the recreational "weekend." By 1920 9 million vehicles traveled the nation's highways, whose planning, construction, and maintenance was assigned to the states by the Federal Highway Act of 1916.

tually codified his expertise in *Principles of Scientific Management* (1911).

Taylor's ideas were understandably unpopular with workers. Many believed that Taylorism reduced them to the status of machines and made their tasks unbearably monotonous. Others feared that a streamlined manufacturing process would precipitate layoffs. "The disciplinary relations within the manufacturing organization must be definite and strict," admitted Taylor, but he insisted that his system would actually improve the lot of labor. He argued that greater efficiency meant greater productivity, thereby making possible shorter hours, higher wages, and lower prices. Smoother procedures also might reduce workers' grievances and improve the relationship between labor and management. Even though Taylor volunteered his services after 1900, workers remained critical of his motives. Their suspicion deepened when industrialists used Taylor's methods to speed up the workflow and eliminate jobs.

Taylor embodied the growing significance of the professional ethic among middle-class graduates of the nation's universities. Optimistic about their ability to manage problems successfully, the new professional class prized order, efficiency, and rationality. These ideas were especially cherished among engineers who shared Taylor's view that scientific concepts could solve social as well as mechanical problems. "The shop (indeed, the whole works) should be managed by the planning department," Taylor insisted. Thus social control and manipulation rather than conscience should be the real basis for reform. "If a man won't do what is right," Taylor said, "*make him.*"

Taylorism transformed the need for social control into the need for planning. Among the first engineers to apply the principles of his profession to society, Taylor prepared the way for other civic-minded engineers such as Herbert Hoover. Like the workers, however, the engineer had no control over how corporate managers might apply his or her techniques. "I have found," Taylor wrote in a paper read before the American Society of Mechanical Engineers in 1909, "that any improvement is not only opposed but aggressively and bitterly opposed by the majority of men."

Taylor died one year after Henry Ford adopted the principles of scientific management to the mass production of automobiles. ■

Corporate investment in machinery, plants, and labor required maximum utilization of resources, which in turn required continuous consumer demand. Not surprisingly, a small number of manufacturing and retail corporations came to dominate the early-twentieth-century marketplace. Consumer market research, the integration of manufacturing and wholesaling, innovative sales programs, and the use of high-volume and low-margin merchandising brought substantial profits to companies such as Ford, Coca-Cola, the American Tobacco Company, the Atlantic and Pacific (A&P) grocery chain, and Sears, Roebuck. Bypassing wholesalers and smaller-scale retailers, the corporate giants created

Exhibit 1-2. Automobile Registration, 1905–1920
(in rounded figures)

1905	77,000
1910	458,000
1915	2,332,000
1920	8,132,000

Source: *Historical Statistics of the United States, Colonial Times to 1970* (1975).

Exhibit 1-3. U.S. Gross National Product, 1890–1920
(in rounded billions of dollars at current prices)

1890	13.1
1900	18.7
1910	35.3
1920	91.5

Source: *Historical Statistics of the United States, Colonial Times to 1970* (1975).

near-monopolies. Advertising, an industry whose expenditures leaped from $52 million in 1870 to $542 million in 1900 to nearly $3 billion by 1920, expanded the influence of the leading retailers.

The urban department store emerged as one of the one most important aspects of consumer culture. Developed in New York, Philadelphia, and Chicago by late-nineteenth-century entrepreneurs such as R.H. Macy, John Wanamaker, and Marshall Field, the all-purpose retail outlet adopted corporate methods of administration and management. In a hierarchical environment, which hid the productive process and the laboring class, male store managers imbued working-class "shop girls" with sufficient gentility to make them effective sales and clerical workers. Department stores cultivated a loyal following of mainly female middle- and upper-class customers by educating consumers about innovations in dress styles and cosmetics, home furnishings, and household appliances. By consolidating retail operations, however, big-city emporiums threatened the competitive viability of independent merchants and neighborhood shops.

IMMIGRANTS AND NATIVISTS

Although department store prosperity initially rested on the patronage of elite Anglo-Protestants, retailers soon tapped the growing number of immigrant shoppers. Nearly 18 million foreign-born people arrived in the United States between 1890 and 1917, all but 3 million during the first fifteen years of the century. Among the newcomers were 130,000 Japanese who arrived between 1900 and 1910 and some 270,000 migrants from Mexico who crossed the border during the century's first two decades. Yet it was the staggering tide of arrivals from Europe that captured national attention and changed the great metropolises of the Northeast and Midwest. By 1910 three-fifths of the residents of the nation's twelve largest cities were "new" immigrants from Europe or their children.

Exhibit 1-4. Net Production of Electrical Energy, 1902–1917
(in billions of kilowatt-hours)

1902	5.9
1907	14.1
1912	24.7
1917	43.4

Source: *Historical Statistics of the United States, Colonial Times to 1970* (1975).

Exhibit 1-5. Telephones per Thousand of U.S. Population

1880	1.1
1890	3.7
1900	17.6
1910	82.0
1920	123.4

Source: *Historical Statistics of the United States, Colonial Times to 1970* (1975).

The great majority of post–Civil War European immigrants came from northern and western Europe, particularly England, Ireland, Germany, and Scandinavia. Beginning in the 1890s, however, more than three-quarters of European arrivals immigrated from the eastern, central, and southern sectors of the continent. Mainly peasants and impoverished rural villagers of Roman Catholic, Eastern Orthodox, and Jewish faiths, few spoke English. Moreover, nearly all the "new" immigrants left societies ruled by repressive and undemocratic governments. They arrived, as social worker Jane Addams put it, "densely ignorant of civic duties."

"New" immigrants frequently were accused of migrating for purely material motives and attacked for reluctance to sever links with their native lands. To some extent, demographic statistics supported such charges. Almost half the Italians, Greeks, and Slavs who came to the United States between 1890 and 1914 returned home. During the peak immigration years in the first decade of the century, about one-fourth as many foreigners departed as arrived. Predominantly male sojourners often planned to earn enough money to return home and buy a small farm or business. Consequently, women constituted only one-third of the Catholic entrants from southern and eastern Europe. Immigrants also returned to their native countries in response to unsatisfying prospects or left during years of economic depression, as in 1908. Other newcomers departed because of rampant discrimination or hostility.

The arrival of a large immigrant population provoked a strong nativist reaction among upper-class patricians and a host of pseudoscientific writers. Some racial theorists applied Darwinian metaphors to posit a hierarchy of national and racial groups, suggesting that Europeans could be divided into Teutonic, Alpine, and Mediterranean "races" in descending order. Applying notions common to animal breeding, some warned that hybrid offspring could reassert the latent characteristics of remote ancestors. Nativists such as Francis A. Walker,

Exhibit 1-6. U.S. Population, 1880–1920
(in rounded millions, based on decennial census)

Year	Population
1880	50.2
1890	62.9
1900	76.0
1910	92.0
1920	105.7

Source: *Historical Statistics of the United States, Colonial Times to 1970* (1975).

Exhibit 1-7. Annual Immigration to the United States, 1870–1920
(in rounded figures)

1870	387,000
1880	457,000
1890	455,000
1900	449,000
1910	1,000,000
1920	430,000

Source: *Historical Statistics of the United States, Colonial Times to 1970* (1975).

president of the Massachusetts Institute of Technology, declared that natural selection now worked against the Anglo-Saxon race. "New" immigrants, charged Walker, were "beaten men from beaten races, representing the worst failures in the struggle for existence."

Nativist anxieties culminated in the notion of "race suicide," popularized by political leaders such as Senator Henry Cabot Lodge and Theodore Roosevelt. Warning that the "higher races" would lose the "warfare of the cradle" by having fewer children, Roosevelt lamented that the "greatest problem of civilization is to be found in the fact that well-to-do families tend to die out." Such notions of racial purity received their most coherent expression in Madison Grant's *The Passing of the Great Race* (1916). The founding president of the New York Zoological Society, Grant celebrated the supremacy of Nordics and Teutonics, "the white man par excellence," as the world's fighters, rulers, organizers, and artists. He warned that the influx of southern and eastern Europeans threatened the older American stock with "mongrelization." New immigrants "adopt the language of the native American, . . . wear his clothes, . . . steal his name . . . and . . . are beginning to take his women," complained Grant, "but they seldom adopt his religion or his ideals."

Antiimmigrant and anti-Catholic sentiment contributed to the strength of the American Protective Association, which in the 1890s pushed for a bill requiring aliens to pass a literacy test in any language. Although President Cleveland vetoed the measure in 1896, a second nativist group, the Immigration Restriction League, rose to power in the early years of the century. In 1903 Congress declared anarchists and prostitutes ineligible for immigration. As nativists continued to insist on the importance of national origins, Congress created the Bureau of Immigration in 1906 to record statistical information on foreign-born arrivals. Castigating immigrants as labor competition and potential criminals, the restriction lobby won passage of the literacy test in 1913 and 1915, although presidential vetoes again prevented the measure from becoming law.

Exhibit 1-8. Immigration from Eastern and Southern Europe as a Percentage
of Total Immigration to the United States, 1890–1910

1890	1900	1910
20.2	45.8	44.6

Source: *Historical Statistics of the United States, Colonial Times to 1970* (1975).

Brown Brothers

Immigrant women sewing clothing in a garment shop in New York City.

Japanese immigrants experienced particularly severe restriction. Because California labor unions perceived Japanese workers as competitors for scarce employment, Japan agreed to a "Gentleman's Agreement" in 1900 that committed it to denying passports to emigrants seeking entry into the United States. Nevertheless, California newspapers continued to shriek about the "yellow peril," and riots against Asians erupted across the state. One year after the Japanese and Korean Exclusion League was organized in 1905, the San Francisco school board voted to place Asian children in segregated schools. When anti-Japanese sentiment became an issue in relations with Tokyo, President Theodore Roosevelt persuaded school authorities to rescind the vote. In exchange, Japan's Gentleman's Agreement of 1907–1908, which remained in force until 1924, promised to further restrict Japanese immigration. In 1913 the California legislature passed an alien land law abolishing the right of Japanese-born farmers to own property.

NATIVE AMERICANS AND NUEVOS MEXICANOS

While Asian immigrants received a cold welcome, Native Americans faced worsening conditions under the Dawes Act of 1887. Poor soil quality and cheating by white speculators made the survival of native farmers on the 160-acre allotments created by the measure extremely difficult. The Burke Act of 1906 accelerated land grants to white purchasers by waiving the government's twenty-five-year trusteeship of native properties. By 1917 Native Americans had lost 62 percent of the lands held thirty years earlier. Washington officials also failed to permit effective self-rule for native peoples. Given the extensive power of federal agents, reservation politics frequently degenerated into contests for bureaucratic favor. Despite the efforts of elders to maintain communal traditions, whites used church-related institutions and reservation public schools to spread Anglo-Protestant values of individual proprietorship. Even after being removed from tribes and sent to boarding schools, however, most native children rejected their education and "returned to the blanket."

Disregard for indigenous people seemed equally blatant in the New Mexico Territory, the home of 60,000 Spanish speakers who had asserted sovereignty rights since the colonial period. As territorial governments transferred lands to Anglo-controlled mining and ranching interests, these Nuevo Mexicano landowners resorted to violence through underground groups such as La Mano Negra (the Black Hand) and Las Gorras Blancas (the White Caps). To resolve the controversy, Congress created a Court of Private Land Claims in 1891. Yet the tribunal upheld Anglo interests in 80 percent of cases, and Nuevo Mexicano landholding fell sharply. Although Hispanics sustained enough strength to mandate bilingualism in the new state constitution, the dominant Anglos ignored these provisions and taught only English in the public schools once New Mexico was admitted to the Union in 1912.

THE TROUBLED SOUTH AND THE RACIAL DIVIDE

African Americans confronted a nation in racial crisis in the early twentieth century, the most severe period of antiblack discrimination and violence since Emancipation. The 1910 Census reported that 80 percent of black Americans lived in the South. Although a small African American middle class of clergy, physicians, educators, funeral directors, barbers, and beauticians served their own communities, southern caste divisions restricted blacks to domestic service, janitorial jobs, or agricultural work. Three-quarters of the South's black labor force languished as tenant farmers or sharecroppers in the declining cotton plantation economy. African Americans "occupy a peculiar place on this land, and must keep it," one southern newspaper explained. As the new century began, white leaders in the South turned to segregation codes and terror to bolster a sense of social place defined by racial supremacy.

Southern racism took a particularly malignant form at the turn of the century when repeated electoral defeats at the hands of Redeemers convinced Populists such as Tom Watson that democracy could not prevail if white conservatives controlled black votes. South Carolina's Ben "Pitchfork" Tillman, Mississippi's James "The White Knight" Vardaman, and Georgia's Hoke Smith rose to power in the Democratic Party through demagogic appeals that fused anxiety over Redeemer support of northern corporations with blatant race-baiting. Vardaman campaigned by dressing in a white suit and riding to political rallies on a white lumber wagon pulled by a team of white oxen. He denounced the black

Library of Congress

Southern lynching victims.

man as "a lazy, lying, lustful animal which no conceivable amount of training can transform into a tolerable citizen." Education, explained Vardaman, "simply renders him unfit for the work which the white man has prescribed, and which he will be forced to perform...the only effect is to spoil a good field hand and make an insolent cook."

To eliminate African Americans from voting rolls, southern populists agreed to support the poll tax, which discouraged political participation by the poor of both races by requiring a rigorous schedule of payments and accounting records. Literacy tests, which demanded an ability to understand a portion of the state constitution read aloud by a county clerk, also disenfranchised potential voters. Poor whites usually avoided the effects of these measures through "grandfather" clauses that suspended voting requirements for those whose ancestors were able to vote before Reconstruction. All-white primaries in the one-party South also purged black voters. Between 1896 and 1904 Louisiana eliminated 99 percent of nonwhite voters from electoral rolls. When Georgia's Hoke Smith campaigned for governor in 1906 by endorsing black disenfranchisement, he won by a 4–1 margin and successfully pushed a state

TOM EDWARD WATSON
1856–1922

Brown Brothers

Georgia's Tom Watson, a dynamic political organizer, embodied the dreams and bitterness of agrarian society. As a boy Watson idolized his grandfather, a plantation owner who worked forty-five slaves on a sizable estate. However, the Civil War destroyed the family's wealth and left the family patriarch dead and Watson's father destitute. The young heir reversed these fortunes and restored the family name through a brilliant career as a criminal lawyer.

A successful man, Watson sought the role of avenger. He directed his wrath toward conservative advocates of a New South who pursued alliances with northern business at the expense of modest southern farmers. Accusing such interests of plots to "betray the South with a Judas kiss," Watson championed small-scale agriculture and proclaimed himself a Populist after election to Congress in 1890.

Still dissatisfied, the irrepressible Watson single-handedly overturned the foundations of southern politics and race relations. First he broke with the Democratic Party of Thomas Jefferson, his spiritual forefather. Then he dared to challenge white solidarity by appealing to white and black farmers to put aside racial differences and vote to further their common interests. "You are kept apart," Watson told the astonished producers of the South, "that you may be separately fleeced of your earnings." The defiant Populist even denounced lynching and once summoned 2,000 poor whites to protect the home of a threatened black supporter.

The aroused political establishment responded ruthlessly to Watson's agenda. To thwart his 1892 reelection plans, conservative Democrats redrew the agitator's congressional district. The strategy worked, and the fiery Populist lost an ugly race marred by violence and fraud. Similar tactics defeated him again two years later. Yet Watson's courage brought national prominence. In 1896 the Populist Party nominated the Georgian to be William Jennings Bryan's running mate. A vigorous opponent of fusion with the Democrats, Watson clung to the dream of a successful third party even as populism evaporated around him. "The sentiment is still there," he mourned shortly after the campaign, "but

constitutional amendment that ended political participation by all but a few African Americans.

Beginning in the 1890s southern legislatures passed "Jim Crow" laws that imposed racial segregation in schools and transportation. In the landmark *Plessy* v. *Ferguson* case of 1896, the Supreme Court ruled that such practices were constitutional if facilities were "separate but equal." Once the court held that blacks did not have the right to use the same accommodations as whites, most southern states adopted even stricter codes that segregated virtually all public areas, including drinking fountains and toilets. Meanwhile, populist demagogues in the Democratic Party learned to win votes by marginalizing African American men as threats to traditional morality and social cohesion. "We would be justified in slaughtering every Ethiop on the earth," proclaimed Mississippi's Vardaman, "to preserve unsulllied the honor of one Caucasian home." Between

confidence is gone." A Republican victory in 1896 and two poor showings as the Populist presidential candidate in 1904 and 1908 sent Watson into political eclipse.

Embittered by the desertion of allies and his belief that rich whites controlled the black vote to destroy southern democracy, Watson increasingly turned to racism and nativism after 1896. By the 1910s his self-published *Tom Watson's Magazine*, *Weekly Jeffersonian*, and *Watson's Jeffersonian Magazine* featured vicious diatribes against blacks, Catholics, Jews, and radicals. Leo Frank, a Jewish factory manager wrongly accused of murdering a young Atlanta girl in 1913, found himself the special target of Watson's vituperation. Denouncing Frank as "the typical young libertine Jew" and a "lascivious pervert," Watson used editorial power to inflame the mob that lynched Frank after the governor of Georgia commuted his death sentence.

Watson's campaign against the "sinister wonders" of Catholicism attracted support from other Georgia newspapers and played a major role in the Atlanta founding of the "second" Ku Klux Klan in 1915. Ironically, Watson had once sent his own daughter to a Catholic school. Nevertheless, anti-Catholic bromides and demands for racial segregation and African American disenfranchisement could be neatly linked to the Progressive movement's obsession with Anglo-Protestant purity. By combining nativist and racist anxieties with grass-roots suspicion of northern corpora-

tions, Watson gradually established a new power base among the small farmers he had once rallied to support reform. By 1917 the Populist leader had refashioned himself into the most important political force in Georgia.

World War I brought still another twist to Watson's tortured odyssey. Siding with anti-corporate critics of Wilson's policy, the Georgia editor joined Mississippi racist Senator James Vardaman to denounce U.S. military intervention in Europe. He now returned to the language of the Populist years and harshly condemned wartime regimentation and centralization as "universal goose-stepping." Watson's scathing attacks on conscription prompted the postmaster general to ban his publications from the mail. The postwar Red Scare, he thundered in 1919, constituted a "deceitful, damnable scheme . . . to convert this republic into a plutocracy."

After losing another race for Congress in 1918, Watson ran for the Senate in 1920. This time he returned to Washington with an overwhelming victory. His triumphant campaign, supported by the Klan, incorporated opposition to the League of Nations with pledges to restore civil liberties.

Barely a year after taking his Senate seat and calling for recognition of the Soviet Union, Tom Watson died. More than any other figure in the South's passionate history, the cantankerous Populist illustrated the tragedy of lost opportunities and squandered energies. ■

1884 and 1914 white vigilantes and mobs lynched some 3,600 black men, many in gruesome public rituals purporting to protect the purity of white women from black sexual assault.

Southern racial practices were legitimized by an outpouring of pseudoscientific literature asserting the biological and cultural inferiority of African peoples. Anthropological works of the period insisted that black people had "primitive nerve impulses" and that their evolutionary development had been retarded by the searing climates of Africa. Psychologists asserted that indolent Africans possessed a "tropical mind without imagination." Such notions led the pioneer psychologist G. Stanley Hall to advise that blacks should be treated by veterinarians instead of physicians. The sociologist Frank Lester Ward speculated that rape involved an unconscious attempt by black men to raise the degraded status of their race. In popular works such as *In the Image of God* and *The Negro a Beast*, early-twentieth-century writers such as Charles Carroll titillated readers by suggesting that black Africans were the result of cross-breeding between humans and apes.

Notions of Anglo-Saxon supremacy found increasing support in the field of history, organized as a profession in the 1880s and 1890s. Academic scholars such as Virginia's Woodrow Wilson now portrayed Reconstruction as a corrupt and misled attempt by northern "carpetbaggers" to integrate former slaves into social and political life on equal terms. Revisionist sentiments reached popular audiences through novels such as Thomas Dixon's *The Clansman* (1905), which romanticized the creation of the terrorist Ku Klux Klan. Ten years after *The Clansman*'s publication, filmmaker D.W. Griffith used the book as the basis for *Birth of a Nation*, Hollywood's first full-length motion picture. Shortly after the movie's White House screening and after personal endorsement by Wilson in 1915, "Colonel" William Joseph Simmons, a former army chaplain, reorganized the Klan as a nostalgic fraternal order in a brief ceremony on Atlanta's Stone Mountain.

Although African Americans in the North generally escaped the codified segregation of the southern states, they regularly encountered discrimination in housing, education, hiring, and union recruiting. As white workers sought to cling to craft jobs threatened by the industrial revolution, black artisans and skilled employees found their livelihoods increasingly in jeopardy. Amid growing racial tensions, African Americans also faced the danger of spontaneous attack by white mobs. Major race riots shook New York City in 1900 and Springfield, Illinois, the home of Abraham Lincoln, in 1908. When a dozen black soldiers stationed in Brownsville, Texas, reacted violently to racial slurs and harassment in 1906, President Theodore Roosevelt issued blanket dishonorable discharges to three companies of their all-black regiment. Six of those discharged had won the Medal of Honor. Meanwhile, pressure increased to segregate the federal civil service by race (see Chapter 3).

ETHNIC ENCLAVES

Despite rampant nativism, Irish Americans, the most populous of the "old" migrants, continued to dominate public life in the cities. By 1900 two-thirds of Irish Americans were citizens, and the group boasted the highest citizenship and voting rates of any immigrant group. Irish workers benefited from positions as skilled blue-collar tradesmen in the construction and industrial crafts and as experienced trade unionists. Moreover, by 1890 40 percent of the native-born Irish had white-collar jobs. As the new century began, Irish Americans attended college in greater proportions than their Protestant counterparts. "What we need is not to dominate the Irish but to absorb them," declared Harvard President Abbott Lawrence Lowell.

Politics and public service provided Irish Americans an indispensable avenue to social mobility and middle-class respectability. By 1890 Irish politicians such as New York's John Kelly had captured control of the Democratic Party in the major urban centers of the North. Four cities—New York, Boston, Chicago, and San Francisco—contained 30 percent of all the municipal employees in the nation. Irish politicians used public payrolls to distribute wealth to communities normally ostracized because of their working-class and Roman Catholic

State Historical Society of Wisconsin

Irish immigrant maids. As they cooked, laundered, and took care of the children, servants were required to wear aprons.

backgrounds. Irish American police officers, firefighters, and civil servants became a mainstay of urban life. By 1910 Irish American women accounted for 20 percent of all city public school teachers in the North (and one-third in Chicago), whereas many others disdained domestic service for better-paying white-collar work as secretaries, clerical employees, and nurses.

Irish politicians, civil servants, and trade unionists acted as Americanizing agents and brokers for "new" immigrants who gravitated to the industrial towns and cities of the Northeast and Midwest. Most pursued trades they had learned in Europe. For example, predominantly male Czech immigrants often served as skilled workers and artisans. Portuguese newcomers were traditionally fishermen, whereas many Greeks and Italians ran fish, vegetable, and fruit markets as well as restaurants and construction companies. In contrast, peasants with Slovakian and Polish backgrounds found jobs in heavy industry. Although men comprised the great majority of non-Jewish migrants from the European continent, immigrant communities sometimes included female workers. Because Italian women maintained a tradition of working in family enterprises, for example, first-generation immigrants from Italy often kept their daughters out of school and allowed them to take in garment piecework or hired them out to factories and mills.

Members of national groups tended to cluster in ethnic neighborhoods that preserved their native cultures through language, food, music, and religion. Immigrant enclaves in cities such as New York, Boston, and Chicago played a crucial role in absorbing newcomers into the flow of urban life. Larger ethnic communities developed their own institutions such as stores and banks to provide education, employment, and capital for residents. In San Francisco A.P. Gianinni created the Bank of Italy (later, the Bank of America) so that non-English-speaking fish and vegetable peddlers might choose a congenial facility in which to do business. Mexican Americans established strong economic and cultural centers with vigorous newspapers in cities such as San Antonio and Los Angeles and even formed cohesive communities in Chicago and St. Paul. Ethnic groups of all nationalities organized fraternal and benevolent orders, burial societies, mutual-aid organizations, and loan and insurance cooperatives.

For Irish, Italian, Polish, Mexican, and some German immigrants, the Roman Catholic church played a crucial role in maintaining cultural traditions that facilitated adjustment to a new social environment. Communal worship provided a sense of personal and collective well-being in a hostile society. While diocesan hospitals, cemeteries, and bookstores solidified Catholic identity, the church created an extensive parochial school system to protect children from Protestant influences. From the 1880s on, Catholic institutions provided education from kindergarten to the university level in every major city. Because parish schools stressed citizenship and English instruction, German, Polish, Italian, and Hispanic Catholics often were denied the use of native languages. Conflicts with the Irish-dominated hierarchy were particularly strong among Italian and Hispanic immigrants, who often felt as if the church showed little respect for their festivals and traditional worship habits.

The Jews of the Lower East Side

Like the Irish, whose native land offered only poverty and political oppression, Jewish immigrants had little choice about return to their places of origin in Russia, Poland, Austria-Hungary, and other areas of eastern Europe. Beginning in the 1880s Jewish communities in the Pale of Settlement, which stretched from the Baltic to the Black Sea, were victimized by a series of pogroms. These campaigns of violence precipitated a mass exodus of more than 2 million Jewish people during the next thirty years. By 1914 one-third of all Jews in Russia and eastern Europe had left. Like the emigrants from Ireland, Jewish immigrants brought entire families and communities to their new homes. Almost half the settlers arriving in the United States were women, and one-fourth were children. Eastern European custom and law had excluded Jews from owning land and had pushed them into mercantile and artisan trades. Significantly, two-thirds of the new Jewish immigrants identified themselves as skilled workers, and more than 70 percent were literate.

More than half of all Jewish immigrants settled in New York City, and half a million clustered on Manhattan's Lower East Side. Using skills learned in eastern Europe, 60 percent of the community's labor force worked in the burgeoning garment industry, mechanized since the Civil War and equipped by Jewish entrepreneurs with electric sewing machines. By 1910 the clothing industry accounted for half of New York City's factories and half of its industrial force. Employers also subcontracted piecework to "sweat shops" whose workers were not covered by union contracts or labor regulations. Because of the demand for

Its curbs lined with food peddlers, Hester Street on Manhattan's Lower East Side lay at the heart of a thriving community of Russian Jewish immigrants.

labor in the needle trades, more than 70 percent of New York's Jewish women older than sixteen worked for wages, and these women accounted for one-third of all garment workers. Although it fostered oppressive labor conditions, the mass production of ready-to-wear garments accelerated the democratization of national dress habits, freed many immigrants from destitution, and accustomed many Jewish women to working outside the home.

Economic necessity on the Lower East Side encouraged more than half the neighborhood's families to take in boarders. In a community of tenements in which children were half the population, overcrowded and unsanitary conditions prevailed. Nevertheless, the enclave fostered a vibrant street life teeming with pushcarts, small trades, shops, and cafes. Yiddish culture found unprecedented freedom of expression in the new environment. A German-based dialect spoken in the ghettos of eastern Europe, Yiddish lent itself to the poetry, song, drama, and socialist writing that molded secular Jewish culture. Immigration also increased the synagogue's role as a center of Jewish communal life and philanthropy and reinforced Zionism, a religious and political ideology that thrived among Russian and Polish Jews who believed that only a national state in Palestine could offer protection from anti-Semitism.

Despite their exclusion from such prestigious fields as corporate business, banking, and the law, German and eastern European Jews experienced more

Holiday crowds spill from the Main Street trolleys in Buffalo, New York, on Labor Day, 1905.

upward mobility than any other immigrant group. Whereas Jewish attorneys specialized in criminal and real estate law, Jewish businessmen extended their expertise in the garment trades into new entertainment enterprises in vaudeville, theater, motion pictures, and popular music. Unlike most immigrants, Jews placed more importance on education than on property ownership. By 1910 the Jewish community contained a higher proportion of people older than sixteen who attended school than any other ethnic group. Jews soon ranked first among immigrants in the percentage of young people attending college, which led several Ivy League colleges to impose quotas on Jewish enrollments. Meanwhile, the Anglo-Protestant elite denied Jews entry into exclusive residential neighborhoods, country clubs and resorts, and many private schools.

LIFE IN THE CITY

"The city has become the central feature of modern civilization," wrote reformer Frederic Howe in 1906. "Man has entered on an urban age." Stimulated by the influx of immigrants and rural migrants, the nation's urban population tripled

Exhibit 1-9. Urban* Population as a Percentage of Total Population, 1880–1920

Year	Percentage
1880	28
1890	35
1900	40
1910	46
1920	51

*According to the Census Bureau, an urban area is one with a population of at least 2,500.
Source: *Historical Statistics of the United States, Colonial Times to 1970* (1975).

between 1890 and 1920—a growth rate ten times that of the rural population. By 1920 more than half the nation's people could be found in a town or city, and nearly two-thirds of urban dwellers clustered in the Northeast. Metropolitan life was substantially changed by more than 800 electric trolley lines and underground railways that integrated residential areas and downtown cores by the early years of the century. By replacing horse-drawn vehicles, streetcars and subways reduced animal waste (ten pounds a day for each horse) and freed thoroughfares of thousands of animal carcasses each year. Improved sanitation contributed to cures for malaria, yellow fever, typhoid, and diphtheria and to a one-third decline in the national death rate after 1900, although life expectancy for whites was only forty-eight years (for nonwhites, thirty-three years).

Although medical and sanitation advances decreased urban death rates, minister and reformer Josiah Strong felt compelled to describe the city as "the grave of the physique of our race." As cities became more densely populated, sewage problems overwhelmed municipal authorities. In 1916 New York City dumped 500 million gallons of raw sewage into its rivers every day. Chicago pumped waste far out into Lake Michigan to minimize contamination of the drinking water it drew closer to shore. Barely half the residents of Rochester and Pittsburgh had sewers, and Baltimore and New Orleans had no sewage system at all. A 1901 survey of tenements in Chicago turned up one city block that contained 82 privies used by 637 people. Many tenements lacked running water. Meanwhile, poor health practices, malnutrition, and childhood diseases contributed to a U.S. infant mortality rate of one in a hundred live births and the lowest public health ranking of any industrialized nation.

Intense overcrowding and deplorable housing characterized the sprawling slums and ghettos of urban-industrial centers. In cities such as Baltimore and Philadelphia, the working class lived in seemingly endless blocks of row houses. Five-story tenements, which featured a narrow central staircase surrounded by four apartments on each level, were the customary form of inner-city residential construction in New York City. One section of Manhattan had a population density of 986 persons per acre, a higher figure than contemporary Bombay, India. One observer noted that even the architecture "seemed to sweat humanity at every window and door." Such settings promoted diseases such as tuberculosis and challenged city officials to respond to the dangers of fire, which extensively damaged four major cities and killed as many as 7,000 people annually between 1870 and 1906. Overcrowding and urban squalor also

Exhibit 1-10. U.S. Life Expectancy, 1900–1915
(in years)

Year	Total	Nonwhites
1900	47.3	33.0
1905	48.7	31.3
1910	50.0	35.6
1915	54.5	38.9

Source: *Historical Statistics of the United States, Colonial Times to 1970* (1975).

contributed to soaring crime rates. By 1893 Chicago averaged one arrest per eleven residents and eight times as many murders as Paris.

The urban environment received extensive coverage in "penny press" newspapers. Publishers such as German immigrant Joseph Pulitzer and the patrician William Randolph Hearst, dubbed practitioners of "yellow journalism" because of their use of color comic strips, provided sensational accounts of crime, gossip, scandal, and corruption. Meanwhile, monthly magazines such as *McClure's* and *Cosmopolitan* followed suit. Ida Tarbell's portrait of the Standard Oil monopoly pioneered the genre. Other examples included Thomas W. Lawson's "Frenzied Finance," a description of insurance company fraud, and Jacob Riis's "How the Other Half Lives," a portrait of life in the tenements of the Lower East Side. David Graham Phillips's "The Treason of the Senate" prompted Theodore Roosevelt to deride journalists as "muckrakers," a name that stuck. Lincoln Steffens's *The Shame of the Cities* (1904), which depicted boss rule, and Upton Sinclair's fictional *The Jungle* (1906), which described conditions in Chicago's meat-packing industry, became muckraking classics.

New Families and Popular Culture

Urban life helped to revolutionize American families, to alter gender roles, and to prepare consumers for a mass popular culture. The trend away from rural farms and small businesses meant that middle-class urbanites relied less on the family as an economic unit of survival. Family size continued to drop as the national birthrate declined from 44.3 per thousand to 27.7 per thousand between 1860 and 1920. The reduction in pregnancies coincided with increased use of contraceptives such as the diaphragm by middle-class women, a practice advanced by birth control advocate Margaret Sanger. Wider economic opportunities for women of the affluent classes also resulted in a gradual increase in the divorce rate from 5 percent in 1880 to 10 percent nearly four decades later. Enhanced personal freedom for women in turn translated into a greater educational opportunity; by 1920 47.3 percent of all college students were women.

The importance of education in the white-collar workplace lengthened the period between physical maturity and economic independence. Elementary school attendance grew steadily between 1898 and 1914, whereas high school and college enrollment more than doubled. By 1917 thirty-eight states had en-

Brown Brothers

The rigid anti-Semitism of Anglo-Protestant elites kept Jewish businessmen and lawyers out of many established areas of business at the turn of the century. Some of the business skills of Jews were therefore directed into the rapidly developing popular culture of the cities such as vaudeville, popular music, and movies. Here is an early moving picture theater in the Jewish section of New York City.

acted laws requiring young people to remain in school until age sixteen. The extended period of schooling encouraged the emergence of a peer culture of "adolescents." The term was conceived by psychologist and child development innovator G. Stanley Hall, whose two-volume work, *Adolescence* (1904), asserted that modern industrial society required an intermediate period of disciplined physical development and postponed sexuality. Hall's work inspired the development of child psychology and greater awareness of the particular needs of young people.

The consumer marketplace helped to draw attention to the place of youth in society. In the influential *The New Basis of Civilization* (1909), economist Simon Patten argued that the replacement of scarcity by market abundance generated new personality traits stressing self-development and individual expression. As the average work week decreased from fifty-six to forty-one hours between

Exhibit 1-11. U.S. Birth Rate, 1900–1920
(estimated live births per thousand of population)

1900	32.3
1910	30.1
1920	27.7

Source: *Historical Statistics of the United States, Colonial Times to 1970* (1975).

1900 and 1920 and child labor declined, a growing number of urban consumers became increasingly attracted to youthful imagery and pursuits. Professional baseball found its way to the major metropolises of the Northeast and Midwest. Meanwhile, amusement parks began to appear on city outskirts. Emulating the midway of the Chicago World's Fair of 1893, the new centers featured arcades, mechanized rides, carousels, roller coasters, food concessions, live orchestras, and dance pavilions. New York's Coney Island, which attracted more than a million people on hot summer days, provided a holiday spirit of exuberant play for working-class families seeking weekend release from jobs.

RAGTIME AND HOLLYWOOD

Middle-class consumers sought more respectable entertainment through the purchase of sheet music designed to be performed on parlor pianos. Beginning in the 1890s, publishers in New York's "Tin Pan Alley" district began to use mass-production techniques to create, print, and market popular songs. By 1915 the industry was selling 200 million sheets of music a year. After 1900 a new form of music called "rag" or "ragtime" began to cross racial, ethnic, and class lines. First played by a German musician in Missouri, ragtime was popularized by the African American composer and pianist Scott Joplin. Fusing syncopated rhythm with European melody, the new music spread from black clubs and brothels to Tin Pan Alley, amusement parks, and dance halls, where it merged with blues and jazz forms emanating from the black South. As urban men and women mixed together in the informal atmosphere of the dance palace, others sought entertainment in the ethnic humor and benign sexuality of the vaudeville stage.

The new century's most revolutionary form of entertainment was the motion picture. Once George Eastman pioneered the photographic process in the 1880s, Thomas Edison developed the movie camera and kinetoscope. Primitive silent pictures like the sixty-second production *The Kiss* (1896) appeared in the penny arcades of urban vice districts. Once films could be projected on walls or screens, director Edwin W. Porter made *The Great Train Robbery* (1903), the first film with a consistent plot line. A group of immigrant Jewish entrepreneurs, including Samuel Goldwyn and Adolph Zukor, then moved exhibitions to "nickelodeon" storefronts in tenement neighborhoods. By 1908 the nation contained nearly 10,000 such establishments. Seeking to expand their audience, exhibitors took over vaudeville stages and built their own theaters. When a lawsuit broke the power of the prevailing film syndicate, several Jewish independents pioneered modern moviemaking by forming their own studios.

Leaving the East Coast for Hollywood to escape harsh weather, high costs, production restrictions, and troublesome labor unions, movie entrepreneurs consolidated casting, production, distribution, and exhibition. By 1913, serials such as *The Perils of Pauline* and *Ruth of the Rockies* were smash hits. Director Mack Sennett also achieved success by featuring the "Keystone Kops" in a series of "slapstick" comedies that parodied police and social authorities. To further cement audience loyalty, filmmakers showcased selected stars such as Lillian Gish, Mary Pickford, and Charlie Chaplin. As movie attendance reached 10 million people a year by the mid-1910s, Chaplin and Pickford negotiated million-dollar contracts.

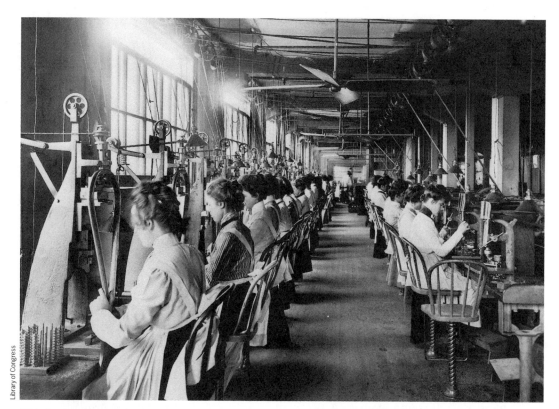

Library of Congress

With the rise of mass production techniques, many women found employment in factories. These women worked for National Cash Register in Dayton, Ohio, 1902.

"Great successes," exclaimed one Hollywood producer, "are those that take hold of the masses, not the classes." Comic heroes such as Buster Keaton, "Fatty" Arbuckle, Harry Langdon, and Chaplin perfectly embodied such insight. Chaplin's brilliant portrait of the "little tramp," an aristocratic underdog and outsider in baggy pants, resonated with millions of immigrants and rural migrants who faced snobbery and middle-class hostility in strange environments. Yet Hollywood also learned to engage middle-class audiences. Although Mary Pickford began her career as "America's sweetheart," the actress and her frequent costar Douglas Fairbanks demonstrated how traditional morality could be synthesized with new styles of indulgence in lavishly costumed and exotic romantic dramas. By 1920 the motion picture industry had become a major influence on popular consumer tastes and values.

THE PLIGHT OF WORKING PEOPLE

The prosperity of early-twentieth-century capitalism rested on the labor of ordinary men, women, and children. Although the incorporation of new technologies created opportunities for engineers, production supervisors, and troubleshooters, corporate mergers and mechanization replaced many traditional craft

Exhibit 1-12. Average Hourly Earnings of U.S. Industrial Workers in Cents, 1890–1914

1890	14.4
1900	15.1
1910	19.8
1914	22.0

Source: *Historical Statistics of the United States, Colonial Times to 1970* (1975).

jobs. Most U.S. workers continued to earn paltry wages for long hours under oppressive working conditions. At the turn of the century, one economist estimated that 60 percent of all men did not earn enough to maintain a family. By 1916 almost two-thirds of the nation's people owned only 5 percent of national wealth.

No event publicized the horrors of industrial work life more vividly than the 1911 fire at the Triangle Shirtwaist Company in New York City. The blaze began on the top floor of a ten-story building one Saturday afternoon as the workers—several hundred Italian and Jewish immigrant women—prepared to leave. The women jammed against the exits, but management had locked the doors to keep employees from stealing fabric and consorting with union organizers. When the elevators filled, some people leaped into the shafts, where their bodies jammed the machinery and stopped the cars. Dozens more climbed to the roof and, holding hands, jumped to their death. The tragedy claimed the lives of nearly 150 young women. A few days later, 80,000 people ignored a steady rain to march in a somber funeral procession. A subsequent investigation blamed company management as well as the building and fire departments, but no one faced criminal charges. Nevertheless, a state investigatory report resulted in passage of some fifty laws designed to improve factory safety.

As the Triangle fire demonstrated, American women often faced harsh prospects in the workplace. The number of women who labored outside the home grew from 5 million in 1900 to 7 million ten years later, making women one-fifth of the nation's gainfully employed work force. Yet social restraints prohibited married women, especially of the middle and upper classes, from entering the labor force. As a result, most women who worked outside the home were either single or lacked any other support. Female employees usually found themselves restricted to low-paying jobs. In 1900 40 percent of the women in the labor force were domestics. Moreover, aside from teaching and nursing, the professions generally remained confined to men. Contemporary critics cited such limited economic choices as the reason some working-class women chose to become prostitutes.

Child labor also proliferated. In 1900 10 percent of all girls between the ages of ten and fifteen and 20 percent of all boys of the same age held jobs. "The most beautiful sight we see is the child at labor," declared Coca-Cola founder Asa Candler. "As early as he may get at labor the more beautiful, the more useful does his life get to be." By 1913 roughly one-fifth of all U.S. children earned their own livings. Asked why he did not play more, one boy replied, "I don't know how." Even when states adopted laws regulating child labor, they typically permitted twelve-year-old children to work ten hours a day (see Chapter 3 for federal child labor legislation).

Exhibit 1-13. Women in the U.S. Labor Force, 1890–1910
(in rounded millions and as a percentage of total labor force)

	Numbers	*Percentage*
1890	4.0	17.2
1900	5.3	18.3
1910	7.4	19.9

Source: *Historical Statistics of the United States, Colonial Times to 1970* (1975).

Some of the nation's worst labor abuses occurred in the South, a region in which 62 percent of the labor force worked in low-wage extractive industries. As consumer demand for ready-made cigarettes spread, producers such as the American Tobacco Company rationalized tobacco processing in the Carolinas and Virginia and employed marginalized farmers in company plants at subsistence wages. The most dramatic development in southern industry occurred in the Piedmont cotton mills of the Carolinas, Georgia, and Alabama. As investment in southern cotton manufacturing leaped seven times between 1880 and 1900, the region surpassed New England as the largest processor of raw cotton into spun fiber and woven fabric. Accordingly, the southern textile work force grew from less than 17,000 to 100,000.

Cotton mill employers initially recruited white women and children from Piedmont farms. During the 1890s child labor increased 130 percent in southern textile mills. Because families survived by acting as working units in an economy with few skilled positions, mill employees resented efforts to regulate the hiring of their children or the enforcement of school attendance laws. Adult women also remained an important part of the mill economy. In 1919 women employees still constituted one-fifth of Georgia's manufacturing workers. Because southern mill wages were among the lowest in the nation, however, male family members were compelled to join the work force so that earnings could be pooled and company housing shared. Living in primitive and racially segregated mill villages that maintained a rural flavor, most southern mill hands worked sixty-hour weeks. Black employees toiled under similar conditions but were assigned the most menial tasks.

Mexican American workers in Texas and the Southwest constituted one of the most abused labor forces in the nation. During the 1890s new state taxation schemes substituted land-value assessments for traditional levies on agricultural income. Consequently, Mexican landowners in the Southwest often were dispossessed of their holdings during years of drought and crop loss. The replacement of the old ranch economy by large-scale commercial operations

Exhibit 1-14. Children Aged 10–15 in the U.S. Work Force, 1890–1910
(in rounded millions)

1890	1.5
1900	1.8
1910	1.6

Source: *Historical Statistics of the United States, Colonial Times to 1970* (1975).

forced many landless Mexicans into agricultural wage labor, tenant farming, railroad construction, or mining. Meanwhile, the federal government initiated a series of dam-building projects to irrigate more than a million acres of southwestern agricultural land. During the first years of the century, commercial interests began to use holdings in Texas, Arizona, and southern California for large-scale cultivation of cotton and vegetables.

Commercial farming in the Southwest benefited from the destruction of the traditional ranching economy. As outside investment promoted the growth of mechanized agriculture and forced Mexican peasants off the land, and as Mexican refugees fled the revolutionary turmoil of the 1910s, agribusiness employers tapped an additional labor supply. The new Mexican Americans, or Chicanos, joined displaced producers above the Rio Grande to become a permanent, migrant work force that traveled across the country cultivating and picking crops as they ripened. Landowners paid the lowest possible wages and housed temporary adult and child field workers in shacks with primitive facilities. To keep wages low and discourage strikes, corporate growers persuaded Congress to waive immigration restrictions on farm workers in 1917. Lower labor costs enabled southwestern farmers to offset land, irrigation, and transportation expenses, thereby assuring profits without raising the price of food and cotton products.

A RISING LABOR MOVEMENT

Seven million American workers participated in 37,000 strikes between 1881 and 1905. Yet the most dramatic growth in union membership occurred during the peak period of corporate mergers between 1897 and 1903, when the number of organized workers in the nation quadrupled. During this period, John Mitchell's United Mine Workers gained recruits with a series of well-publicized walkouts in the Pennsylvania and West Virginia coal mines (see Chapter 2). However, AFL craft unions thrived even more by organizing specialized and skilled workers subject to the reassignments and speed-ups that accompanied mechanization and scientific management strategies. To bolster labor solidarity in an era of corporate consolidation, AFL unions often invoked republican notions of a producers' democracy. For example, the San Francisco building trades supported antimonopolist reforms such as Henry George's single tax and land distribution schemes. By 1917 the AFL had attracted 2 million members and had become a major force in U.S. industrial life.

Although the AFL focused mainly on craft operatives, some of the early twentieth century's most protracted union struggles concerned less privileged workers. In 1900 Jewish labor activists organized the International Ladies Garment Workers Union (ILGWU), which mobilized mainly female apparel employees. The union lost a bitter struggle against the Triangle Shirtwaist Company in 1910 when company guards beat women strikers. After Chicago police killed ten women demonstrators in a citywide walkout later in the year, the ILGWU lost a second strike. Nevertheless, the union prevailed by successfully organizing the garment trade in 1911. Once victorious, the ILGWU brought stability to the industry by pioneering the use of arbitration procedures in labor-management disputes. Meanwhile, socialist Sidney Hillman's Amal-

Brown Brothers

The Triangle Shirtwaist Factory fire, 1911. "They hit the pavement just like hail," a fireman reported.

gamated Clothing Workers combined a conciliatory approach to management with innovative union practices such as cooperative housing and banking.

Common laborers in the South faced greater challenges. In Atlanta, where one-fifth of the labor force was organized, cotton mill workers joined a strike led by the United Textile Workers of America and the AFL in 1914–1915. Subjected to piecework, long hours, low wages, and competition from child labor without the paternalistic benefits offered by Piedmont employers, Atlanta mill workers were unified by kinship ties and republican values. After a walkout precipitated by the discharge of fellow unionists, strikers managed to arrange visits by representatives of the Department of Labor and the U.S. Commission on Industrial Relations. Yet the workers lost the bitter strike when management used blacks to evict them from company-rented housing.

More violent labor conflicts erupted in the West, where the Western Federation of Miners (WFM) became a major force in the 1890s. Expressing the miners'

**Exhibit 1-15. U.S. per Capita Income, 1895–1915
(in rounded dollars)**

1895	200
1900	246
1905	299
1910	383
1915	398

Source: *Historical Statistics of the United States, Colonial Times to 1970* (1975).

**Exhibit 1-16. U.S. Labor Union Membership, 1900–1920
(in rounded millions based on Bureau of Labor Statistics)**

1900	.8
1905	1.9
1910	2.1
1915	2.6
1920	5.0

Source: *Historical Statistics of the United States, Colonial Times to 1970* (1975).

mutuality and an eclectic socialism, the union organized the provision of its own disability and death benefits and ran hospital and ambulance services. When the union struck the Colorado coal fields in 1903, however, the Mine Owners Association launched a campaign of terror, forced the governor to declare martial law, and precipitated a bloody civil war. The next year a confrontation at Cripple Creek resulted in the dynamiting of a train full of strikebreakers. Ironically, mining companies used enhanced resources to implement safety reforms and undertake their own social welfare programs after defeating the union in 1907 and 1908.

Mexican American workers faced even greater challenges in the struggle to gain collective bargaining rights and higher wages. Through *mutualistas*, which were benevolent associations designed to promote ethnic solidarity, Mexican activists sought to organize southwestern farm workers and miners. In 1903 3,500 Mexican miners struck Arizona mining camps. Mexican Americans also joined a WFM union that affiliated with the AFL in 1916 as the Mine, Mill, and Smelter Workers. Yet their most dramatic contribution to western labor conflict was their participation in the fifteen-month strike of Greek, Italian, Slavic, and Mexican miners that the United Mine Workers organized at Ludlow, Colorado, in 1913–1914.

A bitter and protracted struggle, the walkout reached a climax in April 1914 when the Colorado Fuel and Iron Company evicted strikers from company housing and the governor summoned the National Guard. After shootouts between workers and company security forces, Guardsmen exploded bombs above a miners' tent colony and attacked mine families with machine gun fire, killing thirteen adults and five children. Ten days of fighting brought seventy-four more deaths, many of them Mexican American. When 124 strikers were indicted and Guardsmen were acquitted of all charges, union leaders called off the campaign. Nevertheless, the Commission on Industrial Relations blamed Colorado Fuel and Iron for "ruthless suppression of unionism" accomplished by firings, blacklists, armed guards, spies, and "the active aid of venal state, county, and town officials." A shaken John D. Rockefeller, Jr., whose family had a 40 percent interest in the company, adopted public relations tactics and initiated a program of employee representation, union recognition, and higher wages.

The most controversial labor organization of the early century was the Industrial Workers of the World (IWW) or Wobblies, organized in 1903 by WFM leader "Big Bill" Haywood and other socialists. Bluntly declaring that "the working class and the employing class have nothing in common," the IWW rejected the use of labor contracts as well as political action. Instead, charismatic organizers like Haywood and Joe Hill sought to create an all-embracing union of male workers that would employ "direct action" to achieve a classless society. Under Haywood's leadership, the Wobblies mobilized miners, loggers, and migrant workers in the West and used songbooks, hymns, and "free speech" crusades to create worker solidarity and establish a "hobo" subculture. The IWW also spread to the East, where it organized sit-down strikes against General Electric, staged a walkout of silk workers in Paterson, New Jersey, and successfully unionized the textile mills of Lawrence, Massachusetts.

The Wobblies' rhetoric, uncompromising class consciousness, and unwillingness to renounce tactical violence made the organization a symbol of radicalism for citizens and leaders who associated labor unrest with undemocratic threats to social order. Such anxieties worked against widespread support for unions and permitted employers to use federal courts to uphold antilabor injunctions under the Sherman Antitrust Act. The labor movement also suffered from the reluctance of U.S. workers to develop ideological solidarity and class loyalty. In a period in which consumer values stressed personal validation through the promise of upward social mobility, labor collectivism seemed to imply the permanence of a worker's status. As access to the pleasures of popular culture came within reach of millions of working people, efforts to link the labor movement with republican, producer, or socialist values were not always successful.

The ethnic and cultural diversity of the American working class made it even more difficult to forge labor unity. Besides the plethora of mutually antagonistic nationalities and social groups, racial tensions limited the movement, particularly where union solidarity was built on white supremacy. When Japanese and Mexican farm workers struck in Oxnard, California, in 1903, for example, the participation of Asian workers prompted the race-conscious AFL to refuse to charter the union. Most AFL organizations were racially exclusive and rejected women, ethnic minorities, and unskilled labor. Such policies not only limited the potential scope of the union movement but encouraged excluded groups such as African Americans to act as strikebreakers. Gender also affected the struggle because the task orientation and personal nature of female jobs in retail sales, clerical service, and domestic work discouraged collective bargaining.

Socialists, Anarchists, and Cultural Radicals

The growing militance of organized labor generated greater support for a vibrant socialist movement. Organizing the Socialist Party of America in 1900, union activist Eugene Debs brought together industrial workers, urban ethnic minorities, agrarian monetarists, radical intellectuals, and middle-class reformists. "While there is a lower class," declared Debs, "I'm in it. While there is a criminal class, I'm of it. While there's a soul in prison, I am not free." To confront corporate power, the Socialist leader espoused a pragmatic agenda of workplace democracy and participation in elections. Yet theoreticians like Daniel DeLeon argued that revolutionary industrial unions could develop sufficient class consciousness to allow the party to turn government over to working-class syndicates once the party was voted into power. Meanwhile, the skillful Marxist

Eugene Debs in 1904.

oratory of New York's Morris Hillquit appealed to the Socialist Party's autonomous immigrant branches and readers of its foreign-language press.

Socialists won control of the International Association of Machinists in 1907. Yet Samuel Gompers and building trade unions prevented a similar takeover of the AFL. Following Debs's desire to build a mass movement that crossed class lines, the party abandoned its call for the nationalization of land in 1910 and expelled the syndicalist followers of DeLeon two years later. With a membership of nearly 120,000 in 1912, the party sought legitimacy by running a nationwide slate of candidates. By endorsing municipal ownership of public utilities such as gas, water, and sewer systems, Socialists elected 160 city councillors, 145 aldermen, and 56 mayors. The party also placed 33 members in state legislatures and sent Victor Berger, a German American from Milwaukee, to Congress. Running as a fourth-party candidate, Debs received almost a million votes for president (6 percent of the total) in 1912 (see Chapter 2).

Some radicals were attracted to anarchism, a philosophy in which the state is seen as an oppressive instrument serving the propertied classes. Individualist anarchists such as Benjamin Tucker accepted the legitimacy of property when it was the result of personal labor and stressed the importance of educating and persuading workers to support an evolutionary program of pragmatic social change. Yet utopian collectivists such as Emma Goldman, Alexander Berkman, and Johann Most disparaged property ownership and sought to dismantle all power structures. Adhering to the "propaganda of the deed," a few anarchists like Berkman advocated the use of violence or armed rebellion to appropriate property for collective use to create a cooperative society.

A feminist, "free-love" opponent of wedlock, and a pacifist, Goldman carried the spirit of anarchism into the cultural realm. "If I can't dance," she once blurted to a somber gathering of radicals, "I don't want to be part of your revolution." Goldman filled her *Mother Earth* magazine with denunciations of marriage, organized religion, and bourgeois politics as extensions of male power. Women "must no longer keep their mouths shut and their wombs open," she declared. Goldman's stark pamphlet, "Why the Poor Should Not Have Children," resulted in her arrest in 1915 after a birth-control lecture in Portland, Oregon. Meanwhile, Charlotte Perkins Gilman emerged as the new century's leading critic of gender roles. In *Women and Economics* (1898) and *The Man-Made World* (1911), Gilman dismissed housekeeping as the "smallest, lowest, oldest" task in the world and argued that women should be free to join the paid workplace. No economic radical, Gilman nevertheless called for communal meal preparation, cleaning, and child care services provided by professionals.

The 1910s produced an outpouring of political dissent and free-spirited bohemianism that marked the rebellion of a generation rejecting Victorian hierarchy and genteel propriety. Seeking refuge in artistic havens such as New York's Greenwich Village and Taos, New Mexico, middle-class rebels such as Floyd Dell and Waldo Frank deployed Marxist criticism to attack capitalism and adopted Sigmund Freud's notions about sexual repression to discredit "puritanism." "We feel social injustice as our fathers felt personal sin," exclaimed Randolph Bourne, a dissenting essayist who celebrated the potential flowering of youthful idealism in a "trans-national America." Radical poets, novelists, artists, intellectuals, journalists, and cartoonists found a welcome outlet in Max Eastman's magazine, *The Masses*, published between 1911 and 1917.

PRAGMATIST PHILOSOPHERS AND REALIST ARTISTS

As the middle class acknowledged the tensions and dislocations of the urban-industrial frontier, the literary and artistic conventions of the Victorian era began to fade. Although nineteenth-century sentimental, romantic, and moralistic art remained popular, young writers and artists increasingly found such optimism out of place and given to sterile formulations. In literature, a "Little Renaissance" emerged around a cluster of younger writers influenced by the realism and "naturalism" of European novelists like Emile Zola. Naturalism found expression through the work of Theodore Dreiser, the son of a German immigrant. Dreiser portrayed people as animals who abandoned culture and civilization when they pursued private needs. His *Sister Carrie* (1900) exploded the confines of the Victorian novel by realistically depicting a young woman's

A group of artists, the Ashcan school, ceased painting the rural landscape or upper-class portrait and instead created vivid pictures of lower-class life in the growing cities. Here Bellows finds vitality and dignity in the midst of the terrible overcrowding. (Cliff Dwellers, 1913. George Wesley Bellows/American 1882–1925. Oil on canvas, 39½" × 41½").

corruption by city life. Dreiser sustained the book's pessimistic tone and frank sexual themes in works such as *The Financier* (1912) and *The Titan* (1914). Other naturalists included Stephen Crane, Frank Norris, Willa Cather, and Ellen Glasgow.

Similar shifts took place in American poetry. In the 1910s a new generation of young poets rebelled against the Victorian genteel tradition by experimenting with new methods and more contemporary themes. In 1912 Harriet Monroe founded the influential journal *Poetry*, which published works by Robert Frost, Edgar Lee Masters, e.e. cummings, Carl Sandburg, Amy Lowell, and Edna St. Vincent Millay. Although the perspectives of the new poets differed, they drew their material and use of language from the lives and experiences of the common people. Simultaneously, two Americans who spent their careers largely in Europe, T.S. Eliot and Ezra Pound, developed fresh poetic idioms by using new rhythms and common speech.

Modern art also shattered Victorian sensibilities. Painters like John Sloan and George Bellows depicted the harshness and violence of the contemporary world so forcefully and relentlessly that critics named their style the Ashcan school. "Forget about art," realist Robert Henri told his students, "and paint pictures of what interests you." One Ashcan painter, George Luks, claimed to be the best barroom fighter in the country and denounced establishment art figures as "those pink and white idiots." In 1913 the Ashcan artists organized the Armory Show, an exhibition that included work by the Europeans Marcel Duchamp, Henri Matisse, and Pablo Picasso. Introducing such modern art forms as cubism and expressionism, the show dramatized the break with nineteenth-century formalism and heralded the artist's new demand for total freedom to explore the internal and external dimensions of the urban-industrial world.

A similar rejection of nineteenth-century certainties contributed to the development of a distinctively national philosophy: pragmatism. As expressed by its chief proponent, Harvard psychologist and philosopher William James, pragmatism rejected the validity of absolutes and fixed principles. James argued that ideas should be tested by their workability and benefit to the greatest number of people. He insisted that an idea contained meaning only in terms of the consequences precipitated by believing the proposition. "What in short," James asked, "is the truth's cash value in experiential terms?"

Pragmatism found an effective advocate in Columbia University educator John Dewey, who applied its tenets to group activity and social action. Calling himself an "instrumentalist," Dewey considered authoritarian teaching methods such as rote memorization, strict routine, and the mastery of a sharply defined body of knowledge inappropriate to the learning experience. He denounced beliefs in absolute truth as "the ultimate refuge of the stand patter." Instead, Dewey suggested that schools be democratically organized and rooted in direct experience and that they serve as agents of social reform as well as vehicles for transmitting culture. Such ideas reflected a growing faith among urban professionals that public education could help to stabilize the social order. Works by historian Charles Beard and economist Thorstein Veblen also illustrated the faith that "progressive" technicians and reformers could apply rational planning to offset vested interests and mere precedent.

Social Justice and Racial Equality

"Jesus Christ knew a great deal . . . about organizing society," reform-minded minister Washington Gladden observed in the 1890s, "and the application of his law to industrial society will be found to work surprisingly well." Early-twentieth-century reform derived much of its inspiration from Gladden's Social Gospel. The Congregational minister from Ohio sought to recruit laborers to worship by opening branches of his church in working-class districts. Preaching that spiritual regeneration led to social justice, Gladden hoped that class conflict could be reduced by using the government to promote communal property ownership. Protestant theologian Walter Rauschenbusch expanded on Gladden's notions in the influential *Christianity and the Social Crisis* (1907). Arguing that social environment shaped personal character, Rauschenbusch endorsed the call for an activist ministry among the urban poor. Similar views were

By 1900, Booker T. Washington's Tuskegee Institute educated 1200 students. Washington preached cleanliness and etiquette with such fervor that students chuckled about his "gospel of the toothbrush."

embraced by Roman Catholics who adhered to Pope Leo XIII's 1893 encyclical on economic and social justice.

Middle-class women in the cities played the dominant role in the era's social crusades. Liberated by smaller families and increased leisure time, many joined organizations seeking to restore morality to public life. The General Federation of Women's Clubs, which focused on improving working conditions for women and children, grew from a membership of 50,000 in 1898 to more than a million by 1914. The federation's work was paralleled by that of women in the newly developed field of social work. In 1889 Jane Addams, an upper-class college graduate, cofounded Hull House, a pioneer settlement house modeled on London's Toynbee Hall. Addams sought to provide working-class residents of a Chicago neighborhood with a variety of services including child care, a library, meeting rooms, and classes in housekeeping, cooking, music, and art. Attracting women professionals to serve and live with the urban poor, she made the settlement house an advocate of positive social change. By 1910 400 such agencies existed in the United States.

Settlement leaders helped to energize a community of social feminists. Working with the National Child Labor Committee, they lobbied thirty-one state legislatures to prohibit children younger than fourteen from working in factories and those less than sixteen from working in mines. Social feminists also managed to eliminate night work and shifts of more than eight hours a day for some young workers. Reformers broke ground when twenty-two state legislatures established programs that paid child support to widows or abandoned wives. In addition, the coalition of women professionals and purity activists secured the inclusion of the Children's Bureau in the Department of Commerce and Labor in 1912. Meanwhile, Florence Kelley's National Consumers' League and the National Woman's Trade Union League won passage of women's minimum wage bills in fifteen states and maximum hour laws in thirty-nine states. In *Muller* v. *Oregon* (1908), Louis D. Brandeis cited expert testimony on the effect of extended labor on women's health to convince the Supreme Court to uphold a ten-hour daily work limit for female workers.

Reform efforts also touched the sensitive area of race relations. Until 1910 Booker T. Washington remained the undisputed leader of the nation's African American community. Born a slave before the Civil War, Washington graduated from a vocational training school for blacks established by northern philanthropists. As head of Alabama's Normal and Industrial Institute at Tuskegee, he instilled the black student body with middle-class virtues such as hard work, frugality, cleanliness, and proper manners. Convinced that blacks would fare better as southern artisans or farmers than as northern wage earners, the Tuskegee educator encouraged black students to accept a separate social status from whites. As Washington became the conduit for northern contributions to African American schools and the distributor of meager black political patronage, he appeared before the Atlanta Cotton Exposition of 1895 to assure the leaders of the New South that "in all things purely social" the races could "be separate as the fingers, yet one as the hand in all things essential to mutual progress."

As the southern plantation cotton economy stagnated and white racial hysteria escalated, blacks began a migration to the North that would involve more than a million people in the new century's first three decades. Railroad promotions and exhortations by African American newspapers such as the *Chicago Defender* alerted black migrants to new opportunities in auto plants, steel mills, and packing houses, even though most turned out to be menial service jobs. Changing economic circumstances produced new concerns over civil rights. In 1905 W.E.B. Du Bois, a history and economics professor at all-black Atlanta University, organized a conference of community leaders dedicated to "Negro freedom and growth." Meeting on the Canadian side of Niagara Falls, thirty-one conferees endorsed a declaration by Du Bois and Boston activist William Monroe Trotter that racial accommodation had to be replaced by protest.

The first African American to earn a Ph.D. from Harvard, Du Bois accused the powerful Washington of failing to adjust to the urban-industrial age. He taunted the elderly leader by asking if black schools were "training the Negro for his own benefit or for the benefit of somebody else?" Du Bois proposed to challenge racial discrimination under the leadership of a college-educated elite of black Americans he called "the Talented Tenth." He insisted that the race could never achieve economic success without political power. This approach won support from a group of white reformers who hoped to legitimize the idea of civil and social rights for blacks. In 1909 Du Bois joined social worker Lillian Wald, activist Mary White Ovington, socialist William English Walling, Rabbi Stephen Wise, and several reform-minded journalists in organizing the National Association for the Advancement of Colored People (NAACP), the nation's first civil rights organization. As editor of its newspaper, *The Crisis*, the brilliant Du Bois assumed the role of pedagogue to the nation's leading African Americans.

— BOOKER TALIAFERRO WASHINGTON —

1856–1915

Brown Brothers

Nicknamed "the Wizard" for his mastery of political intrigue and power, Booker T. Washington was born into slavery and was the child of a Virginia plantation cook. Never knowing his white father, Washington served as a houseboy until his family moved to West Virginia after Emancipation. After working briefly in salt furnaces and coal mines, the former slave found a position as a house servant for a wealthy general and was taught to read by the officer's wife, a former New England schoolteacher. While attending the Hampton Institute in a Virginia, a teacher training school for "colored" students, he internalized the work ethic that would direct his life efforts.

Washington combined a small grant from the state of Alabama with donations from northern philanthropists to found a "normal" school for African Americans at Tuskegee in 1881. Convinced that slavery had left blacks dependent on whites, he instilled strict discipline and training in skills and crafts to prepare pupils for economic self-sufficiency. As Tuskegee's student body grew, eventually reaching 1,500, industrialists like Andrew Carnegie and John D. Rockefeller consulted the school's director about making donations to other African American vocational institutions. Washington's reputation for reliability generated an invitation to address the Cotton States and International Exposition in Atlanta in 1895.

The Atlanta speech cemented Washington's position as the nation's foremost African American leader. Reiterating calls for hard work, economic improvement, and self-help, the Tuskegee administrator told blacks to "cast down your bucket where you are." By temporarily accepting a separate social status for African Americans and minimizing political demands, Washington offered an accommodationist strategy for southern race relations. Yet his emphasis on black education contradicted racial demagogues like Missis-

sippi's James Vardaman, who believed that schooling was wasted on African Americans. Convinced that political rights would follow economic success, Washington formed the National Negro Business League in 1900. He summarized the self-help strategy in his widely acclaimed autobiography *Up from Slavery* (1901) and won an invitation to dine with President Theodore Roosevelt at the White House.

As segregation laws, voter disenfranchisement, and lynchings spread across the turn-of-the-century South, African American leaders became divided in their response to Washington's strategies. Supporters claimed that the Tuskegee director had wrung essential assistance from northern whites in a period of dangerous racial tension. Yet black professionals and intellectuals asserted that accommodation sacrificed racial pride and that Washington used his patronage powers to ostracize outspoken opponents of white supremacy. Other African American leaders feared that vocational training would permanently relegate black workers to marginal status.

Washington responded to southern racial hysteria by secretly buying stock in black newspapers and financing court challenges to racial segregation. Yet as a consultant on race relations to Presidents Theodore Roosevelt and William Howard Taft, Washington exerted considerable influence on patronage appointments for African Americans and jealously guarded his political power, even hiring a network of informants and agents in black institutions. By 1905 northern leaders such as Boston newspaper editor Monroe Trotter and historian and sociologist W.E.B. Du Bois were mounting open attacks on Washington's accommodationist strategies. Nevertheless, the distinguished principal of Tuskegee remained a symbol of African American aspiration, dignity, and self-mastery long after his death in 1915. ■

WILLIAM EDWARD BURGHARDT DU BOIS
1868–1963

Brown Brothers

"The problem of the twentieth century," W.E.B. Du Bois declared in 1900, "is the problem of the color line."

An African American native of Great Barrington, Massachusetts, Du Bois earned undergraduate degrees from Fisk University and from Harvard University before receiving a Harvard Ph.D. in history after writing a dissertation on the slave trade. Du Bois began his academic career in 1894 by teaching classical languages at Ohio's all-black Wilberforce University. He then became an assistant instructor of sociology at the University of Pennsylvania, where he completed a pioneering study of Philadelphia's African American community. Between 1897 and 1910 Du Bois served as professor of economics and history at Atlanta University, another African American institution.

As a young instructor at Wilberforce, Du Bois had complimented Booker T. Washington's Atlanta Exposition address as "a word fitly spoken." However, traumatized by a well-publicized Georgia lynching in 1899 and moved by participation in the first Pan African Conference in London in 1900, Du Bois eventually rejected accommodationist strategies. In *The Souls of Black Folk* (1903), the scholar melded academic and partisan prose in a penetrating view of U.S. race relations. "The Negro is a sort of seventh son," he wrote, "born with a veil, and gifted with second sight in this American world" because every black was "an American, a Negro; two souls, two thoughts." Du Bois criticized Washington's toleration of disenfranchisement and racial segregation and called for a "talented tenth" to lead African Americans to social inclusion.

Seeking an outlet for political protest, Du Bois convened a 1905 conference dedicated to "Negro freedom and growth." Although the Tuskegee machine organized a boycott of the conference by the black press, delegates issued Du Bois's Declaration of Principles, cowritten with Monroe Trotter, which was the first collective demand for full citizenship rights for African Americans in U.S. history. After several yearly "Niagara movement" meetings, Du Bois joined a group of white reformers and Progressives in 1909 to form the National Association for the Advancement of Colored People.

Designed as an interracial movement to press acceptance of civil and social rights for African Americans, the NAACP chose Du Bois as its director of publicity and research and as the editor of its monthly magazine, *The Crisis*. He used this position to foster political empowerment and racial pride among African Americans participating in the Great Migration from the South. A sign of Du Bois's influence came in 1917 when the brilliant editor organized New York City's silent march against lynching. By then his editorials and articles had helped to spread the NAACP across both the North and the South and to make it the most important African American institution in the nation.

Intent on experiment and self-discovery, Du Bois moved from support of capitalism in the 1890s to brief involvement with the Socialist Party between 1911 and 1912. In subsequent years the great scholar and polemicist embraced Marxian social analyses, joined the Communist Party, and went into self-imposed exile in Ghana. Never a mass leader, Du Bois nevertheless used his intellect to shape modern perceptions of race and civil rights activism. ■

PURITY AND SOCIAL FEMINISM

Social reform often overlapped the ongoing purity crusade. The movement for moral purification had roots in pre–Civil War evangelical, temperance, and antislavery campaigns. Promoted primarily by affluent women, it sought to solve the moral crisis in urban-industrial society by purifying the middle-class home. Moral reformers acknowledged that strong personal character and disciplined families depended on a wholesome social environment. Accordingly, the liquor trade became one of the movement's earliest targets. During the winter of 1873–1874, Frances Willard organized protesting Ohio homemakers into the Women's Christian Temperance Union (WCTU). By 1900 the WCTU's antiliquor petition campaigns, marches, and rallies had enrolled 2 million members. Meanwhile, activists at Ohio's Oberlin College formed the Anti-Saloon League in 1893 as a unified "temperance trust" to take on the liquor industry. The league sought to win passage of an amendment to the U.S. Constitution that would prohibit the sale and distribution of alcoholic beverages.

Prostitution was a second target of the purity crusade. Red-light districts existed openly in post–Civil War cities. Many young female newcomers found themselves either coerced or enticed into prostitution, which could bring six

Norton and Peel, Minnesota Historical Society

These middle-class women in Minneapolis were characteristic of Anglo-Protestant women who endeavored during the Progressive Era to teach social responsibility to the lower class. Later, professional social workers would take over many of these reform activities.

times the earnings of wage labor. Reformers such as Elizabeth Blackwell and Caroline Wilson, two of the first women physicians, and Antoinette Blackwell, the first woman ordained as a Protestant minister, campaigned against the "double standard" that allowed affluent married men to have promiscuous relations with prostitutes but insisted that their wives avoid extramarital liaisons. By abolishing "white slavery," reformers hoped to destroy the sexual marketplace and force men to accept the monogamous standards required of middle-class women. Activists also supported organizations to aid urban newcomers such as the Young Men's Christian Association (YMCA), the Young Women's Christian Association (YWCA), and the Traveler's Aid Society. Extending the germ theory of the biological sciences to the social sphere, urban purity crusaders called for a parental state to administer "preventative medicine" to counteract "social evil."

Prostitution dramatized the seemingly dangerous plight of adolescent males. Although new self-help books often stressed the importance of personality and charm for young men, more traditional guides continued to focus on careers and warn about the hazards of sexual relationships. Adolescents were to avoid the temptations of drink and fallen women and marry partners with the character of their mothers. Virtuous women would provide homes that protected husbands from the pathology of the chaotic city. Although many guides considered women to be more spiritual than men, they also warned that women were controlled by physical appetites instead of intellect. Supposedly deficient in rational capacities, the "weaker sex" was to be excluded from political and public life. Some self-help guides also cautioned that a wife who was overly desirous of sexual pleasure might become "a drag on the energy, spirit, and resolution of her partner."

Disciplined and competitive athletics, played in uniform under the direction of adults, provided one of the most important sanctioned outlets for male adolescents. Turn-of-the-century private schools and universities in the Northeast pioneered participation in football and baseball, as well as in basketball, which was devised by a YMCA youth worker in New England. Football was a particular favorite of a generation that admired the channeling of aggressive energy into team cooperation and collective discipline. Theodore Roosevelt marveled at the "hardihood, physical prowess, and courage" required by the sport. *The New York Times* agreed and remarked that football "educated boys in those characteristics that had made the Anglo-Saxon race preeminent in history." The spread of boxing, fencing, bicycling, and outdoor activity as well as the creation of the Boy and Girl Scouts all attested to middle- and upper-class acceptance of Roosevelt's advocacy of the "strenuous life."

Early-twentieth-century purity crusaders escalated the crusade against prostitution into a public health campaign. As pathologists isolated the organisms that caused syphilis and gonorrhea, blood tests revealed that diseased persons could pass "silent infections" to unsuspecting partners. Physicians also attributed many reproductive tract problems and birth defects to venereal diseases. Social hygienists prevailed upon municipalities to set up venereal disease clinics and marshaled medical evidence to demand that state police power curb commercial prostitution. By 1912 reformers had established vice commissions in most larger cities. In New York, merchants, professionals, social workers, and religious leaders organized a Committee of Fourteen in 1904 to monitor illicit activity. To prevent young women from falling into the vice trade, Portland,

MARGARET HIGGINS SANGER
1883–1966

Culver Pictures

Feminist and birth control advocate Margaret Higgins was the sixth of eleven children born to an Irish-Catholic family in the factory town of Corning, New York. Precluded by financial and social pressures from attending medical school, she became a nurse and then married shortly after graduation, despite her assertion that "marriage was akin to suicide."

As an obstetric nurse, Sanger saw numerous cases of self-inflicted abortion among patients on the poverty-stricken Lower East Side of Manhattan. One woman she nursed to recovery begged her doctor for contraceptive information only to be told, "Tell Jake to sleep on the roof." When the patient died six months later during a second abortion attempt, Sanger said, "[I] came to a sudden realization that my work as a nurse and my activities in social science were entirely palliative and consequently futile and useless to relieve the misery I saw all about me."

"No woman can call herself free who does not own or control her body," wrote Sanger. Convinced that women could take control of their lives only by first achieving reproductive freedom, she dedicated herself to the cause of "birth control," a term she herself coined. Sanger spent a year studying contraception, and then in 1914 began publication of *Woman Rebel*, a journal whose masthead read, "No Gods; No Masters." In its first issue Sanger asserted that a woman would secure "life, liberty and the pursuit of happiness" when she became "absolute mistress of her own body." Only then could the "new woman" gain "the highest possible ful-

Oregon, hired Lola G. Baldwin in 1908 as the nation's first municipally paid policewoman. Reformers won passage of the Mann Act of 1910, which made transporting a woman to another state for immoral purposes a federal crime.

Although concerns about female health framed discourse over prostitution, the debate over contraception proved far more divisive. Public health workers such as Margaret Sanger saw "birth control" as a means of preventing the ill effects of excessive pregnancies. Radical feminists such as Emma Goldman hoped that women could use contraception to gain more control over their lives. Other advocates sought to reduce high birthrates among immigrants and the poor. Yet many purity reformers saw birth control as an affront to women's role as nurturer and feared that carefree sexual intercourse would lead to rampant promiscuity. Accordingly, groups such as the New York Society for the Prevention of Vice campaigned against sending contraceptive or abortion medications through the mail. Sanger was forced to close her first birth control clinic in 1916 when she faced indictment on obscenity charges. Two years later a Supreme Court ruling permitted doctors to distribute birth control information, although state laws still prohibited the sale of contraceptives.

Concerned that new forms of entertainment threatened to facilitate and popularize sexual promiscuity and social irresponsibility, purity crusaders and social workers cooperated in the promotion of wholesome recreation. Their efforts

fillment of her desires on the highest possible plane."

Sanger advocated the diaphragm because it gave women control over reproduction. Her efforts attracted the attention of Anglo-Protestant women eager to limit the size of their own families and anxious to control the growing immigrant population in the cities. Indeed, despite her early radicalism, Sanger consistently received a more sympathetic hearing from the middle class than from the working class. Yet birth control provoked intense opposition from conservative moralists, the Roman Catholic church, and a great many men. "If the women flinch from bleeding," Theodore Roosevelt warned, "the deserved death of the race takes place even quicker." Sanger's use of specific terms such as gonorrhea and syphilis made her early publications even more controversial.

The male-dominated federal legal structure acted quickly to suppress Sanger's work by indicting her on nine counts of sending birth control information through the mail. Those charges carried potential prison terms of forty-five years. Defying feminist purity crusaders by asserting reproductive rights,

Sanger fled to Europe, where she met English psychologist Havelock Ellis and inspected birth control clinics in Holland. The federal government dropped the charges against Sanger when she returned home in 1916, but almost immediately she provoked authorities again by opening the first U.S. birth control clinic in Brooklyn. Although Sanger went to jail for thirty days, her case helped to lay the groundwork for future court rulings permitting contraceptive advice "for the prevention and cure of disease."

Because most states still prohibited the sale of contraceptives, Sanger established the American Birth Control League in 1921 to encourage physicians and social workers to press judges to permit the distribution of information on contraceptives. The struggle to disseminate birth control knowledge consumed the next two decades of Margaret Sanger's life. However, not until 1965 did a Supreme Court decision definitively strike down all laws restricting the use of contraceptive devices. By then the American pioneer of birth control had become an early advocate of the contraceptive pill. ■

resulted in stricter licensing of cabarets, the prevention of liquor sales on dance floors, and the stationing of policewomen at amusement parks and dance pavilions. Motion pictures provided a particularly difficult challenge for reformers concerned about crime, sexuality, and violations of Victorian propriety among immigrants and working-class youth. Social workers John Collier and Jane Addams helped to form the National Board of Review in 1908 to preview films and eliminate objectionable material. The Board soon set national standards for the industry that incorporated Anglo-Protestant standards of propriety. In 1910 San Francisco censors rejected thirty-two films—including *Saved by a Sailor*, *In Hot Pursuit*, and *The Black Viper*—as "unfit for public exhibition." By the early 1920s a hundred American cities and eight states had created similar commissions to monitor the fantasies presented on the screen.

PROHIBITION AND WOMEN'S SUFFRAGE

Purity reformers also crusaded against the dangers of substance abuse. The use of narcotics such as opium, morphine, and cocaine had grown steadily

Three large-girthed Democratic bosses—George N. Lewis, John S. Kelly, and John J. Mahon—enjoy a mug of beer. Many Progressives linked machine politics and saloons.

throughout the nineteenth century. Physicians often prescribed diluted opium, a substance readily available in patent medicine. The popular soft drink Coca-Cola contained small amounts of cocaine until 1903. By the turn of the century the United States had about 250,000 narcotics addicts in a period during which public opinion linked drug use with the Chinese American and African American communities.

The rapidly developing health care professions supported the move to regulate narcotics. Eager to establish professional standards of practice, doctors and pharmacists embraced the idea that widespread drug use was socially harmful. The American Medical Association (AMA) and the American Pharmaceutical Association (APA) insisted that only professionals with the appropriate credentials should dispense drugs. Other groups eager to impose middle-class standards of behavior on immigrant and racial groups joined the crusade. Responding to this pressure, Congress passed the Pure Food and Drug Act in 1906 and initiated federal regulation of the pharmaceutical industry. Three years later, the United States prohibited the importation of smoking opium. In 1914 the Harrison Narcotics Act stipulated that narcotics could be used only for medical purposes and required federal registration of all drug producers, a record of all sales, and a doctor's prescription for all drugs.

Despite the broad scope of the social justice and purity crusades, alcohol remained the main focus of early-twentieth-century reform. In the South, evangelical Protestants denounced the use of liquor as a sin. They were now joined by social service professionals who saw drinking as a social problem requiring state intervention. Throughout the nation, social hygienists and health care professionals depicted alcohol as a destructive drug that brought "serious and permanent" injury to "every function of the normal human body." Industrialists such as Henry Ford portrayed drinking as an obstacle to efficient production. The National Safety Council, founded by corporate interests in 1912, dramatized this point by noting the connection between alcohol use and industrial accidents.

Prohibition had distinct social implications for crusaders eager to universalize Anglo-Protestant notions of rationality, efficiency, and discipline. In northern cities, where reformers tied the liquor trade to ethnic political machines and working-class saloons, the crusade against alcohol targeted European immigrants accustomed to moderate drinking during religious holidays and family celebrations. Midwestern liturgical churches like the Lutherans opposed prohibition because they used wine in their rituals. In the South the drinking controversy intersected with racial politics when white supremacists asserted that abstinence would prevent African American men from raping white women. Yet women's reform groups of both races held inebriated white mobs responsible for most lynchings. Meanwhile, social feminists in all regions used the alcohol issue to initiate discussion of spousal abuse and neglect by drunken husbands.

With evangelical churches as a base, prohibitionists persuaded two-thirds of the counties in the South to "vote dry" by 1907. Supporters like William Jennings Bryan praised antiliquor laws as a triumph of the democratic majority over the corrupt and exploitative liquor interests. Ironically, the movement's power rested on the effectiveness of the Anti-Saloon League, which organized itself as a nationwide lobby and dispersed professional agents to influence public officials. By 1909 six states had passed prohibition laws. Four years later the Webb-Kenyon Act permitted dry states to interdict the transportation of liquor across their boundaries. By 1917, when supporters sought congressional approval for an amendment to the Constitution, nineteen states already had enacted alcohol prohibition legislation.

By pitting the organized power of women's civic groups and purity organizations against liquor interests and urban electoral machines, prohibition brought middle-class women into the political arena and dramatized the power of the women's vote. Within six years of its founding in 1890, the National American Woman Suffrage Association (NAWSA) had seen four western states grant the franchise to women. Yet even as the three Pacific Coast states joined them between 1910 and 1912, national support for women's suffrage grew slowly. As NAWSA's membership surpassed 75,000 in the early 1910s, professional women and female college students began to link the vote to economic independence and sexual freedom. Yet the suffragist cause suffered from the disruptive image associated with a series of confrontational civil disobedience protests conducted in 1913 in the nation's capital by a group led by social worker Alice Paul.

NAWSA sought to reassert leadership over the suffrage crusade in 1915 by electing Carrie Chapman Catt as its president. A veteran campaigner, Catt retreated from attempts to challenge conventional gender roles and social inequality. Joining forces with the purity crusade, suffragists argued that they would be better able to exert a "womanly influence" for reform if they possessed the franchise. Catt had once implored Anglo-Protestants to "cut off the vote of the slums and give it to women." She now expanded this strategy into an appeal to the nativist and racial sentiments of the white middle class. Hostile to the ethnic voters of the industrial cities, NAWSA also rejected requests by black women's groups in the South for inclusion in the suffrage crusade. Although Catt's approach would leave profound ethnic, racial, and class rifts in the women's movement, NAWSA's membership leaped to 2 million by 1917.

Early-twentieth-century Americans sought to create order and stability in a society experiencing pervasive change. As the foundations of a consumer economy and pluralist society emerged in an uneven and chaotic fashion, social, economic, ethnic, racial, and cultural tensions threatened to destroy traditional social ideals. Inevitably, these clashes spilled into the political arena, where they stimulated movements to refashion the state to redress grievances and prepare the nation for future challenges.

SUGGESTED READINGS

Corporate consolidation is explored in segments of Alfred D. Chandler, Jr., *Scale and Scope: The Dynamics of Industrial Capitalism* (1990). For technological developments, see George Basalla, *The Evolution of Technology* (1988), and James R. Beninger, *The Control Revolution: Technologicalization and the Economic Origins of the Information Society* (1986). Taylorization is the subject of Daniel Nelson, *Frederick W. Taylor and the Rise of Scientific Management* (1980). The social implications of corporate innovations are described in Olivier Zunz, *Making America Corporate, 1870–1920* (1990); David F. Noble, *America by Design: Science, Technology, and the Rise of Corporate Capitalism* (1977); and Martin J. Sklar, *The Corporate Reconstruction of American Capitalism, 1890–1916: The Market, the Law, and Politics* (1988). See also the pioneering Robert Wiebe, *The Search for Order, 1877–1920* (1968). Note the relevant segments of William G. Robbins, *Colony and Empire: The Capitalist Transformation of the American West* (1994).

Immigration is described in Alan M. Kraut, *The Huddled Masses: The Immigrant in American Society, 1880–1921* (1982). John Higham, *Strangers in the Land: Patterns of American Nativism, 1860–1925* (1955) is the standard work on anti-immigrant thought but should be supplemented by Ronald Takaki, *A Different Mirror: A History of Multicultural America* (1993). For the Asian American experience, see Sucheng Chan, *This Bittersweet Soil: The Chinese in California Agriculture, 1869–1910* (1987), and Robert A. Wilson and Bill Hosokawa, *East to America: A History of the Japanese in the United States* (1980). Native American history is described in Frederick Hoxie, *A Final Promise: The Campaign to Assimilate the Indians, 1880–1920* (1984), and H. Craig Miner, *The Corporation and the Indian, 1865–1907* (1976). For the use of Chicanos as agricultural labor, see John Moore and Alfredo Cuellar, *Mexican Americans* (1970). The best account of southern racial segregation is C. Vann Woodward, *The Origins of the New South, 1877–1913* (1951), but see Neil R. McMillen, *Dark Journey: Black Mississippians in the Age of Jim Crow* (1989), and Cynthia Neverdon-Martin, *Afro-American Women of the South and the Advancement of the Race, 1895–1905* (1989).

The Irish American experience is explored with insight in Paul Messbarger, *Fiction with a Parochial Purpose: Social Use of American Catholic Literature, 1884–1900* (1970). Among works on immigrant Jews are Gerald Sorin, *A Time for Building: The Third Migration, 1880–1920* (1992); Elizabeth Ewen, *Immigrant*

Women in the Land of Dollars: Life and Culture on the Lower East Side, 1890–1925 (1985); and Susan A. Glenn, *Daughters of the Shtetl: Life and Labor in the Immigrant Generation* (1990). For urban culture, see the relevant segments of Howard Chudacoff, *The Evolution of American Urban Society* (1975). The physical development of cities is surveyed in the appropriate sections of Leland Roth, *A Concise History of American Architecture* (1979). For treatment of the new journalism, see Louis Filler, *Muckraking and Progressivism in the American Tradition* (rev. ed., 1995).

Innovations in family structure are summarized in the relevant segments of John D'Emilio and Estelle B. Freedman, *Intimate Matters: A History of Sexuality in America* (1988). See also Elaine Tyler May, *Great Expectations: Marriage and Divorce in Post-Victorian America* (1980). The growth of consumer culture is treated in Susan Porter Benson, *Counter Cultures: Saleswomen, Managers, and Customers in American Department Stores, 1890–1940* (1986). For amusement parks, see John F. Kasson, *Amusing the Million: Coney Island at the Turn of the Century* (1978). Popular songs are explored in the relevant segments of Ian Whitcomb, *After the Ball: Popular Music from Rag to Rock* (1982). For ragtime, see Peter Gammond, *Scott Joplin and the Ragtime Era* (1976). Dance hall culture is the topic of Kathy Peiss, *Cheap Amusements: Working Women and Leisure in Turn-of-the-Century New York* (1986), and David Nasaw, *Going Out: The Rise and Fall of Public Amusements* (1993). See also Ronald L. Morris, *Wait Until Dark: Jazz and the Underworld, 1890–1940* (1988).

The significance of vaudeville is discussed in Robert W. Snyder, *The Voice of the City: Vaudeville and Popular Culture in New York* (1989). For motion pictures, see Charles Musser, *Before the Nickelodeon: Edwin S. Porter and the Edison Manufacturing Company* (1991) and *The Emergence of Cinema, 1907–1915* (1992), as well as Neil Gabler, *An Empire of Their Own: How the Jews Invented Hollywood* (1988), and Lary May, *Screening Out the Past: The Birth of Mass Culture and the Motion Picture Industry* (1980). See also Charles J. Maland, *Chaplin and American Culture: The Evolution of a Star Image* (1989), and Richard Schikel, *D.W. Griffith: An American Life* (1984).

Descriptions of late-nineteenth-century industrial work culture can be found in William Lazonick, *Competitive Advantage on the Shop Floor* (1990). For a specific study, see Patricia A. Cooper, *Once a Cigar Maker: Men, Women, and Work Culture in American Cigar Factories, 1900–1919* (1987). Southern labor conditions are addressed in David L. Carlton, *Mill and Town in South Carolina, 1880–1920* (1982). See also the relevant segments of Jacqueline Jones, *Labor of Love, Labor of Sorrow: Black Women, Work, and the Family from Slavery to the Present* (1985). Women office workers are the subject of Margery W. Davies, *Woman's Place Is at the Typewriter* (1982).

For the labor movement, see Michael Kazin, *Barons of Labor: The San Francisco Building Trades and Union Power in the Progressive Era* (1987), and the relevant essays in *The Populist Persuasion: An American History* (1995). The AFL is covered in Harold Livesay, *Samuel Gompers and Organized Labor in America* (1978). Regional labor protest can be found in Gary M. Fink, *The Fulton Bag and Cotton Mills Strike of 1914–1915* (1993); Alan Derickson, *Workers' Health, Workers' Democracy: The Western Miners' Struggle, 1891–1925* (1988); and Susan A. Glenn, *Daughters of the Shtetl*.

For the cultural ramifications of labor protest, see John Clendenin Townsend, *Running the Gauntlet: Cultural Sources of Violence Against the IWW* (1986). See also the insightful David Roediger, *The Wages of Whiteness: Race and the Making of the*

American Working Class (1991). For the influence of unions on government policy, see the relevant segments of Melvyn Dubofsky, *The State and Labor in Modern America* (1994). A shop-floor perspective on working-class politics can be found in David Montgomery, *The Fall of the House of Labor* (1987).

The Socialist movement is the subject of Nick Salvatore, *Eugene Debs, Citizen and Socialist* (1990). See also Mary Jo Buhle, *Women and American Socialism, 1870–1920* (1983), and L. Glen Sevetan, *Daniel De Leon: The Odyssey of an American Marxist* (1979). For anarchism, see Candace Serena Falk, *Love, Anarchy, and Emma Goldman: A Biography* (1984), and Marian J. Morton, *Emma Goldman and the American Left* (1992). The spirit of the bohemians is conveyed in Douglas Clayton, *Floyd Dell: The Life and Times of an American Rebel* (1994), and Mary V. Dearborn, *Queen of Bohemia: The Life of Louise Bryant* (1996). See also Robert A. Rosenstone, *A Romantic Revolutionary: A Biography of John Reed* (1990).

Ferment in the visual arts is addressed in Milton Brown, *The Story of the Armory Show* (1963), whereas the rebellion in literature is treated in Jay Martin, *Harvests of Change: American Literature, 1865–1914* (1967). For intellectual change and tradition, see David W. Noble, *The Progressive Mind, 1890–1917* (1970) and *The Paradox of Progressive Thought* (1958). Dewey's ideas are explained in Robert Westbrook, *John Dewey and American Democracy* (1991).

An account of the social gospel movement can be found in Robert Crunden, *Ministers of Reform: The Progressives' Achievement in American Civilization, 1899–1920* (1982), and in the relevant segments of George Marsden, *Fundamentalism and American Culture: The Shaping of Twentieth-Century Evangelicalism, 1870–1925* (1980). For social justice activism, see David B. Danbom, *"The World of Hope": Progressives and the Struggle for an Ethical Life* (1987). Labor reform is outlined in Elizabeth Anne Payne, *Reform, Labor, and Feminism: Margaret Dreier Robins and the Women's Trade Union League* (1988).

Social settlement centers are the subject of Doris Groshen Daniels, *Always a Sister: The Feminism of Lillian D. Wald* (1989); of Mina Carson, *Settlement Folk: Social Thought and the American Settlement Movement, 1885–1930* (1990); and of Rirka Shpak Lissak, *Pluralism and Progressives: Hull House and the New Immigrants, 1890–1919* (1989). For social service professionals, see Elisabeth Israels Perry, *Belle Moskowitz: Feminine Politics and the Exercise of Power in the Age of Alfred E. Smith* (1987), and Gloria E. Myers, *Municipal Mother: Portland's Lola Greene Baldwin, America's First Policewoman* (1995). See also Robyn Muncy, *Creating a Female Dominion in American Reform, 1890–1935* (1991); Theda Skocpol, *Protecting Soldiers and Mothers: The Political Origins of Social Policy in the United States* (1990); and the first half of Don Kirschner, *The Paradox of Professionalism: Reform and Public Service in Urban America, 1900–1940* (1986).

Northern migration by African Americans is portrayed in Nicholas Lemann, *The Promised Land: The Great Black Migration and How it Changed America* (1991), and James R. Grossman, *Land of Hope: Chicago, Black Southerners, and the Great Migration* (1989). For contrasting approaches to black politics, see Louis Harlan, *Booker T. Washington: The Wizard of Tuskegee* (1983), and David Levering Lewis, *W.E.B. Du Bois: Biography of a Race, 1868–1919* (1993).

The martial ethic is explored in segments of Jackson Lears, *No Place of Grace: Antimodernism and the Transformation of American Culture, 1880–1920* (1981). Background on the purity crusade can be found in David J. Pivar, *Purity Crusade: Sexual Morality and Social Control, 1868–1900* (1973). For the movement to abolish prostitution, see Barbara Meil Hobson, *Uneasy Virtue: The Politics of*

Prostitution and the American Reform Tradition (1987), and William Leach, *True and Perfect Union: Feminist Reform of Sex and Society* (1981). The birth control controversy is addressed in David Kennedy, *Birth Control in America: The Career of Margaret Sanger* (1970), and in the relevant segments of Linda Gordon, *Women's Body, Women's Right: A Social History of Birth Control in America* (1976). For the antiliquor crusade, see Richard F. Hamm, *Shaping the Eighteenth Amendment: Temperance Reform, Legal Culture, and the Polity, 1880–1920* (1995); K. Austin Kerr, *Organized for Prohibition: A New History of the Anti-Saloon League* (1985); and Joseph Gusfield, *Symbolic Crusade: Status Politics and the American Temperance Movement* (rev. ed., 1986).

Ties between purity activism and women's suffrage are explored in Janet Zollinger Giele, *The Paths to Women's Equality: Temperance, Suffrage, and the Origins of Modern Feminism* (1995). See also Rosalind Rosenberg, *Beyond Separate Spheres: The Intellectual Roots of Modern Feminism* (1982). The suffrage campaign is the topic of Steven M. Buechler, *The Transformation of the Woman Suffrage Movement: The Case of Illinois, 1850–1920* (1986); of Christine A. Lunardini, *From Equal Suffrage to Equal Rights: Alice Paul and the National Woman's Party, 1910–1928* (1986); and of Linda G. Ford, *Iron-Jawed Angels: The Suffrage Militancy of the National Woman's Party, 1912–1920* (1991). See also Aileen Kraditor, *The Ideas of the Woman Suffrage Movement, 1890–1920* (1965).

2

A dynamic speaker who "seems to throw the word into the air," Theodore Roosevelt addresses a crowd in Brattleboro, Vermont, 1903.

Corbis-Bettmann

THE POLITICS OF PROGRESSIVE REFORM, 1896–1912

The growth of the industrial economy had profound consequences for U.S. politics in the early twentieth century. Anglo-Protestant leaders, corporate modernizers, and middle-class professionals sought to use city, state, and federal governments to promote efficiency, expert rule, and social stability. Yet small farmers and independent business interests relied on politics to regulate corporate power and enhance a competitive economy. Meanwhile, urban social justice activists and ethnic politicians acted to protect working people and expand government social welfare. The result was progressive reform, a political movement of energy and intensity but also of complexity and contradiction. As the nation confronted the consequences of economic concentration, class polarization, and regional specialization, leaders in Washington sought to respond with domestic and foreign policies that simultaneously encouraged prosperity and social stability.

THE ELECTION OF 1896

Once nominated for the presidency, the Populist-Democratic candidate William Jennings Bryan barnstormed the country, traveling 18,000 miles by train to address 3 million people in a sustained plea for tariff and currency reform. Portraying industrial wage earners as independent producers who sold their labor to employers, Bryan used revivalistic rhetoric to persuade voters to join an evangelical crusade for populist and rural values. In contrast, Republican campaign manager Mark Hanna introduced corporate merchandising techniques to erode traditional party loyalty and appeal to voters as independent consumers. After Republican officials tapped the business community for more than $3.5 million in campaign funds, Hanna distributed millions of political pamphlets attacking Bryan as a radical. Instead of campaigning, McKinley stayed at home in Canton, Ohio, and delivered front-porch homilies to 750,000 visitors.

Packaged as the candidate of prosperity and inclusion, McKinley insisted that high tariffs would ensure "a full dinner pail" by protecting industrial workers from underpaid foreign competition. By addressing anxiety about depression, unemployment, and wage cuts, McKinley sought the support of ethnic and urban voters formerly repelled by Republican temperance crusades and anti-Catholicism. The Republicans also courted midwestern farmers who viewed the tariff as protection against foreign agricultural imports. By targeting economic growth, the McKinley campaign demonstrated that free silver and the restoration of traditional social values were not central issues for most of the nation's electorate. Bryan carried twenty-four states and nearly 48 percent of the popular vote. Yet McKinley's popularity among working-class and big-city voters produced a 51 percent majority and a 271–176 victory in the Electoral College.

THE QUEST FOR EMPIRE

McKinley fulfilled the promise to protect domestic industry and agriculture by signing the Dingley Tariff of 1897. Simultaneously, the failure of the European

Republican President William McKinley, who was elected in 1896.

wheat crop and the discovery of gold in Alaska restored prosperity by increasing farm exports, expanding the money supply, and spurring industrial output. Hoping to sustain economic recovery, McKinley turned to foreign policy.

Although nineteenth-century citizens had shown little interest in overseas affairs, corporate leaders became increasingly concerned with foreign markets, raw materials, and investment opportunities. As business and farm groups sought new outlets for the nation's surplus, they brought the domestic economy into a global marketplace. Pressure for a more assertive foreign policy also came from a group of upper-class patricians that included Captain Alfred Thayer Mahan, Theodore Roosevelt, Henry Cabot Lodge, and John Hay. This elite viewed imperialism as a stimulus to both national vitality and the reinvigoration of their own social class. "Americans must now begin to look outward," wrote Mahan, a naval officer and author of *The Influence of Sea Power upon History* (1890). Emphasizing U.S. needs for defense against rival powers, Mahan called for an expansionist foreign policy to secure strategic sea-lanes, overseas markets, and unity at home. Because of Mahan's influence, Washington developed a modern navy by 1898 and continued to expand it during the early twentieth century.

"I should welcome almost any war," declared Theodore Roosevelt, "for I think this country needs one." Roosevelt and his colleagues focused increasingly on the faltering Spanish empire in the Caribbean and the Pacific as an

WILLIAM JENNINGS BRYAN
1860–1925

Brown Brothers

"Money is to be the servant of man," shouted William Jennings Bryan, the foremost adversary of the "privileged classes" in the 1890s. "I protest against all theories that enthrone money and debase mankind."

The "Boy Orator of the Plains" was born in 1860 to a southern Illinois family of evangelical Baptists. His father was a politician and judge. After attending law school in Chicago, Bryan moved to Lincoln, Nebraska, in 1887. Three years later he rode a wave of agrarian unrest to become only the second Democrat in Nebraska history to win a seat in Congress. Opposed to the protective tariff, Bryan inaugurated his congressional career by depicting government "favoritism" toward greedy manufacturers as theft.

Opposition to privileges for wealthy interests dominated his political career. Voting against repeal of the Sherman Silver Purchase Act in 1893, Bryan directed his rage toward the gold standard supported by leaders of both political parties. He portrayed the "eternal war" against a gold currency as a struggle of democratic producers seeking equality before the law. On the other side were "the corporate interests . . . , the moneyed interests, aggregate wealth and capital, imperious, arrogant, compassionless." "The poor man who takes property by force is called a thief," protested Bryan, "but the creditor who can by legislation make a debtor pay a dollar twice as large as he borrowed is lauded as the friend of sound currency." Anticipating important strands of twentieth-century populism, the young politician attacked eastern financial elites for subservience to British finance and for social pretension.

After losing a race for the Senate in 1894, Bryan became editor-in-chief of the pro-silver *Omaha World-Herald* and toured the nation in support of currency-reform Democrats. When depression-weary politicians from the South and West took over the party's convention in 1896, they rebelled against the leadership of President Grover Cleveland and the gold standard. Bryan's political star rose when he used the platform debate to deliver a ringing endorsement of free silver. By fusing Christian evangelism with familiar distinctions between "idle holders of capital" and the "struggling masses," the young Nebraskan made one of the most electrifying speeches in U.S. political history.

"You shall not press down upon the brow of labor this crown of thorns," thundered Bryan. "You shall not crucify mankind upon a cross of gold."

When enthusiastic delegates nominated Bryan for the presidency on the fifth ballot, he was only thirty-six years old. Endorsed as well by the Populist Party, the candidate used rail transit to cross the country in a tireless crusade denouncing "money loaners," "corporate employers," and "trusts and syndicates." Bryan's efforts won him the entire South and most of the West, but his 6.5 million votes fell short of an Electoral College majority.

Undeterred by defeat, Bryan ran again for president in 1900 and 1908. A passionate reformer, he viewed Christianity as a temporal and sacred creed that reflected the democratic wisdom of the people. Although Bryan failed to adjust to changes in the ethnic, religious, and cultural composition of urban life, his association with antiimperialism, corporate reform, labor legislation, aid to farmers, a graduated federal income tax, women's suffrage, the direct election of senators, and the initiative and referendum left a profound impact on the twentieth century. "You cannot deny that I have kept the faith," he once declared. ∎

Exhibit 2-1. Election of 1896

	WASH. 4	MONTANA 3	N.D. 3	MINN. 9		VT. 4	ME. 9

(Map of the United States showing electoral votes by state for the Election of 1896)

State electoral votes shown on the map:

WASH. 4 · ORE. 4 · MONTANA 3 · IDAHO 3 · N.D. 3 · MINN. 9 · WIS. 12 · MICH. 14 · VT. 4 · ME. 9 · N.H. 4 · MASS. 15 · NEV. 3 · UTAH 3 · WYO. · S.D. 4 · NEB. 8 · IOWA · ILL. 24 · IND. 15 · OHIO 23 · PA. 32 · N.Y. 36 · R.I. 4 · CONN. 6 · N.J. 10 · DEL. 3 · MD. 8 · CALIF. 8 · ARIZONA TERRITORY · NEW MEXICO TERRITORY · COLO. 4 · KAN. 10 · MO. 17 · OKLAHOMA TERRITORY · ARK. 8 · TENN. 12 · KY. 12 · W.VA. 6 · VA. 12 · N.C. 11 · S.C. 9 · MISS. 9 · ALA. 11 · GA. 13 · LA. 8 · TEXAS 15 · FLA. 4

	Electoral vote	Popular vote
McKinley (Republican)	271	7,036,000
Bryan (Democrat)	176	6,468,000

Numbers in each state show electoral vote

opportunity for U.S. expansion. Between the 1860s and the 1890s the nation repeatedly expressed popular support for Cuba's revolt against Spanish colonialism. As the fighting on the island raged, the yellow journalism of William Randolph Hearst and Joseph Pulitzer molded national opinion by providing sensationalist coverage of Spanish concentration camps and others methods of pacification. When artist Frederic Remington cabled Hearst from Havana that hostilities were not imminent, the publisher responded, "You furnish the pictures and I'll furnish the war."

Just beginning to recover from the Depression in 1898, corporate and banking leaders feared that a Caribbean war might again destabilize the economy. Yet they also worried about the uncertainty generated by the Cuban Revolution and Spain's inability to deal effectively with the uprising. Long interested in constructing a commercial waterway across the isthmus of Central America to tie Atlantic seaports to the markets of the Pacific and Asia, U.S. officials had important strategic interests in the region. Moreover, the State Department and the military warned that expansion-minded Germany might fill the vacuum left behind if the Spanish retreated from Cuba. While civil war wracked Cuba in 1897, McKinley signed an annexation treaty with a revolutionary regime that had been created by U.S. interests in Hawaii, although a bloc of "antiimperialists" prevented immediate ratification in the Senate.

A sensational contemporary lithograph graphically depicts the sinking of the U.S. battleship Maine *in Havana harbor, an event that helped to initiate the Spanish-American War.*

THE SPANISH-AMERICAN WAR AND THE OPEN DOOR POLICY

After rioting broke out in Havana in 1898, McKinley sent the battleship *Maine* to Cuba. Two weeks later the ship mysteriously exploded and sank, and 260 U.S. sailors were lost. A naval court attributed the explosion to a mine but could not fix responsibility. As newspaper headlines screamed "Remember the *Maine*," the yellow press pictured the blast as the work of Spanish agents. Exasperated by the Cuban situation, McKinley requested a declaration of war, even though Spain was meeting U.S. demands for an armistice and an end to

Exhibit 2-2. U.S. Military Personnel on Active Duty, 1896–1900

1896	41,680
1897	43,656
1898	235,785
1899	100,166
1900	125,923

Source: *Historical Statistics of the United States, Colonial Times to 1970* (1975).

A swaggering Theodore Roosevelt poses with the Rough Riders atop San Juan Hill in Cuba.

concentration camps. In its war resolution Congress recognized Cuban independence and demanded Spain's withdrawal. Through the Teller Amendment, the United States disclaimed any interest in annexation and asserted that control of the island would be left to its people.

Secretary of State John Hay characterized the Spanish-American conflict as a "splendid little war." The U.S. Navy quickly took the strategic initiative when Commodore George Dewey defeated the Spanish fleet in the Philippines. After less than three months of ineffective and poorly organized fighting, Spanish troops surrendered in Cuba, Puerto Rico, and the Philippines. In Cuba a land force of 17,000 soldiers included the "Rough Riders," a cavalry unit under the command of Colonel Leonard Wood and Lieutenant Colonel Theodore Roosevelt. After the celebrated regiment took heavy casualties while storming Santiago's strategic San Juan Hill, the remnants of the Spanish fleet were destroyed by U.S. battleships. Although U.S. war fatalities amounted to a mere 379, more than 5,000 soldiers died from tropical diseases, inadequate sanitation, and rotten meat. Yet the popular crusade stimulated U.S. nationalism and a desire for overseas empire.

Once the Spanish-American War began, McKinley convinced Congress to pass a joint resolution authorizing the annexation of Hawaii. Under the Paris

Exhibit 2-3. The U.S. Pacific Empire, 1899

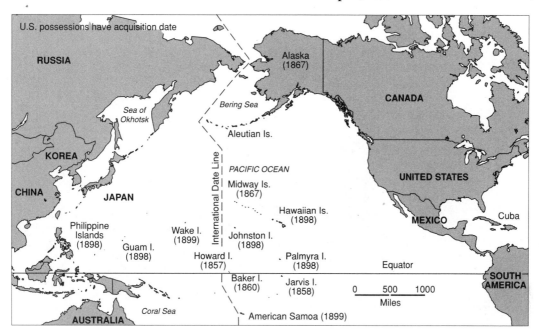

Peace Treaty of 1898 Spain relinquished control of Cuba and ceded the Philippines, Guam, and Puerto Rico to the United States. The nation now stood on the brink of a territorial empire. Yet nineteenth-century traditions of nonintervention and self-determination clashed with the imperialist aspirations of the McKinley administration. The Anti-Imperialist League, organized in 1898, opposed Senate ratification of the Paris Peace Treaty and attempted to build a broad-based coalition opposed to the annexation of overseas territory. Led by William Jennings Bryan, former presidents Benjamin Harrison and Grover Cleveland, industrialist Andrew Carnegie, labor leader Samuel Gompers, and intellectuals such as William James, William Graham Sumner, and Mark Twain, the league denounced the building of an empire as a violation of the nation's most fundamental values.

Antiimperialists feared that a nation with colonial commitments could not preserve liberty at home. Many southern Democrats also objected to the annexation of colonies whose "colored" population might corrupt the purity of the white race. Finally, opponents of territorial expansion argued that U.S. trade could be extended without the acquisition of colonies or the use of military force. However, imperialists insisted that only annexation could provide the military security necessary to pursue trade opportunities against competing nations in the Caribbean, Pacific, and East Asia. The resulting 57–27 vote in favor of accepting the Paris treaty barely met the two-thirds requirement for Senate ratification but steered the nation toward a new emphasis on foreign expansion.

In 1898 the Paris Peace Treaty gave Cuba nominal independence. Three years later, the United States forced Cubans to accept the Platt Amendment to the Cuban constitution. This proviso gave Washington broad authority over Cuban

Four thousand U.S. soldiers died in the four-year struggle to "pacify" the Philippines, a Pacific archipelago McKinley had once dismissed as "those darned islands."

domestic affairs, allowed the United States to establish a permanent naval base at Guantanamo Bay, and permitted U.S. military intervention at will. Meanwhile, in the Philippines, insurgents led by Emilio Aguinaldo turned their struggle against Spain into a war against the U.S. Army. Troops responded with pacification programs, which placed peasants in concentration camps and destroyed their villages and crops. Using the same techniques that the United States once condemned in Spanish-occupied Cuba, the U.S. Army relied on torture to break the morale of rebel leaders and ultimately killed more than 200,000 Filipinos before crushing the persistent uprising.

Although the United States had pacified the Caribbean and had established military outposts in Hawaii, Guam, and the Philippines, its position in East Asia remained weak. In 1899 Secretary of State John Hay issued the first in a series of Open Door Notes. Hay called for Japanese and European governments to refrain from discriminatory trade practices in their spheres of influence in China. When nationalist Chinese students rioted against foreign domination during the "Boxer Rebellion" of 1900, the United States sent 2,500 troops to join the major powers in restoring order. Fearing that the crisis might lead to abandonment of the Open Door policy, Hay issued a second note supporting China as a "territorial and administrative entity" and endorsing "equal and impartial trade." By ruling out U.S. colonial ambitions and an extended presence in China, the secretary sought to assure domestic critics that the Philippine mistake would not be repeated. Although the United States lacked the naval power to enforce the Open Door policy, Europe and Japan acquiesced because they hoped to avoid war over the division of China.

Urban Progressives and Reformers

While national leaders looked to overseas expansion, a group of elite Anglo-Protestants addressed corruption and inefficiency in city government. Reformers confronted powerful patronage machines such as New York's Tammany Hall, which by the 1890s controlled a payroll of $12 million and more jobs than Carnegie Steel. Social worker Jane Addams guessed that 20 percent of all voters in her Chicago district depended upon the goodwill of the ward alderman for employment. By fixing police appointments, machine bosses facilitated pay-offs from liquor, prostitution, gambling, and other vice operations. City officials also sold municipal contracts for public transit lines, road construction, and public utilities. In 1903 corporate bribes for New York City franchises surpassed $470 million.

Although Tammany politician George Washington Plunkitt defended such activity as "honest graft," critics charged that corruption placed intolerable burdens on municipal treasuries and taxpayers. Beginning in the 1870s, urban reformers such as E.L. Godkin, editor of *The Nation*, proposed to attack patronage by using merit examinations for public employees. The Civil Service Act of 1883 established such tests for a small percentage of federal job seekers. When Republicans declined to support expansion of civil service reform in the 1884 presidential election, several so-called "Mugwumps" deserted the party. One Republican patrician, Theodore Roosevelt, remained loyal to the national ticket but embraced the crusade against municipal corruption in 1886 by running for mayor of New York City on a reform platform.

Roosevelt lost the race for mayor but won election to the presidency of the New York Board of Police Commissioners in 1895 as an antivice candidate. Three years later the city of San Francisco received a self-government charter from the California state legislature and instituted civil service testing procedures. Known as "Progressives," municipal activists sought to have government serve the "public interest." Rejecting nineteenth-century notions of a self-regulating and apolitical marketplace, the reformers sought to modernize and rationalize city government by using trained professionals. Advocates of urban revitalization celebrated middle-class ideals of civic virtue, social responsibility, and citizenship, which they hoped to substitute for the ethnic and class loyalties that buttressed the boss system.

Progressive reform received its greatest boost when machine politicians in Galveston, Texas, were unable to deal with the effects of a devastating tidal wave in 1900. The disaster led to the election of a reform ticket and the restructuring of the city charter. Under the Galveston Plan, voters selected at-large city commissioners, each of whom administered a different part of the municipal bureaucracy. Civil service examinations were instituted to place hiring power in government agencies instead of ward syndicates. With its emphasis on efficiency, planning, and expert rule, the Galveston Plan professionalized the administration of urban government and encouraged a citywide perspective among officials.

As the newly organized National Municipal League popularized the commission system and called for the replacement of elected mayors by appointed city managers, muckraking exposes of urban political corruption reinforced the drive for reform. "The misgovernment of the American people is misgovernment *by* the American people," proclaimed Lincoln Steffens in *The Shame of the Cities* (1904). "The spirit of graft and lawlessness is the American spirit." Publicity about the nationwide pattern of corruption helped to strengthen the hand of reform mayors like Seth Low of New York City, Joseph Folk of St. Louis, James D. Phelan of San Francisco, and Mark Fagan of Jersey City. By 1909 one hundred U.S. municipalities had adopted the commissioner or manager form of government. Following the lead of reformers such as Detroit's Hazen S. Pingree, Toledo's Samuel M. Jones, and Cleveland's Thomas L. Johnson, many cities lowered public utility and transit rates. Seeking to minimize costs and reduce graft, two-thirds of the nation's cities owned and operated municipal waterworks by 1915.

Urban reformers introduced city planners, public health officials, sanitary engineers, housing officers, community development advisers, and corporate experts to municipal government. They also initiated the use of the secret ballot, moved voting from saloons to public schools and libraries, created nonpartisan contests, and established residency requirements for voter registration. Yet Progressive electoral reform diluted the voting impact of immigrant and working-class districts and depersonalized urban politics, which helped to produce a 20 percent decline in voter participation in municipal elections between 1890 and 1920. In turn, civil service examinations emphasized loyalty to the impersonal bureaucracy instead of solidarity with class, ethnic, neighborhood, and kinship groups.

Early-twentieth-century progressives soon directed their attention to state capitals. In the South, Democrats supported the direct primary, alcohol prohibition, workers' compensation, and regulation of railroads and other utilities. Yet the most dramatic advances came in the North. Between 1898 and 1910 Republican reform governors in Oregon, South Dakota, Wisconsin, Iowa, and Missouri challenged boss control of legislatures and party conventions by approving such procedural reforms as the direct primary, the referendum, and the voters' initiative. Northern reformers soon passed laws to regulate the labor of women and children while increasing spending for education, public health, and social welfare. The embodiment of state Progressive reform was Wisconsin, where insurgent governor Robert M. La Follette demanded a "new citizenship" to place the "public interest" above corrupt influences. Using university-trained experts to staff regulatory agencies, La Follette laid the groundwork for the "Wisconsin Idea" and the state's reputation as "the laboratory of democracy."

Progressive reform also produced Governor Joseph Folk's "Missouri Idea," a program that used the power of the law to restrain bribery, bossism, and excessive corporate power. Folk's administration passed legislation to regulate lobbyists, railroads, and insurance companies and pressed trusts such as Standard Oil to refrain from monopoly practices or price gouging. Seeking to compel corporations and "selfish" entities to submit to regulation in the public interest, Republican insurgents such as Albert B. Cummins, Albert J. Beveridge, Charles Evans Hughes, and Hiram W. Johnson rode reform waves to the governorships of Iowa, Indiana, New York, and California, respectively. As the arena of progressive reform shifted to national politics, all but Hughes would eventually join La Follette on the floor of the U.S. Senate.

ROOSEVELT AND CORPORATE PROGRESSIVISM

Renominated as the Democratic candidate for president in 1900, William Jennings Bryan sought to make the contest a referendum on imperialism. A self-governing republic "can have no subjects," proclaimed Bryan. "Every citizen is a sovereign, but . . . no one cares to wear a crown." Despite such sentiments, most voters believed the Senate had settled the issue when it approved annexation of the Philippines. Meanwhile, Republicans accepted Theodore Roosevelt as President McKinley's running mate. Returning prosperity and the successful war against Spain brought the incumbents 52 percent of the vote versus the Democrats' 45 percent. Yet six months after his inauguration, McKinley was shot twice at point-blank range by anarchist Leon Czolgosz while attending the Pan-American Exposition in Buffalo. The president died a few days later. "Now look," exclaimed grief-stricken Mark Hanna as Theodore Roosevelt assumed the nation's highest office, "that damned cowboy is president of the United States!"

Theodore Roosevelt brought to the White House a vigor and imagination not seen since the administration of Abraham Lincoln. The son of a wealthy, established New York family, Roosevelt was born to comfort and poor health. He shook off the sickliness of his youth with a vigorous commitment to the strenuous life and grew to adulthood with a conviction that violence and struggle remained the basic ingredients of the human condition. The purpose of a man, Roosevelt declared, was to "work, fight, and breed." Suspicious of the materialism of his era, he welcomed war as "something to think about which isn't material gain." Yet although he was known as a soldier, cowboy, and big-game hunter, Roosevelt also had distinguished himself as an author of historical works on westward expansion and naval history.

The new president brought the same emphasis on manly action to the world of politics. "Roosevelt, more than any other man living . . . was pure act," exclaimed his contemporary, historian Henry Adams. At a time when most patricians of the upper class shunned politics, the energetic New Yorker saw the pursuit of public office as a social responsibility and zestfully embraced his task. He served a term in the New York State assembly and sat on the United States Civil Service Commission. As the head of the New York City Board of Police Commissioners, Roosevelt prowled the city streets at night to observe the police at work and enforced the city's blue laws regulating private morality. After returning from the Spanish-American War, the popular Roosevelt won election as governor of New York. Republican Party bosses, fearful of the governor's energy and progressive leanings, persuaded McKinley to remove Roosevelt from the state by placing him on the 1900 ticket. McKinley's assassination made the forty-two-year-old Roosevelt the youngest president in U.S. history.

IDA MINERVA TARBELL
1857–1944

At a time when social conventions usually bound women to traditional roles, Ida Tarbell rejected domestic life to become a journalist. Fascinated by science from girlhood, she entered Allegheny College as a biology student in 1876 and was determined to pursue a career, but she soon discovered that in science "there was almost nothing . . . open to women." Upon graduation Tarbell became a teacher, entering a profession more accessible to women, but she fled the classroom and its "killing schedule" after two years. She then took a job in a magazine office and began to write. In 1891 Tarbell broke with her comfortable but mundane surroundings and went to Paris, where she met S. S. McClure of *McClure's Magazine*, a successful popular periodical with a large middle-class readership. Throughout the 1890s she published occasional pieces for *McClure's* and worked on anecdotal biographies of Napoleon Bonaparte and Abraham Lincoln.

Brown Brothers

Tarbell's combination of patient study, objective observation, and fair-minded ethics made her a leading muckraker of the early twentieth century. Prodded by the shrewd McClure, she spent five years doing research and interviews for a story about Standard Oil, the "mother" of trusts. The resulting nineteen articles for *McClure's* and the two-volume *History of the Standard Oil Company* (1904) portrayed a pattern of corporate bribery, fraud, coercion, double-dealing, and outright violence that constituted a searing indictment of the morality of the trusts. Tarbell saw herself as a reporter who gathered facts that spoke for themselves. Uncomfortable with characterizations as the "Joan of Arc of the oil industry," she took little interest when the federal government began an antitrust suit against Standard Oil in 1907. As she later remembered in her autobiography, Tarbell found herself "fifty, fagged, wanting to be let alone

---

The new incumbent viewed the presidency as the powerful focal point of the political process and as a national symbol. Roosevelt used the office as a "bully pulpit" from which he could set the national agenda, define the public interest, and mold public opinion. The president realized that a popular and public-relations-minded chief executive could skillfully use the press to build new kinds of political support not available to predecessors. Deliberately personalizing the office, he presented himself as a tribune of the people who was ready to act decisively on their behalf. For example, the White House took the initiative in dealing with Congress by sending drafts of proposed bills to Capitol Hill and then lobbying vigorously for the legislation's passage.

Roosevelt used the presidency to advance a "corporate progressivism" that accepted the existence of big business but used the state to regulate it in the public interest. "Our aim is not to do away with corporations," he told Congress. "On the contrary, these big aggregations are the inevitable development of modern industrialism, and the effort to destroy them would be futile." Yet Roosevelt feared that irresponsible and greedy management would encourage

while I collect trustworthy information for my articles."

The series in *McClure's* brought discussion of trust regulation into the homes of the middle class. Yet Tarbell remained a conservative in many areas. Despite her own experience with gender discrimination, she gave only tepid support to women's issues and criticized assertive feminist leaders for their alleged insensitivity to the importance of home and family. In a 1912 article entitled "Making a Man of Herself," Tarbell warned young women of "the essential barrenness of the achieving woman's triumph, its lack of the savor and tang of life, the multitude of makeshifts she must practice to recompense her for the lack of the great adventure of natural living." Such comments from a woman of her accomplishments sparked angry outcries from women activists. Helen Keller, a young writer who had achieved fame by triumphing over multiple handicaps, denounced Tarbell as too old to understand the changing world.

Stung by such criticism, Tarbell again shifted her interests. Influenced by automobile magnate Henry Ford, she began a new study of business in the 1910s, this time focusing on factory conditions. As she described Ford's mass production methods, wage po-

licies, and treatment of workers, Tarbell became a staunch champion of welfare capitalism. She also praised the scientific management of Frederick W. Taylor as the key to industrial peace. Tarbell released *New Ideals in Business* in 1916. Turning again to biography in the 1920s, Tarbell portrayed U.S. Steel's Elbert H. Gary as an industrial statesman committed to ethical capitalism. A subsequent work treated General Electric chairman Owen D. Young in similar terms.

Some critics, like the reformist *New York World*, spoke of the "taming of Ida Tarbell," but a commitment to the nineteenth-century concepts of individualism and morality molded the journalist's conclusions. Tarbell remained suspicious of what she called "the most dangerous fallacy of our times—and that is that we can be saved . . . by laws and systems." A classic Progressive, Ida Tarbell never abandoned her skepticism toward interest group politics and collective militancy. Believing in personal accountability, she preferred to trust the "fair play" of the great men she described in her biographies. ■

social unrest and radical politics. Accordingly, the president decided to revitalize the Sherman Antitrust Act. In particular, he targeted the Northern Securities Company, a huge holding company that resulted from a bitter stock fight among the Rockefeller interests, J.P. Morgan, and railroad barons James J. Hill and E.H. Harriman. Roosevelt denounced the resulting monopoly of western rail lines as precisely the sort of behavior that big business should avoid. In response, he ordered government attorneys to use the Sherman Act to file suit against Northern Securities for restraint of trade.

Despite protests by Morgan, the administration pursued the antitrust action and won its case before the Supreme Court in 1904. Although the two syndicates ultimately shared control of nearly all western rail lines, the Northern Securities decision modified the *Knight* case and gave new vitality to the Sherman Act. Roosevelt subsequently initiated forty other antitrust actions, thereby earning a reputation as a "trust buster." Nevertheless, he preferred to deal with the trusts through negotiation rather than legal action. In 1903 the president secured legislation that established the Department of Commerce and Labor,

Exhibit 2-4. Timeline of Implementation of the Square Deal

1902	Newlands Reclamation Act
1903	Department of Commerce and Labor created
	Bureau of Corporations created
	Elkins Act (regulates railroad rates)
1906	Hepburn Act (regulates railroad rates)
	Pure Food and Drug Act
	Meat Inspection Act

including a Bureau of Corporations. Roosevelt directed the agency to regulate large corporations instead of breaking them up through antitrust litigation and personally asked the chief executives of U.S. Steel and the International Harvester Company to cooperate with the new bureau.

Through "gentlemen's agreements," firms allowed the Bureau of Corporations to investigate their procedures and recommend more responsible business practices. Those who refused to comply faced the threat of antitrust action. When attorneys for Standard Oil and the American Tobacco Company declined to cooperate with the bureau, Roosevelt turned to the Sherman Act. In 1911 the Supreme Court upheld the dissolution of both companies. Yet under the "rule of reason," the court found that restricted competition did not constitute an illegal restraint of trade unless a company used unfair methods to eliminate competitors or dictated prices that violated the public interest.

Roosevelt hoped to preserve corporate stability and discourage a strong socialist movement by urging business leaders to accept labor unions that worked within the capitalist system. His approach paralleled that of the influential National Civic Federation (NCF). Founded by Mark Hanna in 1900, the NCF sought harmony between labor and management and urged corporations to recognize social responsibilities by promoting trust regulations, workers' compensation, and company welfare programs. To win the support of organized labor, Hanna invited Samuel Gompers of the AFL to serve as vice president of the NCF.

These developments shaped Roosevelt's reaction to the anthracite coal strike of 1902. Under the leadership of John Mitchell and the United Mine Workers (UMW), miners walked off the job and demanded a 10 to 20 percent wage increase, an eight-hour day, and management's recognition of the union. However, mine owners refused to bargain with Mitchell and tried to end the walkout by using strikebreakers and private security forces. Public opinion tilted toward the workers, especially after owner George Baer proclaimed publicly that "God in His Infinite Wisdom has given control of the property interests" to mining entrepreneurs. As the dispute dragged into the fall, the strike threatened coal supplies for the coming winter. Roosevelt stepped in to resolve the matter by summoning both sides to a conference at the White House, an invitation that delighted Mitchell. However, the owners refused to accept mediation. This outraged Roosevelt, who threatened to seize the mines and use the army to mine coal. That warning prompted conservatives such as banker J.P. Morgan to pressure the owners to compromise. Ultimately, the miners received a 10 percent raise and a nine-hour day, but the agreement permitted the owners to raise prices by 10 percent and to shun union recognition.

MARCUS ALONZO HANNA
1837–1904

Stock Montage

Ohio industrialist, corporate progressive, and Republican Party stalwart, Marcus Alonzo Hanna belonged to the party of Lincoln almost from its founding. His mildly reformist Quaker family opposed slavery and supported Republican policies favorable to business. After brief service in the Civil War, Hanna entered the coal and iron business in Cleveland and accumulated extraordinary wealth. The young man's financial dealings increasingly pushed him toward politics. Recognizing the value of close links between industry and politics, Hanna considered personal profits and community profits to be indistinguishable, and he used government power to advance his own financial interests. Accordingly, he campaigned against Cleveland's political bosses to protect his holdings in the city's street railway system. A born politician, Hanna later accepted the bosses as allies to ensure their support in future battles.

Eager for greater influence, Hanna actively sought the role of president maker. He chose Ohio congressional representative William McKinley as his protege in the 1880s. McKinley's scruples and faintly idealistic political style fascinated Hanna. The congressman's support for high tariffs and malleable views on the currency question added to his appeal. One observer noted that Hanna approached McKinley with the deference "of a big, bashful boy toward the girl he loves." Usually a dynamic figure, Hanna became "just a shade obsequious in McKinley's presence." McKinley gave the orders, a mutual associate noted, and Hanna obeyed without question. He managed McKinley's successful drive to win the White House in 1896, contributed vast sums of his own money to the campaign, and raised millions more from his fellow corporate leaders.

Although Hanna remained a staunch McKinley backer, he began pursuing his own ambitions for elective office and won a narrow victory in the 1897 Ohio senatorial contest. He also took an active role in founding the influential National Civic Federation (NCF) as a forum for corporate progressivism. Eager to avoid price competition and to contain the boom-and-bust cycle, the NCF pledged to end the conflict between capital and labor and to achieve the "normal sense of social solidarity which is the foundation stone of democracy." Hanna saw the NCF as a vehicle for spreading the philosophy of corporate capitalism throughout the Republican Party, but the organization also legitimized reforms like trust regulation and workers' compensation among corporate managers.

In the aftermath of McKinley's death, business interests touted Hanna as the logical nominee in 1904, but the ambitious Theodore Roosevelt blocked his path. During the anthracite coal strike of 1902, the president emerged as the spokesman for corporate capitalism, a role the NCF had expected business leaders to assume. In contrast, Hanna failed to influence events. Facing a reelection battle in Ohio, the embattled senator asked J.P. Morgan to pressure the mine owners to settle. "There are several important places where U.S. Steel could do me lots of good," Hanna pleaded. "I am bleeding at every pore already and can't bear the burden." Morgan initially refused, however, and Roosevelt ultimately stepped forward to take credit for resolving the conflict, thereby demonstrating his primacy in the party.

Hanna died in Washington in 1904. His greatest legacy was not his fortune or the McKinley presidency but the progressive agenda of the National Civic Federation. In the name of self-interest, Mark Hanna had helped to move America's corporations toward stability and reform. ■

Roosevelt insisted that he had given both labor and management a "square deal" while protecting the public interest. In a marked departure from government policy in previous industrial disputes, the president had accepted the legitimacy of labor demands and forced the leaders of a major industry to recognize those claims. Nevertheless, Roosevelt did not champion unions, and his involvement in the crisis amounted to an extension of conservative rather than liberal impulses. Exasperated by the shortsightedness of the mine owners, the president asked if they "realize they are putting a very heavy burden on us who stand against socialists; against anarchic disorder?"

Roosevelt's most consistent use of executive power came in the area of natural resources. Emphasizing the efficient use of resources rather than the preservation of virgin wilderness, the president sought to withdraw most federally owned forest lands from unplanned economic exploitation by private interests. Western congressional representatives opposed this scheme because it threatened to slow the rate of economic growth. To reconcile these politicians to his policy, Roosevelt promised that the government would build dams and irrigation systems throughout the West. Accordingly, the Newlands Reclamation Act of 1902 opened millions of acres of desert land to production by using the proceeds from western public land sales to finance construction and maintenance of irrigation projects. Ranchers and growers also accessed cheap water through dams constructed by the Bureau of Reclamation.

Roosevelt's passion for conservation and pride in the nation's heritage led him to dedicate sixteen national monuments, five national parks, and fifty-one wildlife refuges as areas off-limits to economic development. Seeking comprehensive use of natural resources, the president transferred public forest lands from the Department of the Interior to the Department of Agriculture, where his friend Gifford Pinchot headed the Bureau of Forestry. Like Roosevelt, Pinchot believed that timber resources were essential to the nation's economic development but required planned use under the supervision of government professionals. Both leaders insisted that scientific management of forests could maximize their use by loggers, ranchers, and vacationers and could avoid the wasteful exploitation of resources that often accompanied free enterprise.

THE SQUARE DEAL

Roosevelt faced the electorate in 1904 as a president willing to use the federal government to eliminate genuine inequities in national life. Voters responded to the "Square Deal" by giving him 57 percent of the vote and a victory over Democratic candidate Alton B. Parker, a New York state judge. As someone who saw the government as "the most effective instrument in advancing the interests of the people as a whole," Roosevelt moved to expand the federal bureaucracy and the power of the presidency. A prime achievement came in the complex area of railroad regulation, where both agrarian radicals and middle-class reformers had long sought effective control of rates.

Even in his more cautious first term, Roosevelt had supported the Elkins Act of 1903, which outlawed rebates from railroads to large shippers. However, the president preferred to base industry regulation on bureaucratic review rather than on specific legislation. Consequently, he secured passage of the Hepburn Act in 1906, which increased the jurisdiction of the Interstate Commerce Commission and provided the commission with greater authority to set transportation rates. Many railroad executives supported railroad regulation as a step toward greater economic stability. Rates administered by the federal government limited price competition among lines and freed a national industry from inconsistent regulation by the states. Reforms such as the Hepburn Act typified the pursuit of an ordered society by corporate progressives and their allies.

The Roosevelt administration also backed consumer protection legislation. Responding to the efforts of the government's chief chemist, Harvey Wiley of the Department of Agriculture, Congress passed the Pure Food and Drug Act of 1906. The law prohibited the production and sale of adulterated goods and banned false labeling of food and drug items. Well-established concerns accepted the measure because they hoped to reduce competition from specious patent medicine companies and thereby to improve consumer confidence in their own products. Roosevelt also signed the Meat Inspection Act of 1906, which established federal supervision to ensure that packers met sanitation standards set by the government. Consumers had been alerted to industry abuses by the writings of muckraker Upton Sinclair. Yet large meat packers agreed to the new law because it imposed standards of production that they could meet more easily than could smaller competitors and because enhanced quality improved their opportunities in European markets.

Despite such achievements, the Roosevelt presidency faced a crisis when a stock market crash in 1907 brought a rash of business failures and the collapse of major New York banks. When J.P. Morgan organized the financial community to stop the run, the administration allowed Morgan's U.S. Steel Company to violate antitrust laws by absorbing a Tennessee mining subsidiary. Roosevelt signed the Aldrich-Vreeland Act of 1908, which gave national banks additional flexibility in backing their notes and established a National Monetary Commission to study the banking system. By his final year in office, however, the president faced a Congress that had rejected his bills to supervise corporate competition, to regulate railroad securities, to establish income and inheritance taxes, to limit court injunctions against labor unions, and to establish the eight-hour day for federal employees.

Increasingly hostile to the "stalwart" or conservative wing of the Republican Party, Roosevelt attacked conservative judges for hostility to unions, to state workers' compensation laws, and to the regulation of women's working conditions by the states. The president saw himself as the opponent of the "fool radicalism" of socialists and the anarchic selfishness of "malefactors of great wealth." Pressing the nation's people to give up the idealized nineteenth-century marketplace of small farms and independent businesses, Roosevelt urged the acceptance of large corporations and labor unions and the creation of a national bureaucracy to regulate the activities of both. Only energized government, he believed, could fulfill the nation's destiny for greatness.

ROOSEVELT AND
WORLD POWER

Roosevelt came to the White House hoping to consolidate the strategic and commercial gains of the Spanish-American War. One goal was building an

Corbis-Bettmann

Theodore Roosevelt eagerly climbed aboard a steam shovel during a 1906 visit to the Panama Canal Zone.

interocean canal through Central America. The president believed that U.S. and Caribbean peoples shared an interest in peace, democracy, economic development, and security against the incursions of European powers. Roosevelt insisted that a U.S.-controlled canal in a stable Caribbean would permit Latin America to develop as a prosperous region independent of outside forces and capable of upholding "civilized values." In a period of transition spanning the geographic isolation of the nineteenth century and the total warfare of World War I, the president sought to steer U.S. foreign policy toward global modernization.

Working outside formal channels through personal diplomacy, Roosevelt first invited British cooperation in the construction of the Central American canal. Just two months into his presidency in 1901, the United States and Britain signed the Hay-Pauncefote Treaty, in which Britain renounced interest in the isthmus project and sanctioned construction and fortification of a canal by the United States. Roosevelt then signed the Hay-Herran Treaty with Colombia in 1903, thereby securing permanent rights to a canal zone through the middle of the Colombian province of Panama. When proponents of a canal route across Nicaragua joined with those seeking more compensation from Washington, however, the Colombian Senate unanimously rejected the agreement. Furious, Roosevelt complained that "you could no more make an agreement with the Colombia rulers than you could nail currant jelly to the wall."

After meeting with Roosevelt, Philippe Bunau-Varilla, the chief engineer of an earlier French canal venture, convinced Panamanian leaders that the United States would support a move for independence in the long-restless province. Deployment of U.S. warships to the region contributed to the success of the Panamanian rebellion. Washington quickly signed the Hay-Bunau-Varilla Treaty of 1903, which provided the new republic with the same $10 million and supplemental fee schedule that had been offered to Colombia. Congress ratified the agreement the following year. "I took the Canal Zone and let Congress debate," Roosevelt later boasted. After military physicians learned to reduce the incidence of malaria and yellow fever among isthmus construction teams, the U.S. Army Corps of Engineers completed the forty-mile-long lock canal, which opened in 1914. Seven years later, the United States compensated Colombia with $25 million.

The president nourished U.S. assertiveness in the Western Hemisphere with his 1904 announcement of the Roosevelt Corollary to the Monroe Doctrine. Alarmed by the intervention of European nations in Latin America to collect debts and advance competing business interests, Roosevelt broadened the Monroe Doctrine from a statement opposing further European colonization to a sweeping assertion of the U.S. right to intervene in the internal affairs of hemispheric neighbors. "If we intend to say 'Hands off' to the powers of Europe," the president asserted, "then sooner or later we must keep order ourselves." The Roosevelt Corollary declared that the United States would exercise "an international police power" when "chronic wrongdoing" or "impotence" resulted "in a general loosening of the ties of civilized society." Roosevelt applied the corollary for the first time in 1905, when he sent troops to Santo Domingo to forestall a revolution that would benefit German shipping interests.

Concerned with guaranteeing the successful implementation of the Open Door policy, the Roosevelt administration sought to contain the spread of Japanese hegemony in Asia. In 1905 the president grasped the opportunity to mediate the Russo-Japanese War of 1905 by negotiating the Treaty of Portsmouth. Roosevelt's efforts won him the Nobel Peace Prize the following year. Yet his work proved futile when the collapse of the Chinese empire and the swift emergence of Japan subsequently altered the balance of power in the region. To demonstrate U.S. power, Roosevelt sent sixteen battleships on a 45,000-mile voyage that included a stop in Yokohama, Japan. Although the Root-Takahira Treaty of 1908 compelled Washington to accept Japanese restrictions on the Open Door policy in Manchuria, Japan agreed to respect the policy in the rest of China.

Roosevelt also sought to uphold the existing balance of power in Europe by restraining the growing power of Germany. At the Algeciras Conference of 1906, the president mediated a European imperial conflict by supporting British and French interests in North Africa. The resulting agreement not only

Exhibit 2-5. U.S. Involvement in the Caribbean, 1898–1934

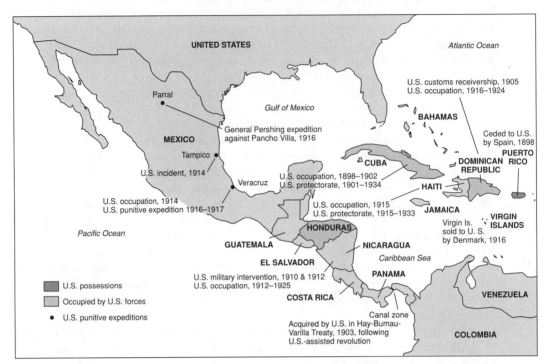

strengthened the informal alliance among the United States, Britain, and France but guaranteed access to the potentially rich region for U.S. business interests. Secretary of State Elihu Root used the conference to remind developing nations of their obligations to ensure life, property, public order, and equal trade opportunities. By combining diplomacy and his self-described "big stick," Roosevelt framed a foreign policy directed toward a stable world order and an open door for U.S. corporations.

TAFT AND THE PROGRESSIVES

When Roosevelt left the White House in 1909, he handed control of the Republican Party and the Progressive movement to William Howard Taft, a talented administrator and lawyer. Taft had won high praise for his performance as governor-general of the Philippines and had served as secretary of war and presidential confidant under Roosevelt. With the enthusiastic backing of his friend, Taft handily won the Republican nomination as the candidate best suited to consolidate the reforms of his predecessor. Meanwhile, the Democrats renominated William Jennings Bryan, who ran a third campaign under the populist slogan "Shall the people rule?" Speaking for the "producing classes," Bryan embraced the direct primary, popular election of U.S. senators, the graduated income tax, federal licensing of corporations, federal guarantees of bank deposits, campaign finance reform, and women's suffrage. Nevertheless, Taft rode Roosevelt's popularity to an easy victory of 52 percent to 43 percent.

The unlikely looking viceroy of the U.S. Pacific empire, William Howard Taft sits ponderously astride a water buffalo during his tenure as governor-general of the Philippines, 1900–1904.

After the election, Roosevelt promptly vanished on a lengthy African safari, where the famous conservationist took dozens of trophies. Unlike the physically fit Roosevelt, Taft weighed more than 300 pounds and was given to nothing more strenuous than golf, a sport not yet popular with the general public. Taft also lacked Roosevelt's gift for public relations and self-promotion. Nor could he stir a crowd or charm the press. Having campaigned on a promise to administer Roosevelt's reform with efficiency, the new president preferred to consolidate existing gains rather than to press new initiatives. "The lesson must be learned," he declared, "that there is only a limited zone within which legislation and governments can accomplish good."

Despite Taft's reluctance to exert government power for reform, the Department of Justice pressed ahead with antitrust activity and filed ninety suits and forty indictments against large companies. The president even proposed that corporations be held to federal licensing standards and that a new agency be created to regulate corporate behavior. Taft further responded to the reform agenda by signing legislation to establish postal savings banks, originally demanded by the Populists. The president also approved the establishment of the Children's Bureau in the Department of Commerce and Labor. Despite such achievements, however, tensions between old guard and progressive elements of the Republican Party tested Taft's limited political skills. At a time when progressive sentiment surged nationally, the chief executive offered the country confused and unproductive leadership that finally destroyed his presidency.

Brown Brothers

Bureau of Forestry head Gifford Pinchot.

The issue of tariff reform illustrated the growing split in the party. Calling Congress into special session in 1909, Taft requested a moderate reduction of the high Dingley Tariff of 1897. However, the president outraged Republican progressives from the Great Plains states when he accepted the Payne-Aldrich Tariff, which actually raised the rates on manufactured goods, thereby threatening crop exports. Taft further offended progressives by replacing James R. Garfield, Roosevelt's conservation-minded secretary of the interior, with western corporate attorney Richard Ballinger. Believing that public lands should either be protected or returned to developers, Ballinger released millions of acres to private ownership or reservoir use against the wishes of Gifford Pinchot, Roosevelt's director of national forests. When Pinchot organized the National Conservation Association to protest such policies, Taft fired him in 1910. Investigated by a Congress that was increasingly hostile to the administration, Ballinger resigned the following year.

The split between the president and congressional progressives deepened because of the controversy regarding House Speaker Joe Cannon, a staunch conservative. Under the leadership of Nebraska's George W. Norris, Republican insurgents sought to weaken Cannon's dictatorial powers. Taft initially supported the revolt and called Cannon "dirty and vulgar." Because he needed the speaker's cooperation for tariff reform, however, the president broke with the insurgents in 1910 and dismissed them as "yelping and snarling" and "rather forward." When the rebels stripped Cannon of his power to make committee assignments, the president's political image suffered.

**Exhibit 2-6. U.S. Exports of Goods and Services, 1898–1910
(in rounded billions of dollars)**

1898	1.3
1902	1.5
1906	2.1
1910	2.2

Source: *Historical Statistics of the United States, Colonial Times to 1970* (1975).

Taft's foreign policy also generated conflict with the progressives. Although Roosevelt had not hesitated to assert U.S. military power in Panama and Santo Domingo, he had always insisted that moral issues were involved in U.S. interventions. However, Taft and Secretary of State Philander C. Knox hoped to minimize European influence in Latin America by encouraging U.S. investment in the region. Consequently, the Taft administration advocated "dollar diplomacy," a foreign policy that unashamedly placed the resources of the Departments of State, War, and the Navy at the disposal of the nation's financial interests. Taft assured the business community that the government would engage in "active intervention to secure for our merchandise and our capitalists opportunity for profitable investment." Acting on such promises, the president sent troops to deal with perceived threats in Nicaragua, Guatemala, Honduras, and Haiti.

By the middle of his term, Taft faced a growing progressive insurgency. One of the most pressing of reform demands was the federal income tax. After repeal of Civil War income taxes in the early 1870s, congressional Democrats and Populists reinstated the provision in 1894 only to have the Supreme Court overturn it the next year. When Democrats and insurgent Republicans managed to add the tax to the 1909 tariff, Republican regulars tried to stall the proposal by turning it into a constitutional amendment that would need approval by the states. Yet the strategy failed when the Democrats captured several key state legislatures in 1910. As a result, enough states ratified the income tax provision to enable it to become the Sixteenth Amendment in 1913.

Congressional interest in reform skyrocketed in 1910 when Democrats gained ten Senate seats and took control of the House for the first time in eighteen years. Working with Republican insurgents like Minnesota's Charles A. Lindbergh, House reformers authorized an investigation of the nation's financial and banking resources in 1912. The sensational Pujo Committee inquiry exposed the interlocking directorates of the Morgan and Rockefeller interests and revealed that control of credit had been consolidated in a "money trust." Insurgents also played a major role in passing the Seventeenth Amendment. Ratified by the states in 1913, the measure finally implemented the Populist proposal that U.S. senators be selected by popular vote rather than by the state legislatures.

Taft's political problems deepened as Roosevelt reentered public life in 1910. The ex-president now embraced the ideas outlined in Herbert Croly's *The Promise of American Life* (1909). Advocating a "new nationalism," Croly accepted large corporations and overseas markets as the key to national prosperity. Nevertheless, he sought a safety net for working people through a federal social welfare state administered by trained professionals. Government business

**Exhibit 2-7. U.S. Gross National Product, 1890–1910
(in rounded billions of dollars)**

1890	13
1895	14
1900	19
1905	25
1910	35

Source: *Historical Statistics of the United States, Colonial Times to 1970* (1975).

regulation and collective bargaining by trade unions would also offset corporate power. Roosevelt expressed these notions in a 1910 speech, "The New Nationalism," in which he described the executive branch of government as the steward of public welfare and proposed to regulate corporations in the national interest. "Our country means nothing unless it means the triumph of a real democracy," he declared.

THE ELECTION OF 1912

Learning that his successor had betrayed the progressive cause, Roosevelt began to distance himself from the Taft regime. The former president finally broke with Taft in 1911 when the White House initiated antitrust proceedings against U.S. Steel, whose merger with a subsidiary had been approved by Roosevelt four years earlier. The president's action not only reversed the promise made to his predecessor but made Roosevelt appear to be a tool of Wall Street instead of a progressive. Enraged by the perceived treachery of his protege, Roosevelt decided to seek the Republican nomination for the presidency. On Lincoln's Birthday in 1912 the former president added a new phrase to the national political lexicon when he announced, "My hat is in the ring."

Roosevelt faced two competitors for the Republican nomination. President Taft represented industrialists, bankers, and stalwart party loyalists who favored high tariffs and a minimum of government interference in the economy. Robert La Follette, the founder of the National Progressive League, was an anticorporate progressive who appealed to small business people and independent farmers. La Follette advocated corrupt-practices legislation to curb the trusts and democratic reforms such as the initiative, referendum, and direct primary. In contrast to his two rivals, Roosevelt embraced corporate progressivism, an approach that accepted large corporations if they were offset by government agencies working to ensure social justice.

As personal problems contributed to the fading of La Follette's campaign, Taft and Roosevelt found themselves in a bitter battle that would leave the Republican Party in shambles. Enormously popular with the rank and file, the former president easily defeated his successor in the thirteen states that conducted presidential primaries, including Taft's native Ohio. At the Chicago convention, however, control rested with the party leadership, most of whom supported the incumbent. When La Follette delegates sought to undercut Roosevelt by siding with Republican stalwarts in a credentials fight, Roosevelt and

Brown Brothers

Woodrow Wilson campaigning for president in the 1912 election.

his backers marched defiantly from the hall, and Taft won the nomination on the first ballot. Roosevelt refused to accept defeat. Arranging for financial backing from newspaper publisher Frank A. Munsey and former Morgan partner George W. Perkins, the former president summoned party dissidents and business and professional reformers to launch a new party, the Progressives.

Insisting that he was eager for the contest, Roosevelt gave the fledgling movement a permanent nickname when he declared himself to be "as strong as a bull moose." With near-religious fervor, delegates roared their unanimous approval of his nomination. "We stand at Armageddon," thundered Roosevelt, "and we battle for the Lord." Progressives chose popular California governor Hiram W. Johnson as their vice presidential candidate. The party platform called for federal regulatory agencies, the prohibition of child labor, the eighthour day, and such democratic reforms as women's suffrage and the popular election of senators. Winning support from luminaries such as social worker Jane Addams, journalist Walter Lippmann, and Herbert Croly, Roosevelt dismissed those "who had taken on the impossible task of returning to the economic conditions that obtained nearly 60 years ago."

Exhibit 2-8. Election of 1912

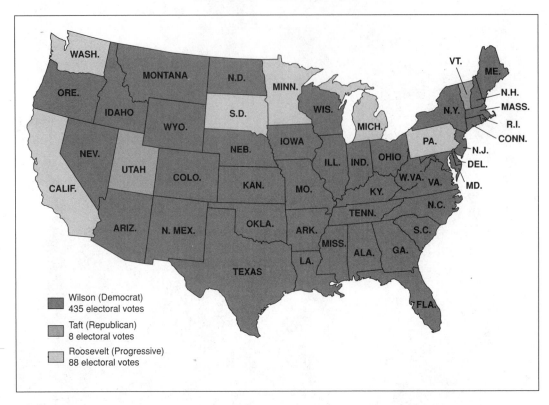

Wilson (Democrat)
435 electoral votes

Taft (Republican)
8 electoral votes

Roosevelt (Progressive)
88 electoral votes

As the party that stood to gain from the Republican split, the Democrats united behind New Jersey reform governor Woodrow Wilson after forty-five ballots. The Virginia-born son of a Presbyterian minister, Wilson followed many talented young southerners of his generation to make a career in the North. Earning a Ph.D. in government at Johns Hopkins University, he began an academic career that led him to the presidency of Princeton University in 1902. Eight years later, embittered by a long struggle over the future of the graduate school, Wilson resigned and ran for the governorship of New Jersey. The candidate of state bosses who saw him as a respectable front man, the governor was also a vigorous progressive. In a state already notorious for its corrupt politics, Wilson built a strong record of reform and established himself as a legitimate contender for national office.

The Democratic nominee drew political support from two contradictory sources. First, he was the candidate of agrarian and small business reformers, often from the South and West, who wished to restrain the growth of large corporations and banks. Wilson promised to restore competition through a "New Freedom" of lower tariffs, banking reform, and government dismantling of unfair and inefficient trusts. "What this country needs above everything else," he declared, "is a body of laws which will look after the men who are on the make rather than the men who are already made." "If America is not to have free enterprise," the candidate proclaimed in defense of small competitors, "then she can have freedom of no sort whatever."

**Exhibit 2-9. Voter Participation in U.S. Presidential Elections, 1896–1912
(in percentages of eligible voters)**

1896	79.3
1900	73.2
1904	65.2
1908	65.4
1912	58.8

Source: *Historical Statistics of the United States, Colonial Times to 1970* (1975).

The second source of Wilson's support came from urban progressives and labor activists who hoped to use government experts to impose efficiency, rationality, and responsibility on large corporations instead of dissolving them. These constituents believed that Wilson's pledge to preserve "free enterprise" was consistent with the candidate's promise to tolerate "reasonable" business combinations. "Nobody can fail to see," he had proclaimed in 1911, "that modern business is going to be done by corporations—the old-time individual competition is gone by." Supporters from both wings of the party nevertheless accepted Wilson's commitment to halt the use of antilabor injunctions by federal courts.

The Socialist Party also competed for the loyalty of reformers. Meeting in Indianapolis, the Socialists nominated Eugene Debs for the presidency and endorsed unemployment insurance and old-age pensions as well as government ownership of railroads, grain elevators, mines, and banks. As a party demanding democratization of the political order, the Socialists advocated a single-term presidency, elimination of the Senate, and removal of the Supreme Court's power of judicial review. With virtually no campaign organization, Debs received more than 900,000 votes, or 6 percent of the popular tally.

Despite Socialist inroads among working-class voters in the industrial cities, the election of 1912 revolved around the two major parties and the Progressives. Significantly, the incumbent Taft only managed to place third by receiving a mere 23 percent of the vote and only the eight electoral votes of Utah and Vermont. Roosevelt finished second by winning 27 percent of the popular ballots and carrying Pennsylvania and Hiram Johnson's California. Wilson received less than 42 percent of the total vote but benefited from strength in the South and growing popularity in the cities to carry the Electoral College by a resounding 435–88.

Through the Republican split and Roosevelt's inability to attract large numbers of progressive Democrats, Woodrow Wilson became only the second nominee of his party to win the White House since the 1850s. However, the dominance of the two reform candidates indicated the extent to which progressive sentiment had penetrated the psyche of the electorate. President-elect Wilson now faced the challenge of translating that often-contradictory impulse into a coherent program that could produce meaningful legislation and policy.

SUGGESTED READINGS

Bryan's role in the pivotal election of 1896 is described in LeRoy Ashby, *William Jennings Bryan: Champion of Democracy* (1987), and in Paolo Colletta, *William*

Jennings Bryan, Political Evangelist, 1860–1908 (1964). The McKinley campaign is covered in Lewis L. Gould, *The Presidency of William McKinley* (1980).

Late-nineteenth-century international relations are explored in Walter LaFeber, *The American Search for Opportunity, 1865–1913* (1993), and in Michael H. Hunt, *Ideology and U.S. Foreign Policy* (1987). See also Kenneth J. Hagan, *The People's Navy: The Making of American Sea Power* (1991). For U.S. expansionism, see Thomas D. Schoonover, *The United States in Central America, 1860–1911: Episodes of Social Imperialism and Imperial Rivalry in the World System* (1991); the relevant portions of Ivan Musicant, *The Banana Wars: A History of United States Military Intervention in Latin America from the Spanish-American War to the Invasion of Panama* (1990); and David Healy, *Drive to Hegemony: The United States in the Caribbean, 1898–1917* (1988).

The Spanish-American War is described in David Trask, *The War with Spain in 1898* (1981). For critical accounts of the conflict, see Philip Foner, *The Spanish-Cuban-American War and the Birth of American Imperialism* (1972); sections of Robert Dallek, *The American Style of Foreign Policy: Culture, Politics, and Foreign Policy* (1983); and the early chapters of William Appleman Williams, *The Tragedy of American Diplomacy* (rev. ed., 1972). The controversy regarding the Philippines is the subject of E. Berkeley Tompkins, *Anti-Imperialism in the United States: The Great Debate, 1890–1920* (1970), and of Robert Beisner, *The Anti-Imperialists, 1898–1900* (1968). See Stuart Creighton Miller, *"Benevolent Assimilation": The American Conquest of the Philippines, 1899–1903* (1982); Glenn May, *Social Engineering in the Philippines: The Aims, Execution, and Impact of American Colonial Policy, 1900–1913* (1980); and Peter W. Stanley and John Curtis Perry, *Sentimental Imperialists: The American Experience in East Asia* (1981).

The rise of Progressive reform in the cities is portrayed by Michael McGerr, *The Decline of Popular Politics: The American North, 1865–1928* (1986), and by Michael H. Ebner and Eugene M. Tobin, eds., *The Age of Urban Reform: New Perspectives on the Progressive Era* (1977). For the conflict between city bosses and reformers, see John Allswang, *Bosses, Machines, and Urban Voters: An American Symbiosis* (1977). Portraits of reform journalists can be found in Louis Filler, *Muckraking and Progressivism in the American Tradition* (rev. ed., 1995). For general accounts of Progressive reform, see Robert Wiebe, *The Search for Order, 1877–1920* (1968); Samuel P. Hays, *The Response to Industrialism, 1885–1914* (1957); and Arthur Link and Richard L. McCormick, *Progressivism* (1983). City reform in the South is explored in Lawrence H. Larsen, *The Rise of the Urban South* (1985).

For progressive reform in the states, see Steven L. Piott, *The Anti-Monopoly Persuasion: Popular Resistance to the Rise of Big Business in the Midwest* (1985), and David Thelen, *Paths of Resistance: Tradition and Democracy in Industrializing Missouri* (1991). The La Follette reform movement is the subject of Thelen's *The New Citizenship: Origins of Progressivism in Wisconsin, 1885–1900* (1972), and of *Robert La Follette and the Insurgent Spirit* (1976). See also Bernard A. Weisberger, *The La Follettes of Wisconsin: Love and Politics in Progressive America* (1994). For the South, see Dewey Grantham, *Southern Progressivism: The Reconciliation of Progress and Tradition* (1983), and William A. Link, *The Paradox of Southern Progressivism, 1880–1930* (1992).

Corporate progressivism is explored in several studies, including Jeffrey Lustig, *Corporate Liberalism: The Origins of Modern Political Theory, 1890–1920* (1982); Morton Keller, *Regulating a New Economy: Public Policy and Economic Change in*

America, 1900–1933 (1990); and Charles Forcey, *Crossroads of Liberalism: Croly, Weyl, Lippmann, and the Progressive Era, 1900–1925* (1961). For the integration of business priorities and reform politics, see Gabriel Kolko, *The Triumph of Conservatism: A Reinterpretation of American History, 1900–1916* (1963), and James Weinstein, *The Corporate Ideal in the Liberal State, 1900–1918* (1969). A more comprehensive application of this thesis can be found in Martin J. Sklar, *The Corporate Reconstruction of American Capitalism, 1890–1916: The Market, the Law, and Politics* (1988), and in *The United States as a Developing Country: Studies in U.S. History in the Progressive Era and the 1920s* (1992).

A good starting point for Roosevelt scholarship is Lewis L. Gould, *The Presidency of Theodore Roosevelt* (1991), and *Reform and Regulation: American Politics from Roosevelt to Wilson* (1986). Biographical treatments include Edmund Morris, *The Rise of Theodore Roosevelt* (1979); David McCullough, *Mornings on Horseback* (1981); John Milton Cooper, Jr., *The Warrior and the Priest: Woodrow Wilson and Theodore Roosevelt* (1983); and John Morton Blum, *The Republican Roosevelt* (1954). For explanations of Roosevelt's foreign policy, see Richard H. Collin, *Theodore Roosevelt, Culture, Diplomacy, and Expansionism* (1985), and *Theodore Roosevelt's Caribbean: The Panama Canal, the Monroe Doctrine, and the Latin American Context* (1990). See also Frederick W. Marks, *Velvet on Iron: The Diplomacy of Theodore Roosevelt* (1982); Raymond Esthus, *Theodore Roosevelt and the International Rivalries* (1970); and Akira Iriye, *Pacific Estrangement: Japanese and American Expansion, 1897–1911* (1972). The building of the Panama Canal is described in David McCullough, *The Path Between the Seas* (1977).

For Taft, see Paolo Colletta, *The Presidency of William Howard Taft* (1973), and the relevant sections of Gould, *Reform and Regulation*, which also summarizes the election of 1912. Wilson's successful presidential campaign is captured in Arthur Link, *Woodrow Wilson and the Progressive Era, 1910–1917* (1954). See also Cooper, *The Warrior and the Priest*, and Sklar, *Corporate Reconstruction of American Politics*.

The Roosevelt and La Follette campaigns are described in the previously listed studies of the two leaders. For the Debs candidacy, see Nick Salvatore, *Eugene Debs: Citizen and Socialist* (1990).

3

The only Ph.D. ever to reach the White House, Woodrow Wilson believed that skillful oratory was a crucial ingredient in presidential power. A renowned classroom lecturer at Princeton, he became the most eloquent political leader of his time.

Corbis-Bettmann

WILSONIAN REFORM AND GLOBAL ORDER, 1912–1920

Progressive reform culminated in the presidency of Woodrow Wilson. As government assumed greater responsibility for social welfare and economic opportunity, political leaders endeavored to balance public interest with the demands of the nation's business community. Federal power also expanded in the realm of global affairs. Building on the Open Door policy of the late 1890s, Wilson blended reformist political ideology and economic imperatives into a quest for international order. Although the dream of collective security remained unfulfilled in his lifetime, this visionary president established the major patterns of twentieth-century foreign policy in an emerging global economy.

WILSON AS CORPORATE PROGRESSIVE

Having prevailed in 1912 under the reformist slogan, "New Freedom," President Wilson sought to unify the country behind the progressive notion of the "public interest." A staunch admirer of the British parliamentary system, the new chief executive believed that the president, like the prime minister, should take a vigorous role in leading his party and securing legislation. "The nation as a whole has chosen him," he said of the president, "and is conscious that it has no other political spokesman. His is the only voice in national affairs." The first White House occupant since John Adams to address Congress in person, Wilson devised his own legislative program and lobbied aggressively for its passage. He installed a private telephone line linking the White House with the capitol and dispatched lobbyists to gain support for administration initiatives. Wilson willingly used the spoils of office to reward backers and punish opponents. He also recognized the press as a crucial link to the people and became the first chief executive to hold news conferences.

On his first day in office the new president boldly summoned Congress into special session and called for downward revision of the tariff. The controversial proposal attracted immediate support from farmers and consumers who had failed to gain tariff reform during the Taft administration and from some industrialists who wanted lower rates for imported raw materials. Exporters and shippers also hoped that rate reductions would encourage reciprocity abroad, thereby stimulating foreign trade. After Wilson's forceful leadership marshaled a solid majority, the Underwood-Simmons Act of 1913 incorporated the first significant tariff reform since the pre–Civil War era.

The new tariff played a key role in changing the national revenue base. Because the Sixteenth Amendment now permitted the institution of federal taxes on incomes, Democratic Representative Cordell Hull of Tennessee proposed a levy on earnings to replace funds lost through tariff reductions. The income tax also served as a symbolic effort to compel the wealthy to pay a large share of government expenses and thereby to reduce class tensions. Imposing a 1 percent personal and corporate tax with a rate of up to 7 percent for earnings greater than $500,000, the measure exempted the first $4,000 in family income from taxation. The graduated income tax gave the federal government unprecedented sources of revenue and prepared the way for an expanded social and military role in the years ahead. Yet only 0.5 percent of the population was

Determined to lead the legislative branch, Wilson presented his agenda in person to joint meetings of the House and Senate.

obliged to file returns (2 percent of the work force), and by 1916 only 9 percent of the government budget came from income levies.

Declaring that "the great monopoly in our country is the money monopoly," the president kept Congress in session to consider banking reform. After the revelations of the Pujo Committee, labor attorney Louis Brandeis had written a series of articles later published as *Other People's Money and How the Bankers Use*

Exhibit 3-1. Wilsonian Domestic Reform, 1913–1916

1913	Underwood Tariff Act
	Federal Income Tax Act
	Federal Reserve Act (created FRB—Federal Reserve Board)
1914	Clayton Antitrust Act
	Federal Trade Commission Act (created FTC)
1916	Adamson Act (eight-hour day for railroad workers)
	Workers' Compensation for Federal Employees
	Rural Credits Act
	La Follette Seamen's Act
	Child Labor Act

Exhibit 3-2. Number of Individual U.S. Income Tax Returns Filed, 1916–1919 (in rounded millions)

1915	.3
1916	.4
1917	3.5
1918	4.4
1919	5.3

Source: *Historical Statistics of the United States, Colonial Times to 1970* (1975).

It (1914), which criticized the nation's concentration of financial resources. Simultaneously, anticorporate progressives such as Robert La Follette demanded government control of a new banking system. In contrast, corporate progressives such as Virginia Senator Carter Glass hoped to decentralize and rationalize the financial apparatus and leave authority with private lenders. Acknowledging that most local banks lacked the resources to provide adequate credit to farmers, Brandeis worked with Wilson to devise a regulatory structure that blended federal supervision with banker control at the regional level.

With the White House deeply involved in the debate, Congress passed the Federal Reserve Act of 1913, the most important domestic legislation of the Wilson presidency. The new system included twelve Federal Reserve banks, which represented the nation's geographic regions. All banks that operated nationally were required to invest part of their capital in the Federal Reserve bank in their district, and state banks could do the same. A Federal Reserve Board, appointed by the president, decided on the rate of interest to be paid to the regional Federal Reserve by investor banks. If the board wanted to encourage expansion, it lowered the interest rate, which made it easier to borrow money; if it wanted to curb inflation, it raised interest rates. The Federal Reserve system also provided reserves to cover local financial crises and established the nation's first coordinated check clearance procedures.

Wilson turned to the explosive issue of the trusts in 1914. By then he had begun to shift his view of supercorporations by replacing the small business ethic of the New Freedom with the corporate progressivism of Theodore Roosevelt's New Nationalism. Again influenced by Louis Brandeis, who was experiencing a similar conversion, Wilson pushed for passage of the Clayton Antitrust Act. The bill sought to close loopholes in existing legislation by barring interlocking directorates, price discrimination, and holding companies among competing firms. The Clayton Act fulfilled the New Freedom promise to discipline monopolistic corporations, but it also demonstrated Wilson's commitment to corporate progressivism. Supported by the National Civic Federation and the Chamber of Commerce, the law targeted the "destructive competition" that prevented corporate planning. To the relief of corporations operating under uncertain state and judicial guidelines, the Clayton Act clarified the limits of business competition by specifying what constituted "unfair practices."

The president also drew a sharp distinction between big business and monopoly. "A trust is an arrangement to get rid of competition," he explained, "and a big business is a business that has survived competition by conquering in the field of intelligence and economy." To regulate those differences, Congress passed the Federal Trade Commission (FTC) Act in 1914, which empowered a new regulatory agency to conduct investigations and issue restraining orders to prevent "unfair trade practices." By stressing administrative regulation of antitrust prosecution, the Wilson administration rejected its earlier commitment to restoring competition. Instead, it embraced the progressive concept of regulation in the public interest through scientific review of data by experts in the field.

Through the Clayton Act and the FTC, the Wilson administration fostered the stability sought by the corporate community but policed the market to prevent flagrant collusion or fraud. By sustaining the distinction between "reasonable" and "unreasonable" restraint of competition, Wilsonian reform institutionalized the Supreme Court's "rule of reason." Antitrust legislation now required prosecutors to prove that corporate offenders were attempting to establish monopolies. Because most of Wilson's FTC appointments were corporate attorneys, the administration initiated few antimonopoly suits and usually encouraged negotiated settlements with private firms. By using government agencies to set predictable ground rules for corporate competition, the Wilson administration effectively ended the debate regarding the legitimacy of big business. Corporate progressives and future advocates of government regulation would continue to base their proposals on the Wilsonian model of reform.

WILSON AND THE LIBERAL STATE

With the creation of the Federal Trade Commission (FTC), Wilson considered his legislative tasks complete, but political pressures forced him to take further reform initiatives. At first the president backed away from proposals that appeared to benefit only special interests as opposed to broader, national concerns. Yet the opposition Republicans fared well in the congressional elections of 1914, and Wilson began to change his position as the 1916 presidential contest approached. The leader of a minority party, he recognized the importance of building a coalition and threw the power of the presidency into that effort. Wilson also saw the White House as a neutral broker among the economy's organized interests. Accordingly, the Clayton Act specifically exempted labor unions and agricultural organizations from antitrust prosecution and restricted the use of court injunctions against union activities.

Wilson built upon this legacy in 1916 by signing laws to improve the conditions of merchant seamen, to regulate child labor, and to provide workers' compensation for federal employees. He also reluctantly approved the Adamson Act, which reduced the workday to eight hours for railroad employees. A federal highway planning bill added to the impressive legislative package. The president set further precedent by establishing the federal government as the source of credit for needy producers. Ironically, the innovation occurred within the relatively prosperous field of agriculture, an area of the economy in which

Exhibit 3-3. Election of 1916

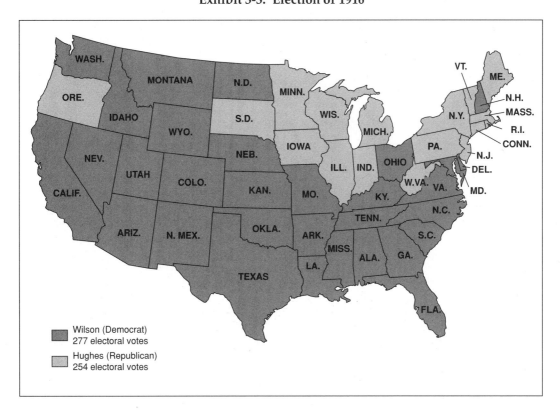

commodity demand exceeded the supply produced by a contracting labor force. Nevertheless, southern congressional representatives and other agrarian reformers persuaded Wilson to sign the Rural Credits Act of 1916. The new law created twelve regions in which credit banks would be supervised and directly subsidized by a Federal Farm Loan Board. Congress also authorized creation of the nation's first agricultural extension service.

As Wilson sought reelection in 1916, he positioned himself as a progressive who sought the involvement of professional experts in government. To bolster this image, the president appointed White House advisor Louis Brandeis to the Supreme Court. By placing the first Jew on the court, the administration sought the support of working-class and ethnic voters in the big cities. Wilson also pursued the votes of Roosevelt Progressives, particularly because the Republicans had nominated Charles Evans Hughes, a progressive and former governor of New York, who had resigned his Supreme Court seat to run for the presidency. Accordingly, the Democratic candidate claimed the mantle of "peace, prosperity, and progressivism." Yet Wilson's campaign may have fallen short if Hughes had not inadvertently snubbed California Republican and former Progressive vice presidential candidate Hiram Johnson. The election produced a narrow 277–254 Democratic majority in the Electoral College. In the closest contest since 1876, Wilson won only 49.4 percent of the popular vote.

LOUIS DEMBITZ BRANDEIS
1856–1941

Brown Brothers

"A lawyer who has not studied economics and sociology is very apt to become a public enemy," declared Louis Brandeis. Born in Louisville, Kentucky, and the son of German-Jewish immigrants, Brandeis reshaped twentieth-century jurisprudence by defending the interests of working people against corporate power. A successful private law practice made him a millionaire by the age of fifty and freed him to devote time to public issues. The bloody Homestead steel strike of 1892 marked a crucial turning point in his life and career. Concluding that "organized capital hired a private army to shoot at organized labor for resisting an arbitrary cut in wages," Brandeis committed himself to assisting the working class.

His most important contribution came in his appearance before the Supreme Court in *Muller* v. *Oregon* (1908). Representing the state of Oregon in a suit challenging the constitutionality of a law setting a maximum workday of ten hours for women, Brandeis brushed aside legal principles with a cursory three-page summary. "There is no logic that is properly applicable to these laws except the logic of facts," he argued. He used one hundred pages to document expert opinion concerning the adverse impact of excessive hours on the health of women. The Brandeis brief marked the first use of sociological data in a Supreme Court case and revolutionized legal argument. "My, how I detest that man's ideas," wrote conservative Justice George Sutherland about Brandeis. "But he is one of the greatest technical lawyers I have ever known."

Politically independent, the progressive Brandeis supported both Republicans and Democrats for national office. In 1912 he ini-

REFORM AND IMPERIALISM IN LATIN AMERICA

"There are times in the history of nations," President Wilson explained, "when they must take up the crude instruments of bloodshed in order to vindicate spiritual conceptions." Wilson initially saw Latin America as the arena where military force might be deployed to sustain moral values. Like Theodore Roosevelt, the president viewed intervention in the nation's historic sphere of influence as a step toward democracy, stability, order, and constitutional government. As a historian who shared Frederick Jackson Turner's theories concerning the importance of expanding frontiers of opportunity, Wilson also appreciated the importance of Latin America for U.S. economic expansion. Accordingly, he viewed the spread of democratic institutions to the "lower peoples" of the area as a component of the political stability and reliability necessary for capitalist development and social progress.

Although the president and Secretary of State William Jennings Bryan repudiated dollar diplomacy, the Wilson administration escalated military intervention in the Caribbean and Central America by sending troops to occupy Cuba,

tially endorsed Robert La Follette for the Republican nomination but later supported Woodrow Wilson when the Republican Party divided. He subsequently became a close adviser to Wilson and a prime architect of the New Freedom. Brandeis played a major role in shaping the Federal Reserve Act of 1913 by insisting that the banking system must ultimately be placed under the control of the federal government instead of the financial community. He also played an important role in the development of the administration's antitrust policy by drafting the Federal Trade Commission Act of 1914.

Wilson risked controversy to nominate Brandeis to a seat on the Supreme Court in 1916. Unlike most justices, Brandeis had held no previous public office, and his legal work on behalf of social causes had given him a reputation as a radical. As the Senate Judiciary Committee spent four months reviewing the nomination, conservative business and political interests strongly opposed confirmation. Seven past presidents of the American Bar Association, including former cabinet officer Elihu Root and former president William Howard Taft, testified in opposition by arguing that Brandeis's career as an advocate

proved his lack of judicial temperament. Ultimately, however, the Senate confirmed the nomination, and Brandeis served on the bench for twenty-three years.

The new justice joined the court in the midst of one of its most conservative periods. He frequently joined Oliver Wendell Holmes in dissenting from the prevailing majority. Brandeis shared the progressive faith that government could solve social and economic problems, and he generally affirmed regulatory and social justice legislation. He considered such laws part of a healthy and desirable process of experimentation in the social sciences. Devoted to the court, Brandeis labored extensively over his richly detailed opinions, drafting everything in longhand without the aid of a secretary.

When the new Supreme Court building opened in 1935, Justice Brandeis refused to move into his new quarters and contended that the authority of the court should rest on the persuasiveness of its opinions instead of on the trappings of institutional power. Brandeis retired in 1939 and was replaced on the court by William Douglas. ■

Santo Domingo, and Nicaragua. Wilson dispatched the marines to Haiti to pressure the government into signing a treaty that ensured U.S. control of the country's finances, public works, army, and foreign relations. Concerned with the security of the Caribbean as war inundated Europe, the president instructed Denmark to sell the Virgin Islands to the United States in 1916 or to face their forcible seizure by U.S. forces.

Wilson's grandest scheme for forcing progress on Latin America involved Mexico, where democratic forces had begun a revolution in 1911. When General Victoriano Huerta led a successful counterrevolution two years later, Wilson refused to recognize the dictatorship on the grounds that it lacked popular

**Exhibit 3-4. U.S. Exports of Goods and Services, 1912–1916
(in rounded billions of dollars)**

1912	2.7
1916	6.0

Source: *Historical Statistics of the United States, Colonial Times to 1970* (1975).

Brown Brothers

General Pershing's troops wind through the Mexican desert in their futile pursuit of Pancho Villa.

support. Demanding that the general relinquish power, the president refused to recognize "a government of butchers." Never before had the United States refused to recognize an existing government. "I am going to teach the South American governments to elect good men," Wilson explained to a British diplomat. He then threw U.S. support behind General Venustiano Carranza and ordered the navy to seize the Mexican port of Vera Cruz to prevent a German steamer from landing with arms for Huerta. When Carranza's army failed to control the chaotic fighting that raged throughout the country, Wilson turned to General Francisco (Pancho) Villa, a charismatic bandit and revolutionary reformer.

Magazine readers in the United States had received firsthand accounts of Villa's romantic exploits, but when Carranza regrouped and pushed Villa into the mountains of northern Mexico in 1915, Wilson again switched sides and recognized the Carranza government. Villa then further confused the situation by shrewdly playing on Mexican resentment of U.S. meddling. In a deliberate act of provocation, Villa crossed the border in 1916 and burned the town of Columbus, New Mexico, killing nineteen people. Outraged, Wilson placed General John J. Pershing in command of a punitive expedition and ordered the army to pursue Villa. Pershing led 7,000 U.S. soldiers 300 miles into Mexico, but President Carranza demanded that Washington respect Mexican sovereignty.

A humiliated Wilson finally called off the futile mission in 1917 as the United States became increasingly concerned with Europe.

NEUTRALITY AND THE EUROPEAN CRISIS

Wilson had ample reason to shift his attention across the Atlantic. Three years earlier, in 1914, Slavic nationalists had murdered Hapsburg Archduke Franz Ferdinand and his wife in the Balkan city of Sarajevo. These assassinations were the first in a rapid series of events that plunged Europe into the first general continental war since the fall of Napoleon. The conflict arrayed the Allies (Britain, France, and Russia) against the Central Powers (Germany and the Hapsburg Empire). Wilson promptly proclaimed a policy of neutrality and called the clash "a war with which we have nothing to do, whose causes cannot touch us." He asked the public to be "neutral in fact as well as in name" and "impartial in thought as well as action."

The president's insistence that the United States had no stake in the European war was far from accurate. Since the 1890s foreign policy leaders had generally seen Germany rather than Britain as the greatest potential threat to U.S. security. Indeed, until the turn of the century, the British fleet served Washington's interests by limiting European involvement in Latin America. Consequently, Theodore Roosevelt and many others expressed alarm at the prospect of a German victory. Strong cultural ties also linked the United States and Britain, particularly among the predominantly Anglo-Protestant officials of the State Department. Wilson himself greatly admired the British people and their institutions. Predictably, within months of the outbreak of hostilities, the president privately admitted that the United States might have to take an active part in the fighting if Germany appeared likely to win.

Wilson also believed that the preservation of democracy and prosperity at home depended upon maintaining an open door to the markets, raw materials, and investments of world commerce. In Asia the Japanese already had thwarted U.S. efforts to invest private capital in major railroad projects in China and Manchuria. As an economic recession deepened in 1914–1915, marketplace issues tended to draw the United States into the Allied camp. Because the war disrupted the productive capacity of Europe, the demand for U.S. industrial and agricultural products increased enormously and boosted trade with the Allies from $825 million in 1914 to $3.2 billion in 1916.

U.S. financiers also supported the war effort by offering huge loans to Britain and France. Proclaiming that money was "the worst of contrabands," the Secretary of State had instituted a ban against loans to the belligerents in 1914. Wilson modified the order by permitting banks to offer short-term credit to the Allies. In September 1915 the president allowed lenders to extend loans to European governments in a controversial decision that he never put in writing. Despite his desire to maintain neutrality, Wilson's convictions concerning the importance of foreign trade led him to permit the Federal Reserve to guarantee these obligations. By 1917 bankers had loaned $2.5 billion to Britain and France.

**Exhibit 3-5. Total U.S. International Investment, 1908–1919
(in rounded billions of dollars)**

1908	2.5
1914	5.0
1919	9.7

Source: *Historical Statistics of the United States, Colonial Times to 1970* (1975).

"Our firm had never for one minute been neutral," a House of Morgan banker later explained. "From the start we did everything we could to contribute to the cause of the Allies." In contrast, U.S. trade with the Central Powers dwindled, and loans to Germany totaled only $300 million.

Meanwhile, Republican leaders pressed the Wilson administration to assert U.S. neutrality rights and to initiate a program of military preparedness. The president hoped that a neutral United States might be in a position to shape the peace. Wilson's approach to foreign policy fused idealism with the imperatives of economic expansion. The president saw the war as an opportunity to end European empires and to open the world to free trade. He hoped that the terrible costs of the war would teach Europe the necessity of ending imperial competition and believed that the United States could provide leadership in forging a peace settlement based on an international Open Door policy. "We are the mediating nation of the world," Wilson declared. "We are compounded of all the nations of the world. We are, therefore, able to understand all nations."

While Wilson awaited the opportunity to initiate a new international community, the actions of the belligerents challenged U.S. neutrality. Once hostilities broke out, Britain and Germany each tried to impose blockades on the other's ports. Just as Britain became an important market for U.S. goods and capital, the Royal Navy mined the entrance to the North Sea and curbed neutral trade with Germany. Yet Washington acquiesced in the British blockade while Wilson denounced the Germans for violating the rights of neutral nations.

Germany's growing reliance on submarine warfare provided the most serious irritant in its relations with the United States. The British blockade mainly relied on surface vessels that used traditional methods of naval warfare and seldom claimed civilian casualties. Unable to meet the British challenge on the open sea, the Germans turned to a new type of naval warfare that employed the U-boat, or submarine. As deadly as it could be to surface vessels, the submarine was extremely vulnerable to attack, especially when it surfaced. Even when it submerged, a skillful sharpshooter could render a submarine helpless by shooting out its periscope. Therefore, the U-boat became a weapon of stealth, and Germany's strategy of submarine warfare resulted in considerable loss of property and numerous civilian casualties.

Berlin's desperate effort to cut supply lines to the British Isles played into the hands of Allied propagandists. Because Britain controlled the only transatlantic cable, it dominated the flow of war news to the United States. The U.S. media readily accepted the British interpretation of events and printed numerous stories of alleged German atrocities, all of which confirmed the image of Germany as an outlaw nation. British propaganda portrayed the Germans as "Huns," a barbaric and savage people who severed the hands of Belgian babies and raped women. Consequently, stories relating the loss of innocent lives to the attacks of German submarines outraged the public.

Wilson's neutrality policy rested on ambiguous and unrealistic assumptions. The president viewed British and German offenses differently. Moreover, he demanded that merchants have the unimpeded right to turn a profit in a war zone while assuming no risks for their actions. The fate of the *Lusitania* illustrated the problems with such a policy. In May 1915 a German submarine sank the British passenger liner within sight of the Irish coast and caused the deaths of 1,198 passengers, including 128 Americans. Theodore Roosevelt denounced the sinking as an "act of piracy," although the *Lusitania* almost certainly used its passengers as a shield for the munitions it carried for the British war effort.

Wilson responded to the sinking by sending a strongly worded note to the German government. Secretary of State Bryan, an adamant neutralist, resigned to protest the president's unwillingness to mount equal criticism of British offenses. The departing secretary criticized the idea that "ammunition intended for one of the belligerents should be safeguarded in transit by the lives of American citizens." Many congressional representatives supported the McLemore Resolution, which warned citizens not to travel to Europe, but Wilson refused to accept any limitations on the rights of neutral nations. By rejecting such restrictions, the president placed himself in a position that required defense of those rights.

In 1915 the Germans acceded to Wilson's demands and promised not to challenge passenger lines, but they increased strikes on armed British merchant vessels, which had been ordered to attack submarines on sight. Germany announced in 1916 that it would fire on Allied shipping without warning. A few weeks later a submarine torpedoed the *Sussex*, an unarmed French passenger ship, and injured several U.S. citizens. When Wilson delivered an ultimatum that called for Germany to stop sinking merchant and passenger ships unless it wished to risk U.S. intervention, Berlin responded affirmatively with the Sussex Pledge. Yet the president realized how precarious the balance between peace and war had become. "Any little German lieutenant can put us into war at any time by some calculated outrage," he admitted.

THE COMING OF WAR

Although Wilson talked of ending the use of military power in foreign affairs, he sought to win respect for U.S. neutrality rights by mobilizing the armed forces. Since the first years of the century, the army and navy had developed comprehensive and centralized staff systems. To professionalize commands and to devise global strategies, both services also established war colleges. The Dick Act of 1903 furthered military consolidation by placing state militias, renamed the National Guard, under federal control. "Let us build a navy bigger" than Britain's, Wilson told an aide in 1916, "and do what we please." The president toured the country to win support for a $500-million preparedness program that included creation of the Reserve Officers' Training Corps (ROTC) on the nation's college campuses. Congress responded by passing the National Defense Act of 1916 and a naval appropriations bill. Rejecting the use of bonds as too burdensome on ordinary taxpayers, Congress financed the package through the Revenue Act of 1916, the first major income and inheritance tax in U.S. history.

By 1916 a coalition of British sympathizers, beneficiaries of wartime prosperity, members of the eastern defense and foreign policy establishments, and belligerent nationalists pressed Wilson to intervene in World War I. Yet many citizens wanted the nation to remain at peace. German Americans who were sympathetic to their homeland and Irish Americans who despised British colonialism constituted the most bitter foes of U.S. involvement. Social justice progressives like Jane Addams and Amos Pinchot also opposed intervention because they feared the war's effects on domestic reform and preferred the peaceful settlement of international disputes. Organizations such as the Carnegie Endowment for International Peace had successfully urged presidents Roosevelt, Taft, and Wilson to sign arbitration treaties with the major powers, which resulted in agreements with all except Germany.

The largest group of noninterventionists consisted of midwestern and western farmers and business interests often aligned with the congressional insurgents. These middle-class citizens did not share the ties to British culture found more prominently in the South and among the eastern upper class. Removed from European financial and trade ties, they saw the overseas conflict as an imperial struggle of corrupt monied interests that had no bearing on small producers and distributors in the domestic economy. Such antiimperial sentiments were best expressed by the Nonpartisan League, a political lobby of agrarian reformers that pressed for state-run banks, grain storage elevators, and hail insurance. By 1918 the league had spread to fourteen north-central and mountain states and boasted a membership of 220,000. Agrarian and nationalist views helped to produce a powerful noninterventionist bloc in Congress and prompted Wilsonians to urge the president's reelection in 1916 with the slogan "He kept us out of war."

As his second term began, Wilson decided to make another effort to mediate the European conflict. Earlier in the war, he twice had sent his personal representative Colonel Edward House to negotiate between the two sides, but to no avail. The Germans resented the pro-Allies bias of the U.S. position, and the British and French believed they would win the war. By 1915 the cost of the conflict had risen so high that neither side would consider a negotiated peace. In late 1916 Wilson tried again by inviting the belligerents to state their terms for peace. Germany made no public response, although it wanted Lithuania, Poland, Belgium, and the Belgian Congo. The Allies insisted on German withdrawal from Belgium, on the return of Alsace-Lorraine to France, on substantial compensation, on an end to Germany's overseas colonialism, and on the division of the Hapsburg Empire.

Frustrated and impatient, Wilson then seized the moment to propose a peace rooted in the ideals and economic imperatives of the Open Door policy. In an address to Congress in January 1917, the president called for a "peace without victory" to preserve a world marketplace guaranteed by freedom of the seas, not huge navies or armies. Although the proposal demonstrated visionary eloquence and enhanced Wilson's global stature, it failed to break the European stalemate, and peace prospects rapidly deteriorated. With the land war deadlocked on the western front and the British blockade creating severe shortages, German leaders met with Kaiser Wilhelm and voted to revoke the Sussex

Pledge and to resume unrestricted submarine warfare. U-boats now would attack the ships of neutral nations as well as those of their adversaries. Germany recognized that this escalation would seriously jeopardize relations with Washington, but it hoped to win the war before the United States could establish a military presence in Europe.

Convinced that domestic democracy and prosperity depended on global freedom of action and sensitive to issues of national honor, Wilson promptly severed diplomatic relations with Germany. The president then asked Congress to pass the Armed Ship bill, which would give him the authority to arm U.S. merchant ships. Seeking to build public support, he released the Zimmerman note, a secret German dispatch recently intercepted by the British. Since 1915 an insurrection against Anglo control of south Texas had resulted in twenty-one U.S. deaths and the summary execution of more than 300 Mexicans by the Texas Rangers. Sent from the foreign secretary of Germany to its Mexican embassy, the Zimmerman note directed Berlin's ambassador to encourage Mexico to attack north of the border if the United States entered the European war. Under the Plan of San Diego, Germany would help Mexico to recover Texas, New Mexico, and Arizona.

One day after publication of the Zimmerman note, the House overwhelmingly approved the Armed Ship bill. Yet in the Senate, a bipartisan coalition of noninterventionists led by La Follette and Norris organized a session-ending filibuster that prevented a vote on the measure. Infuriated at this temporary obstacle to military preparedness and executive prerogative, Wilson announced that "a little group of willful men representing no opinion but their own have rendered the great government of the United States helpless and contemptible." Acting on the advice of Secretary of State Robert Lansing, the president armed the merchant vessels by executive order.

Events proceeded rapidly. In Russia, the March revolution of 1917 toppled the tsarist government and ended 300 years of rule by the Romanov family. As the Russians created a republic, the Allied coalition was no longer tainted by partnership with a despotic ally. In mid-March German submarines sank three U.S. merchant ships in a single day and killed two dozen people. Meanwhile, Wilson received a telegram from the U.S. ambassador to Britain warning that French and British solvency had to be protected to "prevent the collapse of world trade." In early April the president and a cavalry escort rode down Pennsylvania Avenue to ask Congress for a declaration of war. In a powerful address, Wilson told the country that "the right is more precious than the peace." The world, he said, "must be made safe for democracy."

Wilson left the chamber during a roaring ovation. Yet the anguish of the moment surfaced when the president asked an aide why anyone would cheer a message that would bring death to thousands. According to his secretary, the commander in chief wept after he returned to the White House. In Congress a scattering of antimilitarists in the South joined midwestern and western noninterventionists to oppose the war declaration. Denouncing the conflict as an effort to secure the interests of bankers and munition makers, George Norris protested that "we are going to war upon the command of gold." Robert La Follette scoffed at "patriots" who were "back of the thirty-eight corporations most benefited by the war effort." After four days of angry debate, six senators and fifty representatives voted against the declaration of war.

Wilson declares war.

ORGANIZING FOR VICTORY

U.S. involvement came at a crucial time in the Great War. Fighting on the western front had resulted in a bloody stalemate for more than two years, and casualty rates would sap Europe's vitality for a generation. Political unrest in Russia seemed likely to diminish the ability of the Russian army to sustain the eastern front, which would free the Central Powers to divert more forces to the war against the nearly depleted British and French troops. The success of unrestricted submarine warfare compounded Allied problems. In April 1917 Britain had only a six-week supply of food, and the U-boats were sinking 900,000 tons of shipping each month.

Almost immediately, the Wilson administration faced the task of deciding how to finance a war that would ultimately cost $32 billion. With great fanfare that blended modern public relations techniques, the use of prominent entertainment figures, and old-fashioned patriotism, the government launched a series of Liberty Bond drives that netted $23 billion in loans from individual subscribers. This reliance on bonds also limited consumer spending, thus curtailing demand for commodities and cooling inflation. Under pressure from La Follette and other insurgents, Congress raised billions in additional revenue with new taxes on "excess profits," on high incomes, and on luxuries.

Mobilization provided corporate progressives with the chance to create a rationalized economy and a working partnership between government and the private sector. Under the War Finance Corporation headed by treasury secretary and presidential son-in-law William Gibbs McAdoo, the federal government became the ultimate source of private investment capital. In turn, the War In-

Government propaganda used such advertising techniques as sexual themes and innuendo to rally popular support for the war.

dustries Board (WIB) set production goals for corporations in war industries and controlled the flow of raw materials so war output would have top priority. Led by financier Bernard Baruch, the WIB promoted a "new competition" among large firms by sanctioning price fixing, collusive bidding, and

Exhibit 3-6. U.S. Gross National Product, 1916–1920
(in rounded billions of dollars)

1916	48.3
1918	76.4
1920	91.5

Source: *Historical Statistics of the United States, Colonial Times to 1970* (1975).

Exhibit 3-7. Public Debt of the U.S. Federal Government, 1916–1919
(in rounded billions of dollars)

1916	1.2
1917	3.0
1918	12.5
1919	25.5

Source: *Historical Statistics of the United States, Colonial Times to 1970* (1975).

Exhibit 3-8. Percentage of Income Received by Those Earning the Top 1 Percent of Incomes, 1913–1919

1913	15.0
1915	14.3
1917	14.2
1919	13.0

Source: *Historical Statistics of the United States, Colonial Times to 1970* (1975).

guaranteed profits. In blurring the line between government and industry, Baruch adopted a form of corporatism, a European approach to national economic planning in which the state served as the partner and facilitator of business rather than its regulator.

Under Herbert Hoover, a mining engineer turned public servant, the Food Administration took control of agricultural production and distribution. The agency set high prices for commodities to encourage production and then purchased the entire crop. As large harvests of midwestern wheat and southern cotton fed and clothed U.S. and Allied troops, agricultural income jumped 30 percent. Anxious to avoid excessive bureaucratic regulation, Hoover used mechanisms that encouraged the voluntary cooperation of private citizens with a federal agency. Through an elaborate public relations effort, the Food Administration persuaded millions to adopt voluntary solutions to the problems of agricultural distribution by avoiding meat or wheat consumption for several days each week. The success of this campaign enabled the agency to supply domestic, military, and foreign consumers without resorting to compulsory rationing.

Similar forms of centralized planning were applied by the Fuel Administration, which distributed coal to both citizens and defense plants, and by the Railroad Administration, which provided central management of a private system owned by several companies. Wilson also signed the Webb-Pomerene Act

Exhibit 3-9. Unemployment Rates, 1914–1920
(as a percentage of civilian labor force)

1914	7.9
1915	8.5
1916	5.1
1917	4.6
1918	1.4
1919	1.4
1920	5.2

Source: *Historical Statistics of the United States, Colonial Times to 1970* (1975).

of 1918, which authorized corporations to coordinate price and marketing policies in overseas trade. The Edge Act of 1919 allowed bankers to cooperate to control investments abroad. All this seemed to confirm the progressive faith in government planning based on expert leadership.

Progressives also used the war emergency to establish a working relationship with the American Federation of Labor (AFL). Led by Samuel Gompers, the AFL had supported Wilson's preparedness program and hoped that military spending would revive the economy. Once Congress declared war, the federation saw the opportunity to lower unemployment, to increase union membership and wages, to promote shorter hours, and to have a voice in shaping government policy. Gompers achieved most of these goals through the War Labor Board (WLB), a national planning body that encouraged the formation of unions and collective bargaining arrangements in return for labor's cooperation in the war effort. At the recommendation of the WLB, Wilson created the U.S. Employment Service, which placed nearly 4 million workers in war-related jobs. Government intervention prevented discrimination against union employees and preserved employment and wage standards throughout the war.

Cooperation between the Wilson administration and organized labor helped to double union membership to 5 million during the war. As the annual gross national product grew from $48 billion to $91 billion between 1916 and 1920, the average annual wage of workers rose from $600 to $1,400, although the doubling of the cost-of-living index largely negated such increases. Nevertheless, union representation worked with the WLB to prod corporations to institute the eight-hour day and comparable pay for women. Proposals for federal pensions for the elderly and unemployment insurance died, however, because opponents linked them with German welfare policies or with socialism.

THE DOUGHBOYS AND
MILITARY VICTORY

U.S. entry into World War I presented new problems of military recruitment. Believing that the zeal of volunteer fighting men would more than compensate for their lack of training, Theodore Roosevelt offered to raise a volunteer outfit and lead it overseas just as he had done twenty years earlier in Cuba. However, Wilson insisted on a selective service system that would permit the government

**Exhibit 3-10. U.S. Military Personnel on Active Duty
(in rounded figures)**

1916	179,000
1918	2,900,000
1920	343,000

Source: *Historical Statistics of the United States, Colonial Times to 1970* (1975).

to organize human resources for mobilization and deployment. As a progressive, the president also sought to ensure that the fighting forces would be representative of U.S. society and would not simply be drawn from the less privileged classes. The Selective Service Act of 1917 enabled the army to draft 3 million soldiers during the eighteen months of U.S. participation in the war. Although some 300,000 men evaded the draft and 23,000 sought conscientious objector status, another 2 million volunteered for service. For the first time in history, the army used machine-graded intelligence tests to assess the capability of recruits and draftees.

President Wilson appointed General John J. Pershing to command the American Expeditionary Force (AEF). A career professional, Pershing refused to commit troops to combat until they had completed their training. He also was under strict orders from the president to keep the AEF independent of British and French command to preserve U.S. bargaining power in postwar negotiations. On 4 July 1917 a token force of AEF troops landed in France as one officer proclaimed, "Lafayette, we are here!" Yet the army did not expect to be large enough or sufficiently prepared to mount independent operations until 1919.

Exhibit 3-11. U.S. Troops on the Western Front, 1918

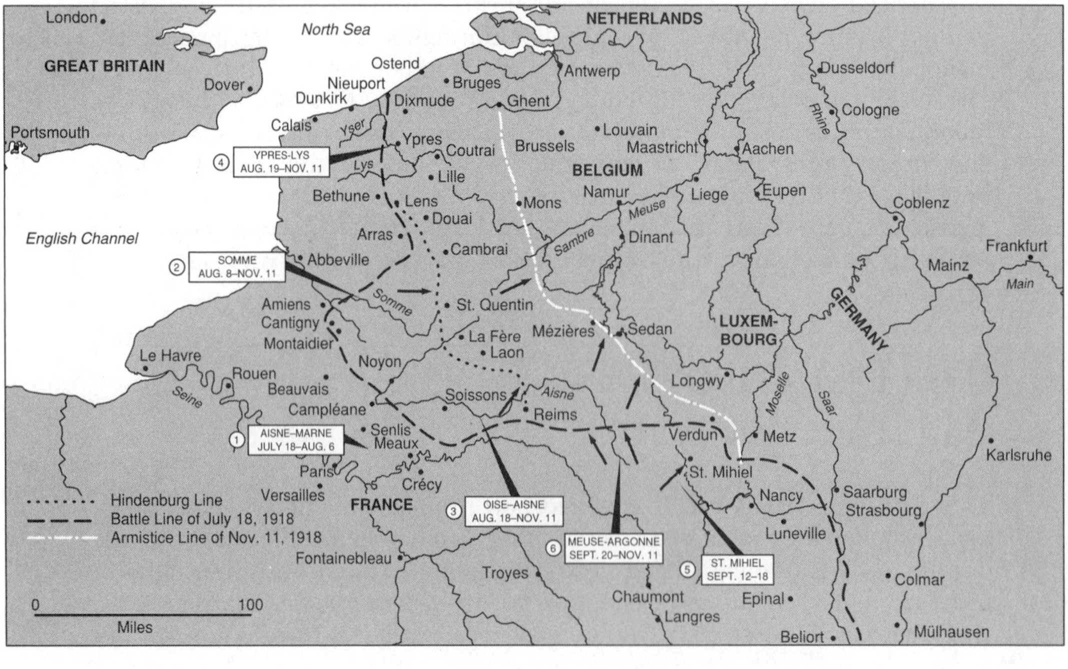

National Archives

A machine gun crew fires on German positions in Belleau Wood. Capable of spewing 450 rounds a minute, the machine gun symbolized the mass killing characteristic of war in the industrial age.

One year after U.S. entry into the war, only 350,000 U.S. troops were in place. Nearly all the AEF's artillery and large amounts of its ammunition were provided by the Allies. Only 40 percent of army supplies came from the United States, but these supplies were shipped by using British transport, as were most U.S. troops. Moreover, the AEF was untrained for mechanized tank warfare and trench combat on the western front.

Anticipating that U.S. troops would not be fully mobilized until the following year, Germany mounted a 1918 spring offensive. Wilson and Pershing agreed to the appointment of French General Ferdinand Foch as supreme commander and allowed the AEF to be deployed in Lorraine, where the possibility of a German breakthrough was minimal. Although the U.S. Army maintained a separate status on paper, AEF soldiers performed more effectively when they fought under seasoned British and French commanders. As the German advance stalled in July 1918, the Allies mounted a counteroffensive, and by September the U.S. First Army pushed the Germans out of the St. Mihiel salient. However, although the AEF held a 9–1 manpower advantage in the southern sector to which it was assigned, Pershing's failure to support infantry attacks with artillery resulted in heavy casualties. In the fall of 1918 1 million U.S. troops participated in the Allied drive along a 200-mile front through the Argonne Forest in the largest battle until that point in U.S. history. After forty-seven days, the Germans were forced to seek a cease-fire when the imperial government dissolved.

GEORGE CREEL
1876–1953

Brown Brothers

As the United States entered World War I, Woodrow Wilson asked George Creel to chair the Committee on Public Information (CPI). Recognizing that the war was unpopular, Wilson hoped that under Creel's leadership the CPI could use new public relations and advertising techniques to build a consensus of support. By establishing the CPI under Creel's leadership, the president authorized the first government propaganda agency in U.S. history.

The son of a former Confederate army officer, George Creel struggled through an early career as a journalist until he founded a Kansas City newspaper early in the century. A staunch Progressive, he threw himself into muckraking by denouncing the city's political machine and demanding a variety of reforms to improve public services, to protect workers, and to make the political process more responsive to middle-class interests. Creel was an admirer of Woodrow Wilson, and he supported the president's reelection bid in 1916 by writing some effective political tracts. Impressed by Creel's Progressive credentials and powers of persuasion, Wilson assigned him the task of interpreting U.S. war aims for audiences at home and abroad.

Creel immediately recruited a core of new public relations professionals and set in motion a campaign of "moral publicity." The CPI distributed 75 million pamphlets, 60,000 press releases, and 14,000 drawings. It assembled a speakers bureau with 75,000 participants and even arranged for 4,000 historians to check the accuracy of their speeches.

Creel also exercised tremendous authority over the export of films and publications and manipulated these cultural products to en-

By the time World War I ended at 11:00 A.M. on 11 November 1918, Germany had lost 1.8 million people and the Hapsburg Empire, 1.2 million. Among the Allies, the Russians suffered 1.7 million deaths, the French nearly 1.4 million, and the British Empire, 947,000. Another 20 million Europeans were wounded. U.S. fatalities totaled 112,432, half from disease. Although the Allies bore the brunt of the fighting, the United States helped to defeat Germany by securing the North Atlantic sea-lanes against the submarine, thereby permitting the shipment of men and supplies to the front. Moreover, the timely arrival of AEF soldiers sustained Allied morale and tipped the balance of power. Most importantly, President Wilson finally was positioned to influence a lasting European settlement.

THE WAR AGAINST DISSENT

The Wilson administration devoted unprecedented resources to the cultivation of public opinion. In a full-scale effort to mobilize the nation's citizens behind the war effort, the president directed progressive journalist George Creel to

sure that the "wholesome life of America" received exposure throughout the world. Creel and his associates painted Americans as virtuous and Germans as villains in films like *The Prussian Cur* and *The Kaiser: The Beast of Berlin*. Through advertisements in such popular magazines as the *Saturday Evening Post*, the CPI encouraged citizens to report anyone who "spreads pessimistic stories, cries for peace, or belittles our efforts to win this war." Creel also persuaded the press to engage in voluntary censorship. Meanwhile, the foreign section of the CPI worked to influence European public opinion by portraying Wilson as a hero who would bring political redemption to the world. As part of this effort, the CPI bribed European newspaper editors, subsidized European publishers, and provided free copies of American propaganda.

Creel turned the CPI into a vehicle for imposing cultural conformity as well as political unity. Like other Anglo-Protestants, Creel feared the cultural pluralism practiced by many European immigrants who tried to continue using their native languages. The CPI clearly conveyed that the use of any tongue other than English was unpatriotic. "When I think of the many voices that were heard before the war," Creel declared, "interpreting America from a class or sectional or selfish standpoint, I am not sure that, if the war had to come, it did not come at the right time for the preservation and reinterpretation of American Ideals." Indeed, Creel's memoir, *How We Advertised America* (1920), celebrated the new professions of advertising and public relations and their ability to create a mass society in which all individuals shared a uniform set of values.

Such concerns for national unity and cultural conformity marked Creel's reaction to World War II and the second Red Scare. Demanding a harsh peace, he spoke of the "blood guilt" of the German and Japanese people and promoted the vicious characterization of enemy civilians that the CPI usually avoided a generation earlier. He also embraced the conspiracy theories of the Republican right wing by charging that a generation of liberal politicians had forged a plot that climaxed in Roosevelt's alleged capitulation to the Soviets during the Yalta conference in 1945. He continued to crusade against dissidents of all types until his death in 1953. ∎

organize the Committee on Public Information (CPI), the nation's first government propaganda agency. Employing 150,000 people, the CPI distributed 75 million pieces of print literature, much of it written by professional journalists and historians. The agency also mobilized popular entertainers such as Charles Chaplin, Douglas Fairbanks, and Mary Pickford to sell war bonds at public rallies. Private groups such as the National Security League, which drew its members from the academic community, supplemented the government's efforts by selling bonds and solidifying support for the European crusade on college campuses.

Despite such efforts, many people continued to criticize the nation's involvement in the European conflict. Socialist Party leader Eugene Debs portrayed the war as a crusade to defend the interests of a transatlantic elite. After the Socialists labeled the war a "crime against humanity," they took 30 percent or more of the vote in the 1917 municipal elections in industrial cities such as Chicago, Dayton, Toledo, and Buffalo. In Oklahoma, where struggling tenant farmers and sharecroppers accounted for the nation's highest proportion of Socialist Party members, more than 400 rioting draft protestors forced the administration to call out federal troops during the Green Corn Rebellion of 1917. Yet socialists were not the only dissenters from wartime policy. The "masses" had not yet accepted the conflict as "an American war," wrote one-time New Jersey governor Edward C. Stokes in the summer of 1917. A former banker and a conservative Republican, Stokes sensed "a widespread feeling that this is a *capitalistic* war, brought on to protect loans abroad."

"War is the health of the state," wrote radical essayist Randolph Bourne in his controversial book *The State* (1918). Opposition to the war was particularly strong in the Midwest, where large numbers of residents quietly resisted bond drives, ignored food pledge campaigns, and sought to evade conscription. Robert La Follette, Idaho senator William E. Borah, and a group of southern representatives bitterly opposed compulsory military service when it was approved by Congress in June 1917. Joining with William Jennings Bryan, La Follette demanded heavy taxation of war profits to conscript capital instead of labor. Both men called for future referenda of the electorate before Congress declared war. Accused of giving aid and comfort to the enemy, La Follette received the condemnation of the faculty of the University of Wisconsin in his home state. He also faced charges that would remove him from the Senate, which were dismissed only after a 51–21 vote of the full body.

World War I heightened concerns about the growing heterogeneity of the nation's people. By the time the United States entered the conflict, foreign-born residents or the children of immigrants accounted for one-third of the nation's population, and many were recent arrivals from the countries that formed the Central Powers. Nativist anxieties surfaced in 1917 when Congress incorporated a literacy test into immigrant processing procedures by overriding a presidential veto. The White House objected to the measure because it did not require personal qualifications of character or fitness on the part of potential entrants. Yet Wilson signed two other immigration laws that permitted authorities to deport aliens who called for the destruction of private property or who belonged to revolutionary organizations. Seeking to forge patriotic unity among the country's wartime ethnic groups, the U.S. Army began to play "The Star-Spangled Banner" for military ceremonies, although the music was not adopted as the national anthem until 1931.

The Wilson administration also responded to dissent with repressive legislation. The Espionage Act of 1917 prohibited any action that might be construed as aiding the enemy or as discouraging military service. The law authorized the postmaster general to prohibit "treasonable" publications from using the mail. Under these provisions, the government imprisoned Debs and prohibited the mailing of Socialist Party periodicals. Movie producer Robert Goldstein received a ten-year prison sentence because his film *The Spirit of '76* showed British soldiers attacking U.S. civilians during the Revolutionary War. In 1918 Congress passed the Sedition Act, which made it a crime to "utter, print, write, or publish any disloyal, profane, scurrilous, or abusive language" about the armed forces. Although the administration rarely enforced this law, the Socialist Party faced indictments and the arrest of more than 1,500 members for criticizing the government.

Radicals and pacifists became special targets of government persecution. Under the leadership of "Big Bill" Haywood, the Industrial Workers of the World (IWW) rejected both the American Federation of Labor's craft unionism and the Socialist Party's commitment to gradual political reform. Woodrow Wilson commented privately that IWW leaders "certainly are worthy of being suppressed," and the government dispatched troops to break strikes led by the

Musician Ernst Kunwald (left), former conductor of the Cincinnati Symphony Orchestra, is taken into custody as an enemy alien.

IWW in Washington and Montana. About 165 IWW leaders faced arrest, and Haywood himself avoided imprisonment only by escaping to Russia. Government repression also led to the imprisonment of 400 conscientious objectors to military service; the administration recognized only members of pacifist churches such as the Quakers and Mennonites as legitimate claimants of conscientious objector status.

The Supreme Court upheld the Wilson administration's attempts to build wartime unity by repressing dissent. In *Schenck* v. *the United States* (1919) the court ruled that constitutional protection of free speech did not apply during wartime. This decision sustained the conviction of a Socialist Party official who had mailed to draft-age men circulars that questioned the constitutionality of conscription. As Justice Oliver Wendell Holmes argued in a unanimous opinion, "The most stringent protection of free speech would not protect a man falsely shouting fire in a crowded theater and causing a panic." Holmes stated that the court could deny free speech when a "clear and present danger" existed to public safety and national security. The high court also upheld the Espionage Act conviction of Eugene Debs, sentenced to ten years in prison for telling an audience that the "master" class made wars while the "subject" class fought them. In *Abrams* v. *the United States* (1919), a split court upheld the Sedition Act as a legitimate attempt to prevent disaffection during wartime.

Institutional efforts to suppress dissent encouraged private citizens to attack critics of the government and of the war effort. In Indiana a jury dismissed charges against a man who had shot someone for yelling, "To hell with the

United States." Occasionally, such vigilantism received semiofficial sanction. When IWW copper miners went on strike in Bisbee, Arizona, in 1917, the county sheriff labeled the 1,200 Mexican Americans subversives and called in vigilantes to deport them to the desert south of the border. Meanwhile, the Justice Department issued cards to the 250,000 members of the American Protective League (APL) that identified the holders as federal agents and permitted them to spy on neighbors and to monitor nonconformists.

German Americans became special targets of wartime harassment. War hysteria translated German measles into liberty measles, dachshunds into liberty pups, and sauerkraut into liberty cabbage. More ominous forms of repression included the suspension of German-language publications, the prohibition of the teaching of German, and physical attacks on German speakers. A Congregational minister denounced the Lutheran Church as "not the bride of Christ but the paramour of kaiserism." Some employers dismissed German Americans from their jobs, and vigilante mobs in Minnesota and Wisconsin sometimes beat suspected "Huns" and intimidated them into purchasing war bonds.

RACE AND GENDER IN WARTIME

The changes of wartime society, new labor demands, and the persistence of progressive ideals broadened opportunities for both women and African Americans. By interrupting immigration from Europe while boosting economic production, World War I created a shortage of workers that was intensified by the conscription of several million young men. Some 1.5 million women entered the labor force as factory workers during the conflict. Moreover, many middle-class and affluent women embraced Wilson's promise concerning the "war to end all wars" and volunteered to support the military effort. While some women served in the Army Nurses Corps or the Red Cross, others helped to implement the voluntary rationing plan organized by the Food Administration or made bandages and clothing for those in the service. Suffragist leaders such as Carrie Chapman Catt and Anna Howard Shaw demonstrated their patriotism by joining the Women's Committee of the Council of National Defense.

World War I provided the context for the fulfillment of women's purity reforms such as the crusade against liquor. Wartime shortages justified reduced consumption of vital grains as beer and whiskey, and economic mobilization underscored the need for efficient production by a sober and healthy work force. The war also intensified the desire to "Americanize" new immigrants by imposing the Anglo-Protestant value of sobriety on them, particularly because German Americans ran most of the large breweries and distilleries. In 1917 Congress approved the Eighteenth Amendment, which ended the sale of alcoholic beverages; the states completed its ratification two years later. Seeking to prevent sexual promiscuity between solders and single women, the American Social Hygiene Association helped to create the Commission on Training Camp Activities. The government agency provided troops with regular medical examinations and venereal disease information but also employed federal agents to place 35,000 women in detention centers for the war's duration on prostitution charges.

Library of Congress

Women defense workers inspect .45 automatic pistol components at Colt's Patent Firearms Plant in Hartford, Connecticut.

The importance of women to the war effort led the administration to endorse women's suffrage. Wilson previously had ordered the arrest of White House picketers, including Alice Paul of the Congressional Union, who protested that no war could be a struggle for democracy as long as women lacked the vote. Officials treated Paul and her supporters roughly and force-fed them in jail when they went on hunger strikes. Although confrontational tactics did little to mobilize the masses of women, they enabled suffrage leaders such as Carrie Chapman Catt to portray the demands of the mainstream movement as more cautious and reasonable. With Wilson's support, Congress approved the Nineteenth Amendment in 1919, which gave women the vote. Within a year, the provision was ratified and nearly doubled the number of citizens eligible to vote.

The onset of World War I also brought new roles for African Americans. Wilson had appealed to black voters in 1912 and even won W.E.B. Du Bois's endorsement, but most administration officials shared the president's southern heritage and made the South's racial mores a part of federal policy. As president, Wilson permitted the dismissal of black government employees on the basis of race and sanctioned the systematic segregation of the federal civil service. When newspaper editor and black activist William Monroe Trotter called at the White House to protest these unprecedented policies, the president quickly ordered him to leave. Despite such reverses, the NAACP continued to test discrimination cases in the courts. In 1915 the organization persuaded the

Exhibit 3-12. Women's Suffrage Before the Nineteenth Amendment

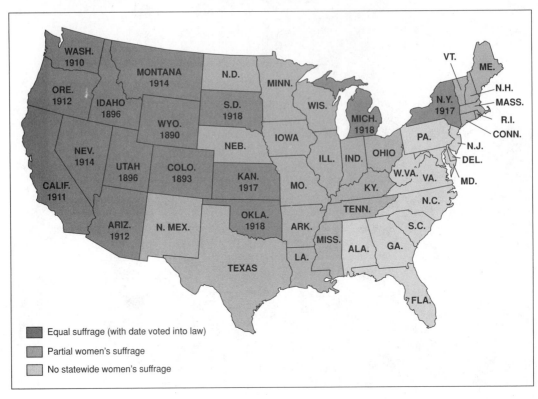

Equal suffrage (with date voted into law)

Partial women's suffrage

No statewide women's suffrage

Exhibit 3-13. U.S. Death Rates by Race, 1900–1920
(per 1000 of population)

	Black	White
1900	25.0	17.0
1905	25.5	15.7
1910	21.7	14.5
1915	20.2	12.9
1920	17.7	12.6

Source: *Historical Statistics of the United States, Colonial Times to 1970* (1975).

Exhibit 3-14. U.S. Life Expectancy by Race, 1900–1920

	Black	White
1900	33.0	47.6
1910	35.6	50.3
1920	45.3	54.9

Source: *Historical Statistics of the United States, Colonial Times to 1970* (1975).

Black infantrymen test their gas masks shortly after arriving in France.

Supreme Court to overturn the grandfather clause in southern voting laws. Two years later the court outlawed residential segregation ordinances.

The war created expanding job opportunities for African Americans in northern centers of steel production, meat packing, and other industries. Such labor demands contributed to the Great Migration, a massive population shift that would relocate nearly half the nation's black population from southern farms to northern and western cities in the next half-century. The Wilson administration also reaffirmed the citizenship of blacks by conscripting them into the military services. Hoping to improve the position of their people, African American leaders such as W.E.B. Du Bois advised followers to "close our ranks shoulder to shoulder with our own white fellow citizens . . . fighting for democracy." Yet the marines accepted no black recruits, and the navy enlisted them only as mess "boys." The army originally intended to use blacks only as laborers, but the NAACP successfully pressured the service into organizing black combat units and establishing a black officers' training camp. Ironically, the first black regiments sent to Europe fought and received decorations as part of the French army.

As more than 400,000 black soldiers served their country during World War I, a new assertiveness emerged among African Americans. Blacks in northern cities were free of the more stifling aspects of southern legal segregation and used the franchise to elect local politicians. More dramatically, the war offered liberation from domestic segregation for black soldiers, some of whom were accepted as social and sexual equals in France. When race riots erupted in twenty-five cities during the bloody summer of 1919, blacks fought back against

DAVID WARK GRIFFITH
1875–1948

Wide World Photos

"The task I am trying to achieve," D.W. Griffith once explained, "is above all to make you see." The founding genius of silent cinema was born in Oldham County, Kentucky, and was the son of a Confederate cavalry officer. After creditors confiscated the family estate, Griffith drifted through a series of odd jobs before entering the entertainment business. He eventually signed a contract with Biograph and became a motion picture director.

Griffith liberated the movies from the conventions of stagecraft and created a fresh idiom of filmic expression. Working with cameraman Billy Bitzer, he developed the visual syntax of motion pictures by drawing on such techniques as close-up and long shots; the *switchback*, or parallel montage; and the fade-out. The talented southerner realized that film was more intimate than the stage, and he encouraged a style of performance that emphasized restraint and subtlety. "I learned more about acting under Griffith's guidance," Mary Pickford confessed, "than I did in all my years in the theater."

Griffith established the director as the principal artistic force in motion pictures. Convinced that the emotional language of film could elevate reason above animality, he used cinematic technique to highlight youthful idealism, saintly women, virtuous producers, and Victorian family values. Once he left Biograph to become an independent in 1913, Griffith bought the rights to Thomas Dixon's *The Clansman* (1905), a popular novel that romanticized the creation of the first Ku Klux Klan. "As I studied the book," he later recalled, "stronger and stronger came to work the traditions that I had learned as a child, all that my father had told me." The "story of the South," he declared, "had been absorbed into the very fiber of my being."

white aggression, and seventy-eight black Americans died. In the South, whites reacted violently to the enhanced sense of pride among many returning black soldiers, some of whom were lynched in uniform. In the North, the riots stemmed from the fear of working-class whites that blacks were taking scarce jobs and that the expansion of black ghettos would destroy white neighborhoods. White repression and black resentment would produce mass movements of African American racial pride and separatism in northern black communities during the 1920s.

THE LEAGUE OF NATIONS AND A NEW WORLD ORDER

President Wilson saw U.S. involvement in World War I as a step toward creating a stable global economic and political order. Yet his vision of postwar peace and prosperity was threatened by a second Russian revolution in 1917 that brought the Bolshevik or Communist Party to power and created the Soviet Union. As a

Ultimately titled *The Birth of a Nation* (1915), the twelve-reel film became Griffith's masterpiece and the most popular movie of the era. Dixon even arranged a White House showing for President Woodrow Wilson, a southern historian sympathetic to the drama's hostile views of Reconstruction. *The Birth of a Nation* mirrored southern stereotypes of blacks as rowdy and untrustworthy sensualists easily exploited by harsh northerners. Accordingly, it aroused the ire of the National Association for the Advancement of Colored People and induced editing by the National Board of Review, a voluntary censor created by the film industry. Yet Griffith perceived himself as a Progressive and as a reform Democrat and insisted that the story pitted the innocence of agrarian virtue against the machinations of Yankee greed and lust. He had intended only to show the plight of small farmers who allowed monopolists to strip them of their land and corrupt the political process.

Determined to strike back at critics and inspire the common people, Griffith used all his profits to produce *Intolerance* (1916), a four-hour, four-part extravaganza shot on 125 miles of celluloid in twenty-two months. Relying on "mental notes" instead of a script, Griffith used the film to depict a pattern of autocracy that reigned from ancient Babylon to industrial society. The director clearly sided with virtuous workers against greedy exploiters. The affluent audiences then attending films had little patience with moralistic denunciations of the rich, however, and the movie failed at the box office.

By the end of World War I the film industry had become a corporate enterprise increasingly controlled by large studios closely linked to investment bankers. Determined to maintain independence, Griffith built his own facilities in Mamaroneck, New York, but the expense proved too great and in 1925 he returned to Hollywood. There Griffith's creative liberties did not mesh with the corporate procedures demanded by the studios. Demoralized by both the working conditions and the waning of the spirit of progressive reform, the outmoded director lost his talent for making successful films.

The architect of the full-length feature and the man responsible for enticing middle-class viewers into movie theaters, D. W. Griffith abandoned the industry in 1931. Deprived of the nineteenth-century folk tradition that gave his work vitality, the great evangelist of the screen found himself without a congregation. ■

prelude to withdrawal from the coalition against the Central Powers, the new Russian leaders published secret Allied treaties for dividing the territorial gains of the war. Calling for peace without victory through international socialist revolution, the Bolsheviks defied the Allies by stating their own terms for peace. Wilson responded to the challenge in January 1918 by going before Congress to outline the Fourteen Points, a prospective settlement. The president's plan called for disarmament, freedom of the seas, open diplomacy, and self-determination for colonized nations and the people of Europe. Most importantly, Wilson proposed the creation of a League of Nations to enforce the new world order.

To dramatize his commitment to the Fourteen Points, the president decided to lead the U.S. delegation to the Versailles Peace Conference. Bolstered by the academic experts of the American Peace Commission, Wilson arrived in Europe in January 1919 amid enormous popular acclaim. Yet British Prime Minister David Lloyd George and French Premier Georges Clemenceau preferred to think in terms of Great Power concerns such as national security and economic compensation. "How can I talk to a fellow who thinks himself the first man in 2,000 years to know anything about peace on earth?" asked the skeptical French

The Big Four, Vittorio Orlando of Italy, David Lloyd George of Great Britain, Georges Clemenceau of France, and Woodrow Wilson of the United States, pose for photographers during the deliberation at Versailles.

leader. Given the enormous financial and human costs absorbed by the Allies, Wilson's only bargaining chip at Versailles remained his personal appeal to the war-weary people of Europe.

Despite the president's insistence on "peace without victory," Wilson shared Allied fears concerning the spread of communism. V.I. Lenin, the Bolshevik leader, had declared that the future of the industrial world belonged to socialism. According to this analysis, capitalist nations would continue to fight wars among themselves as they competed for overseas markets and raw materials until the working class took control and instituted a cooperative global system. This vision of a communist world order challenged Wilson's hopes for an international market economy built on democratic freedoms. As communist uprisings threatened to spread throughout eastern and central Europe, the president sought to contain revolution within Russia and to prevent communism from spreading west. In the summer of 1918 Wilson dispatched U.S. troops to Russia to join military attachments from France, Britain, and Japan. Supposedly sent to keep supplies from falling into German hands, foreign forces occupied northern Russia and Siberia until June 1919 and occupied Manchuria until April 1920.

Although U.S. soldiers took no direct part in the Russian civil war, Wilson clearly hoped that their presence would influence the outcome. The military venture provided an example of the president's vision of international cooperation and interallied unity—a precursor of the collective security he saw as the heart of global order. Wilson's overriding concern with communism also forced

Exhibit 3-15. U.S. Intervention in Russia

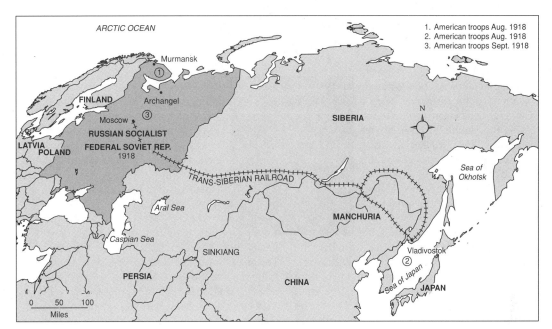

him to compromise with the Allies on his peace plan. The result was the Treaty of Versailles, a document that violated much of the spirit and substance of the Fourteen Points. A peace negotiated in secret by the victors, the settlement ignored freedom of the seas and violated the principle of self-determination. Under its provisions, Britain, France, and Japan divided Germany's colonies among themselves and refused to consider dissolving their own empires. Moreover, whereas Germany and Austria lost sovereignty over non-German peoples of Europe, the treaty's new national boundaries placed many German-speaking people in the newly formed nations of Central Europe and in Italy.

Far from supporting a peace without victors, Versailles imposed harsh penalties on the defeated Germans, who had to accept guilt for the war, to pay $35 billion in reparations, and to limit the size of their armed forces. Marshal Foch suggested that the agreement provided not peace but an armistice for the next twenty years. Yet Wilson accepted the treaty because it included his cherished proposal for a League of Nations. Defining U.S. freedom and welfare in global terms, the president had used military power to ensure the adoption of essential principles of international law and commerce. He now hoped to use the league to create a stable world order in which disputes between nations might be resolved without violence. In a dangerous and revolutionary political environment, Wilson insisted that no international peace mechanism could work without a system of collective security. Accordingly, Article X of the League Covenant required member nations to preserve the territorial integrity and political independence of all participants against external aggression.

Wilson returned to the United States well aware that he faced a difficult struggle to secure Senate ratification of the treaty. Having chosen to lead his country's delegation to France and remain there during the negotiations, the

JOHN REED
1887–1920

Culver Pictures

A rich man's son from Portland, Oregon, John Reed was one of two U.S. citizens to be buried inside the Kremlin Wall in Soviet Russia. "This proletarian revolution will last . . . in history," he proclaimed of the 1917 upheaval that created the Soviet Union, "a pillar of fire for mankind forever."

The strange odyssey of John Reed began at Harvard University, where the ambitious westerner donned a cheerleader's uniform and exulted in the "supreme blissful sensation of swaying 2,000 voices in great crashing choruses." A prolific writer, he drifted to Europe after graduation and later settled in New York City, where he embraced the bohemian lifestyle of Greenwich Village. Influenced by Progressive parents who ardently supported the political career of Theodore Roosevelt and by muckraking journalists like Lincoln Steffens and Ida Tarbell, Reed grew increasingly committed to social causes.

As Reed wrote, the radical intellectuals he met in the Village taught him that "my happiness is built on the misery of others." Moving steadily toward political activism and socialism, he joined the staff of Max Eastman's radical journal, *The Masses*, in 1913. While covering the International Workers of the World (IWW) strike in Paterson, New Jersey, he was jailed with protesting workers. The experience led him to organize artists to help stage the giant Madison Square Garden Pageant for the benefit of the union.

Reed first attracted national attention as a war correspondent for the Hearst publications. He was sent to Mexico to report on the major social revolution of the era. There he spent four months in the desert with Pancho Villa and became known for his ability to match the general's drinking and dancing exploits. Reed sent back a series of brilliant dispatches that captured the tedium and the hor-

president had left no political buffer between himself and the work of the conference. Moreover, because he had failed to appoint prominent Republicans to the delegation, the treaty appeared to be a partisan document. In addition, because the Republicans had exploited war restlessness and discomfort with internationalism to sweep to power in both houses of Congress in 1918, Wilson faced a hostile Senate leadership. The treaty also offended several ethnic groups important to the Democratic Party. Irish Americans, who resented the alliance with the hated British, wanted the treaty to create an independent, united Ireland. Italian Americans in turn wanted larger territorial concessions for Italy.

Three groups of senators impeded the president's quest for league membership. First, eastern Republicans such as Senate Majority Leader Henry Cabot Lodge, a personal adversary of Wilson, opposed ratification for political and tactical reasons. Second, a coalition of sixteen "irreconcilable" eastern Republicans and western progressives refused to endorse the league under any circumstances. Led by La Follette, Borah, and California's Hiram Johnson, these statesmen feared the use of U.S. troops to bolster the "tottering" governments of imperial Europe. "Shall American boys police the world?" asked Johnson in a widely acclaimed Senate speech in 1919. Third, thirty-five Republican "reser-

ror of combat. His book *Insurgent Mexico* (1914) established him as the foremost war journalist of his time. When World War I erupted, Reed immediately left for Europe to report on the western front and returned a second time to visit the eastern war zone. His writing portrayed the bloody conflict as a capitalist civil war.

Reed came home to the United States more committed than ever to the revolutionary struggle. In 1916 he met and subsequently married writer Louise Bryant. The next year the couple sailed for Russia and arrived in Petrograd on the eve of the November revolution, which brought Lenin and the Bolsheviks to power. Reed cultivated a close friendship with the Russian leader and threw himself into the revolutionary process. His classic *Ten Days That Shook the World* (1919), a journalistic diary of the tumultuous events of the November revolution, provided a stirring and optimistic account of the communist revolution.

Back in the United States, Reed's radicalism alarmed government officials, and he returned to a nation that was systematically suppressing dissent. His articles in *The Masses*, especially one under the headline "Knit a Straight-Jacket for Your Soldier Boy," precipitated an indictment of the magazine's publisher for sedition. Two juries failed to return verdicts in the case, but authorities in New York and Philadelphia indicted Reed for "incendiary speeches." Unintimidated, Reed and Bryant insisted on testifying before a Senate committee. While claiming that he "did not know how it was to be attained," he bluntly told his interrogators, "I have always advocated a Revolution for the United States."

Reed worked arduously to build a communist movement in the United States. In mid-1919, however, the national Socialist Convention expelled the journalist and other pro-Bolsheviks. The exiles quickly divided into two factions, the Communist Party and Reed's Communist Labor Party. The novice organizer hoped to build a revolutionary movement of workers outside the mainstream labor organizations, but he soon faced indictment for sedition. He fled the United States on a forged passport only to be deprived of his papers and jailed for three months in Finland. Released as part of a prisoner exchange, Reed finally reached Moscow, where he soon grew impatient with the rigid and remote bureaucracy dominating the revolutionary movement. When he died of typhus in 1920, the Bolsheviks buried Reed in the Kremlin as a hero of their revolution. ■

vationists" hoped to approve membership in the league without Article X. This group maintained that collective security might weaken the United States by tying it to a European status quo when the nation should focus on economic internationalism.

Because public opinion appeared to support Wilson, Lodge offered to recommend league membership with reservations affirming U.S. autonomy. Yet instead of negotiating, Wilson mounted a long and exhausting speaking tour in September 1919 to build public enthusiasm for an unamended treaty. Midway through his trip, the president collapsed. Rushed back to Washington, he suffered a paralyzing stroke. With the president unable to assume his responsibilities for two months, First Lady Edith Galt Wilson and White House physician Cary Grayson became the only links between the president and the outside world. Wilson's physical collapse destroyed the slim chance of compromise with the reservationists. When the Senate considered a resolution to pass the treaty with the Lodge reservations in November 1919, Wilson ordered Democrats to invoke customary party loyalty and to defeat the measure. Although the Senate adopted the treaty with the Lodge reservations in 1920, a bipartisan coalition of Wilson loyalists and irreconcilables prevented ratification by the necessary two-thirds majority. The United States signed a separate peace treaty with Germany two years later. As the nation retreated from internationalism and high-minded idealism, the president's administration and party lay in tatters.

RED SCARE

Social tensions and unrest generated by World War I escalated out of control in the years immediately following the conflict. Concerned that inflation threatened to outstrip wage increases, more than 4 million workers took part in 3,600 strikes in 1919 alone. Early that year the most ambitious general strike in U.S. history gripped Seattle and prompted middle-class fears that European-style class conflict had returned with the doughboys. That fall, coal miners defied the leadership of the United Mine Workers and successfully struck for better wages. Meanwhile, the AFL organized all aspects of steel production and led 375,000 workers in the industry's first strike since 1892. Union organizers focused on better wages, on an eight-hour day, and on improved working conditions; companies such as U.S. Steel portrayed the conflict as having been inspired by radicals and used black and imported Mexican strikebreakers to end the protest. In Boston, police responded to the firing of AFL unionists in their ranks by walking out, prompting Massachusetts Governor Calvin Coolidge to declare, "There is no right to strike against the public safety by anybody, anywhere, anytime."

A series of terrorist incidents and threats coincided with the labor unrest of 1919. In the spring, postal officials discovered several mail bombs addressed to John D. Rockefeller, Supreme Court Justice Holmes, and other powerful political and corporate leaders. Those packages, which were intended for delivery on May Day, came to the attention of authorities because they lacked sufficient postage. The following month, bombs exploded within minutes of each other in eight cities. One of those explosions shook the home of Attorney General A. Mitchell Palmer and startled his neighbor, Assistant Secretary of the Navy Franklin D. Roosevelt. Despite a lack of evidence, the public associated such anarchy with the union movement. By 1919 six heads of states had been assassinated by anarchists.

Labor unrest and threats of terrorism combined with fears arising from the Bolshevik Revolution to bring about the Red Scare. In 1918 two small communist parties emerged in the United States. Suspecting that Soviet doctrines might find fertile ground among working-class immigrants, the Wilson administration organized to fight the "red" threat. Attorney General Palmer named J. Edgar Hoover, a recently hired and obscure Justice Department attorney, to head an antiradical division. Meanwhile, Palmer began to arrest labor leaders, peace activists, socialists, communists, and alien dissenters. On a single evening in January 1920 federal agents detained 6,000 people, held many without charges, and subjected scores to police brutality. Although the government released most of the arrested activists, it deported more than 500 aliens. As thousands of New Yorkers cheered from the docks, the *U.S.S. Buford*, the so-called "Soviet Ark," sailed for Finland with 249 aliens, among them anarchists Emma Goldman and Alexander Berkman.

Brown Brothers

Anarchists Nicola Sacco and Bartolomeo Vanzetti, accused of robbery and murder in Massachusetts, were the most celebrated victims of the Red Scare of 1919–1920.

Palmer's actions were part of a nationwide persecution of radicals that sought to eliminate "alien" influences and ideologies. One Tennessee Democrat urged that citizens with radical ideas be sent to a penal colony in Guam. The New York state legislature expelled five Socialists. Milwaukee Socialist Victor Berger, who once joked that the only results of the war were the influenza epidemic and inflation, was denied his seat in the U.S. House of Representatives despite winning two consecutive elections. Twenty-eight states enacted sedition laws, which resulted in the arrest of 1,400 people and the conviction of 300. Some states required public school teachers to sign loyalty oaths, and local communities banned politically controversial books from their libraries. Radicals also became targets of vigilante violence. After a shoot-out between IWW activists and American Legionnaires killed four people in Centralia, Washington, in November 1919, a mob of angry veterans castrated IWW organizer Wesley Everest and lynched him from a railroad bridge.

Despite such antiradical fervor, the Red Scare ran its course by mid-1920. Palmer appeared ridiculous after his warnings of a May 1 uprising of revolutionaries proved to be unfounded and after he mistakenly identified a design for an improved phonograph as a plan for manufacturing explosives. After labor unrest quieted, as the radical left fell into disarray, and because the Soviet

Exhibit 3-16. U.S. per Capita Income in Dollars, 1914–1920

1914	389
1916	473
1918	740
1920	860

Source: *Historical Statistics of the United States, Colonial Times to 1970* (1975).

threat was no longer perceived as immediate, the public appeared more secure than at any time since 1917. Even the unexplained detonation of a wagonload of explosives on Wall Street in September 1920, which killed thirty-three and injured two hundred, did not shake the new sense of security. Stock prices continued their rise the following day. Yet as the era of Wilsonian liberalism ended, many citizens appeared tired of the burdens of internationalism and of reform at home. Voters selecting leaders for the coming decade would shy away from assertive executives, from reformist rhetoric, and from global commitments.

SUGGESTED READINGS

Wilson's contribution to domestic reform is favorably evaluated in Kendrick A. Clements, *The Presidency of Woodrow Wilson* (1992), which used the chief executive's private papers. Arthur Link, the editor of the Wilson papers, is the author of a multivolume biography titled *Woodrow Wilson* (1947–1965). See also Link's *Woodrow Wilson and the Progressive Era, 1910–1917* (1954), as well as the works listed in Chapter 2 by Cooper, Gould, Keller, Kolko, Sklar, and Weinstein. Another useful account can be found in August Hecksher, *Woodrow Wilson: A Biography* (1991). For Wilsonian income tax reform, see John F. Witte, *The Politics and Development of the Federal Income Tax* (1985) and Robert Stanley, *Dimensions of Law in the Service of Order: Origins of the Federal Income Tax, 1861–1913* (1993).

For Wilsonian Latin American policy, see Frederick S. Calhoun, *Power and Principle: Armed Intervention in Wilsonian Foreign Policy* (1986), and David Healy, *Drive to Hegemony: The United States in the Caribbean, 1898–1917* (1988). U.S. involvement in Mexico is the focus of John S. D. Eisenhower, *Intervention: The United States and the Mexican Revolution, 1913–1917* (1993), and P. Edward Haley, *Revolution and Interventionism: The Diplomacy of Taft and Wilson with Mexico, 1910–1917* (1970). The most thorough examination of Wilson's policy toward Asia is Roy W. Curry, *Woodrow Wilson and Far Eastern Policy, 1913–1921* (1968).

U.S. involvement in World War I has provoked a tremendous outpouring of historical literature. In addition to the previously listed Wilson biographies, see Jan Willem Schulte Nordholt, *Woodrow Wilson: A Life for World Peace* (1991); Paul Fussell, *Woodrow Wilson and World War I, 1917–1921* (1985); and Thomas J. Knock, *To End All Wars: Woodrow Wilson and the Quest for a New World Order* (1992). Neutrality and preparedness are discussed in Manfred Jonas, *The United States and Germany (1984)*; Patrick Devlin, *Too Proud to Fight: Woodrow Wilson's Neutrality* (1975); and Michael Pearlman, *To Make Democracy for America: Patricians and Preparedness in the Progressive Era* (1984). For antiwar sentiment, see

Kendrick A. Clements, *William Jennings Bryan: Missionary Isolationist* (1982), and John M. Cooper, Jr., *The Vanity of Power: American Isolationism and the First World War, 1914–1917* (1969).

Accounts of military affairs can be found in David Trask, *The AEF and Coalition Warmaking, 1917–1918* (1993), and in Eric J. Leed, *No Man's Land: Combat and Identity in World War I* (1979). Other descriptions of the fighting include Edward M. Coffman, *The War to End All Wars* (1969); Russell Weigley, *The American Way of War* (1973); and Henry De Weerd, *President Wilson Fights His War* (1968). For army life, see Laurence Stallings, *The Doughboys* (1973), and A.E. Barbeau and Florette Henri, *The Unknown Soldiers: Black American Troops in World War I* (1974). For wartime dissent, see Christopher C. Gibbs, *The Great Silent Majority: Missouri's Resistance to World War I* (1988); Richard Polenberg, *Fighting Faiths: The Abrams Case, the Supreme Court, and Free Speech* (1987); and Charles Chatfield, *For Peace and Justice* (1971). For the plight of wartime German Americans, see Frederick Luebke, *Bonds of Loyalty* (1974).

The best portrait of the home front appears in David P. Kennedy, *Over Here: The First World War and American Society* (1980). Industrial mobilization is surveyed in Robert D. Cuff, *The War Industries Board: Business-Government Relations during World War I* (1973). For domestic propaganda, see Stephen Vaughn, *Holding Fast the Inner Lines: Democracy, Nationalism, and the Committee on Public Information* (1980). See also George Blakey, *Historians on the Home Front* (1970). The life of women in wartime is assessed in Maurine W. Greenwald, *Women, War, and Work: The Impact of World War I on Women Workers in the United States* (1980), and Barbara Steinson, *American Women's Activism in World War I* (1982). For the war's influence on the African American community, see Barbeau and Henri, *The Unknown Soldiers*.

On the peace process, see Arthur Walworth, *Wilson and His Peacemakers: American Diplomacy at the Paris Peace Conference* (1986), as well as Lloyd E. Ambrosius, *Woodrow Wilson and the American Diplomatic Tradition: The Treaty Fight in Perspective* (1987), and *Wilsonian Statecraft: The Theory and Practice of Liberal Internationalism during World War I* (1991). A more critical perspective can be found in Lloyd C. Gardner, *Safe for Democracy: The Anglo-American Response to Revolution, 1913–1923* (1984). For a more detailed study, see Inga Floto, *Colonel House at Paris* (1980). See also the previously listed Wilson biographies. Noninterventionists are the subject of Thomas N. Guinsburg, *The Pursuit of Isolationism in the United States Senate from Versailles to Pearl Harbor* (1982). See also William Widenor, *Henry Cabot Lodge and the Search for an American Foreign Policy* (1980).

Postwar political repression receives treatment in Robert Murray, *The Red Scare* (1955). See also the relevant segments of Paul L. Murphy, *The Meaning of Free Speech: First Amendment Freedoms from Wilson to FDR* (1972); William Preston, *Aliens and Dissenters: Federal Suppression of Radicals, 1903–1933* (1963); and Polenberg, *Fighting Faiths*. For communism, see Robert A. Rosenstone, *A Romantic Revolutionary: A Biography of John Reed* (1990). Postwar racial tensions are depicted in William Tuttle, *Race Riot* (1970), and in Robert Haynes, *A Night of Violence: The Houston Riot of 1917* (1976).

4

A cherished consumer item available on the installment plan, the automobile helped to spark social and cultural change. As a result, moral traditionalists associated the "flivver" with the "flapper" and the "flask."

THE NEW ERA AND THE ADVENT OF MODERN SOCIETY

As the economy entered a spectacular boom between 1922 and 1929, confident corporate leaders proclaimed a New Era in human affairs. New technologies, rising wages, merchandising and distribution advances, fervid consumer spending, and managerial innovations suggested permanent prosperity and stability. The gross national product increased by 40 percent, and per capita income jumped by 30 percent. Unfortunately, postwar affluence was unevenly distributed and far from permanent. Moreover, the consumer economy brought wrenching cultural issues to center stage. The much-heralded Jazz Age of the 1920s provided the context for one of the most profound cultural confrontations in the nation's history. While modernists and cosmopolitans embraced the stylistic innovations, cultural diversity, and liberating opportunities of mass culture, traditionalists sought to maintain the values of a religiously and ethnically homogeneous society.

THE NEW ERA

At the height of the postwar economic boom, *Nation's Business*, the journal of the U.S. Chamber of Commerce, exulted that ordinary citizens had been "transported to a new world." New Era prosperity drew its vitality from consumerism. After the expansion of wartime metal, chemical, and machine industries, manufacturers learned to apply new technologies to stimulate the domestic market. In the petroleum industry, which generated 1 billion barrels of crude oil annually by 1929, corporate laboratories turned out synthetic petrochemicals such as acetate and Dacron as well as plastics, cosmetics, and synthetic tires. Du Pont, a major military contractor and the world's largest industrial empire, applied wartime expertise to develop rayon, an artificial fiber made by dissolving wood chips in an acetate solution. As synthetic compounds became widespread components of clothing, carpets, and upholstery, Du Pont researchers invented cellophane, which manufacturers used to package many of the mass-produced goods of the growing economy.

"His god was Modern Appliances," Sinclair Lewis wrote of the leading character in *Babbitt* (1922), a satirical novel of small-town life in the consumer era. The technological revolution had its greatest impact in the home. After World War I, producers of electrical products such as General Electric and Westinghouse shifted emphasis from large-scale industrial equipment to smaller consumer items. Accordingly, their amply funded research laboratories developed mass-produced appliances such as washing machines, refrigerators, electric irons, toasters, and vacuum cleaners. Business writers such as Mark Sullivan spoke of "the magic geni of electricity" and promised that the new technology would relieve human drudgery and democratize leisure. Predictably, national electricity consumption nearly tripled between 1917 and 1930.

General Electric played a key role in using vacuum tube technology to develop a revolutionary form of national communication: the radio. Described as "the miracle of the ages" by communication executives, radio won widespread recognition when Pittsburgh's KDKA broadcast the 1920 election-night results. By 1929 annual sales of radio receivers exceeded $800 million. Two years later, the NBC and the CBS radio networks encompassed 150 affiliates, and 12 million families owned their own sets. Radios were among the first mass-produced

**Exhibit 4-1. Net Production of Electrical Energy, 1920–1929
(in billions of kilowatt-hours)**

1920	56.6
1925	84.7
1929	116.7

Source: *Recent Economic Changes* (1929).

**Exhibit 4-2. U.S. Passenger Car Registration, 1920–1928
(in rounded millions)**

1920	8.2
1922	10.9
1924	15.5
1926	19.2
1928	21.6

Source: *Recent Economic Changes* (1929).

**Exhibit 4-3. U.S. Expenditures for Magazine Advertising, 1921–1927
(in rounded millions of dollars)**

1921	95.7
1927	176.8

Source: *Recent Economic Changes* (1929).

goods to be made of plastic. The new medium offered news, commentary, drama, humor, religious services, ethnic shows, and popular music to widely dispersed listeners who could be reached by local and national advertisers. Radio's potential in targeting mass audiences became apparent when the "Grand Ole Opry," a variety show that fused traditional country music with humor, began nationwide broadcasts from Nashville in 1926.

Automobile maker Henry Ford, a leading folk and business idol of the age, confidently described machinery as the "new messiah." Ford's Model-T, which sold for as little as $295 by 1929, offered instant mobility and status to millions of consumers of modest means. "I'll go without food before I'll see us give up the car," a working-class wife in Indiana told researchers. Alfred P. Sloan, Jr., of General Motors revolutionized auto merchandising in the postwar era by changing models annually and offering variably priced cars to different segments of the market. Auto producers sold just fewer than 2 million vehicles in 1919, but by 1929 the industry marketed more than 5.6 million motor vehicles a year. When the decade closed, more than 23 million cars were registered, and two of every three households owned one. Creating millions of jobs in the production of steel, rubber, glass, and electrical parts, automobiles generated one-eighth of the nation's industrial activity. Highway construction alone pumped an annual $1 billion into the economy by 1929.

Half of General Motors' sales and 15 percent of the nation's retail trade were administered through the installment plan. Time purchases in turn often resulted from advertising, the key to the New Era consumer economy. As spending on household goods tripled between 1909 and 1929, advertising revenues surpassed $1.5 billion annually. "The American conception of advertising," industry executive Bruce Barton explained to radio broadcasters in 1929, "is to arouse desires and stimulate wants, to make people dissatisfied with the old and out-of-date." In advancing a self-proclaimed "democracy of goods," merchandisers offered the promise of youth and magical self-transformation through the ritual of purchase. As apostles of modernity, however, advertisers also sought to assuage the anxieties that accompanied progress by marketing therapeutic solutions for intestinal problems, skin irregularities, and body odors.

Chain stores were an essential component of New Era capitalism. Consisting of three or more retail units under common ownership and management, chains were able to charge cheaper prices because they made bulk purchases and provided no credit or delivery services. The Great Atlantic and Pacific Tea Company (A&P) had used the chain idea to revolutionize the grocery trade in the nineteenth century. Postwar retailers such as Boston department store and "bargain basement" innovator Edward A. Filene promoted chains as instruments of consumer democracy in "a Fordized America." Between 1918 and 1929 retail syndicates such as J.C. Penney and Woolworth moved into the variety and sundries fields and increased the nation's number of chain outlets from 30,000 to 160,000. By the end of the decade chain stores accounted for 16 percent of U.S. retail business.

"Today in America we are building a new civilization," announced telephone company executive Walter S. Gifford. In *The Present Economic Revolution in the*

Oregon Historical Society

Chain stores such as this market in Portland, Oregon, played an increasing role in the merchandising strategies of the 1920s. The number of chain outlets increased more than fivefold between 1918 and 1929.

Exhibit 4-4. U.S. Gross National Product, 1920–1928
(in rounded billions of dollars)

1920	91.5
1924	84.7
1928	97.0

Source: *Historical Statistics of the United States, Colonial Times to 1970* (1975).

United States (1925), Harvard's Thomas Nixon Carver asserted that postwar economic democracy gave consumers the freedom to choose among varied and affordable products. *The Magazine of Business* even boasted that the "average woman" prized the vacuum cleaner and electric iron more than the vote and favorably compared the contributions of the corporate economy to the reforms of William Jennings Bryan and Robert La Follette. Former muckrakers like Lincoln Steffens, Ida Tarbell, and socialist John Spargo agreed that scientific management and mass distribution had revitalized society. Business optimism remained so high that General Motors' vice president John J. Raskob proposed democratizing investment by selling stock certificates on the installment plan. "Nobody can become rich by saving," Raskob explained in 1929.

A CORPORATE ECONOMY

New Era leaders envisioned a society in which the surpluses produced by technological change could be dispersed across the social spectrum through lower prices, through better products, and through more leisure time. Such views were a staple of the Harvard Graduate School of Business Administration and other institutions that sought to elevate corporate administration to professional status. Graduate business programs focused on the importance of cooperation, scientific management, and rational planning. Inspired by the ethic of corporate responsibility associated with World War I, a "new generation" of business leaders rose to the forefront of corporate officialdom. Business leaders such as General Electric's Owen D. Young, American Telephone and Telegraph's Walter S. Gifford, and General Motors' Alfred Sloan, Jr., saw themselves as trustees for the public and employees. Acknowledging their obligations to stockholders and the profit motive, professional managers nevertheless sought to tie ethical standards, social responsibility, and the service ethic to corporate goals.

"Service always pays better than selfishness," Henry Ford explained in *My Philosophy of Industry* (1929). Ford insisted that the success of large corporations depended upon the goodwill of consumers. As part of the effort to professionalize corporate management and enhance public relations, 750 companies had subscribed to the U.S. Chamber of Commerce's national code of ethics by 1925. New Era managers also believed that long-range administrative planning and scientific methods ensured the permanent conquest of the business cycle. Large corporations had cooperated with competitors in the commodity committees of the War Industries Board. After the war, business leaders in the oil, cotton textile, lumber, construction, and other industries formed independent trade organizations. Although dominated by industry leaders, the nation's 4000

Exhibit 4.5. U.S. White Collar and Manual Employees, 1920–1930
(in rounded millions)

	White Collar	*Manual*	*All Employees*
1920	10.5	17.0	42.2
1930	14.3	19.3	48.7

Source: *Historical Statistics of the United States, Colonial Times to 1970 (1975).*

trade associations engaged in industry-wide research and market extension campaigns, strove to improve productivity, and framed codes of business ethics.

Trade associations promoted more effective budgeting and forecasting, the elimination of waste, and the standardization and simplification of parts. This application of scientific management contributed to a 70 percent improvement in worker productivity between 1919 and 1929. Trade organizations also insulated large firms from the competitive tactics of new businesses and the risk of government intervention. To the delight of Secretary of Commerce Herbert Hoover, such management techniques suggested how "destructive" competition and economic individualism could be replaced by rational cooperation and planning. Trade associations embodied the hope that harmony, abundance, and progress would prevail over political controversy, social conflict, and class strife. Federal Trade Commission chair William E. Humphrey even claimed that Washington trade representatives spoke "with the voice of the people" and constituted a "sort of parliament."

Innovations in managerial capitalism highlighted the increased importance of white-collar employment. By 1929 200,000 engineers and 300,000 foremen formed an integral part of the industrial apparatus. The New Era economy made its greatest strides in consumer and service fields such as banking and finance, communications, real estate, sales, and utilities. Profits tripled and employment doubled in these key service sectors. By 1929 service occupations accounted for nearly one-fourth of the nation's jobs. A susbstantial proportion of white-collar employees were women, many of whom had recently entered the lower tiers of the work force. The ranks of women workers grew by more than one-fourth in the 1920s. Between 1921 and 1924 alone, the number of employed married women leaped from 1.9 million to 3.1 million. Although one-third of the female labor force continued to work as servants and another one-fourth in low-paying factories and mills, twice as many women labored in clerical and sales jobs as in industry when the decade ended.

Prosperity in the growth sectors of the economy was accompanied by financial concentration and speculation. As entrepreneurs staged 6,000 mergers between 1925 and 1931, monopolies consolidated control of aluminum, salt, sugar, and tropical fruits. Mergers tightened the control of oligopolies consisting of two to four corporations in the provision of petroleum, steel, glass, cement, copper, tobacco, meat packing, milk, and bread. Three companies—General Motors, Ford, and Chrysler—produced 83 percent of the nation's automobiles. The downside of such consolidation resulted in the bankruptcy of nearly 5,000 manufacturing and mining companies in the 1920s. By decade's end the nation's 200 largest corporations controlled just less than half of all nonbanking corporate wealth.

Exhibit 4-6. Percentage of Total U.S. Income Received by Those Earning the Top 5 Percent of Incomes, 1920–1928

1920	22.0
1924	24.0
1928	26.8

Source: *Historical Statistics of the United States, Colonial Times to 1970* (1975).

The uneven pace of economic growth worsened the nation's distribution of wealth. In 1929 the income of the country's richest 0.1 percent equaled that of the poorest 42 percent. Meanwhile, two-fifths of all households lived at what the Brookings Institution described as "subsistence-and-poverty" levels; another 36 percent had "minimum comfort." The difficulties of working-class life were illustrated in 1930 when the federal census reported that one-fourth of the nation's urban homes did not meet minimum government living standards. Two-thirds of the housing units in Indianapolis and nine-tenths of those in Atlanta lacked running water. As the nation's wealthiest 5 percent added to its share of earnings, nearly three-quarters of all families lived on fewer than $2,500 a year.

TROUBLED LABOR

Business leaders of the 1920s sought to apply the management lessons of World War I to labor relations by adopting a "human approach to industry" through "welfare capitalism." "People do the best work when they are best cared for," observed John H. Patterson, a pioneer in corporate welfare at National Cash Register. "Slowly we are learning that low wages for labor do not necessarily mean high profits for capital," preached General Electric's Owen Young. As overall wages rose in the postwar period, managers in some large companies improved working conditions and instituted profit sharing and other fringe benefits. Companies like General Motors, Firestone, and Eastman Kodak provided group insurance, private pension plans, and stock ownership through payroll deductions. Others offered medical services, sports clubs, swimming pools, free classes, and libraries. Larger corporations organized employee shop committees, councils, and company unions and placed psychologists in industrial relations units to help managers maintain worker morale.

Welfare capitalism helped to halve employee turnover in the postwar decade. Yet structural problems in industry prevented such programs from guaranteeing the undivided loyalty of workers. In new areas of mass production such as

Exhibit 4-7. U.S. per Capita Income in Dollars, 1920–1929

1920	860
1923	760
1926	826
1929	847

Source: *Historical Statistics of the United States, Colonial Times to 1970* (1975).

White-collar routine as portrayed in a 1925 film, The Crowd. *Employment in white-collar and service industries jumped by nearly half in the 1920s. Routinization of middle-class labor led to increased emphasis on leisure-time activity.*

automaking and electrical parts manufacturing, the emphasis on productivity, efficiency, and speed often resulted in the replacement of older, experienced operatives with unskilled laborers. Factories began to use age limits when hiring. Despite the enlightened approach of some managers, critics suggested that industrial workers increasingly resembled dehumanized automatons, endlessly repeating specific tasks and losing all control over work rhythms and routines. Meanwhile, management used progressive rhetoric about social efficiency and cooperation to promote company unions and assert management's prerogatives on the shop floor. "I will not permit myself to be in a position of having labor dictate to management," declared Bethlehem Steel's Charles Schwab. Predictably, officials delegated little responsibility to company unions and prevented them from addressing wages and working hours issues.

Increased corporate attention to the workplace also resulted in greater hostility toward organized labor. Wartime tolerance of trade unions evaporated during the Red Scare of 1919–1920, when industrialists believed that

Exhibit 4-8. Productivity of U.S. Manufacturing Workers, 1920–1927
(1899 = 100) (in output per person)

1920	107.9
1923	132.5
1927	149.5

Source: *Recent Economic Changes* (1929).

**Exhibit 4-9. U.S. Employees Engaged in Manufacturing, 1920–1927
(in millions)**

1920	10.7
1922	9.0
1925	9.9
1927	9.7

Source: *Recent Economic Changes* (1929).

revolutionaries had penetrated the labor movement and were seeking to convert immigrant workers to communism. Once the War Labor Board disbanded in 1919, the National Association of Manufacturers (NAM) organized an "open-shop" campaign to overthrow the "closed shop," which required workers to possess union cards before employment. The open-shop movement had a devastating effect on labor solidarity throughout the country. Employers in areas of high economic growth such as the Midwest and the South considered collective bargaining alien to the nation's traditions and unnecessary in a period of rising wages and business confidence.

Organized labor's difficulties coincided with antiunion sentiments among the nation's elites and the decline of blue-collar industries. In 1921 the Supreme Court upheld the use of injunctions against steel unions and ruled that strike picketing by more than one person was illegal. One year later labor faced a similar defeat when 400,000 members of the AFL's railroad shopcraft unions walked off the job, which halted rail transport and constituted the largest strike of the decade. When Attorney General Harry Daugherty won a controversial federal injunction against union picketing, the protest collapsed. Meanwhile, the United Mine Workers (UMW) tried to hold the line against falling demand and lower wages in the coal industry, which resulted from increased use of petroleum for heating and power. West Virginia coal miners struck in 1921 to abolish "yellow dog" contracts that prohibited union membership among new workers, which labor activists viewed as union busting. After U.S. troops crushed the strike, the UMW lost an $8 million legal case to outlaw injunctions enforcing the contracts.

Miners suffered a second legal blow in *United Mine Workers* v. *Coronado Coal Co.* (1922), a ruling that held the UMW liable for damages when strikes affected interstate commerce or involved the destruction of property. Although coal miners gained rights to the eight-hour day and to collective bargaining in the postwar era, unemployment and antiunion violence contributed to a dramatic drop in UMW membership from 450,000 to a mere 150,000 by 1930. Layoffs also hit northern clothing workers, who were adversely affected by the popularity of synthetic fibers and short dresses and by the exodus of small producers to the nonunion South and West. As a result, membership in the predominantly female International Ladies' Garment Workers' Union dropped dramatically in the 1920s.

As factory employment stagnated in the 1920s, labor activists were not prepared to organize white-collar workers in the growing office and service sector. These employees saw themselves as members of the middle class and associated unions with manual laborers with whom they believed they had few ties. Organizers also failed to mobilize unskilled workers who replaced the elite craft

The Archives of Labor and Urban Affairs, Wayne State University

Pennsylvania coal miners on strike. Despite labor militance, declining employment in the depressed coal industry left the United Mine Workers with one-third of their previous membership by 1930.

operatives who had been among the union movement's earliest recruits. In the cigar-making industry that produced AFL leader Samuel Gompers, for example, unskilled immigrant women assumed the jobs of high-wage male workers after the introduction of automatic machinery in 1919. Assembly line industries such as automobile manufacturing drew heavily upon semiskilled immigrants and migrants from the rural countryside, and these workers were ignored by union activists until the 1930s.

The conservative tactics of the AFL hurt the movement's ability to recruit beyond its narrow base in the craft industries and railroads. After the Red Scare of 1919 Gompers led a purge of radicals designed to restore the union's image of respectability. His successor, William Green, continued such policies by presenting the movement as an auxiliary to business that required cooperation, not conflict. Committed to New Era goals of increased output and industrial peace, Green backed away from attempts to organize the southern textile industry when police and Virginia state militia forcibly crushed a cotton mill walkout in the late 1920s. Subsequent strikes in the Piedmont mills of North Carolina and Tennessee brought national publicity about vigilante action against unionists, but the plight of the South's 280,000 cotton mill workers was championed by the Communist Party, not the AFL.

Organized labor was limited by a reluctance to recruit women and minorities. For example, the immigrant women who replaced male cigar makers would have been refused admittance into the AFL craft union that served these workers. Only 3 percent of working women belonged to labor groups in 1929, compared with 11 percent of working men. The constitutions or rituals of twenty-four international unions also excluded African American workers, which forced many to seek employment in open-shop industries such as automaking and steel or to accept work as strikebreakers. Organized labor also discriminated against Mexican Americans. Although Chicano labor activity dated to the early years of the century, AFL recruiters showed no interest in the thousands of migrant workers who served as seasonal laborers in southwestern agriculture. By 1933 economic dislocation, management hostility, and poor organizational strategy had reduced union membership from 5 million in 1920 to fewer than 3 million and had created the worst labor climate since the 1890s.

ETHNIC DIVERSITY

Much of the nation's industrial work force came from immigrant families. By 1929 30 percent of the U.S. population of 122 million was composed of foreign-born residents or their children. Although immigration declined substantially during World War I, most ethnics remained in traditional urban enclaves. In 1920 more than 10 million readers supported more than 1,000 foreign-language newspapers. Meanwhile, religious, benevolent, and mutual aid societies served ethnic communities by maintaining communal rituals, cultural traditions, and sources of investment. Such institutions were particularly important to Roman Catholics, who composed 36 percent of the nation's population by decade's end. Catholic groups such as Slavs, Italians, Irish, and Mexicans continued to center their lives around family, parish, and neighborhood. Only the cohesiveness of Jewish ghettos began to decline in the 1920s as socially mobile Jews moved to newer residential areas and loosened ties to religious and Yiddish organizations.

Ever since the 1880s immigrants had constituted the semiskilled employment pool for industrial expansion. The vast majority of working-class ethnics remained factory laborers or menial service and clerical operators. For example, Italian Americans dominated the construction trades. However, by the 1920s some immigrant families had raised enough capital to open neighborhood stores. Others saw children move up to skilled and supervisory industrial work or join the middle class as educated professionals and managers. For immigrant entrepreneurs, the road out of the working class often lay in machine politics and businesses that thrived on friendly political contacts: construction, utilities, local banking, insurance, and sanitation. Discrimination against Irish Americans and eastern and southern Europeans forced immigrants and their offspring to rely on acquaintances and family connections. As a result, ethnic survival networks in the large cities connected politics, labor unions, entertainment, professional sports, gambling, and crime.

Although World War I disrupted the flow of immigrants from Europe, southwestern agriculture, railroad, and mining concerns encouraged the migration of workers from south of the U.S. border with Mexico. About 10 percent of the Mexican population, or more than 1 million people, migrated north in the first three decades of the twentieth century. The nation's Mexican American population doubled to 1.6 million in the 1920s. Ninety percent of Mexican Americans

Mexican workers in San Antonio, Texas, 1924 (section of panorama).

lived in the Southwest, where many labored as low-wage, temporary workers harvesting cotton, vegetables, and fruits. Exploited by cost-conscious commercial farmers, migrant families were considered outside the realm of government regulation, social agencies, and public schooling. Southwestern employers sustained their control of cheap labor by defeating a 1925 bill to restrict Mexican immigration.

By 1930 55 percent of Mexican immigrants spoke no English, and only 5.5 percent of adults had become U.S. citizens. Yet as two-fifths of the Mexican American population became permanent residents of postwar cities, major centers of Chicano culture emerged in southwestern cities such as San Antonio and Los Angeles, and the "City of Angels" contained the largest concentration of Mexican Americans of any U.S. city. Increasingly concerned with their civil rights as U.S. citizens, urban, middle-class Mexican Americans transformed traditional *mutualistas*, or mutual aid societies, into political lobbies. An important example was the formation in Texas of the League of United Latin American Citizens (LULAC), which mobilized against segregation in public schools. The Mexican American community also extended to the Midwest, where laborers were recruited for jobs in postwar packing houses and rail yards. Chicano workers learned that wages improved more the further one traveled from the source of cheap labor south of the border.

Western employers showed little interest in hiring Asian Americans. Between the time of the first Asian exclusion laws of the 1880s and 1943, the Chinese American population in the United States declined from more than 300,000 to 80,000. Despite strong cultural biases against their presence, however,

West Coast Chinese Americans maintained cohesive family and kinship ties and strong community associations. In contrast, the Japanese American population grew to 275,000 by 1925. Although the Gentleman's Agreement considerably reduced the number of Japanese male immigrants, it did not prevent the arrival of "picture brides" (women who emigrated from Japan to marry husbands to whom they had sent photographs). Yet in the early 1920s nativist anxieties resurfaced in a campaign against the Japanese robe (kimono) as a threat to white women's purity, and sentiment built for formal exclusion. Oregon passed an alien land law in 1923 after its populist governor vowed to discourage "Mongolian races" from gaining a foothold on state soil.

Upheld by the U.S. Supreme Court, alien land laws in Oregon and California contributed to the halving of Japanese American agricultural holdings between 1910 and 1940. Moreover, in the *Ozawa* (1922) and *Thind* (1923) cases, the Court denied citizenship rights to Asian Americans as nonwhites. In setting such precedents, the tribunal cited a 1790 law confining naturalization to "free white persons," an 1870 civil rights statute that excluded non-Caucasian immigrants from its provisions, and the Chinese Exclusion Act of 1882, which specified that Chinese immigrants could not become citizens. Bound by external hostility and historic group cohesiveness, many Japanese nevertheless succeeded as California farmers, orchardists, and merchants by creating a self-contained economy in which 40 percent of participants were self-employed. Japanese Americans sustained such autonomy through traditional institutions such as credit unions, employment agencies, price-setting trade guilds, newspapers, and benevolent societies.

Among the nation's ethnic groups, Native Americans gained the least from New Era prosperity. Anglo reformers in the American Indian Defense Association succeeded in achieving full citizenship for native people through the Snyder Act of 1924. Yet the Bureau of Indian Affairs (BIA) continued to cooperate with developers seeking to exploit reservation lands and resources. Congress created the Pueblo Lands Board in 1924 to compensate native people in New Mexico for lands illegally given to whites. Yet in 1932 Senate investigators revealed that the panel had colluded with speculators, railroad interests, and cattle companies to assess tribal lands below fair market value. In another example of government mismanagement, the Federal Power Commission permitted Montana power interests to develop a hydroelectric site on the Flathead Indian Reservation in 1930 without providing just compensation to native residents. Between 1887 and 1934 the amount of land controlled by Native Americans dwindled from 138 million acres to 47 million acres.

Federal policy in the 1920s concentrated on Americanizing native peoples. Despite tribal resistance, the commissioner of Indian affairs ordered the prohibition of religious dancing, and the Hopi Snake Dance and the Plains Indians' Sun Dance were targeted specifically. Government officials contended that the abolition of "pagan" rituals constituted the first step toward participation in society. Such reasoning led to an increase in annual aid for Native American education in the early 1930s from $3 million to $12 million, yet government boarding schools taught tribal people to despise their heritage. Reformer John Collier led a successful crusade to permit young men to leave the schools for religious rituals. Nevertheless, Native Americans lacked the political power to alter oppressive government policies, and cultural and economic stagnation remained the defining feature of reservation life.

BLACK METROPOLIS

When black nationalist Marcus Garvey proclaimed, "Up, you mighty Race! You can accomplish what you will!" he reflected both the promise and the adversity of African American life in the 1920s. Encouraged by the job opportunities provided by wartime mobilization, the New Era boom, and the advancement of the idea of a "black metropolis" by community leaders and newspaper editors, African Americans left the rural South in unprecedented numbers between 1915 and 1928. The Great Migration brought 1.2 million southern blacks to northern and western cities. By 1930 New York and Chicago contained African American subcities of more than 225,000 each, and at least two-fifths of the nation's black people lived in urban centers.

Nevertheless, the black metropolis offered mixed prospects. Because African Americans were among the last migrants to the industrial cities, many of the available jobs involved menial tasks for low pay. Black workers served as sweepers and firemen in midwestern steel plants. In Detroit, where the African American population increased sixfold in the 1920s, Henry Ford pioneered the hiring of blacks to work on the assembly line, but their jobs were mostly unskilled. Although urbanization produced a black working class adapted to modern industry, African Americans held only 2 percent of the white-collar and skilled jobs in the country in 1930. Racial discrimination also forced black migrants to live in racially defined neighborhoods. Despite the Supreme Court's prohibition of residential segregation ordinances in 1917, white neighborhood associations resorted to restrictive convenants that prevented property holders from selling to blacks.

Northern landlords contributed to the growth of urban ghettos by squeezing profits from declining neighborhoods without improving properties. For example, rents in New York's Harlem doubled between 1919 and 1927. Yet population density approached 336 people an acre, and the district's death rate remained 42 percent higher than that of the rest of New York. Migration and the struggle for economic survival disrupted the stability of black families because, although African American women could find jobs as domestics, black men faced joblessness because of the hiring prejudices of employers and unions. Consequently, African Americans in migrant neighborhoods experienced higher rates of desertion, divorce, and illegitimacy than did whites. Prostitution, gambling, bootlegging, the numbers racket, and narcotics addiction all became part of the impoverished inner-city environment.

Despite these difficulties, black pride, habit, and the need for mutual protection led to efforts to "advance the race" by promoting economic self-sufficiency through racial clubs, fraternal orders, and mutual aid societies. Yet only one organization, the Universal Negro Improvement Association (UNIA), managed to attract major support from working-class African Americans in the northern ghettos. Founded in 1914 by Marcus Garvey, a Jamaican, the UNIA enrolled about 100,000 members at its peak, although Garvey claimed as many as 2 million. The improvement association inspired ordinary people to dream of racial freedom and economic independence under African American leadership.

Garvey's visionary nationalism had been advanced by Wilsonian creeds of self-determination during World War I. Working with black business entrepre-

Stock Montage

Marcus Garvey, the most popular and charismatic black leader of the 1920s. Garvey's Universal Negro Improvement Association preached black pride and economic self-sufficiency. The black nationalist movement attracted more than 100,000 working-class followers.

neurs in the United States and Liberia, the Jamaican leader anticipated that an expanding capitalism could provide the economic basis for racial liberation. Garvey described himself as the provisional president of the African republic and called for an "Africa for the Africans." He suggested that an elite number of African Americans from the United States go to Liberia to teach the skills needed to redeem the continent from European colonialism. Garvey accurately prophesied that a liberated Africa would be an inspiration to black people in the Western Hemisphere. He also preached support of African American businesses in a "buy black" campaign. Accordingly, the UNIA organized grocery chains, restaurants, laundries, a hotel, a black doll factory, a printing plant, and a newspaper called *Negro World*. Its Black Star Steamship Line sought to establish commercial links between the United States, the West Indies, and Africa.

Although condemned by established African American leaders such as W.E.B. Du Bois, Garvey's black nationalism brought hope to a generation embittered by the harsh realities of the urban promised land. After several UNIA businesses failed because of mismanagement, however, federal prosecutors indicted Garvey in 1922 for selling fraudulent stock. Although he protested that white business associates had betrayed him, Garvey alone was convicted. After two years in federal prison, the charismatic leader was deported in 1927 at the insistence of Federal Bureau of Investigation Director J. Edgar Hoover as an alien who had committed a felony.

THE "NEW NEGRO"

While Garvey offered a creed of black nationalism, the National Association for the Advancement of Colored People (NAACP) and the Urban League continued to struggle for justice for blacks in the white community. Under prodding by the NAACP, the Dyer Anti-Lynching Bill passed the House of Representatives in 1921, but southern Democrats filibustered the bill to death in the Senate. Yet the ability of civil rights groups to mobilize members of black voluntary associations, of churches, and of mutual benefit societies bore fruit in 1930, when the Senate blocked the Supreme Court nomination of conservative judge John J. Parker, who had publicly commented about the unpreparedness of African Americans for the "burden and responsibilities of government." The defeat of the Parker nomination, also opposed by the AFL, suggested the formation of a powerful coalition among forces of urban liberalism, labor, and civil rights.

Black activists vigorously pursued equal rights on the local level. In Springfield, Illinois, and Dayton, Ohio, parents and students mounted classroom boycotts when authorities reintroduced school segregation in 1922. Protesters in Gary, Indiana, objected to the building of an all-black public school in 1927. In Chicago and other large cities, African Americans joined white political machines to win jobs and protect community interests. By supporting the machine of Republican Mayor Bill Thompson, for example, African Americans obtained one-fourth of Chicago's postal service jobs. The city's First District elected Oscar DePriest as the North's first black congressional representative. In the South, middle-class college students demonstrated new assertiveness in defending African American interests. When the Ku Klux Klan marched on an all-black veterans hospital in Tuskegee, Alabama, in 1923, students at the nearby Tuskegee Institute defended the institution from potential violence. Students at Nashville's Fisk University mounted campus strikes in 1924 and 1925 to protest administration censorship and the paternalism of the school's white president.

"I am a Negro—and beautiful," exclaimed Harlem poet Langston Hughes at mid-decade. Inspired by the potential of the black metropolis, African American intellectuals, writers, and artists expressed a new racial pride and militancy. The movement spoke of the "New Negro" and depicted the subsequent

JAMES WELDON JOHNSON
1871–1938

UPI/Corbis-Bettmann

In *The Autobiography of an Ex-Colored Man* (1912), James Weldon Johnson's tragic protagonist regretted that he had passed up the opportunity "to have taken part in a work so glorious" as building a new black nation. Yet the versatile and multitalented Johnson accomplished precisely what his fictional hero failed to do and became a central black role model of the Harlem Renaissance of the 1920s.

Born in Jacksonville, Florida, to an immigrant from Nassau and to the headwaiter of a hotel, Johnson attended preparatory school and college at all-black Atlanta University. Returning home in 1894, he became principal of the African American grade school from which he had graduated and added secondary-level classes to the school's curriculum. Johnson also started a black city newspaper, but the enterprise soon suffered financial failure. Pressed for funds and concerned with the improvement of African American living conditions, he studied law with a white attorney and became the first black admitted to the Florida bar by court examination.

Johnson and his musician brother Rosamond began collaborating on black dialect songs and comic operas in 1898. The duo also composed "Lift Every Voice and Sing" for a school assembly dedicated to Abraham Lincoln. By 1915 this stirring song had emerged as the unofficial "Negro National Anthem."

Buoyed by their early success, the Johnson brothers left for New York City in 1902, where they worked with black vaudeville performer Bob Cole. "Under the Bamboo Tree" (1902), a rag-style ditty, became their first hit and sold 400,000 sheet music copies. The trio sought to move beyond the era's popular but demeaning "coon songs" and minstrel shows by introducing what lyricist Johnson called "a higher degree of artistry" to African American music. Yet after completing the words for more than 200 songs and a major musical, the restless songwriter deserted popular culture for new arenas.

Using Republican ties forged through his electoral support of President Theodore Roosevelt in 1904, Johnson won appointments as U.S. consul to multiracial Venezuela and Nicaragua between 1906 and 1913. In his free time, he worked on *The Autobiography of an Ex-Colored Man*, an anonymously published story of a light-skinned black who passed for white and observed the nation's racial foibles with a sense of irony. In 1913 the *New York Times* published Johnson's "Fifty Years," a

outpouring of race-conscious poetry, prose, and art as part of a "Harlem Renaissance." Borrowing from the rich oral traditions of African American culture, the stark verses of Hughes, of Sterling Brown, and of James Weldon Johnson used the rhythms and moods of spirituals, of blues, and of everyday vernacular. Claude McKay brought these techniques to the novel in *Home to Harlem* (1928), an odyssey of the black working class. Jean Toomer's *Cane* (1923) vividly captured the life of poor southern blacks. "Us colored folks is branches without roots," wrote novelist Zora Neale Hurston in *Their Eyes Were Watching God* (1937), "and that makes things come round in queer ways."

Progressive whites rushed to praise the vitality of African American culture. In 1925 the reformist *Survey Graphic* asked Alaine Locke, the nation's first Afri-

rhymed tribute to the Emancipation Proclamation. Hoping to support himself by serious writing, Johnson resigned from government service, changed his middle name from William to the literary-sounding Weldon, and returned to New York City.

Soon the energetic Johnson joined the *New York Age*, the city's oldest African American newspaper, as a leading editorial writer. Moved by W.E.B. Du Bois's call for social activism, he became field secretary for the fledgling NAACP in 1916 and multiplied the organization's branches fivefold within three years. Johnson investigated lynchings and peonage and helped build southern chapter strength from 3 to 131. When war tension led to a massacre of blacks in East St. Louis, Illinois, in 1917, the NAACP field secretary organized a silent parade of nearly 10,000 protesters down New York's Fifth Avenue.

Becoming the NAACP's first African American executive secretary in 1920, Johnson went to Haiti to report on the killing of 3,000 people by U.S. Marines. He soon demanded military withdrawal from the predominantly black nation. As NAACP strength surpassed 100,000, Johnson led the campaign to win House passage of the Dyer Anti-Lynching Bill of 1921, although a southern-led filibuster killed the measure in the Senate. Despite the defeat, NAACP lawyers pressed legal strategies and won a dramatic victory when the Supreme Court took a first step toward guaranteeing black voting rights by outlawing the "white" primary in 1927.

An integrationist, Johnson nevertheless believed that the blending of the races would be more palatable if society acknowledged the cultural contributions of African Americans. He edited an anthology of black poetry in 1922, which emphasized the importance of black folk literature and popular music. Appealing to the growing self-respect among young African American artists and intellectuals associated with the Harlem Renaissance, Johnson issued two collections of Negro spirituals in 1925 and 1926.

In 1927 Johnson published his greatest work of poetry, *God's Trombones—Seven Negro Folk Sermons.* Using the free cadence of an old black preacher, he captured the heart of black idiom by avoiding both dialect verse and strict metric form. "Your arm's too short to box with God," one sermon proclaimed. *God's Trombones* helped to revitalize African American poetry with the rhythm of speech and stimulated pride in black identity. In the same year, publishers issued a new edition of *The Autobiography of an Ex-Colored Man* with Johnson's name on the cover. To further his work as a cultural architect, Johnson also released *Black Manhattan* (1930), an informal history that focused on black contributions to the arts.

A poised, dignified man with an ironic sense of humor, Johnson left the NAACP in 1930 to take up a career as professor of literature at Fisk University. When he issued his autobiography, *Along This Way,* in 1933, James Weldon Johnson could point to his role in moving African Americans from the enforced racial accommodation of the early twentieth century to an emerging assertion of prideful culture and militant politics. ■

can American Rhodes scholar, to edit a special Harlem issue on the New Negro. Meanwhile, the art world opened its doors to young black painters and sculptors whose work incorporated traditional African forms and lines. As integrationists, leaders such as Du Bois and James Weldon Johnson hoped that African American cultural creativity would promote acceptance of their race. Yet urban blacks also found the consumer market highly rewarding. Although radio provided few outlets for African Americans in the 1920s, commercial recording companies tapped a huge market by releasing "race records" by black blues artists such as Ma Rainey, Mamie Smith, Ethel Waters, and Bessie Smith. Similarly, black and white film companies distributed "race movies" made especially for African Americans.

Harlem's jazz nightclubs and revues became symbols of the hedonistic lifestyle in an age of Prohibition. Advertised as an "erotic utopia" where "white people from downtown could be entertained by colored girls," Harlem became a favorite spot for "slumming parties." Establishments such as the Cotton Club attracted exclusively white audiences who sought the "primitive spontaneity" of black entertainers such as dancer Earl "Snakehips" Tucker and vocalist Edith Wilson. African Americans were commodified as an "expressive" and "erotic" people who were untouched by puritanism. Carl Van Vechten's *Nigger Heaven* (1925), a bohemian view of Harlem orgies and seduction, sold 100,000 copies in its first year of publication. While the ghetto festered, Jazz Age tourists enjoyed "a vogue in things Negro."

AUTOMOBILE CULTURE

When workers in New York finished the world's tallest structure, the 1,250-foot Empire State Building, in 1930, the city claimed a fitting symbol of the urban age. The federal census of 1920 had reported that more than half the U.S. population lived in communities of at least 2,500 people. In the following decade, more than 70 percent of the nation's population growth occurred in metropolitan areas, and land values in large urban centers doubled by 1925. The space-saving skyscraper became a dominant feature of downtown areas.

Although central "downtown areas" served the corporate workplace, the 1920s witnessed the growth of widely dispersed "automobile" cities like Los Angeles, Dallas, Detroit, and Kansas City. Hard-surfaced roads, lower taxes and property prices, and readily available electricity promoted the dispersal of urban businesses. Similar enticements encouraged the growth of bedroom settlements within commuting distance of downtown. As middle-class families fled urban filth, noise, overcrowding, crime, and visible poverty, the suburban population doubled in the decade. The homogeneous communities of the suburbs contained bungalows and small homes and replaced the traditional porch with the garage. As suburban families became less dependent on downtown stores, developers constructed suburban shopping centers, where retailers such as Sears, Roebuck built stores featuring free parking and abundant floor space.

Suburban growth and automobile culture exerted a costly influence on older cities. A coalition of auto industry groups, road builders, and land developers convinced municipal authorities that motor vehicles would create new channels of commerce, would open surrounding areas to development, and would reduce congestion in central cities. Consequently, urban governments underwrote the expense of city street paving. Yet road construction destroyed residential

Exhibit 4-10. U.S. Urban and Rural Population, 1920–1930*
(in rounded millions)

	Urban	Rural
1920	54.2	51.5
1930	68.9	53.8

Source: *Historical Statistics of the United States, Colonial Times to 1970* (1975).
*urban = population centers of more than 2,500 people.

neighborhoods by tearing down older homes and by converting community thoroughfares into traffic arteries. As filling stations, auto dealerships, garages, and parking lots cluttered city streets, traffic congestion, exhaust, and noise plagued downtown areas. Already depleted by the flight to the suburbs, city tax bases were stretched further to build and maintain roads that connected to outlying areas, which created a burden estimated at $400 million a year in the 1920s.

Automobile culture also contributed to the decimation of public transit. National ridership on electric streetcars peaked at 15.7 billion passengers in 1923, but trolleys and interurban electric rail lines, which could not maneuver in traffic, were not as attractive as the private motor car. In Los Angeles, where the metropolitan population mushroomed from 50,000 in 1900 to 2.2 million in 1930, residents rebelled against the high fares and poor service of transit companies. One-fourth of the area's population drove cars, and taxpayers in Los Angeles refused to subsidize unreliable private transit companies. By 1925 gasoline-powered buses had replaced trolleys on the outskirts of most substantial cities, and commuters supported the building of public highways. As streetcar lines in major cities went bankrupt in the mid-1920s, urban transit systems were gradually converted to the use of rubber-tire vehicles.

Private motor vehicles had an enormous impact on lifestyle. Car ownership liberated people by increasing personal choices. It afforded mobility to affluent women, customarily restrained from adventure outside the home, and to southern blacks, now free to move beyond white-dominated communities. It gave ordinary people a sense of identity and became as much a symbol of material success and accomplishment as home ownership. Yet as a technological wonder that contained no system for coordinating its movements with others, the automobile remained a perfect symbol of the dual nature of progress. Car advertisements promised to "bring the family together." Yet the recreational aspects of automobility stressed pleasure and individual whim, not family or communal solidarity. Such patterns of individualism emerged when small-town residents neglected the neighborly comraderie of weekend and traditional holidays for auto outings to distant destinations.

The most controversial aspect of automobile culture involved its perceived threat to sexual propriety. Cars enabled young people to interrelate without a chaperone and provided an autonomy and a privacy that disturbed moral critics. One lecturer noted that the once-sacred family had degenerated into a "physical service station." Ministers linked the automobile to rising crime rates and blamed cars for altering sexual mores, for shattering bonds of family life, and for undermining community standards. Joyriding on the Sabbath, for example, upset religious traditionalists. Meanwhile, Nashville's Salvation Army announced that the misfortunes of most of the unwed mothers in its maternity homes were due to "the predatory drivers of automobiles."

HOLLYWOOD, THE FLAPPER, AND THE ROMANTIC IDEAL

In 1920, years before the Jazz Age got its name, more Americans attended movies on Sunday than attended church. By the end of the decade motion pictures

Clara Bow, the "It" girl. Her direct and frank sexuality attracted middle-class urbanites to the movies in the 1920s. Motion pictures forged a new consensus on playful marriage and self-indulgent consumerism.

attracted more than 70 million viewers weekly. Surveys showed that young women went to the movies an average of forty-six times a year. The favorite role models of youth were film idols such as Douglas Fairbanks and Mary Pickford. Enhanced by a glamorous star system, by alluring theater palaces, and by stirring imagery, silent movies profoundly affected social values and consumer styles. Motion pictures became the secular religion of the New Era, and Hollywood was its mecca.

Comic film artists such as Charlie Chaplin, Harold Lloyd, Harry Langdon, and Buster Keaton continued to entertain moviegoers in the postwar era by satirizing pretentious authority and moral hypocrisy. Yet motion picture producers increasingly cultivated middle-class audiences by incorporating sexual and romantic themes. By 1920 the industry had received financial backing from major banks and had organized itself into a consortium of eight major studios that produced, distributed, and exhibited nearly all the nation's films. Early postwar romances featured European stars such as Rudolph Valentino (*The Sheik*, 1920), Erich von Stroheim (*Foolish Wives*, 1922), and Greta Garbo (*The Temptress*, 1926). At the same time, Cecil B. De Mille and other producers worked with homegrown performers such as Clara Bow, Joan Crawford, and Gloria Swanson to express the redefined sexuality of the "flapper," a central character in 1920s film.

As early as 1915, journalist H.L. Mencken had used the term *flapper* to describe brazen and volatile young English women who sought sexual satisfaction, social equality, and personal freedom. Others insisted that the word referred to the youthful fashion of wearing overshoes or galoshes unfastened so the tongues flapped. Flappers of the postwar era wore bobbed hair that concealed the forehead, and they exposed their legs with knee-high skirts or dresses. Abbreviated hemlines, flattened chests, hidden waists, and narrowed hips conveyed the impression of boyish women in energetic motion. To prove their emancipation from Victorian codes of feminine modesty, flappers not only drove cars but frequently wore rouge, lipstick, and eye makeup, used slang, publicly smoked cigarettes, and joined men in illegal speakeasies, jazz clubs, and dance halls. On the screen, they appeared as "modern" and independent women of confident gait and unrestrained energy. Joan Crawford provided a memorable portrait of this type through her frantic version of the Charleston in *Our Dancing Daughters* (1928).

Sociologist Edward A. Ross declared in 1928 that the silver screen had made young people "sex-wise, sex-excited, and sex absorbed." As motion pictures instructed adolescents in techniques of kissing, of eye movement, and of appealing flirtation, they offered a form of rudimentary sex education. Advertisements for films such as *Sinners in Silk* (1924) and *Alimony* (1924) raved about "beautiful jazz babies, champagne baths, midnight revels, petting parties in the purple dawn." Yet Hollywood trod a thin line between sexual sensationalism and moral convention. In 1922 the Big Eight responded to a series of moral scandals involving performers such as Fatty Arbuckle by recruiting Will H. Hays, a Republican fund-raiser and postmaster general, to head the Motion Picture Producers and Distributors Association. Hays coordinated industry censorship by reviewing films and scripts and scrutinizing performers to avoid further scandal. These public relations efforts succeeded in discouraging demands for state and federal censorship by religious and civic groups.

Hoping to pad box-office receipts by titillating audiences without offending moralists, filmmakers perfected the art of skillful compromise. Actresses Gloria Swanson and Joan Crawford frequently played assertive women who used their toughness to protect purity instead of to dispense with it. De Mille productions such as *The Ten Commandments* (1923) and *The Godless Girl* (1929) portrayed immorality but sermonized against promiscuity and youthful sex. Movies like the sensational *It* (1927), starring Clara Bow, depicted the quest of working women for loving husbands, not sexual dalliance. Even provocative features such as De Mille's *The Affairs of Anatol* (1921) brought husband and wife back together in the final reel. De Mille and others repeatedly used these films to emphasize that successful marriages depended upon mutual recognition of sexual and emotional needs.

"They are what people would like to be," commented film actor Stephan Stills about the popularity of 1920s movie stars. Hollywood provided audiences with positive role models for the consumer economy. Both on screen and off, performers such as Douglas Fairbanks, Mary Pickford, and Gloria Swanson personified the promise of freedom in the realm of leisure. Demonstrating that status now came from styles of consumption, their films suggested that discomfort with bureaucratic work routines and loss of autonomy could be alleviated by adopting exciting lifestyles. Moviegoers learned to associate sexiness with apparel, makeup, and perfume as adjuncts to the body. While Fairbanks promoted lines of sports clothes for men of leisure, Swanson endorsed cosmetic and beauty aids for women.

In an age of increasing use of birth control devices, De Mille and other filmmakers suggested a new marital ethic: men would overcome their obsession with work if women would abandon their preoccupation with purity. Redefining success as the means to the good life, Hollywood legitimized the idea of the consumer-age family as an avenue leading to romantic love and personal happiness. Although Swanson married four times during the 1920s, the silver screen taught that relations between husbands and wives could be stabilized by an infusion of dynamic personality, cosmopolitan fun, and healthy beauty and sex. Movies placed new emphasis on youth and innovation instead of age and experience. Old producer virtues such as thrift and frugality could not compete with the new attractions of self-expression, liberation, and fulfillment within the confines of marriage and work. Film stars embodied the grooming, poise, and charm needed to succeed as a personality in the leisure culture of romance and adventure.

THE JAZZ AGE AND YOUTH CULTURE

Popular music reinforced Hollywood's call for qualified hedonism. By the 1920s prewar rag styles had evolved into more carefree and rhythmic jazz forms. Radio listeners learned about the new musical genre through Paul Whiteman, the self-styled "King of Jazz," whose orchestra broadcasts featured the brilliant Iowa cornetist, Bix Beiderbecke, and the relaxed styles of vocalist Bing Crosby. More adventurous fans could trek to New York's Harlem to hear black stride pianists such as James P. Johnson and Thomas ("Fats") Waller or to catch the improvisations of small jazz combos in the district's local clubs. Yet 1920s jazz was mainly dance music. New York City's ballrooms and dance halls admitted 6 million in 1925 alone. Postwar Harlem dance band innovators such as Chick Webb, Duke Ellington, Fletcher Henderson, and Louis Armstrong pioneered the swing music that would become the signature style of the nation's popular music two decades later.

White jazz and popular music dominated the radio waves. Broadcasters favored lighthearted novelty and dance tunes such as "Yes, We Have No Ba-

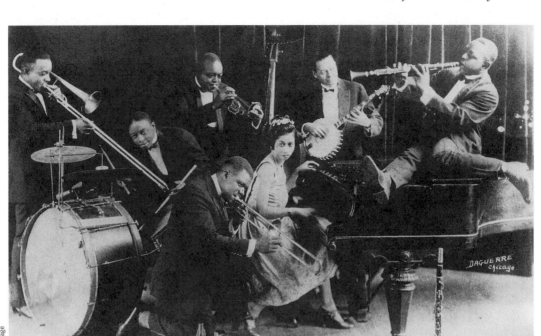

Stock Montage

A new sense of racial pride among blacks in northern cities helped to sustain a rich variety of expression among black musicians and artists. Here blues coronetist Louis Armstrong plays a set with King Oliver's Band.

nanas" (1923), "Somebody Stole My Gal" (1923), and "Yes, Sir, That's My Baby" (1924). Yet a few songwriters like Ira and George Gershwin artfully fused themes of spiritual and sexual love by combining blues influences with introspective lyrics. Songs like the Gershwins' "The Man I Love" (1924) and "Someone to Watch Over Me" (1926), often performed by throaty torch singers, appealed to single women entering the romantic marketplace. Popular music also won favor with middle-class collegiates, whose peer culture sought independence from family influence and traditional mores. College students were frequent patrons of the speakeasies, where a diverse clientele consumed illegal liquor, rubbed elbows with gangsters, danced to "hot" orchestrations, and sought sexual adventure.

The unofficial anthem of the speakeasies was "Making Whoopee" (1928), an irreverent reflection upon marriage and divorce whose title became a common term for having sex. As the movies, radio, popular music, and national magazines popularized new roles and identities associated with the consumer ethic, revised standards of sexual propriety pervaded postwar society. The divorce rate doubled between 1914 and 1929, and the frequency of divorce approached one-sixth that of marriage. More disturbing to moralists, women born after 1900 were twice as likely to engage in premarital sex as those born before the turn of the century. The sexual freedom of the 1920s reflected the increased availability and effectiveness of condoms, contraceptive jellies, and the diaphragm. College students expressed great interest in these birth control techniques. Yet as the

Exhibit 4-11. U.S. Marriage and Divorce Rate, 1920–1928
(per 1,000 population)

	Marriage Rate	Divorce Rate
1920	12.0	1.6
1928	9.8	1.7

Source: *Historical Statistics of the United States, Colonial Times to 1970* (1975).

American Birth Control League sought to contain family size and taught that sexual intercourse need not be limited to procreation, married couples became the leading beneficiaries of the revolution in sexual practices.

Family planning reduced the number of offspring, alleviated sexual guilt, and freed women for life outside the home. Although twenty-two states restricted or forbade the dissemination of contraceptive devices, a 1929 study reported that three-fourths of married women in their early thirties used birth control. Two years later the Federal Council of the Churches of Christ endorsed artificial contraception. By then family size had declined from 4.6 members in 1900 to fewer than 3.8. The trend toward sexual openness received legitimation in *The Revolt of Modern Youth* (1925), by Judge Ben Lindsey, the founder of Denver's juvenile court. In a second book, *The Companionate Marriage* (1927), Lindsey called for the use of contraception and for divorce by mutual consent for childless couples. Although the judge believed that psychological counseling and sex education could prevent broken homes and reduce the chances that youths would commit crime, critics associated his proposals with the antics of a younger generation gone wild and a civilization without ethical bearings.

Concern about changes in moral and sexual codes focused on the behavior of the nation's youth. As occupational specialization extended the period of education and socialization for young people, high school enrollment multiplied sixfold between 1900 and 1930, and college and university attendance tripled to reach 1 million. Although only 12 percent of college-age youth attended institutions of higher learning by the end of the 1920s, campus culture had an enormous influence on social fashions and values. Novelist F. Scott Fitzgerald wrote of campus life in the sensational *This Side of Paradise* (1920). "None of the Victorian mothers," he said, "had any idea how casually their daughters were accustomed to be kissed." An emerging campus peer culture accepted the consumption of liquor and cigarettes as marks of adulthood. Freed from the constraints of family and community, unchaperoned couples explored new freedom in dating and "petting" and coined the terms "boyfriend" and "girlfriend" to replace the cumbersome "lovers" and "sweethearts."

Exhibit 4-12. U.S. Public Secondary School Enrollment, 1920–1930
(in rounded millions)

1920	2.2
1930	4.4

Source: *Historical Statistics of the United States, Colonial Times to 1970* (1975).

THE LOST GENERATION

The most important symbol of postwar youth was the Lost Generation, a name that expatriate Gertrude Stein gave to the self-exiled artists, writers, and intellectuals who flocked to Paris in the 1920s. Writers such as Stein, Ernest Hemingway, F. Scott and Zelda Fitzgerald, John Dos Passos, and Malcolm Cowley drifted to postwar Europe to search for spiritual and artistic roots. They also sought escape from the materialism and puritanism they despised in their home country. As disinherited children of the middle class, they were, in Cowley's words, "strangers in their own land." The rebels berated conventional culture as hopelessly stupid and materialistic. Yet they reserved their most intense wrath for the moral guardians of society, whom they castigated as "philistines" for failing to separate art from morality. *American Mercury* editor H.L. Mencken memorably savaged such targets by calling them the "booboisie."

The brutality of World War I, in which more than 9 million soldiers perished, presented the intelligentsia with a powerful metaphor for disillusionment. Hemingway's bitter novels, *The Sun Also Rises* (1926) and *A Farewell to Arms* (1929), described the Lost Generation's reaction to the ideological sham and cant of its elders. War "kills the very good and the very gentle and the very brave impartially," Hemingway wrote in terse prose. One of the author's protagonists confessed to being "always embarrassed by the words 'sacred,' 'glorious,' and 'sacrifice.'" Only death was an absolute in a world devoid of meaningful political ideology. Such cynicism carried over into views of postwar technology and economic progress. Social critics such as Edmund Wilson, Harold Stearns, Van Wyck Brooks, and Lewis Mumford attacked the monotony of the skyscraper and the assembly line. Meanwhile, imagist poets such as Ezra Pound, T.S. Eliot, Hart Crane, and Amy Lowell portrayed modern existence as an absurd wasteland.

"I love my country, but I don't like it," novelist Sinclair Lewis once explained. The first U.S. author to receive the Nobel Prize for Literature, Lewis published *Main Street* in 1920. "It is dullness made God," the author wrote of life on the Great Northern Plains. His portrait of a married woman's attempt to overcome the conventions of small-town tribalism sold 400,000 copies within weeks. When Lewis's *Babbitt* drew a biting portrait of a complacent midwestern booster two years later, the title introduced a new term of derision into the language. Another midwestern novelist, F. Scott Fitzgerald, dissected the superficial materialism and spiritual poverty of the Jazz Age aristocracy in *The Great Gatsby* (1925).

Following the teachings of Viennese psychoanalyst Sigmund Freud, cultural rebels sought liberation from emotional repression and conformity. Cowley hoped that children could "develop their own personalities" and "blossom freely like flowers." He joined Crane and Stearns in outlining a bohemian code that included momentary gratification, individuality, creative work, self-expression, and female equality. Imaginative people would achieve these, wrote Cowley, even if it meant breaking every law, convention, or rule of art. Bohemian enclaves in places such as New York's Greenwich Village and California's Big Sur brought together like-minded rebels. Despite Crane's suicide and Fitzgerald's alcoholism, the Lost Generation left a rich literary legacy and helped to establish creative artists and writers as cultural critics.

— Francis Scott Key Fitzgerald —
1896–1940
— Zelda Sayre Fitzgerald —
1900–1948

The fiction of F. Scott Fitzgerald—indeed, Fitzgerald's entire career and marriage to Zelda Sayre—epitomized the cultural turbulence that shook traditional values during the Jazz Age of the 1920s. Catapulted to fame by the publication of his first novel, *This Side of Paradise*, in 1920, Fitzgerald depicted "a new generation grown up to find all Gods dead, all wars fought, all faiths in man shaken."

Princeton University Library

Born in St. Paul, Minnesota, Fitzgerald left the wholesome but bland Midwest for the sophistication of the East. First he lived as an undergraduate at Princeton (he quit without graduating in 1917), then as an army officer, and later as an advertising writer in New York. Captivated by wealth, extravagance, and the wholesale rejection of Victorian morality, the novelist and story writer celebrated a younger generation preoccupied with booze, sex, jazz, and easy money. His overnight literary success enabled Fitzgerald to fulfill his version of the American Dream, at least for a while.

Fitzgerald met Zelda Sayre while stationed in her home town, Montgomery, Alabama. Zelda symbolized the rich, beautiful, outrageous flapper type that attracted the young military officer. Wild and zany, she held ambitions of escape as a ballet dancer. Together they set off for Paris, where they lived at the core of an expatriate literary community that included Gertrude Stein and Ernest Hemingway and that embodied the repudiation of the producer values of provincial, small-town America.

The extravagant lifestyle haunted Fitzgerald and compromised his work. "I can't reduce our scale of living and I can't stand this financial insecurity," he complained to his editor. Often—too often, he thought—Fitzgerald wrote popular stories for money (more than 160 short stories in his brief career) while publishing the novels *The Beautiful and Damned* (1922) and *The Great Gatsby* (1925).

Meanwhile, Fitzgerald's success and dominating presence undermined Zelda's confidence. He envied her talent, and his ambivalence about flappers—"brave, shallow, cynical, impatient, turbulent, and empty" he called them—accentuated her frustration. She suffered a series of emotional breakdowns and required hospitalization. While confined, Zelda completed the novel *Save Me the Waltz* (1932), the Gatsby story told from a woman's perspective. She remained institutionalized for the rest of her life.

The economic downturn of the 1930s also undermined F. Scott Fitzgerald's confidence. In 1931 he earned more than $40,000 a year; eight years later his royalties totaled $33! His novel *Tender Is the Night* (1934) received poor critical responses, and his alcoholism became more acute. Fitzgerald moved to Hollywood in 1937 to write movie scripts, but he continued to drink. He died of alcoholism while writing a novel about Hollywood, *The Last Tycoon*, published posthumously in 1941.

Through their work and lifestyles, the Fitzgeralds represented the modern revolt against traditional values while paradoxically lamenting the loss of old certitudes. To the aphorism "You can't repeat the past," Fitzgerald's Gatsby exclaims, "Why of course you can!...I'm going to fix everything just the way it was before...." Yet for all their bravado, F. Scott and Zelda knew otherwise and suffered a relentless sense of failure. ∎

Library of Congress

Suzette Dewey, daughter of Assistant Treasury Secretary Charles Dewey, poses beside her roadster in 1927. The automobile provided new mobility for working-class, black, young, and female Americans and became one of the leading symbols of 1920s culture.

NEW WOMEN, SYMBOLIC HEROES

Flappers and female bohemians offered radical departures from traditional gender roles for young women who rejected the sexual repression and self-denial of Victorian womanhood. Yet cultural innovations did not substantially threaten traditional notions of femininity, which held that normal fulfillment came only through marriage and motherhood. Striving for personal satisfaction, many postwar women hoped to pursue careers while maintaining romantic and emotional attachments to men and families. Significantly, one study of women in eastern Ivy League colleges revealed that, if a conflict arose, 94 percent of the sample intended to choose marriage instead of a career.

Culver Pictures

Clerical work in expanding corporations and government bureaucracies provided new opportunities for women in the 1920s work force. Married women took particular advantage of these openings and increased their participation in the labor force to 3.1 million by the end of the decade.

Although the number of female college graduates tripled in the 1920s, women constituted only 21 percent of the nation's labor force at decade's end. The proportion who worked outside the home remained one in four, a ratio that barely wavered between 1910 and 1940. Women in all occupations averaged less than 60 percent of the earnings of male counterparts. Moreover, they constituted only one-seventh of the nation's professional employment sector in 1929. Confined to the "female" fields of nursing, teaching, and library and social work, women found that most professions and many civil service examinations excluded them outright. As medical schools placed strict quotas on female admissions, for example, the proportion of medical students who were women declined.

Most psychologists, educators, and clergy continued to tell women that their natural place remained the home, where their first task was motherhood. As experts such as the behaviorist John B. Watson insisted that child care required particular training and dedication, high schools and colleges offered women special courses in home economics and child rearing. Such practices were reinforced by advertisers who touted middle-class homemakers as "model consumers" and household business managers. As consumption replaced production as the main activity of the twentieth-century home, corporations targeted the women's market to sell household appliances such as vacuum cleaners and electric irons. Yet the unpaid labor of housework continued to be task oriented, not geared to clock time, and was often unlimited in scope: the work week for 1920s homemakers averaged fifty-six hours. Although merchandisers boasted that technological innovations would liberate women from domestic chores, labor-saving devices simply raised the standards for tedious housework.

The routinized nature of corporate work and increasing family demands moved middle-class men toward vicarious forms of excitement and challenge. Cut off from the physical requirements of rural life and labor, men developed a fascination with spectator sports. College football, with its tribal ritualism and clockwork precision, dominated campus life and provided fans with mythic heroes such as University of Illinois halfback Harold ("Red") Grange. The greatest sports heroes were ethnics and poor whites who gravitated to professional boxing and baseball. Jack Dempsey, an Irish American, thrilled boxing fans with gutsy and ferocious fighting reminiscent of street brawls. Babe Ruth, raised in a Catholic boys' home in Baltimore, helped make baseball the national pastime by hitting a record sixty home runs for the New York Yankees in 1927. The romanticization of athletic heroes was facilitated by the development of national sports media in newspapers and radio.

Both nostalgia and media publicity played key roles in the most celebrated event of the 1920s: Charles A. Lindbergh's solo flight across the Atlantic Ocean in 1927. Lindbergh took off from Long Island's Roosevelt Field and, without instruments, piloted his single-engine *Spirit of St. Louis* nonstop for thirty-three and a half hours. Two continents awaited word of the landing of the tiny plane at an airfield near Paris. The White House immediately ordered a battleship to return the aviator and his craft to the United States. As the front pages of newspapers celebrated the accomplishments of the Lone Eagle, 4 million people turned out to see the twenty-five-year-old Minnesotan parade down New York City's Broadway and be showered with reams of stock exchange ticker tape. Lindbergh's courageous feat stirred the imagination of the media-conscious populace. By combining personal ingenuity with sophisticated machine technology, the youthful adventurer suggested that individual men could still play a dynamic role in society. Moreover, in an era defined by moral uncertainties and changes in social behavior, Lindbergh symbolized the renewal of lost virtue.

SOCIAL PURITY, PROHIBITION, AND FUNDAMENTALISM

"Does Jazz Put the Sin in Syncopation?" Mrs. Marx Obendorfer, national chair of the General Federation of Women's Clubs, asked in 1921. Women's purity activists such as Obendorfer were deeply disturbed by the pervasiveness of postwar popular culture and its alleged influence on youth, women, ethnics, and racial minorities. The like-minded *Ladies' Home Journal* attacked jazz as "cheap, common, tawdry music" that brought "moral ruin." Critics associated the musical style with unruly African rhythms and objected to the sensual appeal of "vulgar" instruments like the "moaning" saxophone. Such agitation led

— George Herman ("Babe") Ruth —
1895–1948

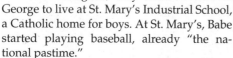

Brown Brothers

Babe Ruth, the nation's first sports superhero, was born in 1895 in a desperately poor and dangerous part of Baltimore near the eventual site of the city's Camden Yards baseball stadium. His father operated a tavern, where George spent much of his time during his preschool years. Yet when his parents gave up on him as incorrigible, they sent George to live at St. Mary's Industrial School, a Catholic home for boys. At St. Mary's, Babe started playing baseball, already "the national pastime."

Ruth began his baseball career at the age of twenty as a pitcher with the Boston Red Sox. Within three years he had led the team to three world championships. Beginning in 1918 the Babe began to show an unusual ability to hit home runs. Yet at the end of that season the Red Sox sold Ruth to the New York Yankees for $100,000 to help finance a Broadway show in which the team owner had an interest. Once in New York, Babe Ruth changed baseball forever.

In his first year with the Yankees, a mediocre team until he arrived, Ruth broke his own record by slugging fifty-four home runs—more than any other *team* hit that year. In 1920 Ruth hit fifty-nine home runs, and New York baseball fans packed the team's stadium at the Polo Grounds. Three years later Yankee management built the larger Yankee Stadium—"the house that Ruth built"—to accommodate the thousands who wanted to see the home run star. Soon most players in baseball were seeking to hit "homers," and this drive gave the game an excitement, heroism, drama, and sense of risk that reflected the exuberant, optimistic, and free-wheeling individualism of the 1920s.

Babe Ruth's personality and behavior off the field added to his attraction for fans across the country. Deprived as a child, Babe indulged himself as an adult and spared no expense. He made more money than any player in baseball and spent every penny of it. Ruth was famous for staying out until dawn, drinking, "chasing women," catching a few hours of sleep, and hitting a home run or two the next afternoon. Babe also had an instinctive public relations sense and a winning way with children. Stories abounded of his visiting hospitals and promising sick youngsters to hit home runs for them—and then doing it. He was mobbed everywhere he went.

Ruth provided good copy for sports writers, who reported and repeated his every exploit on and off the field. He seemed above reproach despite his libertine living habits. Living openly with a woman who was not his wife and drinking illegal liquor did nothing to dim his popularity. After he retired from the field in 1935 Ruth lobbied hard to sign on with a team—preferably the Yankees—as a manager. Yet baseball owners who had put up with his disrespect for their rules when he made them money punished him later by labeling him as too out of control to take responsibility for others. Although Babe Ruth was crushed by such rejection, he remained one of the legendary personalities of the twentieth century when he died of cancer in 1948 at the age of fifty-three. ■

New York to pass the Cotillo Act of 1922, which established municipal regulation of jazz music and dance and prohibited both activities on Broadway after midnight. Sixty other municipalities banned jazz from public dance halls during the decade.

Purity activists were particularly concerned about the movies, a powerful form of communication whose private operators were outside the control of cultural authorities. Although Hollywood public relations curtailed the threat of public censorship, women's clubs and social workers campaigned throughout the 1920s for a federal motion picture commission to protect youthful audiences from commercialized vice and socially harmful pictures. Reacting to the growing impact of popular culture, several states considered the banning of Sunday baseball games, boxing matches, and public dances. Iowa refused to approve legalized boxing in 1929, when politicians condemned the sport as a cheap, commercialized pastime that produced unearned income and encouraged ethnic gambling and crime. Predictably, rural newspaper editors castigated big cities as "death chambers of civilization" whose morally decadent residents were trapped by a "mad craze for sensation."

The "new woman" was particularly dangerous in the opinion of traditionalist critics. In predominantly Mormon Utah, legislators proposed that women's skirts should be three inches above the ankle. Yet even an urbane figure such as California Senator Hiram W. Johnson admitted a preference for "the womanhood of old" instead of "the non-childbearing, smoking, drinking, and neurotic creature who symbolized one of the cracks in the thin veneer of civilization." Seeking to maintain public decorum on sensitive moral issues, the Roman Catholic church cooperated with the Protestant social elite in Boston to maintain strict censorship of books that appeared to legitimate the new social morality. Novels such as Theodore Dreiser's *An American Tragedy* (1925), a realistic portrait of sexuality and amoral ambition, were banned in Boston.

Prohibition constituted the most important and controversial feature of the 1920s purity crusade. The Eighteenth Amendment, which took effect in 1920, outlawed the manufacture, sale, importing, or transportation of intoxicating liquors, defined by the Volstead Act of 1919 as any beverage containing 0.5 percent alcohol. As a "noble experiment," Prohibition sought to unify the nation in support of Anglo-Protestant values of sobriety, social efficiency, and civic virtue. Yet the results were mixed. Beer consumption dropped dramatically, and the consumption of alcohol among working-class drinkers was perhaps halved. Yet by 1927 only eighteen states had provided funds to enforce the federal law. By then bootleggers were providing consumers with $500 million in illicit intoxicants annually by tapping the supply of legal industrial alcohol.

Bootlegging often was associated with organized crime and the colorful antics of Chicago's Al Capone, an Italian American gangster. After open warfare that cost the lives of 400 mobsters between 1923 and 1926, Capone emerged as leader of the city's gambling and prostitution rings. He soon assumed control of a regional network of bootleggers as well. Yet Irish, Jewish, and African American gangsters were as important to the underworld as Italians; most urban liquor suppliers were free-lance entrepreneurs who otherwise obeyed the law. Prosecutors and juries in cities in which ethnics were the majority often refused to challenge the casual use of beer and wine. Federal enforcement also threatened local political alliances, patronage networks, and the prerogatives of local police. As the consumption of hard liquor by affluent drinkers increased by the mid-1920s, critics charged that Prohibition constituted class legislation and promoted more crime and corruption than it deterred.

"The only subjects that are getting any attention from the 'political minded,'" observed a University of California at Los Angeles (UCLA) college newspaper

Brown Brothers

"My rackets are run on strictly American lines," bootlegging syndicate leader Al Capone boasted. Prohibition created a nationwide industry in liquor running and contributed to the growth of organized crime between 1920 and the repeal of Prohibition in 1933. The conflict over the consumption of alcohol bitterly divided the American people.

editor in 1926, "are Prohibition, Birth Control, and the Bible Issue." By the early 1920s a massive revival of traditional faith had come to play a major role in the nation's Protestant denominations. Represented by the World's Christian Fundamentals Association (WCFA), which claimed 6 million members by 1927, evangelicals sought to counter the spread of "modernist" church teachings that accepted rationalist philosophy and Darwinian evolutionary thought. When 155 Baptist ministers agreed to a conference on basic theology in 1920, Curtis Lee Laws, a religious newspaper editor, coined a new term by urging participants "to do royal battle for the Fundamentals." "Two worlds have crashed," the editor of the liberal *Christian Century* noted, "the world of tradition and the world of modernism."

Insisting that the Bible was "inerrant" in its original form, fundamentalists sought to save civilization from wrenching cultural change. One preacher, Presbyterian William ("Billy") Sunday, a former professional baseball player, mixed denunciation of sinners and intellectuals with acrobatics to convert an estimated 300,000 people between 1910 and 1930. Fundamentalist critics complained that postwar biology texts presented Darwinian evolutionary theory as scientific fact and offended those who accepted Genesis as the cornerstone of

AIMEE SEMPLE MCPHERSON
1890–1944

Culver Pictures

When Aimee Semple McPherson opened a Pentecostal temple in Los Angeles on New Year's Day, 1923, she demonstrated that Protestant fundamentalism did not confine itself to the southeastern mountains or to the remote countryside. McPherson's church embodied the compassionate side of a creed that attacked evolutionary theory for promoting a materialistic world ruled by force instead of love.

McPherson fashioned herself into an evangelical faith healer. She had been converted at the age of seventeen by Robert Semple, an itinerant preacher. The two married and left to pursue missionary work in China, but Semple died, and the young widow returned home. After an unhappy marriage to a grocery salesman, McPherson decorated her "gospel automobile" with religious slogans and set out for California.

The "foursquare gospel" of Aimee Semple was an outgrowth of the Protestant pietistic tradition. It appealed to people of little education and small means, to worshipers brought up in the revivalist spirit of the evangelical churches. Most of McPherson's followers were retirees transplanted from the Midwest and elsewhere, who responded enthusiastically to simple sermons of love and faith healing.

McPherson made Los Angeles the headquarters for countless cross-country revival tours. In tents, churches, and public auditoriums nationwide, she spread the word that the Jazz Age was speeding to hell. Endorsed by the mayor of Denver in 1921, she filled that city's coliseum for a month with 12,000 people nightly. The following year McPherson addressed a secret klavern of the Oakland Ku Klux Klan. Once her Pentecostal temple opened in Los Angeles, her religious enterprises expanded to include a Bible college, a publishing house, branch churches, and overseas missions. In 1924 she purchased Los Angeles's third radio station.

The distinguishing feature of McPherson's gospel remained her belief that a Jazz Age preacher must "fight fire with fire." She became the first woman to deliver a sermon over the radio. In San Diego she scattered religious tracts and handbills from an open biplane. The Los Angeles temple provided telephone callers with the time of day as a free service.

McPherson merged the magic of Hollywood with religious ecstasy. She dressed in long white gowns, which dramatically offset her cascading blond hair. Temple services used full orchestras, choirs, elaborate costumes, and colorful pageantry to portray Bible stories in spectacular fashion. Preacher McPherson once illustrated a sermon entitled "The Green Light Is On" by riding a motorcycle down the center aisle.

The evangelist's fusion of traditionalism and modernism brought press outrage when she disappeared in 1926 only to be linked to a Mexican abortion and an affair with the temple radio operator. Nevertheless, her following continued to pay homage to "Everybody's Sister."

After surviving several lawsuits in the mid-1930s, McPherson died in 1944 from the effects of an overdose of barbital sedatives complicated by a kidney ailment. Yet as a response to the secular hedonism of the urban middle class, the Pentecostal movement remained a vital force in Protestantism. Despite her Jazz Age trappings, Aimee Semple McPherson remained a symbol of Anglo-Protestant nostalgia for the purity of a simpler time. Her pioneering fusion of religion and show business anticipated the television evangelists of a later era and gave eloquent voice to grass roots impatience with overintellectualized theology and relativistic moral values. ■

Clarence Darrow (left) and William Jennings Bryan (right), opposing attorneys in the Scopes Trial of 1925. Both men used their legal and oratory skills to mount conflicting arguments over the right to teach evolution in the public schools.

Christian faith. Between 1921 and 1929 organizers introduced forty-one anti-evolution bills in twenty-one statehouses. When one passed in Tennessee as a symbolic gesture, the American Civil Liberties Union (ACLU) objected to the law as an infringement of free speech and sought to challenge it in court. The ensuing trial of high school biology teacher John Scopes pitted Clarence Darrow, the nation's leading defense attorney, against the famed William Jennings Bryan, hired by the WCFA as a prosecutor.

"It is better to trust the Rock of Ages," proclaimed Bryan, "than to know the age of rocks." The Great Commoner already had delivered 3,000 versions of his inspirational address, "The Prince of Peace," to audiences throughout the country. As a committed populist, he hoped to show that the doctrine of evolution paralyzed social reform because it emphasized struggle and conflict instead of Christian love. However, when Bryan testified for the prosecution, he violated his own rule about interpreting scripture when he acknowledged that God may have created the Earth in six time periods rather than six days. The logical inconsistency had no impact on the Scopes conviction. Yet when Bryan died in his sleep five days later, the national press portrayed the heavily publicized "monkey trial" as a triumph of scientific cosmopolitanism over "old-time religion." Once the verdict was reversed on a technicality, the Tennessee law remained in effect until 1966. Nevertheless, evangelicals would not reassert an organizational presence in politics until the late 1970s.

The Ku Klux Klan marches through the streets of Washington, D.C., in 1925. The Klan of the 1920s saw itself as a mass political lobby and used its millions of members to campaign for Prohibition enforcement, immigration restriction, and a strong public school system.

THE KU KLUX KLAN

"One by one," complained Hiram Wesley Evans, imperial wizard of the Knights of the Ku Klux Klan (KKK), "all our traditional moral standards went by the boards. The sacredness of our Sabbath, of our homes, of chastity, and finally even of our right to teach our children in our own schools fundamental facts and truths were torn from us." Most Klansmen were not fundamentalists. Yet Evans spoke for millions of white Protestants when he expressed alienation from the moral relativism of New Era consumerism and Jazz Age innovation. He asserted that the Nordic American was "a stranger in large parts of the land his fathers gave him." To combat this condition, the Klan leader vowed that the Invisible Empire would reclaim its "inherited right" to "maintain and develop our racial heritage in our own, Protestant, American way."

Organized in Atlanta in 1915, the same year in which *The Birth of a Nation* was released, the second Ku Klux Klan admitted "native born, white, gentile Americans" who embraced racial supremacy and patriotic loyalty. Members took secret oaths of allegiance and wore white robes and hoods to fulfill pre-scribed ritual and to maintain anonymity. The Klan initially spread across the Deep South as a pyramid scheme devised by two publicity agents. It gathered support by responding to the influx of black migrants to the region's cities and by reacting to the new pride among returning African American war veterans.

Local klaverns (lodges) organized masked parades to discourage black voting and occasionally directed vigilante threats, whippings, and brandings against African Americans who were considered overly assertive. A series of newspaper exposes and congressional hearings brought the Klan a national following after 1921. When Evans took control as imperial wizard in 1922, he transformed a confederation of local vigilantes into a disciplined national movement that ultimately attracted between 2 million and 6 million followers.

Heralding the flag, the Constitution, and the Bible as its central symbols, the Klan invoked "100 percent Americanism" and "traditional values." KKK rallies, marches, and picnics sought to revitalize community and national life by building a cohesive brotherhood of white Protestants. On the other side were immigrants, who allegedly were prone to crime, poor habits, and disloyalty. Seeking to limit the influence of Roman Catholics, Jews, and others it saw as alien to the nation's institutions, the secret order embraced Prohibition, the public schools, and immigration restriction. In 1922 Klansmen in Oregon helped to pass a voters' initiative requiring children to attend public schools, although the U.S. Supreme Court overturned the law three years later as an invasion of parental rights. Meanwhile, Klansmen used economic boycotts, social ostracism, whispering campaigns, and political patronage to contain adversaries in business and civic life. "You own this country," Evans told regional officers in 1923. "If you propose to allow anyone to take it away from you, it can mean nothing to you."

Although the Klan vowed to destroy the institutional power of the Catholic church, it claimed to support freedom of worship. Evans also insisted that his organization opposed mob terrorism and credited the secret order for nearly eradicating lynching in the South, which declined precipitously in the 1920s. Klan knights saw themselves as guardians of public virtue in a period in which urban commercial and political elites often colluded with vice and criminal syndicates. In cities such as Youngstown, Indianapolis, Dallas, El Paso, Denver, Salt Lake City, and Anaheim, the Klan ignored ethnic targets to focus on Anglo-Protestant business and political elites who impeded its political reform and purity campaigns. By promising to place purity crusaders in control of local government, police, and public schools, the secret order empowered middle-class parents and citizens. Meanwhile, Klanswomen formed their own organizations in states such as Indiana to engage in charity drives and monitor troubled families and public dance halls.

Skillfully consolidating Klan power, Evans organized mass rallies and marches such as the 1926 parade of 80,000 uniformed followers in Washington, D.C. The bipartisan organization helped to elect seven governors and three U.S. Senators and took over nearly every key office in Indiana. Klan political clout prevented the 1924 Democratic National Convention from denouncing the secret order by name by a single vote of 1,038 cast. Yet KKK influence and patronage declined in the late 1920s. Evidence of lingering Klan vigilantism in Alabama revitalized doubts about the organization's commitment to law and order. Equally damaging was the 1925 conviction of Indiana Grand Dragon David C. Stephenson for second-degree murder after the suicide of a secretary Stephenson had abducted. When Indiana's Klan-supported governor refused to pardon him, the defendant produced a "black book" with evidence that sent a member of Congress, the mayor of Indianapolis, a county sheriff, and other Indiana Klansmen to prison.

Exhibit 4-13. Immigration to United States, 1901–1930
(in rounded millions)

1901–1910	8.8
1911–1920	5.7
1921–1930	4.1

Source: *Historical Statistics of the United States, Colonial Times to 1970* (1975).

NATIVISM AND ETHNOCULTURAL POLITICS

By mounting attacks on cultural diversity, the Ku Klux Klan became a disruptive force in national life. Yet much of its message resonated throughout society. Frightened by immigrant involvement in the radical activities of 1919, many native-born citizens joined nervous industrialists in seeking to contain the influx of foreign immigrants. The Immigration Act of 1920 punished aliens for possessing subversive literature or for making financial contributions to seditious groups. By 1920 thirty-five states had legislated criminal syndicalist laws to discourage antistate activity, and thirty ultrapatriotic organizations had mobilized to protect national purity. The American Legion, founded by military officers as a service club in 1919, recruited one-fourth of the nation's World War I veterans to monitor communist and radical influence. Warning that "we have put all the sand into our cement that it will stand," Legion national commander General Leonard Wood initiated a campaign against "hyphenated Americans" of dubious loyalty.

Postwar nativists continued to link immigrants to radicalism, crime, prostitution, machine politics, labor unions, and unseemly tenement life. "Most of the bootleggers...appear to be foreigners," announced sociologist Harry Pratt Fairchild in *The Melting Pot Mistake* (1926). By rejecting U.S. values and customs, immigrants supposedly threatened democracy and social order. Such themes were incorporated in Henry Ford's *The International Jew*, a four-volume tract that sold 500,000 copies when it appeared in the early 1920s. Using forged documents once prepared for the czar of Russia, Ford described a global Jewish conspiracy whose activities ranged from high finance to production of decadent flapper skirts and "skunk cabbage" jazz. Antiimmigrant sentiment also surfaced in the arrest and conviction of Nicola Sacco and Bartolomeo Vanzetti, two Italian American anarchists, for armed robbery outside Boston. Although civil libertarians protested that the defendants' political views had led to their arrest, Sacco and Vanzetti were found guilty and executed in 1927.

Nativist anxieties were reinforced by the reduced need for labor in a mechanized economy. Industrialists who previously opposed immigration restriction now argued that language barriers made foreign-born workers vulnerable to accidents and to costly turnover. A new consensus for immigration restriction resulted in a 1921 emergency measure limiting immigration to an annual 375,000. Three years later, Congress passed the National Origins Act, which created a gradual timetable for limiting migration from outside the Western

Exhibit 4-14. Changing Patterns of Immigration to the United States, 1921–1929 (in rounded figures)

	1921	1925	1929
Northwestern Europe and Canada	204,000	182,000	134,000
Central, eastern, and southern Europe	521,000	69,000	90,000

Source: *Historical Statistics of the United States, Colonial Times to 1970* (1975).

Hemisphere to 150,000 people a year. Using a sliding quota based on the number of each nation's inhabitants living in the United States between 1890 and 1920, the new law drastically reduced immigration from eastern and southern Europe. The statute also formalized the ban on Japanese newcomers. In contrast, the legislation's failure to regulate migration from the Western Hemisphere meant that Mexican and Canadian labor could flow into the United States unimpeded. Canadians soon accounted for 35 percent of U.S. immigration.

By freezing the ethnic proportions of the nation's population, immigration restriction implemented the major goal of twentieth-century nativism. Yet the quota system removed the urgency from the antiimmigrant crusade and stripped groups such as the Klan of their most pressing demand. Nevertheless, ethnocultural tensions continued to play an important role in society. The debate over Prohibition was a case in point. Ethnic voters tolerated urban political machines because ward bosses honored their right to drink and to be free of state supervision of personal behavior. African American, Polish, German, Czech, and Italian voters demonstrated such loyalties when they returned Chicago Republican Bill Thompson to city hall in 1927 after the incumbent Democrat had organized police searches of homes to enforce Prohibition. Only when Thompson uttered a slur about eastern Europeans in 1931 did Chicago voters switch parties to elect Democrat Anton J. Cermak, a Czech immigrant and pioneer in ethnic coalition building.

Ethnocultural conflict surfaced in national politics in 1924, when Governor Al Smith of New York, a Roman Catholic and "wet" opponent of Prohibition, ran for the Democratic presidential nomination. After casting 102 ballots in a stormy convention, delegates refused to endorse the front-running Smith. When the feisty New Yorker succeeded in winning the nomination as a limited-government candidate four years later (see Chapter 5), opponents attacked the governor's views on Prohibition and condemned him as a symbol of urban culture, corrupt machine politics, working-class Catholicism, and ethnic provinciality. Smith threatened the "whole Puritan civilization which has built a sturdy, orderly nation," remarked Kansas newspaper editor William Allen White. Yet by cultivating the vote of urban ethnics, the Democratic politician laid the foundation for the coalition that would change the nation's political alignment in the following decade.

By the close of the 1920s the main foundations of modern society had taken shape. Technological change had brought the national media, the automobile, and consumer advertising—innovations that initially served the secular and ethnically diverse cities. Yet cars, radios, appliances, and movies were universal attractions that also enticed rural residents. As the importance of family, home, church, and local community threatened to recede, people of the postwar era worried that the consumer economy might endanger cherished values and traditional identities. Such anxieties carried over into politics, an arena that addressed not merely social and cultural questions but crucial matters of prosperity, peace, and equity.

SUGGESTED READINGS

Overviews of 1920s cultural history can be found in Paul Carter, *The Twenties in America* (1975) and *Another Part of the Twenties* (1977). See also Roderick Nash, *The Nervous Generation: American Thought, 1917–1930* (1969), and Geoffrey Perrett, *America in the Twenties, a History* (1982). William E. Leuchtenburg, *Perils of Prosperity, 1914–32* (1958), and Gilman M. Ostrander, *American Civilization in the First Machine Age, 1890–1940* (1970), emphasize technology, youth, and moral innovation. Analyses of economic and cultural developments are skillfully integrated in Ellis W. Hawley, *The Great War and the Search for a Modern Order: A History of the American People and Their Institutions, 1917–1933* (1979).

The economic history of the 1920s is outlined in Jim Potter, *The American Economy between the World Wars* (1975). For New Era management philosophy, see the appropriate chapters of Morrell Heald, *The Social Responsibilities of Business: Company and Community, 1900–1960* (1970). Postwar consumerism is described in the relevant sections of Jackson Lears, *Fables of Abundance: A Cultural History of Advertising in America* (1994); Richard S. Tedlow, *New and Improved: The Story of Mass Marketing in America* (1990); Susan Strasser, *Satisfaction Guaranteed: The Making of the American Mass Market* (1989); Roland Marchand, *Advertising the American Dream: Making Way for Modernity, 1920–1940* (1985); and Daniel Horowitz, *The Morality of Spending: Attitudes Toward the Consumer Society in America, 1875–1940* (1985). The effect of consumerism on working-class urbanites is explored with clarity in Lizabeth Cohen, *Making a New Deal: Industrial Workers in Chicago, 1919–1939* (1990).

The best summary of postwar labor conditions and union activity appears in Irving Bernstein, *The Lean Years: A History of the American Worker, 1920–1933* (1960), which can be supplemented by the appropriate segments of Robert H. Zeiger, *American Workers, American Unions, 1920–1985* (1986). For southern mill culture, see the relevant sections of Jacquelyn Dowd Hall et al., *Like a Family: The Making of a Southern Cotton Mill World* (1987), and Jack Temple Kirby, *Rural Worlds Lost: The American South, 1920– 1960* (1987). The role of women in the changing 1920s workplace is covered in segments of Alice Kessler-Harris, *Out to Work: A History of Wage-earning Women in the United States* (1982); Margery Davies, *Women's Place Is at the Typewriter: Office Work and Office Workers, 1870–1930* (1982); and Lisa M. Fine, *The Souls of the Skyscraper: Female Clerical Workers in Chicago, 1870–1930* (1990). See also the relevant chapters of Susan Porter Benson, *Counter Cultures: Saleswomen, Managers, and Customers in American Department Stores, 1890–1940* (1986).

For postwar immigrant life, see portions of Richard Gambino, *Blood of My Blood: The Dilemma of the Italian-Americans* (1975), and Richard Krickus, *Pursuing the American Dream: White Ethnics and the New Populism* (1976). The experience of Jews in the 1920s is explored in the early chapters of Henry L. Feingold,

A Time for Searching: Entering the Mainstream, 1920–1945 (1992), and the later segments of Elizabeth Ewen, *Immigrant Women in the Land of Dollars: Life and Culture on the Lower East Side, 1890–1925* (1985). For Mexican American culture, see the relevant segments of Sarah Deutsch, *No Separate Refuge: Culture, Class, and Gender on an Anglo-Hispanic Frontier in the American Southwest, 1880–1940* (1987), and of David Montejano, *Anglos and Mexicans in the Making of Texas, 1836–1986* (1987). Hispanic, Asian, and Native American communities of the 1920s are portrayed in the relevant chapters of Ronald Takaki, *A Different Mirror: A History of Multicultural America* (1993).

The urbanization of African Americans is explored in the relevant segments of August Meier and Elliot Rudwick, *From Plantation to Ghetto* (1976), and of June Sochen, *The Unbridgeable Gap: Blacks and Their Quest for the American Dream, 1900–1930* (1972). For a case study, see Gilbert Osofsky, *Harlem: The Making of a Ghetto* (1976). The era's most influential African American is described in Judith Stern, *The World of Marcus Garvey: Race and Class in Modern Society* (1986). See also Eugene Levy, *James Weldon Johnson: Black Leader, Black Voice* (1973). Accounts of the Harlem Renaissance include David Levering Lewis, *When Harlem Was in Vogue* (1988); Cary D. Wintz, *Black Culture and the Harlem Renaissance* (1988); and Houston Baker, *Modernism and the Harlem Renaissance* (1987). See also Samuel A. Floyd, Jr., *Black Music in the Harlem Renaissance: A Collection of Essays* (1991).

For auto culture and the suburbs, see Kenneth T. Jackson, *The Crabgrass Frontier: The Suburbanization of the United States* (1985); James J. Flink, *The Car Culture* (1975); and William H. Wilson, *Coming of Age: Urban America, 1915–1945* (1974). Specific studies include Scott Bottles, *Los Angeles and the Automobile: The Making of the Modern City* (1987), and Ed Cray, *Chrome Colossus: General Motors and Its Times* (1980). For the impact of the movies, see the relevant sections of Lary May, *Screening Out the Past: The Birth of Mass Culture and the Motion Picture Industry* (1980), and Robert Sklar, *Movie-Made America: A Cultural History of American Movies* (1975). See also Richard Koszanski, *An Evening's Entertainment: The Age of the Silent Picture, 1917–1928* (1992). Female imagery in film is explored in Billie Melman, *Women and the Popular Imagination in the Twenties: Flappers and Nymphs* (1988), and in sections of Marjorie Rosen, *Popcorn Venus: Women, Movies, and the American Dream* (1973). See also David Stenn, *Clara Bow: Runnin' Wild* (1988).

For 1920s fashions, see segments of Claudia Kidwell and Margaret C. Christman, *Suiting Everyone: The Democratization of Clothing in America* (1986), and Valerie Steele, *Fashion and Eroticism: Ideals of Feminine Beauty from the Victorian Era to the Jazz Age* (1985). The postwar sexual revolution receives treatment in the appropriate chapters of John D'Emilio and Estelle B. Freedman, *Intimate Matters: A History of Sexuality in America* (1988). See also Linda Gordon, *Women's Body, Women's Right: A Social History of Birth Control in America* (1976). For college youth and changing social mores, see Paula Fass, *The Damned and the Beautiful: American Youth in the 1920s* (1977). A more critical approach appears in the appropriate segments of Louis Filler, *Vanguards and Followers: Youth in the American Tradition* (1978). For the significance of the music that gave the 1920s its popular title, see Kathy J. Ogren, *The Jazz Revolution: Twenties America and the Meaning of Jazz* (1989).

Postwar cultural and literary ferment is the topic of Stanley Coben, *Rebellion Against Victorianism: The Impetus for Cultural Change in 1920s America* (1991). See also Caroline Ware, *Greenwich Village, 1920–1930: A Comment on American Civilization in the Postwar Years* (rev. ed., 1976). For the Lost Generation, see Marc Dolan, *Modern Lives: A Cultural Re-reading of the "Lost Generation"* (1996), and John Limon, *Writing After War: American Fiction from Realism to Postmodernism* (1994). Bohemian memoirs include Malcolm Cowley, *Exile's Return: A Literary Odyssey of the 1920s* (1956), and Max Eastman, *Love and Revolution: My Journey Through an Epoch* (1964). The most traditional account of the 1920s literary renaissance is Frederick J. Hoffman, *The Twenties* (1949).

Overviews of women's history include Dorothy M. Brown, *Setting a Course: American Women in the 1920s* (1987), and the first half of Winifred D. Wandersee, *Women's Work and Family Values, 1920–1940* (1981). See also the initial segment of William H. Chafe, *The American Woman: Her Changing Social, Economic, and Political Role, 1920–1970* (1972). For postwar feminism, see Stanley J. Lemons, *The Woman Citizen: Social Feminism in the 1920s* (1973). The influence of social work is depicted in Clarke A. Chambers, *Seedtime of Reform: American Social Service and Social Action, 1918–1933* (1963), and the relevant chapters of Don Kirschner, *The Paradox of Professionalism: Reform and Public Service in Urban America, 1900–1940* (1986).

Evolving male roles are addressed in sections of Peter G. Filene, *Him/Her Self: Sex Roles in Modern America* (1986), and Joe Dubbert, *A Man's Place: Masculinity in Transition* (1979). For sports culture, see Robert W. Creamer, *Ruth: The Legend Comes to Life* (1992), and Marshall Smelser, *The Life that Ruth Built: A Biography* (1975). See also Richard C. Crepeau, *Baseball: America's Diamond Mind, 1919–1941* (1980), and Randy Roberts, *Jack Dempsey, The Manassa Mauler* (1979).

For cultural conflict, see the relevant segments of Coben, *Rebellion Against Victorianism*, and David A. Horowitz, *Beyond Left and Right: Insurgency and the Establishment* (1997). See also Don S. Kirschner, *City and Country: Rural Responses to Urbanization in the 1920s* (1970). The liquor controversy is discussed in Norman H. Clark, *Deliver Us from Evil: An Interpretation of American Prohibition* (1976). For the impact of evangelicalism, see Norman F. Furniss, *The Fundamentalist Controversy, 1918–1933* (1954), and relevant sections of George M. Marsden, *Fundamentalism and American Culture: The Shaping of Twentieth Century Evangelicalism, 1870–1925* (1980). The debate over Darwinism is treated in Edward J. Larson, *Trial and Error: The American Controversy Over Creation and Evolution* (1989). See also Carl Degler, *In Search of Human Nature: The Decline and Revival of Darwinism in American Social Thought* (1991). Bryan's fusion of reform and piety is described in Lawrence W. Levine, *Defender of the Faith: William Jennings Bryan, the Last Decade, 1915–1925* (1965).

Scholarship on the 1920s Ku Klux Klan includes Leonard J. Moore, *Citizen Klansmen: The Ku Klux Klan in Indiana* (1991); Nancy MacLean, *Behind the Mask of Chivalry: The Making of the Second Ku Klux Klan* (1994); Shawn Lay, *Hooded Nights on the Niagara: The Ku Klux Klan in Buffalo, New York* (1995); Robert A. Goldberg, *Hooded Empire: The Ku Klux Klan in Colorado* (1981); and William D. Jenkins, *The Ku Klux Klan in Ohio's Mahoning Valley* (1990). A useful anthology is Shawn Lay, ed., *The Invisible Empire in the West: Toward a New Historical Appraisal of the Ku Klux Klan of the 1920s* (1992). See also Kathleen M. Blee, *Women of the Klan: Racism and Gender in the 1920s* (1991). Older studies include Kenneth T. Jackson, *The Ku Klux Klan in the City, 1915–1930* (1967); Charles C. Alexander, *The Ku Klux Klan in the Southwest* (1965); and David Chalmers, *Hooded Americanism: The First Century of the Ku Klux Klan, 1865–1965* (1965).

For postwar antiimmigrant fervor, see William G. Ross, *Forging New Freedoms: Nativism, Education, and the Constitution, 1917–1927* (1994), and the relevant segments of John Higham, *Strangers in the Land: Patterns of American Nativism, 1860–1925* (1955). Anti-Jewish sentiment in the 1920s is discussed in segments of Frederic Cople Jaher, *A Scapegoat in the Wilderness: The Origins and Rise of Anti-Semitism in America* (1994), and Leonard Dinnerstein, *Antisemitism in America* (1994). The influence of ethnocultural conflict on politics is addressed in David Burner, *The Politics of Provincialism: The Democratic Party in Transition, 1918–1932* (1968), and in the relevant sections of John M. Allswang, *A House for All Peoples: Ethnic Politics in Chicago, 1890–1936* (1971). For a portrait of a key urban politician, see Paula Eldot, *Governor Alfred E. Smith: The Politician as Reformer* (1981).

5

Calvin Coolidge (left) and Herbert Hoover (right), two symbols of Washington's willingness to enhance the business prosperity of the 1920s. Both men saw U.S. capitalism as the road to individual prosperity and social harmony.

THE RISE AND FALL OF REPUBLICAN CONSENSUS, 1920–1932

Postwar voters turned to the Republican Party to sustain economic growth and social stability. As business prospered at home and abroad, 1920s corporate and government leaders forged a successful political consensus. Yet insufficient attention to financial speculation, to decaying industries, and to independent agriculture undermined their strategies. Such neglect provoked frequent protests from small business interests, manual workers, family farmers, and anticorporate insurgents. When business prosperity collapsed after 1929, Republican leaders struggled to mount a response compatible with New Era approaches to government. Their failure brought the most serious political and economic crisis since the Civil War.

HARDING'S NORMALCY

"America's present need is not heroics but healing," declared Republican presidential candidate Warren G. Harding in 1920, "not nostrums but normalcy, not revolution but restoration, not agitation but adjustment." Harding was an undistinguished senator from Ohio, where he had risen to prominence as the owner of a printing establishment in the small town of Marion. He won the presidential nomination when Republican progressives and conservatives settled on a compromise candidate. The nominee presented himself as a "white-haired progressive" who had adopted scientific management in his printing

President Warren G. Harding (left) and Vice President Calvin Coolidge (right), easy victors in the 1920 race for the White House. Harding and Coolidge hoped to build a political consensus based on business prosperity and goodwill.

Exhibit 5-1. Election of 1920

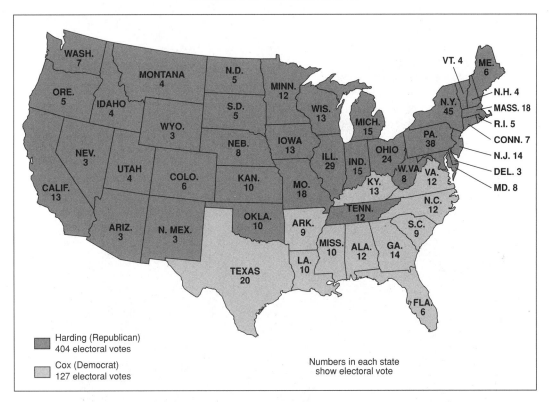

firm. Rank-and-file delegates pushed Harding to accept Governor Calvin Coolidge of Massachusetts as the Republican vice presidential nominee. Coolidge had won national acclaim as an advocate of middle-class interests by denouncing the Boston police strike of 1919.

Harding's campaign tapped a nostalgia for prewar stability and hometown virtue. Mainstream Republicans sensed that middle-class voters had been overwhelmed by the emotional excesses of World War I, by the debate regarding the League of Nations, and by the strains of the Red Scare. "Too much has been said of bolshevism in America," Harding proclaimed. The candidate instead talked about the "Marion Idea" of neighborly cooperation and classless democracy, denounced "executive autocracy" and "government paternalism," and charged that an active government would "make us a nation of dependent incompetents."

The Republican candidate hoped that international peace and corporate prosperity would reduce political strife and would build a national consensus. Although Harding spoke only fleetingly of issues such as lower taxes and a high tariff, his relaxed confidence and goodwill prevailed at the polls. The Republican ticket won 60.4 percent of the popular vote after campaigning against Democratic Governor James M. Cox of Ohio and his running mate, Assistant Secretary of the Navy Franklin D. Roosevelt, Theodore's cousin. Cox's popular tally surpassed Woodrow Wilson's victorious 1916 total, but Harding's 16-million-vote tally was nearly double the amount previously won by the

President Warren G. Harding tosses an opening day baseball into play. Harding sought to bring postwar America back to moderation and consensus. He remained a popular figure until his death in 1923.

Republicans. Winning every state outside the South, and carrying Tennessee as well, Harding and Coolidge won an overwhelming 404–127 victory in the Electoral College.

Beginning in 1920, women's suffrage contributed to the increase in ballots. Yet voter participation never surpassed 57 percent in the presidential elections of the 1920s. Such limited participation was part of a trend toward low turnouts dating back to the early twentieth century. Voting rates were lowest in large industrial cities where working-class ethnics were concentrated. Poor turnout reflected pervasive apathy regarding national political issues and the reluctance of eligible women from immigrant families to cast ballots because patriarchal cultural traditions discouraged their participation. Modest balloting rates among the working class contributed to the Republican plurality of 1.6 million votes in the nation's twelve largest cities and enabled the party to add to its majorities in both houses of Congress. Clearly, Woodrow Wilson's success in unifying the South, the West, and the East behind the Democratic Party had not survived World War I.

Harding sought to fulfill his promise of reduced political discord by pardoning Socialist Party leader Eugene Debs, imprisoned under wartime sedition laws. Despite his incarceration, Debs had run for president in 1920 and had matched the 900,000 votes he had received in 1912 by receiving 3.4 percent of the tally. Harding invited Debs to the White House, where the two reportedly chatted and smoked cigars.

Honoring his commitment to lower taxes, Harding extended a free hand to Secretary of the Treasury Andrew Mellon, a multimillionaire Pittsburgh industrialist and financier. Mellon worked with Budget Director Charles G. Dawes, a Chicago banker, to reduce government expenses and thereby to relieve corporations and wealthy individuals of burdensome taxation. "I have never viewed taxation as a means of rewarding one class of taxpayers or punishing another," explained Mellon. The treasury secretary argued that lower taxes would free investors to use their capital to create jobs and prosperity. In 1921 Mellon persuaded Congress to repeal the wartime excess-profits tax and to decrease the maximum income surtax to 50 percent, although Congress raised postage rates, excise taxes, and licensing fees. Harding chose conservative Republican and former president William Howard Taft to be the chief justice of the U.S. Supreme Court.

[handwritten margin note: Oh, poor little rich people]

HOOVER AND BUSINESS INTERNATIONALISM

Harding's most celebrated appointee was Secretary of Commerce Herbert Hoover, a popular figure who had served as Wilson's wartime food administrator and as coordinator of European relief. As a former mining engineer and international capitalist, Hoover had a strong reputation in the business community. The commerce secretary believed that the nation's corporate structure and democratic heritage could be reconciled through the promotion of voluntary organizations such as trade associations, professional societies, agricultural marketing groups, and labor unions. "We are passing from a period of extremely individualistic action into a period of associational activities," he declared in *American Individualism* (1922), his plan to sustain personal initiative and social efficiency. Hoover sought to develop his "American System" by using the federal government to coordinate and support self-help groups. Through "tempered individualism" and "cooperative" capitalism, the economy could avoid domination by corporations, cartels, or government bureaucracies.

Under Hoover's leadership, the Department of Commerce proposed to regulate the new radio and commercial aviation industries. Hoover also campaigned for the Capper-Volstead Act of 1922, which exempted agricultural marketing associations from antitrust legislation and authorized government loans to farm produce organizations. The secretary had more difficulty promoting cooperation by trade associations. In 1921 the Supreme Court ruled in *American Column and Lumber Co.* v. *the United States* that exchange of information by trade groups constituted restraint of commerce. Yet the court reversed itself four years later in *Maple Flooring Association* v. *the United States* by upholding the right of trade organizations to exchange statistics if they did not control prices or production. The Taft court thus ruled that the flow of trade information was more important than the maintenance of traditional concepts of free competition.

Hoover's most important contribution came when he convinced President Harding to convene the Washington Conference on Unemployment in September 1921. As government spending for wartime necessities ended, industrial output was halved, and unemployment soared to 12 percent. The meeting marked the first time that a president had called attention to joblessness as a national problem. As a result, 225 cities created local emergency committees and voluntary relief groups. Meanwhile, Congress allotted $450 million for state and local public works and passed the Federal Highway Act of 1921, which authorized a national highway system and provided the first matching grants for state road construction. The conference also commissioned an unprecedented analysis of business cycles by the National Bureau of Economics Research, a private council. Released in 1923, the report suggested that economic slumps resulted from waste, extravagance, speculation, inflation, and inefficiency that developed during booms.

The postwar depression stimulated Hoover to obtain increased funds to reorganize the Department of Commerce to focus on the commodities most frequently involved in overseas trade. The department now became a clearinghouse for the collection and dissemination of commercial statistics. Beginning in 1921, the government published a monthly survey of production, prices, and inventories. Hoover also expanded the Bureau of Standards to promote the standardization of industrial weights, measures, sizes, and designs. The secretary's eight years in the Department of Commerce won him praise from the *Magazine of Business* as "the most significant landmark of our age" and a reputation as the "boy wonder" of the Republican Party.

To expand U.S. foreign trade, Hoover also promoted an "open door" to global markets. Dispatching commercial attachés abroad, the Department of Commerce campaigned against foreign cartels that deprived domestic manufacturers of access to raw materials such as rubber and precious metals. The bureau also worked with major oil corporations to gain refining concessions in Venezuela, in the Dutch East Indies (later renamed Indonesia), and in the Per-

Exhibit 5-2. U.S. Gross National Product, 1920–1922
(in rounded billions of dollars at current prices)

1920	91.5
1921	69.6
1922	74.1

Source: *Historical Statistics of the United States, Colonial Times to 1970* (1975).

Exhibit 5-3. U.S. Unemployment, 1920–1922
(percentage of civilian labor force)

1920	5.2
1921	11.7
1922	6.7

Source: *Historical Statistics of the United States, Colonial Times to 1970* (1975).

sian Gulf. To encourage investment in politically stable nations, Secretary of State Charles Evans Hughes directed subordinates to approve foreign loans before private interests were asked to invest in them. Hughes also sent bankers on official missions to negotiate loans to foreign governments. Meanwhile, Congress professionalized diplomatic appointments by passing the Foreign Service Act of 1924.

The Department of Commerce and the Department of State skillfully combined diplomacy with the promotion of U.S. business interests. To free foreign policy from military commitments, the Harding administration sponsored disarmament talks among the major powers. The Washington Armaments Conference of 1921–1922 fixed the number of U.S., British, and Japanese battleships and battle cruisers at a ratio of five to five to three and assigned France and Italy a lesser proportion than Japan. The conference also drafted the Four-Power Treaty, which committed signatories to respect each other's Pacific Island possessions. A Nine-Power Treaty reaffirmed support for the Open Door policy in China and called for the acceptance of existing boundaries in East Asia. The administration anticipated that U.S. economic power ultimately would confine Japanese actions in an area of the world where Washington remained militarily weak (see Chapter 7).

SOCIAL AGENDA

Despite its probusiness stance, the Harding administration carefully addressed the demands of social feminists and women's reform groups. In 1920 female activists had organized the nonpartisan League of Women Voters in hopes of using the power of women's suffrage to gain consumer protection, conservation, family welfare, and child labor legislation. Working with the Women's Joint Congressional Committee, a coalition embracing nearly every important women's organization in the country, the league served as a clearinghouse for social legislation. Even in the traditional South, social feminists helped to institute budget reforms for rapidly growing state governments, created commissions to protect children, and agitated to improve working conditions for women in the textile industry. Meanwhile, consumer advocates exploited fears of a women's voting bloc to win congressional approval of the Packers and Stockyards Act of 1921, which lowered meat, poultry, and dairy prices by banning discriminatory practices by distributors and food marketers.

The most important achievement of the social feminists was passage of the Sheppard-Towner Maternity and Infancy Protection Act of 1921. Concerned about women who failed to meet the means and morals tests for state "mother's pensions," officials in the Children's Bureau sought legislation to permit the federal government to match state spending on medical services to mothers and children. When the American Medical Association (AMA) objected to subsidized health care, Congress limited the bill's coverage to medical education. Nevertheless, the first federal welfare program in U.S. history enabled the Children's Bureau to disburse an average of $1.25 million a year to state health care training clinics. During its eight-year existence, Sheppard-Towner helped decrease national infant and maternal mortality rates.

Social feminists won passage of fifty state minimum wage laws for female workers between 1912 and 1923. Yet in *Adkins* v. *Children's Hospital* (1923), the

Taft court ruled that the contractual rights of laborers were violated when states regulated women's wages. Reformers faced additional frustration in the crusade to ban child labor. One year after the Supreme Court overrode a federal child labor law in 1918, Congress passed a bill that placed prohibitive taxes on products manufactured by children. However, the court cited the Constitution's interstate commerce clause to declare the law an unwarranted regulation of local labor conditions. Stunned into action, social welfare activist Florence Kelley mobilized the National Child Labor Committee in 1924 to win congressional approval of a constitutional amendment authorizing regulation of children's labor. Yet when the Roman Catholic church warned of the dangers of government interference with parental discretion, ratification in key industrial states failed overwhelmingly.

A bitter blow to its supporters, defeat of the child labor amendment revealed deep rifts within the women's movement. Although postwar feminists sought to present a united front as members of a "women's bloc," they were divided between those who sought to aid women as a class and those who hoped to advance women as individuals. Young middle-class women of the 1920s often rejected the demands for sacrifice, social commitment, and sisterhood advanced by older purity crusaders, suffragists, and reformers. Such differences explain why social feminists opposed the efforts of the National Woman's Party to pass an equal rights amendment to the constitution. Brought before Congress by Alice Paul in 1923 and thereafter annually throughout the postwar decade, the pioneering proposal sought to extend equality for women to all areas of law, public policy, and employment. Yet social reformers denounced the measure because it would eradicate remaining protections for female workers and would alienate the public from their efforts to elevate the social morality of the workplace and of the family.

Such divisions relieved politicians of anxieties about a unified women's bloc and legitimized attacks on all strands of feminism. For example, social workers in the Children's Bureau increasingly came under fire as being socialists who sought to collectivize national family life. In 1929 Congress acceded to demands by the AMA and other conservatives and repealed the Sheppard-Towner Act. By the end of the decade most white, middle-class women had rejected the solidarity ethic of prewar feminism and viewed the feminist movement in terms of self-development and individuality. Yet social feminists had laid the foundations for government involvement in labor, health, and social welfare by functioning as an effective political lobby.

THE FARM BLOC

Small and independent farmers did not share New Era prosperity. While the 1920s became the worst decade experienced by southern growers since the 1860s, economic and climatic conditions reduced the rural population of the Northern Great Plains. The agrarian depression of the 1920s lowered the value of the nation's farm properties from $79 billion to $46 billion. While farm bankruptcy affected nearly 18 percent of all operations, total agricultural mortgage debt rose $2 billion during the 1920s. By 1930 42 percent of the agricultural labor force leased farm land as tenants or sharecroppers, and 1 million farm families had left the land.

Exhibit 5-4. U.S. Agricultural Price Squeeze, 1920–1921
(1910–1914 = 100)

	1920	1921
Prices received for farm products	205	116
Prices farmers paid for commodities bought	206	156
Farm wages paid to hired labor	239	150
Taxes on farm property (1914 = 100)	155	217

Source: *Recent Economic Changes* (1929).

Government price supports during World War I and wartime patriotism had motivated producers to expand foodstuff and cotton acreage and to mechanize farm operations with expensive machinery such as tractors. After the conversion of economic capacity to peacetime production, the government abandoned price supports, demand slackened, and farm values dropped. In 1920 cotton prices sank from forty cents a pound to fewer than fourteen cents. Meanwhile, the price of wheat plummeted from $2.57 a bushel to less than a dollar. Corporate agriculture retained sufficient capital to absorb machinery, labor, and freight expenses, as well as to adapt to fluctuations in global commodity rates. Yet independent producers remained subservient to processors and distributors and could not pass on increased costs. In addition, small farmers were vulnerable to rising taxes and higher prices for manufactured goods. Natural disasters such as the boll weevil (beetle) infestation of postwar cotton crops in Georgia and drought in the Dakotas and Montana worsened the prospects for independent growers.

Postwar farm groups and rural politicians insisted that the agricultural depression stemmed from the Federal Reserve Board's 1920 decision to raise the discount (interest) rate charged to member banks. Anticorporate Republicans such as North Dakota's Gerald P. Nye and Wisconsin's Robert La Follette charged that New York bankers had engineered deflation to contract credit and liquidate agricultural loans. Because of greedy speculative interests, they claimed, farmers had experienced a disastrous fall in commodity prices, rural banking had collapsed, and investment capital had deserted the countryside for Wall Street. "The hand that is feeding the world is being spat upon," a Georgia farmer complained bitterly in 1920. "If you burn a man's house, you are punished," a former Republican governor from the East observed of the credit squeeze, "but if you destroy the value of his property through control of the money market, you are regarded as a shrewd financier."

Congressional representatives from farming districts also attacked the Esch-Cummins Transportation Act of 1920, which had returned the railroads to private control after management by the federal government during World War I. The law gave the Interstate Commerce Commission (ICC) power to raise intrastate rates to provide companies a fair return on investment and permitted the commission to administer a revolving fund to distribute profits to weaker rail lines. Although the constitutionality of the statute was upheld by the Supreme Court on two occasions, farm interests bitterly protested that the law allowed the lines to raise their shipping costs to guarantee the value of watered-down railroad securities. Critics like La Follette, Nye, and Iowa Republican Senator

Smith W. Brookhart described the deflation caused by the Federal Reserve and Esch-Cummins as the "twin crimes" of 1920.

Independent farmers tried to compete with agribusiness through cooperative marketing, an idea spread by Aaron Sapiro, a young California lawyer. By 1923 500,000 growers belonged to marketing associations that handled a sales volume of $400 million. Under Sapiro's system, farmers signed contracts to deliver all salable produce to the associations, which then marketed the crops and returned all proceeds to members after deducting costs. Legalized under the Capper-Volstead Act of 1922, marketing groups were most popular among tobacco, wheat, and cotton growers in the South and the West and among some northwestern fruit and dairy producers. By the mid-1920s, however, many of the associations had overextended themselves through poor management, and the farm cooperative movement waned.

The rural depression, an Alabama realtor pleaded with Commerce Secretary Hoover, "will make bolsheviks of the agriculturalists unless some remedy is provided." Faced with the devastation of their way of life, postwar farmers turned to politics as they had in the troubled 1890s. In 1921 southern and northern agrarians formed a congressional farm bloc. The coalition succeeded in passing legislation to assist agricultural marketing associations and worked with social feminists to pass the Packers and Stockyards Act. The Grain Futures Act of 1921, which was promoted jointly with women reformers, limited coercive pricing practices in the grain trade. Once its ranks were increased after the Senate election of two Minnesota Farmer-Labor candidates and several Republican progressives between 1922 and 1923, the farm bloc addressed key economic issues. The agrarians noted that the Fordney-McCumber Tariff of 1922 restored protective rates on industrial goods to pre-1913 levels. To provide similar protection for farm prices, they demanded the creation of a government agency to market agricultural surplus and to recapture European markets.

COOLIDGE ECONOMICS

Farm bloc politicians cooperated with small business interests to attack collusion between the federal government and powerful corporations. After independent oil refiners alerted Robert La Follette, a Senate committee held hearings in 1923 that exposed illegal cooperation between the Harding administration and major domestic oil producers. Testimony revealed that Secretary of the Interior Albert B. Fall secretly had leased valuable government petroleum reserves, including the Teapot Dome area of Wyoming, to private interests. In return, Fall had received more than $300,000 in bribes. A special government prosecution team also discovered multimillion-dollar graft in the newly created Veterans' Bureau and kickbacks to Attorney General Harry Daugherty. The "Teapot Dome" scandal ultimately sent Fall and other officials to prison, forced Daugherty's resignation, and led to the suicide of two presidential appointees.

"I cannot hope to be one of the great presidents," Harding once confided, "but perhaps I may be remembered as one of the best loved." Demoralized by early evidence of betrayal by friends in his "Ohio Gang," the president suffered a stroke while on a West Coast tour in August 1923 and died a few days later in a San Francisco hotel. Many citizens genuinely mourned the popular president's passing. Responsibility for restoring government integrity now fell to

Vice President Calvin Coolidge. A dour, silent, and canny politician, Coolidge kept silent about the Teapot Dome scandal until 1924, when he replaced Attorney General Daugherty with Harlan Fiske Stone, a highly esteemed former dean of Columbia Law School. Stone sought to professionalize government service by appointing J. Edgar Hoover to the directorship of the Federal Bureau of Investigation with a mandate to modernize procedures through the use of fingerprinting and other new techniques. Responding to the relaxation of class tensions in the mid-1920s, Stone also instructed Hoover to discontinue anti-radical surveillance.

As Coolidge prepared for the 1924 election, he consolidated his position within the Republican Party and among the nation's voters. Pressed by northeastern congressional representatives to end an anthracite coal strike that threatened winter fuel supplies in late 1923, the new president permitted Governor Gifford Pinchot of Pennsylvania to arrange a labor settlement favorable to the miners. As a result, Coolidge was not held responsible for the price increases passed on to consumers. The president nevertheless appealed for the support of Republican progressives by publicly embarrassing U.S. Steel into abandoning the twelve-hour work day. Coolidge also signaled his independence from petroleum interests by signing the Oil Pollution Act of 1924, which provided modest fines for polluting coastal waters. He made another gesture to reformers by offering the vice presidential nomination to progressive Idaho Senator William Borah. When Borah declined, the president chose Federal Budget Director and Chicago banker Charles Dawes.

Acknowledging that "the chief business of the American people is business," the Republican nominee sought to ride New Era prosperity to a new term with the slogan "Keep Cool with Coolidge." In an era of easy money and frenzied speculation, Coolidge embodied Yankee austerity and respectability. The president's clear and distinct speaking voice, broadcast in the election year during monthly radio addresses, made him one of the nation's most popular radio personalities. The administration faced little competition from the Democratic Party. Stymied by deep ideological and cultural divisions, the Democrats nominated Wall Street attorney John W. Davis, a political unknown, as their presidential candidate and Charles Bryan, the brother of William Jennings Bryan, as his running mate.

Coolidge's most spirited opposition came from Robert La Follette's Progressives. Rejecting Farmer-Labor or Socialist alternatives, La Follette accepted the new party's presidential nomination in 1924 and named Senator Burton K. Wheeler, a progressive Montana Democrat, as his vice presidential running mate. Unlike Theodore Roosevelt's Progressives in 1912, La Follette's movement attacked large corporations. "The great issue before the American people today," declared the party platform, "is control of government and industry by private monopoly." The Progressives condemned Republican tax policies, denounced the protective tariff, and criticized "mercenary" foreign policy. They also appealed to independent farmers by supporting federal aid to agriculture and by criticizing business control of regulatory agencies. Progressives sought reformist support by calling for government ownership of railroads and of waterpower resources. They also pursued working-class voters by demanding the abolition of labor injunctions and the congressional recognition of collective bargaining rights.

The Progressives easily won La Follette's Wisconsin and finished second in ten midwestern and western states and in sixty-seven industrial counties east

ROBERT M. LA FOLLETTE
1855–1925

Stock Montage

"There were no silk hats and broadcloth suits," a Senate colleague noted of the mourners at the funeral of Robert M. La Follette in 1925. At the age of seventy, the nation's leading crusader and progressive had died only months after capturing one-sixth of the popular vote as a third-party candidate in the 1924 presidential election. La Follette's creed, another colleague told the Senate, was his faith "in the average common sense of the masses." Burton K. Wheeler, the late senator's Progressive Party running mate, later proclaimed that La Follette ranked with Jefferson and Lincoln as one of the three greatest characters produced by U.S. civilization.

Born in a log cabin, La Follette graduated from Wisconsin's new state university and went on to defy the Republican machine by winning three congressional elections in the 1880s. The short, stocky, and square-jawed Republican managed to build his own political organization by using university gradu-

ates and student volunteers to offset the power of the railroad corporations and timber interests. By 1900 La Follette had won the Wisconsin governorship. He proceeded to institute the direct primary, civil service and tax reform, and the innovative use of state regulatory commissions.

Sent to the Senate in 1905, La Follette continued to emphasize the chasm between the "people" and the "interests." By 1917 he was convinced that New York monied interests had taken over transportation, banking, industry, and commerce and that the nation's growing involvement in Europe was a product of "financial imperialism." La Follette bitterly resisted the nation's drift into World War I, then opposed conscription and wartime repression and crusaded for war profits taxes and future referenda on military campaigns. He also helped to defeat U.S. membership in Wilson's League of Nations.

By the time Harding took office in 1921,

of the Mississippi. La Follette and Wheeler won 16.6 percent of the popular vote, which was a strong showing for a poorly funded third party. Yet White House warnings of "Coolidge or Chaos" resulted in a Republican plurality of 1.25 million votes in the twelve largest cities and in an easy victory for the president. Outpolling his Democratic opponent by 54 percent to 29 percent, Coolidge won the Electoral College vote in a one-sided, 382–136–13 contest.

Buoyed by the voters' mandate for conservative economic policies, Secretary of the Treasury Mellon proceeded with his program of tax relief for the affluent. Accordingly, the Revenue Act of 1926 wiped out the gift tax, cut estate taxes by half, and trimmed the surtax on incomes to 20 percent. Two years later Congress reduced taxes by more than $220 million and gave Treasury refunds to large corporations. By the end of the decade government spending had been halved, the national debt had been reduced by one-third, and taxes on the wealthy and corporations had been cut by $350 million annually.

Coolidge's Federal Trade Commission (FTC) further reflected the administration's endorsement of corporate methods and goals. The Supreme Court had ruled in 1920 that U.S. Steel's large size and monopoly status did not violate the

La Follette's opposition to involvement in European rivalries had become an article of national faith. He warned that membership in the World Court would serve international bankers hoping to use U.S. wealth and military power to safeguard their tottering European empires. The irascible senator organized "people's" lobbies to demand that the government retract the rate increases and tax breaks granted to his old adversary, the railroads. Using the detested Esch-Cummins Transportation Act of 1920 as the basis for a new agenda, La Follette assembled two national conferences of Progressives in 1922. During the same year he retained his Senate seat by winning unprecedented statewide margins of three to one in both the Republican primary and in the general election. Buoyed by a fresh confidence and a conviction that the country was returning to its senses, La Follette helped to build a new Progressive Party and became its presidential standard-bearer in 1924.

Tired, aging, without a party apparatus, and outspent twenty to one by Coolidge Republicans, La Follette nevertheless mounted a monumental campaign. His supporters formed a coalition of Republican agrarian insurgents, old Populists, urban liberals and socialists, the railroad brotherhoods and trade unionists, and remnants of the independent middle class. Accordingly, La Follette and Wheeler focused on the broad concerns of the nation's producers by defending private initiative and independent enterprise and by attacking monopoly. Their purpose, the Wisconsinite stated at the climax of the campaign, was "to restore government to the people."

La Follette was the last important presidential candidate to crusade against corporate capitalism. Confronted by an increasingly consumerist economy, the fiery orator continued to evoke the producer values of nineteenth-century entrepreneurs and farmers. Nevertheless, La Follette spoke for a persistent segment of citizens who rejected the dominance of the two major parties by big-money interests.

The Progressive ticket took second place in ten states and sixty-seven industrial counties. More importantly, the La Follette legacy, borne by "Fighting Bob's" son and Senate successor, Robert M. La Follette, Jr., continued to draw the connections between the power of corporate capital at home and pressures for increased military presence overseas. To speak of La Follette was to invoke the spirit of the nation's ordinary people. The New Era was compelled to pay homage to a true giant of the Senate. ■

"rule of reason" because prosecutors had not proven that the corporation engaged in overt coercion or in predatory practices. Once Coolidge appointed corporate attorney and lumber lobbyist William Humphrey as FTC chair in 1925, the regulatory agency investigated only cases in which unfair practices were explicitly detrimental to the public interest and held private hearings. The FTC frequently referred these informal agreements or "stipulations" to trade conferences, thereby providing corporations with "self-rule." Coolidge attempted to balance the FTC's probusiness approach by signing the Watson-Parker Act of 1926, a precedent-setting measure that recognized collective bargaining by railroad workers but prohibited strikes during a sixty-day mediation period.

The administration's greatest accomplishment occurred when Secretary of Commerce Hoover organized the government's response to the Mississippi River flood of 1927. After the river had swollen at points to a fifty-mile width, Hoover created an emergency committee to coordinate relief activity by government agencies and by private groups such as the Red Cross. Volunteer efforts resulted in the construction of 150 refugee camps that housed 325,000

Exhibit 5-5. Election of 1924

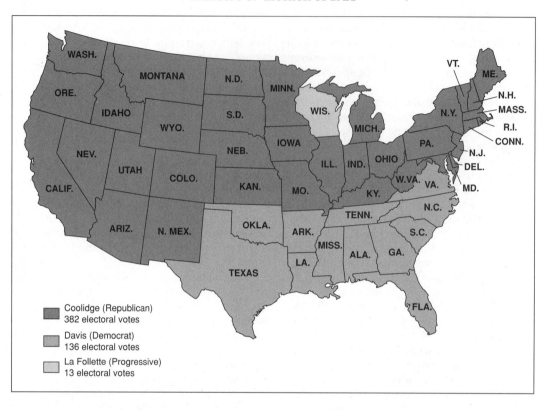

people. Hoover's panel also organized the raising of $17 million by private credit corporations and local chambers of commerce. The "neighborly helpfulness" demonstrated during the Mississippi project remained an important model of voluntarism and local initiative for the ambitious commerce secretary. Meanwhile, Coolidge signed the Jones-Reid Act of 1928, which appropriated $300 million for levees, drainage basins, and spillways and was one of the first steps toward government management of river ecology.

BANKER DIPLOMACY

Like its predecessor, the Coolidge State Department continued to stress financial diplomacy as the alternative to military intervention. In Europe, U.S. priorities focused on friendly relations with Britain and France and the reintegration of postwar Germany into the western community. Under the Dawes Plan of 1924, the former Allies reduced German war reparations, and the United States cut the $10 billion Allied debt by 40 percent. The deal was facilitated by the willingness of J.P. Morgan and other private bankers to offer economic reconstruction loans to Germany. Between 1924 and 1930 U.S. banks loaned more than $1.2 billion to the Germans.

To stabilize global economic growth, the State Department encouraged peace activists to negotiate an international renunciation of war. Pacifists such as Jane

The president and the cabinet, 1923. Throughout his presidency, Coolidge relied heavily on the department heads for advice and assistance.

Addams had a long record of involvement in global affairs. After assuming the presidency of the Women's International League for Peace and Freedom (WILPF) at the league's inception in 1915, Addams organized opposition to U.S. participation in World War I. Like Carrie Chapman Catt, who formed the National Conference on the Cause and Cure of War, social worker Addams believed that the horrors of combat proved the futility of male violence. Although the War Department's Spider Web Chart purported to trace the origins of women's peace groups to bolsheviks, the antiwar lobby played a major role in supporting disarmament at the international peace conferences of the 1920s. Working with activists such as Chicago attorney Salmon O. Levinson and Congregational minister Frederick J. Libby, peace groups approached Secretary of State Frank B. Kellogg with the idea of a treaty to outlaw war.

Neither Kellogg nor the peace advocates believed that a piece of paper could end centuries of bloodshed. Yet pacifists argued that the treaty could strengthen the "machinery" for resolving international disputes and could set an important

**Exhibit 5-6. Total U.S. International Investment, 1919–1930
(in rounded billions of dollars)**

1919	9.7
1924	15.1
1927	17.9
1930	21.5

Source: *Historical Statistics of the United States, Colonial Times to 1970* (1975).

precedent. Kellogg transformed proposals for a U.S.-French nonaggression pact into a multinational treaty that denounced the use of war as an instrument of national policy. Sixty-two nations signed the Kellogg-Briand Pact of 1928, which won a 85–1 vote of approval in the U.S. Senate after intense lobbying by women's peace groups. Although the agreement had no enforcement mechanisms, both Kellogg and Addams later received the Nobel Prize for Peace.

The State Department sought to sustain New Era prosperity by expanding economic activity. Banks and financial interests had channeled billions into overseas loans and investments during World War I, which made the United States the world's leading creditor. As foreign sales leaped by nearly 60 percent between 1922 and 1926, the United States led all other nations in marketing goods. By 1929 the U.S. economy accounted for nearly 16 percent of all global exports, and overseas customers spent $1.5 billion annually on U.S. car parts, oil products, and machinery. Latin America emerged as a major outlet for U.S. goods in the postwar era. Loans to the region, often tied to the purchase of U.S. goods or services, totaled $1.6 billion between 1924 and 1929. By the close of the decade Latin Americans bought nearly half their imports from the United States. In turn, North Americans purchased almost 40 percent of Latin American exports. Multinational U.S. mining concerns like the Guggenheim syndicate and agribusinesses like United Fruit invested heavily in the region, thereby exerting economic and political influence in this underdeveloped part of the world.

The emphasis on long-range stability and criticism from hemispheric neighbors focused attention on military activism as a component of U.S. policy in Latin America. At the Pan American Conference of 1923 the United States defeated Uruguay's attempt to outlaw unilateral intervention under the Monroe Doctrine. The next year President Coolidge withdrew troops from the Dominican Republic yet sent the Marines to Honduras to overcome "a condition of anarchy." Meanwhile, the United States maintained its military occupation of Haiti. In 1925 the president ordered 3,000 Marines to leave Nicaragua but ordered the military back when civil war erupted the following year. This time, however, Coolidge sent Henry L. Stimson, secretary of war under President

**Exhibit 5-7. U.S. Exports, 1922–1928
(in rounded billions of dollars)**

1922	5.0
1924	5.9
1926	6.4
1928	6.8

Source: *Historical Statistics of the United States, Colonial Times to 1970* (1975).

Exhibit 5-8. U.S. Involvement in Central America, 1921–1934

Dominican Republic: Military occupation until 1924. Financial protectorate until 1941.
Haiti: Military occupation until 1934.
Honduras: Military occupation after 1924.
Mexico: Negotiated settlement of subsoil rights, 1927.
Nicaragua: Military occupation until 1925 and 1926–1933.

Taft, to negotiate a settlement that included peaceful elections. By the terms of the 1927 accord, the Nicaraguan rebels agreed to disarm and the Marines would stay long enough to train a nonpolitical national guard.

Coolidge scored his greatest foreign policy success in Mexico, whose government prepared to nationalize oil fields and mines in the mid-1920s. Although independent oil developers talked of a bolshevik threat, Standard Oil and major banks warned that provocative action could "injure American interests" in Mexico in a "period of permanent investment." When the U.S. Senate unanimously recommended arbitration of the controversy in 1927, Coolidge appointed Dwight W. Morrow, a J.P. Morgan attorney, as ambassador and instructed him to bring about a peaceful settlement. Conciliatory efforts resulted in Mexican recognition of mining and petroleum rights granted to foreign companies before 1917. Thus, banker diplomacy had resolved a dangerous dispute without military intervention.

REPUBLICAN INSURGENTS

Western progressives and insurgents in the U.S. Senate were among the foremost critics of Latin American military intervention. Leaders such as

U.S. marines reading comic strips to children during their occupation of Nicaragua in 1927. The military intervention nevertheless produced a bitter legacy among the highly nationalistic Nicaraguans.

Nebraska's George Norris, Montana's Burton Wheeler, and Senate Foreign Relations Committee Chair William Borah of Idaho bitterly opposed colonialism and militarism. Noninterventionists during World War I, the insurgents spoke for western agricultural regions that produced for the domestic market but were subservient to eastern capital. Predictably, Wheeler blamed military intervention in Nicaragua on New York bankers who had "warshipped" a puppet dictatorship to power. Meanwhile, noninterventionists defeated U.S. participation in the Permanent Court of International Justice, an agency created by the League of Nations in 1922 to resolve civil disputes among nations. Although the Senate approved membership in the World Court with reservations in 1926, seven Republican supporters lost their 1926 Senate primaries and thereby deprived the Coolidge administration the votes needed for ratification.

Western noninterventionists and progressives opposed concentrations of economic and financial power and collusion between government and big business. Such views underlay George Norris's successful crusade to keep the federal government from leasing the Muscle Shoals Dam and several nitrate plants on Alabama's Tennessee River to automaker Henry Ford. In 1925 Norris played a key role in the 41–39 Senate vote that defeated sugar lobbyist and Republican fund-raiser Charles B. Warren's nomination for attorney general. Western Republicans also supported the McNary-Haugen bill, the first proposal for government price supports for agriculture in the nation's history. The plan called for a federal marketing corporation to buy surplus commodities at full price and to sell them overseas at reduced rates. Government losses would be com-

Senator George W. Norris, a progressive Republican who led the fight against Henry Ford's attempt to buy the government facilities at Muscle Shoals on the Tennessee River. Norris saw himself as a champion of the independent farmer, worker, and entrepreneur.

pensated through a mandatory "equalization" fee on each farmer's surplus. Although the bill won congressional approval in 1927 and 1928, President Coolidge vetoed it each time and criticized the equalization fee as an unconstitutional tax.

THE ELECTION OF 1928 AND HOOVER'S NEW DAY

When President Coolidge dismissed talk of reelection in 1927 by declaring that "I do not choose to run," Secretary of Commerce Hoover emerged as the logical choice for the Republican nomination. Like the popular Henry Ford, Hoover bridged the gap between corporate capitalism and traditional values. Although the skilled administrator had made a fortune in international mining ventures, his roots lay in the small towns of rural Iowa and Oregon. Raised as a Quaker, he combined humanitarian zeal and organizational skill in widely acclaimed work as wartime food and relief coordinator. Despite Hoover's well-publicized success as commerce secretary, however, most farm state insurgents resented

President Herbert Hoover, Henry Ford, Thomas Edison, and Harvey Firestone (l. to r.) on a Florida vacation, 1929. Hoover hoped to employ corporate techniques of planning and cooperation in his new administration.

Wide World Photos

his opposition to the McNary-Haugen bill. Midwestern corn growers therefore mounted a frantic effort to derail the Hoover candidacy but lost a key convention vote. When Hoover took the nomination on the first ballot, delegates chose Kansas Senator Charles Curtis, a farm bloc leader, to fill the vice presidential spot.

Democrats declared an ideological and sectional cease-fire in 1928 by agreeing to support New York Governor Al Smith. The party nearly had disintegrated four years earlier because of bitter cultural warfare (see Chapter 4), and the Democrats still were divided on political issues. Sustaining the legacy of William Jennings Bryan, southern and western populists like William McAdoo endorsed Prohibition and the expansion of government regulatory and welfare functions. In contrast, Smith and the party's eastern wing opposed the enforcement of liquor laws and objected to the broadening of federal power. Powerful financial interests, including the Du Pont family and John J. Raskob of General Motors, backed the New York governor's bid to become president. Raskob sought to replace the alliance of southern and western Democrats with a coalition embracing the states' rights interests of the South and the East. By proposing nonenforcement of the Fifteenth Amendment, which extended equal voting

New York Governor Al Smith, Democratic candidate for president in 1928. A Catholic and an opponent of Prohibition, Smith represented urban and ethnic constituencies in a period of cultural confusion about the nation's identity.

rights to African Americans, he won southern support for a Smith candidacy committed to the abandonment of Prohibition.

Seeking to balance the ticket, Democrats chose Prohibitionist Joseph T. Robinson, an Arkansas senator, as their vice presidential nominee. The party also emulated the Progressive platform of 1924 by endorsing collective bargaining rights for labor, abolition of antiunion injunctions, federal aid to support farm prices, and government regulation of waterpower. Nevertheless, Raskob's huge campaign contributions allowed the Democratic treasurer to mold the Smith campaign platform to support Republican principles of limited government and a self-regulating economy. Party strategists underestimated the appeal of Hoover's record as an administrator of moderate government in a period of general prosperity. Failing to generate enthusiasm among struggling farmers and manual workers in old-line industries, Smith succeeded in carrying only

FIORELLO H. LA GUARDIA
1882–1947

Stock Montage

Fiorello La Guardia was a short and stocky man with a loud voice. His mother was Jewish, and his father was an Italian American Protestant. La Guardia spoke six foreign languages. He broke into politics as a Theodore Roosevelt Progressive. To win support for a campaign to enter Congress, La Guardia offered free legal services to immigrant pushcart peddlers, to icemen, and to shopkeepers. He mobilized letter carriers and garment workers and pulled flophouse voters out of bed before the Tammany Hall politicians were awake on election day. La Guardia won the Italian-Jewish district of East Harlem by 257 votes and went to Washington as a Republican in 1916.

La Guardia was an urban evangelist. Like all successful politicians, he knew his district. Immigrants from southern and eastern Europe had no tradition of rural individualism in their former villages. Victimized by a dehumanizing industrial system in America, they sought government assistance. Ten years before the New Deal, La Guardia agitated for old-age pensions, unemployment insurance, shorter workdays, workers' compensation, and laws against child labor. The Norris-La Guardia Act of 1932 banned the use of injunctions to prevent strikes and abolished "yellow-dog" contracts that obligated workers to shun unions. La Guardia also campaigned against high prices levied by corporate middlemen. Rising to speak during a House debate about rising profits in the meat industry, La Guardia pulled from his pocket a lamb chop, then a steak, then a tiny roast. "What workman's family can afford to pay three dollars for a roast of this size?" he screamed.

the Deep South and the heavily Catholic states of Massachusetts and Rhode Island. Taking more than 58 percent of the popular vote, Hoover dominated the Electoral College vote by 444–87.

Protestant traditionalists rejoiced that voters had rejected the influence of urban politics. The country was "not yet dominated by its great cities," said the *St. Paul Pioneer Press*. ". . . Main Street is still the principal thoroughfare of the nation." Yet the Smith candidacy proved a turning point in political history. By encouraging the participation of nearly 57 percent of eligible voters, the highest rate since 1916, Smith enabled the Democrats to double their 1924 totals and to embrace the ethnic electorate. For the first time since 1892, Democrats captured more votes in the nation's twelve largest cities than Republicans. By initiating this electoral revolution, Smith and Raskob moved the Democrats toward the politics of urban constituencies. Ironically, the two Catholic conservatives inadvertently facilitated the conversion to political liberalism that would characterize Democratic electoral victories in the 1930s.

Hoover had campaigned on the slogan of the New Day. "We in America are nearer to the final triumph over poverty than ever before in the history of any land," he assured followers. The presidency, declared Hoover, was "the inspiring symbol of all that is highest in America's purposes and ideals." Seeking to balance the interests of producers, trade groups, and consumers, the president

The fiery congressman was not a successful Republican or a cheerleader for the celebrated New Era. Instead, he displayed a streetwise instinct for detecting unwarranted privilege. By 1923 La Guardia had joined rural progressives in denouncing administration friendliness toward corporate monopoly and in opposing high tariffs, instant labor injunctions, and tax benefits for the wealthy. La Guardia led the House attack on Coolidge's plan to sell the Muscle Shoals Dam to Henry Ford by suggesting that "this proposition makes Teapot Dome look like petty larceny." He joined with Senator Norris to campaign for public power, supported Senator Borah's opposition to military occupation of Nicaragua, and demanded the impeachment of treasury secretary Mellon. "I would rather be right than regular," he once explained.

Not surprisingly, the Republican House leadership stripped La Guardia of all committee assignments in 1924. He attended the Progressive Party convention that year and rose to tell the followers of La Follette that "I speak for Avenue A and 116th Street, instead of Broad and Wall." Denied the Republican nomination in 1924, he was returned to Congress by Progressive and Socialist ballots.

La Guardia was the first urban progressive to take his place on Capitol Hill. He worked well with rural insurgents in attacking abuses of power in the Harding and Coolidge administrations. Yet La Guardia broke with many in the progressive coalition when he ridiculed federal censorship of the movies and became one of the House's most passionate critics of immigration restriction. He also dramatized ethnic resentment toward Prohibition by manufacturing beer in his capitol office and defying police to arrest him.

La Guardia's unique contribution was his understanding that the immigrant working class of the large cities constituted a vital component of a new coalition for reform. The man who munched peanuts on the floor of Congress and whose favorite word was *lousy* instigated the separation of progressive reform from the purity crusade of the Protestant elite. By the time La Guardia became mayor of New York City in 1933, urban ethnics were anticipating a "new deal" in Washington and were beginning to flex their political muscle. La Guardia, the Republican progressive from East Harlem, had charted the way. ■

Exhibit 5-9. U.S. Unemployment, 1923–1929 (percentage of civilian labor force)

Year	Percentage
1923	2.4
1925	3.2
1927	3.3
1929	3.2

Source: *Historical Statistics of the United States, Colonial Times to 1970* (1975).

Exhibit 5-10. U.S. Consumer Price Index, 1920–1928 (1967 = 100)

Year	Index
1920	60.0
1922	50.2
1924	51.2
1926	53.0
1928	51.3

Source: *Historical Statistics of the United States, Colonial Times to 1970* (1975).

Exhibit 5-11. Election of 1928

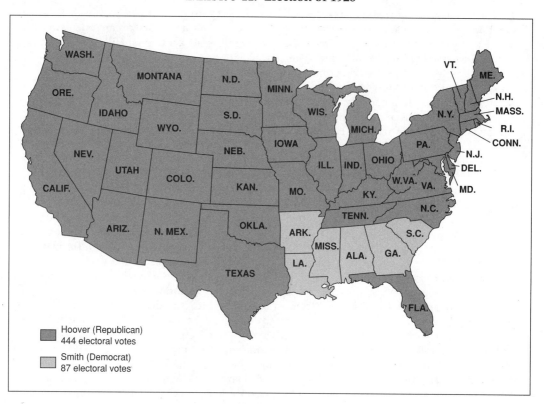

Hoover (Republican)
444 electoral votes

Smith (Democrat)
87 electoral votes

Exhibit 5-12. Voter Participation in U.S. Presidential Elections, 1916–1928 (percentage of eligible voters)

1916	61.6
1920	49.2
1924	48.9
1928	56.9

Source: *Historical Statistics of the United States, Colonial Times to 1970* (1975).

began his term by convening a special session of Congress to address the continuing farm depression. As an alternative to subsidy demands by such groups as the National Grange, the Agricultural Marketing Act of 1929 was enacted. The new law sought to encourage the agricultural merchandising organizations that Hoover had supported as commerce secretary. It established a Federal Farm Board authorized to loan $500 million to agricultural marketing cooperatives and to set up stabilization corporations empowered to buy surplus crops. By interfering directly with farm distribution and prices, Hoover's legislation permitted the most ambitious government involvement ever in the nation's peacetime economy.

Having addressed the contentious farm problem, Hoover sought to heal the nation's divisions over Prohibition. By 1929 the Du Pont family had injected financial aid and new leadership into the Association Against the Prohibition

Amendment, the nation's leading advocate of repeal. Conservative Democrats such as the Du Ponts and John Raskob hoped that eradication of the Eighteenth Amendment would enable the government to reduce income and inheritance taxes and to decrease federal regulation. Hoover asked former Attorney General George W. Wickersham to head a Law Observance and Enforcement Commission. Releasing its report in 1931, the panel acknowledged that administration of the liquor laws had been hindered by illegal syndicates and by public apathy or hostility. Although the commission did not support repeal of the Eighteenth Amendment, most of its members favored revision. Yet Hoover avoided a confrontation with Republican Prohibition supporters by opposing any move to rescind the controversial amendment.

The White House was more comfortable in the foreign policy arena. As an internationalist, Hoover sought to use government policy to encourage the cultivation of global markets and overseas investment. Concerned about the financial stability of Europe, the president sent General Electric's Owen Young to renegotiate the payment of war debts. Under the Young Plan of 1929, Germany received credits from U.S. bankers, and these credits could be used to pay reparations to the Allies during an extended period of fifty-eight years. Officials anticipated that the transfer of capital would enable the Allies to compensate the U.S. government for wartime loans. Yet the Young Plan also signaled that New York had replaced London as the center of international finance and that U.S. capital could now stimulate European purchase of the nation's commodities and farm produce.

The Hoover administration was particularly interested in stabilizing relations with Latin American nations. As president-elect, Hoover conducted a goodwill tour of the region in 1928 and talked of the need for economic and technical cooperation among "good neighbors." The United States soon recognized all de facto Latin American governments and refused to intervene in the Cuban Revolution of 1929–1930. "We cannot slay an idea or an ideology with machine guns," declared Hoover. According to Secretary of State Henry Stimson, the former emissary to Nicaragua, developing nations were to be left alone if they simply honored the "sanctity of contracts" and fulfilled "international obligations." The president also ordered the gradual withdrawal of the U.S. military from Haiti. In Nicaragua, U.S. Marines faced harassment by nationalist guerrillas aligned with General Cesar August Sandino, and Hoover called these troops home in 1933.

THE CRASH OF '29

When Iowa insurgent Smith Brookhart confronted Princeton University economist Joseph Stagg Lawrence, the expert witness at a 1928 Senate hearing, with the prediction that the country was "headed for the greatest panic in the history of the world," Lawrence dismissed the warning as "the curious emissions of a provincial mind." Despite frequent ridicule, critics like Brookhart often denounced the speculative excesses of New Era finance. Henrik Shipstead, a Farmer-Labor Party senator from Minnesota, complained about the 3,500 small banks that went bankrupt in the first half of the postwar decade. Accusing the Federal Reserve of favoring high finance and investors in the stock market, Shipstead and others demanded remedial legislation to avoid a catastrophe.

OWEN D. YOUNG
1874–1962

Stock Montage

On 4 June 1927 General Electric board chairman Owen D. Young stood before 3,000 people to deliver the dedication address for Harvard University's expanded Graduate School of Business Administration. The event symbolized the acceptance of business professionalism and marked a personal triumph for Young, whose complete remarks were printed in the forthcoming *Harvard Business Review.*

Born on an eighty-acre farm in upstate New York, Young attended a one-room schoolhouse before graduating from St. Lawrence University in 1894. He hoped to enter Harvard Law School but settled on attending Boston University when school officials in Cambridge discouraged his plans to attend classes while working part-time. After graduation Young joined a Boston law firm and cultivated clients in the burgeoning electric industry. These contacts led to an offer to join General Electric as general counsel and vice president in 1913.

As a corporate attorney, Young assumed responsibility for negotiating patent disputes and labor conflicts. During World War I he settled a strike at General Electric's plant in Lynn, Massachusetts, and ended the last bout of labor trouble the company experienced until the late 1930s. The young vice president maintained that worker unrest extended beyond wage and hour issues to intangible psychological concerns such as employee powerlessness. His theory influenced the report of the Second Industrial Conference of 1920 and brought Young an appointment to President Harding's Conference on Unemployment. Young soon found that he had a full-time commitment to the developing fields of industrial and public relations. In 1922 General Electric's directors selected the skillful attorney to be corporate chairman of the board.

By the mid-1920s Young not only presided over the largest electric products corporation in the world but sat on the board of powerful General Motors. He also served as executive committee chairman for the Radio Corporation of America (RCA), which he had organized in 1919 by arranging to pool radio technologies developed by several major corporations. With the progressive Gerard Swope as its president and with Young as its chairman, General Electric increased its emphasis on consumer sales of large appliances instead of on capital goods for industry. Young

Although President Hoover worried about excessive speculation, he hoped to rely on White House leadership to balance and stabilize the nation's diverse economic interests. Despite this hope, events moved beyond the president's control and severely tested his faith in national institutions and the principle of limited government. On Black Tuesday, 29 October 1929, securities values dropped by $14 billion, and the loss resulted in the most devastating day in Wall Street's history. Two weeks later, losses rose to a staggering $25 billion, two-fifths of the value of all stock traded on the exchange.

Because stock prices were indicators of investor confidence, the Crash of 1929 was a serious blow to the economy. Ironically, the Wall Street collapse resulted from the same financial practices that had contributed to the speculative boom. Through unregulated margin arrangements, for example, small

stressed a "new capitalism" that fostered cooperation with both government and labor and that reflected General Electric's need to cultivate the long-range goodwill of the public.

Young endorsed Herbert Hoover's concept of corporate self-regulation under government supervision. Moreover, he extended profit sharing, pensions, and life and unemployment insurance to the company's work force. "Business is constantly on the firing line, adopting new methods and exploring new areas," he explained to former muckraker Ida Tarbell. Early in 1927 he appeared on the cover of *System*, the leading management journal in the nation.

"Today and here," Young declared when he spoke at Harvard, "business finally assumes the obligations of a profession." Young noted that 55 percent of Harvard's 1916 graduating class had entered business. Professional business schools would provide the data for enlightened decision making and rational policy in an increasingly complex world, he promised. As Young proclaimed, the "self-imposed rules" of the trade association would shape business morality and enable corporate professionals to honor ideals of service and social responsibility. "Perhaps some day," he told the assembly, corporations might organize cooperative undertakings so that workers could simply buy capital and be entitled to all profits above cost. This would produce a democratic industry without "hired men," Young speculated.

General Electric's chairman saw himself as a trustee for the company's 50,000 stockholders and 100,000 employees as well as for consumers and for the general public. He boasted that the large corporations of the New Era had "completely divorced ownership from responsibility." "I can indict the capitalistic system as well as the bolshevist. I know its failures as well as he," Young told students at Bryn Mawr College in 1928. Yet the resourceful board chairman foresaw "a world of new experiment" that would ensure comfort and economic advancement for consumers as well as a "cultural wage" to permit intellectual self-development by the working class.

Young represented the idealized corporate professional of the New Era. Although admitting that business "provided satisfactory financial rewards," he insisted that the "widening intellectual horizon" of corporate life stretched minds and stimulated the imagination. Young personally embodied such standards by participating in national industrial conferences and by conducting negotiations that resulted in the adoption of the Dawes and Young plans for Europe's postwar financial recovery.

By 1932 Young's insistence on domestic economic revitalization led Democrats to consider him as a possible Democratic candidate for the presidency. More than any single figure of his generation, Owen D. Young personified the consistency between progressive ideals and the imperatives of the corporate economy. ■

---

investors had generated market inflation by purchasing stocks for as little as 10 percent of their face value. Many then borrowed additional funds by using stock as collateral, thereby inviting disaster if the value of securities fell. In 1927 Wall Street floated nearly $19 billion worth of new stocks with only $3 billion in assets.

Serious structural weaknesses also played a role in the market collapse. New England and the agricultural areas of the South, Midwest, and mountain states never shared 1920s prosperity. Indeed, the postwar economy experienced substantial declines in coal mining, cotton, manufacturing, shipbuilding, shoe and leather production, and the railroad industry, and these losses were compounded by the contraction of foreign markets that accompanied the period's high tariffs. Poor distribution of purchasing power also contributed to the

**Exhibit 5-13. Percentage of Total U.S. Households
in Diverse Income Categories, 1929**

Annual Income	Percentage
Less than $2,000	65
$2,000–$2,999	17
$3,000–$4,999	12
$5,000–$9,999	5
$10,000 or greater	1

Source: *Historical Statistics of the United States, Colonial Times to 1970* (1975).

disaster. As profit gains exceeded wage hikes in the 1920s, those who received the top 1 percent of incomes increased their share of national earnings from 12 percent to 19 percent. Yet three-fifths of the nation's families earned incomes that only allowed the purchase of basic necessities. Given the limits on consumption potential, investment surpassed the capacity of sales to return profits. Residential construction, auto manufacturing, and road building all declined by the late 1920s. Despite rhetoric to the contrary, New Era management and government regulation failed to keep up with changes in technology, world markets, and international finance.

THE SEARCH FOR SOLUTIONS

Hoover first described the economic decline as a "depression" instead of a "panic" or "crisis" because he hoped to allay public fears. The president believed that corporate maintenance of employment, production, high wages, and labor peace would sustain the morale necessary for renewed prosperity. Within weeks of the crash, he called leading officers of the major corporations to the White House to win promises of cooperation. He also created a host of emergency federal agencies and bureaus to address unemployment and the need for relief. Declaring in 1930 that "we have passed the worst," Hoover expanded federal outlays for municipal and state public works and requested $150 million for the construction of government buildings.

The administration first focused on confidence as the key to recovery. "There is more to fear from frozen minds than frozen assets," lectured Secretary of the Treasury Ogden L. Mills. Yet several developments sabotaged the government's recovery strategy. Pressed by the farm bloc for protection from foreign competition, Hoover signed the Hawley-Smoot Tariff of 1930, which raised the import duties on farm products by 70 percent while increasing the rates on industrial goods to a hefty 40 percent. More than 1,000 professional economists urged the president to veto the bill as a detriment to foreign trade and economic recovery. Yet Republican partisan interests and nationalist impulses prompted Hoover to approve the risky tariff.

The Federal Reserve Board also complicated the road to prosperity. Reacting belatedly to excessive stock market speculation and debt, the panel decided to raise interest rates in 1931. Just as the administration anticipated economic recovery, circulating currency decreased. Between 1930 and 1932 tight monetary

Exhibit 5-14. Hoover's Recovery Program

1930	Agricultural commodity stabilization corporations created by Federal Farm Board
1931	$2.25 billion public works program
1932	Federal Home Loan Bank Act (created Federal Home Mortgage Board)
	Glass-Steagall Banking Act
	Emergency and Relief Construction Act ($2.3 billion in public works and relief loans to states)
	Reconstruction Finance Corporation (RFC), $2 billion capitalization
	Norris-LaGuardia Anti-Injunction Act

policies reduced the money supply by one-third. The results were disastrous. Anticipating slackened consumer demand, major industries disregarded voluntary promises to sustain output and began to cut production and to lay off workers. Moreover, investors lost faith in financial institutions and began to withhold capital from the marketplace. "We are going through a period when character and courage are on trial," declared Hoover, "where the very faith that is within us is under test."

To worsen matters, the president faced a collapse of the European credit system. Attention shifted to Europe in the spring of 1931 when France called in German and Austrian loans and Austria's largest bank collapsed. In the ensuing panic, investors withdrew gold from German and Austrian banks. Hoover issued a one-year moratorium on the collection of German and Austrian debts. Nevertheless, the financial crisis spread to France and Britain, both of whom joined other European nations in repudiating the gold standard. European investors now sold off their U.S. investments and demanded payment in gold. The resulting withdrawal of capital from New York stock and money markets led to the failure of nearly 2,000 U.S. banks in the second half of 1931. Meanwhile, national employment dropped 12 percent, and wages tumbled a demoralizing 30 percent.

Faced with a deteriorating economy and Democratic congressional majorities after 1930, Hoover became the first president to apply federal power to meet an economic emergency. In 1931 he asked Congress to appropriate $2.25 billion for public works and thereby created the most costly federal program to that point in history. Among the approved projects was a massive Colorado River dam soon named after the president. Yet Hoover's preference for balanced budgets and limited government moved him to veto George Norris's bill to build government power facilities at Muscle Shoals. The president also rejected a program of industrial stabilization and compulsory economic and welfare planning proposed by General Electric's Gerard Swope. The Swope Plan of 1931 sought to give federally supervised trade associations the power to fix prices, control production, and regulate business practices. It also included federal programs for old-age, life, and unemployment insurance. Yet Hoover objected that such assertions of government power would create a permanent socialist bureaucracy.

By 1932 the stock market crash had brought the nation into a full-scale depression. Nearly 6,000 banks with assets of $4 billion had failed, and more than 100,000 businesses had gone bankrupt. Unemployment, almost 16 percent at the start of the year, surged toward 25 percent. Meanwhile, the gross national product was barely half its 1929 level and exports a mere 35 percent of

Exhibit 5-15. U.S. Unemployment, 1929–1932
(percentage of civilian labor force)

1929	3.2
1930	8.7
1931	15.9
1932	23.6

Source: *Historical Statistics of the United States, Colonial Times to 1970* (1975).

Exhibit 5-16. U.S. Gross National Product, 1929–1933
(in rounded billions of dollars)

1929	103
1933	56

Source: *Historical Statistics of the United States, Colonial Times to 1970* (1975).

Exhibit 5-17. U.S. Imports and Exports of Goods and Services, 1929–1932
(in rounded billions of dollars)

Year	Imports	Exports	Trade Surplus
1929	5.9	7.0	1.1
1930	4.4	5.4	1.0
1931	3.1	3.6	0.5
1932	2.1	2.5	0.4

Source: *Historical Statistics of the United States, Colonial Times to 1970* (1975).

their precrash high. Hoover also discovered that his farm program had collapsed. Lacking the power to limit production, the Federal Farm Board tried to rescue growers from a depressed global market by purchasing large wheat and cotton surpluses. When major losses occurred, the agency abandoned the purchasing program in 1931. As national agricultural income was halved again in the following year, the farm board found itself $500 million in the red.

Hoover once again expanded the scope of federal activity. He increased the nation's credit supply by approving the Glass-Steagall Act of 1932. By permitting the government to use commercial paper as partial backing for U.S. Treasury certificates, the measure freed $750 million in gold formerly used as collateral for government bonds and securities. The president also signed the Federal Home Loan Bank Act of 1932. Modeled on the Federal Reserve Act, the law created a home mortgage board in Washington and awarded $125 million to twelve regional banks to encourage ownership of residences and to provide loans to distressed lenders and mortgage companies. To please industrial workers, Hoover signed the Norris-La Guardia Act of 1932, which fulfilled organized labor's historic desire to prohibit court injunctions against strikes, boycotts, and union picketing.

The president's most important actions directly addressed the deflationary crisis in agriculture and industry and the frightening collapse in employment and purchasing power. In 1932 Congress agreed to create the Reconstruction Finance Corporation (RFC), the first federal agency ever mobilized to fight an economic depression. Capitalized at $500 million, the government corporation was authorized to borrow $2 billion through tax-exempt bonds to provide emergency loans to banks, insurance companies, railroads, farm mortgage associations, and other private institutions. Months later, the Emergency and Relief Construction Act extended the RFC's borrowing capacity and authorized the agency to loan $1.5 billion to local and state governments for public works projects. Pushed by congressional Democrats, the measure responded to the relief crisis by empowering the RFC to loan another $300 million to the states to assist the needy.

THE BURDEN OF THE GREAT DEPRESSION

Although $1.2 billion in RFC funds were awarded to financial institutions within six months of the RFC's creation, the agency proved unable to stimulate economic growth. Significantly, the RFC spent only 10 percent of the monies earmarked for state relief. Despite its dramatic abandonment of the laissez-faire or noninterventionist approach to government economic policy, the Hoover administration continued to insist that recovery would follow the restoration of business confidence. It emphasized that investor morale depended upon balanced budgets and government fiscal integrity. Accordingly, the White House insisted on raising taxes to offset government spending, and this strategy further depleted investment capital and purchasing power.

"No president must ever admit he has been wrong," Hoover once confided to a Chamber of Commerce official. Yet by 1932 the Great Depression had plunged some 40 million of the nation's people into poverty. In single-industry cities such as Akron and Toledo, unemployment skyrocketed to a paralyzing 60 to 80 percent. Landlords evicted 200,000 families from their apartments in New York City in 1931 alone. By the end of the following year, at least 1 million transients, including 200,000 homeless children, roamed the nation's highways, railroad yards, and migrant camps. In Chicago, a journalist described "a crowd of some fifty men fighting over a barrel of garbage." An economist from a New York investment house worried that the economic order threatened to revert to the "feudalism and barter which ensued upon the breakup of the Roman Empire."

The unprecedented economic disaster created profound insecurity for people of all social classes. "I sat in my back office, trying to figure out what to do," newspaper publisher J. David Stern remembered of the crash. "To be explicit, I sat in my private bathroom. My bowels were loose from fear." As more than 100,000 workers lost jobs every week between 1929 and 1932, employment no longer was part of the natural order of life. Fear, noted a writer in *The Atlantic* magazine, had become "the dominant emotion of contemporary America—fear of losing one's job, fear of reduced salary or wages, fear of eventual destitution and want." Jobless graduates of eastern professional schools formed the Association of Unemployed College Alumni. Meanwhile, the International Apple

A Depression breadline in New York City. Such demoralizing scenes became symbols of the breakdown of the U.S. economic system after 1929.

Shippers' Association began to sell apples on credit to unemployed men who resold them at five cents apiece. The ubiquitous street corner apple peddlers of the great cities provided one of the most enduring images of the Great Depression.

As unemployment, homelessness, and hunger increasingly burdened municipal agencies and charities, recovery programs appeared utterly inadequate. By 1932 more than one hundred cities had no resources to assist the needy. Yet President Hoover consistently opposed all direct federal relief. Clinging to traditional notions of Anglo-Protestant personal accountability, the White House warned that direct aid to the jobless would invite bureaucratic control by Washington and would ensure bankruptcy of the U.S. Treasury. Hoover's experiences as European relief administrator and coordinator for the Mississippi flood emergency had strengthened his sincere belief in interclass harmony, voluntarism, and local control. However, as a president who was willing to provide feed for farm animals but not food for needy children, Hoover found his credibility damaged. Residents of the shanty towns that sprung up in many cities sarcastically referred to their migrant settlements as "Hoovervilles"; newspapers used to protect sleeping vagrants became "Hoover blankets."

Independent producers were some of the president's most virulent critics. Stung by the free fall of commodity prices, midwestern growers organized the militant Farmers Holiday Association in 1932. The movement's first actions occurred in Iowa, where angry dairy farmers barricaded highways to stop underpriced milk and other produce from going to market. Meanwhile, the National Farmers Union pressed Congress for cost-of-production price guarantees. Oregon's Charles L. McNary, the Senate agriculture committee chair who had coauthored the McNary-Haugen bill, sought to address agrarian discontent in 1932 by amending the Agricultural Marketing Act. McNary proposed that the

Federal Farm Board set domestic prices of farm goods and place an equalization fee on exported surpluses. In turn, growers would receive government credits (debentures) to buy imported goods. After a close vote, however, the Senate returned the amendments to committee.

– NOT PASSED

When retail sales were halved after 1929, independent merchants blamed chain stores for perpetuating the Depression. Organizing their own associations, newspapers, and radio stations, small retailers mounted 400 trade-at-home campaigns in the year after the stock market crash. The independents argued that chain stores were a product of Wall Street speculation, that chain syndicates drained capital from local communities, and that chain monopolies would produce higher retail prices. By 1931 ten states had passed taxes on chain outlets, and 175 additional bills remained to be considered. Meanwhile, the House of Representatives passed a measure to regulate resale prices, but the proposal died in the Senate. In 1932 North Dakota Senator Gerald Nye pressed for legislation to require the Federal Trade Commission (FTC) to prosecute chains that violated trade rules.

The Depression increased populist suspicion of governmental and financial elites. Texas Democrat Wright Patman compelled the House Judiciary Committee to consider the impeachment in 1932 of Treasury Secretary Andrew Mellon, accused of a conflict of interest for advancing favors to a petroleum conglomerate. The controversy only abated when President Hoover appointed Mellon as ambassador to Great Britain. Meanwhile, auditors revealed that Swedish entrepreneur Ivar Krueger, who had shot himself in Paris, had forged $100 million in bonds sold to investment houses in the United States. California Senator Hiram Johnson soon conducted a Senate inquiry into the role of graft, fraud, and unethical practices in the depreciation and default of foreign bonds and securities. As popular radio commentator Charles E. Coughlin, a Roman Catholic priest from Michigan, began to refer to bankers as "banksters," Hoover asked the Senate Committee on Banking and Currency to investigate the New York Stock Exchange.

Banking and currency panel counsel Ferdinand Pecora subjected some of the country's most powerful financial figures to grueling public questioning. Testimony from stock exchange president Richard Whitney, from leading bankers Charles Mitchell and Albert Wiggin, and from other witnesses revealed that bull market operators had organized stock pools for "insiders," had allowed associates to buy securities at special discounts, had "pegged" certain stocks at artificially high prices, had provided lucrative bonuses for themselves, and had used improper publicity to induce investors to buy questionable stock. Committee chair Peter Norbeck, a South Dakota insurgent and a former well-driller, told a radio audience that Wall Street "was the worst crap game in the country." Panel investigators soon discovered that the thirty-two-state public utility–holding empire of financier Samuel Insull, which had recently collapsed, likewise had been built on deceit and fraud.

As President Hoover prepared for reelection during the summer of 1932, more than 15,000 unemployed World War I veterans marched on Washington, D.C., as part of the Bonus Expeditionary Force. The protesters hoped to convince the Senate to approve Wright Patman's House bill authorizing immediate payment of a veterans' bonus scheduled for payment in 1945. Once the Senate followed the president's lead and rejected the bonus, 2000 marchers remained in their shanty town on government property at the Anacostia Flats. After clashes killed two veterans and two local police officers, Hoover ordered the army to disassemble the encampment. Chief of Staff Douglas MacArthur disobeyed the president's order for restraint and used tanks, tear gas, infantry, cavalry, and machine guns to forcibly eject the veterans and burn the settlement. The routing of the "Bonus Army" and the placement of locks on the White House gates created the impression that the embattled Hoover had become a prisoner of the presidency.

THE ELECTION OF 1932

Sensing victory at the polls, the Democratic Party turned to New York's Franklin Delano Roosevelt as presidential nominee in 1932. A distant cousin of Theodore, Roosevelt was graduated from exclusive Groton and Harvard, studied law at Columbia, served as assistant secretary of the navy in the Wilson administration, and ran unsuccessfully as the Democratic candidate for the vice presidency before the Harding landslide of 1920. The following year, Roosevelt suffered an attack of poliomyelitis, and he remained unable to walk without assistance for the rest of his life. After Roosevelt was redirected into political life through the persistence of his wife, Eleanor, and his longtime aide, Louis Howe, the ebullient aristocrat twice won election as governor of New York, in

The Bonus Expeditionary Force, dispersed by federal troops in Washington, D.C., in the summer of 1932. The rout of the Bonus Army worked against President Hoover's political fortunes in that year's election campaign.

1928 and in 1930. As a progressive governor, Roosevelt sponsored unemployment relief, labor and banking reform, aid to farmers, state hydroelectric power, and conservation measures. Despite minor opposition, Roosevelt won the Democratic nomination for president on the third ballot.

The Democratic platform called for active government aid to the unemployed but demanded a 25 percent cut in federal spending. To offset the deficit and to satisfy fiscal conservatives, the Democrats proposed to repeal Prohibition and to collect revenues from the sale of liquor. Roosevelt focused his quest for the presidency on the "forgotten man at the bottom of the economic pyramid" and the need for "bold, persistent experimentation." Breaking precedent, he flew to the Chicago convention to accept the Democratic nomination personally. "I pledge you," he told the delegates, "I pledge myself, to a new deal for the American people." Always indirect about his political philosophy, Roosevelt described himself as "a Christian and a Democrat." He assured the business community that he would address the need for economic growth. The candidate also promised lower tariffs and relief for the unemployed. Demonstrating the progressive belief in planning by professionals, Roosevelt announced that he would use a "brains trust" of university experts to establish government policy.

Herbert Hoover responded to the Democratic campaign by warning that the party's low tariff policies would guarantee that "the grass will grow in the streets of a hundred cities" and "weeds will overrun the fields of a million farms." Although Roosevelt never presented a clear program to end the Depression and even criticized Hoover's spending, voters responded to the New Yorker's warmth, assertiveness, and willingness to experiment. Described by contemporary reports as not so much rebellious as drifting, voters rejected the apparent impotence of Hoover's leadership and gave Roosevelt and vice presidential candidate John N. Garner of Texas 57 percent of the popular ballot. Hoover carried only six states for a total of fifty-nine votes in the Electoral College.

By the start of 1933 nearly one-fourth of the normal work force was unemployed. Wages had declined from a high of $53 billion in 1929 to $31 billion. Farm receipts had dropped from $12 billion to $5 billion. In the four years since the Crash, both industrial production and national income had been cut in half. Investment in capital goods had decreased 88 percent. Two indicator industries —automobile manufacturing and construction—lay in ruins: annual car sales had plummeted from 4.5 million to 1.1 million, and building outlays had tumbled from $8.7 billion to $1.4 billion. As Roosevelt prepared to assume the presidency in 1933, the economic decline approached catastrophe. After thousands of financial institutions had declared bankruptcy, depositors began to participate in bank "runs" to withdraw savings before they were lost. The disaster prompted twenty-nine states to declare banking moratoriums and to place severe restrictions on the withdrawal of assets. Meanwhile, three midwestern states suspended foreclosures on farm mortgages.

As Roosevelt learned from New York financiers, the collapse of the nation's credit system had produced an emergency that "could not be greater." "It is impossible to contemplate the extent of the human suffering and the social consequences of a denial of currency and credit to our urban populations," one banker emphasized in a confidential memo. As Franklin Roosevelt rode to his inauguration, the weight of the economic and political system rested on his

Exhibit 5-18. Election of 1932

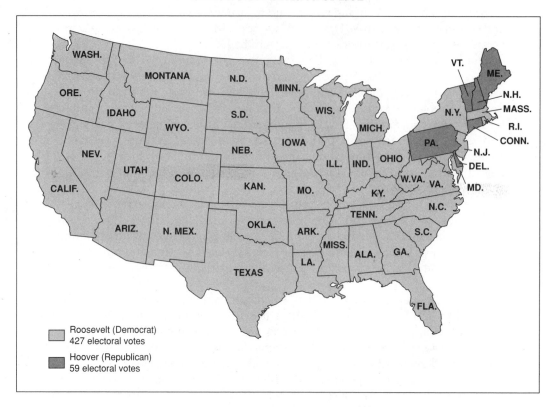

Roosevelt (Democrat)
427 electoral votes

Hoover (Republican)
59 electoral votes

shoulders. The promise of New Era prosperity and consensus nurtured during three Republican presidencies now lay in ashes. A demoralized public veered between apathy and fury at discredited business leaders. The nation waited to see how the Democrat Franklin Roosevelt would respond.

SUGGESTED READINGS

The standard overview of 1920s political history is John D. Hicks, *The Republican Ascendancy, 1921–1933* (1960). For Harding, see Eugene Trani and David L. Wilson, *The Presidency of Warren G. Harding* (1977). See also Robert K. Murray, *The Politics of Normalcy: Government Theory and Practice in the Harding-Coolidge Era* (1973) and *The Harding Era: Warren G. Harding and His Administration* (1969). The Harding scandals are described in Burl Noggle, *Teapot Dome: Oil and Politics in the 1920s* (1962).

Hoover's role as secretary of commerce is emphasized by Joan Hoff Wilson, *Herbert Hoover: The Forgotten Progressive* (1975). See also the relevant segments of David Burner, *Herbert Hoover: The Public Life* (1978), and Ellis W. Hawley, *The Great War and the Search for a Modern Order: A History of the American People and Their Institutions, 1917–1933* (1979). Revised assessments of Hoover's political career appear in Carl E. Krog and William R. Tanner, eds., *Herbert Hoover and the Republican Era: A Reconsideration* (1984). Robert F. Himmelberg, *The Origins*

of the National Recovery Administration: Business, Government, and the Trade Association Issue, 1921–1933 (1975), depicts the evolving government response to
trade groups.

For Harding-era social legislation, see the works on social feminism listed in
Chapter 4. For a revisionist approach to 1920s Republican reform, see the appropriate chapters of Martin J. Sklar, *The United States as a Developing Country:
Studies in U.S. History in the Progressive Era and the 1920s* (1992). Postwar agrarian
discontent is the subject of James H. Shideler, *Farm Crisis, 1919–1923* (1957), and
the relevant segments of Theodore Saloutos and John D. Hicks, *Twentieth Century Populism: Agricultural Discontent in the Middle West, 1900–1939* (1951). For
the South, see portions of Pete Daniel, *Breaking the Land: The Transformation of
Cotton, Tobacco, and Rice Cultures Since 1880* (1985).

The Coolidge years are portrayed in Murray, *The Politics of Normalcy*, and
Donald B. McCoy, *Calvin Coolidge: The Quiet President* (1967). For postwar for-
eign policy, see Warren I. Cohen, *Empire Without Tears: America's Foreign Rela-
tions, 1921–1933* (1987). Diplomatic ties with Europe are the focus of Frank
Costigliola, *Awkward Dominion: American Political, Economic, and Cultural Rela-
tions with Europe, 1919–1933* (1985). For business internationalism, see Joan Hoff
Wilson, *American Business and Foreign Policy, 1920–1933* (1985), and segments of
Akira Iriye, *The Globalizing of America, 1913–1945* (1993). The roots of Central
American intervention can be found in Walter LaFeber, *Inevitable Revolutions:
The United States in Central America* (1983). For noninterventionist sentiment, see
Robert David Johnson, *The Peace Progressives and American Foreign Relations*
(1995), and Thomas N. Guinsburg, *The Pursuit of Isolationism in the United States
Senate from Versailles to Pearl Harbor* (1982).

Expressions of 1920s insurgence are described in segments of Saloutos and
Hicks, *Twentieth Century Populism*; Russel B. Nye, *Midwestern Progressive Politics:
A Historical Study of Its Origins and Development, 1870–1958* (1959); and David A.
Horowitz, *Beyond Left and Right: Insurgency and the Establishment* (1997). A good
case study is Millard L. Gieske, *Minnesota Farmer-Laborism: The Third Party Alternative* (1979). For the dilemmas of postwar progressivism, see LeRoy Ashby, *The
Spearless Leader: Senator Borah and the Progressive Movement in the 1920s* (1972),
and Eugene M. Tobin, *Organize or Perish: America's Independent Progressives,
1913–1933* (1986). See also David B. Danbom, *"The World of Hope": Progressives
and the Struggle for an Ethical Public Life* (1987).

For the Democrats and the 1928 election, see Douglas B. Craig, *After Wilson:
The Struggle for the Democratic Party, 1920–1934* (1992), and David Burner, *The
Politics of Provincialism: The Democratic Party in Transition, 1918–1932* (1968). The
role of Catholicism is emphasized by Allan J. Lichtman, *Prejudice and the Old
Politics: The Presidential Election of 1928* (1979). Charles W. Eagles, *Democracy
Delayed: Congressional Reapportionment and Urban-Rural Conflict in the 1920s*
(1990), argues that political ideology was more important than ethnocultural
conflict.

The standard account of the 1929 stock market collapse is John K. Galbraith,
The Great Crash, 1929 (1961). Structural problems in the postwar economy are
addressed by Peter Fearon, *War, Prosperity, and Depression: The U.S. Economy,
1917–1945* (1987), and Jim Potter, *The American Economy between the World Wars*
(1975). For obstacles to recovery, see Michael Bernstein, *The Great Depression:
Delayed Recovery and Economic Change in America, 1929–1939* (1987). The social
consequences of the disaster are described in Robert S. McElvaine, *The Great*

Depression, 1919–1941 (1984), and in John A. Garraty, *The Great Depression* (1986). See also Caroline Bird, *The Invisible Scar* (1966); Studs Terkel, *Hard Times* (1970); and Robert S. Lynd and Helen M. Lynd, *Middletown in Transition* (1937).

Hoover's response to the Depression is the subject of Martin L. Fausold, *The Presidency of Herbert C. Hoover* (1985), and Fausold and George T. Mazuazan, eds., *The Hoover Presidency: A Reappraisal* (1974). See also previously listed works by Wilson, Burner, Hawley, and Krog and Tanner. Critical portraits of the president include Gene Smith, *The Shattered Dream: Herbert Hoover and the Great Depression* (1970), and Albert U. Romasco, *The Poverty of Abundance: Hoover, the Nation, the Depression* (1965). Revisionists who place Hoover in the New Deal tradition include William J. Barber, *From New Era to the New Deal: Herbert Hoover, the Economists, and American Economic Policy, 1921–1933* (1985); Elliot A. Rosen, *Hoover, Roosevelt, and the Brains Trust: From Depression to New Deal* (1977); and Alan Dawley, *Struggles for Justice: Social Responsibility and the Liberal State* (1991).

6

Franklin D. Roosevelt campaigning in 1932.

ROOSEVELT, THE NEW DEAL, AND DOMESTIC SECURITY: 1932–1940

The New Deal, proclaimed Franklin D. Roosevelt, involved a "changed concept of the duty and responsibility of government toward economic life." Roosevelt embodied the nation's will to recover. His relief and reform programs brought unprecedented participation by the federal government in the lives of ordinary people. New welfare structures and bureaucratic regulation of the marketplace were two of the more controversial legacies of the Roosevelt administration. Critics maintained that New Deal reform came at the expense of small farmers and of independent business interests and that Roosevelt's expansion of federal power would prove irreversible. Nevertheless, the desire to restore stability and order in the economic emergency pushed the nation toward consensus.

The New Deal

"The only thing we have to fear is fear itself—nameless, unreasoning, unjustified terror," Franklin Roosevelt declared in his inaugural address in 1933. Seeking to reassure an uneasy nation, Roosevelt promised to ask for "broad executive power to urge war against the emergency, as great as the power that would be given to me if we were in fact invaded by a foreign foe." To stop the run on the banks, the president proclaimed a national bank "holiday," a moratorium on transactions in gold and silver. He also convened a special session of Congress. Both houses responded immediately by overwhelmingly passing the Emergency Banking Act of 1933, which gave the chief executive extraordinary powers to regulate the currency and which authorized the U.S. Treasury to grant licenses and federal loans to sound banks. Eight days after the inauguration, the president took to the radio to deliver his first "fireside chat." Roosevelt assured 60 million listeners that returning savings to the reorganized banks was safe. Deposits immediately began to exceed withdrawals. "Capitalism was saved in eight days," White House advisor Raymond Moley later recalled.

Roosevelt's New Deal operated on the assumption that society could be reconstructed along just, rational, and efficient lines through the intelligent use of government power to serve the general welfare. The president sought to restore balance to the economy by remedying defects in the private market. His first one hundred days in office provided an indication of the New Deal's approach. Weeks after taking power, the chief executive announced that he had taken the currency off the gold standard by prohibiting the export of gold. Roosevelt later signed the Gold Reserve Act of 1934, which set the price of gold at $35 an ounce and gave the president the authority to devalue the dollar. Through such actions, the White House hoped to restore deflated prices, to stimulate production, and to facilitate economic recovery.

As the Senate continued its investigation of the stock exchange, Roosevelt signed legislation to regulate the financial markets. The Securities Act of 1933 required that information on stocks be filed with the Federal Trade Commission and that company directors be liable for improper practices. Congress created the Securities and Exchange Commission (SEC) in 1934 to regulate and license stock exchanges. The administration also sought to reform banking practices. The Glass-Steagall Act of 1933 separated commercial from investment banking, expanded the Federal Reserve Board's ability to discourage speculation, and

Exhibit 6-1. First One Hundred Days of the New Deal
(March–June 1933)

- Abandonment of Gold Standard by Executive Action
- Civil Conservation Corps Reforestation Relief Act (created **CCC**—Civilian Conservation Corps)
- Federal Emergency Relief Act (created **FERA**—Federal Employment Relief Administration)
- Agricultural Adjustment Act (created **AAA**—Agricultural Adjustment Administration)
- Tennessee Valley Authority Act (created **TVA**—Tennessee Valley Authority)
- Federal Securities Act
- Home Owners Refinancing Act (created **HOLC**—Home Owners Loan Corporation)
- Glass-Steagall Banking Act
- Farm Credit Act (created **FCA**—Farm Credit Administration)
- National Industrial Recovery Act (created **NRA**—National Recovery Administration and **PWA**—Public Works Administration)

established the Federal Deposit Insurance Corporation (FDIC) to insure bank deposits of as much as $5,000. Congress created the Federal Savings and Loan Insurance Corporation in 1934 to regulate home loan interest rates and to ensure the solvency of mortgage lenders. Another measure, the Banking Act of 1935, allowed the Federal Reserve Board to set reserve requirements and to review the interest rates of member banks.

Declining farm prices presented the Roosevelt administration with as severe a challenge as the banking crisis. The Senate had passed a bill to set crop prices above the "cost of production," but administration fears of inflation led to the measure's defeat in the House. One day before a scheduled protest strike by the Farmers Holiday Association in 1933, Congress passed the Agricultural Adjustment Act. The law established government price supports to ensure parity for basic commodities, thus providing a guarantee that farm prices would maintain the same relation to nonfarm prices that had existed in the prosperous years from 1909 to 1914. To deal with overproduction, the Agricultural Adjustment Administration (AAA) awarded subsidies to limit cultivated acreage. "Kill every third pig or plow every third row under," advised the AAA. The agency distributed $100 million in payments in its first year in return for the slaughter of 6 million pigs and the destruction of one-fourth of the nation's cotton crop.

The administration also sought to provide capital for needy farmers. The Commodity Credit Corporation, created in 1933, enabled growers to borrow money for crops they agreed to take out of production. Another new bureau, the Farm Credit Corporation, consolidated all federal agencies dealing with agricultural loans and refinanced one-fifth of all farm mortgages. By 1935 prices for basic crops and national farm income both had doubled, and agricultural debt had decreased by $2 billion. Yet production quotas forced more than 300,000 poor black and white sharecroppers off the land. Roosevelt responded with the Resettlement Administration, which relocated a few tenants and poor farmers in experimental homestead communities. Meanwhile, Congress created the Soil Conservation Service, which sent out government teams to promote contour plowing, rotation of crops, fertilizing, and gully planting.

Home mortgage bankruptcies presented another major crisis. Facing 1,000 residential foreclosures daily, New Deal officials asked Congress to create the Home Owners Loan Corporation (HOLC) in 1933. The agency protected home ownership by issuing government bonds to refinance more than 1 million

Farm Holiday Association activists blocking highways outside of Sioux City, Iowa, to restrict the marketing of agricultural goods during the price depression of 1932–1933.

mortgages. Within two years, the HOLC spent $3 billion to rescue 10 percent of the nation's owner-occupied residences from default or foreclosure. Congress sought to finance single-family housing construction in 1934 by creating the Federal Housing Administration (FHA). The FHA insured long-term mortgages and lowered down payment requirements. By focusing on building single-family units, New Deal agencies promoted suburban housing at the expense of the inner cities. Moreover, the Resettlement Administration, created in 1935, implemented a program to build model "greenbelt towns" in suburban communities.

Roosevelt's greatest challenge lay with the millions of people desperate for immediate relief. In 1933 the administration convinced Congress to create the Federal Employment Relief Administration (FERA). The agency granted $500 million to states and municipalities to aid the jobless. Initiating the federal

Exhibit 6-2. The New Deal, 1934

- Gold Reserve Act
- Farm Mortgage Refinancing Act (created FFMC—Federal Farm Mortgage Corporation)
- Export-Import Bank
- Securities Exchange Act (created SEC—Securities and Exchange Commission)
- Communications Act (created FCC—Federal Communications Commission)
- Frazier-Lemke Farm Bankruptcy Act
- National Housing Act (created FHA—Federal Housing Administration)

Relief administrators Harry Hopkins, Harold Ickes, and Frank Walker, key participants in the emergency bureaucracy created by Franklin Roosevelt's New Deal.

government's first direct relief effort, FERA director Harry L. Hopkins provided $4 billion in cash stipends and work programs to more than 20 million recipients. Not satisfied, Roosevelt placed Hopkins in charge of a second agency, the Civil Works Administration, which spent $1 billion to hire 4 million unemployed workers during the winter of 1933–1934. Another jobs program, the Civilian Conservation Corps (CCC), combined employment relief and conservation principles. After its creation in 1933, the CCC hired 2.5 million men between the ages of eighteen and twenty-five for reforesting, road construction, flood control, land reclamation, range improvement, and soil erosion efforts. Organized along military lines, the corps stressed discipline, outdoor experience, and national service and became a recruitment pool for noncommissioned army officers.

A second conservation agency, the Tennessee Valley Authority (TVA), involved an ambitious public power project embracing a seven-state river basin. First promoted by Republican reformer George Norris, the massive undertaking coordinated the construction of nine government dams. The dams produced inexpensive power for fertilizer and explosives factories and created reservoirs for flood control. An independent public corporation, the TVA used resource experts to promote soil conservation and reforestation. Although private utility firms opposed the project, the TVA showed that government electric power could stimulate private investment, agricultural development, and consumption. Under its auspices, thousands of isolated homesteads became consumers of electric appliances. The TVA also provided a yardstick for setting reasonable and fair utility rates.

Federal innovation also addressed industrial recovery after the Senate approved a proposal to spread work among the unemployed by creating a thirty-hour week. When business opposed the measure, the administration substituted the National Industrial Recovery Act of 1933, which Congress passed. Based on World War I industrial coordination and the 1931 Swope Plan, the bill freed corporations from antitrust provisions and created the National Recovery Administration (NRA) to supervise the enforcement of self-regulating industrial codes. These agreements allowed competing corporations to curtail production, raise prices, regulate business practices, set minimum wages and maximum working hours, and ban child labor. Section 7(a) of the legislation extended union collective bargaining and the forty-hour work week to about half the nation's labor force. Roosevelt appointed New York Senator Robert F. Wagner to head the National Labor Board to mediate labor code disagreements.

THE WELFARE STATE

Impatient with the slow pace of recovery by 1935, President Roosevelt accelerated New Deal efforts to provide jobs for the unemployed. The administration sought to achieve this goal by using a $5 billion emergency appropriation from Congress to create the Works Progress Administration (WPA). While the states distributed cash relief, the WPA organized a massive jobs program for 3.5 million people. WPA jobs paid less than prevailing wages, and private sector positions were excluded from WPA control. State and local governments also were required to administer strict means and eligibility tests for recipients, including a 16 percent ceiling on jobs for women. Despite such limitations, the WPA rebuilt a decaying national infrastructure of highways, bridges, sewers, airports, post offices, and other public facilities. The program also provided the first federal sponsorship of the arts through projects that hired dramatists, writers, musicians, and artists. Under its auspices, the National Youth Administration offered jobs, vocational training, citizenship classes, and educational stipends to relieve the effects of youth unemployment. By 1942 the WPA had spent $11 billion to hire 7 million people in the largest public works program in history.

While the work relief program expanded, the NRA collapsed. Designed to raise prices, end destructive competition, and introduce industrial planning, the recovery agency disappointed competing interest groups. Consumers objected to high prices. Union leaders argued that corporations evaded labor guarantees. Corporate officials complained of excessive government interference. Small businesses charged that domination of code authorities by large corporations led to fixed prices and monopoly practices. Such criticism became moot, however, when in 1935 the Supreme Court ruled in the *Schecter* case that the establishment of the NRA involved an invalid transfer of legislative power from

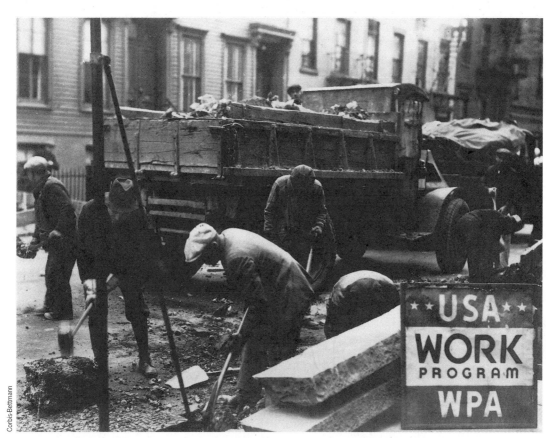

Corbis-Bettmann

The WPA in action. The Works Progress Administration employed more than 7 million Americans between 1935 and 1942 at a cost of $11 billion. Its projects ranged from aid to the arts to the reconstruction of bridges and sewers.

Congress to the president and an unconstitutional attempt to regulate industry within individual states.

Infuriated at the court, Roosevelt snapped that "we have been relegated to a horse and buggy definition of interstate commerce." To replace the NRA's labor provisions, the president supported Senator Wagner's bill to outlaw "unfair labor practices" as "must legislation." Considered the Magna Carta of organized labor, the National Labor Relations Act of 1935 upheld the right of workers to join unions and to bargain collectively through representatives chosen in federally supervised elections. The law bound employers to recognize duly elected bargaining agents and forbade them from firing workers for union activity. It prohibited company unions, yellow dog contracts, employer blacklists, and labor spies. The National Labor Relations Board supervised elections,

Exhibit 6-3. U.S. Public Secondary School Enrollment, 1932–1940 (in rounded millions)

1932	5.1
1940	6.6

Source: *Historical Statistics of the United States, Colonial Times to 1970* (1975).

Exhibit 6-4. The New Deal, 1935

- Emergency Relief Appropriation Act (created WPA—Works Progress Administration)
- Soil Conservation Act (created Soil Conservation Service)
- Resettlement Administration (RA), created by executive order
- Rural Electrification Administration (REA), created by executive order
- National Youth Administration (NYA), created by executive order
- National Labor Relations Act (created NLRB—National Labor Relations Board)
- Social Security Act
- Banking Act of 1935 (created Open Market Committee of Federal Reserve System)
- Public Utility Holding Company Act
- Frazier-Lemke Farm-Mortgage Moratorium Act
- Wealth Tax Act

investigated unfair employer practices, issued cease-and-desist orders, and reviewed arbitrary firings. Although the statute did not initially apply to workers in agriculture, domestic service, public employment, or intrastate commerce, it initiated a historic shift in the relations between management, labor, and government.

Roosevelt's agenda for 1935 also included protections against old age, unemployment, and economic dependency. By the mid-1930s, twenty-nine states had established old-age pension programs to supplement charity aid. However, social security advocates such as Dr. Francis E. Townsend pushed for a comprehensive federal program. The president's Committee on Economic Security, headed by Secretary of Labor Frances Perkins, warned that declining death rates, a contracting economy, and smaller families had increased the dependency of the elderly on their families. Accordingly, the Social Security Act of 1935 provided those older than age sixty-five with monthly federal pensions from a self-supporting Social Security Administration. Unlike social welfare plans in other industrial nations, old-age insurance in the United States rested on a contributory system of payroll taxes for both employers and workers. The law also established the first federal unemployment insurance. Funded by payroll taxes on employers, the state-administered unemployment program covered those who worked for wages and salaries in commerce and industry.

By emulating contributory private insurance plans, old-age and unemployment programs qualified as legitimate benefits for deserving employees. In contrast, Aid to Dependent Children (ADC), another Social Security program, treated poor women and mothers as social dependents rather than as deserving workers. Designed by social work professionals in the Children's Bureau, ADC provided federal matching funds to states to continue "mother's pension" payments to single beneficiaries who maintained "suitable homes." Because planners underestimated the number of poor, female-headed households,

Exhibit 6-5. U.S. Gross National Product, 1933–1936
(in rounded billions of dollars)

1933	55.6
1936	82.5

Source: *Historical Statistics of the United States, Colonial Times to 1970* (1975).

FRANCES PERKINS
1880–1965

Corbis-Bettmann

An interviewer frustrated by Frances Perkins's caution once described Roosevelt's labor secretary as a "colorless woman who talked as if she had swallowed a press release." Yet the first female cabinet member in U.S. history was a passionate reformer who exemplified the integration of the social service professions into government.

As a young Mount Holyoke College student at the turn of the century, Perkins was electrified by a speech made by Progressive social activist Florence Kelley. The experience inspired her to join the crusade against child labor led by the National Consumers' League. A professional social worker who joined Jane Addams at Hull House, Perkins became executive secretary of the New York City Consumers' League in 1910. As the organization's key lobbyist, she worked closely with the legislature in Albany, where she met future patrons of her career such as Alfred E. Smith and Franklin D. Roosevelt.

Perkins soon found herself involved in Progressive crusades to secure workers' rights, to negotiate labor-management conflicts, and to secure safer working conditions. Until Al Smith assumed the New York state governorship in 1918, she considered her work nonpartisan. However, Smith named the dynamic social worker to the State Industrial Commission, and his successor, Franklin Roosevelt, made her his chief advisor on labor matters. Perkins played a major role in persuading Roosevelt to act vigorously to combat the economic slump following the stock market crash of 1929. The governor's program of unemployment relief helped launch him toward national office. Once elected, Roosevelt named Perkins to his cabinet.

Aware of her pioneering role, Perkins intended to be taken seriously. "Many good and intelligent women ... dress in ways that are very attractive and pretty," she once commented, "but don't invite confidence in their common sense, integrity, or sense of justice." Regularly outfitted in a plain black dress, a white bow, and a trim hat, Perkins took pride in colleague Harold Ickes's remark that she was "the best man in the cabinet." Despite her own career, the secretary of labor denounced affluent women who sought outside employment during the Depression. "Any woman capable of supporting herself without a job," she declared in 1930, "should devote herself to motherhood and the home."

A strong advocate of unemployment relief through public works, Perkins headed Roosevelt's Committee on Economic Security in 1934. Convinced that social insurance was a "great forward step" in the "liberation of humanity," the labor secretary pushed the panel toward endorsement of a national old-age and survivor's insurance plan, a prototype of Social Security. She also drew upon female colleagues in the Progressive era's children's welfare movement to write the child employment provisions of the Fair Labor Standards Act of 1938.

Perkins reacted coolly to the Wagner Act's endorsement of unionization and of collective bargaining. In her own words, she "never lifted a finger" for the measure because she had "very little sympathy" for organized labor. Despite aloofness from union activists and feminists, however, Perkins helped to transform liberalism into a creed serving working people. An able New Deal administrator, she demonstrated that women had an important role to play in government in a period in which society rarely acknowledged such accomplishments. ∎

**Exhibit 6-6. U.S. Exports of Goods and Services, 1933–1936
(in rounded billions of dollars)**

1933	2.4
1936	3.4

Source: *Historical Statistics of the United States, Colonial Times to 1970* (1975).

**Exhibit 6-7. U.S. Unemployment, 1933–1936
(percentage of civilian labor force)**

1933	24.9
1934	21.7
1935	20.1
1936	16.9

Source: *Historical Statistics of the United States, Colonial Times to 1970* (1975).

inadequate appropriations led to strict means and morals screening. ADC also failed to include national health coverage for needy families, although the Social Security Act provided public health services and medical funds for mothers and children in economically distressed areas and federal aid to physically disabled children.

As Roosevelt looked to the 1936 election, he addressed issues of wealth redistribution and corporate reform. In response to the popularity of Huey Long of Louisiana, the president supported the Wealth Tax of 1935. When congressional committees changed the bill into a minor revenue measure, however, Roosevelt meekly retreated. The White House had more success with reform of the electric utility industry, in which twelve large companies controlled almost half the nation's power. The president signed the Public Utility Holding Act of 1935, which created the Federal Power Commission to regulate interstate electric rates and business practices and authorized the Federal Trade Commission (FTC) to supervise interstate sales of natural gas. The law also authorized the Securities and Exchange Commission to prevent utilities from maintaining financial interests in other companies through "pyramid" schemes. Firms had five years to demonstrate the local nature of their operations, or they would face dissolution.

THE TRIUMPH OF INDUSTRIAL UNIONISM

For working people who dreamed of social mobility in the 1920s, the Great Depression brought a terrifying loss of economic security. Workers sought to improve their position by turning to the union movement. Labor organizers benefited from Section 7(a) of the National Industrial Recovery Act, which compelled business codes to incorporate collective bargaining procedures. The law enabled union leaders to tell workers that the president wanted them to form unions to fight the Depression. The shared experience of the economic crisis

**Exhibit 6-8. U.S. Labor Union Membership, 1936–1940
(in rounded millions)**

1936	4.1
1938	6.1
1940	7.3

Source: *Historical Statistics of the United States, Colonial Times to 1970* (1975).

provided industrial laborers with the opportunity to unite. By 1934 1,700 national and local labor organizations thrived in mass production industries such as automobiles, steel, lumber, rubber, and aluminum.

Nevertheless, union success varied by geographic region and by industry. On the West Coast, predominantly northern European maritime workers resorted to "direct action" on the docks to win a bitterly contested 1934 strike. In the East, where longshore locals were racially and ethnically divided and often dominated by racketeers, workers resisted calls for industrial solidarity. In the southern textile industry, low wages, reduced hours, layoffs, and speed-ups prompted a massive walkout of Georgia and Piedmont mill workers in 1934. Yet managers in this labor-intensive and competitive industry, whose costs could not easily be passed on to consumers, were bitterly antiunion. When the work force split over unionization, one of the most militant strikes in southern history ended in failure.

The Congress of Industrial Organizations (CIO) emerged as the most important vehicle of labor discontent. The CIO was formed in 1935 by John L. Lewis, whose United Mine Workers (UMW) had gained collective bargaining rights for the entire soft-coal industry under the auspices of the NRA. Instead of enrolling workers on the basis of the AFL's craft divisions, the CIO organized participants on an industry-wide basis and targeted mass production fields such as steel, rubber, automobiles, and radio appliances. The industrial unions stressed grass roots organization and recruited blue-collar ethnics, southern whites, African Americans, and women in all phases of factory and mill work. Sensitive to problems on the mechanized assembly line, the CIO responded to grievances with immediate direct action.

The industrial union movement provided a major outlet for Depression militancy. Whereas unemployment produced passivity and demoralization, blue-collar workers who retained their jobs rose against the arbitrary policies of corporate management. When industrial corporations refused to honor the Wagner Act's provisions for collective bargaining, a series of worker rebellions erupted. Between 1936 and 1937 500,000 industrial laborers joined CIO sit-downs in which strikers stopped production by occupying plants and factories. A major turning point in the campaign occurred when President Roosevelt pressured General Motors to negotiate with the CIO's United Auto Workers. Shortly thereafter, U.S. Steel, a bitter opponent of industrial unionism in 1919, settled with the CIO steelworkers union.

Although corporations like General Motors and U.S. Steel reluctantly accepted collective bargaining, smaller firms felt more threatened by union wage demands and labor participation in hirings and promotions. When the CIO's Steel Workers Organizing Committee sought to unionize smaller companies in the Little Steel Strike of 1937, strikers met brutal resistance. The climax came at

Strikers riot at Fisher Body plant, Cleveland, 1937.

the Republic Steel plant in Chicago when city police fired on a thousand workers and their families, killed ten, and injured fifty-eight. Industrial unions abandoned sit-downs after they lost the Little Steel Strike and the Supreme Court declared the protests illegal. Nevertheless, CIO strength reached 2.8 million by 1941 as nearly one-fourth of the nonagricultural work force joined the ranks of organized labor.

Organizational clout, support from the Roosevelt administration, and the protections of the Wagner Act provided unionized workers with seniority rights, grievance mechanisms, freedom from arbitrary firings, and better wages. Labor solidarity also sustained pride and dignity in a period of economic adversity and social insecurity. Yet few CIO members saw their organizations as agents of revolutionary change. Viewing dues payments as a guarantor of workplace protections and stability, most employees accepted narrow "business unionism." As labor negotiators increasingly viewed workers as consumers and focused on pay scales and fringe benefits, unions retreated from demands for participation in production planning or for a shorter work week. Contractually responsible for maintaining shop discipline and for preventing spontaneous walkouts, labor officials insulated the rank and file from decision making. Such marginalization increased worker apathy and limited commitment to the union movement.

AFRICAN AMERICANS
AND THE DEPRESSION

At the 1936 Olympics held in Nazi Berlin, African American track star Jessie Owens disproved Adolf Hitler's racial theories by winning four gold medals (although in deference to Nazi hosts, the U.S. team benched two Jewish runners). Two years later, heavyweight boxing champ Joe Louis, an African American, defeated German Max Schmeling with a first-round knockout in a boxing match promoted by Hitler as a test of Nazi racial superiority. The success and popularity of these black athletes testified to a growing acceptance of African American achievement. Yet for most black Americans, the Depression and the New Deal brought limited opportunities for racial integration, economic advancement, and social acceptance.

Blacks fared most poorly in the rural South, where nearly half of African Americans lived. As cotton prices sank to the lowest levels since the 1890s, banks and insurance companies foreclosed on one-third of the region's cotton farms. By promoting mechanized operations and by encouraging reduction of

Plantation overseer and field hands in the Mississippi delta, 1936. This photograph was taken by Dorothea Lange for the Farm Security Administration.

cultivated acreage, federal programs such as the Agricultural Adjustment Administration led landlords to evict tenants. The Roosevelt administration's Committee on Farm Tenancy described the standard of living of southern sharecroppers and tenants as "below any level of decency." Despite this finding, farm laborers were initially excluded from receiving Social Security benefits. Moreover, as conditions worsened, both blacks and whites fled the countryside in increasing numbers.

As the southern labor market narrowed, white leaders tightened control of a racial caste system that segregated public accommodations, schools, churches, and even movie theaters. State laws excluded blacks from jury service, and poll taxes, literacy tests, and white primaries kept them from voting. Outside the legal system, strict rules of conduct strove to eliminate interracial contact. Whites addressed African Americans by their first names or insisted that black servants or messengers use the rear door. Physical contact between black men and white women was strictly prohibited. Southern communities often enforced racial segregation through intimidation, violence, and lynching. In 1931 national attention focused on Scottsboro, Alabama, where local authorities used thin evidence to convict nine African American teenagers of raping two white female prostitutes. As eight of the defendants faced death penalties, the Communist Party took up the case, which led to a reversal of the convictions in 1935 by a U.S. Supreme Court ruling that the defendants had been denied fair trials because African Americans were excluded from Alabama juries.

Marginalized by southern white society, black tenants and sharecroppers received the attention of 1930s political radicals. The biracial Alabama Sharecroppers Union (ASU), initiated by white Communist Party organizers, claimed 12,000 members by 1935 and engaged in several violent confrontations with county deputies. In Arkansas, the Socialist Party helped to form the racially integrated Southern Tenant Farmers Union (STFU), which eventually claimed 25,000 followers. The STFU not only attacked evictions and low wages but also demonstrated against racist practices such as the poll tax, inferior education, and denial of civil liberties. The activities of the ASU, STFU, and the Communist Party prompted southern leaders to associate all civil rights activities with radical agitation.

Although African Americans faced less repressive conditions outside the South, blacks were excluded from many positions in deference to jobless whites. National black unemployment rates were triple those of whites: in the depths of the Depression, about half of all black workers had no work. High unemployment enabled urban African Americans to receive relief at three times the rate of urban whites. In part because of prodding by the NAACP and the Urban League, blacks also received WPA and CCC jobs. Yet demoralizing conditions in segregated neighborhoods fostered profound resentment. When the Home Owners Loan Corporation began to "red-line" or undervalue older and racially mixed neighborhoods, black homeowners were unable to refinance mortgages or improve properties. Police abuse also worsened tensions in African American communities and led to major race riots in Harlem and Detroit. The bitterness and incipient violence of northern black life was detailed in black novelist Richard Wright's *Native Son* (1940).

Although African American voters supported the New Deal at the polls through substantial Democratic majorities in 1936, the Roosevelt administration remained indebted to white political leaders in the South and rejected federal enforcement of civil rights. When a series of racially motivated vigilante murders in the Deep South prompted the NAACP to reintroduce federal antilynching legislation in 1933, the president refused to support the proposal. Without such help, northern liberals such as Senator Robert Wagner were unable to break a filibuster by southern Democrats espousing states' rights. Civil rights groups also failed to eradicate racially segregated housing and public facilities in southern CCC camps and TVA model towns.

Despite difficulties, whites and African Americans often cooperated to advance racial justice. The biracial Association of Southern Women for the Prevention of Lynching mounted a national campaign to expose the horrors of antiblack violence. To foster unity between New Deal liberals, industrial unions, and African American interests, labor organizer A. Philip Randolph created the National Negro Congress in 1936. Eleanor Roosevelt, the president's wife, also supported African American efforts to end discrimination. When the Daughters of the American Revolution refused to rent Washington, D.C.'s only concert stage to African American opera singer Marian Anderson in 1939, Eleanor Roosevelt resigned from the organization and arranged for a recital on the steps of the Lincoln Memorial. The resulting Easter Sunday gathering attracted 75,000 people in the first mass demonstration for civil rights in the nation's history.

Mexican Americans and Native Americans: Hard Times

Depression conditions pushed more than half the Mexican American population of 1.4 million to the cities, where economic pressures remained severe. Fearing increased job competition, President Hoover's Department of Labor had endorsed the deportation of illegal immigrants in 1929. Local authorities subsequently broadened the sweep to include all Mexican laborers. In Texas, where the Agricultural Adjustment Administration destroyed 40 percent of the cotton crop after 1933, farmers were encouraged to call immigration authorities to arrest hired Mexican hands and sharecroppers. In Los Angeles, police round-ups forced members of the nation's largest Chicano community to flee the country. Colorado declared martial law to turn away Mexican job seekers at state borders. With support from the AFL and the American Legion, midwestern officials shipped half the region's Mexican community south of the border. By 1940 the campaign to "repatriate" Mexican Americans had victimized nearly 600,000 people, and two-thirds of them were born in the United States.

The repressive atmosphere placed great strains on Mexican American unions. As the rural migrant labor pool increased and as agricultural wages declined, Mexican workers turned to labor organizations for protection. During the early 1930s farm workers in large California orchards won partial victories by using roving pickets, but when the Cannery and Agricultural Workers Industrial Union (CAWIU) sought to organize California cotton fields between 1933 and 1934, large farmers deported union activists, burned strikers' shacks, forcibly dispersed rallies, and murdered several activists. The bitter farm

National Archives

Chicano laborers shelling pecans in San Antonio, Texas, in the 1930s.

worker strikes led growers to form the Associated Farmers, an organization that frequently resorted to vigilante activities. Meanwhile, the Communist-led CAWIU disbanded in 1934 after police raided its Sacramento headquarters and charged fifteen party loyalists with criminal syndicalism. In one Jewish community a Communist Party labor organizer was kidnapped and tarred and feathered by irate orchard owners.

Mexican American women participated in farmworker strikes but played a more important role in organizing the southwestern food processing industry, three-quarters of whose employees were women. In 1937 these union workers in Texas and California formed the seventh-largest CIO affiliate. Using rank-and-file leaders, the union negotiated benefits such as maternity leave, company-provided day care, and paid vacations and organized women workers in San Antonio's pecan-shelling industry. By the 1930s most of the nation's 1.4 million Mexican Americans had been born in the United States. Community leaders increasingly focused on issues such as public education, voter registration, civil rights, and entrance into the professions. Seeking to develop middle-class Chicano leaders who could align the Mexican American labor movement with New Deal reform, CIO organizer Luisa Moreno founded the Spanish-Speaking Congress in 1938.

Spurred by the "Indian New Deal" of Commissioner of Indian Affairs John Collier, the federal government reversed detribalization programs and sought to preserve Native American culture and resources. Collier encouraged tribal organization, economic self-sufficiency, and self-management. His Emergency Conservation Work Program, organized in 1933, functioned as an "all-Indian CCC." Collier persuaded Congress to pass the Indian Reorganization Act of 1934, a measure that guaranteed the principle of reservation home rule through tribal constitutions written and ratified by each tribe. The law also provided government financial aid to support the college education of native people and to promote the study of Native American culture. Its most controversial provision was the reversion of land-holding to tribal title. Since the Dawes Act of 1887, Native American land had been held by individuals. By 1934 almost half such property included semiarid or desert lands, and only half the Native Americans in the country owned any land. Average native income in 1934 amounted to $48 a year.

Many Native Americans distrusted Collier's reforms, but more than two-thirds of the tribes voted to participate. Conservative critics condemned the tribal property arrangement as "sovietization" of reservation life and claimed that the Bureau of Indian Affairs (BIA) relegated Native Americans to a reservation existence. In contrast, Collier believed that tribal cooperative and communal experience provided an alternative to the atomization of urban industrialism. Despite reduced bureau appropriations, the New Deal administrator directed the BIA to assist self-governing tribal corporations in using conservation techniques and in establishing cooperative businesses. Although federal land policies frequently clashed with tribal traditions, Native Americans won freedom of contract and no longer needed government approval of tribal agreements. Yet in practice the BIA continued to deny legal rights to tribal governments.

WOMEN AND THE RETREAT TO SECURITY

Although the Depression economy pushed women into the labor force, conservative social values encouraged married women to stay at home. Women remained in the work force in the 1930s in about the same proportion as in the 1920s. Yet three-quarters of female professionals continued to work as teachers and nurses, and women's share of the professional labor market dropped. In industry, women workers earned between one-half and two-thirds of male wages and were concentrated in low-paying textile mills and clothing factories. The willingness of women to perform menial tasks lowered their

Exhibit 6-9. U.S. Women Workers, 1930–1940
(in rounded millions)

Year	Female	Male	Total
1930	10.7	38.1	48.8
1940	12.1	37.5	49.6

Source: *Historical Statistics of the United States, Colonial Times to 1970* (1975).

unemployment rates in comparison to men. White women also benefited when corporations replaced old machinery and converted skilled "male" tasks into routine labor.

More rapid economic recovery in light industry, in the service sector, and in clerical work provided enhanced opportunities for female employees. In addition, New Deal labor laws and union activity established hour and wage standards for both sexes. Nevertheless, social mores still frowned on female job holding. Psychologists reported alarming rates of sexual impotence among men no longer able to assert the male breadwinner role. A 1936 Gallup poll found 82 percent of the sample opposed to women taking jobs if their husbands worked. Secretary of Labor Frances Perkins, the first female cabinet member in history, characterized women who worked "without need" as a menace to society. Twenty-six state legislatures considered bills prohibiting the employment of married women. Federal law stipulated that only one member of a family could work in a civil service job.

Although marriage and birth rates declined during the Depression and the divorce rate doubled, young women continued to romanticize motherhood and home. Three-fifths of female college students told one pollster that they hoped to marry within a year or two of graduation. Although organizations such as the League of Women Voters pursued civic and social reform, little support emerged for a separate women's agenda. Social feminists like Perkins and Democratic Party leader Molly Dewson fought for slum clearance, abolition of child labor, unemployment insurance, public housing, and federal regulation of working conditions. Yet as New Deal activists, they separated such campaigns from gender issues and saw workers as male breadwinners.

The most important advocate of human rights in national politics was Eleanor Roosevelt. A crusader for social legislation in New York in the 1920s, she lobbied her husband the president for civil rights and for government assistance to African Americans, the poor, women, and children. The president's wife also influenced the appointment of women to federal diplomatic posts and other positions. Although such efforts stirred controversy, Roosevelt's political activism and public profile refashioned the previously ceremonial role of "first lady."

PUBLIC CULTURE AND THE RADICAL INTELLIGENTSIA

"There is no longer I, there is WE," exclaimed essayist and wit Dorothy Parker, as intellectuals, writers, and artists searched for meaning during the social and economic crisis. Celebrating the struggle of the masses of society, creative writers transformed the documentary into the most important art form of the 1930s. Literary figures like Edmund Wilson, Theodore Dreiser, and Sherwood Anderson compiled eyewitness reports of mining, factory work, and strikes. The WPA's Federal Writers Project produced oral narratives, state guidebooks, and community histories. Performers in the Federal Theater Project worked contemporary events into improvised dramas called "living newspapers." Conservation-minded film documentaries like Pare Lorentz's *The River* (1937)

Corbis-Bettmann

California refugees from the Dust Bowl drought of the mid-1930s. This photograph was taken by Dorothea Lange for the Farm Security Administration. It is an example of the best of the documentary art sponsored by government agencies during the Depression.

and *The Land* (1941) received funding from the Farm Security Administration (FSA). The FSA also sponsored publication of James Agee and Walker Evans's *Let Us Now Praise Famous Men* (1941), a photo-essay on Alabama sharecroppers, as well as of the stunning portraits of photographic artist Dorothea Lange.

New Deal agencies used documentary art to create an uplifting public culture focusing on ordinary people. Hoping to democratize the arts and to make them self-supporting, the WPA created community arts centers, mounted traveling gallery exhibits, provided free concerts, and offered classes in regional folklore and handicrafts. Federally supported artists created murals in post offices, schools, and public institutions. Agency grants also underwrote the work of composer Aaron Copland, who incorporated traditional folk motifs into suites, ballets, and symphonies.

Some of the nation's leading painters joined the rush to document ordinary life. Trained by Ashcan school artist Robert Henri, realist Edward Hopper

Edward Hopper's Nighthawks, *1942; oil on canvas, 30 × 56¹¹⁄₁₆.*

The Art Institute of Chicago

portrayed the solitude and alienation of urban dwellers in late-night restaurants and theater lobbies. The work of Reginald Marsh depicted seedy venues like dance halls, honky-tonks, and downtown movie houses. Alice Neel's bleak portraits of New York's Spanish Harlem captured the despair of Depression families. Drawn to political activism, Ben Shahn produced paintings, posters, and murals that satirized the elite and celebrated the martyrdom of working-class radicals like Sacco and Vanzetti. Regionalists like Iowa's Grant Wood and Missouri's Thomas Hart Benton applied realist perspectives to the natural landscape, whereas Georgia O'Keeffe used the bleached bones of animals to accent a colorful, surrealistic, New Mexican motif. Numerous artists, writers, and musicians joined the Communist Party's "John Reed Clubs," which attempted to merge creative work with a commitment to social justice.

Depression fiction hardly could be separated from social issues. Communist novelists like Jack Conroy and Robert Cantwell saw literature as a weapon of class warfare and produced "proletarian" novels such as *The Disinherited* (1933) and *Land of Plenty* (1934). Early feminist writers such as Tillie Olsen and Meridel Le Sueur depicted the burdens of women in hard times. Ernest Hemingway's highly acclaimed *For Whom the Bell Tolls* (1941), an account of the antifascist struggle in Spain (see Chapter 7), illuminated the conflict between personal integrity and political action. Similar concern for personal endurance appeared in *Tobacco Road* (1932), Erskine Caldwell's popular story of Georgia sharecroppers. In the *Studs Lonigan* trilogy (1936), James T. Farrell portrayed the struggle of Irish Catholics in Chicago's slums. Another trilogy, John Dos Passos's *U.S.A.* (1930–1936), used a montage of imagery, vernacular language, and historical texts to depict the assault on individual values. John Steinbeck's acclaimed *The Grapes of Wrath* (1939) suggested that life lost meaning when capitalism severed traditional ties to the soil and to the community.

Intellectuals were among society's most radical critics. In the name of the working class, writers such as philosopher Sidney Hook, theologian Reinhold Niebuhr, educator John Dewey, and popular economists George Soule and Stuart Chase embraced the notion of a collectivist economy and a planned commonwealth. Socialist Norman Thomas, a Presbyterian minister, received nearly 900,000 votes in the 1932 presidential contest. Two years later, California Democrats nominated Socialist Upton Sinclair for governor, although the author's pledge to use welfare payments to "end poverty" brought defeat when business and movie industry leaders warned that the state would be swamped with unemployed migrants. More militant activists were attracted to the revolutionary Socialist Workers Party, whose leader was former Bolshevik Leon Trotsky.

As writers and artists struggled to forge a revolutionary community with working people, the Communist Party emerged as the most important agent of social change. Party discipline offered intellectuals the opportunity to abandon "class privilege" and cultural isolation and to participate in the historic struggle for a workers' state. Literary critics such as Edmund Wilson, Harvard's Granville Hicks, and *New Masses* editor Michael Gold demanded that "bourgeois" individualism make way for collectivist ideas and a commitment to "class conscious" political action. In 1932 fifty-two "brain workers," including Wilson and journalist Malcolm Cowley, publicly pledged to stand with "muscle workers" in supporting Communist electoral candidates as the first step toward building a new order of justice and equality.

As the threat of fascism spread from Italy and Germany at mid-decade (see Chapter 7), however, Communists made little headway against the New Deal, and party leaders embraced the Soviet Union's call to build coalitions with liberals in an international "popular front." Acknowledging the evolutionary nature of social change and of the humane values of democratic capitalism, Communists like Granville Hicks now supported Roosevelt's reforms. "Communism is twentieth-century Americanism," party head Earl Browder declared in 1936. By expressing traditional national values, the Communist Party attracted the children of European immigrants seeking a place in the U.S. melting pot. Communists also did labor organizing among marginalized African Americans and Chicanos and constituted 10 percent of CIO industrial union hierarchy by decade's end. Many Jewish refugees who fled Nazi persecution in Europe identified with the militant antifascism of the Communist Party. Although the party's membership never surpassed 55,000 in the 1930s, its members became the leading exponents of antifascism and economic justice around the world.

Despite the Communist Party's influence, its manipulative tactics stirred controversy. AFL leaders resented Communists who voted as members of secret factions or "dual unions" in the labor movement. When white Communists sought to take over the prolabor and liberal National Negro Congress, A. Philip Randolph and other African American leaders walked out of the organization. Communist reverses overseas also hurt the party's image. Having rushed to defend the republican government of Spain against a fascist uprising in 1936 (see Chapter 7), the movement was stung by the victory of the reactionary rebels. Equally demoralizing were Soviet leader Josef Stalin's "purge" trials, which sought to demonstrate that the surviving leaders of the Bolshevik revolution were traitors to the communist movement. A final crisis for U.S.

Communists came when Stalin signed a nonaggression pact with Nazi Germany in 1939.

GRASS-ROOTS RADICALS

The radicalism of small business activists and agrarian reformers differed sharply from that of urban workers and the intelligentsia. Adhering to revered notions of free enterprise and individualism, these activists sought to turn New Deal policy against high finance and big business. Reformers included progressive crusader William Borah, who attacked the National Recovery Administration for permitting large monopolies to dominate industry-wide codes. Suspicion of big business led to passage of the Robinson-Patman Act of 1936, which outlawed manufacturers' discounts to large distributors and chain stores. The Miller-Tydings Act of 1937 permitted states to pass fair-trade laws controlling chain store price cutting. By 1939 twenty-seven states had singled out chain stores for special regulation or taxation, although attempts to enact a national chain store tax never succeeded.

Independent farmers experienced similar frustration with New Deal liberalism. In Minnesota, Governor Floyd Olson, heading the Farmer-Labor Party, persuaded the reluctant legislature to enact relief for growers facing foreclosures. In Wisconsin, Philip La Follette formed a new Progressive Party in 1934 and used the governorship to introduce economic reforms, including mortgage relief, property tax reduction, and unemployment insurance. North Dakota Representative William Lemke pushed Congress to enact legislation to refinance bankrupt farm mortgages in 1934 and 1935. Congress also responded to farmers' demands for higher agricultural prices by authorizing the president to remonetize silver. When Roosevelt announced that the nation had abandoned the gold standard, agrarian reformers passed the Silver Purchase Act of 1934 to enable the Treasury to use silver to back U.S. currency.

Inflationary schemes frequently met the needs of special interests. After years of controversy regarding the payment of World War I veterans' bonuses, Congress overrode Roosevelt's veto in 1936 to require the government to issue new currency to pay the stipends. California physician Dr. Francis E. Townsend sought similar payments for the elderly when he proposed an old-age revolving pension fund that would grant $200 a month to every retired person over the age of sixty if they spent the entire sum each month. Although the Townsend Plan was to be financed by a 2 percent tax on business transactions, its supporters argued that the program would stimulate spending and end joblessness by cutting the labor force. Organizing along evangelical and patriotic lines, Townsendites gathered millions of signatures on national petitions and pushed Roosevelt to endorse social security legislation.

A more radical attack on the New Deal came from Father Charles E. Coughlin, a Michigan Roman Catholic priest with a national radio audience of 30 to 40 million. An early Roosevelt supporter, Coughlin turned against the New Deal by accusing the administration of simultaneously advancing the interests of finance capital and communism. Forming the National Union for Social Justice in 1934, the radio priest attracted lower-middle-class support among ethnic Catholics in the urban Northeast and Midwest. His weekly radio commentaries

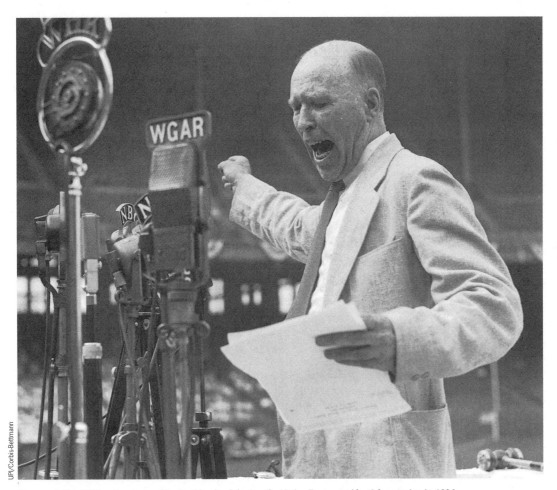

Representative William Lemke speaking in Cleveland during the Union Party presidential campaign in 1936.

denounced conspiratorial bankers and industrial union leaders while extolling the dignity of working people and small entrepreneurs. Like monetary radicals such as Lemke and Wright Patman of Texas, Coughlin called for Congress to charter a publicly owned national bank to replace the Federal Reserve.

Louisiana's Huey Long, nicknamed "The Kingfish," was the most colorful and effective opponent of the New Deal. Elected to the Senate in 1930 and assuming his seat two years later, Long launched an ambitious "Share Our Wealth" proposal. He focused upon maldistribution of wealth as the key issue before the nation. His economic program called for the liquidation of all personal fortunes greater than $5 million through a capital tax. Long also planned to use the income tax to prohibit families from earning more than $1 million a year. He promised every family a guaranteed annual income that would provide enough money to buy a $5,000 homestead, a car, and a radio. Pensions would be distributed to the elderly, and "worthy youth" would receive free college educations. Long pledged that a massive public works program would combine with a federal minimum wage and a thirty-hour week to bolster purchasing power.

—— HUEY ("THE KINGFISH") LONG ——
1893–1935

Stock Montage

Louisiana's Huey Long was the revered leader of the most popular rural insurgency since the Populist crusades of the 1890s. As a folk hero to poor southern farmers and villagers, Long focused on Depression issues to broaden his appeal until he appeared to threaten Roosevelt's reelection to the White House in 1936. His earthy sarcasm and impatience with privilege created nightmares for vested interests from Baton Rouge to Washington.

Long came out of the pine-studded uplands of northern Louisiana, the home of pious Baptists with a long tradition of populism. At the age of twenty-five, he won election as Louisiana's public service commissioner. Long used his power to decrease streetcar and telephone rates and to penalize Standard Oil. He attacked the greed of the oil colossus in an effective campaign for governor in 1924, but the Ku Klux Klan's opposition denied him victory. Four years later, after Klan power had diminished, the brash upstart captured the populist vote and won the governorship.

Long used a phrase from an old speech by William Jennings Bryan as his campaign slogan: "Every Man a King." His program consisted of massive highway and hospital construction and of free school textbooks and night classes for poor whites and blacks. To finance these reforms, Long resorted to deficit spending and levied heavy taxes on the oil refineries. Meanwhile, he established an awesome patronage machine.

The Louisiana House of Representatives charged Governor Long with unauthorized use of state funds and impeached him in 1929, but the state senate failed to convict him. Long claimed that Standard Oil had persecuted him, and he tightened control over the state. By 1934 he had prevailed on the legislature to abolish local government and had taken personal control of police and teaching appointments, the militia, the courts, election agencies, and tax-assessing bodies. Critics charged him with running a dictatorial police state that terrorized political enemies.

By 1935 27,000 Share Our Wealth clubs had sprouted up across the country, and the campaign had a mailing list of millions. Long won national support with his folksy ridicule of corporate interests and his parodies of urbane New Deal administrators. Calling "Every Man a King," he planned to run for president in 1936. Democratic tacticians feared that Long might capture 3 or 4 million votes on a third-party ticket and might throw the election into the House of Representatives. In September 1935, however, Long was assassinated by the enraged relative of a Louisiana political adversary.

THE SECOND TERM

Republicans hoped to exploit anti–New Deal fervor. Within a year after the repeal of Prohibition through the passage of the Twenty-first Amendment in 1933, opponents of the "noble experiment" sought to rally conservative Demo-

When Long came to Washington as a senator in 1932, he said he intended to cut the great American fortunes down to "frying size." An early supporter of Roosevelt, he now turned bitterly against the National Recovery Administration and called the president "a liar and a faker." Like Borah of Idaho, Long believed that the recovery agency only helped large producers to organize a controlled market. He pointed out that Agricultural Adjustment Administration crop reductions compelled rich landlords to force black tenants off the land, and he attacked farm corporations as the source of agricultural impoverishment. The senator praised Roosevelt's "death sentence" for public utilities but complained that "we might as well try to regulate a rattlesnake."

Huey Long made redistribution of wealth a focal point of 1930s politics. From the Senate floor, the Kingfish advanced a "Share Our Wealth" program that intended to use tax reform and a guaranteed income to alleviate the inefficient distribution of purchasing power in the Depression. Long savagely attacked plutocrats like the Rockefellers and the Du Ponts by noting that 600 U.S. families controlled 90 percent of the nation's wealth. He compared the rich to cannibals and predicted that they would let the country "go slap down to hell" before they surrendered their mastery.

Long's emphasis on stock ownership neglected the corporate structure and ignored capital investment that could not be easily liquidated and redistributed. Yet concentration of wealth remained an undeniable defect in the national economy. Long addressed the concerns of marginal members of the lower-middle class who felt unable to control their own destiny in a world of distant and remote centers of power. Share Our Wealth promised a cooperative solution by using government taxing ability to protect communities from encroaching financial power. Long's followers in the rural South and West assumed that the protective government would not become an intrusive power itself.

In 1935 a secret poll by the Democratic Party indicated that Long might take 4 million votes as a third-party competitor in the coming presidential race. Just a month after he announced his candidacy, however, the Kingfish was assassinated by the son-in-law of an embittered victim of Long's state patronage manipulations.

Critics condemned Long as an ignorant demagogue and a dangerous totalitarian. Yet as a North Dakota congressman observed, Huey Pierce Long "had more friends among the common people than any man who has lived in this country in the last half century." ■

crats against New Deal social welfare programs, high taxation, and regulatory controls. The Du Pont family reorganized the Association Against the Prohibition Amendment into the American Liberty League and encouraged former presidential candidate Al Smith to lead the charge against government-fostered collectivism. Republicans took up the anti-big-government cry when they nominated Governor Alfred Landon of Kansas to thwart Roosevelt's quest for a second term in 1936.

Claiming that regulated monopoly had replaced free enterprise, the Republican platform characterized New Deal legislation as blatantly unconstitutional. The Republicans demanded a balanced federal budget and the transfer of relief programs to nonpolitical local agencies. By 1936 stories were circulating that wealthy Republicans were expressing their rage at Roosevelt by refusing to utter his name and by often referring to the occupant of the White House as "that man." Conservative Democrats like Smith joined them in charging that the New Deal fostered class animosity and minority-bloc politics. "The trouble with this recognition of class war," complained Wilsonian Newton Baker, "is

Exhibit 6-10. U.S. Voter Participation in Presidential Elections, 1932–1936
(percentage of eligible voters)

1932	56.9
1936	61.0

Source: *Historical Statistics of the United States, Colonial Times to 1970* (1975).

that it spreads like a grease stain and every group . . . demands the same sort of recognition."

Roosevelt adamantly rejected such attacks. Discarding ideological party labels, the president professed faith in "the capitalist system." "The true conservative," he proclaimed in his acceptance speech at the 1936 Democratic National Convention, "seeks to protect the system of private property and free enterprise by correcting such injustices and inequities as arise from it." The president had a responsibility to save business "from the selfish forces which ruined it," he stated, and he referred repeatedly to "economic royalists" who hid behind a professed defense of the nation's interest to protect their own power. In a bitter speech in New York's Madison Square Garden at the climax of the 1936 presidential campaign, Roosevelt remarked that the forces of "organized money are unanimous in their hate for me—and I welcome their hatred." If "the forces of selfishness and lust for power" had met their match in his first term, Roosevelt cried, the second term would certainly confront them with "their master."

As two-thirds of the country's major newspapers endorsed Landon, the conservative *Literary Digest* predicted a sweeping Republican victory. Despite these predictions, Roosevelt convinced voters that a competent and caring administration had set economic recovery in motion. By defining liberalism as a populist philosophy of government generosity, the Democrats won broad support, particularly in the South, the region where voters most often identified themselves as liberals. Roosevelt won 61 percent of the popular vote in the 1936 election in a landslide in which he prevailed in every state except Maine and Vermont. The Union Party, which mobilized followers of Huey Long, Father Coughlin, and Dr. Townsend behind the candidacy of William Lemke, won only 2 percent of the vote. Democrats captured a 76–16 majority in the Senate and swept to a 331–89 victory in the House. The New Deal coalition won the allegiance of farmers and southerners as well as urban union workers, white ethnics, and middle-class liberals. A majority of African Americans also voted for a Democrat for the first time.

"I see one-third of a nation ill-housed, ill-clad, ill-nourished," Roosevelt declared in his second-term inaugural address. Promising to eliminate poverty and make every person the subject of government concern, the president proclaimed that the Depression had produced a "rendezvous with destiny." Roosevelt believed that voters had given him a mandate to extend New Deal reforms to needy groups such as sharecroppers, tenant farmers, and industrial workers. Accordingly, in 1937 he asked Congress to establish the Farm Security Administration (FSA), which built county health care facilities and sanitary camps for rural migrants and provided $500 million in long-term, low-interest loans to tenants, sharecroppers, and farm laborers.

The White House and Congress also replaced the AAA, which had been invalidated by the Supreme Court in 1936. The Agricultural Adjustment Act of

Exhibit 6-11. The New Deal, 1936–1938

1936	• Soil Conservation and Domestic Allotment Act
	• Robinson-Patman Anti-Price Discrimination Act
1937	• Bankhead-Jones Farm Tenant Act (created FSA—Farm Security Administration)
	• Miller-Tydings Enabling Act
	• Wagner-Steagall National Housing Act (created USHA—United States Housing Authority)
1938	• Agricultural Adjustment Act (created FCIC—Federal Crop Insurance Corporation)
	• Fair Labor Standards Act

1938 guaranteed federal price supports with U.S. Treasury funds instead of the processing tax. By using the Commodity Credit Corporation, the administration allowed farmers to receive government loans if they took surplus crops off the market. The Soil Conservation Service provided stipends to growers who cultivated soil-conserving crops. Another agency, the Federal Crop Insurance Corporation, provided security for wheat and cotton producers by accepting crop payments as insurance premiums against future crop losses.

THE ANTI–NEW DEAL COALITION

Roosevelt hoped to expand government resource planning to include six more TVAs, but the president faced strong resistance in his second term from an increasingly independent Congress. Roosevelt's political woes first surfaced during a bitter controversy regarding the Supreme Court. Stung by a reversal of the laws creating the NRA and AAA and fearing that the entire New Deal might be invalidated, the White House introduced a judiciary reorganization bill in 1937. The proposal authorized the president to appoint an additional Supreme Court judge for each justice who did not retire at age seventy. Because six court members already had reached that age, the administration plan could have increased the panel's membership from nine to fifteen. Many Democrats joined both progressive and conservative Republicans in opposing the measure as a presidential attempt to "pack" the court and to destroy the balance of power among the branches of government. After Democrat Burton Wheeler produced a letter in which Chief Justice Charles Evans Hughes asserted the court's ability to manage its caseload without added help, the Senate returned the judicial plan to committee by a lopsided vote.

By asking Congress for unprecedented power over another branch of government, Roosevelt lent credence to attacks on his "dictatorial" methods. Conservative critics reasoned that a subservient court might legitimize threats to private property such as labor sit-downs. Progressives like Burton Wheeler worried about the growing power of New Deal agencies. Such anxieties underlay congressional defeat of the administration's executive reorganization bills in 1937 and 1938. Recommended by a presidential committee on administrative

Charles Evans Hughes, chief justice of the Supreme Court, 1930–1940. Hughes played a major role in the effort to defeat Roosevelt's attempt to restructure the court in 1937.

management, the proposals sought to increase government efficiency by regrouping and simplifying federal agencies. Once the court fight destroyed Roosevelt's invincibility, the National Committee to Uphold Constitutional Government and other conservative groups targeted executive reorganization as an example of the president's "dictatorial ambitions." By the time an amended version of the bill passed in 1939, Roosevelt's reputation had been badly damaged.

Emboldened by controversy regarding Roosevelt's governing methods, an anti–New Deal coalition emerged in Congress by 1938. Composed of progressive and conservative Republicans as well as rural Democrats, the powerful bloc represented nonurban and small-business interests who resented the costs of government aid to big-city workers and relief recipients. Roosevelt adversaries attacked wasteful government bureaucracy and asserted that emergency measures had deteriorated into permanent schemes for social experiment and collectivism. Political resistance from Senate Democrats such as Georgia's Walter F. George, South Carolina's "Cotton Ed" Smith, and Maryland's Millard Tydings prompted Roosevelt to campaign for New Deal loyalists in the 1938 primaries. Yet critics accused the president of attempting to "purge" his own party, and the strategy backfired wherever the White House intervened. The president's political woes deepened during the general election when Republicans scored substantial gains in the House and Senate.

Increasingly committed to budget retrenchment, private enterprise, and states' rights, Congress attacked political radicalism in 1938 by recreating the

House Un-American Activities Committee (HUAC). First established in 1934, the committee had investigated the activities of the German-American Bund, a Nazi group that espoused Adolf Hitler's anti-Semitic and fascist agenda. Yet under the chairmanship of Texas Democrat Martin Dies, HUAC investigated allegations of Communist infiltration of New Deal agencies such as the WPA's Federal Theater Project. Congress responded to charges that WPA officials had engaged in political campaigning by passing the Hatch Act of 1939. The law prohibited election activity by federal employees and prevented them from soliciting political contributions from relief recipients. Anti–New Deal fervor also surfaced in reduced appropriations for the WPA and in the elimination of the Federal Theater Project. Meanwhile, Wisconsin Governor Philip La Follette's National Progressives of America attacked the New Deal for fostering political bossism, citizen dependence, and an unproductive monetary system.

THE NEW DEAL LEGACY

Concerned that government spending might induce inflation and inflame political opponents, Roosevelt cut public works as his second term began. Soon the most precipitous economic decline in history sent unemployment soaring from 7 million to 11 million between August 1937 and March 1938. Jobless rates exceeded 50 percent for those between the ages of sixteen and twenty. As the government foreclosed on 100,000 mortgages—10 percent of those it had refinanced—the stock market lost two-thirds of the ground it had gained since 1933.

The White House responded to the recession with antimonopoly rhetoric and a series of antitrust suits initiated by Assistant Attorney General Thurman Arnold. In an economy in which six industrial firms accounted for almost one-fourth of the profits of the nation's 1,000 largest corporations, small business leaders pressed for a outright ban on monopoly practices. Instead, Roosevelt created the Temporary National Economic Committee in 1938 to investigate corporate consolidation. Yet the panel failed to agree on a definition of "monopoly" and recommended mere technical changes in existing legislation. Meanwhile, administration leaders followed the advice of Federal Reserve Board Governor and Utah banker Marriner Eccles, who opposed disciplinary regulation of business or reliance on taxation as a means of redistributing wealth. Accordingly, the last phase of the New Deal employed fiscal management to rehabilitate capitalism through full employment and sustained purchasing power.

Looking to the business community as the source of economic vitality, Roosevelt agreed to a reduction of corporate taxes in 1938. Yet, in addition, he signed the Fair Labor Standards Act, the long-awaited replacement for the wage and hours guarantees of the defunct NRA and the last important piece of New Deal legislation. The law enhanced consumer purchasing power by legislating the nation's first industrial minimum wage (forty cents an hour) and a forty-hour work week, but both were to be implemented gradually as a concession to constituents in the South, which had lower living costs. Banning workers between the ages of sixteen and eighteen from occupations declared hazardous by the Children's Bureau, the law also prohibited interstate shipment of most

Exhibit 6-12. U.S. Government Social Welfare Spending, 1933–1939
(in rounded billions of dollars)

Year	Welfare Spending	Percentage of Gross National Product
1933	4.5	7.9
1939	9.2	10.5

Source: *Historical Statistics of the United States, Colonial Times to 1970* (1975).

Exhibit 6-13. U.S. Federal Budget Deficits, 1933–1939
(in rounded billions of dollars)

1933	2.6
1936	3.4
1939	2.8

Source: *Historical Statistics of the United States, Colonial Times to 1970* (1975).

goods produced by employees less than sixteen years old. Another provision banned home work in the garment trades.

To further bolster consumer spending, Roosevelt requested an extra $3 billion for the WPA and other relief programs. In addition, Congress created the Federal Surplus Relief Corporation in 1939 to distribute unsold produce to state welfare agencies and thereby inaugurated the nation's first food stamp program. The president equated such policies with liberalism, which he considered to be a philosophy of generous welfare for the many, in contrast with conservatism, which he defined as limited government by the selfish few. In establishing the welfare system as a permanent safety net for the needy, New Deal leaders consciously adopted deficit spending as a tool of economic planning. The use of government expenditures as a substitute for private investment coincided with the ideas of British economist John Maynard Keynes, who argued that government manipulation of capital investment could forever end Depressions. Federal spending, which hovered at $2 billion in 1933, leaped to $5.2 billion by 1939.

Despite Roosevelt's recovery programs, 40 percent of family incomes remained below the poverty line in 1940. Almost 8 million workers, mostly in agriculture, earned less than the minimum wage. Working-class citizens also felt the disproportionate burden of sales and gasoline taxes enacted by states suffering budget deficits. Yet Roosevelt built support for the New Deal system of state capitalism by equating the needs of ordinary people with the requirements of the consumer economy. Subsidies and labor protections bolstered mass purchasing power and aided consumer-driven industries such as food products, chemicals, petroleum, and home construction. Annual housing starts, which were fewer than 100,000 in 1933, leaped to more than 600,000 by 1941. As the banker of last resort, government agencies loaned capital to commercial and mortgage lenders and invested in regional and agricultural development. In the South and the West, for example, federal dams, hydroelectric power plants, and land reclamation projects freed entrepreneurs from dependence on outside capital and prepared the way for recovery.

Exhibit 6-14. U.S. Exports of Goods and Services, 1936–1939
(in rounded billions of dollars)

1936	3.5
1939	4.4

Source: *Historical Statistics of the United States, Colonial Times to 1970* (1975).

By pioneering government management of the peacetime economy, New Deal reform centralized federal power. For example, creation of the Federal Deposit Insurance Corporation inadvertently made most bank robberies federal crimes under the jurisdiction of the Federal Bureau of Investigation (FBI). Highly publicized arrests of bank robbers such as John Dillinger accustomed citizens to the idea of a federal police force. After the son of Charles and Anne Lindbergh was abducted and murdered in 1932, Congress gave the FBI jurisdiction over kidnaping. Roosevelt furthered government police powers when he requested secret investigations of Nazis and communists for "subversive activities." Although the Federal Communications Act of 1934 made telephone wiretapping illegal, presidential memos authorized FBI electronic eavesdropping during security investigations. Roosevelt also centralized government management by creating the Executive Office of the President and by retaining his own staff and assistants. Moving the budget bureau from the Department of the Treasury to the White House, he set the precedent for placing agencies under direct presidential control.

The Supreme Court played a major role in legitimizing the growth of federal authority. During the bitter judicial reform debate, the tribunal reversed past practice and validated New Deal laws such as the Wagner Act and the Social Security Act. Fashioning a constitutional revolution, the court accepted government intervention in the economy and recognized the power of Congress to shape federal involvement. By invoking a broad definition of "stream of commerce," the court stepped aside to let the elected branches of government regulate private property in the public interest. Government management of the economy now became a matter of political choice instead of constitutional controversy. The change was facilitated by deaths and retirements that allowed Roosevelt to make four Supreme Court appointments between 1937 and 1939. The new justices included liberals Hugo Black, Felix Frankfurter, and William O. Douglas and extended the New Deal's influence on government for another generation.

Enhanced executive powers gave Roosevelt greater latitude in hemispheric relations. Starting in 1934 Congress agreed to a series of reciprocal trade acts that empowered the president to halve tariffs on Latin American imports in return for rate reductions on U.S. exports. Roosevelt also established the Export-Import Bank, which lent government funds to Latin American nations that pledged to purchase U.S. products. Calling for a hemispheric partnership based on mutual respect, the White House announced the Good Neighbor Policy in 1933. As the U.S. Marines left Nicaragua and Haiti, Washington abandoned the interventionist Platt amendment in Cuba and promised Panama not to deploy troops outside the Canal Zone. Moreover, the United States ratified the Buenos Aires Convention of 1936, which obligated it to arbitrate regional conflicts. In

Franklin Delano Roosevelt Library

Nicaraguan dictator Anastasio Somoza Garcia (left) riding with President Roosevelt. The United States supported Latin American strongmen such as Somoza and Cuban dictator Fulgencio Batista because it hoped to promote business interests and stability in the region.

1938 the Roosevelt administration refused to intervene in a dispute between U.S. oil companies and the government of Mexico. Nevertheless, Roosevelt pursued hemispheric stability by maintaining friendly ties with corrupt dictators in Nicaragua and Cuba.

THE CULTURE OF SCARCITY AND HOPE

Depression scarcity put a premium on austerity. Jobless workers continued to consider unemployment as a sign of individual failure. Economic dependence forced young couples to postpone weddings and led to a dramatic drop in marriage rates. As children became an economic burden on families, the sale of contraceptives boomed and birthrates sank to their lowest point in the nation's history. As men and women struggled to feed families with as little fanfare and waste as possible, the psychological strain of scarcity lowered tolerance of social deviance. After the repeal of Prohibition, eight states remained dry, and others adopted the local option for counties. Purity reform also resurfaced in Narcotics Bureau Director Harry J. Anslinger's campaign against marijuana use, which he tied to crime, vice, and degeneracy.

Despite such inhibitions, most people found ways to deal with the demoralizing aspects of the Depression. The end of Prohibition reinvigorated big-city

**Exhibit 6-15. U.S. Gross National Product, 1936–1939
(in rounded billions of dollars)**

1936	82.5
1939	90.5

Source: *Historical Statistics of the United States, Colonial Times to 1970* (1975).

**Exhibit 6-16. U.S. Unemployment, 1937–1941
(as a percentage of the civilian labor force)**

1937	14.3
1938	19.0
1939	17.2
1940	14.6
1941	9.9

Source: *Historical Statistics of the United States, Colonial Times to 1970* (1975).

**Exhibit 6-17. U.S. White Collar and Manual Employees, 1930–1940
(in rounded millions)**

Year	White Collar	Manual	All Employees
1930	14.3	19.3	48.7
1940	16.1	20.6	51.7

Source: *Historical Statistics of the United States, Colonial Times to 1970* (1975).

nightclubs and popularized the great African American "swing" bands of Duke Ellington, Count Basie, Fletcher Henderson, and Chick Webb. Radio networks carried white versions of the swing sound to mass audiences through live broadcasts of combos led by Benny Goodman, Glenn Miller, and Tommy Dorsey. Unable to pay for live entertainment, small stations hired "disc jockeys" to play the recordings of Tin Pan Alley songwriters such as Irving Berlin, Jerome Kern, and George and Ira Gershwin. Love ballads and novelty tunes sustained fantasy, romance, and hope in hard times. Radio news, dramas ("soap operas"), comedies, and variety shows also unified the nation through shared standards of speech, taste, and humor. By the end of the 1930s 40 million owners of radio receivers could access this national network of popular culture and information.

Despite radio's popularity, Hollywood remained the nation's primary creator of unifying myths and dreams. By 1939 nearly two-thirds of the population went to the movies at least once a week. Yet the Depression brought major challenges to the film industry. With the advent of sound in the late 1920s, motion pictures began producing provocative films that questioned sexual propriety and social decorum. While female stars such as Marlene Dietrich and Jean Harlow explored dark sexual themes, the irreverent comedies of W.C. Fields, Mae West, and the Marx Brothers reworked vaudeville routines into anarchic parodies of middle-class conventions. The early years of the

The Duke Ellington Orchestra, Chicago, 1932. Ellington helped to revolutionize urban popular music with swing rhythms originating in black jazz. Enthusiasm for his music reflected increasing musical sophistication among urbanites of the 1930s.

economic crisis also produced a series of horror films, including *Dracula* (1931), *Frankenstein* (1931), and *King Kong* (1933), which graphically explored anxieties about civilization's survival. In turn, gangster films such as *Public Enemy* (1931) and *Little Ceasar* (1930), featuring actors like James Cagney and Edward G. Robinson, dramatized the need for toughness in overcoming adversity.

The predominance of sex and crime in the movies of the early 1930s brought a sharp reaction from purity crusaders. Aligning themselves in 1933 with Protestant film reformers and women's club activists, Roman Catholic bishops organized the Legion of Decency. As a result, 11 million Catholics signed pledges to boycott "indecent" motion pictures. Concerned with falling box office receipts, Hollywood expanded the breadth and enforcement powers of the Hays Code. Elements of "good" in film scenarios now were to balance those of "evil," and "bad" acts were to result in punishment or reform. The enhanced code prohibited portraits of homosexuality, interracial sex, abortion, incest, or drug use and eliminated profanity, including the word "sex," from screen language.

Hollywood's response to the Hays Code resulted in the "golden age" of motion pictures. Walt Disney cartoons, comedies starring child actress Shirley Temple, and productions like the *Our Gang* series and *The Wizard of Oz* (1939) stressed themes of youthful innocence and play that delighted moviegoers. Audiences also escaped Depression worries through extravagant musicals facilitated by sound technology. Directors like Busby Berkeley brought the Broadway revue and musical theater to the screen by combining lush orchestration, intricate choreography, and arresting visuals. Musical comedies produced new stars such as Bing Crosby, Dick Powell, and Alice Faye. Screen dancers included Fred Astaire and Ginger Rogers, who combined intimacy and grace to provide the perfect complement to the work of Tin Pan Alley masters like Cole Porter and Irving Berlin.

WALT DISNEY
1901–1966

The Granger Collection

Two months after President Roosevelt told the nation that "the only thing we have to fear is fear itself," Americans started humming, whistling, and singing a hit tune entitled "Who's Afraid of the Big Bad Wolf." The song came from the sound track of Walt Disney's animated cartoon *The Three Little Pigs* (1933) and served as a metaphor for the national resolve to overcome the Depression. Disney's extraordinary success during this period of crisis reflected his skill in defining popular anxieties and in resolving them with Hollywood-style happy endings.

Disney was born in Chicago but spent several impressionable years on a farm in Missouri. Lonely as a boy, he befriended the barnyard animals and later relied on those childhood friendships as the inspiration for his cartoon animation. In the 1920s Disney produced crude animated films in Kansas City, mostly for commercial advertisers, but could not succeed financially. He moved to Hollywood in 1923 and established an independent production company to make a variety of animated cartoons, including *Oswald the Lucky Rabbit* (1927) and the Mickey Mouse series, which debuted in 1928.

At a time when national culture was torn between modern values and nostalgia for a rural society, Disney's characters embraced both worlds. A society of domesticated animals with anthropomorphic gestures and human problems evoked a lost age of farming communities. Yet the cartoons themselves depended on new, sophisticated technologies including synchronized sound (1928) and color (1932), which distinguished Disney's creations. Moreover, the first Mickey Mouse cartoon, *Plane Crazy* (1928), mirrored the nation's fascination with the exploits of Charles Lindbergh.

The popularity of Disney cartoons in the 1930s illuminated the subliminal anxieties produced by the economic crisis. In a typical cartoon plot, rooms fell apart, houses exploded, or, as in *The Sorcerer's Apprentice,* inanimate objects developed a mind of their own and created utter chaos, but the familiar order was eventually restored. Disney fantasies also provided psychological escape. In such movies as *Snow White and the Seven Dwarfs* (1937) or *Fantasia* (1940), viewers found refuge from the sobering world outside the theaters. Yet even films like *Bambi* (1942) hinged on an underlying anxiety about the precariousness of life in the modern world.

During World War II Disney made propaganda cartoons to support the war effort and mixed animation and live action in movies produced for the military. His films of the postwar era blended sentimental fantasy (*Cinderella*, 1950) with a celebration of traditional mythologies (*Davy Crockett—King of the Wild Frontier*, 1955). Disney entertainment now expanded rapidly into television, into collateral brand-name products, and into the thematic amusement park, Disneyland, which opened in 1955. Disney also planned another recreational park in Florida but did not live to see the opening of Disneyworld. He died in 1966.

These various enterprises were founded on a consistent theme. Disney, a product of the white, Anglo-Protestant Midwest, remained committed to traditional values and assumptions despite rapid social change. His creative work depended on his characters' ability to establish control over chaos; however irrational their means, reason always prevailed in the end. Similarly, Disney's amusement parks, known for their cleanliness and orderliness, offered conservative, prepackaged entertainment with neither surprise nor spontaneity. His sentimental vision appealed to a people uncertain about the country's values and worried about its future. Like many of the nation's cultural pioneers, Disney expressed his genius through an uncanny synthesis of modernism and tradition. ■

FRANK CAPRA
1897–1991

Archive Photos

"Dreams hung in fragments at the far end of the room," F. Scott Fitzgerald wrote of a movie producer's projection facility in *The Last Tycoon* (1941). The description aptly captured the work of Frank Capra, Hollywood's most popular film director of the 1930s.

Capra immigrated from Sicily with his family at the turn of the century and worked his way through the California Institute of Technology, where he received a chemical engineering degree. Surviving as a cardsharp and salesman in San Francisco, he experimented with moviemaking before relocating to Hollywood in the 1920s. As a novice film editor, writer, and director of silent slapstick features, Capra learned the fundamentals of comedy, timing, and character.

Signing on with Columbia Pictures, a marginal studio, Capra directed Jean Harlow in his first sound feature, *Platinum Blond* (1931), but his reputation did not take hold until the appearance of *It Happened One Night* (1934), a comic drama that starred Claudette Colbert and Clark Gable and won five Academy Awards. Placing a wealthy socialite and a tough newspaper reporter in the commonplace scenes of ordinary life, the film fascinated and charmed audiences struggling to survive the Depression. Capra also touched viewers by conveying a central faith in the American dream and the recurring theme of his creative work: the idea that character, not wealth, determined social class.

By boosting morale to alleviate Depression-era shame and anxiety, Capra taught Hollywood how to achieve cultural legitimacy and how to restore profits as well. In *Mr. Deeds Goes to Town* (1936), the director molded Gary Cooper into a small-town hero who ignored urban cynicism, greed, and pretension to distribute an inherited fortune to small farmers. Capra also scored a hit with *You Can't Take It with You* (1938), a lighthearted comedy about a rich man who discovered his human-

ity and let his compassion prevail against selfishness.

The classic Frank Capra work of the 1930s was *Mr. Smith Goes to Washington* (1939), a political morality play starring James Stewart as a junior senator fighting a dictatorial and corrupt political machine that threatened democratic ideals. Its climactic scene placed Stewart's Jefferson Smith at the Lincoln Memorial to confide in the fallen president, "We're the people and we're tough. A free people can beat the world at anything . . . if we all pulled the oars in the same direction." The road out of social crisis lay in "plain, ordinary, everyday kindness, a little looking out for the other fella, loving thy neighbor."

Capra was less sure of the outcome when fascism became the enemy in *Meet John Doe* (1941), another Gary Cooper vehicle. Yet Capra's movies never departed from a populist faith reflected in his depictions of ordinary individuals pitted against corrupt rackets and governments, dictatorial bosses, and sleazy politicians. Capra's fantasies called for more responsible and compassionate people in positions of power, but the director's folk heroes also needed help from the common people, who gave his protagonists the strength and imagination to carry on.

By celebrating the commonsense lessons of everyday life, Capra involved viewers in his stories and sustained them with hope in hard times. Addressing the burdens of citizenship, he conveyed the idea that democracy belonged to everyone. *Why We Fight*, a series of six documentary films produced for the Office of War Information during World War II, reasserted this message in a new context. The postwar *It's a Wonderful Life* (1946) generated only mild box office success, although the director's synthesis of sentimentality and melancholy ultimately achieved cult status as a Hollywood classic. ■

Exhibit 6-18. U.S. Annual per Capita Income in Dollars, 1929–1941

1929	847
1932	465
1935	567
1938	651
1941	934

Source: *Historical Statistics of the United States, Colonial Times to 1970* (1975).

Film producers occasionally tackled social issues, as in the prolabor *Black Fury* (1935) and *The Grapes of Wrath* (1940). Yet Depression movies more often offered generous doses of optimism and populist social morality. "Screwball comedies" such as *It Happened One Night* (1934), *Bringing up Baby* (1938), and *The Philadelphia Story* (1940) parodied the rich and suggested that social class was defined by character instead of wealth. Similarly, historical and political dramas like *Gone With the Wind* (1939) and *Mr. Smith Goes to Washington* (1939) stressed the importance of humility, common sense, decency, and toughness of spirit. Depression audiences bonded with characters who conveyed such "American" qualities and made stars of performers such as Jimmy Stewart, Henry Fonda, Cary Grant, Carole Lombard, and Katharine Hepburn.

As Stalinism, fascism, and the prospect of war dominated Europe in the late 1930s, intellectuals in the United States also reasserted national values. Former radicals like literary critic Alfred Kazin, novelist John Dos Passos, and poet Archibald MacLeish now concluded that capitalism did not face extinction and that human rights were better protected at home than overseas. Seeking to establish consensus and common ground, the nation's leading writers looked to the past to celebrate traditions of democracy and individualism. As the Depression decade ended, the intelligentsia identified with government efforts to promote economic recovery, social stability, national security, and democracy.

Franklin Roosevelt perfectly conveyed the goals of democratic pluralism. As immigration restriction resulted in reduced anxieties regarding the influx of southern and eastern Europeans, Democratic officials rewarded the electoral support of Irish Americans, Jews, and European ethnics with political patronage. Under Roosevelt, one of every nine government jobs went to a Catholic or Jew, as opposed to one of every twenty-five under Hoover. Non-Protestants also received 30 percent of the president's federal judiciary nominations, which resulted in the Supreme Court appointment of Felix Frankfurter, a Jew, and Frank Murphy, a Catholic. Yet Roosevelt went beyond mere politics in celebrating national unity and ethnic diversity. Mastering the press conference and delivering sixteen "fireside chats" broadcast on the radio in eight years, Roosevelt became the first president to convey the concept of multiple "American faiths" and the "Judeo-Christian" heritage.

Although inclusion rarely embraced African Americans and Hispanics by name, ethnic and cultural solidarity became one of the hallmarks of New Deal reform and the Roosevelt legacy. As the administration began to prepare citizens for challenges overseas, pluralism would become an ever more central facet of the U.S. identity and the national mission.

SUGGESTED READINGS

Overviews of the New Deal include Anthony Badger, *The New Deal: The Depression Years, 1933–1940* (1989); William E. Leuchtenburg, *Franklin D. Roosevelt and the New Deal* (1963); and Paul K. Conkin, *The New Deal* (1967). See also George Wolfskill, *Happy Days Are Here Again! A Short Interpretive History of the New Deal* (1974). Studies focusing on Roosevelt's influence are Arthur Schlesinger, Jr., *The Age of Roosevelt*, 3 volumes (1957–1960); Frank Freidel, *Franklin D. Roosevelt*, 4 volumes (1952–1973); James M. Burns, *Roosevelt: The Lion and the Fox* (1956); and Wilbur J. Cohen, *The Roosevelt New Deal* (1986). For recovery efforts, see the works by Garraty, M. Bernstein, and Fearon listed in Chapter 5.

Roosevelt's approach to big business is analyzed in Ellis W. Hawley, *The New Deal and the Problem of Monopoly: A Study in Economic Ambivalence* (1966), and Donald R. Brand, *Corporatism and the Rule of Law: A Study of the National Recovery Administration* (1988). For the New Deal's most popular public agency, see Walter L. Creese, *TVA's Public Planning: The Vision, the Reality* (1990). Government environmental activity is treated in A.L. Owen, *Conservation under FDR* (1983). The welfare state is the focus of William Ranulf Brock, *Welfare, Democracy, and the New Deal* (1988), and of the appropriate segments of Linda Gordon, *Pitied but not Entitled: Single Mothers and the History of Welfare, 1890–1935* (1994). For the politics of the National Youth Administration, see Richard A. Reiman, *The New Deal and American Youth: Ideas and Ideals in a Depression Decade* (1992).

Roosevelt's approach to unions is the subject of Stanley Vittoz, *New Deal Labor Policy and the American Industrial Economy* (1987), and James A. Hodges, *New Deal Labor Policy and the Southern Cotton Textile Industry, 1933–1941* (1986). See also J. Joseph Hutchmacher, *Senator Robert E. Wagner and the Rise of Urban Liberalism* (1971). The labor movement's relationship with the administration is outlined in David Milton, *The Politics of United States Labor: From the Great Depression to the New Deal* (1981).

Union activism in the 1930s is described in the relevant chapters of Robert H. Zeiger, *American Workers, American Unions, 1920–1985* (1986). For the CIO, see Zeiger, *The CIO: 1935–1955* (1955), and *John L. Lewis: Labor Leader* (1988), and see Daniel Nelson, *American Rubber Workers and Organized Labor, 1900–1941* (1988). Contrasts between eastern and western dock workers are drawn in Bruce Nelson, *Workers on the Waterfront: Seamen, Longshoremen, and Unionism in the 1930s* (1988), and in Howard Kimeldorf, *Reds or Rackets? The Making of Radical and Conservative Unions on the Waterfront* (1988). For Communist Party influence in the labor movement, see Roger Keeran, *The Communist Party and the Auto Workers Unions* (1980). Working-class culture is the subject of John Bodnar, *Workers' World: Kinship, Community, and Protest in an Industrial Society, 1900–1940* (1982), and Lizabeth Cohen, *Making a New Deal: Industrial Workers in Chicago, 1919–1939* (1990).

For the social transformation of the South, see the relevant segments of Jack Temple Kirby, *Rural Worlds Lost: The American South, 1920–1960* (1987), and of Pete Daniel, *Breaking the Land: Transformation of Cotton, Tobacco, and Rice Cultures Since 1880* (1985). Westward migration from the Great Plains is the subject of James N. Gregory, *American Exodus: Dust Bowl Migration and Okie Culture in California* (1989).

The African American experience in the 1930s is portrayed in John B. Kirby, *Black Americans in the Roosevelt Era: Liberalism and Race* (1980), and in Harvard Sitkoff, *A New Deal for Blacks: The Emergence of Civil Rights as a National Issue* (1978). See also Nancy J. Weiss, *Farewell to the Party of Lincoln: Black Politics in the Age of Franklin D. Roosevelt* (1983). The emergence of civil rights is depicted in Sarah E. Wright, *A. Philip Randolph: Integration in the Workplace* (1990), and Paula F. Pfeffer, *A. Philip Randolph: Pioneer of the Civil Rights Movement* (1990). For southern blacks and the Communist Party, see James M. Goodman, *Stories of Scottsboro* (1994), and Robin D.G. Kelley, *Hammer and Hoe: Alabama Communists during the Great Depression* (1990).

The repression of the Mexican American community is the focus of Abraham Hoffman, *Unwanted Mexican Americans in the Great Depression: Repatriation Pressures, 1929–1939* (1974), which can be supplemented by the relevant sections of Rodolpho Acuna, *Occupied America: A History of Chicanos* (rev. ed., 1988). See also later sections of Sarah Deutsch, *No Separate Refuge: Culture, Class, and Gender on an Anglo-Hispanic Frontier in the American Southwest, 1880–1940* (1987). An excellent case study is Vicki L. Ruiz, *Cannery Women, Cannery Lives: Mexican Women, Unionization, and the California Food Processing Industry, 1930–1950* (1987). See also portions of David Montejano, *Anglos and Mexicans in the Making of Texas, 1836–1986* (1987). For the growth of the Mexican American civil rights movement, see Mario T. Garcia, *Mexican-Americans: Leadership, Ideology, and Identity, 1930–1960* (1989).

Government policy toward Native Americans is the subject of Lawrence C. Kelly, *The Assault on Assimilation: John Collier and the Origins of Indian Policy Reform* (1983), and Graham D. Taylor, *The New Deal and American Indian Tribalism: The Administration of the Indian Reorganization Act, 1934–1945* (1980). For the Depression experience of immigrants and racial and ethnic minorities, see the relevant segments of Ronald Takaki, *A Different Mirror: A History of Multicultural America* (1993).

An extensive literature on 1930s women includes Susan Ware, *Beyond Suffrage: Women in the New Deal* (1981), and *Holding Their Own: American Women in the 1930s* (1982). See also the relevant chapters of Sheila Rothman, *Woman's Proper Place: A History of Changing Ideals and Practices, 1870 to the Present* (1978), and of Winifred D. Wandersee, *Women's Work and Family Values, 1920–1940* (1981). Useful portraits of the First Lady's activism can be found in William Chafe, *Without Precedent: The Life and Career of Eleanor Roosevelt* (1984), and in Lois Scharf, *Eleanor Roosevelt: First Lady of American Liberalism* (1987). For the contradictions of social feminism, see Gordon, *Pitied but not Entitled*.

Socially conscious art and journalism are described in William Stott, *Documentary Expression and Thirties America* (1973). For government sponsorship of the arts, see Marlene Park and Gerald E. Markowitz, *Democratic Vistas: Post Offices and Public Art in the New Deal* (1984), and the innovative James Curtis, *Mind's Eye, Mind's Truth: FSA Photography Reconsidered* (1989). See also Barbara Melosh, *Engendering Culture: Manhood and Womanhood in New Deal Public Art and Theater* (1991). For 1930s art history, see the relevant segments of Donald Goddard, *American Painting* (1990). A cross-disciplinary approach to 1930s culture appears in Alice G. Marquis, *Hopes and Ashes: The Birth of Modern Times, 1929–1939* (1986), which supplements the more conventional Charles C. Alexander, *Nationalism in American Thought, 1930–1945* (1969).

The aspirations and dilemmas of 1930s intellectuals are surveyed in Richard Pells, *Radical Visions and American Dreams: Culture and Social Thought in the Depression Years* (1973). See also Terry A. Cooney, *The Rise of the New York Intellectuals*: Partisan Review *and Its Circle* (1986); Alexander Bloom, *Prodigal Sons: The New York Intellectuals and Their New World* (1987); and Alan Wald, *The New York Intellectuals: The Rise and Decline of the Anti-Stalinist Left from the 1930s to the 1980s* (1987).

An extensive literature on 1930s communism includes portraits by Fraser Ottanelli, *The Communist Party of the United States: From the Depression to World War II* (1991); Robbie Lieberman, *"My Song is My Weapon": People's Songs, American Communism, and the Politics of Culture, 1930–50* (1989); and Peter N. Carroll, *The Odyssey of the Abraham Lincoln Brigade: Americans in the Spanish Civil War* (1994). See also Malcolm Cowley, *The Dream of the Golden Mountains: Remembering the 1930s* (rev. ed., 1980), and Daniel Aaron, *Writers on the Left: Episodes in American Literary Communism* (1961). More critical assessments include Harvey Klehr, *The Heyday of American Communism: The Depression Decade* (1984), and David Shannon, *The Decline of American Communism* (1959). For Communist Party influence in the labor movement, see Keeran, *The Communist Party and the Auto Workers Unions*. Communist involvement in farm cooperatives and unions is described in Lowell K. Dyson, *Red Harvest: The Communist Party and American Farmers* (1982).

For agrarian unrest, see Theodore Saloutos, *The American Farmer and the New Deal* (1982), and the relevant segments of Saloutos and John D. Hicks, *Twentieth Century Populism: Agricultural Discontent in the Middle West, 1900–1939* (1951). The social views of independent producers are examined by Cartherine McNicol Stock, *Main Street in Crisis: The Great Depression and the Old Middle Class on the Northern Plains* (1992), and in several chapters of David A. Horowitz, *Beyond Left and Right: Insurgency and the Establishment* (1997). Useful biographical accounts include Alan Brinkley, *Voices of Protest: Huey Long, Father Coughlin, and the Great Depression* (1982); Glen Jeansonne, *Messiah of the Masses: Huey P. Long and the Great Depression* (1992); William Ivy Hair, *The Kingfish and His Realm: The Life and Times of Huey P. Long* (1991); and John E. Miller, *Governor Philip F. La Follette, the Wisconsin Progressives, and the New Deal, 1930–1939* (1982). See also the relevant portions of Leo P. Ribuffo, *The Old Christian Right: The Protestant Far Right from the Great Depression to the Cold War* (1983), and of Michael Kazin, *The Populist Persuasion, an American History* (1995).

Anti–New Deal politics is explored in Clyde P. Weed, *The Nemesis of Reform: The Republican Party During the New Deal* (1994). See also Ronald L. Feinman, *Twilight of Progressivism: The Western Republican Senators and the New Deal* (1981), and Ronald A. Mulder, *The Insurgent Progressives in the United States Senate and the New Deal, 1933–1939* (1979). Other monographs include James T. Patterson, *Congressional Conservatism and the New Deal: The Growth of the Conservative Coalition in Congress, 1933–1939* (1967), and David L. Porter, *Congress and the Waning of the New Deal* (1980). See also R. Alan Lawson, *The Failure of Independent Liberalism, 1933–1941* (1971). For the Supreme Court controversy, see Leonard Baker, *Back to Back: The Duel between FDR and the Supreme Court* (1967). The New Deal constitutional revolution is explained in sections of Arthur S. Miller, *The Modern Corporate State: Private Governments and the American Constitution* (1976), and of Jeffrey D. Hockett, *New Deal Justice: the Constitutional Jurisprudence of Hugo L. Black, Felix Frankfurter, and Robert H. Jackson* (1996).

The legacy of deficit spending is the subject of Mark Hugh Leff, *The Limits of Symbolic Reform: The New Deal and Taxation, 1933–1939* (1984), and of Alan Brinkley, *The End of Reform: New Deal Liberalism in Recession and War* (1995). For the consequences of fiscal policy for development in the South and the West, see Jordan A. Schwarz, *The New Dealers: Power Politics in the Age of Roosevelt* (1993). The limits of New Deal reform are explored in Theodore Rosenof, *Patterns of Political Economy in America: The Failure to Develop a Democratic Left Synthesis, 1933–1950* (1983), and the implications of Keynesian fiscal policies and of labor consensus are explored in several essays in Steve Fraser and Gary Gerstle, eds., *The Rise and Fall of the New Deal Order, 1930–1980* (1989). For Latin American policy, see Irwin F. Gellman, *Good Neighbor Diplomacy: United States Policies in Latin America, 1933–1945* (1979), and Earl R. Curry, *Hoover's Dominican Diplomacy and the Origins of the Good Neighbor Policy* (1979).

The movie industry's responses to the Hays Code are described in segments of Leonard J. Leff and Jerold L. Simmons, *The Dame in the Kimono: Hollywood, Censorship, and the Production Code From the 1920s to the 1960s* (1990). See also the relevant chapters of Douglas Gomery, *The Hollywood Studio System* (1986); Garth Jowett, *Film, the Democratic Art* (1976); and Robert Sklar, *Movie-Made America: A Cultural History of American Movies* (1975). For the studio-audience relationship, see John Izod, *Hollywood and the Box Office, 1895–1986* (1988). Comedies of the early 1930s are described in Henry Jenkins, *What Made Pistachio Nuts? Early Sound Comedy and the Vaudeville Aesthetic* (1992), and in June Sochen, *Mae West: "She Who Laughs, Lasts"* (1992). The social function of 1930s film is the subject of Richard Maltby, *Harmless Entertainment: Hollywood and the Ideology of Consensus* (1983). See also Joseph McBride, *Frank Capra: The Catastrophe of Success* (1992).

For radio, see Hugh G.J. Aitken, *The Continuous Wave: Technology and American Radio, 1900–1932* (1985) and Fred J. MacDonald, *Don't Touch that Dial! Radio Programming in American Life from 1920 to 1960* (1979). Popular musical tastes of the era are described in the relevant portions of Ian Whitcomb, *After the Ball: Popular Music from Rag to Rock* (1982). For jazz, see John Edward Hasse, *Beyond Category: The Life and Genius of Duke Ellington* (1993).

7

Women workers contributed much to advance the war effort during World War II.

WORLD WAR II: THE CRUSADE AGAINST FASCISM AND THE SEARCH FOR GLOBAL ORDER

The war against fascism—from the German invasion of Poland on 1 September 1939, through the Japanese surrender on 2 September 1945—emerged as a watershed in modern U.S. history, separating the prewar economic crisis from postwar affluence and dividing prewar neutrality from postwar interventionism. The magnitude of the war effort involved more private citizens—soldiers, civilian employees, workers, and consumers—in government activities than ever before. Total warfare saw U.S. industrial production double, increasing from $91 billion to $166 billion, and created 15 million new jobs. The war also expanded the sweep of federal government powers. These changes laid the foundation for the postwar national security state, which demanded large military budgets and political consensus on the home front. The war had immense costs in terms of dollars, casualties, and disruption of ordinary lives. Yet ultimate victory not only served to justify the losses but also resulted in growing U.S. responsibility for global stability. For the next generation, World War II stood both as a warning against military weakness and as a reminder of U.S. industrial power.

THE OPEN DOOR AND THE ORIGINS OF GLOBAL CONFLICTS

Author Claire Booth Luce once observed that each of the major figures of World War II had his typical gesture: Hitler had the upraised arm, Churchill the "V" sign, and, as for Roosevelt, Luce wet her index finger and held it up in the air. As the gesture suggested, President Franklin D. Roosevelt was a master politician who liked to test which way the public winds were blowing before acting. He also liked to avoid commitments and allow decisions to drift. Often the president hesitated to explain his thinking publicly lest it narrow the range of future options or offend domestic opinion. He frequently changed his mind and contradicted himself. In addition, he insisted on maintaining personal control over major policy decisions, especially in foreign affairs. Despite his many deficiencies, Roosevelt enjoyed tremendous prestige at home and abroad, and his leadership stamped an indelible mark on U.S. relations with the world.

Roosevelt's ambiguous comments about foreign affairs brought a rude awakening. At the outbreak of World War II in Europe in 1939, the president assured a worried nation that U.S. citizens were the "best informed" in the world. On 7 December 1941, however, the country was stunned by news that Japanese aircraft had executed a devastating attack against U.S. bases at Pearl Harbor in the territory of Hawaii. "Every single man, woman, and child is a partner in the most tremendous undertaking of our American history," said Roosevelt as he led the nation into war. Yet one year later opinion polls found that one-third of the public lacked a clear understanding of U.S. war aims. Avoiding the complexities of international relations, the president had urged the nation to focus on one goal: winning the war.

U.S. involvement in World War II resulted from long-standing economic and political commitments. Throughout the twentieth century, a guiding principle of U.S. foreign relations was the Open Door policy, which advocated free trade for all nations with equal access to raw materials and foreign markets. During

Exhibit 7-1. Manchuria and Adjacent Area, 1931

the Depression, Roosevelt had come to believe that the nation's economic prosperity depended on finding markets for U.S. products. Moreover, he feared that failure to develop international trade would create severe social dislocations that would imperil U.S. democratic traditions. Roosevelt also worried about the emergence of strong nationalist states, especially Nazi Germany, which threatened U.S. trade overseas. This distrust of Germany also reflected the historic

U.S. friendship with Great Britain and France, which dated to the 1890s and had brought the United States into the Allied camp during World War I.

The Open Door policy and pro-Allied sentiment shaped U.S. foreign policy, even after the Senate rejected the Versailles Treaty and the League of Nations in 1919 and 1920. At the Washington Arms Conference of 1921–1922, for example, the United States persuaded Japan to accept the principles of the Open Door policy embodied in the Nine Power Pact. Japan promised to restore sovereignty over the Shantung Peninsula to China and to remove Japanese troops from southern Siberia, although the agreement allowed Japanese troops to remain in China. Because the United States had a limited stake in Asia in the 1920s, Washington raised no objections to such a Japanese presence.

During the Depression, however, U.S. business leaders searched for new markets around the globe—Latin America, the Soviet Union, and Asia—and assigned greater importance to China. Although U.S. commerce with Japan exceeded the value of trade with China, the vast potential of the China market suggested a permanent solution to recurrent depressions. Meanwhile, Japan followed its own expansionist plans. In 1931 the Japanese easily defeated Chinese armies in Manchuria and converted the province into a Japanese protectorate the next year. Because the Japanese occupation violated international law as well as the Open Door policy, Secretary of State Henry Stimson responded with a formal protest. Reaffirming a commitment to the Open Door policy, the Stimson Doctrine announced that the United States would not recognize the Japanese puppet government in Manchuria. Even this minimal protest outraged the nation's neutralists. "The American people," stated *The Philadelphia Record*, "don't give a hoot in a rain barrel who controls North China." When the League of Nations adopted the U.S. policy of nonrecognition in 1933, moreover, Japan refused to change policies and withdrew from the international organization.

Germany departed from the League in 1933. Under the leadership of Adolf Hitler, who assumed absolute power in that year, German National Socialists demanded a revision of the Versailles Treaty to reestablish their nation as a world power. Yet French rejection of military equality in Europe convinced the Germans to act independently, and Hitler announced a rearmament program in 1934. By subsidizing German corporations and winning bilateral agreements from trading partners, Hitler's National Socialism (Nazism) intensified economic competition with the United States in Latin America and caused U.S. exports to Germany to decrease drastically. Meanwhile, Italy, led by the fascist Benito Mussolini, further disrupted peace and international order. Seeking glory and conquest in Ethiopia, Mussolini took advantage of a military clash at a desert oasis in 1934 to demand compensation for military losses. As the European arms race escalated in 1935, Japan proposed a revision of the Washington agreement to obtain naval equality. The United States and Britain rejected the request; Japan decided to expand its navy anyway.

THE NONINTERVENTIONIST CRUSADE

Militaristic rumblings abroad reinforced strong traditions of nonintervention at home. Since the disillusionment of World War I, most citizens believed the

United States had been tricked into participation in World War I. During the mid-1930s, investigations headed by North Dakota's Republican Senator Gerald P. Nye revealed extensive wartime profiteering by munitions manufacturers and bankers, which implied close connections between the arms industry, international financiers, and presidential foreign policy. Walter Millis's best-seller, *Road to War* (1935), popularized the idea that the nation had been lured into the war by a combination of business profiteering and Allied propaganda.

Public distrust of bankers and arms interests directly affected U.S. foreign policy. When Roosevelt requested power to stop arms sales to selected aggressor nations, Congress blocked any increases in executive power. Instead, a noninterventionist Congress passed the Neutrality Act of 1935, which required the president to establish an arms embargo against all warring countries and to notify U.S. citizens that they sailed on ships owned by warring nations at their own risk. These provisions attempted to shield the country from becoming involved even accidentally in foreign wars by eliminating the very factors that many people believed had drawn the United States into World War I. The law deliberately narrowed the president's options. In signing the measure, Roosevelt warned that its "inflexible provisions might drag us into war instead of keeping us out."

Despite U.S. policy, Mussolini invaded Ethiopia in 1935. Although the League of Nations condemned Italian aggression, Britain and France chose not to intervene in the war. Roosevelt called for a "moral embargo" on the shipment of oil to Italy, but such gestures were merely symbolic, and U.S. exports to Italy increased. Even so, Mussolini withdrew from the League of Nations and signed a treaty of alliance with Hitler in 1936.

As Europe moved closer to war, Congress attempted to protect the United States from military involvement. Roosevelt's effort to add a discretionary clause to the Neutrality Act, allowing the president to apply the embargo more flexibly, raised stiff opposition. Congress forced the president to accept the 1935 regulations and established a new ban on loans to warring countries. Caught between a popular wave of noninterventionist sentiment and developing aggression abroad, Roosevelt assured the public during the 1936 presidential campaign that "We are not isolationists except insofar as we seek to isolate ourselves completely from war."

Noninterventionism shaped Roosevelt's response to the Spanish Civil War, which erupted in 1936 when the reactionary General Francisco Franco led a rebellion against the republican government of Spain. Although Hitler and Mussolini provided crucial military support for Franco, and the Soviet Union and Mexico aided the Spanish republic, Britain and France adopted a policy of nonintervention. Roosevelt followed their lead. The effect was to deny supplies to the legally elected Spanish republic. In the United States, the Spanish Civil War aroused public opinion. As Hitler and Mussolini supported the Spanish generals, liberals and leftists saw Spain as a moral battleground between the forces of democracy and the legions of fascism and demanded U.S. support for the elected government of Spain. However, conservatives and Catholics saw Franco as a defender of the traditional social order against a government committed to land reform, secularism, and social democracy. Although U.S. Gallup polls of the American people found that sympathy toward the Spanish republic greatly exceeded support of Franco, Roosevelt feared offending U.S. Catholics by supporting the socialist Spanish republic. State Department officials also perceived the republic as a potential threat to U.S. investors.

Hostile to any movements for social revolution, the Roosevelt administration imposed an embargo on arms shipments to Spain and forbade civilians from traveling to that embattled country. Congress endorsed that policy in 1937. Violating the law, 2,800 young U.S. men and women volunteered for the Abraham Lincoln Brigade in an attempt to defend the Spanish republic in a crusade that won wide support from intellectuals like Ernest Hemingway, Langston Hughes, and Lillian Hellman. One-third of the U.S. volunteers died in Spain. U.S. businesses also broke the law by selling war materiel to Franco. With superior arms, the fascist allies triumphed in Spain in 1939. Neither Congress nor Roosevelt viewed the survival of the Spanish republic as vital to U.S. national interests.

The U.S. public overwhelmingly supported neutrality laws and hoped to keep the nation out of foreign wars. Yet business interests tied to international trade feared that neutrality would interfere with the development of Depression-era markets. Seeking to balance those counterpressures, presidential adviser Bernard M. Baruch suggested a revision of the Neutrality Act that would incorporate the principle of "cash and carry." As enacted by Congress in 1937, "cash and carry" permitted the sale of nonmilitary products to nations at war, but warring countries had to pay cash (to avoid the debt entanglements associated with U.S. entry into World War I), and goods had to be transported in non-U.S. ships (to avoid the problems posed by neutral rights on the high seas). The "cash and carry" policy favored nations with strong navies and large cash reserves, and Roosevelt understood that Britain and France, not Germany, would benefit from the new provisions. The law also required a mandatory embargo on arms sales to all warring countries.

While Congress tried to perfect neutrality law, decisions made abroad raised the cost of strict neutrality. In 1937 Japan attacked the northern provinces of China. Appealing to Asian nationalism, the Japanese promised to create an East Asia Co-Prosperity Sphere that would exclude the European colonial powers from Chinese markets and resources. Such a sphere of influence paralleled Nazi expansion in central Europe, British control of the Commonwealth nations, and U.S. dominance of Latin America. Yet Roosevelt remained committed to the Open Door policy in Asia and supported an independent China. Backed by strong anti-Japanese public opinion, the president bypassed neutrality law by refusing to acknowledge that a state of war existed between Japan and China. This decision enabled the Roosevelt administration to extend trade credits to Chiang Kai-shek's Nationalists to finance anti-Japanese resistance. Yet such assistance remained limited. With Europe heading for war, the administration wished to avoid a break with Japan.

Roosevelt worried nonetheless about the inhibiting effect of noninterventionist sentiment. To counteract what he called "isolationism," the president spoke out in 1937 against the "epidemic of world lawlessness" and called for a "quarantine" of aggressor nations. Although he offered no specific plan, Roosevelt publicly admitted for the first time that war might become a necessary tool of foreign policy. Although interventionist newspapers praised the president, the quarantine speech also brought negative comments that were strong enough to prevent any change of policy. "It's a terrible thing," Roosevelt later said, "to look over your shoulder when you are trying to lead—and to find no one

Exhibit 7-2. Countdown to World War II, 1931–1939

1931	Japan occupies Manchuria
1933	Japan withdraws from League of Nations
	Adolf Hitler's National Socialists assume power in Germany
1934	German rearmament
1935	Italy invades Ethiopia
	U.S. Neutrality Act invokes arms embargo
	Nye Munitions Investigation convenes
1936	Italy withdraws from League of Nations and enters alliance with Germany
	Germany reoccupies Rhineland
	Spanish Civil War begins
1937	Japan attacks northern China
	U. S. Neutrality Act invokes "cash-and-carry" nonmilitary aid
	Roosevelt "quarantine" speech
1938	Munich Conference accepts German Annexation of Austria and parts of Czechoslovakia
	Germany annexes all of Czechoslovakia
1939	Russo-German Nonaggression Pact
	Germany invades Poland
	Great Britain and France declare war on Germany
	U.S. Neutrality Act invokes "cash and carry" for military aid

there." When Japanese planes attacked the U.S. gunboat *Panay* on the Yangtze River in late 1937, the president accepted a Japanese apology and promise of compensation for the damage. Meanwhile, noninterventionists backed a controversial amendment to the Constitution sponsored by Democratic Representative Louis Ludlow of Indiana to require a public referendum before Congress could declare war. Under extreme pressure from the Roosevelt administration, the House of Representatives returned the measure to committee early in 1938 by a close vote of 209 to 188.

The United States watched nervously as conditions deteriorated in Europe. Conservatives in Britain and France, fearing another war, hoped that Nazi Germany would serve as a barrier against Soviet communism. In what became known as a policy of "appeasement," Britain and France accepted Germany's takeover of Austria in March 1938. Six months later, Hitler demanded portions of Czechoslovakian territory, and the world veered toward war. Again, France and Britain, led by Prime Minister Neville Chamberlain, signed an agreement with Hitler and Mussolini at Munich that ceded areas of Czechoslovakia to Germany. The Munich Pact demoralized antifascists throughout the world and persuaded the Soviet Union that the Western Allies wanted Germany to expand eastward. Britain and France issued no protest when German armies occupied the rest of Czechoslovakia early in 1939, although they did guarantee to protect Poland and began to rearm.

As German expansion threatened the world order, Roosevelt increased the U.S. military arsenal, particularly the air forces, beginning in 1938. Such rearmament, although haphazard and underfunded, reflected the president's belief that air power would deter Nazi aggression without requiring a large and unpopular army. Roosevelt also realized that the United States might become a supplier of military equipment to France and Britain, and the president secretly approved U.S. manufacture of French warplanes. Yet Roosevelt's plans remained ambiguous, partly because he feared that public disclosure would arouse congressional opposition. Potential conflict between the executive and legislative branches thus encouraged presidential vacillation and secrecy. White House requests for military appropriations remained small. In turn, the lack of military power made Roosevelt wary of becoming involved in European controversies. Meanwhile, Germany began to threaten Poland in 1939, which prompted the Western Allies to abandon appeasement. Hitler then signed a nonaggression pact with Soviet leader Josef Stalin in August 1939 to eliminate the danger of a two-front war. Five days later, on 1 September 1939, Germany invaded Poland. Within two days, Britain and France declared war on Nazi Germany.

THE FAILURE OF NEUTRALITY, 1939–1941

The outbreak of World War II intensified the contradictions in Roosevelt's foreign policy—his belief that France and Britain must defeat Germany to preserve stability in Europe and his commitment to stay out of war. To reconcile these contradictions, the president emphasized that support of Britain would protect U.S. interests without embroiling the nation in European hostilities. Accordingly, Roosevelt called Congress into special session in September 1939 to repeal the arms embargo.

"Keep America out of the blood business" read just one of hundreds of thousands of letters that poured into Congress as the nation engaged in a dramatic debate about U.S. interests in World War II. Senate defenders of neutrality, such as Gerald Nye and Robert M. La Follette, Jr., warned that any revisions of the law would bring the United States into the war. Yet interventionists in both political parties organized well-funded lobbying groups to press for change. The massive press and radio campaign and intense lobbying by the Roosevelt administration persuaded Congress to repeal the arms embargo in 1939. The new Neutrality Act still prohibited U.S. vessels from entering war zones but permitted belligerents to purchase military supplies on a cash-and-carry basis. Because of their naval strength and geographic position, Britain and France benefited most from these provisions. The law in effect placed the United States in the Allied camp.

Once German armies invaded Norway, Denmark, the Low Countries, and France in the spring of 1940, the battle between U.S. interventionists and neutralists intensified. As Nazi troops blitzed toward Paris, Roosevelt warned against "the illusion that we are remote and isolated." Noninterventionists such as Democratic Senator Burton K. Wheeler of Montana derided the notion that Germany could ever mount an invasion of the Western Hemisphere. Yet while Wheeler and noninterventionists in both parties called for a negotiated peace, Congress approved increased defense appropriations to prepare for a war. The president sought bipartisan support by appointing two leading Republican internationalists to the cabinet: Henry Stimson, as secretary of war, and Frank Knox, the Republican vice presidential candidate in 1936, as secretary of the navy. The fall of France in June 1940 brought a dramatic rise in pro-British sentiment, but U.S. public opinion polls showed that 82 percent of those

This noninterventionist poster of 1941 depicts the U.S. policy of convoying supplies and war materiel to Great Britain as one bound to involve the nation in the European war.

surveyed still opposed U.S. intervention in the war. Like Roosevelt, the public clung to the hope that military assistance would enable Britain to defeat Germany without further U.S. involvement.

As German planes bombed British cities and German submarines sank vessels in the Atlantic during the summer of 1940, Prime Minister Winston Churchill pleaded for U.S. naval assistance. Roosevelt responded with an "executive agreement," trading fifty overage navy destroyers for British bases in the Western Hemisphere and a promise that Britain would never surrender the fleet. The "destroyers for bases" deal had less military value than symbolic importance because it dramatized the U.S. commitment to the British cause. Eager to show noninterventionists that he was strengthening U.S. defenses, Roosevelt proclaimed that the arrangement was "the most important action in the reinforcement of our national defense since the Louisiana Purchase." Yet noninterventionists such as the popular aviator Charles Lindbergh argued that Roosevelt had failed to consult Congress and that aid to Britain weakened the national defense. A bipartisan coalition of congressional noninterventionists now warned that Roosevelt was dragging the country into a European war whose outcome was not vital to U.S. interests.

Months earlier, interventionists led by Kansas newspaper editor William Allen White had set up a Committee to Defend America by Aiding the Allies. Noninterventionists responded by creating their own organization, the America First Committee, in September 1940. With financial backing from business interests that served the domestic market, America First quickly enrolled more than 800,000 Americans, mostly midwesterners. Public speakers like Lindbergh and Nye spread the antiwar message through mass rallies and radio broadcasts, warning that involvement in the European war would lead the country to militarism, dictatorship, and collectivism.

Despite the popularity of the noninterventionist position, the brutality of the German war machine, Nazi violence against civilians, and the persecution of Jews helped win support for Roosevelt's interventionist policies. Twelve days after the creation of America First, Congress approved the first peacetime draft in U.S. history. The profound sense of national crisis permitted the president to seek an unprecedented third term in 1940. Within the Republican Party, a bitter fight between interventionists and noninterventionists resulted in the nomination of Wendell Willkie, a Wall Street lawyer who supported both the destroyers-for-bases agreement and the peacetime draft. In the campaign, Roosevelt denounced noninterventionists as "appeasers" and pictured the struggle against Nazi aggression as one of "people versus dictatorship." As German aircraft hurled bombs on British cities and the Royal Air Force fought brilliantly in the skies, live radio broadcasts from London by Edward R. Murrow focused sympathy on the Allied side. Yet Roosevelt promised to keep out of European hostilities. "Your boys," he reaffirmed on the eve of the election, "are not going to be sent into any foreign wars." One week later, Roosevelt took nearly 55 percent of the popular vote. He was the first president to serve more than two terms.

Once reelected, Roosevelt announced that a British victory was essential for U.S. "national security" and that the United States must become "the great arsenal of democracy." In his State of the Union address of January 1941, the president continued to lead the nation away from a policy of strict neutrality and condemned the "so-called new order of tyranny which the dictators seek to create with the crash of a bomb." Roosevelt appealed for the defense of "Four Freedoms"—freedom of speech and expression, freedom of religion, freedom from want, and freedom from fear. For most citizens this rhetoric defined World War II as a conflict between freedom and tyranny rather than a defense of national interest.

CHARLES A. LINDBERGH
1902–1974

Stock Montage

Perhaps the most prominent of the noninterventionist advocates in the years before World War II was aviation pioneer Charles Lindbergh. Since winning international acclaim for his solo flight from New York to Paris in 1927, the flier had been the object of almost unceasing public scrutiny. Always wary of both the public and the press, Lindbergh felt his suspicion was confirmed by the spectacle surrounding the kidnap-murder of his son in 1931. Four years later he and his wife, writer Anne Morrow Lindbergh, fled to Europe, where they lived until the eve of World War II. During the 1930s he made five trips to Nazi Germany to inspect the German air industry and came away highly impressed by what he found. "The German aviation development is without parallel," he wrote. By 1938 he considered Germany "probably the strongest air power in Europe, . . . greater than that of all other European countries combined."

With war imminent, the family returned in mid-1939 to the United States, where Lindbergh threw himself into the public debate over U.S. involvement in the European conflict. The origins of his noninterventionist sentiments were complex. For one thing, his father, a member of the House of Representatives, had strongly opposed U.S. involvement in World War I, and the younger Lindbergh probably inherited some midwestern skepticism about European entanglements. Second, Lindbergh's conservative leanings and Republican connections made him deeply suspicious of Franklin Roosevelt. Lindbergh regarded Roosevelt as a devious and deceitful man who was exploiting the world crisis to expand his own power.

More troubling, however, was Lindbergh's thinking about the comparative merits of the United States and Nazi Germany. He felt considerable resentment toward his native country, which he believed had given him a celeb-

With Britain running out of capital and the United States forbidden by neutrality law to extend credit, Roosevelt faced the problem of moving supplies across the Atlantic. In response, the president decided, as he put it, to "eliminate the dollar sign." If your neighbor's house were on fire, Roosevelt explained, it would be prudent to lend him an old garden hose to put out the fire before it spread to your house. Afterward the neighbor would return the hose or, if it were damaged, replace it. Such was the logic of the "Lend-Lease" proposal, which the administration introduced early in 1941. This sweeping package gave the president unprecedented power to sell, transfer, exchange, lend, or lease military equipment and other goods to any nation whose defense he deemed essential to U.S. security. In one of the most intense debates in U.S. history, noninterventionists insisted that Roosevelt was asking for dictatorial power that would eventually lead the nation into war. In a bitter reference to Roosevelt's New Deal farm policy, Senator Wheeler warned that Lend-Lease would plough under every fourth American boy. Despite these warnings, Congress approved Lend-Lease in March 1941 and authorized $7 billion to send supplies to Britain and its allies.

rity he had never sought and then exploited his family's tragedy. "We Americans are a primitive people," he told *Life* magazine. "We do not have discipline. Our moral standards are low. It shows up in the private lives of people we know—their drinking and behavior with women. It shows in the newspapers, the morbid curiosity over crimes and murder trials." He viewed Germany as marked by "a strength and vigor which it is impossible to overlook." In addition, he claimed to have "found the most personal freedom in Germany." Compounding all this was Lindbergh's rabid anticommunism. "An alliance between the United States and Russia should be opposed by every American, every Christian, and by every humanitarian in this country," he declared shortly after Hitler invaded the Soviet Union.

Convinced that the democracies were deteriorating morally and that German technology would dominate the future, Lindbergh first advocated appeasement and then a negotiated peace with Germany. He saw British defeat as imminent and inevitable, a view doubtless influenced by his own confidence that air power would determine the outcome of modern war. Some also saw a tinge of anti-Semitism in his assertion that Jewish groups were working with the British and the Roo-

sevelt administration to push the United States into war through their "large ownership and influence in our motion pictures, our press, our radio, and our government."

The disturbing nature of such statements detracted from Lindbergh's legitimate criticism of interventionist policies. He noted the irony of demanding involvement in Europe to defend democratic principles while the Roosevelt administration resorted to subterfuge to advance a policy that public opinion clearly was not yet ready to support. He warned that the delicate balance of power between the executive and legislative branches was being permanently tipped by Roosevelt's undeclared naval war in the North Atlantic without the approval of Congress. Lindbergh also feared that participation in the war would change the character of U.S. life. To defeat Germany, the nation must become a "uniformed and regimented nation," possibly for generations to come. Such questions about the legitimate scope of U.S. involvement in conflicts abroad, the formulation of foreign policy under cover of secrecy, and the growing militarization of public life would all become crucial in the decades after World War II. ■

As the critics predicted, Lend-Lease destroyed the fiction of U.S. neutrality. The success of German submarines in sinking Allied vessels placed increasing pressure on the United States to assure the delivery of goods to Britain. Roosevelt now assumed unprecedented presidential powers. In the face of negative public opinion, he would not allow naval convoys to escort Lend-Lease material. Instead he devised a new fiction, the idea of "hemispheric defense," which extended the neutral zone halfway across the Atlantic. He ordered the navy to report the presence of German ships and planes in this zone to the British. Roosevelt also signed an executive agreement with the Danish government in exile that provided for U.S. bases in Greenland.

Roosevelt's disregard for strict neutrality infuriated his opponents. Criticism escalated when the president extended Lend-Lease to the Soviet Union after Hitler's invasion of that nation in June 1941. Charles Lindbergh announced his preference for an alliance with Germany "with all her faults" rather than one "with the cruelty, Godlessness, and the barbarism that exist in the Soviet Union." Senator Harry S Truman expressed a third view: "If we see that Germany is winning the war we ought to help Russia," he stated; "if Russia is

Exhibit 7-3. The Road to War, 1940–1941

1940	Germany occupies Denmark, Norway, Low Countries, and France
	Japan occupies French Indochina (Vietnam)
	U.S. establishes economic sanctions against Japan
	Germany, Italy, and Japan sign Axis military pact
	U.S. builds two-ocean navy and enacts first peacetime draft
	Roosevelt wins third presidential term
	Battle of Britain
1941	Lend-Lease Act provides U.S. aid to Britain
	Germany invades Soviet Union
	United States and Britain sign Atlantic Charter
	Extension of U.S. draft
	Escalation of Battle of the Atlantic
	Repeal of U.S. neutrality law permits arming of merchant ships
	Japanese attack on Pearl Harbor

winning we ought to help Germany and that way let them kill as many as possible."

The controversial support of the Soviet Union put strains on the U.S. political system that would last for years. However, Roosevelt believed that only a total defeat of Germany could prevent Hitler's Third Reich from conquering the world, and the president advocated providing generous aid to all enemies of Germany. As German submarines continued to attack Atlantic shipping (and sank a U.S. vessel in May 1941), the president feared that Britain might lose the war. He resolved to move ahead of public opinion. In July Roosevelt extended the range of U.S. convoys to Iceland, a policy that brought the merchant marine directly into conflict with German warships.

A close brush with war occurred in September 1941 when the U.S. destroyer *Greer* exchanged fire with a German submarine and attempted to sink the German vessel. Roosevelt concealed that fact from Congress and the public when he announced a major change of policy: U.S. ships, he ordered, could "shoot on sight" German ships in the so-called neutral zone. "It is time for all Americans," Roosevelt declared, "to stop being deluded by the romantic notion that the Americas can go on living happily and peacefully in a Nazi-dominated world." By concealing all the facts in the *Greer* case, Roosevelt gained wide public support for his undeclared war in the Atlantic. In the aftermath of the *Greer* incident, German submarines continued to attack U.S. ships. In November Congress revised the Neutrality Act to permit the arming of merchant vessels and to allow them to enter the war zone.

These decisions effectively terminated U.S. neutrality. It was now only a matter of time before naval confrontations would create a crisis similar to that of 1917. Equally portentous, the arming of merchant ships demonstrated that Roosevelt no longer believed that diplomacy could protect U.S. interests. However, Hitler was too involved in the European war and too afraid of U.S. military potential to accept the challenge. Yet ironically the German invasion of the Soviet Union had altered the military situation in Asia, encouraging Japan to make new threats. Hitler opposed Japanese policies that might draw the United States into the war, but the German dictator no more controlled Japanese foreign policy than did Roosevelt.

To Pearl Harbor

Although the United States had protested Japan's invasion of China in 1937 and had extended credit to Chiang Kai-shek, U.S. businesses continued to trade with Japan. In July 1939, however, Roosevelt moved to increase pressure on Tokyo by terminating the U.S.-Japanese trade agreement. Yet the president hesitated to create a crisis. China was not considered important to U.S. interests, especially in light of the German threat to European stability.

The war in Europe nevertheless had important implications for Asia. German victories in western Europe weakened British, French, and Dutch control of their colonial empires in Southeast Asia. To Japan's leaders, those territories offered economic and political opportunities. Believing that national self-sufficiency was essential to Japan's political and cultural survival, Japanese leaders turned to expansion to guarantee access to markets and raw materials such as oil, rubber, and tin. The Japanese military also believed that occupation of areas such as Manchuria in northern China would provide the assets and geopolitical strength to deter outside challenges to their regional ambitions. As Japan's military prepared to enter northern Indochina in the fall of 1940, Roosevelt responded to this threat to European interests by placing an embargo on the sale of aviation gasoline and high-grade scrap iron to Japan. When Japan nevertheless occupied northern Indochina, the president tightened the economic screws by embargoing all iron and steel but permitting the export of certain petroleum products to Japan. By applying pressure through such gradual means, Roosevelt hoped to stop Japanese expansion. Instead, Japan signed a tripartite military assistance pact with Italy and Germany.

Economic pressure led Japan to open diplomatic negotiations with the United States in the spring of 1941, but neither nation was prepared to submit to the other's terms. Adhering to the Open Door policy, Washington insisted that Japan depart from Indochina and China before full trade relations could be restored. In contrast, Japan's pursuit of the Asian Co-Prosperity Sphere prevented acceptance of a policy that would deprive Japan of crucial resources. Japanese leaders refused to leave the Asian mainland under U.S. pressure. While negotiations dragged on, the German invasion of the Soviet Union in June 1941 altered the Asian balance and gave Japan the opportunity to attack Siberia or to move southward into the Malay Peninsula and the Dutch East Indies, both areas rich in oil and rubber. In July 1941 the Japanese invaded southern Indochina, and Roosevelt promptly embargoed oil shipments and froze Japanese assets in the United States, which limited Japan's ability to purchase supplies.

The Japanese now faced a crucial choice. They could either abandon plans for Asian expansion or attempt to seize oil from the British and Dutch colonies. Given the militaristic values of Japanese leaders, the first alternative was unacceptable. The Japanese also realized—and Roosevelt confirmed to the British—that the United States would not tolerate an attack on British possessions in Asia. In other words, further Japanese expansion would mean war with the United States. Even by their own estimates, Japanese military leaders realized that they could not defeat U.S. forces. Yet they also knew that Roosevelt was committed to a "Europe-first" strategy. Faced with the possibility of humiliating surrender in 1941 and U.S. insistence that withdrawal from China precede any

Exhibit 7-4. Japanese Expansion, 1937–1942

1. Panay bombed, Dec. 12, 1937
2. Occupied Feb. 10, 1939
3. Occupied N. Indochina Sept. 22, 1940
4. Occupied S. Indochina July 24, 1941
5. Landings Dec. 8, 1941
6. Landings Dec. 10, 1941
7. Landings Dec. 16, 1941
8. Landings Dec. 20, 1941
9. Landings Dec. 24, 1941
10. Hong Kong falls Dec. 25, 1941
11. Singapore falls Feb. 15, 1942

SOVIET UNION

Sakhalin

Kurile Is. (Jap.)

NORTH PACIFIC OCEAN

Khabarovsk

Karafuto

MONGOLIA

Harbin

MANCHUKUO

Vladivostok

INNER MONGOLIA

Sea of Japan

SINKIANG

Peking

Tientsin

Dairen

Tokyo

JAPANESE EMPIRE

Huang Ho R.

TIBET

CHINA

Nanking

Shanghai

Chungking

Yangtze R.

East China Sea

Foochow

Amoy

Burma Road

INDIA

Canton

③

⑩

SOUTH PACIFIC OCEAN

JAPANESE MANDATE

(Br.) BURMA

Mekong R.

Hanoi

⑥

Rangoon

Hainan

②

Luzon

THAILAND

FRENCH INDOCHINA

Philippine Islands (U.S.)

Marshall Is.

Bangkok

④

Camranh Bay

Kra Isthmus

⑤

Saigon

BR. N. BORNEO

⑨

Mindanao

Yap

⑥

Gilbert Is.

⑧

Palau

Guam (U.S.)

MALAY STATES (Br.)

SARAWAK (Br.) ⑦

Caroline Is. (Japanese Mandate)

Sumatra

⑪

Borneo

New Guinea

Batavia

Celebes

(Austr. Mandate)

INDIAN OCEAN

DUTCH EAST INDIES

Java

Timor (Port.)

PAPUA (Austr.)

0   500   1000

Miles

AUSTRALIA

serious negotiations, the Japanese opted to preserve their pride and gambled on a German victory. By the fall of 1941 U.S. intelligence had broken some of Japan's diplomatic codes. Despite Japan's public affirmation that it sought peace, Washington strongly suspected that war was imminent. Yet where would the attack begin?

On Sunday morning, 7 December 1941, Japanese airplanes targeted U.S. forces at Pearl Harbor. Catching the base by surprise, the Japanese destroyed or damaged 8 battleships, 3 cruisers, and 347 aircraft and inflicted nearly 3,500 U.S. casualties while sustaining minimal losses. The next day, Roosevelt told

Beachhead assaults accounted for most American battle casualties in the Pacific theater of the war. These marines discard their lifejackets as they charge from a landing craft to form a secure line.

a joint session of Congress that a state of war existed and promised to lead the country to "absolute victory." With one dissenting vote by Republican pacifist Jeannette Rankin, Congress promptly issued a formal declaration of war. Three days later, Germany and Italy joined Japan and declared war on the United States, and the same day, 11 December, Congress responded in kind.

THE GRAND ALLIANCE

Four months before the United States entered the war, Roosevelt and Churchill signed the Atlantic Charter on a battleship off Canada's Newfoundland coast. Because Hitler's armies had recently invaded the Soviet Union, Roosevelt hoped to forestall any agreement under which Churchill and Stalin might divide Europe into spheres of influence and thus imperil U.S. foreign trade after the war. According to the charter's provisions, the United States and Britain denied any desire for territorial gain and expressed universal principles of self-determination. The 1941 agreement also asserted the right of all nations to "equal terms to the trade and to the raw materials of the world." Roosevelt and Churchill dramatized this commitment to the Open Door policy by pledging to create a postwar system of collective security to enforce it.

U.S. wartime policy followed similar lines of national interest. Although U.S. public opinion polls showed that a majority wanted prompt vengeance against Japan for attacking Pearl Harbor, the president insisted that Germany represented the greater threat. Yet, even without such a Europe-first military strategy,

Japanese advances put the United States on the defensive in the Pacific. One week after Pearl Harbor, U.S. forces surrendered Guam and, a week after that, capitulated at Wake Island. Japanese forces then moved quickly into the Dutch East Indies, conquered the British naval base at Singapore, and advanced into the Gilbert and Solomon Islands. These setbacks climaxed in the capture of U.S. troops at Corregidor and Bataan in the Philippines—a strategic and psychological blow. The Japanese then compelled U.S. prisoners of war to march fifty-five miles to prison camps, which resulted in thousands of deaths. When confirmed publicly in 1944, such atrocities intensified anger against Japan and justified total warfare against the Japanese people.

Despite the cataclysm at Pearl Harbor, however, the Japanese failed to destroy aircraft carriers and vital shore installations. Within months, the U.S. Navy assembled a fleet that successfully engaged the Japanese during the Battle of the Coral Sea (May 1942) and at Midway (July 1942) and used air power effectively to destroy Japanese aircraft carriers, cruisers, and destroyers. These important victories limited Japanese expansion in the Pacific. By 1943 U.S. forces, backed by Australians and New Zealanders, began to reverse Japanese conquests. In a series of bloody island encounters, U.S. troops drove the Japanese from Guadalcanal in the Solomon Islands (January through February 1943), from Tarawa in the Gilbert Islands (November 1943), and from the Marianas (summer 1944). By February 1945 forces under the command of General Douglas MacArthur fulfilled his 1942 promise, "I shall return," and recaptured the Philippines. However, military confidence in an easy defeat of the Japanese abated suddenly after ferocious combat on the islands of Iwo Jima (where more than 4,000 Americans and 21,000 Japanese were killed) and Okinawa (where more than 11,000 Americans and more than 110,000 Japanese were killed). Such bloodbaths suggested that Japanese soldiers would fight to the death to save Japan's home islands.

Each advance brought U.S. aircraft closer to Japan, and Japanese cities became sitting targets for mass bombardments. As early as 1942, General James Doolittle led an air raid on Tokyo, boosting U.S. morale. By mid-1944 U.S. bombers began attacking strategic targets such as aircraft factories. Weather conditions often prevented accurate targeting, and the incendiary bombs created dreadful firestorms that killed thousands of civilians. Such tactics served both to punish what was perceived as a fanatical enemy and to soften Japan for an amphibious landing after the defeat of Germany.

Meanwhile, in the European theater political considerations proved more subtle. Within the Grand Alliance each nation saw its own national interest as paramount. Reeling under the German advance, the Russians desperately needed Allied assistance and urged the creation of a second front in western Europe. Stalin also wanted a postwar settlement that would protect the Soviet Union from future invasions from central Europe. Churchill was determined to preserve the British colonial empire as well as trade advantages with Commonwealth nations and the Middle East. Roosevelt wanted above all a quick defeat of Germany and Japan with minimal U.S. casualties; politically, he hoped to replace European spheres of influence—whether British or Soviet—with equal access to international trade for all nations.

These differences had important effects on military strategy. While Stalin pleaded for a second front, U.S. generals advised a concentrated buildup of forces in Europe until an invasion of the continent could be mounted. However,

Exhibit 7-5. The War Against Japan, Final Phase, 1944–1945

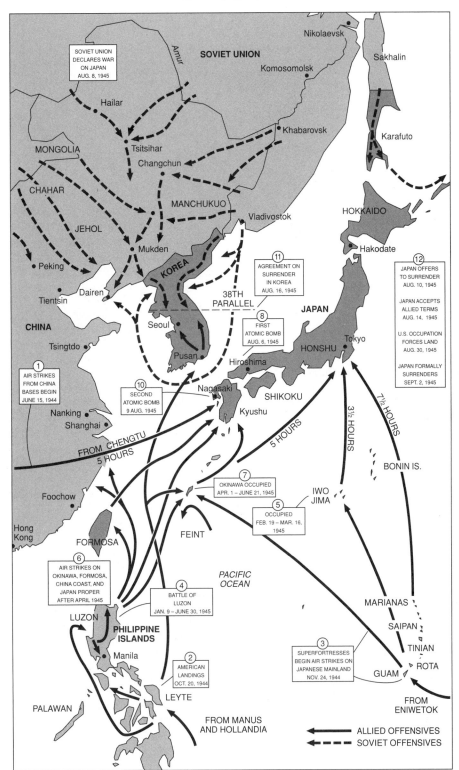

AUDIE MURPHY
1924–1971

Wide World Photos

For Audie Murphy, as for thousands of other young people his age, the formative experiences of his life were the Great Depression of the 1930s and the Great War of the 1940s. One of eleven children born to a family of Texas sharecroppers, Murphy grew up amid tragedy and poverty. As the Dust Bowl destroyed his land, Murphy's father abandoned the family, and his wife, a woman Murphy described as "a sad-eyed, silent woman" who "toiled eternally," died soon after. The family then broke up; the younger children went to an orphanage, and sixteen-year-old Murphy drifted through a series of dead-end jobs. A kid with nothing to lose, Murphy saw World War II as his chance to make something of his life, and he tried to enlist on his eighteenth birthday. The Marine Corps and Army Air Corps rejected him because he was too small, but he finally got a place in the infantry. The new private assured himself that his assignment was only temporary until he could find a more suitable and more daring role as a glider pilot.

Instead, Murphy spent a harrowing two and a half years as a combat infantryman in North Africa, Italy, and France. His most celebrated moment came in February 1945 when he climbed atop a burning tank and turned its machine guns on an advancing wave of German attackers. Holding the position almost single-handedly, Murphy killed about 240 Germans and blunted the assault. His heroics earned him the Medal of Honor and a host of other decorations as well. By the end of the war Murphy had achieved the rank of second lieutenant and was the most decorated U.S. combat veteran. His brief, sparsely written memoir, *To Hell and Back*, attracted attention in Hollywood and became a movie of the same title. Murphy portrayed himself in the film and launched a career in Grade B films in which he usually played a cowboy or a soldier.

The young man who had gone to war seeking glory, however, was acutely aware that he had found very little of it. For him, the reality of war was brutal and inescapable. "I see war as it is," he later wrote, "an endless series of problems involving blood and guts." Of his original company of 235 men, only Murphy and one other man escaped the war without injury. As he later affirmed in his GI catechism, "I believe in the force of a hand grenade, the power of artillery, the accuracy of a Garand. I believe in hitting before you get hit, and that dead men do not look noble." His return to civilian life was marked by the stress and disillusionment a later generation considered unique to Vietnam War veterans. The war had "branded" him, Murphy said, and for years afterward he was unable to sleep at night without a pistol under his pillow. The medals he had won were meaningless to him, and he gave most of them away to children.

Searing as it was, Murphy's experience was atypical for U.S. soldiers of his era. At least in a limited sense, the Roosevelt administration continued the prewar policy of arming others to do its fighting, thus spending U.S. wealth to conserve U.S. lives. Although 16 million men and women served in the armed forces, only one in eight saw combat duty. U.S. casualties were relatively low: 405,000 Americans died in military service, and another 800,000 were wounded. The other belligerents suffered much higher losses, most notably the Soviet Union, which lost 25 million. ∎

Churchill, anxious for any victory and desiring to protect the Mediterranean, persuaded Roosevelt to support an amphibious invasion of North Africa in November 1942. After gaining early victories, U.S. military leaders opted to keep casualties low by accepting a negotiated settlement. General Dwight Eisenhower proceeded to negotiate an armistice with French Admiral Jean Darlan that permitted the pro-Nazi French to remain in power. By allowing Nazi collaborators to go unpunished, the deal outraged the U.S. public, although Darlan was soon assassinated by French patriots.

The successful North African campaign eliminated German threats to Middle Eastern oil, protected shipping in the Mediterranean, and provided a base for the invasion of Italy. Soon afterward, Roosevelt and Churchill met at Casablanca in January 1943 and announced a policy of "unconditional surrender"—partly to divert criticism of the Darlan deal and partly to thwart any secret negotiations between Stalin and Hitler. Military advisers criticized the term "unconditional surrender" because they feared it would harden enemy resistance. However, Roosevelt wanted to demonstrate his sincerity to Stalin despite the delay in implementing the second front. Indeed, although U.S. and British troops suffered light casualties in North Africa, Soviet armies engaged in savage warfare on the eastern front. Long before the Western Allies engaged major German forces, the Russian army had devastated the German military, and the Soviet Union lost more than 25 million people. Still, the United States hoped for Soviet aid in the war against Japan after the defeat of Germany.

U.S. and British forces finally invaded Europe in the summer of 1943. Landing in Sicily and Italy, Allied troops engaged in a series of bloody battles along the Italian coast. Mussolini soon fell from power and was replaced by Marshal Pietro Badoglio, who conditionally surrendered in September 1943. In agreeing to negotiate with Badoglio, U.S. and British leaders recognized his potential importance as an anticommunist force in postwar Italy. Indeed, the Western Allies excluded the Soviet Union from the Allied Control Commission in Italy and answered Stalin's protests by arguing that the Soviet Red Army had not participated in the Italian campaign. This decision became an important precedent for Soviet policy in eastern Europe. Meanwhile, after the surrender of Italian forces, German units entered Italy, where they fought against Allied troops until 1945.

Buoyed by successes in Italy, the Big Three—Roosevelt, Churchill, and Stalin—met at Teheran in November 1943 and agreed to open a second front in France next spring. They also agreed to a temporary division of postwar Germany into zones and prepared to claim reparations for the cost of the war. In addition, Stalin promised to declare war on Japan soon after the German defeat.

As the Allies prepared to invade France in the spring of 1944, U.S. and British aircraft began bombing factories and transportation routes on the European continent, a policy that caused thousands of civilian deaths. Although postwar studies found that these raids barely disrupted German industry, bombing acquired a popular mystique as the ultimate military solution. The air war proved more successful in destroying Germany's air forces and greatly facilitated the Allied landing on the beaches of Normandy on D-Day, 6 June 1944, during the largest amphibious military operation in history. After tough fighting in northern France, the Allies moved eastward, racing to destroy German armies. Meanwhile, the Red Army pressed into Germany from the east, killing or capturing more Germans in the two months after D-Day than were stationed in all of western Europe.

Exhibit 7-6. Western European Theater, 1942–1945

1. Allied landings, North Africa, Nov. 8, 1942
2. Surrender Tunisia, May 13, 1943
3. Allied landings Sicily, July 10, 1943
4. Allied landings Italy, Sept. 9, 1943
5. Italian surrender, Malta, Sept. 29, 1943
6. Allied landings Normandy, June 6, 1944
7. Allied landings southern France, Aug. 15, 1944
8. Paris liberated, Aug. 25, 1944
9. German surrender, Reims, May 7, 1945

As the Allies approached victory in Europe, the Big Three met at Yalta in February 1945 to plan a postwar political settlement. At a time when the defeat of Japan seemed both difficult and remote, Stalin repeated his promise to enter the Pacific theater. This move lessened the importance of China in ending the war. No longer worried about Chinese contributions to the war, Roosevelt and Churchill agreed to compensate the Soviets with the Kurile Islands north of Japan as well as economic rights in Manchuria. The Allies also reaffirmed the temporary partition of Germany, including the division of Berlin into occupied zones. Yet they failed to agree about the amount or the nature of German war reparations.

The main problem at Yalta involved Poland—the country whose defense had triggered World War II in 1939. To protect the Soviet Union's western boundary,

Franklin D. Roosevelt Library

At Yalta, the "Big Three"—(left to right) Prime Minister Winston Churchill, President Franklin Roosevelt, and Soviet Premier Josef Stalin—searched for a consensus on Poland, war reparations, and the United Nations while protecting their separate national interests.

Stalin demanded recognition of territory taken from Poland during his alliance with Hitler from 1939 through 1941. To compensate Poland, Germany would surrender areas of eastern Prussia. Stalin also demanded a friendly Polish government on his vulnerable border, an idea Roosevelt and Churchill reluctantly accepted. However, the Western Allies convinced Stalin to broaden the Polish government to include some Poles who had established a noncommunist government in exile in London and to permit "free and unfettered elections" as soon as possible. Yet in Poland as in Italy, the Allies did not have an equal stake. Roosevelt understood that the Soviet Union would dominate eastern Europe, particularly because the delayed opening of the second front had contributed to the Red Army's exclusive control of the territory east of Germany.

Although the Big Three made major decisions without consulting all the affected nations, Roosevelt believed that an international organization, the United Nations, was essential to keep the peace. As a disillusioned disciple of former president Woodrow Wilson, Roosevelt believed that collective security would be meaningless without the participation of the great powers. Whereas Wilson had envisioned a league of all nations, Roosevelt suggested that "Four Policemen"—the United States, the Soviet Union, Great Britain, and China—

would provide greater stability and called for their permanent seating in what would become the United Nations Security Council. Unlike Wilson, Roosevelt worked to gain bipartisan support for the United Nations in Congress. Indeed, Roosevelt's hope of winning congressional approval of the United Nations led him to conceal the pro-Soviet Polish settlement, which he knew would be unpopular. By the end of World War II public opinion strongly supported U.S. leadership in the United Nations. Plans for the international organization were first drafted at the Dumbarton Oaks Conference in Washington in 1944. The new international league included a Security Council in which each of the Big Four held veto power. By assuring no infringement of U.S. sovereignty, this power helped win congressional support of the United Nations.

Roosevelt's vision of the postwar world reflected not only the realities of military power but also his view of U.S. self-interest. As a proponent of free international trade, he opposed returning Indochina to France and expected Britain to move toward decolonization. Yet the defeat of Japan would create a power vacuum in Asia. To assure stability, Roosevelt envisioned the rise of an independent China free from European imperialism and strong enough to provide a buffer against the Soviet Union. In elevating China to a world power, Roosevelt exaggerated the role of Chiang Kai-shek as a force for national unity. Numerous U.S. diplomats in China had condemned the ineptitude of Chiang's regime and had stressed the importance of creating a coalition government with Chinese communists. However, Roosevelt distrusted the State Department bureaucracy and rejected this advice. His decision assured the continuation of the civil war that had raged in China since the 1920s. Roosevelt's dislike of diplomatic formalities also undermined his plans for decolonization. His unwillingness to issue clear directives about Indochina, for example, gave his subordinates no guidelines for future policy. These omissions assumed critical importance when Roosevelt died suddenly on 12 April 1945.

WARTIME MOBILIZATION

"If you...go to war...in a capitalist country," said Secretary of War Henry Stimson, "you have to let business make money out of the process or business won't work." For more than a decade before Pearl Harbor, the U.S. economy had languished in Depression conditions, but the nation possessed a mighty industrial potential that soon exceeded all expectations. Once war began, a convenient marriage between government and business achieved magnificent results. One year after Pearl Harbor, the United States was producing more war materiel than all its enemies combined. With 1943 levels of production, replacing all the aircraft lost at Pearl Harbor would take only two days. Such achievements helped restore public confidence in U.S. business and undermined Depression-era critics who doubted that capitalism could survive without major changes. In turn, corporate leaders learned to appreciate the advantages of cooperation with the federal government. Indeed, Washington provided two-thirds of the $26 billion spent on wartime plants and equipment.

Although Roosevelt had recognized the importance of preparing industry for war as early as 1938, his administration had not adopted a development plan or delegated authority to a single commission. In 1939 the president ap-

Exhibit 7-7. National Defense Spending, 1941–1945
(in rounded billions of dollars)

1941	14.0
1943	78.9
1945	95.2

Source: *Historical Statistics of the United States, Colonial Times to 1970* (1975).

Exhibit 7-8. Gross National Product, 1941–1945
(in rounded billions of dollars)

1941	124.5
1943	191.6
1945	211.9

Source: *Historical Statistics of the United States, Colonial Times to 1970* (1975).

Exhibit 7-9. Individual Income Tax Paid, 1940–1943
(in rounded billions of dollars)

1940	1.4
1941	3.8
1942	8.8
1943	14.4

Source: *Historical Statistics of the United States, Colonial Times to 1970* (1975).

pointed a War Resources Board, but noninterventionist opinion prompted him to ignore its report. Other bureaucracies followed: an Advisory Commission for National Defense, which was later replaced by the Office of Production Management; the Office of Price Administration, which supervised price controls; and the Supply Priorities and Allocations Board, which dealt with problems of industrial conversion. These agencies started moving the economy toward wartime production. During 1941 arms manufacturing increased 225 percent.

Roosevelt's efforts to administer the wartime economy mirrored the improvisational strategy of the New Deal. After Pearl Harbor, the president created the War Production Board (WPB), which set production goals and priorities for the allocation of natural resources and raw materials. Other administrative decisions involved coordinating supplies for the civilian economy, the military, and Lend-Lease. Amid considerable bureaucratic struggling, the military managed to bypass civilian oversight of procurement and obtained control of supply purchases, which created relationships between the Pentagon and private business that endured into the postwar era. Meanwhile, Lend-Lease accounted for nearly $50 billion in materiel shipped overseas (60 percent to Britain; 20 percent to the Soviet Union; the rest to other countries).

In developing the war economy, the Roosevelt administration had to convince private business to set aside peacetime production. Many industrialists feared that conversion to war-related manufacturing would cause overproduction, leading to a postwar depression. Others were reluctant to abandon

**Exhibit 7-10. Federal Budget Deficits, 1940–1945
(in rounded billions of dollars)**

1940	2.9
1945	47.6

Source: *Economic Report of the President* (1988).

civilian-oriented production that was stimulated by wartime jobs and consumer spending. To win business confidence, the White House appointed corporate leaders to "dollar-a-year" positions on the War Production Board and other agencies and encouraged administrators to adopt policies that would reduce the risks associated with conversion to a wartime economy.

Headed by Donald M. Nelson of Sears, Roebuck, the War Production Board awarded $175 billion in "cost-plus" contracts that guaranteed fixed profits. The federal government also financed some $800 million a year in private research and development programs at businesses and universities. More than fifty firms and schools received contracts worth $1 million or more. Government funds supported expensive technological projects at Cal Tech's Jet Propulsion Laboratory as well as the top-secret atomic energy programs at Los Alamos, New Mexico; Hanford, Washington; and Oak Ridge, Tennessee. Wartime scientists and engineers in government-funded university research laboratories achieved breakthroughs in electronic digital computing that would lay the foundation for an enormous postwar industry.

Government policy also encouraged industrial mobilization by abandoning antitrust actions against war-related businesses and offering contractors generous tax deductions. Under a five-year amortization plan, defense contractors were allowed to take possession of commercial assets leased from the government and were awarded tax write-offs for expenses incurred in reconverting the property to civilian production. Moreover, wartime excess profits collected by the Internal Revenue Service were returned to companies to defray reconversion costs. Such subsidies amounted to the greatest capital expansion in U.S. history and provided the foundation for economic growth in the postwar era.

Wartime production and investment policies generally favored big businesses over small firms. For example, two-thirds of military contracts went to just one hundred companies. Large corporations had greater access to government agencies and more experience with extensive procurement contracts. Although the Roosevelt administration responded to complaints by creating the Smaller War Plants Corporation, the government's primary objective remained maximum industrial efficiency. During World War II, industrial production increased 96 percent, while net corporate profits doubled. Equally important, half a million small businesses disappeared, some of them absorbed by 1,600 corporate mergers.

The war inevitably demanded tremendous quantities of natural resources such as petroleum. One armored battalion, for example, used 17,000 gallons of gasoline to move one hundred miles; the Fifth Fleet consumed 630 million gallons of oil in less than two months. The U.S. oil industry was prepared to meet these huge demands in return for protection from government interference, including immunity from antitrust suits, and a dominant voice in national oil policy making. Petroleum corporations also expanded production in the Middle East to lessen the drain on domestic oil reserves. This decision required direct government support such as Lend-Lease aid to Saudi Arabia to keep British companies from challenging U.S. development. The State Department also backed private efforts to penetrate British and Soviet control of oil in Iran. Such government assistance stimulated the industry to produce 6 billion barrels of oil during the war. However, postwar petroleum policy, including increasing dependence on foreign oil, remained in private hands.

MOBILIZING LABOR

Ending a decade of work shortages, the wartime economy set the work force in motion. Between 1940 and 1947, 25 million people (21 percent of the population) left home for another county or state. Most dramatic was the surge in westward migration. As the federal government invested $70 billion in wartime industries in the West, 7 million Americans moved across the Mississippi, half of them going to the Pacific Coast. California gained 3.5 million residents during the 1940s. The search for wartime jobs drew 750,000 African Americans from their home states in the South, reducing the region's share of the black population from 77 percent to 68 percent. Some 340,000 African Americans moved to California. Meanwhile, 25,000 Native Americans left their reservations for military service, while another 40,000 found war-related work. This remarkable movement permanently changed the character of all regions.

The sheer number of new jobs effectively ended the Great Depression. Although 8 million workers (17 percent of the labor force) remained unemployed in 1939, the wartime economy soon absorbed the active work force. By 1942 other previously unemployable workers—teenagers, the elderly, minorities, and women—also began to find work. The armed services absorbed 15 million men and women. Another 7 million found jobs on the home front.

Despite wartime urgency, however, opportunities for better jobs encouraged frequent worker turnover and shortages in crucial industries. To oversee such problems, Roosevelt created a War Manpower Commission, but the agency lacked enforcement powers, and absenteeism and job mobility remained common. In 1944 the turnover rate in manufacturing industries was 82 percent. As in the Depression, however, disruptions in the labor force were more than offset by time-saving machinery that increased individual productivity. The Department of Agriculture estimated that farm productivity increased 25 percent per work hour between 1939 and 1945 because of mechanization, land consolidation, and increased use of chemical fertilizers. In the Southwest the need for

Exhibit 7-11. Civilian Unemployment Rates, 1939–1945

1939	17.2%
1941	9.9%
1943	1.9%
1945	1.9%

Source: *Historical Statistics of the United States, Colonial Times to 1970* (1975).

farm and railroad workers led the government to negotiate with Mexico to recruit contract laborers. This "bracero" program brought the United States more than 200,000 Mexicans, who accepted low wages for temporary work.

The shortage of labor also provided opportunities for people who had been underrepresented in the work force. African American agricultural workers, for example, displaced by farm machines or seeking better jobs, moved in great numbers to urban centers. Yet as the war began, many still confronted racial discrimination in employment, even in government programs and within the armed services. "While we are in complete sympathy with the Negro," declared the president of North American Aviation in a typical statement, "it is against company policy to employ them as aircraft workers or mechanics . . . regardless of their training. . . . There will be some jobs as janitors for Negroes."

Challenging such discrimination, A. Philip Randolph, president of the Brotherhood of Sleeping Car Porters, called for a protest march on Washington in 1941. The proposal deeply embarrassed the president and forced Roosevelt to issue Executive Order 8802 in June 1941 prohibiting job discrimination in war industries and creating a Fair Employment Practices Committee to investigate complaints. Throughout the war years, the FEPC successfully challenged numerous cases of racial discrimination. Yet Roosevelt worried about antagonizing southern Democrats in Congress and the military and therefore declined to order the desegregation of the armed services, government departments, or labor unions. The California Supreme Court finally outlawed segregated unions in 1945, but West Coast African Americans continued to encounter racial restrictions in housing and public accommodations. Despite these disadvantages, some 2 million blacks eventually found work in war industries.

The labor crisis also catapulted women into new jobs. Although women constituted 25 percent of the prewar work force, middle-class opinion disapproved of working women. Even as the nation prepared for war, private contractors often refused to hire women. To encourage women's employment, the Office of War Information supported a domestic propaganda campaign to make women's work appear patriotic. Most women worked because they needed the wages and appreciated the opportunity to take better-paying jobs normally reserved for men. A considerable proportion of black women also moved from domestic to industrial occupations, although they remained in the lowest wage brackets. Between 1941 and 1945 6.5 million women entered the labor force, a 57 percent increase. By the war's end 36 percent of all civilian workers were women.

Although women were entitled to the same pay as men for the same work, employers routinely ignored such rules. Most women earned no more than the minimum wage and were usually excluded from management positions. Businesses also preferred to segregate women into "female" jobs, which paid less than "male" jobs. These practices reflected the prevailing belief that war work was temporary, intended not to encourage women's economic independence, much less accelerate their working careers, but simply to support the men at war. Although a government survey showed that 75 percent of women wished to retain their jobs, business and union leaders agreed that women should give up their jobs to returning veterans. "Americans may no longer believe that a woman's place is in the home," sociologist Jerome Bruner observed, "but more important, we believe even less that a man's place is on the street without a job."

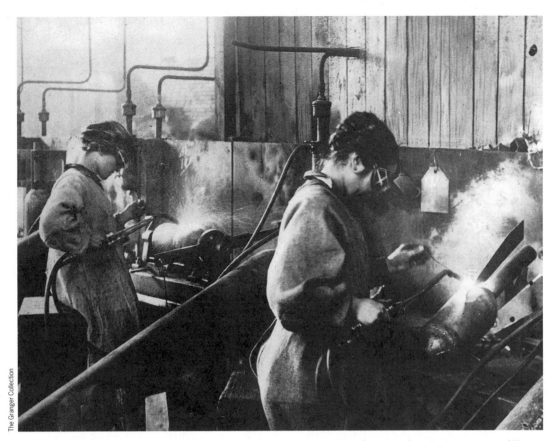

The Granger Collection

The war economy opened new vistas for women and minorities, even in munitions factories, where these women are welding bomb casings.

Taking advantage of pervasive worker shortages, organized labor aggressively enrolled new union members. Between 1939 and 1945 union membership nearly doubled, and unions claimed 15 million organized workers. The number of women union workers quadrupled to 3 million by 1944. After the Japanese attack on Pearl Harbor, labor unions adopted a "no-strike" policy but continued to press for higher wages. To deal with labor disputes, Roosevelt created new government agencies that regulated wages, hours, and working conditions. The National War Labor Board attempted to control wage inflation by establishing a cost-of-living standard, but wage limits did not apply to overtime work. Although hourly wages increased 24 percent during the war, weekly earnings rose 70 percent. In exchange for the no-strike agreement and wage limits, organized labor accepted a "maintenance of membership" arrangement that encouraged workers to join unions.

Despite these gains, numerous unauthorized "wildcat" strikes occurred, even in war industries, and affected 3 million workers in 1943. A strike among the nation's coal miners that year threatened the entire economy. Such walkouts intensified antilabor sentiment. In 1943 Congress responded by passing, over Roosevelt's veto, the Smith-Connally Labor Act, which imposed a thirty-day cooling off period before workers could go on strike, prohibited strikes in war

ASA PHILIP RANDOLPH
1889–1979

Stock Montage

A. Philip Randolph, a dignified and soft-spoken man who served as president of a small union of sleeping car porters, ranked as the nation's single most important black leader of the 1930s and 1940s. By 1941 Randolph's efforts to build a mass movement of black working people elicited the first federal proclamation concerning African Americans since the Civil War.

Born in Jacksonville, Florida, Randolph departed on a steamboat for New York City in 1911. A devout follower of civil rights advocate W.E.B. Du Bois, Randolph believed himself to be among the "talented tenth" of African Americans that Du Bois had described. Randolph took night classes at City College and gravitated toward socialism. In 1915 he helped to launch the *Messenger*, a radical black magazine that opposed participation in World War I until African Americans achieved equality at home. These efforts resulted in his questioning by the Justice Department for violations of the Espionage Act.

Randolph's career took a new direction when black railroad porters asked him to organize a union in 1925. Ever since Emancipation the Pullman Company had hired black men only as porters, believing that subservient and congenial former slaves would accept insults and demands from white passengers. Pullman was the largest private employer of blacks in the nation, and Randolph hoped to show that his people could build and sustain an organization to pursue their own economic survival without permitting whites to choose their leaders. The Brotherhood of Sleeping Car Porters organized half the Pullman porters and maids within three years and won higher monthly salaries, respectful treatment, and an end to demeaning tipping.

Randolph's success catapulted him into national black leadership in the 1930s. As president of the National Negro Congress, he called for a "new deal" for the nation's "submerged tenth" and urged African Americans to join the burgeoning union movement. Randolph reasoned that black struggles for social

industries, and banned union contributions to political parties. Despite such hostility toward organized labor, U.S. workers participated in nearly 10,000 spontaneous walkouts between 1944 and 1945.

THE HOME FRONT

With business booming and workers bringing home big paychecks, the economy faced the risk of runaway inflation. In 1942 the Office of Price Administration froze most consumer prices, based on March 1942 levels. However, food prices continued to climb. Congress then passed the Anti-Inflation Act of 1942, which regulated agricultural prices and wages and stabilized the economy. During the last two years of the war, consumer prices increased by less than 2 percent.

justice paralleled the efforts of white workers and liberal allies. Yet he also pointed out that "the salvation of the Negro, like [that of] the workers, must come from within." Accordingly, when the Roosevelt administration failed to heed protests against racial discrimination in government and defense jobs, Randolph prepared to lead a march of 100,000 black working people to the capital in 1941. "Power and pressure," he told the nation's civil rights organizations, "are at the foundation of the march of social justice and reform."

Despite pleas for restraint from white liberals such as Eleanor Roosevelt and New York City Mayor Fiorello La Guardia, Randolph insisted that "there are some things Negroes must do alone." His strategy worked brilliantly. When Roosevelt summoned the black leader to the White House in June 1941, the president asked whether Randolph could actually deliver the 100,000 protestors he promised. Looking the chief executive straight in the eye, Randolph calmly answered that he could assure a huge turnout. The polite and measured confrontation marked one of the few times that the master politician in the White House had ever been out-bluffed. One week before the scheduled demonstration Roosevelt agreed to issue Executive Order 8802, which forbade discrimination in government-related hiring and created a Fair Employment Practices Committee. Randolph considered the president's actions a substantial gain and called off the march.

African Americans understood the government's desire to maintain racial harmony at home in contrast to Nazi Germany's espousal of Aryan supremacy and other racial ideologies. Yet, although Executive Order 8802 represented the most dramatic gesture that Washington had ever made on behalf of black citizens, enforcement proved to be no easy task because of war mobilization and the Roosevelt administration's dependence on southern political allies. Randolph also faced disappointment when his hopes of engaging the African American masses in a permanent March on Washington movement foundered because of disunity and organizational jealousy. Nevertheless, he helped lay the foundations of the postwar civil rights revolution by popularizing the concept of mass demonstrations led and organized by blacks. Twenty-two years later he saw the fruits of his pioneering efforts when he introduced Martin Luther King, Jr., to a crowd of 250,000 during the celebrated 1963 March on Washington. From Du Bois to King, A. Philip Randolph's remarkable career helped provide continuity in African American leadership in the twentieth century. ∎

The government also instituted a rationing program for scarce materials such as canned goods (because of tin shortages), rubber, gasoline, coffee, shoes, sugar, meat, butter, and fuel oil. Rationing programs forced consumers to accept these government regulations. Most saw personal sacrifices as part of the patriotic war effort, although people with cash could often circumvent the rules in an illegal black market. The government also organized scrap campaigns to collect used goods such as old tires and tin cans. These community drives

Exhibit 7-12. Consumer Price Index, 1941–1945
(1967 = 100)

1941	44.1
1943	51.8
1945	53.9

Source: *Historical Statistics of the United States, Colonial Times to 1970* (1975).

People of all ages and from diverse ethnic backgrounds supported the war effort by buying United States defense bonds.

UPI/Corbis-Bettmann

served both patriotic and practical purposes. Even more effective were mass campaigns sparked by Hollywood celebrities to encourage the public to buy war bonds. Through payroll deduction plans and bond drives, bond sales reached $135 billion, $40 billion of which was purchased by small investors. Bond sales also discouraged inflation by absorbing consumer dollars.

During the four years of war, the federal government spent $321 billion, ten times as much as World War I cost. Taxation financed more than 40 percent of the total bill (and further reduced consumer purchasing power). The Revenue Act of 1942 both increased tax rates and broadened the tax base to include

Exhibit 7-13. Gross Federal Debt, 1939–1945
(in rounded billions of dollars)

1939	48
1941	57
1943	143
1945	260

Source: *Economic Report of the President* (1996).

lower-income workers for the first time. The measure increased corporate taxes to 40 percent and raised excess profits taxes to 90 percent, although loopholes and generous legal interpretations frequently lowered these rates in practice. The law also instituted the payroll withholding tax to keep dollars out of consumers' hands. Taxes on high personal income and excess profits produced a substantial although temporary redistribution of personal income. The top 5 percent income bracket declined in relative economic worth as its control of disposable income diminished. At the same time, full employment and the increase in two-income families brought greater purchasing power to poorer people. The number of families earning less than $2,000 a year was halved, whereas the number of those making more than $5,000 a year increased fourfold.

Commodity shortages and rationing also cut across class lines: people with money could not always find what they wanted to buy. In 1942, for example, the government ordered the automobile industry to stop making cars and light trucks and switch to manufacturing tanks and airplanes. Additional income thus went into personal savings accounts, which would later provide the capital for heavy postwar consumer spending. Wartime advertising also directed attention from shortages to postwar opportunities. "Ordnance Today, Washers Tomorrow," boasted the Easy Washing Machine Company. The Cessna Aircraft Company predicted that the "Family Car of the Air" would enable weekend golfers to tee off 500 miles from home "after the war."

Without available consumer goods, people with money to spend shopped for entertainment. By 1945 Hollywood movie attendance reached 80 million customers a week. The government's Office of War Information, using the power to censor overseas screenings, supported prowar movies while eliminating unfavorable portrayals of the U.S. war effort. One successful collaboration was Frank Capra's documentary *Why We Fight* series, which disseminated an official version of the war effort. The political content of Hollywood movies appeared blatantly patriotic—celebrating U.S. allies, deprecating the enemy, and inspiring sacrifices on the home front. War films—*Sahara* (1942) and *Lifeboat* (1944), for example—depicted U.S. soldiers in a melting pot of nationalities. Innumerable movies presented the "ethnic" platoon, stressing the contributions of white ethnics and nonwhite minorities in combat roles. A series of movies—*Mission to Moscow* (1943), *The North Star* (1943), and *Song of Russia* (1944)—praised the heroism of the Soviet people. Yet in *Casablanca* (1943), Humphrey Bogart starred as a nonideological individualist who comes to see the war as a unifying struggle for common decency. Hollywood not only reinforced morale at home but provided the nation's fighting forces with personal appearances by performers and with screenings throughout the world.

Popular images of U.S. enemies paralleled the course of the war. In 1942 600,000 Italian Americans had not become naturalized citizens and legally were "enemy aliens," but only a few suspected fascists were arrested for the duration of the war. Roosevelt, aware of the ethnic antagonism of World War I, hoped to reduce racist hysteria against white ethnics. He also appreciated the power of the Italian vote in the 1942 congressional elections. On Columbus Day, therefore, the president revoked the enemy alien status of most Italian Americans and eased procedures for naturalization. In a similar election situation in 1944, Roosevelt announced both a loan and relief supplies for the defeated Italian enemy, now viewed as an ally against the German occupiers. The desire to

To inspire support on the home front, this 1942 poster exaggerated the danger of enemy attacks on civilian property.

differentiate between the Italian people and Italy's fascist government emerged clearly in Hollywood films. In *Sahara*, for example, an Italian prisoner was described contemptuously as a "pot of spaghetti," but the film also suggested that loyal Italian Americans had manufactured the steel for U.S. tanks. "Italians are not Germans," the film concluded; the fascist uniform covered only the body, not the soul. Such notions helped prepare the public for the relatively lenient treatment of Italy in 1943.

In contrast, the mass media portrayed Nazis and Japanese as ruthless barbarians. Because the Roosevelt administration played down anti-German feeling, the mass media distinguished between Nazis and other Germans. "They despise the world of civilians," said *Life* magazine of the German military. "They wear monocles to train themselves to control their face muscles." Hollywood used such stereotypes to scoff at Nazi stupidity, a recurring screen phenomenon that addressed wartime anxieties by encouraging audiences to laugh at the world conquerors. Depictions of the Japanese were utterly humorless. Partly because of the anger aroused by Japanese atrocities and partly because of anti-Asian racism, movies and advertisements portrayed this enemy as subhuman. In dehumanizing the Japanese, however, the mass media took pains to distinguish between them and friendly Asian peoples, especially the Chinese and Filipinos. Hereafter, not all Asians would be lumped together as "Orientals."

POLITICS IN WARTIME

Although the popular media emphasized national unity and ethnic cooperation, political disagreements undermined Roosevelt's search for consensus, especially after the 1942 elections increased conservative strength in Congress. This conservative majority proceeded to dismantle such New Deal agencies as the Civilian Conservation Corps, the National Youth Administration, and the Works Progress Administration. At a December 1943 press conference, Roosevelt announced what he could not prevent: "Dr. New Deal" had been replaced by "Dr. Win the War." By 1945 federal spending had leaped nearly ten times above prewar levels to $95 billion, and the number of civilian employees in the federal government had tripled to more than 4 million. After numerous investigations, Congress attempted to reverse government growth by limiting Office of Price Administration spending and by abolishing the National Resources Planning Board, an executive bureau that supported deficit spending to fund a postwar social welfare state.

Despite his difficulties with Congress, the president continued to hope for postwar reform. In January 1944 Roosevelt proposed an economic "bill of rights," arguing that the nation could not "be content if some fraction of our people . . . is ill-fed, ill-clothed, ill-housed and insecure." The president also demanded legislation for liberal veterans' benefits. By 1944 about 1 million veterans had returned from the armed services, many of them injured or otherwise unable to adjust to civilian life. Congress responded by enacting the Servicemen's Readjustment Act, known as the "GI Bill of Rights," a landmark measure that provided unemployment, Social Security, and educational benefits to veterans. By providing college scholarships, home loans, and life insurance, the GI Bill reintegrated veterans into civilian society and helped stimulate postwar prosperity by increasing their purchasing power.

Roosevelt's problems with conservatives dominated the 1944 presidential election. Vice President Henry A. Wallace, an outspoken liberal, had offended regular party bosses as well as southern Democrats. Roosevelt prudently dropped Wallace and chose Senator Harry S Truman of Missouri as his running mate. Truman had gained popularity as chairman of the Senate War Investigating Committee, which had exposed government waste and war profiteering.

President Franklin Delano Roosevelt, famous for his soothing radio oratory, raises a hand to test the political winds during his successful 1944 campaign for an unprecedented fourth term.

With the popular conservative Robert A. Taft of Ohio running for reelection to the Senate, the Republicans turned to Governor Thomas E. Dewey of New York, often identified with the party's Wall Street wing, to challenge Roosevelt's bid for a fourth term. Dewey endorsed a bipartisan foreign policy, including a postwar United Nations, and accepted such New Deal programs as Social Security, unemployment benefits, and collective bargaining. In the election the Democrats benefited from the campaign support of the Congress of Industrial Organizations' Political Action Committee, which brought out the labor vote. This urban electorate provided Roosevelt's margin of victory. Although the president's popular vote slipped below 54 percent of the total, Roosevelt took advantage of the wartime mood of crisis to win an unprecedented fourth term.

BATTLES ON THE HOME FRONT

Roosevelt's efforts to minimize political disturbances nevertheless accentuated important divisions in U.S. political and cultural life. Concerned about threats to national security from pro-Nazi, profascist, and procommunist groups, the

White House approved an FBI domestic intelligence program that violated traditional civil liberties, arranged for the possible arrest of so-called subversives, and permitted the military to discriminate against political radicals. The Roosevelt administration also engineered a "Brown Scare" to preserve the "free world" from Nazi subversion. Roosevelt pressed the Catholic hierarchy to silence the acerbic anti-Semitic broadcasts of radio priest Father Charles Coughlin. The Department of Justice mounted a mass sedition trial and accused thirty defendants of conspiring with the Third Reich to undermine the loyalty of the armed forces. Yet the proceedings were marred by insufficient evidence and ended in an embarrassing mistrial in 1944. Although the Soviet Union fought as an ally, the government suspected—correctly in some cases—that communist sympathizers were working with spies to acquire military and diplomatic secrets. Making no distinctions between criminal activities and political dissidence, the FBI and the military treated all communists as dangerous, which laid the foundation for the postwar "Red Scare."

Government indifference to civil rights in wartime appeared most blatantly in the arrest of more than 110,000 West Coast Japanese Americans. Alarmed by Pearl Harbor and Japanese victories in the Pacific, journalists falsely reported that California Japanese had conspired with the Japanese enemy and planned further subversion at home. When none occurred, California Attorney General Earl Warren used this demonstrable loyalty as counterproof: "We are just being lulled into a false sense of security," he told a congressional committee, "and the only reason we haven't had disaster in California is because it has been timed for a different date." Racism played a large role in this disregard for Japanese American civil rights. "It's a question of whether the white man lives on the Pacific or a brown man," admitted one farmer anxious to get rid of Japanese American competition. The commanding general of the area, John DeWitt, offered a simple explanation: "A Jap's a Jap.... It makes no difference if he is an American citizen." However, the army assumed that the 150,000 Japanese Americans in Hawaii, so necessary to the islands' wartime economy, were loyal and need not be detained or removed.

Roosevelt shared this distrust of Japanese Americans. In 1942 he issued Executive Order 9066, which required the internment and relocation of all Japanese in the region. Two-thirds of the affected people were U.S. citizens by birth (under the Naturalization Act of 1924, Japanese immigrants were barred from citizenship). Many second-generation Japanese Americans, or Nisei, wished to prove their loyalty by complying with the order. Others protested vigorously: "Has the Gestapo come to America? Have we not risen in righteous anger at Hitler's mistreatment of the Jews? Then, is it not incongruous that citizen Americans of Japanese descent should be similarly mistreated and persecuted?"

Forced to sell their property at short notice—usually to unscrupulous buyers—the Japanese were herded into detention centers and then relocated into ten concentration camps in remote, often bleak parts of the country. Despite serious constitutional questions concerning the rights of citizens, the American Civil Liberties Union hesitated to defend the Japanese. Moreover, government officials conspired to present tainted evidence to the Supreme Court, which in the *Korematsu* case of 1944 upheld the relocation on grounds of military necessity. In the *Endo* decision, however, the court ruled that citizens could not be detained once their loyalty had been established. By then the Roosevelt administration understood that incarceration was no longer necessary. Yet the

Presidential Executive Order 9066 required all Japanese Americans, including U.S. citizens such as this family, to evacuate their homes and move into concentration camps, where they lived under armed guard.

president delayed closing the concentration camps for five months because he feared that release of Japanese American prisoners might hurt his reelection bid in 1944. Litigation would continue into the 1980s, when surviving Japanese American prisoners received economic compensation from the federal government for a wartime loss of $400 million in property. Despite these abuses of government power, 18,000 Nisei volunteered for military service and fought heroically in a segregated unit in the European theater of war. However, several thousand Japanese Americans, angered by their treatment, disavowed U.S. citizenship and returned to Japan after the war.

In contrast to the internment program, the desire for national unity enabled African Americans to challenge racial prejudice. Whereas the theme for blacks in World War I had been W.E.B. Du Bois's summons to "close ranks," African American leaders in World War II launched a "Double V" campaign: "Declarations of war do not lessen the obligation to preserve and extend civil liberties" at home. Randolph's March on Washington movement did not disband but persisted as an all-black, mass pressure group. Meanwhile, the NAACP increased its membership ninefold to 450,000 during the war. In 1942 nonviolence advocate James Farmer founded the Congress of Racial Equality (CORE), which used sit-ins to desegregate public facilities in Chicago and Washington, D.C. "Not since Reconstruction," concluded Gunnar Myrdal's massive study of racism, *An American Dilemma* (1944), "has there been more reason to anticipate fundamental changes in American race relations."

Changes came slower than Myrdal predicted. In the military, African Americans, like Japanese Americans, served in segregated units, and the Red Cross separated "colored" blood from "white." (Ironically, a black physician, Charles Drew, had originally developed blood transfusion techniques.) Military policy, explained one general, "is simply transferring discrimination from everyday life into the Army." Believing that African Americans were too docile to make good soldiers, the army initially assigned blacks to labor units and denied them the opportunity for promotion and prestigious duties such as flying. Moreover, despite proven battlefield valor, no African Americans received Medals of Honor during World War II (although in 1997 President Bill Clinton belatedly awarded the nation's highest military honor to seven African American heroes of that war). To their humiliation, black soldiers discovered that Nazi prisoners of war could use public eating facilities in places where African American soldiers in uniform were denied service. Such treatment did not go unchallenged in the military. Numerous race riots occurred both on and off base, and in one notorious case, the black athlete Jackie Robinson was court-martialed—and acquitted—for refusing to sit in the back of a bus.

African Americans on the home front also faced racist attitudes. A public opinion poll taken at the beginning of the war found that 18 percent of blacks admitted pro-Japanese feelings; in a similar poll, when asked to choose between complete racial equality or a German victory, the vast majority of southern white industrialists preferred a Nazi victory. Similar sentiments emerged in the North. In 1942 white crowds rioted in Detroit to prevent blacks from living in a federally funded housing project. Whites also initiated "hate" strikes to protest the entry of blacks into factories and shipyards. In 1943 Detroit exploded in a two-day riot that left 35 dead and more than 700 injured. In Philadelphia, trolley car workers went on strike to protest integration and forced the federal government to send armed troops to break the strike. During the war major race riots also occurred in Texas, Ohio, Massachusetts, and New York City.

Despite these conflicts, World War II represented an ideological turning point in U.S. race relations. The repudiation of Nazi racism, reinforced at the war's end by the discovery of the infamous death camps, challenged all racist assumptions. In 1943 the American Bar Association admitted its first black member. That year Congress passed legislation accepting Chinese immigration and naturalization, a reversal of racial exclusion policies established in 1882. In 1944 the Supreme Court overturned the white primary, which had served to disenfranchise black voters in most southern states. In Hollywood movies, the Sambo stereotypes of the 1930s were replaced by serious depictions of African Americans, and Chinese were shown as responsible allies. Within the military, moreover, religious chaplains of diverse faiths cooperated in providing spiritual care for soldiers, stressing interfaith toleration. These precedents provided a solid bedrock for civil rights movements of the postwar era.

Just ten years before Pearl Harbor, the Supreme Court referred to the country as a "Christian nation." Although Roosevelt had appointed many Jews to important positions in government before the war, Jewish Americans faced open prejudice in business, social life, and education. Immigration laws established quotas that discriminated against Jews even when Jewish refugees from Nazi persecution faced death as the only alternative. Despite growing evidence that Germans were systematically destroying European Jews as well as other "undesirables" such as gypsies and homosexuals, Roosevelt did not move to facilitate the admission of Jewish refugees from Europe until 1944.

Complacency about Nazi treatment of Jews ended abruptly with revelations of the European Holocaust in 1945. Images of Nazi concentration camps—the emaciated look of survivors, the piles of dead and naked victims, the sickening display of mountains of human hair, eyeglasses, shoes—demonstrated the full horror of racism and modern war. This massive evil defied easy explanation. In 1945 most citizens recognized that the nation had reached a watershed in racial attitudes. Nazi anti-Semitism undermined U.S. anti-Semitism and discredited all public assertions of racial "inferiority." To be sure, racial prejudice did not disappear from the land, but no longer did public racist assertions seem acceptable, at least against whites.

Other forms of ethnic antagonism endured. Spanish-speaking, brown-skinned Mexican Americans of the Southwest and southern California continued to face segregated housing, higher unemployment, and lower wages. "Why teach them to read and write and spell?" a Los Angeles elementary school principal remarked in a typical dismissal; "they'll only pick beets anyway." Although most Mexican Americans lacked familiarity with such government agencies as the Fair Employment Practices Committee, middle-class activists in the League of United Latin American Citizens saw the war as an opportunity to advance civil rights for their constituents. Adopting the slogan "Americans All," a new generation of Mexican American leaders identified with the democratic aspirations of their adopted country and discarded old attachments to Mexico. In similar fashion, thirty Native American tribes organized into the National Congress of American Indians in 1944.

During the war, younger Mexican Americans formed teenage *pachuco* gangs and dressed in lavish outfits known as "zoot suits." Such costumes, like teenage slang and music, offered a visible protest against conformity to white standards. "The zoot suit was not a costume or uniform from the world of entertainment," explained Harold Fox, the Chicago retailer who first introduced the fashion. "It came right off the street and out of the ghetto." Yet in July 1943 rumors that *pachucos* had beaten a sailor provoked a four-day race riot in Los Angeles as white servicemen raided the barrios, attacked zoot suiters, and stripped them of their clothing. The fiasco showed that Mexican Americans, like Japanese Americans, lacked the power to defend their communities. Yet Mexican American and African American youth—including the young Malcolm X—continued to wear zoot suits to assert their cultural independence.

Hostility toward the zoot suiters revealed not only the problem of ethnic antagonism but also a more general anxiety about the nation's youth. As opportunities in the work force improved, educators noted a simultaneous increase in teenage runaways, truancy, and high school dropouts. Police reported a dramatic rise in teenage sexual crimes. Such trends paralleled an increase in teenage marriages, the tendency for adolescents to "go steady" at a younger age, and the finding that more younger women were becoming sexually active. Indeed, sex researcher Alfred Kinsey found that infidelity increased in only one

Wide World Photos

Racial tensions between military personnel and Mexican Americans erupted in violence in Los Angeles in June 1943, when sailors attacked these eighteen-year-olds and slashed their "zoot suit" trousers.

social group: very young married women. These changes reflected the pressures of wartime—the shortage of young men, opportunities for independence, and fears associated with military service.

The liberalization of sexual behavior reinforced a conservative counter-trend—the celebration of the traditional family. After the Depression decade, wartime prosperity encouraged an increase in marriage and birth rates. Although war mobilization brought more married women into the work force, women of childbearing age tended to remain at home. Moreover, the appeal for women workers emphasized the temporary nature of wartime employment. "Mother, when will you stay home again?" asked a daughter in one industrial ad campaign; "some jubilant day mother will stay home again, doing the job she likes best—making a home for you and daddy, when he gets back." Even when war undermined traditional expectations about women and the family, ideal sexual roles remained unchanged.

"Home," wrote the front-line journalist Ernie Pyle, "the one really profound goal that obsesses every one of the Americans marching on foreign shores." Whereas the "doughboys" of World War I were seen as heroic adventurers, the soldiers of World War II appeared as civilians in uniform who were eager to resume prewar activities. Yet the war profoundly disrupted traditional family life. With 16 million men and women in the military, more than 18 percent of U.S. families had at least one relative in the armed forces, and the 400,000 U.S. war dead meant that more than 180,000 children had lost their fathers. On the home front, child care centers remained inadequate, and conservatives criticized working mothers for threatening the stability of the home. Yet, unlike World War I, World War II demanded family sacrifice. Even the fictional heroes were different. The outstanding novel of World War II, Norman Mailer's *The Naked and the Dead* (1948), used the flashback device to accentuate the temporary nature of soldiers' status. Such attitudes encouraged the notion that life would revert to prewar conditions after the defeat of the enemy.

World War II nevertheless altered the relationship between government and the ordinary citizen. Bureaucratic control of the economy, the broadening of the tax base, government-funded advertising campaigns, federal support of technological research and development, the vast expansion of the armed services—these developments did not disappear at the war's end. Equally important, the conflict inspired a new definition of national security. The defeat of noninterventionism between 1939 and 1941 produced a new consensus that the national interest had a global dimension. To most citizens, the two oceans no longer protected the republic from its enemies; an adverse event anywhere in the world could be a threat to national security. This redefinition in turn demanded a strong and vigilant government dominated by an alert executive branch.

TRUMAN AND TRUCE

One month before World War II ended in Europe, the sudden death of Franklin D. Roosevelt thrust Harry Truman into the White House. Although he lacked Roosevelt's experience and skill, Truman inherited the delicate diplomatic responsibility for settling the peace. Unlike Roosevelt, Truman hoped to obtain postwar concessions from the Soviet Union. Roosevelt had pragmatically accepted the vague language of Yalta, but the new president insisted that the Soviet Union adopt the U.S. interpretation of wartime agreements. Truman offended the Allies further when, after the formal German surrender on 8 May 1945 (V-E Day), the president abruptly halted Lend-Lease and ordered ships in the middle of the Atlantic Ocean to turn around, although British and Soviet protests persuaded Truman to reverse the order.

Worried about the deterioration of U.S.-Soviet relations, the new president eagerly anticipated another summit conference with Allied leaders. Expecting fresh information about the top-secret military project to build an atomic bomb, Truman speculated that the weapon might give the United States greater leverage in winning concessions from the Soviets. Truman arranged to meet at Potsdam in mid-July 1945, the same week the first atomic bomb would be tested in New Mexico. As scientists developed the atomic bomb, Roosevelt had shared the secret with the British, who made important scientific contributions, but he refused to divulge the secret project to Stalin, even though he knew that spies already had passed information to the Russians. Roosevelt's decision indicated his belief that Britain would be a postwar ally, whereas the Soviet Union might not. Truman shared that assumption. The Truman administration never doubted that the atomic bomb would be used against the enemy. Military and

Brown Brothers

Ground zero, Hiroshima, symbolized the awesome power of atomic bombs.

political leaders predicted that the new weapon would forestall an invasion of Japan and save many U.S. lives. Moreover, they ignored the moral issues; fire bombings of Dresden and Tokyo already had claimed more victims than would die in atomic blasts.

The Potsdam conference failed to resolve U.S.-Soviet disagreements. With news of the successful atomic bomb test, Truman tried to persuade Stalin to alter the political arrangement in eastern Europe, where procommunist parties prevailed in areas occupied by the Red Army. Stalin refused to change these governments and viewed Truman's request as a betrayal of the Yalta agreements. At Potsdam, the Big Three did agree to partition Germany but again failed to resolve the question of German reparations for war damages. Final treaties were delayed until a later meeting of foreign ministers.

By the time the Potsdam conference was held, the Japanese cause seemed hopeless. In July 1945 the Japanese premier made overtures through the Soviet Union that indicated a willingness to sue for peace. Truman replied with demands for unconditional surrender and warned that Japan faced imminent destruction. When the Japanese did not accept those terms, the president allowed military decisions to proceed. On 6 August 1945 a single atomic bomb incinerated the Japanese city of Hiroshima and killed about 100,000 civilians. On 9 August the Soviet Union entered the war in the Pacific. The same day, the United States dropped another atomic bomb on Nagasaki. The Japanese now sought immediate peace and agreed to surrender on 14 August, provided only that the Japanese emperor be retained. When Truman accepted that condition, World War II was over. In a ceremony held aboard the U.S. battleship *Missouri* on 2 September 1945, Japan signed a formal treaty of surrender.

Black American soldiers view remains in the Nazi crematorium at Ebensee.

"Ours is the supreme position," exulted the *New York Herald Tribune*. "The Great Republic has come into its own; it stands first among the peoples of the earth." Such confidence nevertheless belied a certain dread of what World War II had wrought. The tremendous slaughter of human beings, the destruction of whole cities, the ravishing of the earth—all stood as solemn warnings about human survival. World War II proved the genuine possibility of annihilation—not just of national enemies but of all humanity. "Never again" became the watchword of the nation's leaders, a worldview that would shape U.S. policy for the next half century.

The difficulty in reaching international agreements at Yalta and Potsdam contrasted with Allied unanimity in punishing German war criminals. During World War II, Nazi Germany had violated accepted rules of warfare by indiscriminately killing civilians, by instituting reigns of terror in occupied countries, and by implementing horrible genocidal policies, including the murder of 6 million European Jews. The Allies convened an International Military Tribunal at Nuremberg, Germany, in August 1945 to bring Nazi war criminals to trial. The national interests of the judges—U.S., Soviet, British, and French—precluded a completely fair accounting. Yet in rendering judgment against twenty-two Nazi defendants, the Nuremberg tribunal established the basic principles of modern warfare: wars of aggression, violations of traditional warfare, and inhuman acts constituted war crimes; individuals accused of crimes were entitled to judicial trials; and individuals remained accountable for their criminal actions even though they were only following the orders of superiors. These legal precedents promised to protect civilian populations from military terror. Since then, history has shown the limitations of the Nuremberg precedent. The Grand Alliance of World War II did not long outlive the circumstances that had created it.

Suggested Readings

An outstanding introduction to the political problems of this period is Doris Kearns Goodwin, *No Ordinary Time: Franklin and Eleanor Roosevelt: The Home Front in World War II* (1994). The most comprehensive treatment of Roosevelt's foreign policy is Robert Dallek, *Franklin D. Roosevelt and American Foreign Policy, 1932–1945* (1979). More critical of Roosevelt is Frederick W. Marks III, *Wind Over Sand: The Diplomacy of Franklin Roosevelt* (1988), as is Arnold A. Offner, *American Appeasement: United States Foreign Policy and Germany, 1933–1938* (1969). U.S. policy is placed in its global context in Arnold A. Offner, *The Origins of the Second World War: American Foreign Policy and World Politics, 1917–1941* (1975). The final steps toward war are well described in Waldo Heinrichs, *Threshold of War: Franklin D. Roosevelt and American Entry into World War II* (1988).

A brief but thorough introduction to the major issues of foreign policy on the eve of World War II is Robert A. Divine, *The Reluctant Belligerent: American Entry into World War II* (1965). More detailed is a two-volume study by William L. Langer and S. Everett Gleason, *Challenge to Isolation, 1937–1940* (1952) and *The Undeclared War, 1940–1941* (1953). These surveys may be supplemented by John E. Wiltz, *From Isolation to War, 1931–1941* (1968).

The economic assumptions of U.S. foreign policy are explained in Patrick J. Hearden, *Roosevelt Confronts Hitler: America's Entry into World War II* (1987), and in Lloyd C. Gardner, *Economic Aspects of New Deal Diplomacy* (1964). For a thorough account of the politics of noninterventionism, see Wayne S. Cole, *Roosevelt and the Isolationists, 1932–45* (1983), which can be supplemented by two older works: John E. Wiltz, *In Search of Peace: The Senate Munitions Inquiry, 1934–1936* (1963), and Manfred Jonas, *Isolationism in America: 1935–1941* (1966). The background to noninterventionism in the Spanish Civil War emerges in Douglas Little, *Malevolent Neutrality: The United States, Great Britain, and the Origins of the Spanish Civil War* (1985), and in Richard P. Traina, *American Diplomacy and the Spanish Civil War* (1968). For the American volunteers in that war, see Peter N. Carroll, *The Odyssey of the Abraham Lincoln Brigade: Americans in the Spanish Civil War* (1994), and Danny Duncan Collum and Victor Berch, editors, *African Americans in the Spanish Civil War: "This Ain't Ethiopia, But It'll Do"* (1992). Roosevelt's perception of the national interest emerges in David Reynolds, *The Creation of the Anglo-American Alliance, 1937–41: A Study in Competitive Co-operation* (1981).

A thorough study of U.S. relations with Japan is Dorothy Borg, *The United States and the Far Eastern Crises of 1933–1938* (1964), which should be supplemented by Herbert Feis, *Road to Pearl Harbor* (1950). The ideological nature of the war is emphasized in John W. Dower, *War Without Mercy: Race and Power in the Pacific War* (1986), and in Akira Iriye, *Power and Culture: The Japanese-*

American War, 1941–1945 (1981). Roosevelt's China policy is the subject of Michael Schaller, *The U.S. Crusade in China, 1938–1945* (1979). For the Japanese context, see Robert J. Butow, *Tojo and the Coming of the War* (1961). The attack on Pearl Harbor is examined thoroughly in Gordon W. Prange, *At Dawn We Slept* (1981).

The issues of wartime diplomacy are described in Gaddis Smith, *American Diplomacy During the Second World War, 1941–1945* (1965), and in John Snell, *Illusion and Necessity: The Diplomacy of World War II* (1963). Also illuminating is Warren F. Kimball, *The Juggler: Franklin Roosevelt as Wartime Statesman* (1994). An outstanding study of international relations pertaining to Asia is Christopher Thorne, *Allies of a Kind: The United States, Britain and the War Against Japan, 1941–1945* (1978). Gabriel Kolko's *The Politics of War: The World and United States Foreign Policy, 1943–1945* (1968) stresses the inherent contradictions in national interest within the Grand Alliance. The origins of the United Nations are covered well in Robert A. Divine, *Second Chance: The Triumph of Internationalism in America During World War II* (1967). The relation between oil and foreign and domestic policy is studied in Michael B. Stoff, *Oil, War, and American Security: The Search for a National Policy on Foreign Oil, 1941–1947* (1980). Roosevelt's limited interest in Nazi genocide is documented in David S. Wyman, *The Abandonment of the Jews: America and the Holocaust, 1941–1945* (1984). Wartime diplomacy involving the atomic bomb is described in Gar Alperovitz, *The Decision to Use the Atomic Bomb and the Architecture of an American Myth* (1995), and in Martin J. Sherwin, *A World Destroyed: The Atomic Bomb and the Grand Alliance* (1975). For an analysis of the termination of the war in the Pacific, see Leon V. Sigal, *Fighting to a Finish: The Politics of War Termination in the United States and Japan, 1945* (1988).

The relation between military and diplomatic affairs is emphasized in A. Russell Buchanan, *The United States and World War II*, 2 volumes (1964). More specific is Raymond G. O'Connor, *Diplomacy for Victory: FDR and Unconditional Surrender* (1971). For U.S. military leadership, see two fine biographies: Stephen E. Ambrose, *Eisenhower*, volume 1 (1983), and Forrest C. Pogue, *George C. Marshall*, volumes 4–5 (1968, 1973). A brilliant analysis of U.S. air strategy is Michael S. Sherry, *The Rise of American Air Power* (1987). For the U.S. combat role in Europe, see Stephen E. Ambrose, *D-Day, June 6, 1944: The Climactic Battle of World War II* (1994). The view of the war from the perspective of the average soldier is presented in Lee Kennett, *G.I.: The American Soldier in World War II* (1987). A wonderful anthology of wartime journalism is the two-volume Library of America's *Reporting World War II* (1995).

Domestic issues during World War II are best described in Richard Polenberg, *War and Society: The United States, 1941–1945* (1972). For a brilliant study of American workers' experience, see George Lipsitz, *Rainbow at Midnight: Labor and Culture in the 1940s* (1994). How the war affected New Deal thinking is the subject of Alan Brinkley, *The End of Reform: New Deal Liberalism in Recession and War* (1995). Business values are treated in Howell John Harris, *The Right to Manage: Industrial Relations Policies of American Business in the 1940s* (1982). A fine study of the Office of War Information is Allan M. Winkler, *The Politics of Propaganda* (1978). For Roosevelt's presidential role, see James MacGregor Burns, *Roosevelt: The Soldier of Freedom* (1970). John Morton Blum, *V Was for Victory: Politics and American Culture During World War II* (1976), explores the cultural context of wartime decision making. Fresh approaches to the war at home appear in Lewis A. Erenberg and Susan E. Hirsch, editors, *The War in American Culture: Society and Consciousness During World War II* (1996). It may be supplemented by Geoffrey Perrett, *Days of Sadness, Years of Triumph* (1973), by Richard Lingeman, *Don't You Know There's a War On?* (1970), and by a compilation of oral histories, Studs Terkel, *The Good War* (1984). A superb study of military censorship of the mass media is George H. Roeder, Jr., *The Censored War: American Visual Experience During World War II* (1993). American advertising during World War II is the subject of Frank Fox, *Madison Avenue Goes to War: The Strange Military Career of American Advertising, 1941–1945* (1975). For the movie industry, see Clayton R. Koppes and Gregory D. Black, *Hollywood Goes to War: How Politics, Profits, and Propaganda Shaped World War II Movies* (1987); Allen L. Woll, *The Hollywood Musical Goes to War* (1983); and Thomas Doherty, *Projections of War: Hollywood, American Culture, and World War II* (1993).

The impact of the war on American society is summarized in the relevant chapters of Richard Polenberg, *One Nation Divisible: Class, Race, and Ethnicity in the United States* (1980). For the role of organized labor, see Nelson Lichtenstein, *Labor's War at Home: The CIO in World War II* (1983). Excellent studies of the war's impact on specific regions include Alan Clive, *State of War: Michigan in World War II* (1979); Marc Scott Miller, *The Irony of Victory: World War II and Lowell, Massachusetts* (1988); and Marilynn S. Johnson, *The Second Gold Rush: Oakland and the East Bay in World War II* (1993). Broader in scope is Gerald D. Nash, *The American West Transformed: The Impact of the Second World War* (1985). The position of the U.S. Communist Party is described in Maurice Isserman, *Which Side Were You On: The American Communist Party During the Second World War* (1982).

The experience of Japanese Americans is examined by Roger Daniels, *Concentration Camps USA: Japanese-Americans and World War II* (1971), as well as by Edward Spicer et al., *Impounded People: Japanese-Americans in the Relocation Centers* (1969), a report originally written in 1946 for the War Relocation Authority. Critical reappraisals of the internment program are Peter Irons, *Justice at War* (1983), and Richard Drinnon, *Keeper of Concentration Camps: Dillon S. Myer and American Racism* (1987). The Roosevelt administration's treatment of political dissenters emerges in the relevant chapters of Leo P. Ribuffo, *The Old Christian Right: The Protestant Far Right from the Great Depression to the Cold War* (1983). The imprisonment of other victims of the war is the subject of John Christgau, *"Enemies": World War II Alien Internment* (1985), and of Stephen Fox, *The Unknown Internment: An Oral History of the Relocation of Italian Americans During World War II* (1990). For the government's surveillance programs, see the relevant chapters of Richard Gid Powers, *Secrecy and Power: The Life of J. Edgar Hoover* (1987), and Athan G. Theoharis and John Stuart Cox, *The Boss: J. Edgar Hoover and the Great American Inquisition* (1988).

The experience of blacks emerges in Richard Dalfiume, *Desegregation of the Armed Forces, 1939–1953* (1969). The March on Washington movement is described in the later chapters of Harvard Sitkoff, *A New Deal for Blacks* (1978). Also illuminating are the memoirs of black soldiers compiled by Mary Penick Motley in *The Invisible Soldier* (1975). A good study of Native Americans is Alison R. Bernstein, *American Indians and World War II: Toward a New Era in Indian Affairs* (1991).

The best sources for the impact of the war on women are the relevant chapters of William H. Chafe, *The American Woman* (1972). The intellectual and social implications of women's wartime experiences are explored in Ruth Milkman, *Gender at Work: The Dynamics of Job Segregation by Sex during World War II* (1987); in Maureen Honey, *Creating Rosie the Riveter: Class, Gender, and Propaganda during World War II* (1984), and in Karen Anderson, *Wartime Women: Sex Roles, Family Relations, and the Status of Women During World War II* (1981). A good comparative study is Leila Rupp, *Mobilizing Women for War: German and American Propaganda, 1939–1945* (1978). The war's impact on children is the subject of William M. Tuttle, Jr., *"Daddy's Gone to War": The Second World War in the Lives of America's Children* (1993). For the pacifist movement, see Lawrence S. Wittner, *Rebels Against War: The American Peace Movement, 1941–1960* (1969). For religious thought, see the relevant chapters of Martin E. Marty, *Modern American Religion*, volume 3, *Under God, Indivisible, 1941–1960* (1996).

For the Nuremberg trials, see Bradley F. Smith, *Reaching Judgment at Nuremberg* (1977), and Telford Taylor, *Nuremberg and Vietnam: An American Tragedy* (1970).

8

Truman delivering Truman Doctrine speech, March 12, 1947.

Stock Montage

TRUMAN, THE COLD WAR, AND THE ANTICOMMUNIST CRUSADE, 1945–1952

S ix days after the atomic bombing of Hiroshima, radio commentator Edward
R. Murrow observed, "Seldom, if ever, has a war ended leaving the victors
with such a sense of uncertainty and fear, with such a realization that the future
is obscure and that survival is not assured." Although the United States
emerged from World War II virtually undamaged and prepared to assume leadership in world affairs, divisions within the Grand Alliance left many unsolved
problems to threaten the peace. Within two years of victory, President Harry S
Truman brought the nation into another global war—the "Cold War"—which
altered the scope of government activity and inevitably affected political life on
the home front.

PROBLEMS OF RECONVERSION

"The ultimate duty of government," declared Truman in September 1945, was
"to prevent prolonged unemployment." Identifying with Roosevelt's New
Deal, the president promptly asked Congress for full-employment legislation
as well as a package of liberal measures, such as a permanent Fair Employment
Practices Commission (FEPC), public housing, higher minimum wages, and
urban redevelopment. This ambitious program soon collided with a conservative Congress of southern Democrats and northern Republicans opposed to
government intervention in the economy. "It is just a case of out-New Dealing
the New Deal," complained one House Republican leader. Fearing "creeping
socialism," Congress opted for "maximum" rather than "full" employment. Although the Employment Act of 1946 committed the federal government to maximize employment, neither Truman nor his successors supported the creation
of government jobs to ease unemployment. Indeed, the abrupt layoff of women
workers after World War II brought no government response. Likewise, when
Truman requested an extension of wartime economic controls in 1946, the conservative Congress resisted granting additional economic powers to the
president.

Truman's efforts to control the rash of postwar labor strikes nevertheless
alarmed liberals more than conservatives. Responding to a national railroad
workers strike in May 1946, Truman first seized the railroads, then asked Congress to authorize court injunctions to keep workers on the job, to allow the
army to operate the trains, and to permit the drafting of strikers into the military to force them to work. Although the walkout ended before Congress could
act, Truman's proposal brought wide criticism. "In his angry determination to
get the trains running on time again," protested the liberal *Nation*, "Truman
[took] . . . a leaf from the book of another man who made railroad history, Benito
Mussolini." Nonetheless, Congress approved the use of court injunctions to
stop certain strikes.

Truman soon used government power to end a coal strike by John L. Lewis's
United Mine Workers (UMW). Several times during the war, this union had
broken labor's "no-strike" pledge. When Lewis called another strike in 1946,
Truman seized the mines and ended the walkout by accepting an inflationary
settlement. Six months later, the UMW defied the government again by calling
a strike. Unlike Roosevelt, who in wartime had met Lewis's demands, Truman
obtained an injunction and a $3.5 million judgment against the union (and

another $10,000 judgment against Lewis), which forced the UMW to surrender. According to a Gallup poll, the president's antiunion stand increased his popularity.

Although liberals scorned Truman's failure to maintain price controls and his hostility to unions, Republicans criticized him for promoting big government, for administrative ineptness, and for laxity in protecting federal agencies from communist influence. "The choice which confronts Americans this year," advised the Republican national chairman, "is between Communism and Republicanism." New Republican candidates, such as Joseph R. McCarthy of Wisconsin and Richard M. Nixon of California, openly appealed to popular fears of communist subversion. Their allegations gained credibility from two highly publicized scandals: the discovery in 1945 of stolen secret documents in the offices of *Amerasia*, a left-wing diplomatic journal, and the capture of Soviet spies in Canada the following year. Republican red-baiting, as well as public disapproval of strikes, inflation, and bureaucracy, fueled criticism of the White House. With the simple campaign slogan "Had Enough?" Republicans won a landslide in 1946, obtaining a congressional majority in both houses for the first time since 1928. McCarthy and Nixon stood among the victors.

Once in control of the Eightieth Congress, Republicans reestablished a working alliance with southern Democrats to thwart civil rights legislation and to block Truman's other liberal measures, such as public housing, federal aid to education, higher Social Security payments, and certain farm benefits. Conservatives of both parties joined to pass the Taft-Hartley Act of 1947, which limited labor union activities. (For more on Taft-Hartley, see Chapter 9.) Criticizing such "vindictive" legislation, Truman vetoed the bill, but in a show of conservative muscle, Congress easily overrode the veto. The president's opposition, however, helped return organized labor to the Democratic camp.

POSTWAR FOREIGN POLICY

Although the public widely approved of U.S. participation in the United Nations, demands for rapid demobilization and military budget cuts in 1946 showed a limited commitment to global involvement. Public pressure forced Truman to reduce the size of the armed forces from 12 million to 3 million within months of V-J Day. The president's failure to reach postwar agreements with the Soviet Union contributed to his loss of popularity, but public suspicion of the Soviet Union and world communism enabled Truman to develop an increasingly militant and internationalist position. The president's primary postwar goal was to secure the nation from any foreign threat—military or economic. "We must face the fact that peace must be built on power," said Truman in 1945, "as well as upon good will and good deeds." Such power hinged not only on military preparedness but also on a stable world economic environment. The huge expenditure of natural resources during World War II underscored the importance of protecting U.S. access to raw materials.

"Our foreign relations inevitably affect employment in the United States," explained Secretary of State James F. Byrnes in August 1945. "Prosperity and depression in the United States just as inevitably affect our relations with other nations of the world." Such assumptions echoed the Open Door policy first formalized in 1900, which proposed free international trade with China as an alternative to imperialist spheres of influence. To ensure access to markets and resources and to prevent economic stagnation at home, postwar leaders advocated a worldwide system of free trade. "Peace, freedom and world trade are indivisible," Truman later remarked. "We must not go through the thirties again."

This economic approach to foreign affairs partially reflected the social background of many of the nation's policymakers in the postwar period. Leading State Department officials like Dean Acheson and John Foster Dulles often had personal ties to the nation's largest corporations and held powerful positions as corporate lawyers, financiers, or big-business executives. For example, the names of five of the six secretaries of state between 1945 and 1960 and of five of the six secretaries of defense between 1947 and 1960 appeared in the Social Register of the nation's richest families. Such men, appointed by both Democratic and Republican presidents, formulated a foreign policy that expressed and protected the values of the corporate elite. "I am an advocate of business," conceded Secretary of Defense James Forrestal in 1947. "Calvin Coolidge was ridiculed for saying . . . 'The chief business of the United States is business,' but that is a fact."

The International Monetary Fund and the World Bank, both created at the Bretton Woods Conference of 1944, sought to stabilize international currency and trade for postwar economic expansion. Leaders in Washington sought to direct a new economic order that would dissolve prewar economic blocs and assure economic growth. Although foreign trade comprised only 6 percent of the gross national product in 1945, State Department planners hoped to use U.S. economic power to force Great Britain, France, and the Soviet Union to open their trading blocs to U.S. business. When these nations applied for U.S. loans in 1945 to replace the wartime assistance provided under the Lend-Lease Act, negotiators delayed action to win trading concessions. Such pressure forced Britain to open its empire to U.S. trade before receiving a $3.75 billion loan in 1946. Nearly bankrupted by the war, Britain had no choice but to accept U.S. conditions. The French made similar concessions, but the Soviet Union, although devastated by the war, refused to accept U.S. conditions.

Although Soviet leaders continued to advocate the Marxist-Leninist doctrine of worldwide communist revolution, Josef Stalin primarily sought to rebuild his war-ravaged country with German reparations. Stalin also established "friendly governments" in eastern Europe to prevent another invasion of Russia. Given historic conflicts between the Soviet Union and anticommunist nationalists in eastern Europe, Stalin rejected "free and unfettered elections" in some areas occupied by Soviet troops. In Poland, for example, the Red Army repressed political freedom to promote a pro-Soviet regime. During the war, Roosevelt had minimized the problem of Soviet expansion in eastern Europe, largely because he could do nothing about it and wanted to preserve the Grand Alliance against Hitler. Although he remained suspicious of Stalin and refused to share information about the atomic bomb, the president tried to treat the Soviet Union as a "normal" state that was only protecting its national interests.

Roosevelt failed to attract public support for his foreign policy. Fearful of a resurgence of isolationism, he hesitated to move ahead of public opinion. Nor did he challenge the popular view that the United Nations, like the League of Nations, would be based on the Wilsonian principle of equal representation for all nations. Yet Roosevelt believed that the organization could succeed where the League of Nations had failed only if the Big Powers dominated international diplomacy. He assumed that the Big Four (Britain, China, the United States, and the Soviet Union) would use their veto power in the Security Council to protect their national interests. At Yalta, for example, Roosevelt and Churchill acknowledged Soviet dominance in eastern Europe, the British claimed special privileges in the Mediterranean, and the United States sought to maintain power in Latin America. Such spheres of influence contradicted Wilsonian internationalism as well as the Open Door policy. Roosevelt accepted these limitations because he understood the special interests of each Allied nation.

At Roosevelt's death, Truman knew nothing about these foreign policy assumptions. Instead, the new president viewed the Soviet presence in eastern Europe as an infringement of the principle of national self-determination and a violation of the Yalta agreements. Determined to prove his strength in the diplomatic arena, Truman clashed angrily with Soviet Foreign Minister V.M. Molotov in April 1945 about the undemocratic character of the Polish government and decided to withhold U.S. economic aid until Stalin retreated.

The new administration also shifted U.S. policy toward the British, Dutch, and French empires, most significantly in French Indochina. Opposed to French imperialism, Roosevelt had proposed that Indochina be placed under international trusteeship until the French colony achieved full independence. Although the leader of the Indochinese national liberation movement, Ho Chi Minh, drafted a declaration of independence in 1945, British pressure forced Roosevelt to accept the return of French troops—but with the goal of ultimately granting Indochinese independence. Truman dropped that essential qualification. Pressed by Churchill, who feared that the liberation of French colonies would set a precedent for the British empire, Truman agreed to return Indochina to France. Ho's sympathy toward communism had alarmed State Department officials. Equally important, Truman wished to retain French support in Europe, where France could join Britain as an ally against the Soviet Union. In 1945 the United States provided ships and military assistance to transport French troops back to Indochina. Thereafter, the U.S. State Department ignored Ho Chi Minh's appeals for support.

While restoring French imperialism in Southeast Asia, Truman proceeded with prewar plans to grant independence to the Philippine Islands, first seized from Spain in 1898. Yet, before departing from that strategic region, the United States negotiated long-term treaties providing for military bases and the stationing of U.S. troops in the Philippines. Besides ensuring military security, such treaties protected U.S. economic investments and reinforced the rule of conservative elites. Similar arrangements brought the United States a string of military bases in Iceland, in North Africa, in Okinawa, an island near Japan, and the Azores, a group of islands in the Atlantic Ocean. In Spain, the United States accepted the fascist dictator Francisco Franco as a defender against socialist revolution and Soviet influence.

THE COLD WAR BEGINS

The Big Three met in Potsdam in July 1945 but failed to settle their differences. Stalin, concerned primarily with obtaining German reparations, expressed little

Despite basic disagreements, the Big Three—(left to right) Prime Minister Winston Churchill, President Truman, and Premier Josef Stalin—pose amicably at the Potsdam conference in 1945. Days later, Churchill's defeat at the polls forced his replacement by Clement Atlee.

interest in reducing Soviet influence in eastern Europe, but Truman, emboldened by the first successful test of the atomic bomb that month, rejected such a Soviet sphere of influence. He also proposed smaller reparations from Germany in hopes of maintaining Soviet dependence on U.S. exports. Failing to reach agreement, the Big Three postponed resolution of these issues until the Foreign Ministers Conference in London in September 1945. Frustrated by Soviet stubbornness, Truman decided to exclude the Soviet Union from participation in the occupation of Japan.

The atomic bombings of Japan in August 1945 reinforced Truman's confidence but aroused Soviet suspicions. At the London conference, the Soviets offered minor concessions on elections in Bulgaria and Hungary, but the Truman administration demanded Western-style political contests. Again, the diplomats could not reach an agreement. This failure showed the futility of atomic bomb diplomacy. When Molotov asked jokingly whether U.S. Secretary of State Byrnes had an atomic bomb in his pocket, Byrnes replied, "If you don't cut out all this stalling . . . I am going to pull an atomic bomb out of my hip pocket and let you have it!" To the surprise of U.S. negotiators, the Soviet Union would not be coerced into accepting Truman's demands. Secretary of War Stimson, who had once viewed the bomb as a diplomatic lever, now saw an opportunity to ease tensions by sharing atomic secrets with the Soviet Union. "If we fail to approach them now and merely continue to negotiate with them, having this weapon rather ostentatiously on our hip," he warned, "their suspicions and

Exhibit 8-1. Origins of the Cold War, 1945–1949

Year	Event
1945	Yalta Conference
	V-E Day: Germany surrenders
	Potsdam Conference
	Atomic bombings of Japan and Japanese surrender
1946	Kennan telegram
	Churchill's "Iron Curtain" speech
	Soviet occupation of northern Iran
	Acheson-Lilienthal and Baruch Plans for Atomic Energy
	Atomic Energy Act (creates AEC—Atomic Energy Commission)
1947	Truman Doctrine
	Federal Employee Loyalty Program
	National Security Act
1948	Communist coup in Czechoslovakia
	Marshall Plan—European Recovery Program
	Berlin airlift
1949	NATO
	Soviet A-bomb detonated
	Communist victory over Chinese Nationalists

their distrust . . . will increase." Yet after a high-level policy debate, the president chose to maintain the U.S. atomic monopoly.

Despite doubts about further negotiations, Secretary of State Byrnes met with Stalin in Moscow in December 1945, producing tentative agreements about portions of eastern Europe, about Korea, and especially about a United Nations Atomic Energy Commission. Yet pressure from congressional conservatives, who opposed any concessions to Stalin, forced Truman to adopt a more rigid position, and he abruptly disavowed Byrnes's agreements. "Unless Russia is faced with an iron fist and strong language another war is in the making," he declared. "I'm tired of babying the Soviets."

Truman's firmness won support within the State Department from George F. Kennan, a longtime analyst of Soviet affairs. "We have here," Kennan cabled from Moscow in February 1946, "a political force committed fanatically to the belief that . . . it is desirable and necessary that the internal harmony of our society be disrupted, our traditional way of life destroyed, the international authority of our state be broken if Soviet power is to be secure." Kennan's "long telegram" confirmed the president's belief that there could be no compromise with communist nations. One month later, Truman accompanied Winston Churchill to Fulton, Missouri, where the former prime minister attacked the Soviet Union for drawing an "iron curtain" around eastern Europe. The speech, approved by Truman, brought wide editorial criticism but publicized the change in foreign policy.

The United States also challenged the Soviet Union within the United Nations. The first major crisis involved Soviet occupation of northern Iran in 1946. The problem was oil. During the war, the Soviets, the British, and the Americans had occupied Iran jointly, but the Soviets hesitated to leave until they received oil concessions similar to those won by the British. Fearing a Soviet attempt to control vital oil resources, the White House supported Iran in the Security Council, where the United States controlled a preponderance of

Exhibit 8-2. Iran, 1946

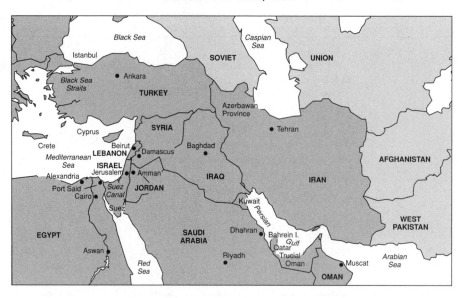

votes. Such diplomatic pressure forced Iran and the Soviet Union to negotiate oil concessions in exchange for a Soviet withdrawal. Afterward, however, Iran repudiated the agreement. Using U.N. institutions, the United States had thwarted Soviet expansion.

The United Nations also sanctioned the U.S. decision to maintain a monopoly on atomic weapons. In 1946, to ease public fear of atomic war, the Truman administration announced the Acheson-Lilienthal plan, which proposed that atomic energy be made an internationally shared technology. The United States would relinquish control of atomic weapons in stages. During the transition, the United States would maintain an atomic monopoly, and other countries would be required to allow international inspection. The United States "should not under any circumstances throw away our gun until we are sure the rest of the world can not arm against us," said Truman. In presenting the program to the United Nations, Truman's advisor, financier Bernard Baruch, added other conditions, including the surrender of the U.N. Security Council veto on atomic energy issues and the imposition of "condign punishments" against violators of the plan by a majority vote (which was controlled by U.S. allies). Although fearful of the U.S. atomic monopoly, the Soviet Union was rushing to build its own atomic bombs and rejected the Baruch plan. Instead, the Soviets suggested immediate nuclear disarmament and sharing of atomic secrets. Truman considered the Soviet alternative unacceptable.

Frustrated by Soviet negotiators, U.S. leaders accused Stalin of violating every wartime agreement. Yet most diplomatic quarrels involved arguments about the ambiguous language of the original agreements. No less than Truman, Stalin sought to protect his nation's best interests. Truman's inability to appreciate Soviet concerns, especially about atomic bombs, reflected the uncompromising anticommunism that dominated Cold War thinking. Defining Soviet communism as "red fascism," U.S. leaders were determined to avoid a repetition of the "appeasement" that had allowed Germany to control Europe in the

1930s. "The language of military power is the only language which disciples of power politics understand," presidential adviser Clark Clifford assured Truman in 1946. Moreover, in identifying the Soviet Union with Nazi Germany, Truman broadened support for his policy. Under the principle of "bipartisanship," Republicans, led by Senator Arthur Vandenberg and foreign policy expert John Foster Dulles, supported Truman administration diplomacy, at least in Europe.

As a Cold War consensus crystallized in Washington, one former New Dealer emerged as a major critic—Henry A. Wallace, secretary of agriculture during the 1930s, Roosevelt's third-term vice president, and now Truman's secretary of commerce. In September 1946, after gaining Truman's approval, Wallace spoke publicly at Madison Square Garden, arguing that the United States had "no more business in the political affairs of Eastern Europe than Russia had in the political affairs of Latin America, Western Europe, and the United States." Yet when other members of the administration protested the speech, Truman abruptly fired Wallace. "The Reds, phonies, and the 'parlor pinks,'" Truman wrote, "seem to be banded together and are becoming a national danger."

Fear of communist influence permeated the nation. Preparing for a Soviet attack, FBI Director J. Edgar Hoover developed a Custodial Detention Program and compiled lists of suspected subversives who would be arrested at the outbreak of war. When the White House tried to minimize the communist threat, Hoover aligned with more militant anticommunists in Congress. "Communism," Hoover told the House Committee on Un-American Activities (HUAC), "is . . . an evil and malignant way of life." Persuaded by such testimony, Congress voted to provide more funds for FBI investigations of government workers. These political pressures pushed Truman toward a more militant anticommunist position.

The dismissal of Wallace revealed the administration's growing intolerance of positions that had seemed acceptable only one year before. After conservative Republican victories in the 1946 elections, some liberals deserted Truman and formed a coalition group, Progressive Citizens of America (PCA). Complaining that the Democratic Party had departed from the tradition of Roosevelt, the PCA urged a return to liberal principles or the creation of a third party. Although the PCA did not discriminate against members of the Communist Party, most liberals bitterly opposed communism and especially resented conservative accusations that liberals were tools of Soviet foreign policy. In January 1947 these anticommunist liberals formed Americans for Democratic Action (ADA). Like the PCA, the ADA endorsed expansion of the New Deal, the United Nations, and civil rights, but the ADA explicitly rejected "any association with Communists or sympathizers with communism."

THE TRUMAN DOCTRINE

Early in 1947 U.S. intelligence detected a relaxation of Soviet policy in changes ranging from military demobilization to a willingness to negotiate about Germany. The State Department concluded that such changes were deliberately deceptive. This mistrust was reinforced by growing concern about the slow pace of economic recovery in Europe. The State Department feared that economic unrest both encouraged communist expansion and undermined U.S.

exports. The problem climaxed in February 1947 when Great Britain announced it could no longer provide support for Greece, a client state it had supported since World War II in a civil war against communist guerrillas. Truman welcomed the opportunity to replace Britain in the area, but U.S. intervention required congressional approval at a time when conservatives sought to cut government expenses. Moreover, the public appeared uninterested in Greek affairs.

Truman decided, in the words of Vandenberg, to "scare hell out of the American people." In an impassioned speech, the president personally presented the "Truman Doctrine" to a special session of Congress in March 1947, requesting $400 million in economic and military assistance to Greece and Turkey. Condemning a communist system based on "terror and oppression, a controlled press and radio, fixed elections and the suppression of political freedoms," Truman depicted an emergency situation that forced the U.S. to "support free peoples who are resisting attempted subjugation by armed minorities or by outside pressures."

The Truman Doctrine represented a major turning point in foreign policy—the announcement that the United States would initiate unilateral action without consulting the United Nations or the Soviet Union. The Truman Doctrine also abandoned the idea of effecting changes within the Soviet sphere of influence and instead stressed the importance of containing Soviet expansion. This decision divided the globe into areas of "freedom" and zones of "terror and oppression." Such divisions allowed no room for compromise: all communists were evil, and all communist threats became equally critical. Furthermore, the Truman Doctrine expanded the definition of "national security" to encompass regions throughout the entire world. "Wherever aggression, direct or indirect, threatened the peace," Truman later explained, "the security of the United States was involved." George Kennan elaborated on this idea of containment in an influential article, "The Sources of Soviet Conduct," published anonymously in the journal *Foreign Affairs* in 1947.

Truman's belief that communism represented a monolithic threat placed the United States on the side of authoritarian governments in Greece and Turkey. Viewing Greek communists as minions of Moscow, Truman supported a conservative monarchy that had little popular support. In Turkey, the United States backed a repressive regime that had cooperated with the Germans during World War II and continued to crush internal dissent. The administration justified these alliances by articulating what later became known as the domino theory: "If Greece and then Turkey succumb," one State Department official advised, "the whole Middle East will be lost. France may then capitulate to the communists. As France goes, all Western Europe and North Africa will go." Such logic alarmed conservatives and liberals alike. Republican Senator Robert Taft protested that Truman had made fundamental policy choices without adequately consulting Congress. Meanwhile, the liberal Wallace broadcast a scathing critique: "There is no regime too reactionary" to receive U.S. aid, he said, "provided it stands in Russia's expansionist path."

Truman believed that international politics was too complex for average voters, whom he considered overly idealistic. Rather than risk divisive partisan debates, the president preferred to rely on foreign policy experts and then seek public support. Conservative Republicans such as Taft objected that Congress and the public were left to ratify Cold War policies instead of formulating them.

Exhibit 8-3. Greece, Turkey, and the Mediterranean, 1947

The administration's attempt to influence public opinion proved effective, however, and the announcement of the Truman Doctrine raised the president's approval rating from 49 percent to 60 percent in two months. Yet U.S. aid neither suppressed the Greek rebellion nor made the monarchy less oppressive. "There is no use pretending . . . that for $400 million we have bought peace," admitted Vandenberg. "It is merely a down payment."

Although the Truman Doctrine addressed U.S. fears of communist subversion, the slowness of postwar economic recovery in Europe created conditions that encouraged communist criticism of capitalism. Seeking to end economic shortages in Europe, stabilize economic growth, and stimulate U.S. trade, Secretary of State George C. Marshall unveiled the administration's innovative European Recovery Program in a highly publicized speech at the Harvard University commencement in June 1947. Describing severe economic problems in Europe, Marshall called for a massive program of economic aid offering assistance to all European nations, including communist governments. "Our policy is directed not against any country or doctrine," he stated, "but against hunger, poverty, desperation, and chaos." However, Marshall's purportedly unselfish offer of aid to the Soviets was deceptive because the plan threatened the independence of the Soviet economy. In addition, the program attempted to return to prewar conditions that left eastern Europe far less industrialized than the West. Instead of receiving reparations, the Soviet Union might have to contribute food to other countries. Finally, the plan would rebuild the German economy and hasten German integration with western trade.

The State Department correctly predicted the effect of these proposals: the Soviets rejected participation in what came to be known as the Marshall Plan

GEORGE CATLETT MARSHALL, JR.
1880–1959

The Granger Collection

When Indiana Senator William Jenner opposed George Marshall's nomination as secretary of defense in 1950 by dismissing the general as a "living lie . . . a front man for traitors," it was as if someone had attacked the integrity of George Washington. Described by President Truman as "the greatest living American," Marshall had designed and coordinated the Normandy invasion. Serving as Truman's army chief of staff and principal military advisor, he was the highest-ranking general when World War II ended. A veteran whose distinguished career dated back to service in the Philippines in 1902, Marshall became secretary of state between 1947 and 1949 and headed the Defense Department from 1950 to 1951. The key architect of the European Recovery Program, known as the Marshall Plan, in 1953 he became the first career soldier to win the Nobel Peace Prize.

"We are now concerned with the peace of the world," Marshall declared as World War II concluded. One day after the general resigned from the military, Truman appointed him special presidential emissary to China with orders to seek an accord between warring Nationalists and Maoist communists. U.S. officials worried that a victory by Maoists would strengthen Soviet influence in Asia. Arriving in China in 1946, Marshall used the lever of U.S. aid to compel the Nationalist government of Chiang Kai-shek to cease troop movements and institute democratic reforms. Meanwhile, he tried to convince the communists to agree to a coalition government and unified army under Chiang's leadership.

Aware that domestic political pressures prevented a complete cessation of U.S. aid to an anticommunist ally, Chiang ignored Marshall's pleadings and launched a major military offensive. Perceiving that negotiations had "reached an impasse," Marshall warned Washington that "the Communists have lost cities and towns but they have not lost their armies." After more than 300 meetings with the disputing parties, Marshall returned home in 1947, citing "complete, almost overwhelming" mutual suspicion as "the greatest obstacle to peace" in China.

The failure of the China mission underscored the lessons Marshall had drawn from nearly half a century of military experience. First, power was not limitless and could not be equated with moral purity. Second, armed strategy was to serve policy, not drive it. These principles prompted Truman's most trusted military advisor to recommend the firing of Korean War commander General Douglas MacArthur in 1951. Months later, Senator Joseph McCarthy denounced Marshall as an accessory to the 1949 victory of the Chinese Maoists and a coconspirator in the communist quest for world domination.

"God bless democracy," Marshall once had exclaimed. "I approve of it highly but suffer from it extremely." A tall, erect, and decisive leader, the general embodied the techniques of professional administration in molding postwar military life. Marshall understood how economic, political, social, and psychological conditions provided the context for military effectiveness. Such insight allowed him to popularize the Marshall Plan as a fight against the enemies of "hunger, poverty, desperation, and chaos." Yet the "fall" of China challenged the U.S. plan for global peace, prosperity, and democracy, and the principal architect of the postwar world became the centerpiece of recriminating debates that tore at the Cold War consensus. ∎

and forced its client states in eastern Europe to do the same. The Russians also moved to tighten political control in eastern Europe. Meanwhile, sixteen nations drafted a four-year program of economic recovery and gladly accepted $17 billion in U.S. aid. Wielding this economic power, Washington persuaded political leaders in Italy and France to exclude the Communist Party from participation in their coalition governments.

Despite the anticommunist aspects of the Marshall Plan, the conservative majority in Congress remained suspicious of executive power, foreign aid, and potential benefits to large exporters rather than domestically oriented small firms. Moreover, as late as November 1947, 40 percent of the public had never heard of the Marshall Plan, but as economic conditions in western Europe continued to deteriorate and Communist Parties throughout Europe organized protests, street demonstrations, and strikes, the White House moved quickly to arouse domestic opinion. Mustering big-business executives, organized labor, the ADA, and the Farm Bureau, the administration launched a public relations campaign to lobby Congress.

"We'll either have to provide a program of interim aid relief until the Marshall program gets going," Truman warned a group of congressional leaders, "or the governments of France and Italy will fall, Austria too, and for all practical purposes, Europe will be Communist." Drawing on his personal standing among Republican leaders, Marshall sold Congress on the idea. Pleas that Europe be saved from communism undermined conservative scruples about government spending abroad. Summoning a special session, Truman played down the economic basis of the plan and returned to the militant anticommunist rhetoric of the Truman Doctrine. The strategy worked, and Congress passed an interim aid measure. By 1950 the program had delivered $35 billion in government grants and loans to European countries and was credited with restoring European morale and revitalizing Europe's political centrism.

RED SCARE

Anticommunist foreign policy paralleled an anticommunist crusade at home. Believing that the Soviet Union was a hostile and expansionist foreign power, Washington assumed that the U.S. Communist Party served as Stalin's domestic agent. After the Republican election victories in 1946, Truman had attempted to defuse the explosive issue of communist influence in government by creating a Temporary Commission on Employee Loyalty. Nine days after enunciating the Truman Doctrine, the president created a permanent Federal Employee Loyalty program to eliminate subversives from government. The announcement reflected continuing pressures from congressional conservatives as well as anticommunist feelings within the administration. In 1947 the House Un-American Activities Committee (HUAC) resumed investigation of communist infiltration of government, Hollywood, education, and labor unions. HUAC's inquiry into the movie industry resulted in contempt charges against the "Hollywood Ten," a group of writers and directors who refused on First Amendment grounds to answer questions about their political activities. After the Supreme Court refused to hear their appeals, the Hollywood Ten went to prison.

Attempting to preempt similar investigations of government employees, a presidential Executive Order mandated loyalty investigations of all federal

Truman meets with his fourth secretary of state, Dean Acheson, whose connections with the cosmopolitan corporate "Establishment" infuriated Republican conservatives.

workers and job applicants. The president also ordered dismissal of workers for whom "reasonable grounds" for suspicion of disloyalty existed. Truman instructed Attorney General Tom Clark to publicize a list of "subversive" organizations, and ninety-one groups were so designated in 1947. The Justice Department contended that groups on the attorney general's list were "fronts" for the Communist Party. Federal investigators were to treat membership in such organizations as grounds for further disloyalty inquiries for suspected individuals. "There are many Communists in America," the attorney general declared. "They are everywhere—in factories, offices, butcher shops, on street corners, in private businesses—and each carries with him the germs of death for society." The list stigmatized opponents of government policy, encouraging public and private discrimination against members.

"What," asked a HUAC pamphlet, "is the difference in fact between a Communist and a Fascist? Answer: None worth noticing." In 1947 J. Edgar Hoover published a widely circulated article, "Red Fascism in the United States Today," warning of the imminent danger of communist subversion. Seeking judicial sanction for surveillance and detention programs, Hoover pressed the Department of Justice to prosecute leaders of the Communist Party for violating the Smith Act of 1940, which made it a crime to advocate the overthrow of government by force or to belong to a group with such a goal. In 1948 the Justice Department charged twelve leading communists with violations of the Smith Act, winning convictions and stiff prison sentences.

Despite claims of Soviet espionage, Truman's Loyalty Program found no government spies. Domestic communism did not represent a political threat as much as a suspect ideology. Many eastern European ethnic groups hated Soviet communists for invading their homelands and attacking Christian churches. However, the core of anticommunism lay in public perceptions of Stalinist Russia. The popular novels of Mickey Spillane, Hollywood films like *The Iron Curtain* (1948), and a spate of magazine articles all portrayed communism as the epitome of heartless atheism, deadening bureaucracy, and ruthless totalitarianism. Hostile to Soviet expansion, many Americans believed that communism jeopardized traditional views of religion, family, individual liberty, and personal initiative. "Communism is secularism on the march," J. Edgar Hoover told a Methodist gathering. "It is a moral foe of Christianity."

Ironically, the growth of government bureaucracy, big corporations, and impersonal, homogenized communities already threatened traditional values. "Our problem is not outside ourselves," admitted Republican presidential candidate Thomas E. Dewey in 1948. "Our problem is within ourselves." Anticommunist spokesmen such as Joseph McCarthy, J. Edgar Hoover, and Richard Nixon saw themselves as defending individualism, religion, and free enterprise. Their wrath focused not so much on actual communists as on the sophisticated, cosmopolitan State Department elites who tolerated communists in government and accommodated the Soviet Union. "I look at that fellow," Senator Hugh Butler of Nebraska remarked about Secretary of State Dean Acheson. "I watch his smart-aleck manner and his British clothes and that New Dealism, everlasting New Dealism in everything he says and does, and I want to shout, 'Get out, Get out. You stand for everything that has been wrong with the United States.'"

Conservative Republicans like Nixon and McCarthy exploited the anticommunist crusade to attack Democrats and the New Deal tradition. Meanwhile, public distrust of elites who were unaccountable to voters—government bureaucrats, intellectuals, scientists, media and entertainment leaders—encouraged loyalty oaths, "naming names" of alleged communist associates, blacklists, and legal persecution. Spillane's detective novel *One Lonely Night* (1951), which sold 7 million copies, advocated another method to eliminate communists: "Don't arrest them, don't treat them with the dignity of the democratic process of courts of law . . . do the same thing that they'd do to you! Treat 'em to the inglorious taste of sudden death."

Backed by public opinion and the courts, law enforcement officials and anticommunist activists faced few obstacles in purging "red" elements from American life. As the FBI budget increased from $35 million in 1947 to $53 million in 1950 to $130 million by 1962, the agency's watchdogs processed nearly 5 million loyalty forms between 1947 and 1954. Under Truman, more than 7,000 federal government employees lost their jobs; thousands more were never hired in the first place. State and municipal governments adopted similar programs barring "subversives" from public employment. Workers and managers in private industry cooperated to harass suspected employees. Teachers, union leaders, even factory workers were forced to sign loyalty oaths; refusal usually meant dismissal. New York City high school students had to sign loyalty oaths to collect their diplomas. Meanwhile, the U.S. Post Office intercepted and opened mail from certain communist countries. "If ignorant people read it," said one censor, "they might begin to believe it."

J. Edgar Hoover
1895–1972

Stock Montage

Without question, J. Edgar Hoover was the most successful bureaucrat in U.S. history. A man whose entire life centered on Washington, D.C., he was the son of a bureaucrat, born and raised a few blocks from the Capitol. After graduation from George Washington University, he took a job with the Department of Justice, beginning a half-century career that ended only with his death in 1972. The young Hoover was assigned to the Enemy Alien Registration Section of the Bureau of Investigation and played an important role in investigating and deporting radicals during the Red Scare of 1919–1920. He also played a part in federal probes of black activist Marcus Garvey, which ultimately led to Garvey's conviction and deportation. During the Harding presidency, the Bureau of Investigation became so corrupt and ineffective that Hoover considered resigning, but after Harding's death, a new attorney general, Harlan F. Stone, offered the twenty-nine-year-old attorney the directorship. Hoover accepted with the stipulation that he be given the authority to professionalize the bureau and to insulate it from politics.

Energetic and capable, Hoover applied modern management techniques to the bureau (it became the Federal Bureau of Investigation in 1935) with remarkable results. He hired agents with backgrounds in law or accounting and schooled them in the application of scientific principles to law enforcement. He supervised the assembling of a huge centralized fingerprint file, the creation of a sophisticated crime laboratory, and the establishment of the National Police Academy to train other law enforcement officers in scientific investigation. Simultaneously, Hoover recognized the enormous value of good public re-

Such excesses might have been checked by an independent judiciary, but Truman's appointments to the Supreme Court, including Attorney General Clark, consistently voted against civil liberties. In the *Dennis* case (1951) the Court upheld the convictions of eleven Communist Party leaders, ruling that "communist speech" was not protected by constitutional guarantees because communists participated in an international movement. As a result of 141 indictments and other harassment, many Communist Party leaders went "underground," and the party lost half its membership.

The Military Crisis

The sense of national emergency stimulated the reorganization of the military services. The National Security Act of 1947 unified command over the armed services within the new Department of Defense, formalized the Joint Chiefs of Staff, and created an independent air force prepared to incorporate the newest advances in technology. The law also established the National Security Council (NSC) and the Central Intelligence Agency (CIA) as secret bureaus responsible

lations and steadily built the image of the G-man through shrewd manipulation of popular culture. The image was enhanced by well-publicized and successful manhunts for such celebrated gangsters as John Dillinger and "Machine Gun" Kelly. This concern for image also led Hoover to impose on the bureau a code of conduct rooted in the Victorianism of his upbringing in turn-of-the-century Washington. Special agents should wear dark suits and white shirts; women did not smoke; and FBI employees did not take coffee breaks.

After World War II, Hoover's tenure at the FBI became increasingly controversial. Some critics charged that the FBI focused on sensational but episodic criminal activity while ignoring organized crime and white collar crime. In addition, the FBI zealously investigated communist subversives, an activity that broadened considerably as first the civil rights movement and later the antiwar movement stirred the Director's disapproval. In the process of conducting extensive domestic surveillance of political dissidents, the FBI collected a set of files on literally millions of Americans, files which Hoover was willing to use ruthlessly. Most notorious was the bu-

reau's attempt to destroy Martin Luther King, Jr., with a tape recording of sexual activity involving the civil rights leader. Although the effort failed, the King incident illustrates the enormous power Hoover derived from domestic surveillance. As a former aide put it, "I'm afraid of him. I can't imagine what he'd do to me, but I'd rather not mess with him."

Even presidents felt the same way. His relationship with John Kennedy was tense, but his position remained secure, perhaps in part because Hoover had a potentially embarrassing tape of a Kennedy sexual liaison during World War II. His disdain for both Kennedy brothers was plain, however. When Hoover telephoned Robert Kennedy to report that President John F. Kennedy had been killed, Kennedy later remembered that Hoover sounded, "not quite as excited as if he were reporting the fact that he had found a Communist on the faculty at Howard University." Kennedy's successor, Lyndon Johnson, delighted in the bits of scandal that Hoover regularly passed along, and both he and Richard Nixon waived mandatory retirement rules to enable Hoover to remain on the job until his death in May 1972. ∎

only to the president. The NSC would coordinate and refine foreign policy for the White House and act as the president's liaison to the security bureaucracy. The CIA would preside over the gathering of intelligence information. The agency's congressional charter also provided for "such other functions as the Director of Central Intelligence shall, from time to time, deem appropriate." This loophole allowed the agency to develop secret military and political projects overseas. Amendments to the charter in 1949 exempted the CIA from budgetary accounting requirements, thereby releasing the agency from strict congressional oversight.

By rationalizing decision making, the National Security Act consolidated the power of the executive branch. Foreign policy decisions increasingly became insulated from external scrutiny and confined to a narrowing group of advisers. In a critical choice of military strategy, Truman opted in 1948 for an "air-atomic" plan that made strategic bombing, including nuclear weapons, the primary military force. Yet the United States possessed few atomic bombs or technicians capable of assembling more. To the budget-conscious president, however, air-atomic technology seemed an inexpensive way to build an unassailable defense. The plan had the additional advantage of reducing the need for a huge fighting army.

The decision to rebuild U.S. military strength faced opposition from both conservatives and liberals. Wallace, who announced his presidential candidacy as leader of the new Progressive Party, chastised Truman for ignoring the United Nations and provoking the Soviet Union. More powerful opposition came from Republicans like Taft who denounced the swollen federal budget and argued that the war with communism was ultimately a contest of ideas, not military might. When the president requested funds for the air-atomic plan in January 1948, Congress seemed uninterested. "The outlook for greatly increased aviation budgets is not bright," the trade journal *Aviation Week* lamented early in 1948.

Congress abruptly snapped to attention, however, when communists seized power in Soviet-occupied Czechoslovakia in February 1948. Although the State Department had treated Czechoslovakia as part of the Soviet bloc, news of the communist coup shocked the public, confirming fears of Soviet aggression through internal subversion. Truman resolved not to repeat the Munich sellout of Czechoslovakia of 1938, when British and French "appeasement" had permitted Hitler to occupy Czechoslovakian territory. Looking to the past, Truman responded quickly when U.S. military officers stationed in Germany reported a change in Soviet attitudes.

Speaking to a joint session of Congress in March 1948, the president warned that the United States was on the verge of war. The Soviet Union had "destroyed the independence and democratic character of a whole series of nations," said Truman, and so revealed "the clear design" to conquer "the remaining free nations of Europe." "There is some risk involved in action–there always is," he admitted, "but there is far more risk in failure to act." The somber speech persuaded Congress to approve the Marshall Plan and to reestablish the military draft. Conservatives managed to defeat a proposal for universal military training, but Congress allocated an extra $3.5 billion for military purposes, which was 25 percent more than the White House had requested.

Military confrontation came one step closer when the Soviet Union blockaded Berlin in June 1948. Since the end of the war, the great powers had failed to sign a final peace settlement. While the United States and the Soviet Union argued about German reparations, their former enemy remained divided into occupied zones. As the United States and Britain planned to integrate their occupied zones and initiate currency reform, Stalin realized that the Western allies were hastening German independence to bring Germany into the Western alliance. In response the Soviets blocked access to Berlin through East Germany.

Truman saw war on the horizon. Determined to support Berlin, Truman ordered a massive airlift of food and supplies that lasted eleven months. Unwilling to go to war, Stalin had to accept U.S. plans for West Germany. Yet the crisis escalated the level of conflict. In July 1948 Truman ordered B-29 bombers to England. These were the only planes capable of dropping atomic bombs in Europe, although (unknown to the Soviets) they were not modified for such work until 1949. For the first time, atomic weapons had become an explicit instrument of foreign policy.

The Cold War crisis enabled Congress to reverse administration policy in Asia. The corruption of Chiang Kai-shek's Nationalist regime in China and the success of Mao Zedong's communists had persuaded the president to allow the Chinese Civil War to run its course, but the Truman Doctrine had suggested that any communist expansion threatened U.S. interests. Influenced by a well-

Exhibit 8-4. Berlin Blockade, 1948

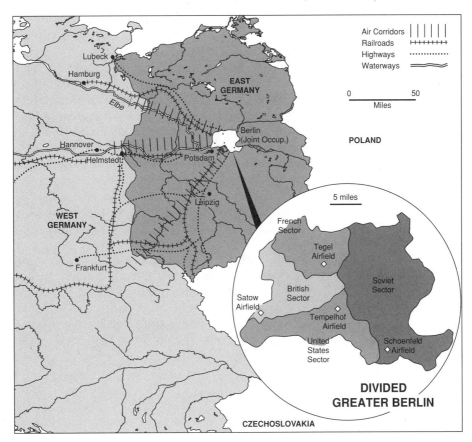

funded pressure group known as the China Lobby, congressional conservatives led by Republican Senator William Knowland of California insisted on a literal interpretation of the Truman Doctrine. Contrary to administration intentions, Congress proceeded to appropriate funds to support Chiang's regime, committing the United States to a repressive but noncommunist government and influencing subsequent foreign policy in Asia for three decades. Meanwhile, Truman's decision to abandon Chiang accelerated accommodation with Japan, which now appeared to be a likely noncommunist ally. In 1947 Truman extended economic assistance to Japan and strengthened U.S. military forces there.

Washington also solidified its sphere of influence in Latin America. The Rio Pact of 1947 provided for collective self-defense of the Western Hemisphere. The following year, the Bogota Treaty created the Organization of American States to coordinate policy, and the United States disavowed intervention in the affairs of other states. In creating this alliance, the administration avoided economic commitments, preferring to support private development. Yet in a series of bilateral agreements, Washington offered military assistance, including the training of Latin American armies. Such support stabilized military and landed elites throughout Latin America and increased their dependence on U.S. trade.

THE ELECTION OF 1948

As the nation faced a series of foreign policy crises, political pundits questioned Truman's leadership. A March 1948 Gallup poll showed that the Democrats would lose the presidential election to any one of several Republican challengers: Dewey, Vandenberg, former Minnesota Governor Harold Stassen, or General Douglas MacArthur. Meanwhile, Henry Wallace announced an independent candidacy. "There is no real fight between a Truman and a Republican," said Wallace. "Both stand for a policy which opens the door to war in our lifetime and makes war certain for our children." Yet military mobilization against Soviet communism worked to the president's advantage. By identifying Wallace as procommunist, the president kept most liberals in the Democratic Party. Moreover, Truman's endorsement of African American civil rights, including an executive order to desegregate the military, appealed to northern liberals. Truman also improved his standing among Jews by promptly recognizing the new state of Israel in 1948.

The Wallace insurgency emboldened Republicans. Renominating Dewey for president, Republicans adopted a moderate platform that called for federal support of housing, farm payments, abolition of poll taxes, a permanent FEPC, and increases in Social Security benefits. Confident of an election victory, Republicans deliberately excluded foreign policy issues from debate, which freed Truman from having to defend his positions. The president then undermined

Exhibit 8-5. Election of 1948

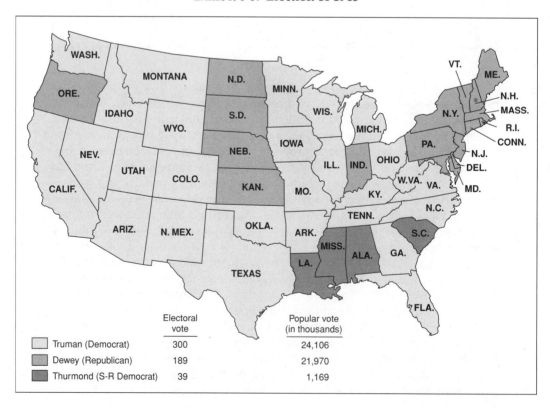

	Electoral vote	Popular vote (in thousands)
Truman (Democrat)	300	24,106
Dewey (Republican)	189	21,970
Thurmond (S-R Democrat)	39	1,169

Stock Montage

President Harry Truman gloats at an erroneous headline on the morning after his upset victory in 1948. Convinced that Truman would lose, pollsters had halted their public opinion surveys prematurely!

the Republicans by calling the Eightieth Congress into special session and daring the Republican majority to enact the party platform.

Truman also confronted divisions within the Democratic Party. Liberals, led by Minneapolis Mayor Hubert Humphrey, demanded a commitment to civil rights legislation. "The time has arrived for the Democratic party to get out of the shadow of states rights," Humphrey told the Democratic National Convention, "and walk forthrightly into the bright sunshine of human rights." Democrats responded by backing a strong civil rights plank. Angry southern delegates who opposed this plank promptly bolted from the convention. Three days later, these Dixiecrats met in Birmingham, Alabama, formed the States' Rights Party, and nominated South Carolina's Strom Thurmond for president. Other southern Democrats simply ignored the party platform. Running in Texas for the Senate, Lyndon B. Johnson attacked the FEPC ("because if a man can tell you whom you must hire, he can tell you whom you cannot employ"), anti-poll-tax proposals, and federal antilynching laws.

Supporters of Henry Wallace proceeded to organize the Progressive Party and launched another independent campaign. Although communists held important positions in the party, the platform primarily reflected liberal principles. Offering a genuine alternative to Truman's Cold War and Dewey's bipartisanship, the Progressives argued that "ending the tragic prospect of war is a joint responsibility of the Soviet Union and the United States." Yet the Progressives could never overcome their association with communism. "Politicians of both major parties have tried to pin the Communist tag on the followers of . . . Wallace," observed pollster George Gallup. "Apparently their efforts have succeeded." The Wallace campaign encountered harassment, mob violence, and denial of public meeting places, particularly in southern states that refused to permit racially mixed gatherings.

While Dixiecrats and Progressives attacked Truman, the special session of the Eightieth Congress convened. If Republicans enacted their platform, Truman would get credit for goading them to act; if not, they would appear hypocritical. After much discussion, Congress adjourned without passing significant legislation. The decision gave Truman campaign ammunition against "do-nothing" Republicans. While preelection polls forecast a Republican victory, Truman took to the stump, launching a whistle-stop campaign that covered more than 20,000 miles. "Give 'em hell, Harry!" became a rallying cry as Truman appealed to anxious farmers about Republican threats to the price support program and became the first president to campaign for the African American vote in Harlem.

The results brought a surprise Democratic victory in November when Truman topped Dewey by more than 2 million votes. "The publishers' press is a very small part of our population," gloated Truman. "They have debauched [their] responsibility . . . to the country and the people have shown them just how they like it." The electoral college gave Truman 304 votes, Dewey 189, Thurmond 34 (all in the South), and Wallace none. Each third-party candidate attracted slightly more than 1 million votes, but Truman did best among farmers, organized labor, and blacks, all groups that supported Roosevelt's New Deal.

THE FAIR DEAL

"Every segment of our population and every individual," Truman told the Eighty-first Congress, "has a right to expect from our Government a fair deal." Working again with a Democratic majority in Congress, the president called for increased Social Security benefits and minimum wages, civil rights legislation, federal aid to education, national health insurance, and repeal of the Taft-Hartley Act. However, White House proposals soon met resistance from the true majority in Congress—a conservative coalition of southern Democrats and midwestern Republicans. By controlling the congressional committee system, these groups prevented consideration of Truman's program. Although Congress passed the Housing Act of 1949, providing for slum clearance and federally funded low-income housing, insufficient appropriations limited implementation of the program. In addition, civil rights legislation died in committee, and, choosing to avoid a hopeless skirmish, Truman avoided pursuing its passage.

Truman's support of civil rights appeared ambiguous. Despite the president's 1948 order to desegregate the armed services, the military evaded enforcement. In Truman's inauguration parade of 1949, African American soldiers

Republican leaders Robert Taft (left) and Arthur Vandenberg endorsed a bipartisan foreign policy, while disagreeing about overseas military commitments.

marched with whites, but the army blocked full integration by segregating platoons, a policy that persisted during the Korean War. Truman's Department of Justice supported civil rights suits, but the Federal Housing Authority continued to accept residential segregation, even after the Supreme Court outlawed restrictive covenants. (For the legal issues, see Chapter 9.) As for equal employment opportunity, the president hesitated to reestablish the FEPC, then failed to halt discrimination in war industries. Nonetheless, African Americans praised Truman's moral support. "No occupant of the White House since the nation was born," wrote the NAACP's Walter White in 1952, "has taken so frontal or constant a stand against racial discrimination as has Harry S Truman."

The limitations of Truman's Fair Deal reflected basic changes in liberal thinking. After the defeat of Wallace, liberals repudiated associations with communism and moved away from radical positions. Anticommunist liberals, including theologian Reinhold Niebuhr and historian Arthur M. Schlesinger,

Exhibit 8-6. Federal Budget Deficits, 1945–1950
(in rounded billions of dollars)

1945	47.6
1950	3.1

Source: *Economic Report of the President* (1988).

Jr., argued that the search for a perfect society such as a communist utopia appeared naive and self-deceptive, and led to totalitarian excesses. At a time when more middle-class citizens were enjoying personal prosperity, supporting the baby boom, and celebrating conformity, U.S. liberalism understandably supported the status quo.

LIMITING BIPARTISANSHIP

Although political disagreement eventually undermined the foreign policy consensus, a bipartisan spirit prevailed on European issues until 1951. In June 1948 the Senate passed the Vandenberg Resolution, which permitted participation in a peacetime military alliance with the nations of western Europe. The next year, the United States signed the North Atlantic Treaty, a pact which provided for a collective defense against the Soviets by forming the North Atlantic Treaty Organization (NATO). At the same time, the administration moved to create a new West German state, and in 1949 the Federal Republic of Germany joined the Western alliance. Although the treaty obligated the United States to send military assistance to European allies, its purposes appeared less military than political. First, NATO served as a diplomatic deterrent to Soviet expansion. Second, the alliance ensured U.S. domination of western Europe by obliging its members to adopt a united, U.S.-influenced approach to the region's security. Third, the pact linked German industrial and military power with the rest of western Europe to avoid renewing old rivalries. Opposed to permanent military commitments, Taft led the fight against the treaty's ratification but could not overcome the president's policy. The House, however, hesitated to allocate funds to implement the treaty's provisions. Then, in September 1949 the president announced that the Soviet Union had exploded an atomic bomb. Within a week, the House gladly provided funding for NATO.

Perceiving the Soviet Union as a relentless enemy that now possessed devastating weapons of destruction, Republicans and Democrats alike felt increasingly vulnerable to attack both at home and abroad. Although Soviet spies accelerated the development of a Soviet atomic bomb (probably by fewer than two years), fears of domestic subversion assumed nightmarish proportions. Allegations that government "traitors" such as former State Department official Alger Hiss passed secret documents to communist agents reinforced the climate of suspicion. Yet Washington recognized that the Soviet Union lacked the military capacity to launch an atomic attack. Even so, Truman opted to strengthen U.S. military power. Despite unanimous objections by scientists and civilians on the Atomic Energy Commission's General Advisory Council, commission head Lewis Strauss, backed by physicist Edward Teller, urged the development of a super bomb—the hydrogen bomb. In January 1950 Truman ended the debate by ordering development of the bomb. By the end of the next year the United States had successfully tested the new weapon; within two years the Soviet Union did the same.

Although he had strengthened the U.S. arsenal, Truman faced Republican criticism for neglecting China's Chiang Kai-shek. Despite appropriations exceeding $1 billion for the Chinese Nationalists, communist armies steadily destroyed Chiang's crumbling forces. By August 1949 the State Department

ARTHUR H. VANDENBERG
1884–1951

Stock Montage

"The Old Guard dies but never surrenders," wrote journalist Milton S. Mayer of the last-ditch noninterventionists in 1940; "Vandenberg surrenders, but never dies." Michigan Senator Arthur H. Vandenberg stood for many other conservative Americans when he made the transition from prewar antiinterventionism to postwar internationalism. Although staunch Old Guard Republicans such as Robert Taft of Ohio refused to compromise their "America-first" principles, Vandenberg believed that national security required a new internationalist commitment. Insisting that the Soviet Union constituted a threat to U.S. interests around the world, he worked with the Truman administration to build a national consensus in support of the Cold War.

Born in Grand Rapids, Michigan, Vandenberg embraced the conservative middle-class midwestern values of his surroundings. As editor of the *Grand Rapids Herald*, he backed Woodrow Wilson's decision to seek intervention in World War I but opposed U.S. entry into the League of Nations. Appointed to the Senate in 1928, Vandenberg supported Hoover's efforts to end the Depression and later backed early New Deal programs in the interests of bipartisanship. By 1935, however, he rejected Roosevelt's leadership and became an outspoken critic.

Vandenberg also dissented vigorously against Roosevelt's foreign policy. In 1933, for example, he was one of only two senators to oppose U.S. recognition of the Soviet Union. During the 1930s he favored strict neutrality legislation. With other antiinterventionists, he attacked the Lend-Lease plan, arguing that it would hasten U.S. entry into the European war. The trauma of Pearl Harbor changed Vandenberg's position. Embracing internationalism, he appealed to Roosevelt to establish a joint congressional-executive committee to forge a united foreign policy. (Roosevelt, unwilling to share foreign policy with anyone, ignored the plea.) Then, in January 1945 Vandenberg presented a widely hailed speech, announcing his support of a postwar United Nations organization.

To win Republican backing of the postwar settlement, Truman chose Vandenberg to attend the first United Nations conference in San Francisco in 1945. Vandenberg succeeded in persuading the delegates to adopt Article 51 of the U.N. Charter, providing for regional alliances. Intended to protect U.S. influence in Latin America, this article later provided the basis for NATO and other regional pacts.

Considered the leading internationalist in the Republican Party, Vandenberg demanded a voice in foreign policy in exchange for bipartisan support of the Cold War. Criticizing any sign of "appeasement" of the Soviet Union, he denounced negotiations to internationalize atomic energy in 1946. Yet Vandenberg was personally vain and easily subject to flattery and pressure. Using the principle of bipartisanship, the administration won his support of the Truman Doctrine, Marshall Plan, and NATO. Vandenberg also intervened with Republican leaders to prevent any serious debate of foreign policy in the 1948 presidential election.

Unlike Taft, Vandenberg did not question the high cost of the Cold War or the growth of a national security state. Taft's opposition to the military state prevented him from winning the Republican nomination in 1948 and 1952. Yet Vandenberg, whose foreign policy position seemed more popular, failed to win the respect of his colleagues and never became a party leader. ■

Exhibit 8-7. The North Atlantic Treaty Organization (NATO)

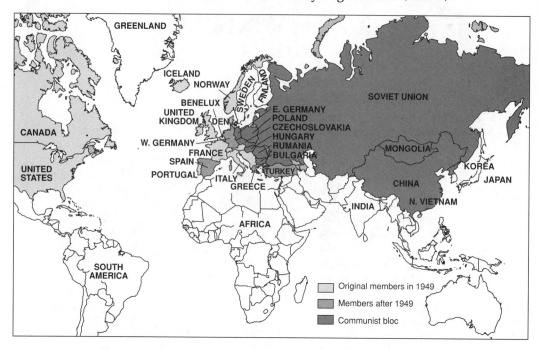

predicted a communist victory and halted further assistance. "The only alternative open to the United States," asserted a State Department "White Paper," "was full-scale intervention in behalf of a government which had lost the confidence of its own troops and its own people." Yet, although it conceded the inevitability of a communist victory, the Truman administration rejected accommodation with the Chinese insurgents. Four months later Mao Zedong's communist forces swept into power, forcing Chiang to abandon the mainland and flee to the island of Taiwan (Formosa).

Given the logic of containment, the communist victory in China could only be seen as a defeat of U.S. policy, especially after Mao signed a mutual assistance pact with the Soviet Union in 1950. The China Lobby, including such leading Republicans as former president Herbert Hoover, Taft, and Knowland, attacked the administration for failing to support an anticommunist ally. Such criticism reinforced Truman's reluctance to negotiate with Chinese communists. Instead, the United States adopted a policy of nonrecognition that lasted for more than two decades. Meanwhile, the CIA secretly supported anticommunist Chinese in an ineffective effort to disrupt the mainland regime.

FEAR OF SUBVERSION AND THE RISE OF MCCARTHY

Anxieties over the "loss" of China and the Soviet explosion of an atomic bomb escalated in January 1950 when a jury found Alger Hiss guilty of perjury for denying that he had passed classified documents to erstwhile communist

Former State Department official Alger Hiss denied allegations of communist ties, setting the stage for a dramatic perjury trial. After one hung jury failed to reach a verdict, a second trial convicted Hiss in 1950.

Whittaker Chambers in the 1930s. For anticommunists, the sensational case proved an inseparable link existed between Hiss's New Deal liberalism and communist influence in government. The case particularly embarrassed the Democrats because Truman had labeled HUAC's investigation of Hiss "a red herring" and issued a 1948 executive order barring Congress from access to government loyalty files without presidential approval. Traumatized by the possibility that Hiss may have been "duped" by communist spies, liberals henceforth took pains to disassociate themselves from political activities that might prove embarrassing. The Hiss case and the arrest of other spies in Britain solidified the Cold War truism that association with the U.S. Communist Party was equivalent to service to the Soviet state. Indeed, the Soviets found willing agents among U.S. Communist Party members. However, most U.S. communists attempted to affect policy through more conventional political activities such as participation in labor groups, elections, or public events. Except in the extremely ambiguous Hiss case, investigators never found communist agents in government. Nonetheless, HUAC's Richard Nixon, who had sparked the Hiss investigation, denounced "high officials" for concealing a larger subversive "conspiracy."

One month after the Hiss conviction, Senator Joseph McCarthy captured national attention by claiming to have proof of a communist conspiracy in government. "I have in my hands," he told the Women's Republican Club in Wheeling, West Virginia, "a list of 205 [government employees] that were made known to the Secretary of State as being members of the Communist party and who nevertheless are still working and shaping policy in the State Department." In later versions McCarthy changed the number of alleged communists, but he vigorously defended the charge that subversives permeated the federal government.

McCarthy's attacks on communism mirrored the national mood. The arrest of Julius and Ethel Rosenberg in June 1950 on charges of transmitting atomic bomb secrets to the Soviet Union during World War II underscored the domestic threat. New evidence suggests that Julius Rosenberg provided proximity fuses and sketches of an atomic bomb to Soviet agents, although the value of such information to Soviet physicists was slight. Yet, without specific information, Nevada's conservative Democratic Senator Patrick McCarran introduced the Internal Security Act, which authorized the president to declare an "internal security emergency" and to detain suspected dissidents. The law banned communists from employment in defense industries, established a Subversive Activities Control Board, required communists to register with the attorney general, and excluded communists from obtaining passports. Truman vetoed the bill "because any governmental stifling of the free expression of opinion is a long step toward totalitarianism." Congress overrode the veto by an overwhelming margin. Terrified by the prospect of an atomic war with the Soviet Union, the public supported such anticommunist measures.

McCarthy's accusations concerning communists in government attracted the support of conservative Republicans, who, despite occasional misgivings, endorsed these attacks on the Truman administration. In 1950 a Senate investigating committee chaired by Maryland Democrat Millard Tydings found no evidence to support McCarthy's charges and concluded that the allegations were "a fraud and a hoax." Yet the Senate responded to the report along strict party lines. Such party loyalty enabled McCarthy to remain a presence if not a decisive factor in the 1950 congressional elections. In Maryland, McCarthy smeared Tydings as a procommunist and contributed to Tydings's defeat. Meanwhile, in California, Nixon defeated Helen Gahagan Douglas, whom he dubbed the "Pink Lady," to win election to the Senate.

After the 1950 elections, McCarran's Senate Internal Security subcommittee focused on communist influence at the United Nations, and HUAC resumed investigations of Hollywood figures in 1951. Meanwhile, McCarthy's accusations that communists were employed in the State Department gained wide public attention. Truman called McCarthy a liar. Yet the administration reacted to the charges not by defending the civil liberties of the accused but by affirming its own anticommunist credentials. In April 1951 Truman issued an executive order introducing a new standard for ferreting out subversives: a federal employee could be fired not when there were "reasonable grounds" but rather when there was "reasonable doubt" about the person's loyalty. The burden of proof thus shifted from the accuser to the accused.

In 1952 Congress endeavored to protect U.S. borders by establishing new rules for immigration. The McCarran-Walter Immigration Act, passed over Truman's veto, gave the president power to exclude any foreigner deemed "detrimental" to the national interest. Continuing previous immigration policies, the law favored immigrants from northern and western European countries but sharply limited newcomers from colonies of those countries. While slightly increasing Asian immigration quotas and permitting wider immigration from

Millard Tydings (right) faces Joseph McCarthy at a March 8, 1950, Senate foreign relations subcommittee hearing bearing on McCarthy's charges that a communist spy ring was operating in the State Department.

Latin America, these rules reduced immigration from the West Indies and Africa. Consistent with the anticommunist crusade, the McCarran-Walter Act also limited immigration from countries under communist control and facilitated expulsion of undesirable aliens and even naturalized citizens.

THE KOREAN WAR

By 1950 the sense of an impending international crisis led the National Security Council to develop a comprehensive analysis of U.S. foreign policy in a secret document labeled NSC-68. Asserting that "the Soviet Union . . . is animated by a new fanatic faith . . . and seeks to impose its absolute authority over the rest of the world," the report emphasized the possibility of immediate war and recommended that the United States be prepared to halt Soviet expansion throughout the world. Such a goal demanded a global defense system that included hydrogen bombs, expansion of conventional military forces, and a network of international alliances. To finance this policy, NSC-68 recommended a quadrupling of the $13 billion national defense budget. This costly plan faced considerable opposition in Congress, particularly because the Soviet Union had avoided any overt action since 1948 that justified U.S. military intervention. Meanwhile, in secret meetings, the administration debated plans to defend Taiwan from invasion by Chinese communists.

Exhibit 8-8. The Korean War

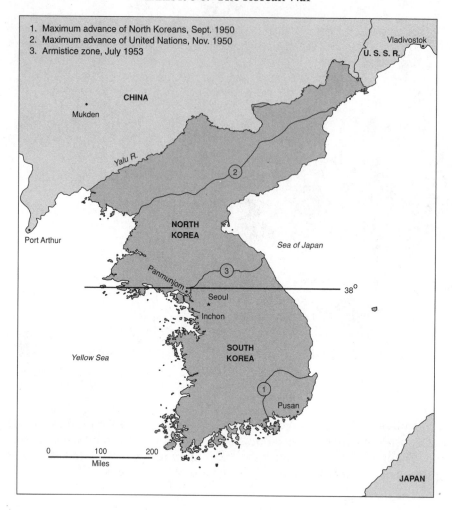

1. Maximum advance of North Koreans, Sept. 1950
2. Maximum advance of United Nations, Nov. 1950
3. Armistice zone, July 1953

The tense peace was shattered on 25 June 1950, when North Korean troops suddenly invaded South Korea. Six months earlier, Acheson had remarked in a speech to the National Press Club that Korea and Taiwan lay beyond the U.S. "defense perimeter" in the Pacific. The statement, challenged by Republican conservatives, justified a reduction of aid to Chiang Kai-shek, but as North Korean armies advanced quickly, Truman ordered military assistance to South Korea and directed the Seventh Fleet to sail between mainland China and Taiwan to prevent an invasion of the Nationalist-held islands. The next day the United States called an emergency session of the U.N. Security Council, which branded North Korea an aggressor. (The Soviet delegation, boycotting the Security Council on another matter, missed the critical vote.) As South Korean armies collapsed, Truman ordered U.S. troops into action. "The attack upon Korea," he declared, "makes it plain beyond all doubt that communism has passed beyond the use of subversion to conquer independent nations." The United Nations later approved Truman's action, giving international sanction to U.S. policy. Sixteen nations eventually participated in the war, but the United States provided most of the resources and leadership.

Intervention in Korea stemmed from the conviction that the United States had to "draw the line" against communist aggression and demonstrate its willingness to fight the Soviets anywhere in the world. As with earlier decisions to challenge the Berlin blockade and develop hydrogen bombs, the president bypassed consultation with congressional leaders, thereby setting important precedents for successors. Although Taft denounced Truman's "complete usurpation . . . of authority to use the armed forces," public opinion supported the president's action. Indeed, Truman's claim to be enforcing U.N. policy won favor among liberals, even though the U.S. military commander, General Douglas MacArthur, took orders directly and exclusively from Washington.

U.S. forces arrived in Korea just in time to stop a complete North Korean victory. After hard fighting near the southern port of Pusan, the U.N. Allies forced the enemy to retreat. At the start of the war, the administration insisted that fighting was "solely for the purpose of restoring the Republic of Korea to its status prior to the invasion." In September 1950, however, Truman authorized a military advance north of the thirty-eighth parallel, the border between North and South Korea, in an effort to liberate North Korea from communism before U.S. congressional elections. General MacArthur promised victory by Christmas. In October Truman conferred with MacArthur at Wake Island and agreed to allow Allied troops to proceed to the Yalu River, which bordered China. Even before these decisions, China had decided to protect North Korea. By November Chinese forces had stopped U.S. advances, driving the U.N. armies into a retreat south of the thirty-eighth parallel.

Confrontation with Chinese troops also raised the possibility of another world war, including the use of nuclear weapons. Truman, however, exercised his power as commander-in-chief to restrain MacArthur and prevent an attack on China. By 1951 battle lines again stabilized around the thirty-eighth parallel, but MacArthur criticized the limits of U.S. involvement. "There is no substitute for victory," he declared. Unfamiliar with the concept of limited war, public opinion appeared ambivalent, showing both strong support for the use of atomic bombs and a desire to withdraw from the war altogether. When Truman announced a stalemated "cease fire," MacArthur, harboring his own presidential ambitions, publicly criticized the president's "no-win" policy.

Exasperated by MacArthur's insubordination, Truman fired the general in April 1951. The decision infuriated conservatives, who spoke of impeaching the president and welcomed MacArthur home with parades and a unique address to a joint session of Congress. The general took the opportunity to condemn the idea of limited war. Yet the removal of MacArthur facilitated the opening of truce negotiations that began in 1951. These talks lasted for two years, while the fighting continued under the command of General Matthew Ridgeway. Truman's refusal to repatriate communist prisoners of war who declined to return to their homelands stalled negotiations. The impasse ended only after the inauguration of the next administration in 1953. The limited war had cost 34,000 U.S. lives.

The Korean War justified the military buildup envisioned in NSC-68. Wartime appropriations expanded the armed forces and nuclear arsenal and increased the number of overseas bases. Funding for aircraft research and development escalated from $1.8 billion to $3.1 billion. Furthermore, the CIA

General Douglas MacArthur greets President Truman at Wake Island in the Pacific to discuss Korean War strategy in 1950. It was the only time the two met. Truman fired his general the next year.

expanded in size and scope of operations and increased its staff from fewer than 5,000 in 1950 to 15,000 by 1955. The war led the president to hold regular meetings with the National Security Council, setting a precedent for Truman's successors. To check inflation, Congress gave Truman authority to establish wage, price, and rent controls. In December 1950 the president declared a "national emergency" and implemented those economic powers, stabilizing the cost of living index for the remainder of the war. The military crisis emboldened Truman to seize operations of the steel industry to end a strike in 1952, but the Supreme Court ruled the act unconstitutional.

The Korean crisis also prompted the Truman administration to proceed with plans to rearm Germany. When France objected, Truman offered to station U.S. troops in Europe permanently to ensure stability. Congressional conservatives protested these unprecedented peacetime military commitments. In the "Great Debate" of 1951, Republicans leaders ended the bipartisan foreign policy that had characterized Cold War politics since 1947. Attacking the poorly executed land war in Korea and expressing frustration that Chiang Kai-shek had not been permitted to enter the fray, Republicans focused on the unilateral nature of Truman's military decisions and insisted that Congress have a role in the formation of foreign policy. Dramatizing these concerns, Republicans sponsored a Senate resolution that blocked U.S. troops from being sent to Europe without approval from Congress. Although testimony from NATO's supreme commander, General Dwight D. Eisenhower, blunted some of the Republicans' criticism, Congress passed a compromise version of the resolution that limited troop deployments to four divisions.

The Korean War also stimulated a more aggressive policy in Asia. Although the Truman administration had been prepared to accept a communist Chinese invasion of Taiwan in early 1950, the Korean conflict provided an excuse to send the Seventh Fleet to protect the besieged island. Truman also deepened U.S. involvement in Indochina. When Ho Chi Minh, leader of the anti-French liberation movement, accepted support from China and the Soviet Union in 1949, the United States increased aid to France. After the Korean War began, Truman permitted U.S. military personnel to assist French forces. "If Indochina went," explained a State Department official in 1951, "the fall of Burma and the fall of Thailand would be absolutely inevitable." These would be followed by communist victories in Malaysia and India. Such assumptions led to increasing commitments in Southeast Asia that culminated in the Vietnam War.

Investment in the French empire contrasted with lack of support for colonized peoples. In his 1949 inauguration address, Truman introduced the "Point Four" program, asserting that the United States had a responsibility to spread "the benefits of our scientific advances and industrial progress" to the "underdeveloped areas" of the world. Yet Point Four foreign aid offered no alternatives to existing economic relations: "underdeveloped areas" were seen only as suppliers of raw materials and consumers of industrial goods. Rather than a humanitarian program, Point Four funded economic studies to facilitate private business investment. Even so, the administration could not persuade Congress to appropriate more than a token $27 million in 1950.

Such priorities reflected the overwhelming emphasis on using procapitalist countries as allies in the Cold War. Japan's U.S.-dictated Constitution of 1947 sought to uproot traditional militarism and ultranationalism by disavowing war. The United States also brought Japan's rebuilt economy into an Asian anticommunist network, including South Korea, Taiwan, and Indochina, to stabilize relations in the Pacific. A new treaty of 1951 then restored Japanese control of their home islands but allowed U.S. occupation of Okinawa and the stationing of troops on Japanese territory. To overcome objections from Japan's former enemies in the Pacific, the United States promised to protect Australia and New Zealand from attack, an agreement formalized in the ANZUS treaty of 1951. With such alliances, Washington established an anticommunist barrier against Chinese and Soviet expansion in the Pacific.

Alliances with former enemies also promoted support of Italy and Spain. In 1951 the Western allies lifted military restrictions imposed on Italy at the end of World War II. At the same time, Truman entered negotiations with Franco's Spain, which culminated in a 1953 treaty that allowed U.S. military bases in Spain in exchange for economic and military assistance. (Meanwhile, on the home front, the attorney general placed Veterans of the Abraham Lincoln Brigade, whose members had fought against Franco in the Spanish Civil War, on a list of subversive organizations.) In supporting Spain, Italy, Germany, and Japan against China and the Soviet Union, Truman had ironically reversed the Grand Alliance of World War II.

By 1952 the Truman administration had lost control of foreign and domestic policy. Truman's commitment to Soviet containment had wrecked earlier State Department hopes for an international extension of the Open Door policy;

U.S. trade with eastern Europe and China remained minimal. Even worse, containment had bogged down in the "limited" Korean War, which promised neither victory nor an early end. In domestic affairs, the Fair Deal lacked a political base to overcome the opposition of congressional conservatives. Seeking support for his foreign policy, Truman allowed his liberal domestic programs to founder. Meanwhile, McCarthy continued a campaign to expose alleged communists in government. Revelations of corruption by administration officials compounded Truman's difficulties. Republican leaders expected to change government policy by capturing the White House in 1952.

SUGGESTED READINGS

The major issues of the Truman years are explored in Alonzo L. Hamby, *Beyond the New Deal: Harry S Truman and American Liberalism* (1973). A conventional and sympathetic account of the Truman presidency is Robert J. Donovan's two-volume study, *Conflict and Crisis* (1977) and *Tumultuous Years* (1982). Two good biographies are Robert H. Ferrell, *Harry S Truman: A Life* (1994), and Alonzo L. Hamby, *Man of the People: A Life of Harry S Truman* (1995). Also useful as an introduction to the period is an anthology, Barton J. Bernstein, ed., *Politics and Policies of the Truman Administration* (1970). A convenient collection of primary sources is Barton J. Bernstein and Allen Matusow, eds., *The Truman Administration* (1966). See also Gary W. Reichard, *Politics as Usual: The Age of Truman and Eisenhower* (1988).

For Truman's farm policies, see Allen Matusow, *Farm Policies and Politics in the Truman Years* (1967); for labor, see R. Alton Lee, *Truman and Taft-Hartley* (1966). Analysis of a landmark case involving the relation between government and business appears in Maeva Marcus, *Truman and the Steel Seizure Case* (1977). The Wallace candidacy is described in Richard J. Walton, *Henry Wallace, Harry Truman, and the Cold War* (1976), which contains many primary sources, and in Norman D. Markowitz, *The Rise and Fall of the People's Century: Henry A. Wallace and American Liberalism* (1973). James T. Patterson's *Mr. Republican: A Biography of Robert A. Taft* (1972) examines the career of the leading conservative. For the early career of Lyndon B. Johnson, see the second volume of Robert Caro's *The Years of Lyndon Johnson: Means of Ascent* (1990).

The domestic anticommunist crusade is described by Richard M. Fried, *Nightmare in Red: The McCarthy Era in Perspective* (1990). The political consequences of anticommunism are explored in Francis H. Thompson, *The Frustration of Politics: Truman, Congress, and the Loyalty Drive, 1945–1953* (1979); in Athan Theoharis, *Seeds of Repression: Harry S Truman and the Origins of McCarthyism* (1971); and in Alan D. Harper, *The Politics of Loyalty* (1969). The impact of the Red Scare is thoroughly documented in David Caute, *The Great Fear: The Anti-Communist Purge Under Truman and Eisenhower* (1978). Also illuminating is Les Adler, *The Red Image: American Attitudes Toward Communism in the Cold War Era* (1991). The investigations of Hollywood are detailed in Larry Ceplair and Steven Englund, *The Inquisition in Hollywood: Politics in the Film Community, 1930–1960* (1980), and in Victor Navasky, *Naming Names* (1980). An oral history exploring these issues is Griffin Fariello, *Red Scare: Memories of the American Inquisition* (1995).

There are numerous books about the dramatic political trials of the era: Allan Weinstein, *Perjury: The Hiss-Chambers Case* (1978), contends that Hiss was guilty, whereas John Chabot Smith, *Alger Hiss: The True Story* (1977), avers his innocence; Ronald Radosh and Joyce Milton, *The Rosenberg File* (1987), asserts the guilt of Julius Rosenberg (not Ethel Rosenberg), whereas the Rosenbergs' innocence is defended by Walter and Miriam Schneir, *Invitation to an Inquest* (1983). For the harassment of U.S. Spanish Civil War veterans, see Peter N. Carroll, *The Odyssey of the Abraham Lincoln Brigade: Americans in the Spanish Civil War* (1994). McCarthy's attack on one State Department official is told in Robert P. Newman, *Owen Lattimore and the "Loss" of China* (1992). A good background to such trials is Stanley Kutler, *The American Inquisition: Justice and Injustice in the Cold War* (1982). More sympathetic to the anticommunist crusade is Richard Gid Powers, *Not Without Honor: The History of American Anticommunism* (1995). The role of the FBI is detailed in Richard Gid Powers, *Secrecy and Power: The Life of J. Edgar Hoover* (1987), and in Athan G. Theoharis and John Stuart Cox, *The Boss: J. Edgar Hoover and the Great American Inquisition* (1988).

For Joseph McCarthy, the best starting point is David M. Oshinsky, *A Conspiracy So Immense: The World of Joe McCarthy* (1983), but also see the titles listed at the end of Chapter 10. The close relation between domestic anticommunism and foreign policy is presented in Richard M. Freeland, *The Truman Doctrine and the Origins of McCarthyism* (1972). For the split between liberals and radicals, see William O'Neill, *A Better World: The Great Schism: Stalinism and the American Intellectuals* (1983), and Mary Sperling McAuliffe, *Crisis on the Left* (1978).

The literature on the Cold War is vast. A sensible and readable introduction is Walter Lafeber, *America, Russia, and the Cold War* (1985), as is Bernard Weisberger, *Cold War, Cold Peace* (1984). More detailed on the origins of postwar foreign policy is Melvyn P. Leffler, *A Preponderance of Power: National Security, the Truman Administration, and the Cold War* (1992), which can be supplemented with Daniel Yergin, *Shattered Peace: The Origins of the Cold War and the National Security State* (1977). A valuable analysis of foreign policy issues is John Lewis Gaddis, *Strategies of Containment: A Critical Appraisal of Postwar American National Security Policy* (1982). The importance of the atomic bomb in foreign policy and military planning is analyzed carefully in Gregg Harken, *The Winning Weapon: The Atomic Bomb in the Cold War, 1945–1950* (1980). The role of key personalities in policy-making emerges in Robert L. Messer, *The End of an Alliance: James F. Byrnes, Roosevelt, Truman, and the Origins of the Cold War* (1982). See also Michael J. Hogan, *The Marshall Plan: America, Britain, and the Reconstruction of Western Europe* (1987). The persistence of isolationism is the subject of Justus D. Doenecke, *Not to the Swift: The Old Isolationists in the Cold War* (1979). A useful anthology on the dissenters from Truman's policies is Thomas G. Paterson, ed., *Cold War Critics* (1971).

The Cold War in Asia is described in Robert M. Blum, *Drawing the Line: The Origin of the American Containment Policy in East Asia* (1982); in William Whitney Stueck, Jr., *The Road to Confrontation: American Policy Toward China and Korea, 1947–1950* (1981); and in Nancy Tucker, *Patterns in the Dust: Chinese American Relations and the Recognition Controversy, 1949–1950* (1983). A good analysis of postwar Asian policy is Gordon H. Chang, *Friends and Enemies: The United States, China, and the Soviet Union, 1948–1972* (1990). The background of the Korean War is best studied in James Irving Matray, *The Reluctant Crusade: American Foreign Policy in Korea, 1941–1950* (1985), in Jian Chen, *China's Road to the*

Korean War: The Making of the Sino-American Confrontation (1994), and in William Whitney Stueck, Jr., *The Korean War: An International History* (1995), which may be supplemented by Bruce Cumings's two-volume study, *The Origins of the Korean War* (1981–1990), and Rosemary Foot, *The Wrong War: American Policy and the Dimensions of the Korean Conflict, 1950–1953* (1985). Still valuable is Ronald Caridi, *The Korean War and American Politics* (1968). For U.S. policy in Indochina, see the relevant chapters of Lloyd C. Gardner, *Approaching Vietnam: From World War II Through Dienbienphu, 1941–1954* (1988).

U.S. policy in the Middle East is presented in Aaron David Miller, *The Search for Security: Saudi Arabian Oil and American Foreign Policy, 1939–1949* (1980); in Barry Rubin, *Paved with Good Intentions: American Experience in Iran* (1980); and in Zvi Ganin, *Truman, American Jewry, and Israel, 1945–1948* (1979). For international economic affairs, see Fred L. Block, *The Origins of International Economic Disorder* (1977). Also insightful is Ernest R. May, *"Lessons" of the Past: The Use and Misuse of History in American Foreign Policy* (1973).

9

A big, gleaming new car was one of the supreme status symbols of the affluent society. Here a 1954 Buick Super Riviera shines in all its glory.

TROUBLED AFFLUENCE: POSTWAR SOCIETY, 1945–1960

"Nobody's job is safe," a woman salesclerk learned in Hollywood's classic 1946 film, *The Best Years of Our Lives.* With the demobilization of 12 million soldiers and the loss of 10 million war-related jobs, Americans in all economic classes feared the return of another Great Depression. Instead, the economy entered an era of unprecedented growth characterized by a dramatic rise in production and productivity, expanded corporate profits, increased personal income, and soaring consumer spending. By 1955 the 6 percent of the world population that lived in the United States made two-thirds of the world's manufactured goods. Real income doubled for families in all economic brackets between 1947 and 1973. Yet as 22 million people migrated from rural areas into the cities in the 1940s and 1950s, postwar affluence spread unevenly and at a social cost. Material abundance also provoked concern about a loss of spiritual values and the pace of social and technological change. The tensions between prosperity and its consequences provided the context for the new postwar generation.

REBUILDING A CIVILIAN ECONOMY

Wartime government relied on the expertise of corporate leaders—"dollar-a-year" men—who remained on the payrolls of their private corporations while making economic decisions for the nation. Their primary commitment to big business triggered a bitter debate about the reconversion to a civilian economy. As the need for war materials declined in 1944, the War Production Board (WPB) recommended that small businesses that were losing war contracts reconvert to peacetime production while larger corporations continue to meet military needs. Corporate leaders vigorously resisted this proposal because they opposed small firms gaining advantages in the transition to civilian production. Unwilling to slacken war manufacturing, military leaders backed the major war contractors. This alliance delayed economic reconversion until 1945, thereby protecting the wartime expansion of big business but also extending the shortage of civilian goods past the end of the war.

Ignoring the problems of small business, the War Production Board lifted wartime regulations as soon as the war ended. The abrupt termination of government control over scarce resources benefited larger corporations that had stockpiled such materials. Unable to obtain basic manufacturing resources, many small businesses folded or sold out to bigger firms. Large corporations also took advantage of Washington's generous reconversion sales and bought government-built plants and resources at a fraction of their cost. Such subsidies ensured that the biggest companies would continue to dominate the economy. The Federal Trade Commission (FTC) reported in 1947 that 2,450 independent mining and manufacturing firms had disappeared since 1940 because of mergers and acquisitions. Concentrated economic power, the FTC declared, was "the greatest dramatic challenge to the American theory of competitive enterprise." Although Congress eventually responded to small business pressure by creating the Small Business Administration in 1953, most government contracts still went to large corporations.

Exhibit 9-1. Gross National Product, 1946–1958
(in rounded billions of dollars)

1946	212
1950	288
1954	372
1958	457

Source: *Economic Report of the President* (1988).

Exhibit 9-2. Consumer Price Index, 1945–1949
(1967 = 100)

1945	53.9
1947	66.9
1949	71.4

Source: *Historical Statistics of the United States, Colonial Times to 1970* (1975).

Postwar business decisions worsened consumer shortages. Because companies made greater profits from expensive goods than from cheaper ones—for example, gowns rather than house dresses—manufacturers preferred to produce high-priced goods. The resulting shortage of necessities led to skyrocketing prices and an illegal black market. Lifting controls on building materials stimulated construction of profitable industrial plants without alleviating residential housing shortages. Builders and real estate brokers made enormous profits as house prices soared overnight. Shortages and inflation soon became political footballs as congressional conservatives opposed extension of wartime regulations, and President Truman demanded consumer protection. The resulting compromise retained some price controls until mid-1947, but the consumer price index increased 30 percent between mid-1946 and 1948.

Wartime agricultural trends also persisted in the postwar era, bringing fundamental changes in U.S. food production. Recognizing the profitability of mechanization and land consolidation, food producers invested in new equipment and new hybrid crops that could be handled by machines; increased the use of chemical fertilizers, pesticides, additives, and antibiotics; and acquired ever-larger holdings. Cotton became the leading California agricultural crop once growers discovered that the flat, dry San Joaquin Valley permitted cultivation with large planting and harvesting machines, but mechanized farming required substantial capital investment and therefore stimulated the emergence of agribusiness corporations. Between 1949 and 1959 farm production increased 6 percent per year as the farm population declined and the number of farms dwindled.

Such changes benefited from government assistance to corporate farming. In the early postwar years, federal loans to war-torn Europe subsidized the export of farm surpluses. After European farming recovered, the Agricultural Acts of 1948–1949 established government price supports for sales of basic crops. In 1956 Congress authorized payment for not planting certain crops, and the Soil Bank Act of 1956 provided reimbursements for converting crop land into noncommercial conservation acreage. Larger farms gained most. "The majority of farm people derive little or no benefit from our agricultural price support legislation," stated the Economic Report of the President in 1959; "those with the higher incomes are the main beneficiaries." The reduction in government rice allotments and the replacement of cotton sharecroppers by hired labor and tractors stimulated an exodus of millions of poor whites and African Americans from the rural South.

Technological agriculture encouraged consumption of mass-produced food. As consumers used more processed and frozen foods, food processors such as Birdseye dictated which crop strains would be planted, resulting in a decline in the number of available seed and food varieties. Franchise restaurant chains, which also proliferated in this period, preferred standardized menus, which created another vast market for single strains of produce. Meanwhile, average per capita consumption of dairy products, fresh fruits, and fresh vegetables declined. Yet processed food relied on nutritional additives and preservatives to maintain food value, which added as much as 30 percent to the cost of each edible pound. Corporate consolidation similarly affected beverage consumption. In the beer industry the number of breweries dropped from 450 in 1950 to 170 in 1960 to 70 in 1970. Soft drink manufacturers dramatically increased sales by using advertising to encourage users to consume their products in the living room instead of the kitchen. Such changes encouraged a homogenization of U.S. eating and drinking habits.

THE TECHNOLOGICAL FRONTIER

Wartime engineering and scientific achievement provided the model for postwar technological development. The introduction of radar and jet propulsion, the use of pesticides such as DDT, the effectiveness of "miracle drugs" like penicillin, and the emergence of synthetic compounds to substitute for scarce resources like rubber all testified to the importance of scientific research for social progress. In popular wartime imagery the scientist and the engineer appeared as heroic figures.

Atomic bombs dwarfed these technological accomplishments. Although the atomic bomb often was associated with the victory over Japan and Cold War security, the use of nuclear weapons raised profound dilemmas about uncontrolled scientific investigation. During the war the government had classified atomic energy research (the "Manhattan Project") as top-secret, although physicists around the world understood the theoretical basis of the bomb. In 1945 U.S. scientists predicted that other countries could develop similar weapons in three to five years. However, President Truman preferred to believe the opinion of military leaders who claimed the United States could monopolize atomic bombs for at least twenty years. The president therefore rejected recommendations to share atomic research with the Soviet Union. This decision was supported by public opinion and Congress. The Atomic Energy Act of 1946 established the Atomic Energy Commission (AEC) and placed control of nuclear research and development in civilian hands.

Stock Montage

Symbolizing "troubled affluence" in the atomic age, a cake shaped like an atomic mushroom cloud is cut by Vice Admiral and Mrs. W.H.P. Blandy to celebrate (with Admiral F.J. Lowery) "Operation Crossroads," the first peacetime atomic bomb testing in 1946.

J. Robert Oppenheimer, head of the Los Alamos research team that developed the atomic bomb, expressed widely held anxieties about the future of scientific investigation: "In some sense, which no vulgarity, no humor, no overstatement can quite extinguish," he said, "the physicists have known sin; and this is a knowledge which they cannot lose." Such concern appeared on a popular level in postwar science fiction, which enjoyed a remarkable revival. Authors such as Isaac Asimov and Ray Bradbury developed futuristic themes involving human beings seeking to avert ultimate catastrophe. The serious scientist appeared as an ambivalent character, simultaneously capable of bringing salvation or annihilation. "To the average civilized man of 1950," concluded *Scientific American*, "science no longer means primarily the promise of a more abundant life; it means the atomic bomb."

Despite civilian control of atomic energy, nearly all nuclear research and development involved military work. To counter popular fears, the AEC launched a public relations division in 1947 to stress that "atomic energy is already at work for good." With private contractors such as General Electric and Westinghouse, the AEC sponsored public exhibitions and educational programs, which suggested that atomic energy would be used for social betterment. Worried that the public might not be willing to make sacrifices in the emerging Cold War, government agencies minimized the harmful effects of bomb testing and radiation fallout.

These deceptions protected the expansion of the nuclear arsenal from public criticism. After the Soviet Union's first atomic bomb test in 1949, Truman ordered the development of the vastly more powerful hydrogen bomb the next year. Research for this super bomb in turn stimulated government interest in sophisticated mathematical calculators. Meanwhile, H-bomb tests in the Pacific and A-bomb tests in the western states showered radiation on unsuspecting civilians and may have increased cancer and mortality rates, although the federal government denied responsibility. Truman also created the Federal Civil Defense Administration to prepare the public for a nuclear holocaust. President Dwight D. Eisenhower continued these policies. In 1953, for example, he advised the AEC to keep the public "confused" about the hazards of radiation. Civil defense programs served less to protect the public than to soothe its fears.

Despite pervasive anxieties about atomic research, the public generally welcomed technological innovations such as synthetic goods. Rayon, nylon, and Dacron increasingly replaced cotton and wool. In home furnishings, plastics supplanted wood and leather. Artificial flavors, colors, and preservatives became staples of the U.S. diet. Most synthetics were derivatives of petroleum products, which depleted nonrenewable resources while contaminating the environment with nonbiodegradable waste. Only exceptional cases of pollution aroused public attention. For example, scientists disclosed during the 1950s that radioactive strontium 90, a "fallout" of atomic bomb testing, might be poisoning milk.

Technological innovation usually appeared more beneficial. The fluoridation of water, for example, considerably reduced tooth decay, particularly among children. When given the choice of voting for fluoridation, however, nearly all local communities initially rejected the proposals, but by 1963 50 million people—25 percent of the population—were drinking fluoridated water. During the postwar decade, the United States replaced Europe as the prime manufacturer of precision scientific instruments. New medical technologies included kidney dialysis machines (1945), artificial heart valves (1953), and electronic heart pacemakers (1957). By 1960 U.S. surgeons were successfully performing 5,000 open-heart operations each week. Meanwhile, the introduction of "miracle" antibiotics such as streptomycin and aureomycin helped to control infectious diseases. Most dramatically, the introduction of Dr. Jonas Salk's poliomyelitis vaccine in 1955 effectively eliminated a dreaded disease that had claimed 55,000 victims each year.

Advances in technology reinforced public optimism about the possibility of unlimited progress. Consumers supported both the automobile industry's high-horsepower engines and the petroleum industry's high-octane gasoline, although with added auto body weight, automobile fuel efficiency fell as low as ten miles per gallon. Although a few ecologists such as William Vogt and Fairfield Osborn warned about the limits of available resources, the public accepted corporate assurances that applied science would eventually solve such technological problems.

Jet aircraft and missiles, electronic transistors and computers testified to the expanding technological frontiers of the postwar era. Committed to military preparedness, the federal government sponsored $12 billion in research and development (R & D) between 1950 and 1959, including $300 million per year for university research. Aircraft manufacturing, one of the leading growth industries, drew 80 percent of its business from military contracts. The government also backed electronics, which grew 15 percent per year, making it the fifth largest industry by 1960.

Secret military programs for nuclear weapons, missiles, and cryptography demanded complicated mathematical calculations that sparked the computer industry. The first World War II–era computers occupied 15,000 square feet and used 18,000 radio tubes. The introduction of the transistor by Bell Laboratories in 1947 paved the way for miniaturization. Although most electronics were purchased by the federal government for military programs, computers entered the industrial marketplace in 1951. By the end of the 1950s such devices enabled the electrical power and petroleum refinery industries to use electronic data to monitor and control the production process. During the 1950s computerized manufacturing still depended on human operators to perform adjustments based on electronic data; during the next decade closed loop systems increasingly replaced the human element.

Military weapons programs directed the flow of most R & D expenditures. To protect military secrets, the government separated the artificial satellite project from military research and prepared to launch an earth satellite by 1958. In October 1957, however, the Soviet Union surprised the world by sending the 184-pound satellite Sputnik into space. The event sent psychological shock waves across the nation, suggesting both a technological defeat for U.S. science and a military threat to the nation. "The time has clearly come," said one Republican critic, "to be less concerned with the depth of pile on the new broadloom rug or the height of the tail fin on the car and to be more prepared to shed blood, sweat, and tears if this country and the Free World are to survive." Although military intelligence understood that U.S. rocketry remained competitive with the Soviet achievement, public fears stimulated greater government support for scientific research. In 1958 Congress created the National Aeronautics and Space Administration (NASA), a civilian space program, and increased appropriations for missile and satellite research. Government expenditures for R & D jumped from $6.2 billion in 1955 to $14.3 billion six years later, a 131 percent increase.

Highlighting the glamorous space program, NASA unveiled Project Mercury, a program for manned space flight, and introduced the first seven astronauts to the public in 1959. In the international "space race," however, U.S. rocketry seemed to lag behind Soviet successes. Early Soviet missiles carried more than a ton of cargo (and even a dog), whereas the first U.S. satellite, the army's Explorer, launched in January 1958, weighed only thirty pounds. Soviet leader Nikita Khrushchev derisively called it a "grapefruit." However, in the next decade, electronic miniaturization and the development of intercontinental ballistic missiles (ICBMs) brought primacy to U.S. rocketry. The space program remained a secondary beneficiary of military defense.

Military superiority also justified generous government help for the petroleum industry. Accepting the industry's argument that the national interest depended on preserving domestic reserves while exploiting foreign oil, the federal government waived antitrust regulations to permit profitable development of Middle Eastern oil and devised generous tax credits to subsidize private arrangements with Saudi Arabia. Under the Truman administration's Marshall Plan of 1947, the United States refinanced a major shift in western European energy consumption from coal to petroleum. This step provided a $384 million subsidy to U.S. oil companies and made the Western Allies dependent on imports. In addition, Congress enacted mandatory petroleum import quotas in 1950, which kept cheap foreign oil from lowering domestic oil prices.

In supporting the oil industry, government agencies continued the World War II practice of awarding contracts to the largest corporations. Only 4 percent of R & D funds reached small businesses. Although convenient for government administrators, this support of big business did not reduce costs. Without competitive bidding, federal budgets routinely absorbed business cost "overruns." There was little irony, therefore, when Eisenhower's secretary of defense Charles E. Wilson, the former president of General Motors, said: "For years I thought what was good for the country was good for General Motors, and vice versa."

THE SUBURBAN BOOM

As the economy prospered, the nation's landscape shifted dramatically during the postwar years thanks to the federal government's veterans' benefits program established under the "GI Bill of Rights," which Congress passed in 1944. The law provided unemployment insurance ($20 a week for one year), life insurance, home mortgage insurance for single family dwellings, and educational scholarships. With such subsidies, life insurance became one of the great growth industries of the postwar period. Between 1950 and 1960 sales of individual policies increased by more than 200 percent. Meanwhile, the GI home mortgage program proved a boon to families seeking first houses as well as to land developers and real estate agents. As early as 1947 more than 1 million veterans obtained government-insured home loans without the usual down payments, which enabled most to purchase houses for the first time. Government-financed scholarships also gave veterans unprecedented opportunities for educational advancement. Between 1945 and 1950 6 million veterans (half the nation's total) used government money to enroll in colleges, universities, and vocational training programs. By 1952 the federal government had spent $13.5 billion for these purposes.

Postwar surveys found that as many as one-fifth of college-bound veterans would not have returned to school without federal aid. Women also entered colleges in high numbers, but without veterans' benefits women formed a smaller percentage of college students than they did before the war. Surveys found that women students saw college less as an opportunity to launch careers than to find suitable mates, and many women quit school to get married. Still, the influx of students encouraged colleges to expand facilities, open branch campuses, offer evening instruction, and adjust their curricula to accommodate older students, many of whom held jobs and supported families. By underwriting tuition bills, federal funds boosted the expansion of academia and established a precedent for later support of education. In addition, the appearance of ethnically diverse students—mostly the children of early-twentieth-century European immigrants—eroded the cultural homogeneity that had dominated elite campuses.

Ex-servicemen and their wives also produced the most remarkable population explosion in U.S. history. Taking their cue from a popular 1945 song "Gotta

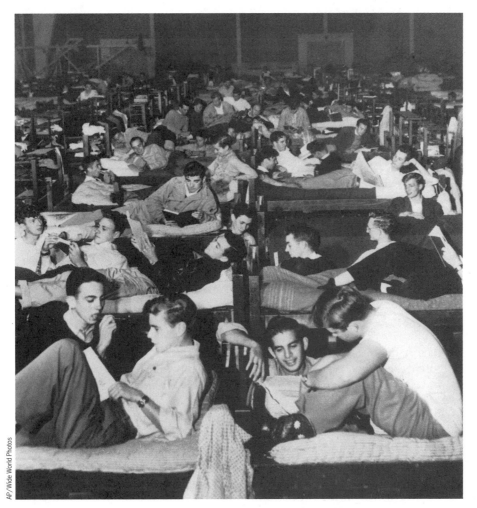

Because of typical postwar overcrowding on college campuses, these former soldiers had to bunk in double-deckers while enrolling at the University of Maryland. Most had their tuition paid under the GI "Bill of Rights."

Make Up for Lost Time," veterans rushed to get married and settle down with their families. The national birth rate had begun to rise as prosperity returned in 1940, but in May 1946, nine months after V-J Day, the number of births soared and remained high until 1957. Demographers found that the "baby boom" resulted from couples marrying younger, thereby increasing the years of marital fertility and producing more third and fourth babies. Yet the number of families with five or more children declined, which suggested a greater willingness to use birth control. Pushed by the baby boom, the nation's population grew from 140 million in 1945 to 152 million in 1950 and exceeded 179 million by 1960. Such growth also reflected the slightly declining death rate, which resulted from medical advances. Between 1950 and 1959 life expectancy for whites rose from 69.1 to 70.5 years and for nonwhites, from 60.8 to 63.5 years.

The rising population accelerated long-term patterns of geographic mobility. Attracted by industrial expansion during World War II, workers and their

Exhibit 9-3. Birth Rates, 1940–1960

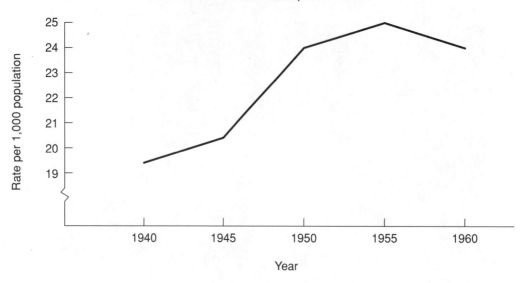

families had flocked to the southwestern and western states. In Texas the growth of the petrochemical industry, stimulated by the increased use of oil and natural gas, encouraged population to increase by one-third. In Arizona, Tucson and Phoenix mushroomed into sizable cities and continued war-induced growth by selling the advantages of a warm, sunny climate. Yet when asked in 1956, "Which city would you most like to live in?" more Americans responded: "Los Angeles." California, home of the prospering aircraft and electronics industries, attracted more than 5 million people between 1940 and 1960, doubled in size, and surpassed New York as the most populous state in 1963. Reflecting the westward movement was the admission into the union of Alaska and Hawaii in 1959.

The baby boom soon underscored what many considered the nation's most serious domestic problem: a shortage of housing. During the Depression and World War II residential construction had virtually ended, and by 1945 the nation's housing was worth 7 percent less than in 1929. Returning veterans often had to live with other families, camp out in public facilities, or accept substandard rooms in converted chicken coops or Quonset huts. Postwar shortages of building materials and the inflation of real estate prices perpetuated the shortage. Responding to the need to reduce housing costs, builders began to construct new dwellings on the suburban fringes of cities. With apartments unavailable, families discovered that purchasing a house was often cheaper if they obtained a home mortgage backed by the federal government under the Federal Housing Authority (FHA) or Veterans Administration.

Mass production techniques soon transformed home construction. To meet the tremendous demand, New York builder William J. Levitt drew on his experience as a war contractor and developed a system of producing standardized housing units at affordable prices. Using specialized work crews, interchangeable designs, prefabricated materials, and package deals that included interior appliances, landscaping, and legal fees, Levitt produced 4½-room, Cape Cod–

This aerial photograph of Levittown, New York, in the 1950s shows the rapid transformation of rural areas into densely populated suburbs. Critics lamented the uniformity of such housing and warned about the demoralizing effects of social conformity.

style houses for $8,000 in 1949. Many were financed by veterans' loans, which required minimal down payments and offered government-protected finance charges. To keep prices down, the new designs eliminated dining rooms, basements, and attics as well as unnecessary trim. Efficient production methods enabled the builder to erect one four-room house every sixteen minutes!

Between 1947 and 1951 Levitt built more than 17,000 dwellings in Levittown, Long Island, and converted a potato field into a community of 75,000 residents. When critics complained that the structures were monotonously repetitious, the developer offered different exterior paints, curved streets, and homes placed at slightly different angles. Such housing, imitated by builders around the nation, benefited from new standardization within the appliance and home-furnishing industries. Credit for the construction of housing was advanced through the growing savings and loan industry. Yet the suburban boom rested on government financing of housing loans, highways, and sewer systems. Federal tax deductions for mortgage interest, which totaled $2.9 billion in 1962 alone, also played a big role. The mixture of private enterprise and government policy enabled most of the nation's families to own their residences for the first time in U.S. history. Between 1945 and 1961 the number of homeowners increased by 12 million.

The growth of suburbia accentuated individual mobility, but as workers now commuted to their jobs in the cities, housewives and children remained isolated from urban life. Consumer commodities such as air conditioning, television, and phonographs encouraged suburbanites to spend more time alone or with families than with neighbors. Moreover, new housing developments initially lacked community institutions such as libraries, schools, hospitals, mass transportation, and even common gathering places, and few older residents were attracted to suburban regions. Social critics lamented the bland uniformity of suburban lifestyles, but promoters stressed the value of individual home ownership. "No man who owns his own house and lot can be a Communist," Levitt declared. Suburbia also reinforced the ideology of family "togetherness."

Distance from downtown areas made the use of automobiles a suburban necessity. Auto registration jumped from 26 million in 1945 to 40 million in 1950 to 62 million by 1960. The popularity of motorized vehicles spawned the proliferation of fast-food restaurants, drive-in theaters, shopping centers, motels, mobile home parks, and gasoline service stations. Although fuel prices remained low (about twenty-five cents per gallon), automobiles brought other costs: increased national dependence on foreign oil and worsening air pollution. In 1947 journalist John Gunther boasted that Los Angeles used electricity to produce "clean industry" and uncontaminated air. Yet within one decade the city's auto exhausts had created a lingering smog that was a serious hazard to public health. Despite such problems, passage of the Interstate Highway Act in 1956 committed the federal government to spend $26 billion to develop a continental freeway system, and this figure reached $37 billion five years later.

In suburbia, mobility became more valued than community attachments. As families grew, suburbanites readily moved to larger homes. Residential change often mirrored the interchangeability of jobs in an increasingly white-collar and service economy. By 1960 nearly two-fifths of the U.S. labor force worked for organizations with at least 500 employees. The proliferation of chain stores reflected this trend. As chains increased their share of total food sales from 29 percent to 44 percent in the ten years after 1948, nearly 100,000 independent groceries disappeared. Retail consolidation often meant that management relocated employees at its own convenience, which destroyed the intimacy between small merchants and their customers. Corporate managers, Gunther noted, never became "a real ingredient in the life of a community." "Ever since the war," complained TV's fictional Alice Kramden on "The Honeymooners," "the butchers don't treat a woman with respect."

CONSUMER CULTURE AND CONSENSUS

Spurred by the baby boom, suburban growth, and the expansion of white collar jobs, corporate prosperity stimulated tremendous confidence in the economic future. "Not only do the younger people accept the beneficent society as normal," reported sociologist William H. Whyte, Jr.; "they accept improvement, considerable and constant, as normal too." Although recessions occurred in 1948–1949, 1953–1954, and 1957–1958, private consumption steadily increased each year. In the immediate postwar years consumers exhausted their savings to buy durable household goods such as appliances, furniture, and automobiles—some 21 million cars, 20 million refrigerators, 5 million stoves, and 12 million TVs. Then they relied on borrowed money to purchase disposable goods and services such as insurance, entertainment, and travel. In 1950 Diner's Club introduced the credit card to allow businessmen to charge their meals. By the end of the decade Carte Blanche, American Express, and Bankamericard extended easy credit to predominantly male members. (Married women could not obtain personal credit until the 1970s.) Installment credit soared from $4 billion in 1954 to $43 billion in 1960. Some of this spending reflected the age-specific demands of the baby boom: children's clothing, toys, "family-size" products. In 1956 for the first time the airline industry attracted as many passengers as railroads did; two years later the Boeing 707 brought jet speed to commercial aviation. Planned obsolescence made consumption appear to be an end in itself. Men's clothing styles began imitating women's fashions by undergoing annual changes that made serviceable wardrobes outmoded. By emphasizing cosmetic innovations like fender "fins," annual changes in automobile models encouraged frequent trade-ins.

Advertising, not coincidentally, became one of the major growth industries of the postwar period. Although best-selling books such as Vance Packard's *The Hidden Persuaders* (1957) publicized the psychological techniques of advertising, market research found that consumers remained more responsive to emotional appeals than to product substance. As advertising touted consumer disposables and luxuries such as tobacco, beverages, drugs, amusements, and extra home furnishings, annual advertising expenditures exceeded $10 billion by 1960. Postwar advertising relied increasingly on national media, facilitating product recognition for a population that increasingly migrated around the country. TV advertisers geared their pitches to market segments identified by demographic factors such as age, income, education, and life-style. "Let's clean up the mess in Washington!" declared General Dwight Eisenhower in the first political advertising to appear on television in 1952. Coached by Hollywood actor Robert Montgomery and inspired by the Batten, Barton, Durstine, and Osborn advertising agency, Eisenhower's campaign proved the political value of the new media.

The growth of advertising paralleled the expansion of all service industries. Each year consumers spent ever-larger sums for insurance, utilities, automobile repairs, medical care, and travel. Expanding service industries also altered the nature of work. As part of a long historical trend, technological innovation increased individual worker productivity, which in turn reduced the number of blue-collar jobs. Meanwhile, the growth of corporations created new managerial jobs for employees who administered the bureaucracies rather than producing commodities. In 1956 the number of people employed in service industries exceeded the number of producers for the first time, which heralded the post-industrial society. For these "organization men," tasks became increasingly technical, specialized, and separated from any tangible product. In the growing bureaucracies of the corporate economy, expertise and teamwork became core values. Government bureaucracies also swelled on all levels. Employment in state and local government increased by 2 million during the 1950s, an increase of 52 percent. By 1960 nearly 8.5 million employees drew government paychecks, largely for white-collar employment.

The requirements of the corporate workplace contributed to an emphasis on consensus in postwar society. College students appeared greatly concerned about the need to conform and to "get along." Dubbed the "silent generation," many young people preferred courses in business administration and education to those in the liberal arts. In the social sciences, sociologist William H. Whyte observed a "bias against conflict" among scholars who viewed terms such as "disharmony, disequilibrium, maladjustment, disorganization" as "bad things." Sociologists and political scientists stressed social "pluralism," a belief that a diversity of interest groups competed on an equal basis and adjusted their differences through reason and compromise. Liberal theory held that democracy was unworkable if people maintained loyalties to social classes, ethnic groups, or ideologies. Indeed, sociologist Daniel Bell declared that ideology was "dead." Historians Louis Hartz, Richard Hofstadter, and Daniel Boorstin described the national past in terms of a homogenized culture that succeeded because it avoided major social conflicts.

Postwar consensus also emerged in the resurgence of church membership in all denominations—from 64 million in 1940 to 115 million in 1960, or from 50 percent to 63 percent of the population. This interest in spiritual security partly reflected the underlying anxieties of a rootless society and the search for identity amid new communities. Appropriately, Congress added the words "under God" to the Pledge of Allegiance in 1954. Yet religious leaders of the 1950s offered less a promise of salvation than a sense of secular reassurance and solace. "Believe in yourself!" the Reverend Norman Vincent Peale proclaimed in the popular tract, *The Power of Positive Thinking* (1952). "Have faith in your abilities! Without a humble but reasonable confidence in your own powers you cannot succeed." Evangelicals like the Baptist Billy Graham also flourished in this religious renaissance, particularly in the urban South and boom towns of the Southwest. Worshippers spent $1 billion building churches in 1960 alone.

The postwar consensus also influenced the values of young people. "I would like to be able to fly if everybody else did," a twelve-year-old girl told sociologist David Riesman, "but it would be kind of conspicuous." Critics contended that conformity had worked its way into the public schools through progressive education, a spinoff of John Dewey's philosophy that rejected rote learning and stressed the life experience of students. "The best thing about contemporary education," wrote psychologist Paul Woodring in 1952, "is that a great many classroom teachers ignore the gobbledygook and pedagogese and go right ahead and do a sensible job of teaching." Progressive education became the target of further attacks when the Soviet Sputnik launch of 1957 abruptly challenged the pedagogical status quo. Shocked by this Cold War "defeat," educational reformers scurried to improve academic standards. Congress quickly passed the National Defense Education Act of 1958, the first major federal aid to education, to encourage the study of science, mathematics, and foreign languages. This government support, which later included such subjects vital to the "national defense" as U.S. history, financed the vast expansion of higher education in the next decade.

LABOR UNIONS AND ECONOMIC STABILITY

Despite remarkable economic growth, inflation and unemployment remained endemic problems. In the immediate postwar years workers faced rapid price inflation, which reduced real wages and purchasing power. Organized labor responded with a series of prolonged strikes, including several "general" strikes

BILLY GRAHAM
1918–

Stock Montage

The most famous religious figures of the 1950s were two southerners in the Baptist tradition, Billy Graham and Martin Luther King, Jr., but whereas King challenged U.S. society with a stinging moral critique on behalf of the dispossessed, Graham won access to the rich and powerful with a message palatable to political and economic elites. Handsome, charismatic, and committed, Graham threw himself into evangelism early in life, honing his skills while traveling the country after World War II for a fledgling fundamentalist group, Youth for Christ. His big break came during the fourth week of a 1949 Los Angeles revival, when the powerful newspaper publisher William Randolph Hearst sent a blunt telegram to the editors of his newspapers: "Puff Graham." Attracted to the anticommunist themes 'of Graham's sermons, Hearst was the first of many powerful figures eager to use the preacher's sincerity and popularity to advance their own agendas. Within a year, Graham had been the subject of major articles in *Time*, *Life*, and *Newsweek*, and within a decade, he was the most popular religious figure in the country.

Like evangelists before him, Graham blended familiar hymns and an altar call with a dynamic and polished pulpit style. Cutting through the apparent complexities of the "age of anxiety," he called on his listeners to heal their lives through a personal commitment to Jesus. To a nation that had survived depression and war only to find itself in the midst of the Nuclear Age, the simplicity and directness of Graham's message had enormous appeal. Although Graham traveled constantly, conducting six major crusades a year, he and his associates soon realized that print, films, radio, and especially television offered enormous opportunities to broaden their ministry even further. His direct-mail techniques were so sophisticated that representatives of both political parties visited his headquarters to study them. This pioneering work in marketing and media techniques helped pave the way for the televangelists of the 1980s.

Although Graham has declared himself to be "completely neutral in politics," his fundamentalist, eschatological theology has long made him a particular favorite of conservative Republicans. Called by some a "Gabriel in Gabardine," Graham spent much of his career preaching a gospel that upheld traditional values and justified existing elites while calling for domestic consensus against communist expansion. Although he insisted that his crusade audiences be integrated even before the Supreme Court's *Brown* decision, Graham typically emphasized otherworldly solutions to both personal and social problems. "My message is so intensely personal," he explained, "that people miss the overwhelming social content." However, as a longtime friend of Richard Nixon, Graham clearly supported Nixon's political career despite advice to avoid politics. (His wife once kicked him under the table when he started to give political advice during a White House dinner.) Deeply shocked by the Watergate scandal and its revelations of Nixon's coarse personal manner, Graham subsequently isolated himself more carefully from politics, ironically doing so at a time when the religious right was just beginning to become a major force under the leadership of other religious broadcasters. ■

Police and strikers confronting each other in Los Angeles during one of many postwar strikes in 1946. Employers wanted to lower wages, and workers refused to give up the higher living standard achieved during the war.

that involved whole communities. The year after V-J Day brought more labor protests than any twelve months in U.S. history. Such actions won substantial wage increases as well as "cost-of-living" adjustments to offset inflation. Businesses passed these increases on to consumers, however, thereby feeding the inflationary cycle.

Although labor unions continued to seek higher wages, better working conditions, and job security, corporations steadfastly rejected efforts by unions to influence management decisions. Corporate leaders used the Cold War atmosphere to silence labor activism by identifying labor radicals with communist enemies. Sharing anticommunist views, labor leaders preferred to cooperate with business. "We have no classes in this country," explained CIO head Philip Murray in 1948. "The interests of farmers, factory hands, business and professional people, and white collar toilers prove to be the same." As organized labor purged communists from its ranks, the CIO expelled eleven unions that refused to do so.

Labor-business relations took new forms under the Taft-Hartley Act of 1947. Aimed at protecting the public from labor-management disputes, the law allowed government to seek an injunction against strike action and provided for a sixty-day "cooling-off" period during which federal mediators would try to settle disagreements. Between 1947 and 1959 Presidents Truman and Eisenhower called for strike injunctions seventeen times. Taft-Hartley also prohibited "closed" shops (which forced employers to hire only union members) but permitted "union" shops (in which all employees had to join a union after being hired). Responding to the threat of community-wide general strikes, Taft-Hartley prohibited secondary boycotts, jurisdictional strikes, and certain "unfair labor practices." The law required union leaders to certify that they were not members of the Communist Party or other subversive groups. On the state level Taft-Hartley encouraged passage of "right-to-work" laws that permitted "open" shops, in which workers did not have to join a union.

Recognizing the destabilizing costs of labor strife, corporate leaders increasingly negotiated long-term, industry-wide contracts that included cost-of-living increases and other welfare benefits. "We need the union to insure enforcement of the contract we have signed," acknowledged a business executive, "to settle grievances, to counsel employees in giving a fair day's work, . . . to help increase productivity." By the early 1950s union membership reached the highest level in U.S. history. At the end of the decade the most rapid increase in manufacturing productivity since the late nineteenth century was attributed to peaceful labor-management relations and moderated class conflict.

The emphasis on industry-wide stability often led union leaders to ignore the local problems of rank-and-file workers. Unauthorized "wildcat" strikes frequently attacked not only employers but also unresponsive union leaders. Worker participation in union elections declined from 82 percent before World War II to 58 percent in 1958, and this trend continued throughout the next decades. While critics complained about labor leaders' "passion for respectability," congressional investigation unearthed widespread corruption in managing union funds. The Landrum-Griffin Act of 1959 required unions to file economic statements with the Department of Labor.

In seeking agreements within unionized industries, labor leaders neglected the problems of unorganized workers, especially in the new white-collar jobs. Many unions also ignored women workers, who were seen as a threat to male jobs, and all-white local unions opposed opening membership to racial minorities. Instead, rival AFL and CIO unions debated jurisdictional issues and raided each other's membership. Although union membership increased from nearly 15 million in 1945 to 18 million a decade later, the proportion of unionized workers declined 14 percent by 1960. Meanwhile, the desire for worker stability minimized the differences between the AFL and the CIO. In 1955 the two federations merged into the AFL-CIO. Yet five years later organized labor accounted for less than one-third of all nonfarm workers. By 1960 the militant labor movement of the 1930s had virtually disappeared.

New Issues of Gender and Sexuality

Although many women workers were replaced by returning veterans in 1945–1946, female employment rose sharply in 1947 and returned to World War II levels by 1950. Between 1940 and 1960 the number of women workers doubled, and by 1960 nearly 40 percent of the adult female population participated in the labor force. This increasing female employment rate reflected new social patterns. The average age of women employees in 1960 was forty-one, and

60 percent of women workers were married. Households in which both husband and wife worked numbered 10 million by 1960. These two-income families included a growing number of mothers with young children. Before World War II, working wives and mothers usually came from the poorest classes of society, but, in the postwar period, an increasing number of middle-class women found jobs even when their husbands earned substantial incomes.

Working women emphasized financial necessity as a motive for their employment. Widows, unmarried mothers, and women who were divorced, separated, or deserted headed one-twelfth of U.S. households in 1956. Most worked as secretaries, sales clerks, or semiskilled workers—occupations that labor unions usually ignored—and earned lower salaries than men did for similar tasks. Then as now, female-headed households were among the poorest in the nation. Moreover, because postwar real wages remained lower than wartime earnings until 1955, families needed additional incomes to acquire goods and services. In middle-class households the demand for luxury items or a private home encouraged two-income families.

The higher her level of education, the more likely a woman was to enter the labor force. Finding satisfaction in occupational roles and careers rather than in traditional domestic work stimulated a growing awareness of women's independence. The rise in female employment challenged the prevailing view that a woman's place was in the home. According to conventional psychological theories, women were naturally passive, unassertive, and therefore ill-equipped to cope with the problems of business. Women who appeared competitive or who ventured into public life were by definition unnatural. "I Denied My Sex," the title of a popular magazine story about a woman's career in police work, typified a pulp literature that advocated domesticity. The most popular TV comedy of the 1950s, "I Love Lucy," consistently parodied the housewife's craving for success outside the home while making light of male ineptitude on the domestic front. Even sensitive films like *The Snake Pit* (1949) portrayed rebellion against domesticity as unusual. Middle-class magazines like *Good Housekeeping* urged women to value the satisfaction of raising children while providing moral support for male breadwinners. Despite such arguments, the increasing number of working women indicated deep stresses within the nation's family life.

TV programs with titles like "The Honeymooners," "Make Room For Daddy," and "Father Knows Best" ostensibly portrayed marital bliss, but the plots usually emphasized intense family conflicts. TV commercials also appealed to an unending battle of the sexes. In addition, postwar films such as *Picnic* and *The Seven Year Itch* focused on family tensions and repression of the individual. Although families were the one place where many people believed they could control their destinies, troubles at home brought many middle-class patients into psychiatrists' offices. Indeed, after World War II the psychiatric profession shifted its attention from psychotic patients who required hospitalization to neurotic clients who simply required "adjustment" to the strains of modern life. Chemical tranquilizers emerged as standard therapy for frustrated spouses. Psychological depression also provoked self-destructive behavior such as alcoholism and shoplifting. Such evidence helps explain why, despite all the propaganda in support of domesticity, marriage rates steadily declined, and divorce rates rose.

Dissatisfaction with traditional marriage also reflected a conflict between sexual values and sexual behavior. In 1948 Alfred Kinsey of Indiana University published a major research study, *Sexual Behavior in the Human Male*, followed five years later by a similar study of women. Both became best-sellers. Kinsey tilted his research sample to support the unconventional conclusions he wished to dramatize. Yet at a time when popular values advocated premarital virginity, the Kinsey report suggested that most men and nearly 50 percent of the women interviewed had experienced premarital intercourse. Fully 95 percent of the study's adult white males claimed to have violated at least one law to have an orgasm. Half the men and 26 percent of the women interviewed reported that they had experienced extramarital sexual relations. Kinsey concluded that two-thirds of the marriages studied had serious sexual problems, and he speculated that sexual incompatibility caused 75 percent of divorces.

Kinsey's studies were among the first to point to a sexual revolution among affluent men. Because of larger discretionary incomes and a rising divorce rate, middle-class men were increasingly free to indulge hedonistic fantasies without being burdened with family responsibilities. These values began to surface in magazines such as *Playboy*, which claimed half a million readers by 1956. With sexually provocative photographs of young women, stories that ridiculed domesticity, and advertisements that idealized the life-style of the single male consumer, such magazines offered an alternative to marriage and family stability.

Literature also reflected the sexual revolution. Grace Metallious's best-selling novel of 1957, *Peyton Place*, emphasized sexual themes while exposing the hypocrisy of small-town life. The next year Vladimir Nabokov's novel *Lolita* aroused further controversy with its artful account of the seduction of a preadolescent girl. Public tastes had changed. Ten years earlier Norman Mailer had to invent the nonword "fug" to get *The Naked and the Dead* past the censors. However, in 1959 the Supreme Court prevented censorship of D.H. Lawrence's *Lady Chatterly's Lover* to preserve freedom of speech. Although inconsistently enforced, the decision opened the door to other unconventional sexual literature.

The Kinsey report also pointed to surprising patterns of homosexual behavior: 37 percent of the men and 13 percent of the women interviewed said they had participated in at least one postadolescent homosexual encounter. Such figures reflected the growth of homosexual communities in most major cities after World War II. Yet the proliferation of gay life-styles did not produce greater tolerance of homosexuals. Police raids and blackmail plagued the gay population, and the federal government viewed homosexuals in the military as susceptible to compromise by foreign agents. Thousands of homosexuals lost government jobs during the 1940s and 1950s. Although homosexuals formed self-protective groups such as the Mattachine Society (1951) and the Daughters of Bilitis (1955), fear of exposure prevented homosexuals from effectively defending their rights.

Free expression of sexuality among youth prompted social conservatives to warn about the collapse of traditional morality and a new national malaise—juvenile delinquency. Newspapers luridly described teenage crimes, most of which involved underage drinking, premarital sex, and driving without a license. Critics such as FBI Director J. Edgar Hoover blamed juvenile delinquency on working mothers and warned that youth crime would not be contained unless society strengthened the family, home, church, and local community. President Truman joined a chorus of politicians who urged working mothers to end the crime wave by returning to the home. In fact, however, New York City arrest rates for children under the age of sixteen lagged far behind those reported in the first two decades of the century. Sociologists insisted that poverty caused juvenile crime and advocated slum clearance and social welfare programs as solutions. In addition, Dr. Kinsey said that teenage sexuality appeared normal and healthy and called for greater tolerance from parents and law enforcement authorities.

Kinsey's advice reinforced the message adults received from the most popular pediatrician of the postwar era, Dr. Benjamin Spock, whose book, *Baby and Child Care*, published in 1946, sold more than 22 million copies. "Trust yourself," Spock told anxious parents. "Don't be overawed by what the experts say. Don't be afraid to trust your common sense." Although earlier government child-rearing pamphlets had recommended strict regimens, Spock called for flexibility. His respect for children led critics to denounce his "permissiveness." Yet Spock advocated firm parental control based on love and understanding.

RACE, POVERTY, AND THE URBAN CRISIS

"The saving grace of the American social system," boasted *Life* magazine in 1949, "is . . . the phenomenon of social 'mobility'—the opportunity to move rapidly upward through the levels of society." In an influential 1958 book Harvard economist John Kenneth Galbraith described America as "the affluent society." Family earnings among all postwar recipients of income increased by at least 2.4 percent per year until 1973. Yet even in the prosperous 1950s unemployment rates remained between 3 and 8 percent, and unemployment insurance reimbursed only 20 percent of lost income. While touting middle-class success, social commentators usually ignored what Michael Harrington called "the other America"—the numerous subcultures of poverty.

Among the poorest people were those more than sixty-five years of age. A 1960 Senate report found that "at least one-half of the aged—approximately 8 million people—cannot afford today decent housing, proper nutrition, adequate medical care, preventive or acute, or necessary recreation." Mandatory retirement programs drove many able-bodied workers into poverty. During the 1950s the number of people entitled to Social Security benefits increased fivefold to 9.6 million. Government assistance filled a small fraction of their needs. More than half of the households headed by people over sixty-five had incomes less than $3,000 a year in 1960.

On Thanksgiving Day 1960 Edward R. Murrow's TV broadcast, "Harvest of Shame," stunned the nation by revealing the poverty of landless rural workers. In 1959 1.5 million farmers, five-sixths of them white, had net incomes less than $3,000. Most lived in the South in dilapidated housing without electricity and plumbing. These migrant farm workers of every nationality had virtually no protection from illegal labor practices that kept them poor and dependent. Mi-

Indian Health Service, Public Health Service, Dept. of Health and Human Services

Many Native Americans like this man in a remote village in Alaska still obtained water from unsafe or contaminated sources in the 1950s despite the increasing affluence of other social groups.

nority peoples such as Puerto Ricans, Mexican Americans, Native Americans, and Asian Americans earned extremely low incomes in occupations unprotected by minimum wage laws. Eighty percent of New York City's Puerto Rican families earned less than the government's estimated minimum levels for "modest but adequate" living standards. In California the average income of Japanese and Chinese American families in 1959 was a lowly $3,000, but even that was higher than the income of Spanish-speaking workers. Native Americans appeared poorest of all nonwhites and lived in such squalor that their death rate was three times the national average.

Native American tribes continued to struggle with poverty and assimilation. Stimulated by wartime migrations, the urban Native American population had more than doubled during the 1940s and reached 56,000 by 1950, but many Native Americans faced severe economic hardships and discriminatory policies. In two southwestern states, Native American citizens were denied the vote until 1948, and officials routinely prevented them from receiving veterans' benefits and from making other civil claims. Hoping to end Native American dependence on government, Congress passed the Indian Claims Commission Act of 1946, which allowed native tribes to bring legal action against the federal government for violations of previous treaties. The Bureau of Indian Affairs (BIA) and congressional conservatives saw the measure primarily as an opportunity to terminate government responsibility for native peoples. Although many assimilated Native Americans welcomed the opportunity to claim compensation for past wrongs, traditionalist tribal leaders warned that termination would leave native people vulnerable to economic problems and cultural isolation. Yet Congress embraced detribalization by passing a series of termination laws in 1954 to dissolve tribal structures, disburse tribal assets, and end federal assistance. For the Menominee of Wisconsin and the Klamath of Oregon as well as one hundred smaller tribes, the policy created severe economic and social dislocation.

Unemployment rates on reservations were staggering: more than 70 percent among the Blackfeet of Montana and the Hopi of New Mexico and more than 86 percent among the Choctaw of Mississippi. Many job-seekers moved to nearby cities, where they lived in poverty. Off the reservations, traditional tribal rituals became less important, and the number of spoken Native American languages declined. Yet traditionalists also mobilized resistance to white culture. Thus the postwar period also saw a revitalization of Native American religion and identity, particularly among Native American youth. Assertions of American Indian pride helped block the termination program in the 1960s.

The plight of African Americans was more complex. As middle-class whites assumed new life-styles in the suburbs between 1940 and 1970, 5 million blacks left southern farms for the North and West. By 1960 half the nation's African American people lived in central cities. Migration to industrial areas helped to increase their incomes. Although less than 17 percent of the nation's blacks were in the middle-income category in 1940, nearly 47 percent were middle-income earners by 1970. Black social mobility was symbolized by the eradication of the color barrier in organized sports. African American Joe Louis, the heavyweight boxing champion, had struck a blow against white supremacy in 1938 by defeating German champion Max Schmeling, pride of the master race. In 1947 Jackie Robinson joined the Brooklyn Dodgers and became the first African American to play major league baseball in more than sixty years. By 1960 professional basketball and football had joined baseball as racially integrated sports followed by millions of television viewers.

Despite such dramatic gains, black migrants to the cities often found that the number of blue-collar jobs had been reduced by technological advances and that white-collar opportunities were shifting to the suburbs. Moreover, African American women earned less as factory workers than white women and continued to be relegated to unskilled or semiskilled jobs such as housekeeping, waitressing, and practical nursing. Although Congress passed the Housing Act of 1949, which authorized slum clearance and construction of 810,000 units of low-rent housing, the federal program was undermined by budget cutbacks and by uncooperative real estate interests, which blocked loan programs in inner cities. City planners also found loopholes in the law that permitted the destruction of old buildings without replacement by low-cost rentals. One million postwar residential units faced the wrecking ball, but fewer than 350,000 took their place.

Urban renewal saw old neighborhoods, often with homogeneous ethnic populations, uprooted to make way for convention centers, office buildings, parking lots, and other nonresidential units. Such practices worsened homelessness. During the postwar period every large city had a "skid row" with from 5,000 to 10,000 homeless people. Newcomers to the city also confronted patterns of racial discrimination supported by government policy. Through "restrictive covenants," white property owners and real estate agents adopted legal agreements to avoid selling or renting dwellings to minorities. "If a neighborhood is to retain stability," advised an FHA underwriting manual, "it is necessary that properties shall continue to be occupied by the same social and racial classes."

FHA regulations also denied insurance coverage to racially integrated housing projects. In 1948 the Supreme Court responded to an NAACP-sponsored lawsuit, *Shelley* v. *Kraemer*, by ruling that restrictive covenants were illegal. However, residential segregation persisted and affected African Americans and other minorities. Levittown, for example, did not accept African Americans until 1960. Of the nearly 1 million Puerto Ricans residing in New York in 1960, 40 percent lived in inadequate dwellings, yet rent absorbed as much as one-third of their incomes. In higher income brackets, residential segregation affected such groups as Jews, Chinese Americans, and Japanese Americans, who tended to cluster in homogeneous communities.

City dwellers also found that the suburbanization of middle-class taxpayers shrank the urban tax base and curtailed municipal services. Because of increased use of automobiles, mass transit deteriorated for want of passengers. In cities such as Los Angeles, St. Louis, Philadelphia, and Salt Lake City, municipal officials accepted bribes from General Motors to replace inexpensive electric trolley cars with the company's gas-consuming buses. The resulting traffic congestion could not be eased even by the construction of new freeways in most major cities.

African Americans in southern states faced far harsher conditions than their northern counterparts. Under the 1896 *Plessy* doctrine of "separate but equal," seventeen states required segregated public school facilities in 1951. Southern boards of education typically spent twice as much to teach white children as black children, and whites were four times as likely as blacks to finish high school. During the postwar era, civil rights groups led by NAACP lawyer Thurgood Marshall initiated a series of legal suits to end academic discrimination. Benefiting from postwar criticism of racism, Marshall won legal victories against segregated law schools and graduate schools by arguing that the alternative black institutions were unequal in quality to white schools. Emboldened by these legal victories, the NAACP attacked public school segregation by denying that educational systems could be racially separate and still equal.

Using psychological evidence to argue that "prejudice and segregation have definitely detrimental effects on the personality development of the Negro child," Marshall persuaded the Supreme Court to reconsider the *Plessy* doctrine. In a historic ruling delivered on 17 May 1954 in *Brown* v. *Board of Education of Topeka*, the Supreme Court acknowledged that segregating children "because of their race generates a feeling of inferiority . . . that may affect their hearts and minds in a way unlikely ever to be undone." In public education, the Court concluded, "'separate, but equal' has no place. Separate educational facilities are inherently unequal." The Brown ruling landed like a bombshell on the political scene, forcing complacent politicians to rethink the goals of U.S. education and heralding a new era of civil rights protest. (See Chapter 10 for details of the civil rights movement.)

MASS CULTURE AND THE YOUTH CULT

Rising personal consumption brought larger postwar recreation expenditures, which jumped from $11 billion in 1950 to more than $18 billion in 1959. Professional baseball truly became the national pastime in 1958 when major-league teams moved to San Francisco and Los Angeles. Television became the major innovation in postwar entertainment. In 1947 ten TV broadcasting stations reached about 20,000 TV sets. The next year TV sales suddenly skyrocketed. By 1957 U.S. households owned 40 million TV sets and could select programs from as many as seven broadcasting channels at a time. TV quickly became part of family life—seen by promoters as a modern "hearth" to encourage "togetherness" and by critics as an omnipresent salesman's foot in the door. Although a new industry, television was controlled by the same corporations that dominated radio. Advertising rather than programming content determined the broadcast schedule. In 1951 the first coaxial cable linked the East and West Coasts and enabled national audiences to see the same thing at the same time. That year TV commercial sales surpassed radio advertising revenue for the first time. Although a host of young writers and performers produced brilliant examples of "live" drama and spontaneous comedy, the pressure to increase network ratings mostly generated formulaic series, variety programs, and quiz shows. The introduction of TV film in the mid-1950s crushed the remaining creative spontaneity. Even national news programs ran for only fifteen minutes.

Television nonetheless eclipsed the other popular media—radio, newspapers, magazines, and motion pictures. During the immediate postwar years, Hollywood had examined such controversial subjects as racism (*Home of the Brave*, 1948); anti-Semitism (*Crossfire*, 1947; *Gentlemen's Agreement*, 1947); and mental illness (*The Snake Pit*, 1949). Yet the investigation of Hollywood for communist subversion in 1947 sent a chill through the industry that discouraged social criticism. Hollywood also suffered from declining movie attendance. By 1953 ticket sales were a scant half of their 1946 record highs. The postwar baby boom, which tended to keep young adults at home, contributed to the drop. However, the crowning blow was that by 1953 more than 43 percent of U.S. families owned TV sets. Hoping to recapture audiences, Hollywood introduced production innovations—3-D, wide screens, and more color—that were unavailable on TV, but as movie mogul Sam Goldwyn predicted in 1949, people were "unwilling to pay to see poor pictures when they can stay at home and see something which is, at least, no worse."

Hollywood's recourse was to concentrate on psychological themes, daring sex, and films geared to the youth culture. TV's family audiences limited sexual content to vague double-meanings or slapstick comedy. Yet, although the motion picture industry still prohibited nudity or explicit sexuality, movies exploited the pseudosexuality of stars like Marilyn Monroe, who combined skin-tight costumes with an uncanny sense of humor. Although many of Monroe's films portrayed sexual pleasure as a reward of affluence, the actress was a complex figure. A working-class woman who had escaped the dreariness of Los Angeles factory life, Monroe resented being judged by appearances even as she mastered the art of cinematic seduction.

Brown Brothers

In the 1955 film Rebel Without a Cause, *teenage delinquents in leather jackets seemed more concerned with social conformity than alternative life-styles.*

Hollywood achieved greater success in exploiting a growing youth culture with sensitive and brooding young actors such as James Dean, Montgomery Clift, and Marlon Brando. "What are you rebelling against?" a teenage waitress asked a motorcycle tough in the Hollywood epic, *The Wild One* (1954). "What do ya got?" replied Brando. Popular movies about youth culture such as *Rebel Without a Cause* (1955) portrayed a young generation that rejected the materialistic values of its parents. Because adults made the films, however, they also expressed a lack of confidence in the older generation's ability to guide the young. "No longer is it thought to be the child's job to understand the adult world as the adult sees it," complained David Riesman in his classic study, *The Lonely Crowd* (1950).

Searching for peer approval and a sense of belonging, many adolescents turned to clubs, cliques, and gangs that experimented with cigarettes, alcohol, and sex. The antiauthoritarian *Mad* magazine, scoffing at mainstream culture, politicians, teachers, and parents, emerged as an instant hit among high-school and college students. However, the primary form of social rebellion among postwar youth involved rock and roll music, a derivative of black rhythm and blues that was introduced to wider audiences by Cleveland disc jockey Allan Freed. Records by African American performers such as Chuck Berry and Little Richard often contained themes that rejected adult authority and assumed knowledge of sexual matters. By 1956 Elvis Presley, a sideburned white southerner whose music was based on the country "rockabilly" tradition, had

Frank Driggs/Archive Photos

Elvis Presley dazzles a crowd of teenagers in Long Beach, California, in 1956. Flaunting sexuality and defiance of adult attitudes, Presley built an enormous following among the nation's youth, who dubbed him the "king" of rock and roll.

achieved cult status by blatantly mixing pelvic thrusts with knowing grins and raunchy blues shouts. The introduction of a new dance, "the Twist," by Chubby Checker in 1959 turned suggestive body expression into a national fad and hinted at the social integration of blacks and whites in postwar society.

Clergy and moral authorities professed shock at the frankness of rock and roll and its roots in the working-class cultures of blacks and southerners. In Boston police banned a live show staged by Freed and claimed that the loud and heavy beat excited teenagers to violence and delinquency. Yet for all its symbolic rebellion, rock and roll served more as a collective ritual for adolescents experiencing the traumas of puberty. Even "delinquents" in black leather jackets and motorcycle boots emulated the adult world by participating in consumer culture. Moreover, when *Blackboard Jungle* (1955) became the first film to use rock and roll in its soundtrack, Hollywood began to tailor its products to the burgeoning youth market. Other youth-oriented commodities included clothing and shoes, jewelry, cosmetics, soda pop, and even automobiles. Meanwhile, white country music performers such as Hank Williams, Patsy Cline, and Bob Wills and the Texas Playboys expressed the joys and hardships of sexual love for working-class audiences. By 1955 annual record sales in the United States reached $225 million.

— King Hiram ("Hank") Williams —
1923–1953

Wide World Photos

"Don't worry," country singer Hank Williams once confided to a stage-show crowd, "nothing's gonna turn out right no how."

Embodying the rising popularity of postwar country music, Williams grew up in small Alabama towns during the Depression. The son of a part-time farmer and log-train engineer who spent the 1930s in a veterans' hospital, he was raised by a strong-willed mother who worked for a WPA cannery and introduced him to the hymns and gospel tunes of the fundamentalist Baptist church. Meanwhile, Williams sold peanuts and newspapers and shined shoes. Forming his own "hillbilly" band when he was fourteen years old, he imitated the commercial sound of stars Roy Acuff and Ernest Tubb but also was influenced by black street musicians. After Williams won an amateur-night contest in Montgomery by singing his "WPA Blues" in 1937, he formed the Drifting Cowboys and played the "blood buckets"—the rough southern Alabama honky-tonks.

After failing his military physical, Williams gave up music during World War II for more lucrative work in the Mobile, Alabama, shipyards. In 1946 he traveled to Nashville to become a songwriter. As the war relocated southern blacks and whites to defense plants and military bases and as jukeboxes spread across the country, rhythm and blues and country music became national phenomena. Fusing gospel, blues, and honky-tonk, Williams won a recording contract in 1947 and produced his first hit, "Move It On Over." The next year he joined the "Louisiana Hayride," a country music radio show from Shreveport, Louisiana, that played for workers in the booming regional oil and gas industry. After his smash 1949 hit, "Lovesick Blues," Williams reached the top of his profession and made regular guest appearances on Nashville's "Grand Ole Opry."

Selling 11 million records and earning $200,000 a year between 1949 and 1953, Williams used his unpolished, light voice to master blues techniques such as falsetto singing and call-and-response. Williams won the devotion of working-class fans because he appeared to "live" his music. "When a hillbilly sings a crazy song," he once explained, "he feels crazy . . . He sings more sincere than most entertainers because the hillbilly was raised rougher . . . You got to have smelt a lot of manure before you can sing like a hillbilly."

Williams bonded with audiences by sharing the sense of betrayal and abandonment that romance often inflicts. By honestly conveying the loneliness, frustration, and despair involved in the search for love, songs like "Your Cheating Heart" and "Cold Cold Heart" excused listeners from postwar insistence on domestic bliss. Williams expressed another form of release through drinking songs like "Jambalaya," which celebrated immediate pleasure over the rigors of delayed gratification and middle-class propriety.

As the singer poured out his marital problems in music, however, he was unable to stop a descent into alcoholism, abusive behavior, and physical deterioration. On New Year's Day 1953, eight months before his thirtieth birthday, Hank Williams suffered a fatal heart attack. A biracial crowd of more than 20,000 mourners gathered at the city auditorium in Montgomery, Alabama, as leading country music stars conducted a gospel tribute to the fallen performer. By portraying pain and joy as the common denominators of life, Williams became a legendary figure in working-class culture and had an enormous impact on popular music. ■

LENNY BRUCE
1926–1966

A stand-up nightclub performer, Lenny Bruce emerged as the most controversial comedian of the postwar era. Using a jazz soloist's style, Bruce blended plain street talk with Yiddish and black idiom to satirize and demystify social conventions. His most scathing routines focused on religious hypocrisy, the artificiality of traditional sexual relationships, and racial prejudice. Because of his brutal honesty, the established media labeled Bruce and such colleagues as Mort Sahl "sick" comedians. "I'm not a comedian," Bruce retorted. "And I'm not sick. The world is sick and I'm the doctor. I'm a surgeon with a scalpel for false values. I don't have an act. I just talk." Even the title of his autobiography—*How to Talk Dirty and Influence People*—made fun of the popular homilies for success.

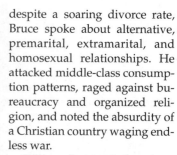

Dennis Stock © Magnum Photos

Born Leonard Schneider in New York, he joined the navy at the age of sixteen and saw active service in the Mediterranean. After the war Bruce hustled as a con-artist for phony charities before drifting into comedy work in sleazy nightclubs and dance halls. By the mid-1950s Bruce's brand of comedy captured national attention. He appeared on network television, made popular records, and captivated audiences at top nightclubs across the country.

Bruce's comic routines illuminated the anxieties and unspoken assumptions of postwar society. Although middle-class ethnic groups embraced homogenized suburban values (including, as in Bruce's case, the changing of ethnic names), the comedian's sketches reaffirmed the vitality of ethnic, religious, and racial identity. As middle-class media celebrated traditional monogamous marriage despite a soaring divorce rate, Bruce spoke about alternative, premarital, extramarital, and homosexual relationships. He attacked middle-class consumption patterns, raged against bureaucracy and organized religion, and noted the absurdity of a Christian country waging endless war.

"All my humor is based on destruction and despair," he admitted. "If the whole world were tranquil, without disease and violence, I'd be standing on the breadline right in back of J. Edgar Hoover and . . . Dr. Jonas Salk." Bruce's insistence on creative freedom led him to attack legal censorship of free speech. "What's wrong with appealing to the prurient interest?" he wanted to know. "We appeal to the *killing* interest." His use of explicit language brought police reprisals, and he faced a series of arrests and court trials in several cities on charges of obscenity. He was also accused of using illegal drugs. The endless litigation drained his energy, and the subject of legal harassment came to dominate his nightclub act. "The halls of justice," quipped Bruce. "That's the only place you see the justice . . . in the halls."

As police departments worked with municipal courts to silence the irreverent comedian, Bruce died of a heroin overdose. His obscenity conviction, however, was overturned posthumously. Bruce's quarrel with censorship provided an important basis for the free speech movements that spread across many college campuses in the 1960s. Moreover, in merging humor about sex, race, and politics, Bruce's comedy foreshadowed the radical synthesis of the New Left and the counterculture of the 1960s. ∎

VOICES OF DISSIDENCE

Just as the irreverent youth culture rebelled against middle-class standards, social critics and artists began to question the premises of the postwar consensus. "The religion that actually prevails among Americans today has lost much of its authentic . . . content," observed Will Herberg, author of the popular *Protestant Catholic Jew* (1956). The blandness of spirituality reflected a larger problem of alienation. "When white-collar people get jobs," cautioned sociologist C. Wright Mills in *White Collar* (1951), "they sell not only their time and energy but their personalities as well." Similar warnings came from such works as David Riesman's *The Lonely Crowd* (1950), Herbert Marcuse's *Eros and Civilization* (1955), and William H. Whyte's *The Organization Man* (1957). These books attacked the prevalence of social conformity, the decline in individual initiative, and the obsession with security in business and private life. Poet Sylvia Plath put it succinctly by describing herself as living inside a "bell jar" of conformity. In a prophetic essay, "The White Negro," novelist Norman Mailer predicted an explosion of violent rebellion led by hipster-outlaws against a repressive society.

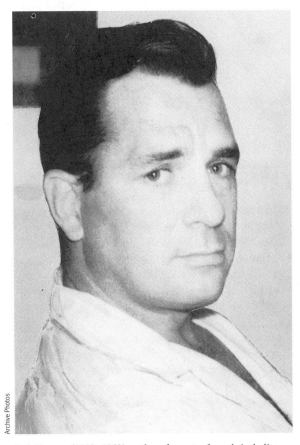

Jack Kerouac (1922–1969), author of a spate of novels including the classic On the Road *(1957), personified the frenetic energy of young intellectuals searching for spiritual meaning in a society of extravagant materialism.*

Alternative voices also emerged in art, music, and comedy. Although the public preferred the representational painting of Thomas Hart Benton, Grant Wood, and Grandma Moses, a new group of "abstract expressionists" turned New York into an international center of nonrepresentational Action Painting. Jackson Pollock, Willem de Kooning, and Mark Rothko painted with vigorous line and color that compelled viewers to find meaning in the work on their own. Abstract painters also celebrated traditional national subjects: Larry Rivers's tongue-in-cheek version of "Washington Crossing the Delaware" (1953), for example, or Jasper Johns's numerous depictions of the American flag. In music, teenagers danced to rock and roll while their parents worked and shopped to Muzak. The "bebop" sound of Charlie Parker and Dizzy Gillespie brought new vitality to jazz by offering hard-driving rhythms and complex, nonlinear harmonies. Nightclubs featured a new breed of "sick" comedians—Mort Sahl, Lenny Bruce, Dick Gregory—who savagely derided social convention.

The strongest voices of protest came from a group of "Beat" poets and writers who congregated in San Francisco. Jack Kerouac, William Burroughs, Lawrence Ferlinghetti, and Gary Snyder decried the alienating effects of bureaucratic culture and called for a new spiritualism that merged the body and the spirit. Emphasizing the spoken word, the Beats celebrated the human voice as an alternative to mass media. Most eloquent was poet Allen Ginsberg. In "Howl," read aloud in 1955 and published the next year, he indicted a sterile society that watched "the best minds of my generation destroyed by madness." Strong, rolling cadences condemned "scholars of war" with their "demonic industries" and "monstrous bombs." Ginsberg pleaded with America to "end the human war." Here in the cultural underground lay the roots of protest and transcendence that would puncture middle-class illusions of stability and security in the 1960s.

SUGGESTED READINGS

A detailed social history of the postwar period is Geoffrey Perrett, *A Dream of Greatness: The American People, 1945–1963* (1979), which can be supplemented by Marty Jezer, *The Dark Ages: Life in the United States, 1945–1960* (1982). Also useful are David Halberstam, *The Fifties* (1993); Douglas T. Miller and Marion Nowak, *The Fifties: The Way We Really Were* (1977); and Paul A. Carter, *Another Part of the Fifties* (1983). The intellectual context emerges in Richard H. Pells, *The Liberal Mind in a Conservative Age: American Intellectuals in the 1940s and 1950s* (1985).

The relation between government and the economy is illuminated in Elizabeth A. Fones-Wolf, *Selling Free Enterprise: The Business Assault on Labor and Liberalism, 1945–1960* (1994). For a fine study of the relation between technology and industrial development, see David F. Noble, *Forces of Production: A Social History of Industrial Automation* (1986). Government support of science and technology is the major theme of three valuable studies: Walter A. McDougall, *The Heavens and the Earth: A Political History of the Space Age* (1985); Richard Rhodes, *Dark Sun: The Making of the Hydrogen Bomb* (1995); and Kenneth Flamm, *Creating the Computer: Government, Industry, and High Technology* (1988). For the impact of the atomic bomb on American society, see Paul Boyer, *By the Bomb's Early Light: American Thought and Culture at the Dawn of the Atomic Age* (1985), and Spencer

R. Weart, *Nuclear Fear: A History of Images* (1988). The ordeal of one physicist is described in Peter J. Goodchild, *J. Robert Oppenheimer: Shatterer of Worlds* (1981), and the contributions of a mathematical genius are the subject of William Aspery, *John von Newmann and the Origins of Modern Computing* (1990). The impact of Sputnik is described in Robert A. Divine, *The Sputnik Challenge* (1993).

The consequences of the high postwar birthrate are described in Landon Y. Jones, *America and the Baby Boom Generation* (1980). For a good overview of social and economic trends, see William Issel, *Social Change in the United States, 1945–1983* (1985). For the broader problems of economic class and wealth, see the later chapters of George Lipsitz, *Rainbow at Midnight: Labor and Culture in the 1940s* (1994). Michael Harrington, *The Other America* (1962), remains a valuable study of poverty. For the housing problem in the postwar years, see Richard O. Davies, *Housing Reform During the Truman Administration* (1966). A vast literature examines suburbia in the 1950s. A good starting point is Kenneth T. Jackson, *The Crabgrass Frontier: The Suburbanization of the United States* (1985). Still useful is Robert C. Wood, *Suburbia: Its People and Their Politics* (1959), but it should be supplemented with Scott Donaldson, *The Suburban Myth* (1969).

An excellent survey of women's history is Elaine Tyler May's *Homeward Bound: American Families in the Cold War Era* (1988), which can be supplemented with Rochelle Gatlin, *American Women Since 1945* (1987). For the status and problems of women in postwar society, see Barbara Ehrenreich, *Hearts of Men: The Flight from Commitment* (1984). Women's political activity in the 1950s is described in Leila J. Rupp and Verta Taylor, *Survival in the Doldrums* (1987). For popular images of women in film, see Molly Haskell, *From Reverence to Rape* (1974); Brandon French, *On the Verge of Revolt* (1978); and Michael Wilson, ed., *Salt of the Earth* (1978). The origins of the sexual revolution are treated in the relevant chapters of John D'Emilio and Estelle B. Freedman, *Intimate Matters: A History of Sexuality in America* (1988).

For surveys of the postwar civil rights movement, see Harvard Sitkoff, *The Struggle for Black Equality: 1954–1980* (1981), and Manning Marable, *Race, Reform, and Rebellion: The Second Reconstruction in Black America, 1945–1982* (1991). The legal struggle to end racial discrimination is brilliantly described in Richard Kluger, *Simple Justice: The History of Brown v. Board of Education and Black America's Struggle for Equality* (1976). Also valuable are the early chapters of Taylor Branch, *Parting the Waters: America in the King Years, 1954–63* (1988), and the first two volumes of *The Papers of Martin Luther King, Jr.*, edited by Clayborne Carson (1992–1994). An excellent study of the relation between sports and race is Jules Tygiel, *Baseball's Great Experiment: Jackie Robinson and His Legacy* (1983). See also the relevant titles listed after Chapter 10.

Government policy toward Native Americans is described in Donald L. Fixico, *Termination and Relocation: Federal Indian Policy, 1945–1960* (1986); in Vine Deloria, Jr., *Custer Died for Your Sins: An Indian Manifesto* (1969); and in the relevant chapters of Richard Drinnon, *Keeper of Concentration Camps: Dillon S. Myer and American Racism* (1987). The emergence of homosexual communities is well treated in John D'Emilio, *Sexual Politics, Sexual Communities: The Making of a Homosexual Minority in the United States, 1940–1970* (1983). See also Stephanie Coontz, *The Way We Never Were: American Families and the Nostalgia Trap* (1992).

The problems of youth are described in James Gilbert, *A Cycle of Outrage: America's Reaction to the Juvenile Delinquent in the 1950s* (1986). An imaginative treatment of rock and roll is Greil Marcus, *Mystery Train: Images of America in*

Rock 'n' Roll (1975). An examination of TV's impact on postwar society is Lynn Spigel, *Make Room for TV: Television and the Family Ideal in Postwar America* (1992). Erik Barnouw's *The Image Empire* (1970) describes the television industry. Also interesting is Jeff Kisseloff's *The Box: An Oral History of Television, 1920–1961* (1995). For the movies, see Peter Biskind, *Seeing is Believing: How Hollywood Taught Us to Stop Worrying and Love the Fifties* (1983), and Thomas Doherty, *Teenagers and Teenpics: The Juvenilization of American Movies in the 1950s* (1988). James Gunn, *Alternative Worlds: The Illustrated History of Science Fiction* (1975), surveys the genre. For the bebop revolt and social attitudes of black musicians, see the relevant chapters of Ben Sidran, *Black Talk* (1981). The fine arts are the subject of two excellent books, Serge Guilbaut, *How New York Stole the Idea of Modern Art: Abstract Expressionism, Freedom, and the Cold War* (1983), and Sidra Stich, *Made in USA: An Americanization in Modern Art, the '50s and '60s* (1987).

An overview of religious thinking is Martin E. Marty, *Modern American Religion*, volume 3, *Under God, Indivisible: 1941–1960* (1996). For a survey of dissident intellectuals, see Andrew Jamison and Ron Eyerman, *Seeds of the Sixties* (1994). Postwar novels and novelists are discussed in Josephine Hendin, *Vulnerable People: A View of American Fiction Since 1945* (1978). For the Beat writers, see Lawrence Lipton, *The Holy Barbarians* (1959); John Tytell, *Naked Angels* (1976); Dennis McNally, *Desolate Angels* (1979); and Michael Davidson, *The San Francisco Renaissance: Poetics and Community at Mid-century* (1989).

"I Like Ike": Candidate Dwight D. Eisenhower and his wife, Mamie, greet a seven-year-old polio survivor during the 1952 campaign in Syracuse, New York.

UPI/Corbis-Bettmann

10

THE EISENHOWER CONSENSUS, 1952–1960

P artisan conflict in the last years of the Truman era gave way to a politics of consensus after 1952. Although Republicans had criticized the cost and futility of Truman's containment policy, the continuation of the Cold War resulted in an expansion of overseas commitments and a large military establishment. The anticommunist consensus left little room for disagreement concerning management of the conflict with the Soviet Union. Conservatives who hoped to dismantle the New Deal confronted powerful liberal forces in Congress and the nation that protected social welfare benefits and labor rights. By the end of the 1950s both political parties accepted an active federal government at home and abroad.

THE ELECTION OF 1952

The Republican campaign slogan of 1952 summarized the troubles of the incumbent administration—"KlC2": Korea, Communism, Corruption. The phrase offered a convenient formula for tapping voter dissatisfaction. According to opinion polls, the limited war in Korea remained the primary public concern. As part of the Cold War, moreover, the Korean conflict intensified fear of atomic war. Congress appropriated $3 billion for bomb shelters, but officials admitted that less than 1 percent of the population would be protected from an atomic strike. In New York and San Francisco, public schools routinely issued dog tags to pupils to help identify victims of nuclear war. "I cannot tell you when or where the attack will come or that it will come at all," Truman admitted. "I can only remind you that we must be ready when it does come." Such vague warnings fed a remarkable popular interest in flying saucers and mysterious invaders. The Hollywood science fiction film *The Thing* (1951) ended by advising audiences to "Watch the skies!"

Republicans expected to benefit from this climate of fear. The party's front-runner, Senator Robert Taft of Ohio, appealed to conservatives by demanding a retreat from expensive international commitments and a reduction in the size and scope of government programs. "The greatest enemy of liberty," he declared, "is the concentration of power in Washington." Taft's conservatism attracted midwestern and western Republicans, but his strident hostility to big government alarmed more liberal eastern Republicans, particularly big-business leaders. These "corporate liberals" preferred an internationalist foreign policy to stabilize world trade and recognized that New Deal programs such as Social Security bolstered purchasing power and helped to prevent social unrest at home.

Fearing that Taft's conservatism would doom the party at the polls, eastern Republicans led by Massachusetts Senator Henry Cabot Lodge, Jr., and former Governor Thomas Dewey of New York turned to a candidate who claimed to have no interest in presidential politics: General Dwight David "Ike" Eisenhower. As supreme commander of NATO forces in Europe, Eisenhower's political views appeared sufficiently ambiguous for Truman to offer him the Democratic nomination in 1952. Eisenhower was too conservative to run as a Democrat. Yet, unlike Taft, the general believed in the importance of the U.S. military presence in Europe. After a series of successful primary showings, including a surprise victory in New Hampshire, Eisenhower came home from

Europe in June 1952 to seek the presidential nomination. Benefitting from his immense popularity and some astute maneuvering at the convention by Lodge, the general captured a first-ballot nomination. As a concession to conservatives, Eisenhower chose as his running mate the conservative Californian Richard Milhous Nixon.

While Eisenhower grandiosely offered "to lead a great crusade . . . for freedom," KlC2 dictated the Republican platform. "There are no Communists in the Republican Party," it boasted, whereas Democrats "shielded Traitors . . . in high places." Denouncing Truman's containment policy as "negative, futile, and immoral," Republicans vowed to bring "genuine independence" to the "captive peoples" of eastern Europe, a promise that appealed to eastern European ethnics, who usually voted for Democrats. The platform also adopted a conservative position on civil rights by insisting that state governments had primary responsibility in that area.

The Democratic spotlight flashed briefly on Tennessee's Senator Estes Kefauver, who won a series of primary contests, but Democratic leaders, including Truman, feared that Kefauver's investigations of organized crime would hurt the party in the cities and turned to Governor Adlai Stevenson of Illinois. A cultivated liberal, Stevenson presented himself as a voice of reason, criticizing McCarthyism ("we want no shackles on the mind . . . no iron conformity") and promising to "talk sense to the American people." To balance the ticket in the South, Stevenson chose Senator John Sparkman of Alabama as his running mate.

Despite the Democratic candidate's efforts to distance himself from the Truman administration, Stevenson stood for a continuity of the party's principles and policies. He defended the Korean War as "a long step toward building a security system in Asia" and echoed the White House attack on domestic communism. Unlike Truman, Stevenson took a moderate position on civil rights by emphasizing the importance of state sovereignty. Only after intense criticism from liberals did he endorse a permanent Fair Employment Practices Commission (FEPC). This belated gesture cost Stevenson support among African Americans while offending white southern Democrats. Stevenson further angered Gulf Coast Democrats by opposing state control of offshore oil wells. The candidate's hesitancy to attack the Taft-Hartley labor law also offended his traditionally Democratic labor constituency.

Eisenhower, meanwhile, stood as a candidate above parties, a middle-of-the-road moderate with leadership experience that reflected caution, restraint, and common sense. After making peace with Taft, Eisenhower scrupulously avoided antagonizing Old Guard Republicans. Although personally insulted by Senator Joseph McCarthy's attack on General George Marshall, Eisenhower's former superior officer, the nominee quietly deleted a defense of Marshall when speaking in McCarthy's home state of Wisconsin. Eisenhower avoided direct attacks on Truman and left the partisan oratory to Nixon, who denounced "Adlai the appeaser . . . who got a Ph.D. from Dean Acheson's College of Cowardly Communist Containment."

Nixon's verbal ammunition suddenly exploded when newspapers reported that the Republican vice presidential candidate had a secret "millionaire's" fund to defray his Senate political expenses. When Democrats used the issue to reply to Republican accusations about a "mess in Washington," Eisenhower's advisers urged him to drop Nixon from the ticket, but while the presidential nominee

Exhibit 10-1. Election of 1952

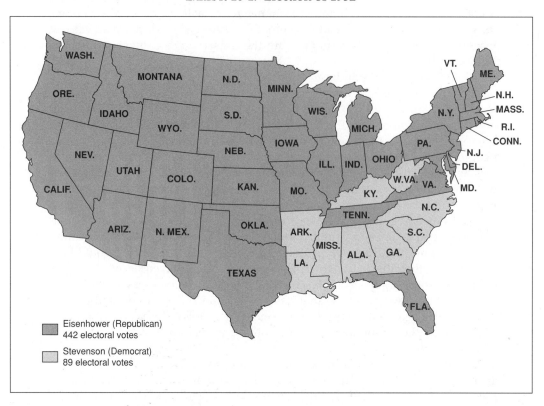

Eisenhower (Republican)
442 electoral votes

Stevenson (Democrat)
89 electoral votes

delayed action, Nixon seized the initiative, buying television time to defend his personal honesty. Emphasizing that his family had not profited from politics, Nixon said his wife still wore a "plain Republican cloth coat" and that despite criticism he would not return a gift his daughter had received, a cocker spaniel named Checkers.

The sentimental performance proved effective. As public support for Nixon increased, Eisenhower decided to keep him on the ticket. For the first time, political pundits saw the immense power of television. This recognition highlighted the importance of a candidate's image and suggested that a politician could effectively appeal to the voters over the heads of party leaders. As for Nixon, the speech gave him confidence in the medium of television. In later years he returned to the small screen to win vindication of other aspects of his career, although seldom with the success of the 1952 effort.

Supporting the basic premises of Truman's Cold War, Eisenhower avoided the militant rhetoric of the Republican platform on matters of foreign policy. He approved of Truman's intervention in Korea but opposed General MacArthur's call for all-out war. When Stevenson argued that the only "answer" to Korea was to "keep it up as long as we have to," Eisenhower hinted at alternative policies. His military experience enabled him to speak with authority. In a late campaign speech in Detroit, Eisenhower suggested that ending the war required his personal presence in Korea. "I shall make that trip," he declared. "I shall go to Korea." Eisenhower's promise ignited the hopes of a war-weary nation.

Portraying himself as a nonpartisan soldier, Eisenhower achieved a stunning victory. He captured nearly 34 million votes (55 percent) to Stevenson's 27 million (44 percent) and swept the Electoral College 442–89. The Republican ticket carried four southern states, breaking the Democrats' "solid South" for the first time since Al Smith's defeat in 1928. Eisenhower attracted traditional Democrats in the big cities—African Americans, Catholics, and ethnics. On his coattails, he pulled a Republican majority into both houses of Congress.

Republicans exulted in the destruction of the New Deal coalition. The reelection of conservatives like McCarthy and the defeat of several of McCarthy's critics seemed to vindicate the anticommunist crusade. However, statistics also showed that Eisenhower ran far ahead of other Republicans, including McCarthy. The election of 1952 was an Eisenhower victory, not a Republican one, and the party controlled the House by only eight seats, the Senate by one. During the 1950s voting behavior generally followed party lines. Voters seemed less interested in political ideology and appeared more sensitive to short-term issues or party affiliation. Yet Eisenhower managed to attract independent voters and Democrats, including a well-funded "Democrats for Eisenhower" organization headed by Hollywood actor Ronald Reagan. The breadth of Eisenhower's support reflected not only his personal popularity but also a political consensus based on internationalism abroad and minimum social welfare at home.

THE GENERAL TAKES COMMAND

Eisenhower's success among Democrats reinforced his political philosophy of consensus. As a career military officer, the former general represented the new managerial middle class of the twentieth century. In a world dominated by large corporate bureaucracies he emphasized the importance of voluntary cooperation between government and business. Nearly all the members of his cabinet—including Secretary of State John Foster Dulles, Secretary of Defense Charles E. Wilson, Secretary of the Treasury George M. Humphrey, and Attorney General Herbert Brownell, Jr.—came from the highest ranks of corporate management and law. (The exception was Secretary of Labor Martin Durkin, a plumber, who soon resigned and was replaced by a department store personnel manager.) Eisenhower believed these leaders could apply conservative principles to the management of government without turning back the clock or canceling promises of social justice.

To streamline administration, Eisenhower relied more heavily than Truman on the National Security Council (NSC), but the president frequently overrode the advice of the Joint Chiefs of Staff. Eisenhower distrusted special interests, partisan conflicts, and mass movements. Contrary to the wishes of Old Guard Republicans, he preserved the New Deal and even established a cabinet-level Department of Health, Education, and Welfare in 1953. However, the president initiated no social welfare legislation because he believed that expansion of government services would stultify a free, capitalist society. "We cannot risk living all our lifetime under emergency measures," he said in ending economic controls established by Truman during the Korean War.

Courtesy Dwight D. Eisenhower Library

The president looks right but points left: During presidential press conferences Eisenhower demonstrated considerable skill in deflecting questions and keeping reporters from probing too deeply into White House affairs.

Eisenhower envisioned a world order based on free trade and protected by restrained military power. On many occasions, he resisted pressure from military and civilian advisers to increase the Pentagon budget or to rush rashly into war. "I just don't believe you can buy 100 percent security in every little corner of the world," the president said in 1954. Yet Eisenhower permitted the nuclear arsenal to expand from hundreds to thousands of weapons and ordered the deployment of nuclear weapons overseas. He also relied increasingly on covert operations by the CIA, headed by Allen Dulles, brother of the secretary of state. Always the cold warrior, Eisenhower assumed that the United States should maintain military superiority over communist nations. "Forces of good and evil are massed and armed and opposed as rarely before in history," the president explained in his inaugural address. "Freedom is pitted against slavery; lightness against the dark. . . . In the final choice, a soldier's pack is not so heavy a burden as a prisoner's chains."

These metaphors of morality and struggle reflected the new administration's approach to foreign policy. Determined to take the initiative in the Cold War, Eisenhower and Secretary of State Dulles replaced the Democratic strategy of containment with a new doctrine of "massive retaliation." Dulles argued that neither public opinion nor the nation's economy could sustain a series of limited conventional wars like the Korean War. Instead, he echoed conservative policy

Exhibit 10-2. U.S. National Defense and Veterans Outlays, 1955–1960
(in billions of dollars)

1955	47.4
1960	53.5

Source: *Statistical Abstract of the United States* (1987).

by calling for reliance upon air and naval superiority, a position Eisenhower supported. The nations of the "free world," the president proclaimed, would be prepared "to retaliate instantly" against the Soviet Union "by means and at places of our own choosing." Nuclear weapons aimed at the Kremlin—not at some border area—would deter further communist expansion. In military terms, massive retaliation merely reaffirmed the air-atomic strategy approved by Truman and updated his policy of containment with the doctrine of nuclear deterrence. Eisenhower never intended to go to war to overturn communist control of "captive nations" in eastern Europe. However, his administration hoped to use the nuclear arsenal as a symbolic weapon—and an ever-present threat—in the political crusade for anticommunist liberation.

A policy of massive retaliation had distinct domestic advantages. Conservative Republicans led by Taft had long opposed soaring military budgets. Eisenhower shared these sentiments, although he believed that cost-cutting should not compromise the nation's strength. Air power and nuclear weapons provided a cheaper solution. Eisenhower's "New Look" in military policy enabled the Pentagon to reduce the size of conventional forces. This policy cut $7 billion from Truman's projected budget. Subsequent opinion polls found wide support for these reductions.

Eisenhower's enormous prestige as a military leader as well as his electoral popularity enabled him to accomplish in Korea what Truman had been reluctant to suggest. After fulfilling his campaign promise to visit Korea in December 1952, the new president recognized that a continuation of the ground war would only bleed the army and the federal budget. Secretary Dulles joined conservative senators such as Styles Bridges and William Knowland in advocating complete victory. Yet Eisenhower, primarily concerned with reaching a political settlement, rejected the use of atomic weapons. The president instead used a show of force to persuade the enemy to negotiate. In his inaugural address Eisenhower announced the removal of the Seventh Fleet from the area separating Taiwan from the Chinese mainland and hinted that he might "unleash" Chiang Kai-shek against the communist stronghold. The White House also used diplomatic channels to notify China that the United States might use nuclear weapons if negotiations failed. The death of Josef Stalin in March 1953 added to China's uncertainties about Soviet support.

Both China and Eisenhower understood and accepted the limits of military struggle. The main stumbling block now involved the return of prisoners of war. Hoping to discourage communist China's future reliance on its troops, the United States refused to require the repatriation of communist prisoners who did not wish to go home. After the United States made additional threats to use atomic weapons, China accepted the idea of voluntary repatriation of prisoners of war. At the last minute, South Korea's dictator, Syngman Rhee, nearly thwarted the truce by suddenly releasing 27,000 prisoners, who promptly disappeared into the countryside. The move violated the armistice agreement, but Eisenhower ignored Rhee's action, and the United States signed a truce in July 1953. "We have won an armistice on a single battlefield—not peace in the world," Eisenhower reminded the nation. "We may not now relax our guard nor cease our quest."

The end of the Korean War brought not a sense of celebration but plain relief. Thirty-three thousand U.S. soldiers had died to defend an area that in 1950 Secretary of State Dean Acheson had acknowledged lay beyond the nation's strategic defense perimeter. Sensitive to criticism from conservatives about selling out Korea to the communists, the White House reiterated the possibility of massive retaliation against any further aggression. The retention of U.S. military bases in Korea provided the muscle behind those threats. The Eisenhower administration also adopted a multibillion-dollar program of economic and military assistance to bolster South Korea. The Korean armistice, then, formalized Truman's policy of communist containment in Asia.

Frustrated by the Korean compromise, conservative Republicans criticized Eisenhower's version of containment. In 1951 Republican Senator John Bricker of Ohio had introduced a constitutional amendment requiring congressional approval of all international agreements. Through this partisan move, Bricker sought to limit Truman's executive independence, but the measure never came to the Senate floor. The 1952 Republican Party platform kept the issue alive by promising to "repudiate all commitments contained in secret understandings such as those of Yalta which aid Communist enslavements." This position reflected strong congressional opposition to presidential control of foreign policy, but Eisenhower, distrustful of congressional critics, refused to compromise his presidential powers. Nevertheless, in 1954 Bricker reintroduced his constitutional amendment. Eisenhower strongly opposed the proposal. Yet because the president believed in a rigid separation of powers, he exercised minimal leadership in the Senate debates. Democrats led by Lyndon Johnson saved the president from his own party's militants. Although the Bricker amendment won a 60–31 majority, it fell one vote short of the necessary two-thirds required for the passage of constitutional amendments. The White House, not Congress, would continue to control foreign policy.

Eisenhower's European policies revealed basic continuities with those of his predecessor. Although the Eisenhower administration talked about liberating eastern Europe, the principles of massive retaliation appeared too inflexible to respond effectively to minor crises. When East German workers staged anticommunist protests in June 1953, Dulles could offer only moral encouragement and $15 million in food. Like Truman, Eisenhower worked instead to strengthen U.S. allies in western Europe. When Stalin's successor, Georgi Malenkov, proposed a treaty that would make Germany a neutral country, Eisenhower saw the plan as a ruse to divide the Western Alliance and rejected the Soviet overture. More concerned with bringing Germany into the western political camp, the administration urged the formation of a European Defense Community. When France objected to rearming Germany, however, the president chose an alternative policy that enabled Germany to rearm under NATO. "These agreements are founded upon the profound yearning for peace which is shared by all the Atlantic peoples," Eisenhower declared. "The agreements endanger no nation." Yet the entry of West Germany into NATO assured a long-term division of central Europe. In 1955 the Soviet Union created the Warsaw Pact, a military alliance that attempted to balance the power of NATO.

SECRET FOREIGN POLICY

While exercising restraint in Korea and Europe, Eisenhower pursued an aggressive but secret foreign policy beyond the scrutiny of Congress and the public. Under the Central Intelligence Agency Act of 1949, the CIA had a multibillion-dollar, top-secret budget that was exempt from congressional accountability and control. Between 1950 and 1955 the agency tripled in size to 15,000 personnel. Initially intended as an intelligence-gathering body, the CIA under Eisenhower became an interventionist organization as well. In one secret mission, for example, the agency built an underground tunnel beneath East Berlin and used wiretaps and recording devices to obtain an intelligence windfall. Besides establishing spy networks around the world, the CIA performed secret, illegal operations that promoted the State Department's formal policy. For example, the CIA regularly supported disruptive raids launched from Taiwan onto the Chinese mainland. When such activities were discovered, the United States denied all allegations and used the episodes to denounce its enemies. In 1955 Democratic Senator Mike Mansfield proposed the creation of a congressional intelligence oversight committee, but the White House effectively

Allen W. Dulles, director of the Central Intelligence Agency, after appearing at an executive session of the Joint Congressional Atomic Energy Committee in 1958.

blocked such interference with foreign policy management by the executive branch.

CIA intervention proved especially effective on the new battlefronts of the Cold War in the developing ("third") world. In 1953, for example, the United States instigated a coup d'etat in Iran, then denied complicity in the affair. Two years earlier, the premier of Iran, Dr. Mohammed Mossadegh, had attempted to end British exploitation by nationalizing Iran's oil wells. Western-owned companies retaliated by boycotting Iranian oil. Mossadegh appealed to Eisenhower for assistance, but the president rebuffed him, stating, "It would not be fair to American taxpayers." Mossadegh then turned to the Soviet Union. In response, Eisenhower ordered the CIA to intervene in Iran's internal affairs. In August 1953 U.S. agents provided crucial military support that enabled the hereditary Shah to topple the Mossadegh regime and return to power. In the ensuing negotiations, the nationalized oil wells were replaced by an international consortium in which U.S.-owned companies held a 40 percent interest. The western oil companies then agreed to limit Iranian oil production to maximize their profits at the expense of Iran. By overthrowing Mossadegh, the United States not only broke the British oil monopoly but also placed Iran safely in the noncommunist camp. Continued economic and military aid to the Shah strengthened this realignment. Yet the CIA never acknowledged its role in the coup; even today, the relevant documents remain classified.

The CIA also implemented Eisenhower's foreign policy in Guatemala in 1954. As in Iran, a popular leader, Colonel Jacobo Arbenz, attempted to improve economic conditions by enacting land reform and nationalizing the holdings of the United Fruit Company. Arbenz offered compensation for the expropriated property, but United Fruit, backed by the State Department, rejected the sum. The administration then began planning the overthrow of Arbenz with the help of a CIA invasion army trained in Nicaragua and Honduras.

Justifying this new version of dollar diplomacy, the United States falsely described Arbenz as a front man for "international communism," who imperiled the entire hemisphere. In March 1954 Washington sponsored a resolution at the Tenth Inter-American Conference, declaring that communist control of "any American State" endangered "the peace of America." Guatemala alone voted against this new interpretation of the Monroe Doctrine. Two months later, Arbenz received a shipment of arms from Czechoslovakia, which confirmed administration fears. The next month a CIA-backed rebel army and mercenary force invaded and bombed Guatemala and defeated Arbenz. At the same time, U.S. military officers in Germany blockaded Soviet shipments to Guatemala. This action violated international trade agreements. Despite British protests, administration policy won bipartisan approval at home. "There is no question here of United States interference in the domestic affairs of any American State," insisted Senator Lyndon Johnson.

Claiming to have saved Guatemala from an international conspiracy, the administration supported the regime of Colonel Carlos Armas with $90 million in economic and military aid. Armas returned the nationalized land to United Fruit, provided tax benefits for the corporation, crushed the labor union movement, and disenfranchised illiterate people, who constituted 70 percent of the population. By using force to restore conditions favorable to U.S. investment, the administration supported reactionary military government in Central America.

BUILDING A CORPORATE COMMONWEALTH

In domestic affairs Eisenhower attempted to steer a middle course between unregulated capitalism and an activist state. The president believed that government should be used to moderate economic conflict and sustain growth without threatening private enterprise or becoming too burdensome. Eisenhower saw the administrative state as a mediator among society's interests and hoped that cooperation and consensus, not coercion, would direct the nation toward social harmony. Instead of prosecuting violations of antitrust laws, for example, the

Charlie Wilson, shown with models of some of the Pentagon's best toys, went from being head of General Motors to a job that seemed much the same—head of the defense department.

administration preferred negotiated settlements between government and business. The president also resolved to reduce the scope of federal government activities and supported Secretary of the Treasury George Humphrey's efforts to balance the federal budget by reducing expenses. However, Eisenhower would not agree to drop basic New Deal programs such as Social Security and minimum wages. To balance the budget, therefore, the White House reluctantly delayed a tax cut. Despite Humphrey's efforts to promote frugality and the sharp criticism of conservative Republicans, government expenditures remained a basic prop of the economy.

Although Eisenhower joined "corporate liberals" in retaining New Deal regulations and social welfare nets, he sided with conservatives in defending the petroleum industry against federal regulation. The president strongly believed that a prosperous oil industry reinforced national defense. For more than a decade, the federal government had contested the claim of several coastal states, particularly Texas, Louisiana, and California, to jurisdiction over offshore oil. Because the major petroleum companies expected beneficial legislation from state governments, they supported the state claims. Conservative Republicans opposed federal control of private business and also supported the states' claims. So did southern Democrats, who saw state control of oil as not only in their economic interests but also as a defense of states' rights. In 1946 and again in 1952 Congress passed legislation giving control of offshore oil to the states. Truman vetoed both measures and before leaving office reserved offshore oil for the navy, but Eisenhower reversed his predecessor's position, and Republicans cooperated with southern Democrats to pass a measure giving control of offshore oil to the states in 1953.

THE ANTICOMMUNIST CRUSADE

Eisenhower's personal popularity failed to silence criticism of communist influence in government. The president's efforts to stand above controversy strengthened the most fervent congressional anticommunists, particularly Joseph McCarthy. The appointment of Scott McLeod, a McCarthy supporter, to head the State Department's personnel program in 1953 accelerated the dismissal of alleged subversives. Soon after taking office, Eisenhower revised Truman's loyalty program, issuing Executive Order 10450, which established new standards for dismissal of government employees. Although Truman required evidence of disloyalty or subversion, Eisenhower authorized dismissal on the grounds that an individual's employment "may not be clearly consistent with the interests of national security." Under the new guidelines, Eisenhower removed 2,200 "security risks" in his first year in office. Few were actually charged with disloyalty.

The administration's definition of security risks revealed the underlying cultural assumptions within the Cold War consensus. Besides obvious cases of negligence, criminality, and insanity, Eisenhower's criteria for dismissal included "notoriously disgraceful conduct, habitual use of intoxicants to excess, drug addiction, or sexual perversion." Persons practicing such acts were considered risks because they were vulnerable to blackmail, and government loyalty boards frequently dismissed homosexuals (making such individuals *more* vulnerable to blackmail). In a single case in 1960 the National Security Agency fired twenty-six employees for alleged homosexuality.

The insistence on conformity also demanded the suppression of political dissent. Shortly after moving into the State Department, Dulles fired several career diplomats, including prestigious China experts such as John Carter Vincent and John Paton Davies, who had predicted Mao's victory in 1949. Dulles also encouraged the departure of George Kennan, viewed as the architect of containment. To replace Kennan as ambassador to the Soviet Union, the administration supported Charles E. Bohlen. However, rigid anticommunists questioned the nomination, pointing out that Bohlen had acted as presidential translator at Yalta. Rumors of the nominee's homosexuality also surfaced. Unwilling to drop one of his first appointees, Eisenhower accepted a compromise, permitting two senators to examine Bohlen's confidential FBI file. Their favorable report led to senatorial confirmation. Nonetheless, Taft warned the president: "No more Bohlens."

J. Robert Oppenheimer, the celebrated physicist who had directed the development of the atomic bomb, also fell victim to the loyalty controversy (see the accompanying biography). Fearing that Oppenheimer's moral doubts about the hydrogen bomb might influence other scientists, Eisenhower supported the AEC's decision to lift the scientist's security clearance. In yet another controversial case, the president refused to provide clemency to the convicted atomic spies Julius and Ethel Rosenberg, exaggerating their activities by claiming that the couple "may have condemned to death tens of million of innocent people all over the world." Despite ambiguous evidence about Ethel Rosenberg's espionage activities, the unrepentant couple was electrocuted in 1953.

"In America," protested the playwright Arthur Miller in *The Crucible,* a 1953 version of the Salem witch trials, "any man who is not reactionary in his views is open to the charge of alliance with the Red hell." During the anticommunist crusade, the nation's foremost witch hunter was Senator Joseph McCarthy, a crude, intemperate inquisitor who disregarded formalities in his search for communist sympathizers. Even after Eisenhower's inauguration, McCarthy continued to attack communist influence in government. As chairman of a Senate subcommittee on government operations, McCarthy held public hearings in 1953 about the Voice of America and claimed that the State Department's propaganda organ served as a front for communists. With the tacit consent of Secretary Dulles, McCarthy meddled in other State Department affairs. Two members of McCarthy's staff, Roy Cohn and G. David Schine, embarked on a chaotic investigation of the United States Information Agency (USIA) in Europe. Their scrutiny of USIA libraries unearthed innumerable "subversive" works by authors such as novelist Theodore Dreiser and historian Arthur M. Schlesinger, Jr. Fearing McCarthy's wrath, the agency removed several thousand volumes from library shelves.

"I will not get into the gutter with that guy," said Eisenhower, avoiding direct confrontation with the vitriolic senator. Wishing to prevent a split in Republican ranks, the president hoped that if he ignored McCarthy the senator would recede from the limelight. Instead, McCarthy felt emboldened to attack the Eisenhower administration. In September 1953 he launched an investigation of army security procedures at Fort Monmouth, New Jersey. Concerned about the

Brown Brothers

Ethel and Julius Rosenberg, convicted in a controversial Cold War trial of passing atomic bomb "secrets" to the Soviet Union during World War II, were sentenced to death in 1951.

routine promotion of a communist dentist, McCarthy clashed with General Ralph Zwicker, chastising the officer for defending "Communist conspirators." The army responded by releasing documents showing that McCarthy attempted to obtain special privileges for Cohn's coworker Private David Schine. McCarthy then ordered a full investigation of the army, including Eisenhower's Secretary of the Army Robert Stevens.

The president now entered the conflict, refusing to cooperate with the Senate investigation. "In opposing Communism," he told a March 1954 press conference, "we are defeating ourselves if we use methods that do not conform to the American sense of justice." Although Attorney General Brownell could find no legal precedents for denying subpoenaed documents and personnel, Eisenhower invoked the right of "executive privilege" to block McCarthy's access to his staff. In taking this stand, Eisenhower expressed concern that McCarthy's indiscriminate investigations would uncover the continuing Oppenheimer controversy and disturb scientific work on hydrogen bombs. "We've got to handle this so that all our scientists are not made out to be Reds," Eisenhower remarked. "That goddamn McCarthy is just likely to try such a thing." Such fears reflected the desire of many modern presidents for secrecy in

Republican Senator Joseph R. McCarthy, flanked by his aides, captured national attention by claiming to have "proof" of communist subversion inside the federal government.

matters of nuclear policy, CIA activities, and internal disagreements. To Eisenhower's alarm, McCarthy was threatening to penetrate the secrets of the national security state.

As McCarthy pursued the investigation of army security procedures and the army made accusations against McCarthy, Democratic Minority Leader Lyndon Johnson demanded that the public hearings be televised. Beginning in March 1954 the three major television networks broadcast the much-heralded Army-McCarthy hearings. The spectacle once again demonstrated the new medium's power to influence public opinion. For thirty-six days viewers witnessed McCarthy's erratic, stormy behavior. While the senator attacked colleagues, threatened witnesses, and ignored legal procedures, his favorable public opinion ratings declined from 50 percent to 34 percent. The hearings climaxed when McCarthy chastised a young army lawyer for once belonging to the National Lawyers Guild, which was in McCarthy's words, "the legal bulwark of the Communist Party." Chief Army Counsel Joseph Welch used the episode to strike back at the senator from Wisconsin. "Little did I dream you could be so reckless and so cruel," Welch berated McCarthy before the cameras. "Have you no sense of decency, sir, at long last? Have you left no sense of decency?"

When McCarthy amended his denunciation of "twenty years of treason" to "twenty-*one* years," thus implicating Eisenhower in a cover-up of communism, his reach exceeded his grasp. "Were the junior Senator from Wisconsin in the pay of Communists," Republican Senator Ralph Flanders of Vermont declared, "he could not have done a better job for them." In July 1954 Flanders introduced a resolution to strip McCarthy of his committee chairmanships. However, the proposal violated the Senate tradition of seniority in committee matters, and Flanders modified his bill to call for McCarthy's censure by the Senate instead. In a carefully orchestrated proceeding, a panel of conservative senators chaired by Republican Arthur Watkins of Utah recommended censure for conduct that "tended to bring the Senate into dishonor and disrepute." McCarthy continued to rage against his adversaries, accusing the Senate of serving the communists, but half the Republicans joined the unanimous Democrats to censure McCarthy by a vote of 67–22. Vice President Nixon, presiding in the Senate, deleted the word *censure* from the final document. It was a formality that made no difference. McCarthy had lost his power. He remained in the Senate, politically ineffective, until his death in 1957.

McCarthy's fall created an illusion that communist witch hunts had ended, but the attack on communism extended beyond Congress and assumed the power of a national obsession. Libraries removed controversial books; school boards and universities fired radical teachers; industries established blacklists to prevent employment of suspected communists. Such activities won wide support even from liberals. Minnesota's Hubert H. Humphrey sponsored the Communist Control Act of 1954, which outlawed the Communist Party. "We liberals," added Illinois's Paul Douglas, "must destroy the Communists if this dirty game is to stop."

Encouraged by the anticommunist consensus, FBI Director J. Edgar Hoover stepped up his attacks on the Communist Party. The conviction of leading communists for violating the Smith Act had been upheld by the Supreme Court in the *Dennis* case of 1951 (see Chapter 8). Because the Communist Control Act stated that the Communist Party was "not entitled to any of the rights, privileges, and immunities . . . [of] legal bodies," Hoover moved to disrupt the organization with a Counterintelligence Program (COINTELPRO) introduced in 1956. Using informants, infiltrators, wiretaps, and a variety of "dirty tricks" (forged letters, anonymous telephone calls, police harassment), the FBI doggedly attacked the dwindling communist movement. FBI harassment, together with revelations of Stalin's totalitarianism and Soviet aggression in eastern Europe, drastically reduced the party's membership. From a peak membership of 75,000 during World War II, the party dwindled to fewer than 3,500 members by the end of 1957, and more than half the subscriptions to the party's *Daily Worker* newspaper were received by FBI agents. By then the Supreme Court agreed to reconsider the *Dennis* decision and ruled in the 1957 *Yates* case that violation of the Smith Act required proof not merely of revolutionary beliefs but of incitement to revolutionary action.

An Age of Consensus

Republican leaders expected the anticommunist crusade to remain an effective campaign weapon in the 1954 congressional elections. True to his dispassionate style of leadership, Eisenhower avoided the emotionally charged issue. Nixon repeated his performance of 1952 and attacked the Democrats for tolerating communists in government. Yet neither Eisenhower's prestige nor Nixon's rhetoric could overcome the political effects of an economic recession. Although Eisenhower could attract independent voters, other Republicans were linked with traditional party labels. In the end, Democrats won small majorities in both houses of Congress.

Instead of creating partisan conflict between the branches of government, the Democratic congressional victories actually encouraged cooperation. Senate Majority Leader Lyndon Johnson and House Speaker Sam Rayburn accepted a political consensus and a balance of power between the parties. Because congressional committee assignments depended on seniority, southerners, who came from a one-party region, enjoyed advantages. Patterns of congressional representation also strengthened conservative groups. Urban areas, which usually supported liberals, were underrepresented in Congress because state legislatures divided voting districts to suit local needs. The principle of "one-person, one-vote" required a Supreme Court ruling (*Baker* v. *Carr*) in 1962.

Yet Eisenhower rejected rigid antigovernment attitudes, acknowledging that the federal government "must do its part to advance human welfare and encourage economic growth with constructive actions." Thus the administration continued to subsidize farm prices, even though Secretary of Agriculture Ezra Taft Benson persuaded Congress to lower the level of supports. The president backed a slight expansion of Social Security to include self-employed workers and approved modest housing legislation. Using the justification of "national security," Eisenhower signed legislation in 1954 to build the St. Lawrence Seaway to connect the Great Lakes to ocean ports. On the same grounds, the White House endorsed the 1956 Interstate Highway Act (see Chapter 9).

Committed to such "modern Republicanism," Eisenhower presided over a consensus that unified moderates in both political parties through vigorous pursuit of the Cold War. A 1956 survey found no correlation between political opinions on domestic issues and support for a tough stand against international communism. Democrats and Republicans alike shared a belief in the communist menace and agreed to seek military superiority. The correlation between military expenditures and economic prosperity also assured minimal resistance to administration requests for large Pentagon budgets.

FOREIGN POLICY IN ASIA

A rare assertion of congressional independence prevented U.S. military intervention in the political crisis of Indochina in 1954. Since the Korean War, the United States had supported French attempts to suppress the Viet Minh rebels led by Ho Chi Minh. By 1954 Washington had spent $1.2 billion on military assistance and was financing nearly 80 percent of France's total war costs. These expenses included several hundred "technical" advisers. The administration justified intervention on the grounds that Vietnam provided valuable raw materials such as tin and rubber and remained a vital strategic link in the attempt to halt communist expansion. Yet, although Washington supported its NATO ally in Southeast Asia, administration leaders repeatedly expressed frustration at France's failure to develop support among noncommunist Vietnamese.

J. ROBERT OPPENHEIMER
1904–1967

Brown Brothers

The security status of one of the nation's leading atomic physicists provoked a dramatic closed-door clash in 1954 between traditional freedom of scientific inquiry and Cold War demands for limited political association. The ensuing top-secret hearings into the matter of J. Robert Oppenheimer revealed both changing standards of political propriety and a growing concern about "national security" in an age of fundamental insecurity.

A secular Jew who studied quantum mechanics at Harvard, Cambridge, and the University of Gottenburg, Oppenheimer helped to make the University of California at Berkeley the global center of theoretical physics in the 1930s. Yet the Depression-era poverty of his students and anti-Semitism in Nazi Germany encouraged the affluent bachelor to support progressive social causes. As a "fellow traveler" of the communist movement popular in intellectual circles, Oppenheimer contributed generous sums to the Communist Party because he believed the communists could effectively mobilize resources to defeat the fascist uprising in Spain. Yet the Roosevelt administration viewed such activity as dangerous "premature antifascism."

Both Oppenheimer's socialite wife and his brother had communist affiliations. However, once appointed head of the Los Alamos Laboratory in 1942 and given responsibility for developing the atomic bomb, the scientist cooperated with security investigators by providing the names of program applicants he knew had communist backgrounds. Convinced that advancement of the project depended on keeping communists out of sensitive positions, the Los Alamos director won a reputation as a man with "unusual discretion with secrets."

As the first nuclear weapon exploded at the Trinity test site in New Mexico in July 1945, Oppenheimer remembered the Sanskrit cry of the Bhagavad-Gita: "I am become Death. The shatterer of worlds." Yet the physicist never regretted his role in the development of the atomic bombs that devastated Hiroshima and Nagasaki. Nevertheless, he agreed with most scientists that eventually the Soviet Union

Despite U.S. aid, the French military position worsened. By the spring of 1954 Viet Minh guerrilla forces had surrounded a garrison of French troops at Dien Bien Phu. Facing a military disaster, France appealed for U.S. intervention. The loss of Dien Bien Phu would doom the French empire in Indochina (Vietnam, Cambodia, and Laos). In this crisis situation, the White House faced critical choices. Sensitive to the limited success in Korea, Eisenhower hesitated to commit forces unilaterally. Although the CIA flew relief missions to the embattled garrison and conducted reconnaissance flights, the doctrine of massive retaliation reduced U.S. options to tactical air strikes, perhaps with atomic weapons. This prospect alarmed the British, who worried about Chinese intervention, particularly against Hong Kong and Malaysia. The allies also feared Soviet retaliation in an atomic war. Without British support, moreover, congressional Democrats led by Senator Richard Russell of Georgia refused to sanction military action. As Russell's protege Lyndon Johnson told Dulles, "No more Koreas with the United States furnishing 90 percent of the manpower."

would develop the ability to produce nuclear weapons and recoiled at the unmonitored spread of atomic technology. During 1946 Oppenheimer helped to write politically unpopular proposals for international control of nuclear energy. As chief advisor to the Atomic Energy Commission, the physicist led efforts to oppose the development of the hydrogen fusion bomb, which he regarded as a "weapon of genocide." Accordingly, Oppenheimer called for the use of tactical nuclear weapons for continental defense instead of the massive strategic bombing preferred by the air force. He also insisted that it was technically premature to build nuclear-powered aircraft and opposed construction of atomic submarines.

The AEC gave Oppenheimer security clearance in 1947, but in late 1953 a former congressional staffer sent the FBI a detailed list of accusations against Oppenheimer. The subsequent bureau report prompted President Eisenhower to demand that a "blank wall" be erected between the physicist and sensitive information. Eisenhower feared that the highly respected scientist might persuade other researchers to abandon the super-bomb project. The president also wished to head off potentially embarrassing investigations by Joseph McCarthy. Consequently, the White House asked the AEC to initiate hearings on Oppenheimer's security clearance.

The agency's Personnel Security Board ruled in a 2–1 vote that as a security risk Oppenheimer should not have access to government secrets. The scientist depicted his associations with "fellow travelers" as naive and apologized for occasional lapses of candor, but physicist Edward Teller testified that although Oppenheimer's loyalty was unquestioned, he lacked the "wisdom and judgment" for a security clearance. Soon the full AEC upheld the security panel's findings. By continuing to associate with known communists and by withholding information, the AEC explained, the father of the atomic bomb had "consistently placed himself outside the rules that govern others" and "repeatedly exhibited a willful disregard of the normal and proper obligations of society."

By focusing on Oppenheimer's character, the AEC rejected the view that intellectuals and scientists should be judged differently than military and government personnel. By 1954 many Americans distrusted intellectual cosmopolitans such as Oppenheimer and believed that loyalty to the struggle against communism was the most important qualification for public service. Without a security clearance, Oppenheimer returned to teaching at Princeton University. In a friendlier political climate, the AEC gave the physicist the prestigious Fermi Award in 1963, but Oppenheimer never again performed government work. ■

For Eisenhower, Vietnam held the future of Asia. In 1954 a special NSC committee called for military victory "to provide tangible evidence of Western strength and determination to defeat Communism." At a press conference that year the president buttressed this position with the "falling domino" theory: "You have a row of dominos set up, you knock over the first one, and what will happen to the last one is the certainty that it will go over very quickly." The fall of Vietnam would mean that "many human beings pass under a dictatorship that is inimical to the free world." It would interfere with the acquisition of precious resources, imperil Japanese trade, and force that ally "toward the Communist areas in order to live."

Eisenhower never wavered from this belief that the Viet Minh represented not an anticolonial force but an instrument of world communism. Consequently, he failed to distinguish between Asian nationalism and an international communist conspiracy. Yet Eisenhower had benefited from the Korean experience. Without British support and explicit approval from Congress, the

Exhibit 10-3. Indochina after the Geneva Accords of 1954

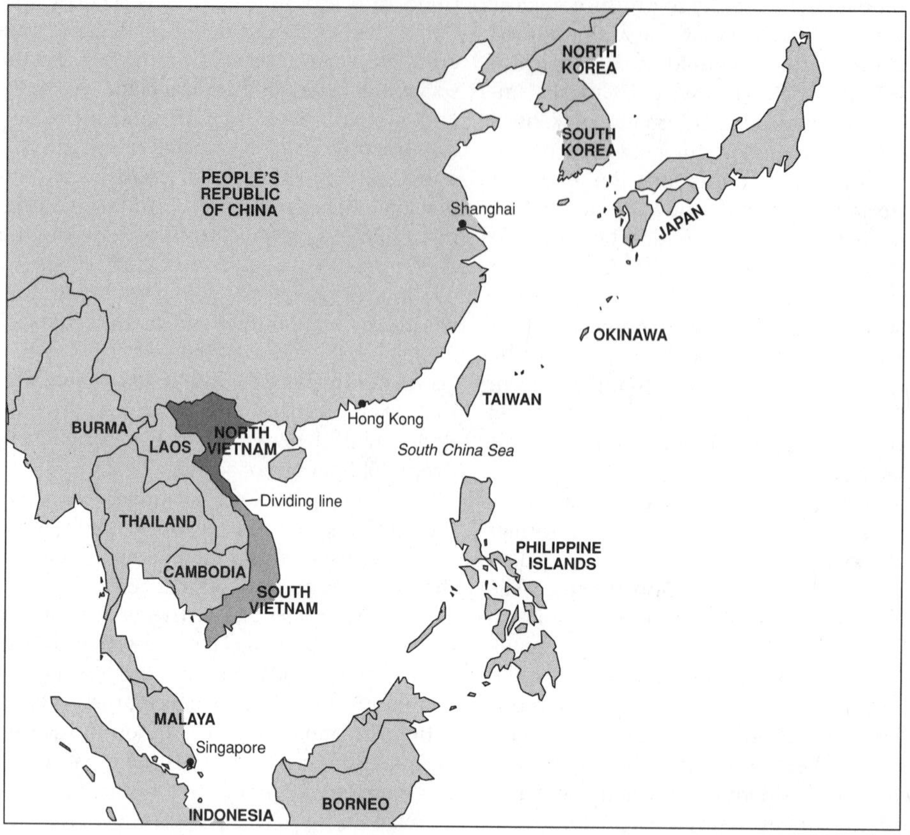

Source: Thomas A. Bailey, *A Diplomatic History of the American People* (Prentice Hall, rev. ed., 1980).

president refused to commit ground forces to another war in Asia. Yet when the French finally surrendered to the Viet Minh in May 1954, Lyndon Johnson criticized the White House's failure to act. "American foreign policy had never in all its history suffered such a stunning reversal," he declared. "We have been caught bluffing by our enemies."

The French defeat made a diplomatic settlement imperative. In July 1954 France signed the Geneva Accords and ended eight years of war by accepting the independence of Vietnam, Laos, and Cambodia. The agreement divided Vietnam militarily at the seventeenth parallel, but this temporary line did not imply a political separation. The agreement also called for national elections, supervised by an international commission, to be held within two years. By acknowledging a Viet Minh government, if only in North Vietnam, the Geneva settlement represented a defeat of Eisenhower's anticommunist foreign policy. The United States announced it would respect the Geneva Accords, but the administration refused to sign the document, and Dulles referred to South Vietnam as a "country." More seriously, the United States began to violate the Geneva agreements by continuing the secret war against the Viet Minh. Instead of accepting a communist Vietnam, Washington worked to build an anticommunist nationalist movement led by Ngo Dinh Diem, a U.S.-educated Catholic

President Eisenhower, determined to block national unification under Ho Chi Minh in Vietnam, personally welcomed South Vietnamese President Ngo Dinh Diem in Washington, D.C., in 1957.

seminarian. Installed as premier of the French-controlled portion of the country, Diem welcomed a U.S. military mission, which organized a South Vietnamese army and launched acts of sabotage and a propaganda campaign against the Viet Minh in the north. Meanwhile, the CIA distributed $12 million to bribe Diem's rivals into neutrality.

Besides engaging in these military activities, the United States moved to supplant France's role in Vietnam. Bypassing French officials, Washington transmitted aid directly to Diem, thus avoiding the appearance of supporting French colonialism. Such policies led France to withdraw from Vietnam before the 1956 election deadline. Quickly stepping into the power vacuum, U.S. advisers began to train a large Vietnamese army "to deter Viet Minh aggression." Acknowledging that Ho Chi Minh would win national elections, the administration worked to stop national unification under the terms of the Geneva Accords.

Diem made these policies explicit in 1955 by announcing his rejection of national elections. Unlike France and Britain, Eisenhower backed Diem and welcomed him in Washington, where the two leaders reaffirmed the struggle against "continuing Communist subversive capabilities." During the next five years, when Vietnam seldom attracted media attention, the United States sent nearly $1.5 billion in economic and military aid to finance most of Diem's government expenses. Such support enabled the dictator to suppress political rivals as his soldiers arrested communists and noncommunists alike. Diem also subverted land reforms begun by the Viet Minh. By 1959 these repressive policies triggered a guerrilla revolt. Although the United States urged Diem to institute political and social reforms, the South Vietnamese leader refused, prompting the U.S. ambassador to suggest "it may become necessary . . . to begin consideration of alternative courses of actions and leaders." Eisenhower passed this unresolved predicament to the next U.S. presidential administration in 1961.

While adopting unilateral action in Vietnam, Eisenhower instituted collective security plans to prevent the spread of communism in Asia. In 1954 the United States signed a Southeast Asia Treaty Organization (SEATO) pact with Britain, France, Australia, New Zealand, Thailand, Pakistan, and the Philippines. This accord provided for mutual defense against armed attack, subversion, or indirect aggression. "An attack on the treaty area would occasion a reaction so united, so strong, and so well placed," Dulles declared, "that the aggressor would lose more than it could hope to gain." Yet the SEATO agreement had inherent limitations—the refusal of neutral India to participate and the difficulty of implementing massive retaliation against subversion. The Senate ratified the treaty with little dissent, but the military provisions were never invoked, and the agreement ended in 1977.

Even as Dulles was flying to Manila to negotiate the SEATO pact in 1954, the weaknesses of the treaty became apparent. Without warning or obvious provocation, Chinese shore batteries suddenly began to bombard Quemoy, one of the islands (along with Matsu and the Tachen Islands) between China and Taiwan. The attacks quickly moved Washington to prepare for war, including an atomic bombing of China. Although Eisenhower recognized that the islands were not crucial to the defense of Taiwan, the president defined the Chiang regime as part of the "backbone" of international security. Meanwhile, the government of mainland China began to prepare for an atomic attack. As war fever rose, Dulles negotiated a mutual defense pact with Taiwan but made no mention of the disputed islands.

When China captured one of the Tachen Islands, Eisenhower asked Congress for authority to use armed forces to defend Taiwan and the nearby islands. Approved by nearly unanimous votes of both houses of Congress in 1955, the so-called Formosa Resolution gave the president discretionary power to declare war, a virtual blank check for future presidential foreign policy. As China continued to bomb the islands, Eisenhower reiterated the threat of atomic attack. At the same time, however, the Soviet Union was seeking a relaxation of global tensions and hoping for an arms control agreement in Europe. Soviet pressure, combined with Eisenhower's threats, persuaded China to break the deadlock. As abruptly as it began, the crisis passed.

U.S. threats to use atomic bombs moved the People's Republic of China to develop its own nuclear capacities. Meanwhile, the Taiwanese government proceeded to strengthen fortifications on the disputed offshore islands. Tensions between the two Chinas kept the world on edge. Then, in 1958, the People's Republic abruptly reopened the crisis by launching a steady bombardment of Quemoy. This time, as the administration rushed military aid to Taiwan, Eisenhower avoided reference to nuclear weapons. By then both the United

Exhibit 10-4. Taiwan and the People's Republic of China

States and the Soviet Union were discussing an arms control agreement, and scientists meeting in Geneva had announced "a workable and effective control system for the detection of violations." The refusal of the Soviet Union to support China's attack intensified the rift between the communist allies. Yet neither the United States nor the Soviet Union could abandon their rival Chinese ally. The result was the preservation of the two-China status quo. Eisenhower and Dulles had accomplished no more than Truman's policy of containment.

EUROPEAN DIPLOMACY

Reluctant to risk his personal prestige, Eisenhower avoided presidential diplomacy during his first years in office. While allowing Dulles to negotiate in public, the president preferred to issue broad policy statements. In December

1953, for example, Eisenhower addressed the United Nations General Assembly, presenting a dramatic "atoms for peace" proposal that urged international control of atomic weapons. In offering to join the Soviet Union in pooling nuclear resources for peaceful purposes, the president hoped to overcome the mutual hostility that set the two powers on a deadly course. Yet Eisenhower knew, as did the Soviets, that his proposal would preserve U.S. nuclear superiority. When the Soviet Union reacted unfavorably, the president settled for the propaganda advantages and made no counteroffer.

Two years later Eisenhower again captured international attention with an "open-skies" plan, which would permit overflights of foreign countries to prevent surprise attacks. The president had tried to avoid a direct meeting with world leaders, but Democrats urged some gesture of reconciliation. Eisenhower insisted that the former allies first sign a peace treaty with Austria. When the Soviets agreed in 1955, Eisenhower flew to a summit meeting in Geneva with British, French, and Soviet leaders. The main topics on the agenda—the status of Germany and disarmament—could not be settled. However, the open-skies proposal was intended to break the stalemate of suspicion and relax global tensions. Yet, as with atoms for peace, the plan offered more advantages to the less-secretive United States than to the closed Soviet Union. The Russians rejected the scheme. Eisenhower then proceeded with plans to use a secret spy plane—the U-2—to achieve the goal of the open-skies plan. Although the United States continued to test hydrogen bombs and intercontinental missiles, the summit meeting eased world tensions. "Communist tactics against the free nations have shifted," observed Eisenhower in 1956, "from reliance on violence to reliance on division."

The "thaw" in the Cold War had obvious limits. As Poland and then Hungary tried to establish more liberal communist governments in 1956, the United States hailed the collapse of the Soviet empire. However, when Soviet tanks crushed the uprising in Budapest, massive retaliation proved worthless. Although Radio Free Europe broadcast moral support and inspired suicidal resistance to Soviet tanks, the president settled for condemnations of Soviet cruelty and allowed 20,000 Hungarian refugees to enter the country.

CRISES IN THE MIDDLE EAST

The importance of oil in the postwar world underscored the strategic value of the Middle East. Although the United States supported the independence of Israel, both Truman and Eisenhower encouraged U.S. oil companies to provide Arab states with subsidies, which were tacitly repaid by the federal government in the form of tax deductions. Eisenhower also backed British influence in the Middle East to check Soviet expansion and supported a British plan for regional cooperation through the Baghdad Pact of 1955. This alliance alarmed Egyptian leader Gamal Abdel Nasser, who sought economic and military assistance to strengthen his country. As Nasser negotiated the purchase of arms from Czechoslovakia, the United States offered to finance the Aswan Dam, a giant hydroelectric project that promised to modernize Egypt. The plan collapsed when Nasser announced his recognition of the People's Republic of China in 1956.

Exhibit 10-5. The Middle East, 1956–1958

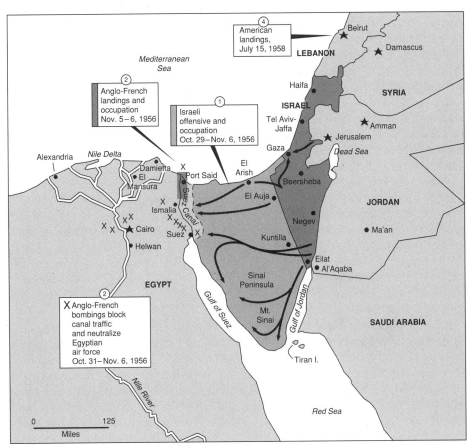

"Do nations which play both sides get better treatment than nations which are stalwart and work with us?" asked Dulles angrily. Eisenhower promptly withdrew the offer to build the dam. The reversal humiliated Nasser. One week later, the Egyptian leader nationalized the Suez Canal, thereby jeopardizing western Europe's access to oil and Israeli shipping rights. Although Britain and France threatened military reprisal, Eisenhower opposed a reassertion of colonialism. U.S. allies then resolved to take bilateral action with Israel. In October 1956 the Israelis launched a surprise attack on Egypt, which provided Britain and France with an excuse to intervene to protect the Suez Canal. The invasion coincided with the Soviet suppression of the Hungarian uprising. Faced with a double crisis, Eisenhower demanded the withdrawal of troops from Egypt. So did Soviet leader Nikita Khrushchev, who warned the western nations of a retaliatory attack and expressed interest in a Soviet presence in the Middle East. To prevent such Soviet expansion, Eisenhower increased pressure on the allies, by halting oil shipments to western Europe. The embargo forced the British and French to remove their forces from the Middle East by the end of the year.

The "Eisenhower Doctrine," presented to Congress in January 1957, attempted to fill the power vacuum in the Middle East. Asking Congress to approve unspecified economic and military assistance, the president also requested a resolution announcing that "overt armed aggression from any nation controlled by international Communism" would be met by U.S. military force. After subtle changes in wording, Congress adopted the measure. By confusing Arab nationalism with communist expansion, the Eisenhower Doctrine gave the White House extensive authority to intervene in the Middle East. In April 1957, for example, Jordan's King Hussein claimed that a pro-Nasser rebellion constituted a communist attack. Understanding the duplicity of this language, Eisenhower nevertheless sent the Sixth Fleet to protect the political status quo. In July 1958 a similar distortion of events led the president to order the Marines into Lebanon. This dramatic gesture served notice to Arab nationalists that the United States was determined to protect access to Middle Eastern oil.

"What makes the Soviet threat unique in history," the president stated in 1958, "is its all-inclusiveness. . . . Trade, economic development, military power, arts, science, education, the whole world of ideas—all are harnessed to the same chariot of expansion." Fear of Soviet influence in economically underdeveloped countries stimulated a reappraisal of U.S. economic foreign policy. As a proponent of international free enterprise, Eisenhower hoped that foreign trade and private investment would assure U.S. influence without adding to government expenditures. Foreign aid remained largely military and was justified on grounds of national security.

By mid-decade increased Soviet competition persuaded the president to endorse foreign aid as a way of accelerating economic development of other countries and linking their interests to the West. In 1957 Congress established the Development Loan Fund and two years later created the Inter-American Loan Bank for Latin America. Both projects provided relatively small sums and emphasized private investment. Eisenhower defined such assistance not as an attempt to reduce poverty but rather as a defense of national security in the fight against communism. Moreover, foreign military aid far exceeded economic assistance and caused a severe imbalance in international payments that weakened the dollar abroad. Yet Eisenhower's commitment to foreign economic development provided a precedent for later administrations.

THE POLITICS OF MODERATION

Surveying the political spectrum in 1956, Adlai Stevenson concluded that "moderation is the spirit of the times." Although liberals like Hubert Humphrey and Paul Douglas spoke eloquently about social reform, Democrats worked closely with Eisenhower's "modern" Republicans to enact minimal welfare legislation. In 1955, for example, Eisenhower proposed a ninety-cent-an-hour minimum wage, thirty-five cents less than organized labor desired, and extension of coverage to include certain unorganized workers, but conservatives opposed giving the minimum wage to unskilled workers. Congress then enacted a compromise that raised the minimum wage to one dollar an hour but ignored unorganized workers. Similarly, Eisenhower requested the construction of 140,000 units of public housing, but Congress reduced that number to 75,000. Political leaders in both parties dismissed proposals for national health insurance as socialized medicine.

The White House also opposed public control of electric power projects. In 1954 Eisenhower recommended a revision of the Atomic Energy Act to allow private manufacture and operation of atomic reactors. This legislation led to the first privately run nuclear power plants. The administration's decision to bypass the Tennessee Valley Authority (TVA) in providing electricity for AEC facilities proved more controversial. By ignoring the TVA, long a symbol of New Deal liberalism, the policy attacked federal support of public power. Hints of political corruption weakened the president's position, however, and a compromise ended the controversy. The administration did succeed in blocking public power projects in other parts of the country, such as Hell's Canyon on the Snake River.

Eisenhower, the grandfatherly former soldier, remained extremely popular. Although the president's heart attack in September 1955 shook public confidence, he recovered rapidly and resolved to seek a second term. After slight hesitation, Eisenhower agreed to keep Vice President Nixon on the ticket. Democratic chances seemed slim. Stevenson won a first-ballot nomination and then, in a dramatic moment, opened the vice presidential choice to the whole Democratic National Convention. In the exciting floor fight, Estes Kefauver managed to defeat Senator John Kennedy of Massachusetts. The Democrats then adopted a moderate platform. Hoping to regain the South, the party waffled on support of the Supreme Court's school desegregation decision (see Chapter 9). Democrats echoed Eisenhower's Cold War principles, although Stevenson did introduce two controversial proposals into the campaign by calling for an end to the military draft and suggesting a moratorium on hydrogen bomb testing. However, both issues played to Eisenhower's strength as a military expert. "The butchers of the Kremlin," said Nixon, "would make mincemeat of Stevenson over a conference table."

Eisenhower's margin of victory exceeded the totals of 1952. Capturing 58 percent of the popular vote, he carried all but seven states. Other Republican candidates ran far behind, and Democrats strengthened their control of both houses of Congress. This anomalous situation reflected the persistence of party voting habits (50 percent more voters had registered as Democrats than as Republicans in 1956). Unlike congressional candidates, Eisenhower could attract voters from all parts of the political spectrum because specific issues appeared relatively unimportant. One exception to the rule was the African American vote. In 1956 40 percent of black voters, including Martin Luther King, Jr., supported the party of Abraham Lincoln against Democratic racists who controlled southern politics.

DOMESTIC DEBATE: BUDGETS, CIVIL RIGHTS, SPUTNIK

Emboldened by the congressional elections, Democrats moved to clarify their political position. Eisenhower's success in the black neighborhoods of northern cities goaded congressional liberals into action. "I don't think a party should run on 'trouble,' on economic difficulty," declared Hubert Humphrey. "We must design a new liberal program." Led by Humphrey and Paul Douglas, liberal

ESTES KEFAUVER
1903–1963

Stock Montage

In an era of political consensus and corporate expansion, Tennessee's Senator Estes Kefauver flourished as a maverick politician and a champion of the ordinary citizen against big business and political corruption. Running for the Senate in 1948, he broke with Tennessee's political machine and adopted a coonskin cap as a symbol of his frontier independence. The folksy style became his political trademark. Kefauver's image as a populist, enhanced by televised broadcasts of his Senate hearings on organized crime in 1950 and 1951, catapulted him to national fame and made the senator a strong Democratic presidential contender. Yet his individualism created many enemies, who thwarted his ambitions. In the end, he was deemed too much a southerner for liberals, too much a liberal for southerners.

Kefauver was born in eastern Tennessee, studied law at Yale, and worked as a corporation lawyer in Chattanooga, where he supported the Tennessee Valley Authority. Elected to Congress in 1939, he defended the embattled New Deal, supported small business interests against corporate concentration, and advocated congressional reform, coauthoring the book *A Twentieth Century Congress* (1947). Sensitive to civil liberties issues, he opposed the Taft-Hartley labor law and voted against refunding the House Committee on Un-American Activities. Yet, as a southern representative, he opposed a federal Fair Employment Practices Commission and antilynching legislation. Unlike most racial opportunists, however, Kefauver urged repeal of poll taxes because they disenfranchised the poor of both races, and he opposed the use of the filibuster to kill civil rights legislation. Indeed, after the Supreme Court overturned school segregation in 1954, he readily accepted the idea of racial integration.

Kefauver's investigation of organized crime during the first Senate hearings ever televised

senators presented a sixteen-point "Democratic Declaration" that advocated civil rights legislation, public housing, unemployment compensation, and other progressive reforms. Meanwhile, Democratic Party chairman Paul Butler organized a Democratic Advisory Council distinct from the congressional leadership of Johnson and Rayburn to press for a liberal agenda. Such maneuvers assured greater conflict with the Republican administration.

The first controversy erupted when the president presented a $73.3 billion budget request, the highest appropriation ever requested in peacetime, for fiscal year 1958. Committed to a balanced budget, Treasury Secretary George Humphrey blundered by predicting that such expenditures would cause a depression "that will curl your hair." Eisenhower complicated the situation by inviting Congress to reduce government expenditures. The result was a bitter legislative "battle of the budget" as Congress picked apart the president's entire program, shaving the budget by $4 billion, including $1 billion in foreign aid. For Eisenhower, said presidential advisor Sherman Adams, the outcome was "a serious and disturbing personal defeat."

Contrary to Secretary Humphrey's predictions, instead of boosting the economy, the reduction in government expenditures slowed economic growth.

created a national sensation in 1950. Exposure of national crime networks and widespread political graft underscored an abiding fear in the Cold War era that secret forces—"government-within-a-government," as Kefauver put it—were threatening national values. For Kefauver, it was crime and corruption, not communism, that was the prime menace. Significantly, he opposed provisions of the 1954 communist control bill that made Communist Party membership a felony. Kefauver's crime hearings also showed the political power of television. In his book, *Crime in America* (1951), Kefauver estimated that more than 20 million people watched the hearings; in New York City, the Consolidated Edison electric company had to install a new generator to handle the demand. As a result, Kefauver suddenly became a nationally known politician.

Capitalizing on this popularity, Kefauver donned his coonskin cap in 1952 and entered a series of Democratic presidential primaries as the first major candidate to recognize the potential of grassroots support. He surprised the country by defeating President Truman in New Hampshire, but his unorthodox style precluded building a national organization, and despite his many victories at the polls, Kefauver controlled few delegates at the Democratic convention. His nonpartisan investigations of organized crime alarmed the Democratic leadership, which feared a loss of party strength in the cities. Meanwhile, Kefauver's spotty record on civil rights weakened his support among liberals, and his opposition to filibusters cut into his southern base. Defeated by Adlai Stevenson in 1952 and 1956, Kefauver staged a dramatic floor rally to win the vice presidential nomination over Massachusetts Senator John F. Kennedy in 1956. Ironically, the televised spectacle increased Kennedy's visibility in the next election.

As his presidential ambitions waned, Kefauver focused on problems of corporate capitalism. As chair of the Senate Antitrust and Monopoly Subcommittee, he headed investigations of price-fixing and monopolistic practices in the electrical equipment, steel, and drug industries. The Kefauver-Harris Drug Control Act (1962), a landmark consumer measure, encouraged competition and instituted safety requirements in the prescription drug industry. While attacking the Kennedy administration's monopolistic Communications Satellite Act, Kefauver collapsed on the Senate floor in 1963. He died two days later of a ruptured aneurysm. ■

By mid-1957 industrial production had dropped and unemployment had increased. Eisenhower remained skeptical about the ability of government spending to stimulate the economy. Congress had fewer reservations. Increased appropriations, including public works projects, added more than $8 billion to the budget and halted the recession. Yet continued government spending resulted in large budget deficits.

While politicians wrangled about the budget, the nation headed toward a major civil rights crisis. As the issue emerged during the 1950s, Eisenhower, a product of the segregated military and a friend of numerous southern

**Exhibit 10-6. U.S. Government Spending as Percentage of
Gross National Product, 1949–1959**

1949	23.0
1959	26.9

Source: *Historical Statistics of the United States, from Colonial Times to 1970* (1975).

The southern states enforced racial segregation in a variety of public accommodations, including schools, restaurants, toilets, drinking fountains, laundries, and other places where body contact might occur. Such "Jim Crow" laws were not outlawed until 1964.

conservatives, showed no leadership. In his first year in office, the president continued Truman's efforts to end segregation in the armed forces, the federal government, and the nation's capital but otherwise stressed the role of states and cities in resolving these questions. Then in 1954 the Supreme Court desegregation decision created a new climate of opinion (see Chapter 9). "We hail the decision," declared the Conference of Negro Education in the language of the Cold War, "because it dramatically distinguishes our way of life in a democracy.... Here in the United States great social wrongs can be and are righted without bloodshed and without revolutionary means."

While African Americans and liberals heralded the imminent end of racial segregation in all aspects of social life, conservatives warned about the dangers of rapid upheaval. Responding to concern about implementing the *Brown* decision, the Supreme Court issued a second decree in 1955 ordering compliance with desegregation not immediately but "with all deliberate speed" and gave the responsibility for desegregation to federal district courts, which were dominated by traditional segregationist judges. The ruling opened a broad loophole for local defiance. "You are not required to obey any court which passes out such a ruling," advised Mississippi Senator James Eastland. "In fact, you are obligated to defy it." Some southerners opposed any alteration of traditional race relations; others resented the expansion of federal power over states' rights. Either way, segregationists endorsed "massive resistance" to public school integration.

EARL WARREN
1891–1974

Brown Brothers

Of his eight years in the White House, President Eisenhower later said that the nomination of Earl Warren as Chief Justice of the Supreme Court in 1953 was "the biggest damnfool decision I ever made." For the Republican White House, Warren produced a number of constitutional surprises. In making the choice, Eisenhower had fulfilled a political debt. As the three-term governor of California, Warren represented the liberal wing of the Republican Party. He had run for vice president (with Thomas Dewey) in 1948 and remained an important "dark horse" candidate four years later.

Warren's political background had offered few clues to his subsequent career. As a California district attorney and state attorney general, he earned a reputation as a tough law enforcement officer. During World War II he advocated the confinement of all Japanese Americans regardless of their political beliefs. His position reflected an undisguised racism that viewed "Orientals" as essentially unassimilable. Elected governor in 1942, Warren supported liberal legislation in such areas as health insurance and prison reform.

Warren's appointment to the Supreme Court led to dramatic reversals of legal precedent. In his first major decision, *Brown* v. *Board of Education* (1954), the Chief Justice dismantled the doctrine of separate but equal and paved the way for fundamental changes in race relations. Eight years later he carried the principle of democracy further by mandating the reapportionment of all legislative districts according to the principle of one person, one vote in *Baker* v. *Carr*. As in the *Brown* ruling, the decision attacked traditional political structures—in this case, state legislatures—that had enabled rural interests to ignore numeric majorities.

Warren also emerged as a strong defender of individual civil liberties. In the *Yates* decision (1957) he concurred in reversing the conviction of leading communists by differentiating between the theory of subversion and its actual practice. This position led to the eventual overthrow of certain loyalty oaths and state laws against communists. Under the principle of due process of law, he defended the rights of criminals to legal counsel (*Escobedo*, 1964) and to fair treatment by police (*Miranda*, 1966). The Warren-led court tightened the interpretation of obscenity to protect the rights of free speech and freedom of the press from censorship. In 1962 the court supported a rigid separation of church and state by denying prayer and Bible reading in public schools. Such opinions earned Warren the hatred of right-wing groups such as the John Birch Society, which called for his impeachment and stimulated the rise of populist conservativism after the 1960s.

Despite the unpopularity of some of his rulings, Warren was widely respected for personal integrity, and President Lyndon Johnson named the chief justice to head a commission to investigate the assassination of President John Kennedy. Viewing his task as one of evaluating the evidence rather than gathering it, Warren did not pursue a vigorous investigation. Yet his personal reputation helped persuade political leaders to accept the commission's controversial report in 1964.

The decisions of the Warren Court contributed to the liberal climate of the 1960s, and Warren's retirement in 1969 heralded the end of a liberal, "activist" judiciary. In the 1970s the court would modify its rulings about pornography, criminal rights, and capital punishment. However, *Brown* and *Baker* v. *Carr* had forever changed the constitutional landscape of American politics. ■

The Montgomery police fingerprint Rosa Parks after her arrest for failing to vacate her seat on a segregated bus.

While southern leaders defended segregated institutions, African American dissidents seized the initiative by organizing a grass-roots civil rights movement that changed the face of American life. The crusade began on a public transit bus in Montgomery, Alabama, in December 1955, when Rosa Parks, a local NAACP worker, refused to obey a law requiring segregated seating. Overnight, her arrest produced an organized, carefully orchestrated citywide bus boycott led by Baptist minister Martin Luther King, Jr. "We have known humiliation, we have known abusive language, we have been plunged into the abyss of oppression," King declared from the pulpit of the Dexter Avenue Baptist Church. "And we decided to rise up only with the weapon of protest. It is one of the greatest glories of America that we have the right to protest." The year-long boycott unified the African American community, but the Supreme Court had to intervene before municipal officials accepted bus desegregation. Montgomery showed the power of organized black protest and inaugurated the mass actions of the civil rights movement.

As African Americans adopted direct action against racial discrimination, southern resistance increased. State legislatures passed new laws making voter registration more difficult, harassed civil rights organizations (the NAACP was outlawed in several states), and sanctioned police violations of legal rights. Whites also created local "Citizens Councils," which implemented economic reprisals against blacks who attempted to exercise their rights to vote or register their children in integrated schools. The rejuvenated Ku Klux Klan responded to any sign of dissent with violence, and a rash of bombings, targeting integrated schools, black churches, and Jewish synagogues, erupted throughout the South. Fourteen-year-old Emmett Till, a Chicago youth visiting relatives in Mississippi, was kidnapped and murdered for whistling at a white woman in 1955. The acquittal of his accused killers showed that local law enforcement had failed. Yet Eisenhower refused to assert federal power.

Despite occasional pleas for reason, 101 defiant southern congressmen issued a "Declaration of Constitutional Principles" in 1956 that denied the power of the federal government to order desegregation in the states. Eisenhower, who personally opposed the *Brown* ruling, declared, "The final battle against intolerance is to be fought—not in the chambers of any legislature—but in the hearts of men." The president firmly rebuffed suggestions that he take a stand supporting the desegregation of public schools, but in response to appeals from Harlem Congressman Adam Clayton Powell, the White House ordered the desegregation of employment in southern navy yards and worked quietly to desegregate public facilities such as movie theaters in the District of Columbia. In 1956 Attorney General Herbert Brownell proposed legislation to protect African Americans' voting rights, but the measure died in a southern-controlled committee in the Senate. In the absence of clear support from the federal government, violence and coercion *reduced* the number of registered black voters in some southern states.

"Give us the ballot," declared Martin Luther King, "and we will no longer have to worry the federal government about our basic rights." On the third anniversary of the *Brown* ruling in 1957, African American leaders organized a "Prayer Pilgrimage" to Washington that attracted more than 30,000 protesters against racial discrimination. That year Eisenhower again requested legislation to protect the right to vote. This time the proposal won support from Lyndon Johnson, who sought to broaden his national political appeal. Working behind the scenes, Johnson persuaded southern leaders to drop the filibuster in exchange for a mild bill. The new law called for a relatively weak Civil Rights Commission and authorized the attorney general to seek injunctions for violations of voting rights. The measure was the first significant civil rights legislation since Reconstruction, but in 1960 only 25 percent of eligible African Americans could exercise their right to vote.

Direct action by blacks forced the president to support desegregation. In September 1957 Governor Orval Faubus of Arkansas mobilized the National Guard to prevent the integration of Central High School in Little Rock, an action that violated a federal court order. While armed soldiers prevented nine black students from attending the school, Eisenhower remained aloof. Faubus's defiance of federal authority threatened the constitutional system of government, and national protests aroused Eisenhower to action. "Law cannot be flaunted with impunity by any individual or mob of extremists," he conceded. The president federalized the National Guard and ordered paratroopers to enforce the court decision. Despite continuing mob violence, black students began attending the school under the protection of the federalized National Guard. Faubus managed to close the school the next year, but a court order ended Little Rock school segregation in 1959. Elsewhere in the South, school desegregation

RICHARD B. RUSSELL, JR.
1897–1971

AP/Wide World Photos

One of the great barons of the United States Senate at mid-century was Richard Russell. Styled as the "boy wonder" of Georgia politics, he was elected governor in 1930 at the age of thirty-three (he had already served ten years in the state legislature) and two years later was elected to the Senate, where he remained for the rest of his life. A bachelor who had spartan habits, Russell devoted himself completely to the Senate, and over the years as his seniority and his shrewdness grew, he became one of its most powerful members. Always mindful of details, he read every line of the *Congressional Record* daily and was an acknowledged master of parliamentary maneuver. Although he rejected an opportunity to become majority leader in 1953, Russell functioned as "Dean of the Senate Establishment," presiding over the informal inner club that largely dominated Senate affairs.

Russell's career illustrates both the power and the frustration of ambitious southern politicians in an era of segregation. The systematic disenfranchisement of blacks, poor whites, and city dwellers produced a political system that generally did not challenge entrenched leadership. Once elected, southern congressmen and senators could expect a long tenure. Consequently, Russell, like many other southerners, steadily accumulated great power in a legislative branch that stressed seniority of membership and the committee system. When seniority made them chairs of major committees, they could channel federal dollars to their constituents, something Russell did extremely well. An advocate of military preparedness almost from his earliest days in Congress, he became chairman of the Senate Armed Services Committee in 1951, and by 1960 Georgia had some fifteen military installations employing 40,000

continued to provoke mob violence. By 1960 less than 1 percent of African American children attended integrated schools in southern states. In the North the Supreme Court decision did not address de facto segregation.

Organizing religious allies, Martin Luther King helped build a coalition of black activists, the Southern Christian Leadership Conference (SCLC), in 1957. Committed to nonviolent civil disobedience, such groups emphasized the spiritual righteousness of their cause and endeavored to touch the conscience of whites. A new generation of African Americans educated after World War II rejected compromise with racial injustice and demanded the full rights of citizens. Many were encouraged by the emergence of the new nations of black Africa in the late 1950s, which inspired hopes of freedom at home.

"All of Africa will be free," exclaimed novelist James Baldwin, "before we can get a lousy cup of coffee." Such anger and frustration provoked a series of disciplined nonviolent "sit-in" protests by African American college students at the lunch counters of Greensboro, North Carolina, in February 1960. The idea spread like wildfire through the southern states. Instead of waiting for legislative or judicial sanction, young blacks simply violated segregation laws and went to jail. These actions won support among white liberals, who joined Afri-

people and was home to the major defense contractor Lockheed Aircraft as well.

Although the southern political system was an important element in Russell's power, it ultimately thwarted his broader ambitions by making him unacceptable to a national Democratic constituency. Russell came to Washington in 1933 as a strong New Dealer, but as New Deal policies began to pose challenges, however limited, to southern elites, Russell grew steadily more conservative. He was a liberal in a depression, he explained, but "I'm a reactionary when times are good." After World War II he was increasingly uncomfortable in a Democratic Party dominated by New Dealers and Fair Dealers, especially as civil rights emerged as a major national issue. To change the focus of the party, he sought the Democratic presidential nomination in 1952 but was resoundingly defeated. His appeal was limited almost exclusively to the Deep South, and his main effect on the contest was to frustrate the ambitions of his more moderate fellow southerner, Senator Estes Kefauver. A disappointed man, Russell increasingly devoted his energy and talents to opposing civil rights legislation in Congress. Russell's power began to erode after the Civil Rights Act of 1964 was passed, despite his stalwart opposition, although he remained a major force in the Senate until his death in 1971.

Richard Russell was the product of political arrangements in the South and in Washington designed to maximize the power of archconservatives like himself. His skills as a legislator enabled him to exploit the potential of that conservative system, but he was unable to reach beyond his heritage to offer constructive leadership in dealing with the most pressing issues of his time. His often astute judgment on military affairs was blighted by a chauvinism that was jarringly discordant in the nuclear era. "If we have to start over again with another Adam and Eve," he told the Senate, "then I want them to be Americans and not Russians, and I want them to be on this continent and not in Europe."

His unswerving commitment to segregation made him the champion of a demeaning system of economic exploitation and social control. If the integrationists "overwhelm us," he declared, "you will find me in the last ditch." Tragically, both for his region and his own career, too much of his talent and energy went into a misguided defense of what he considered to be "the Southern way of life." ■

can Americans in a national crusade for civil rights. During the next decade, these protests would alter forever the nation's political and cultural landscape (see Chapter 11).

The astounding news of 4 October 1957 abruptly shifted public attention from Little Rock to the heavens: The Soviet Union had launched the first artificial satellite, called "Sputnik." "The Soviets have beaten us at our own game," declared Lyndon Johnson, "—daring scientific advances in the atomic age." Besides the philosophic shockwaves caused by the triumph over the earth's gravitation, Sputnik aroused fear that the communist enemy was now able to deliver intercontinental ballistic missiles armed with nuclear weapons before the United States could muster sufficient retaliatory power. This belief in a missile gap fed widespread fear of nuclear annihilation. Best-selling books such as Nevil Shute's *On the Beach* (1957) and Walt Miller's *A Canticle for Leibowitz* (1959) dramatized the imminence of holocaust.

Eisenhower remained calm, denied military weakness, and rejected plans to build fallout shelters around the country. The United States was actually prepared to match the Soviet achievement. After a few highly publicized failures, the army lofted its own satellite into orbit in 1958. Moreover, Sputnik effectively ended the debate about "open skies," although in the absence of spy satellites Eisenhower continued to rely on the secret U-2 planes. The president also created a White House Science Advisory Committee headed by the Massachusetts Institute of Technology's James Killian. By bringing scientists into the administration, Eisenhower for the first time had access to authoritative opinions about a range of technological issues. These scientists would later contradict the advice of the Atomic Energy Commission (AEC) and the Pentagon and suggest that the nuclear arms race could be controlled. Democratic leaders nonetheless criticized the president's leadership. In the Senate Johnson backed legislation to establish a civilian-controlled space agency, the National Aeronautics and Space Administration (NASA), in 1958.

The combination of Sputnik, Little Rock, and the recession brought landslide victories for the Democrats in the elections of 1958 and shifted the political balance in a liberal direction. Controlling the House by seventy votes and the Senate by thirty, Democrats rejected the president's fiscal austerity and promptly voted to increase the military budget. Congress also admitted Alaska and Hawaii to the union in 1959 but carefully reversed the administration's priorities by welcoming the Democratic Alaska first. For the first time since 1925 the Senate rejected a White House cabinet nominee, Lewis Strauss, Eisenhower's choice to head the Department of Commerce, because of political disagreements. Despite these disputes, however, the administration worked with Congress to enact the National Defense Education Act of 1958 and the Landrum-Griffin labor law. (For details of these measures, see Chapter 9.) Congress also voted to increase support of state unemployment programs and to reorganize the Pentagon.

PRESIDENTIAL DIPLOMACY

After the death of Secretary of State Dulles in 1959, Eisenhower engaged more openly in personal diplomacy. In 1958 he had sent Nixon on a goodwill tour of Latin America, but the vice president had been met by hostile crowds protesting U.S. economic and political exploitation. The administration dismissed these demonstrations as examples of communist infiltration of the hemisphere. Democrats disagreed. "It is foolish . . . to attribute anti-Americanism just to Communist agitation," explained Adlai Stevenson after a trip to Latin America in 1960. Rather, the Eisenhower administration "has been basically concerned with making Latin America safe for American business, not for democracy," especially by supporting "hated dictators."

The issue soon focused on Cuba. After backing dictator Fulgencio Batista since 1952, the White House reacted cautiously to the revolutionary government established by Fidel Castro in 1959. Although the United States offered Castro economic aid, the Eisenhower administration opposed Castro's agrarian reform laws because they nationalized private U.S. holdings. Eisenhower therefore quickly cut aid to Cuba and demanded immediate compensation. As relations between the two nations worsened in 1960, Castro announced the sale of sugar to the Soviet Union in exchange for economic and military assistance.

Eisenhower responded with a two-pronged attack. In 1960 the president ordered the CIA "to organize the training of Cuban exiles mainly in Guatemala

Moscow, 1959. Soviet Premier Nikita Khrushchev and Vice President Richard Nixon at the American National Exhibition.

against a possible future day when they might return to their homeland." Meanwhile, the president exerted economic pressure by decreasing purchases of Cuban sugar. Castro protested that the reduction in U.S. sugar imports was a prelude to an invasion, and Soviet leader Khrushchev announced that his country would protect the Cuban government. Frustrated by Castro's audacity, Eisenhower severed diplomatic relations with Cuba in January 1961 and left the problem for his successor.

Eisenhower attempted nonetheless to reduce conflict with the Soviet Union without jeopardizing U.S. strength. Since his "atoms for peace" proposal of 1953, the president had emphasized inspection and control as a precondition for disarmament. In 1956 he had sneered at Stevenson's call for a halt in nuclear testing, but a diplomatic conference among U.S. and Soviet scientists in Geneva in 1958 indicated that controls could be implemented. Domestic science advisors also had warned Eisenhower that strontium 90, an element of radioactive fallout from atomic testing, was threatening to poison the nation's food chain. Consequently, the president announced in 1958 that the United States was ending further nuclear testing. The Soviet Union performed a final series of tests before it too halted such explosions.

Despite these accommodations, Eisenhower vigorously resisted Khrushchev's demands that Allied forces depart from Berlin. "Any sign of Western weakness at this forward position," he declared in 1958, "could be misinterpreted with grievous consequences." Both powers now spoke about World War III, but in the next year tensions abated when Khrushchev and Eisenhower agreed to engage in personal diplomacy. In 1959 the Soviet leader toured the United States and met amicably with the president at Camp David. Although substantive issues remained unresolved, the two powers were close to agreement about nuclear arms.

The loss of a U-2 airplane destroyed those hopes. In May 1960, on the eve of a summit conference to discuss arms control, Khrushchev announced that the Soviet Union had shot down a U.S. spy plane. The administration immediately denied the charge and claimed that a "weather plane" had merely strayed off course. To Eisenhower's embarrassment, Khrushchev produced the CIA pilot, Francis Gary Powers, which revealed the president's lie. While the whole world watched anxiously, the State Department acknowledged the U-2 mission and justified such flights with the open-skies reasoning that the Soviets had rejected in 1955.

Eisenhower still hoped to salvage the summit conference. By claiming ignorance of the U-2 program, the president could escape complicity. Yet Eisenhower's disavowal of knowledge of the spy mission implied that subordinates were controlling crucial foreign policy decisions. The situation threatened the president's credibility as a political leader and negotiating partner. Reluctantly, Eisenhower acknowledged his involvement. "It is a distasteful but vital necessity," he declared, reminding the public of the lessons of Pearl Harbor. Eisenhower's admission destroyed the summit meeting. At the Paris session, Khrushchev denounced the president and refused to negotiate.

The intensification of the Cold War had a profound effect on public opinion. Democratic politicians criticized the president's clumsy diplomacy. More fundamentally, the U-2 affair shocked the public by revealing the government's dishonesty. Eisenhower, who strove to rise above parties, had lied not only to Khrushchev but to his own citizens. The notion of a credibility gap between the people and their government would haunt politicians for the next two decades.

SUGGESTED READINGS

A thorough and sympathetic account of the Eisenhower administration appears in the second volume of Stephen E. Ambrose, *Eisenhower* (1984). For a fine analysis of the president's political ideology, see an important article, Robert Griffith, "Dwight D. Eisenhower and the Corporate Commonwealth," *American Historical Review*, volume 87 (1982). The traditional view of Eisenhower as a laissez-faire president can be found in Peter Lyon, *Eisenhower: Portrait of a Hero* (1974). This view has been challenged persuasively in Blanche Wiesen Cook, *The Declassified Eisenhower: A Divided Legacy* (1981), and Fred Greenstein, *The Hidden Hand Presidency: Eisenhower as Leader* (1982). A detailed collection of primary sources is Robert L. Branyan and Lawrence H. Larsen, *The Eisenhower Administration*, two volumes (1971).

Numerous biographies offer insight into domestic politics. For the workings of congressional power, see Rowland Evans and Robert Novak, *Lyndon B. Johnson: The Exercise of Power* (1966). Good studies of the leading Democrat include Jeff Broadwater, *Adlai Stevenson and American Politics: The Odyssey of a Cold War Liberal* (1994), and John Bartlow Martin's more detailed two-volume *The Life of Adlai Stevenson* (1976–1977). For the vice president's career, see Stephen E. Ambrose's biography, *Nixon: The Education of a Politician* (1987), as well as the superb analysis by Garry Wills, *Nixon Agonistes* (1970). The liberal perspective emerges in Carl Solberg, *Hubert Humphrey: A Biography* (1984). Voting behavior in the 1950s is explained in Norman H. Nie et al., *The Changing American Voter* (1976).

The civil rights movement is surveyed in the books by Sitkoff, Marable, and Branch listed after Chapter 9. The question of African American voting is treated in two books by Steven F. Lawson: *Black Ballots: Voting Rights in the South, 1944–1969* (1976) and *Running for Freedom: Civil Rights and Black Politics in America Since 1941* (1991). The problem of federal jurisdiction is analyzed in Michael R. Belknap, *Federal Law and Southern Order: Racial Violence and Constitutional Conflict in the Post Brown South* (1987). Other studies include William Chafe, *Civilities and Civil Rights: Greensboro, North Carolina, and the Black Struggle for Freedom* (1980); Robert F. Burk, *The Eisenhower Administration and Black Civil Rights* (1980); and Juan Williams, *Eyes on the Prize: America's Civil Rights Years, 1954–1965* (1987). For an excellent single-state study, see John Dittmer, *Local People: The Struggle for Civil Rights in Mississippi* (1994). The Montgomery bus boycott is abundantly documented in the third volume of *The Papers of Martin Luther King, Jr.*, edited by Clayborne Carson (1997). For the origins of the Southern Christian Leadership Conference, see Adam Fairclough, *To Redeem the Soul of America: The Southern Christian Leadership Conference and Martin Luther King, Jr.* (1987). A detailed study of southern politics is Jack Bass and Walter DeVries, *The Transformation of Southern Politics: Social Change and Political Consequence Since 1945* (1976). For the Warren Court, see the relevant chapters of Paul L. Murphy, *The Constitution in Crisis Times: 1918–1969* (1972), and two fine biographies: G. Edward White, *Earl Warren: A Public Life* (1982), and Bernard Schwartz, *Super Chief: Earl Warren and His Supreme Court: A Judicial Biography* (1983).

White House anticommunism is the theme of Jeff Broadwater, *Eisenhower & the Anti-Communist Crusade* (1992). For the larger McCarthy phenomenon, see David M. Oshinsky, *A Conspiracy So Immense: The World of Joe McCarthy* (1983); Thomas C. Reeves, *The Life and Times of Joe McCarthy* (1981); Mark Landis, *Joseph McCarthy: The Politics of Chaos* (1987); and Robert Griffith, *The Politics of Fear: Joseph R. McCarthy and the Senate* (1988). For the impact of McCarthyism in academia, see Ellen W. Schrecker, *No Ivory Tower: McCarthyism and the Universities* (1986). An interesting collection of case studies appears in Bud Schultz and Ruth Schultz, eds., *It Did Happen Here: Recollections of Political Repression in America* (1989). Also helpful in understanding McCarthy's support are Michael Paul Rogin, *The Intellectuals and McCarthy* (1967), and David M. Oshinsky, *Senator Joseph McCarthy and the American Labor Movement* (1976). The role of Senator Pat McCarran is documented in the relevant chapters of Stanley Kutler, *The American Inquisition: Justice and Injustice in Cold War America* (1982). See also the titles listed after Chapter 8.

A good introduction to Eisenhower's foreign policy is Walter Lafeber, *America, Russia, and the Cold War* (1985). A more favorable account is Robert A. Divine, *Eisenhower and the Cold War* (1981). These works should be supplemented by the suggestive articles in Richard A. Melanson and David Mayers, *Reevaluating Eisenhower: American Foreign Policy in the 1950s* (1987). The origin of the space race is analyzed in Walter A. McDougall, *The Heavens and the Earth: A Political History of the Space Age* (1985), as well as in Divine, *Sputnik Challenge* listed in Chapter 9. For the disarmament question, see Robert A. Divine, *Blowing on the Wind: The Nuclear Test Ban Debate, 1954–1960* (1978). African American views about international affairs are discussed in Brenda Gayle Plummer, *Rising Wind: Black Americans and U.S. Foreign Affairs, 1935–1960* (1996).

Eisenhower's economic foreign policy is the subject of Burton I. Kaufman, *Trade and Aid: Eisenhower's Foreign Economic Policy, 1953–61* (1982). U.S. intervention in Central America is described in R.H. Immerman, *The CIA in Guatemala: The Foreign Policy of Intervention* (1982), and in Stephen C. Schlesinger and Stephen Kinzer, *Bitter Fruit: The Untold Story of the American Coup in Guatemala* (1982). The Vietnam issue is described in James R. Arnold, *The First Domino: Eisenhower, the Military, and America's Intervention in Vietnam* (1991); in Melanie Billings-Yun, *Decision Against War: Eisenhower and Dien Bien Phu, 1954* (1988); and in the relevant chapters of Lloyd Gardner, *Approaching Vietnam* (1990), listed after Chapter 8. For China and the offshore island issue, see Gordon H. Chang, *Friends and Enemies* (1990), also listed in Chapter 8.

11

President John F. Kennedy and Vice President Lyndon B. Johnson view the crowd at their inauguration ceremony.

U.S. Army in the John F. Kennedy Library

KENNEDY, JOHNSON, AND LIBERAL ACTIVISM, 1960–1968

The 1960s heralded a new era of liberalism. Rejecting Eisenhower's belief in limited government, Democrats John F. Kennedy and Lyndon B. Johnson advocated an active federal government to achieve economic and social progress. As African Americans and other minorities pleaded for political equality, liberal programs brought greater government benefits to disadvantaged groups, but, ironically, government favors also accentuated conflicts between competing interests. Meanwhile, an assertive foreign policy intensified disagreements about U.S. intervention abroad, triggering an aggressive antiwar movement. By the end of the decade, the Cold War consensus had been replaced by bitter strife about the proper uses of U.S. power.

THE ELECTION OF 1960

"The American people are tired of the drift in our national course," said Massachusetts Senator John Kennedy in launching his run for the presidency. For eight years Eisenhower had extolled the warrior virtues of strength and power. Yet, at the age of seventy, the grandfatherly Ike, then the oldest man to serve as president, seemed helpless against Khrushchev's indignation, the eruption of liberation movements in Asia and Africa, and anti-U.S. protests in Latin America and Japan. At home, voters blamed the administration for the recession of 1957–1958. "Wind up the Eisenhower doll," ran a popular joke, "and it does nothing for eight years."

Kennedy was only forty-two years old when he announced his candidacy. Youthful in appearance (and concealing serious chronic illnesses), he symbolized strength, vigor, and energy. In the Senate, Kennedy attacked the administration for creating a "missile gap" between Soviet and U.S. arsenals. "This is not a call of despair," he stated. "It is a call for action."

Kennedy's ambition benefitted from great personal wealth, but his Roman Catholicism loomed as a major handicap. Only one Catholic, Al Smith, had run for president, and he had suffered a devastating defeat in 1928. Kennedy challenged religious prejudices directly, entering a series of primaries against his major rival, Minnesota Senator Hubert H. Humphrey. Kennedy won their first contest in Wisconsin, but voting analysis showed that he carried Catholic districts, whereas Humphrey attracted Protestants. The race moved to West Virginia, an impoverished state with a 95 percent Protestant population. Humphrey shamelessly used the theme song, "Give Me That Old-Time Religion." Kennedy responded with an expensive campaign that emphasized his commitment to New Deal liberalism. A decisive victory over Humphrey overcame the issue of religion, and Kennedy went on to win a first-ballot nomination for the presidency. To balance the Democratic ticket in the South, he chose as his running mate Senate Majority Leader Lyndon Johnson of Texas.

Kennedy's Catholicism remained a controversial issue in the campaign against Vice President Richard M. Nixon. "I am not a Catholic candidate," Kennedy insisted. "I am the Democratic Party's candidate, . . . who happens also to be a Catholic." Vowing to maintain the separation of church and state, the nominee expressed disbelief that 40 million citizens "lost their chance of being president on the day they were baptized." Although since 1945 white ethnics had penetrated most educational, business, and social organizations, religious

Brown Brothers

John F. Kennedy responds to opponent Richard M. Nixon at their televised debate during the 1960 presidential contest.

prejudices still influenced political behavior. In the election, Kennedy won a high proportion of Catholic supporters but lost among Protestants. One exception was Kennedy's appeal to black evangelicals. When civil rights activist Martin Luther King, Jr., was sentenced to prison for trespassing in a segregated restaurant in Georgia, a much-publicized telephone call from Kennedy to King's wife, Coretta, revealed the candidate's genuine compassion as well as astute political calculation. By appealing both to African Americans and white ethnics, Kennedy restored the New Deal coalition, but subsequent voting analysis suggested that the issue of religion probably cost him more votes than it won him.

Religion seemed important in 1960 because the differences between Kennedy and Nixon remained fairly small. Four nationally televised debates, which attracted more than 100 million viewers, spotlighted their similarities. Both candidates were Cold Warriors who vowed to end communist expansion and disagreed only about whether to defend the islands between mainland China and Taiwan. Both stressed the importance of economic growth. Both used the phrase "new frontiers" to evoke a spirit of opportunity and expansion. "Mr. Nixon says, 'We never had it so good,'" Kennedy stated in a typical remark. "I say we can do better."

Despite these common assumptions, television illuminated not the candidates' words but their manner of presentation. Radio listeners, who were not distracted by visual appearances, reacted favorably to Nixon's speeches, but the television cameras accentuated the vice president's heavy "five o'clock shadow" and dripping makeup. In contrast, Kennedy had a dramatic flair and projected self-confidence. Polls indicated that the debates may have swayed 4 million voters, three-quarters of whom supported Kennedy.

Such intangible factors had immense significance because the balloting was extremely close. With nearly 69 million people voting, Kennedy obtained a popular majority of only 118,000—a margin of one-tenth of 1 percent. The

Exhibit 11-1. Election of 1960

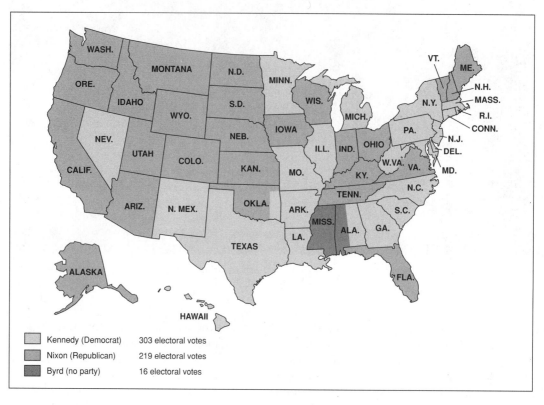

	Kennedy (Democrat)	303 electoral votes
	Nixon (Republican)	219 electoral votes
	Byrd (no party)	16 electoral votes

Electoral College vote was 303–219, but these figures concealed paper-thin majorities and probable fraud in such key states as Illinois and Texas. Kennedy also trailed behind Democratic congressional candidates. Although the Democrats held control of both houses of Congress, most of the sixty-three new legislators subsequently voted against the White House on important issues. Because southern Democrats frequently aligned with Republicans, the Kennedy administration lacked a working majority in Congress.

LAUNCHING THE
NEW FRONTIER

"Let the word go forth that the torch has been passed to a new generation of Americans," the new president declared. With his slender political majority, however, Kennedy's inaugural speech avoided domestic topics and focused exclusively on the international peril. Kennedy exaggerated the Soviet threat. Although Khrushchev had recently advocated wars of national liberation, the Russian leader was addressing criticism from his Chinese ally rather than the United States. To Kennedy, however, Khrushchev's speech had brought the nation to "its hour of maximum danger," and he stressed the "burden" of "relentless struggle." Said Kennedy: "Ask not what your country can do for you—ask what you can do for your country," but despite his dynamic language, Kennedy lacked the political base to initiate bold policy departures.

Reflecting the era's distrust of emotionalism and ideology, Kennedy's leadership extolled the virtues of scientific management and cold reason. "Most of the problems . . . that we now face are technical problems, are administrative problems," he said in 1962. "They are very sophisticated judgments which do not lend themselves to the great sort of 'passionate movements' which have stirred this country so often in the past." Matters of foreign policy, the president suggested, "are so sophisticated and so technical that people who are not intimately involved week after week, month after month, reach judgments which are based on emotion rather than knowledge of the real alternatives."

Secretary of Defense Robert S. McNamara typified the liberal leadership. Taking charge of the Pentagon, the former head of the Ford Motor Company initiated a program of rigorous "cost-benefit" accounting to determine military priorities. In place of Eisenhower's "massive retaliation," the new administration preferred flexibility, conventional arms for "brushfire" wars, and the elite Special Forces (Green Berets) for counterinsurgency and guerrilla warfare. Kennedy also demanded additional nuclear missiles even after learning soon after taking office that no "missile gap" existed. Within a month of the inauguration, the White House requested funds for missiles, warheads, and electronic support systems such as computer data bases and orbiting communications and spy satellites. This emphasis on technological developments in turn encouraged a managerial revolution within the Pentagon. Under McNamara, the defense department centralized research and development and created a Defense Intelligence Agency to coordinate military assessments.

Enthusiasm for technical management flourished in the space program. Five months after taking office, Kennedy used the continuing Cold War to call for a human landing on the moon by the end of the decade. "No single space project," he said, "will be more impressive to mankind." Vice President Johnson, author of the 1958 legislation that established the National Aeronautics and Space Administration (NASA), now served as chair of the National Aeronautics and Space Council and shared Kennedy's zeal. To Secretary McNamara, moreover, the space program promised to compensate the aerospace industry for cuts in military contracting demanded by cost-benefit analysis, thus blunting some of the expected unemployment. Concerned about winning support from big business, Kennedy and Johnson endorsed private ownership of a communications satellite corporation and worked vigorously to overcome a 1962 Senate filibuster led by Tennessee's Estes Kefauver to block this federally supported private monopoly.

A carefully orchestrated public relations program reinforced popular support for space travel. The mass media portrayed the first astronauts as all-American pioneers and heralded John Glenn's 1962 flight around the globe as a Cold War victory. As NASA planned Project Mercury (the circumnavigation of Earth by single astronauts, 1962); Project Gemini (multimanned flights, rendezvous in space, and spacewalks, 1964–1965); and Project Apollo (moon landing, 1969), the space budget leaped fivefold to more than $5 billion by 1964. The space program accounted for 78 percent of all U.S. research and development, but, although the White House emphasized the prestige of space exploration, expenditures served essential military functions involving ballistic missiles, communications, and intelligence gathering. For national security reasons, this

JOHN H. GLENN, JR.
1921–

"We have stressed the team effort in Project Mercury," said the nation's newest hero three days after becoming the first American to circumnavigate the Earth from outer space on 20 February 1962. "It goes across the board . . . sort of a crosscut of Americana, of industry and military and civil service, government workers, contractors—a crosscut of American effort in the technical field." At this moment of awesome technological achievement, however, astronaut John Glenn also symbolized the vitality of traditional earthbound virtues: love of family, religion, and patriotism.

Born and raised in small-town Ohio in the 1920s and 1930s, Glenn left home to become a Marine aviator during World War II and remained in the military as a combat flyer in Korea and later as a test pilot of jet aircraft. In 1957 he set the coast-to-coast speed record (three hours, twenty-three minutes, 8.4 seconds) in a Chance Voight F8U-1 Crusader that required three midair refuelings with high-

flying tankers. Such technical proficiency and iron-willed self-discipline qualified Glenn to become one of the seven original astronauts.

Yet he deliberately blended his enthusiasm for modern technology with old-fashioned "Manifest Destiny." "I take my religion very seriously," the Presbyterian stated at the first Project Mercury press conference in 1959. "We are placed here with certain talents and capabilities. . . . I think we would be most remiss in our duty if we didn't make the full use of our talents in volunteering for something . . . as important as this is to our country and to the world in general right now."

Framed by the Cold War with the Soviet Union, the "space race" pitted free-enterprise capitalism against state-supported technological planning. The U.S. astronauts presented the human side of the competition. To the public's dismay, however, the nation appeared to be running second. Soviet cosmonaut Yuri Gagarin circumnavigated the globe

aspect of the space program remained secret. Moreover, although the Outer Space Treaty, signed by sixty-two nations in 1967, prohibited nuclear weapons in space and declared the moon a demilitarized zone, the defense strategy of both superpowers depended on continuing military operations in space.

THE POLITICS OF ECONOMIC GROWTH

As Kennedy took office in 1961, a Gallup poll found that 42 percent of the public hoped the president would pursue moderate policies; 24 percent hoped he would be conservative; and 23 percent desired a liberal position. This middle-of-the-road climate reinforced the cautious congressional leadership, which jealously guarded its power. To assist the new president, House Speaker Sam Rayburn agreed to expand the powerful Rules Committee to weaken the con-

in April 1961, a month before Project Mercury's Alan Shepard's first suborbital flight. Thus, despite serious technological malfunctions aboard Glenn's *Friendship 7* space capsule, the mission restored national confidence in the space program. "This is the new ocean," declared President John Kennedy moments after Glenn splashed down in the Atlantic, "and I believe the United States must sail on it and be . . . second to none."

The public spontaneously embraced the sunny-faced astronaut. "I still get a hard-to-define feeling inside when the flag goes by," Glenn told a joint session of Congress, which interrupted his patriotic remarks twenty-five times with applause. Four million people—equivalent to half the population of New York City—lined the streets of lower Manhattan to form the largest ticker-tape parade crowd in history. "Freedom, devotion to God and country are not things of the past," the astronaut assured a luncheon audience at New York's Waldorf Astoria Hotel. During the next year Glenn received more than half a million letters of encouragement from around the country. He won medals from a variety of organizations. He was named Father of the Year, and the Daughters of the American Revolution saluted him "for demonstrating that patriotism is not old-fashioned." Even the many journalists and photographers who covered these events eventually broke ranks to ask for his autograph.

Treated as a prophet of the space age, Glenn felt emboldened to offer opinions on a multitude of subjects, including politics. Spurred by the Kennedy brothers, he ran for the Ohio Democratic senatorial nomination in 1964, but an accidental injury forced his withdrawal. Robert Kennedy's ill-fated campaign of 1968 drew him back into politics. By then, however, the political mood demanded more cogent policy positions, and Glenn's homilies failed him. He narrowly lost a Senate bid in 1970. Then, after Watergate, as voters sought confirmation of traditional virtues, Glenn won election to the Senate by more than 1 million votes. The former astronaut expressed higher ambitions but competed unsuccessfully for the vice presidency in 1976 and for the presidency four years later. His personal fame, obvious sincerity, and diligence on technical issues involving nuclear power and nuclear weapons could not compensate for bland political rhetoric and a penchant for boring detail. The hard-working Glenn kept his seat in the Senate. "I have a very big ego," he admitted, "but for me the glitter, the glamour, the attention mean very little now. I've had it all. I've had the ticker-tape parades." ∎

servative majority. Despite strong opposition from southern conservatives, Rayburn managed to push the change through on a very narrow vote. Yet southern legislators, who defended states' rights and regional economic interests, later took revenge by killing or diluting liberal proposals such as higher minimum wages and federal aid to education.

Despite growing public concern about poverty, especially after the publication of Michael Harrington's influential book, *The Other America*, in 1962, Congress thwarted social reform. In 1961, for example, legislators responded favorably to Kennedy's request for an Area Development Agency to stimulate industrial development in depressed areas such as Appalachia. Yet, while approving road construction and cheap loans to entice business to relocate, Congress provided insufficient funds to implement the program. By 1963 the entire state of West Virginia had gained only 350 jobs. Similarly, public housing legislation in 1961 permitted the razing of slums but failed to mandate adequate replacement housing. By 1967 some 400,000 buildings had been demolished, which resulted in more than 1.4 million displaced residents. Kennedy lacked

The first Mercury astronauts, including John Glenn, third from left, and Alan Shepard, second from right.

enough political support even to introduce legislation providing hospital insurance for the elderly.

During the presidential campaign, Kennedy promised to produce a 5 percent annual rate of economic growth. This goal seemed especially relevant because the unemployment rate was 7.7 percent in January 1961. White House economic advisors, particularly the liberal Walter Heller, urged more vigorous federal spending. However, except for military appropriations, the president declined to request additional programs. Instead, Kennedy proposed a tax credit to encourage business investment in new plant equipment. By stimulating capital investment, the measure would simultaneously attack unemployment and stimulate long-term growth. To compensate for the loss of tax revenue, Kennedy requested reforms to close corporate tax loopholes such as expense accounts and tax-exempt foreign income. Yet these reforms adversely affected influential corporate leaders, and Congress delayed action until 1962. Meanwhile, large military expenditures boosted the sagging economy.

Concern about recession was soon supplanted by fear of inflation. In 1962 the Council of Economic Advisers announced wage-price "guideposts" to discourage inflationary increases. However, corporate leaders resisted efforts to regulate business costs and profits. The disagreement climaxed in a major clash between the White House and the nation's largest industry—steel—in the spring of 1962. As part of the antiinflation program, the White House had persuaded the steelworkers' union to accept modest pay increases by assuring workers that the industry would hold the price line, but in April 1962 U.S. Steel

President Kennedy's televised press conferences provided a showcase for his personal charisma—as well as his spontaneous humor, intelligence, charm, and what the media called "the Kennedy style."

notified Kennedy that the company would increase prices 3.5 percent, an amount the administration considered inflationary. Other steel companies said they would follow U.S. Steel's lead. "My father once told me that all business-men were sons of bitches," Kennedy remarked. The president proceeded to exert maximum executive pressure to force the steel industry to retreat. McNamara instructed the Department of Defense to purchase steel only from noninflationary companies, and Attorney General Robert F. Kennedy ordered investigations of industry price-fixing. These pressures led one company to reject the price increase, a retreat that spread throughout the industry. Kennedy had effectively defended his economic strategy.

Although lower steel prices reduced costs for other manufacturers, business leaders bitterly resented this show of government economic power. A slumping stock market intensified their anger. In May 1962 Wall Street prices reached their lowest point since the Crash of 1929. The downturn reflected the belated impact of the 1960–1961 recession, which had reduced corporate earnings. However, the president's stand on steel prices disheartened elements of the business com-munity, which blamed the administration for the slump. Kennedy responded to this crisis in confidence by emphasizing his support of business. At the Yale commencement in June 1962 the president requested an end to "sterile acri-mony." Kennedy also denied the evils of deficit spending. "What is at stake is not some grand warfare of rival ideologies," he declared, "but the practical management of a modern economy."

The administration moved quickly to support corporate prosperity. A lowering of margin requirements stimulated the stock market. The Treasury Department liberalized depreciation allowances for business equipment, thereby encouraging the replacement of older machinery. Congress finally enacted the proposed tax credit for new investments as well as tax reforms that gave business specific benefits. Kennedy endorsed new legislation favorable to the drug industry and lobbied Congress to permit private control of space communications. This commitment to business culminated in the president's support of foreign trade. Since the late 1950s the economy had suffered imbalances of foreign payments, largely because of heavy spending for military bases abroad. In 1961 Kennedy created a new position in the Pentagon to encourage sales of U.S. arms to foreign nations. By 1962 the White House persuaded Congress to pass a foreign trade expansion bill.

Departing from the tradition of strict balanced budgets, Kennedy also embraced the "new economics" of John Maynard Keynes, who advocated deficit spending to stimulate the economy. Taking the advice of Keynes's disciples on the Council of Economic Advisers, Kennedy gradually accepted the theory that a tax cut would increase consumer spending, curtail the "fiscal drag," and increase the rate of economic growth. In 1963 the president submitted a bill calling for a $13.6 billion reduction in taxes, mostly on individual incomes, as well as reforms that would shift the tax burden to upper-income brackets. The move set the stage for unprecedented economic growth.

THE CIVIL RIGHTS CRISIS

While seeking the approval of the business community, Kennedy dragged his feet on civil rights. Recognizing the power of southern Democrats, the White House appeased regional demands for patronage by awarding federal construction projects to southern states, raising price supports on cotton, and declining to introduce civil rights legislation. Instead, the president took moderate executive actions such as creating the Commission on Equal Employment Opportunity (CEEO) in 1961. Headed by Vice President Johnson, the CEEO endeavored to end employment discrimination in work done under government contract. However, the commission preferred voluntary compliance and seldom punished violators. Moreover, although Kennedy claimed during the 1960 campaign that Eisenhower could eliminate federal support of segregated housing "with the stroke of a pen," the president became remarkably silent when that power passed into his own hands. Civil rights leaders began sending pens to the White House—without altering policy. Hoping to win congressional approval for a Department of Urban Affairs, Kennedy refused to challenge segregated housing. Only after Congress defeated his efforts in 1962 did the president act to end segregation in federally funded housing. More than previous presidents, however, Kennedy appointed African Americans to government positions and allowed them to work in areas other than race relations.

Kennedy showed a similar lack of interest in women's rights. Notorious for his affairs with attractive women, the president never connected changing sexual values with issues of power. The "new woman," according to Helen Gurley Brown's 1962 best-seller, *Sex and the Single Girl*, "took the pill and lived in an apartment with a double bed. She spent money on herself and men spent attention on her. She was the old feminist ideal of the independent woman with a new twist—she was sexy." Rising female employment and the sexual revolution bolstered a growing sense of female autonomy. By 1960 nearly 40 percent of women more than sixteen years old held jobs outside the home. Yet women workers earned only three-fifths of what men received and seldom held political power. Working women well understood these limitations.

Although the radical National Woman's Party continued to press for an equal rights amendment to the Constitution that would guarantee legal equality to both sexes, Kennedy, like his predecessors, listened primarily to the liberals in the government's Woman's Bureau who advocated economic gains without threatening the existing laws that provided specific protections for women workers. Kennedy made few important appointments of women, but in 1962 the White House created the President's Commission on the Status of Women, charged with making economic and social policy recommendations. "Equality of rights . . . for all persons, male or female, is . . . basic to democracy," the commission reported in 1963. Yet the president's advisors insisted that the Fourteenth Amendment, not a new equal rights amendment, would serve as the basis for reforms. That year Congress passed the Equal Pay Act, which provided equal wages for "equal work." However, the law excluded numerous jobs and lacked enforcement provisions, and the traditional segregation of occupations by gender further eroded the concept of "equal work." Still, at a time when the proportion of women in the work force continued to increase, the federal government had begun to address widespread economic inequalities.

Kennedy's limited support of equal rights reflected the values of liberal reformism. Believing that changes in social relations could not be forced on the nation, the White House intended to follow rather than lead public opinion, but, although issues of gender equality were largely ignored, problems of race moved to the forefront of the national agenda. Kennedy had hoped to limit government action to enforcement of the voting rights provisions of the Civil Rights Acts of 1957 and 1960. Yet his fear of white southern political power led him to appoint segregationist judges to federal courts in the South. One appointee openly referred to blacks as "niggers" and "chimpanzees."

African American activists resolved to move ahead of the White House to challenge legal segregation and force the federal government to protect equal rights. Following the nonviolent, direct action strategy of Martin Luther King, Jr., and the sit-in demonstrators of 1960, the Congress of Racial Equality (CORE) embarked on interracial "freedom rides" in 1961 to desegregate interstate travel and commerce. As expected, violent mobs throughout the South viciously attacked the travelers, and local and state law enforcement authorities failed to provide minimal protection. The raw violence, coming on the eve of a summit meeting between Kennedy and Khrushchev, embarrassed the White House and compelled the federal government to intervene in areas of law enforcement that traditionally had been handled by the states. The president responded by ordering federal marshals into the South and obtained court injunctions against interference with interstate travel. At the same time, however, the president's brother, Attorney General Robert F. Kennedy, asked the freedom riders for a "cooling-off period." "If we got any cooler," protested James Farmer, organizer

BETTY FRIEDAN
1924–

Michael Ginsburg © Magnum Photos

At a time when psychologists insisted that a normal woman would achieve maximum fulfillment as wife, mother, housewife, and homemaker, author Betty Friedan challenged the cult of domesticity in her bestselling 1963 book, *The Feminine Mystique*. According to Friedan, middle-class women responded to traditional expectations of domestic bliss with a bewildered "Is that all?" Her book sold 3 million copies, reached an estimated readership five times as large, and provoked a fundamental reexamination of women's place in U.S. society. Scarcely a single family was unaffected by its message.

The daughter of immigrant Jewish parents from Peoria, Illinois, Friedan had studied psychology and social science at Smith College and the University of California at Berkeley. "I didn't want to be like my mother" she later recalled. She worked as a journalist during World War II but lost her job to a returning war veteran. Despite a union contract for-

bidding such actions, she was fired from another job because of pregnancy. In 1949, she explained, no term existed to describe "sex discrimination."

During the 1950s Friedan lived in the suburbs of New York, where she raised three children and continued to pursue a journalism career as a free-lancer by writing articles for such magazines as *Harper's*, *Good Housekeeping*, *Redbook*, and *Mademoiselle*. For a piece about her Smith College classmates fifteen years after graduation, she conducted a survey of their attitudes and feelings. Her research revealed a profound unhappiness among college-educated, middle-class women, but the article contradicted the assumptions of the day, and the editors of women's magazines refused to publish her findings.

Friedan decided to write a book. "Something is very wrong with the way American women are trying to live their lives today," she began. "It is no longer possible to . . . dis-

of the freedom rides, "we'd be in a deep freeze." Meanwhile, the attorney general petitioned the Interstate Commerce Commission (ICC) to end segregation in interstate travel. Administration pressure led to the desired ICC ruling in 1961.

Despite Kennedy's effort to remain aloof from the civil rights controversy, black activism and white intransigence continued to force presidential intervention. In 1962 James Meredith, an African American air force veteran, won a federal court order to enter the all-white University of Mississippi. Governor Ross Barnett spoke for the southern leadership when he announced his refusal to comply with the ruling. Following the precedent of Eisenhower in 1957, Kennedy federalized the National Guard and sent federal marshals and soldiers into the university town of Oxford. After a night of violence and bloodshed, Meredith gained entry into the university. However, Kennedy tried to avoid further antagonism of southern leaders by limiting federal interference to minimal legal protection and by refusing to take responsibility for local law enforcement.

While the White House sought to avoid racial confrontations, the Student Nonviolent Coordinating Committee (SNCC) proceeded with a voter registra-

miss the desperation of so many American women." Friedan proceeded to demolish the "happy housewife" image of postwar society, arguing that middle-class women required a source of personal fulfillment, a career, to achieve satisfaction.

Having identified a major social problem, Friedan joined other feminists in seeking a solution. Her philosophy was quintessentially liberal. She demanded that women be given opportunities equal to those of men to achieve economic and political citizenship. In 1966 Friedan helped found the National Organization for Women (NOW) "to bring women into full participation in the mainstream of American society now" and served as its first president until 1970. Besides demanding employment opportunities and legal rights, NOW advocated child care centers and "the right of women to control their reproductive rights." Working within the liberal consensus, Friedan also helped establish the National Women's Political Caucus in 1971 to pressure the major political parties to accept greater female participation.

Friedan's liberal agenda clashed not only with sexist values but also with more radical feminism. Viewing politics in traditional terms, she rejected the radical idea that "the personal is political." When lesbians demanded political recognition within the women's movement, Friedan denounced the "lavender menace" as internally divisive and a needless provocation for a conservative counterattack. Yet during the 1970s, a time of significant although mixed advances for women in terms of education, employment, and legal rights, Friedan enjoyed considerable stature as a foremother of contemporary feminism.

Never comfortable with radical feminism, Friedan used the backlash against women's rights in the late 1970s and 1980s (the defeat of the equal rights amendment and the attack on abortion rights) to address the frustrations of younger women seeking to balance public careers with private needs. In her controversial 1981 book, *The Second Stage*, Friedan denied an antagonism between women's equality and the family. Urging feminists to accept the responsibilities and joys of childbearing and nurturing, she stressed the diversity of contemporary family types, the blurring of traditional gender roles involving work and child care, and the growing equality within U.S. families. "We have to break through our own *feminist* mystique now," she declared, "to come to terms with the new reality of our personal and political experience." ■

tion campaign among disenfranchised blacks. This Voter Education Project, funded by northern liberal foundations but implemented primarily by courageous white students and black students, soon provoked a violent reign of terror—beatings, bombings, and murders—to prevent the expansion of the African American electorate. As in the case of the freedom rides, civil rights workers discovered that the federal government failed to provide adequate protection on the grounds that it lacked a statutory right to intervene. As northern liberals and black activists protested White House inertia, the president introduced a civil rights bill in February 1963 that called for prosecution of voting rights violations, federal funds to encourage school desegregation, and extension of the Civil Rights Commission. "We are committed to achieving true equality of opportunity," said Kennedy, "because it is right."

African American leaders, looking for more fundamental changes, rejected Kennedy's modest proposal. In the spring of 1963 King's Southern Christian Leadership Conference (SCLC) carried the civil rights crusade to Birmingham, Alabama, purportedly "the most thoroughly segregated big city" in the nation. The movement's nonviolent strategy aimed at producing so much "creative

The Reverend Martin Luther King, Jr., addressed 250,000 demonstrators in front of the Lincoln Memorial on 28 August 1963 and demanded jobs, civil rights, and racial justice.

tension" that segregationist leaders would feel compelled to negotiate a peaceful settlement. As noisy but peaceful marchers paraded downtown, local police chief "Bull" Connor ordered violent arrests that filled the jails. After weeks of futile demonstrations, civil rights leaders feared the crusade would fail for want of volunteers who could afford to be rearrested. African American leaders decided to find recruits among the city's youth, some as young as six years old. When police attacked these children with clubs, fire hoses, and vicious dogs, the nation's conscience was shaken. The brutality not only steeled the nerves of black protesters, but, because of wide television coverage, sent waves of outrage throughout the land.

"We face . . . a moral crisis as a country and as a people," Kennedy told a television audience in June 1963. "It cannot be met by repressive police action. It cannot be left to increased demonstrations in the streets." The president then introduced a new civil rights bill to prohibit racial discrimination in public accommodations, to authorize the justice department to initiate suits to desegregate public schools, to improve black employment opportunities, and to protect voting rights. Although African American leaders questioned loopholes in the proposal, few doubted the clarity of Kennedy's moral position.

While Congress began to consider the civil rights bill, black leaders staged a show of strength by organizing a March on Washington. The president initially discouraged the demonstration, but civil rights activists refused to retreat. On 28 August 1963, 250,000 marchers converged in the nation's capital and heard Martin Luther King, Jr., proclaim, "I have a dream . . . that the sons of former slaves and the sons of former slave owners will be able to sit together at the table of brotherhood." King's passionate language electrified the crowd.

Other voices in Washington, however, indicated deep rifts within the African American community. SNCC's John Lewis attacked the administration for its "immoral compromises" with conservative politicians. "If any radical social, political, and economic changes are to take place in our society," he said, "the people, the masses must bring them about. . . . We must seek more than mere civil rights; we must work for the community of love, peace, and true brotherhood." Three months later Lewis's words were echoed in a speech by black nationalist leader Malcolm X. Recognizing the importance of achieving political power as a precondition for racial progress, Malcolm rejected the limited horizons of racial integration. "A revolutionary," he asserted, "is a black nationalist."

THE COLD WAR ON NEW FRONTIERS

In continuing the global Cold War against communism, Kennedy kept his eye closely fixed on Moscow and Bejing, but the president also believed that the nations of Asia, Africa, and Latin America held the key to victory. To energize the nation's youth for that struggle, Kennedy created the Peace Corps in 1961, encouraging volunteers to serve "on a mission of freedom" around the world. Kennedy also launched a Food for Peace program to send surplus food to poor countries. By 1963 the plan was feeding 93 million people each day. Nor did Kennedy, unlike Eisenhower, insist that neutral nations take sides in the Cold War. In the former Belgian colony of the Congo, for example, the United States supported a United Nations peace mission to back a neutral government, although the White House allowed the CIA to provide secret payments and military aid to friendly Congolese politicians.

Kennedy also proposed "a new alliance for progress" in Latin America. Promising technical expertise and capital investment, the president envisioned major agrarian reform and public welfare within democratic institutions. In 1961 the administration pledged $20 billion to alleviate endemic poverty and bring social reform, but, although these funds boosted U.S. prestige, the White House had no intention of altering Latin American politics. Instead, Washington continued to cooperate with conservative landed elites and their military allies.

U.S. corporations also hesitated to invest in unstable countries. In 1962 Congress approved the Hickenlooper Amendment, which stopped foreign aid to countries that nationalized or excessively taxed corporate property. The next year the Foreign Assistance Act established an investment guaranty program that required recipients of U.S. aid to insure investors against losses due to nationalization, but most aid to Latin America went in the form of loans, rather than grants, and had to be repaid with interest and service charges (usually amounting to half the face value of the loan). Even these limited funds had to be spent within the United States at prevailing prices.

The Executive Committee of the National Security Council deliberating during the Kennedy Administration.

The Alliance for Progress promised nonetheless to blunt the appeal of Fidel Castro's revolutionary Cuba. During his last days in office, Eisenhower had broken diplomatic relations with Cuba and ordered the CIA to plan a military coup. As a presidential candidate, Kennedy endorsed the overthrow of Castro. Believing that Castro did not represent the Cuban people and could be toppled with sufficient pressure, Kennedy urged business leaders to boycott Cuba and banned the importation of Cuban sugar.

Anti-Castro activities culminated in a military invasion of Cuba at the Bay of Pigs in April 1961 by 1,400 Cuban exiles trained and organized by the CIA. But the CIA planned badly, choosing an indefensible landing position and mismanaging air attacks. Recognizing an imminent disaster, the White House refused to provide additional air support, which doomed the mission. Most seriously, the president had underestimated the strength of Castro's political base.

Although U.S. media had received unofficial leaks about the Bay of Pigs operation, the administration persuaded publications such as *The New York Times* to suppress the story. "There will not be, under any conditions, an intervention in Cuba," the president told a press conference five days before the mission. Secretary of State Dean Rusk lied blatantly: "The American people are entitled to know whether we are intervening in Cuba or intend to do so in the future," he said on the morning of the invasion. "The answer to that question is no. What happens in Cuba is for the Cuban people to decide." In justifying the invasion, Kennedy saw Castro as a pawn in the Cold War. "We are opposed around the world by a monolithic and ruthless conspiracy," he told the nation's leading news editors, "that relies primarily on covert means for expanding its sphere of influence." The president urged the news media to limit reporting of world events. "Every democracy," he claimed, "recognizes the necessary restraints of national security."

In the aftermath of the Bay of Pigs fiasco, the president permitted the CIA to conduct illegal military activities against Castro, provided they were "plausibly deniable." The CIA proceeded to disrupt Cuban trade with the Soviet Union, in one case contaminating a shipload of sugar with bad-tasting chemicals. Secret CIA operations included support of anti-Castro exiles and underworld gangsters who attempted to assassinate the Cuban leader. Kennedy also exerted economic pressure by prohibiting trade with the island. Such destabilization efforts drew Castro closer to the Soviet Union.

Having failed in Cuba, however, Kennedy resolved to prove his strength on the issue of Germany. Although the Soviet Union wanted to formalize the existence of two German states— one linked to the communist bloc, the other to the West—and thereby force the Western Allies to leave Berlin, Washington demanded the unification of Germany through free elections (in which the larger population of West Germany would predominate). Soon after taking office, Kennedy asked Congress for increased military appropriations to build a preponderance of power that would force the Kremlin to accept U.S. terms. In this spirit he agreed to meet Khrushchev in Vienna in June 1961.

Kennedy underestimated Soviet resolve. In a blistering encounter, Khrushchev reminded the president that World War II had ended sixteen years earlier and demanded that the Western powers sign a final peace treaty that recognized the two German states and terminated the military occupation of Berlin. Kennedy rejected the proposal and insisted that the United States could not abandon West Berlin. Instead of easing international tensions, the summit conference intensified the Cold War.

The president returned from Vienna bearing "sober" news and promptly asked Congress for another $3 billion military appropriation, which increased the total military spending package to $6 billion in his first six months in office. Kennedy also called up the military reserves and extended the draft. Finally, in a gesture that spread horror throughout the land, the president requested increased appropriations for civil defense and bomb shelters. Khrushchev then ordered the erection of a military barrier between East and West Berlin in August 1961, which ended the flood of refugees from East Germany and showed his determination to preserve two German states. Despite an extreme atmosphere of crisis, Kennedy resolved to test Soviet strategy by ordering 1,500 battle-ready troops to drive from West Germany into West Berlin, where they would be met by Vice President Johnson. Khrushchev decided not to worsen the situation. After U.S. troops entered West Berlin, Khrushchev scrapped his deadline for settling the Berlin question, and the crisis passed.

The Cold War intensified that same month when the Russian leader announced the resumption of Soviet nuclear bomb testing. Within a week, Kennedy declared the United States had "no other choice" but to resume underground testing. Two days later *Life* magazine published an article, endorsed by Kennedy, asserting (erroneously) that a national program of fallout shelters would ensure a 97 percent survival rate in case of nuclear war. The news precipitated the first major protests against nuclear testing by peace organizations such as the National Committee for a Sane Nuclear Policy (SANE) and the

Student Peace Union. As Soviet tests escalated to the fifty-megaton level, the White House heightened tensions by revealing to Khrushchev that U.S. intelligence knew the extent of Soviet military weakness. The president then proposed disarmament talks that would preserve the U.S. advantage. When the Russians objected to international inspection, Kennedy ordered a resumption of atmospheric tests.

THE CUBAN MISSILE CRISIS

In admitting the nonexistence of a "missile gap," Kennedy increased Soviet concerns about the imbalance of power. The White House accentuated the issue by announcing a shift in nuclear strategy in June 1962. Hereafter, U.S. missiles would be aimed not at Soviet cities but at nuclear missile sites. Such targets meant that a U.S. first strike could destroy Soviet power to retaliate. This disadvantage may have influenced Khrushchev's decision to place less expensive short-range missiles in Cuba. In the aftermath of Sputnik, the United States had pursued a similar policy by establishing missile bases in Turkey and Italy. Khrushchev also sought to discourage further U.S. military action in Cuba.

During the summer of 1962, the Russians began building sites in Cuba to base missiles with a striking range of 2,000 miles, sufficient to reach East Coast cities or the Panama Canal. In addition, the Soviets had placed nearly one hundred nuclear warheads on the island—most attached to tactical rockets with a fifteen- to twenty-mile range. The United States did not learn about the presence of the warheads until the 1990s, but when U-2 spy planes confirmed intelligence reports, Kennedy summoned a top-level executive committee in October 1962 to consider U.S. responses. The choices ranged from immediate military attack— a "Pearl Harbor in reverse," objected Robert Kennedy—to a diplomatic retreat by closing U.S. missile bases in Turkey if the Soviets removed theirs from Cuba. A consensus eventually emerged that considered armed intervention only as a last resort. Yet the administration rejected the possibility of negotiating the removal of the missiles. To Kennedy, Soviet power in the Western Hemisphere was not negotiable.

The president finally accepted a third strategy that did not completely rule out the other two. In a dramatic televised speech, Kennedy described Soviet intervention as "deliberately provocative" and demanded the removal of all missiles. "We will not prematurely or unnecessarily risk the cost of worldwide nuclear war in which the fruits of victory would be ashes in our mouth," he promised, "but neither will we shrink from that risk at any time it must be faced." As the world approached a nuclear holocaust, Kennedy announced the establishment of a "quarantine"—a naval blockade—to exclude offensive weapons from Cuba.

Khrushchev had not anticipated Kennedy's outraged reaction. In a private letter to the president, the Soviet leader protested the demand for unconditional surrender. Yet Khrushchev did not want to start a war that "would not be in our power to stop." In a second, emotional letter, the Russian leader emphasized that Soviet ships in the mid-Atlantic carried nonmilitary goods and that the missiles had already arrived in Cuba. He then offered to remove the weapons provided that the United States end the blockade and agree to respect Cuban

Exhibit 11-2. Cuban Missile Crisis

independence. "Only a madman," Khrushchev wrote, "can believe that armaments are the principal means in the life of a society."

The next day, however, the president received still another message from Khrushchev that stiffened the terms for removal of the missiles. The Soviet leader now demanded the withdrawal of missiles from Turkey in exchange for withdrawal of those in Cuba. Months earlier, Kennedy had questioned the value of those outmoded weapons, but during the Cuban crisis, the White House refused to negotiate the question, fearing to suggest a wavering of national policy.

Other administration officials saw a solution to this new dilemma. The United States would ignore Khrushchev's last letter and answer only the more conciliatory message that preceded it. Kennedy's formal reply therefore made no mention of the bases in Turkey (although the administration privately agreed to remove the missiles from Turkey and Italy). Khrushchev then accepted the arrangement, and the crisis passed. Two months later, Kennedy admitted that the Cuban missiles would not have changed the military balance of power. "But it would have politically changed the balance of power," Kennedy explained.

"It would have appeared to, and appearances contribute to reality." Although Khrushchev's retreat enhanced the president's reputation, the diplomatic victory obscured Washington's failure to change the government of Cuba. While Castro remained in power, the frustrated administration continued a secret program to assassinate the Cuban leader and overthrow the communist regime.

TOWARD DETENTE

The brush with nuclear war convinced both Kennedy and Khrushchev to seek an end to nuclear testing. At the same time, the international balance of power shifted dramatically when Soviet and Chinese leaders split over the issue of the future of world communism. The breakup of the Sino-Soviet alliance, although still incomplete, persuaded the Russians to seek accommodation with the West. One remaining stumbling block was Khrushchev's refusal to allow on-site inspections to verify compliance with a test ban treaty. As the two superpowers resumed negotiations, Kennedy placed his faith in U.S. technology—satellite photographs and distant seismography. In a dramatic speech at American University in June 1963 the president introduced a major reevaluation of the Cold War. Explaining that the United States did not seek "a Pax Americana enforced . . . by American weapons of war," he assured the nation that "we can help make the world safe for diversity."

Kennedy then announced he was sending a mission to Moscow to negotiate a test ban treaty, and in an act of "good faith" he ordered a halt on nuclear testing. Having set aside questions of inspection and underground testing, negotiators quickly reached agreement. Yet the treaty required the approval of Congress, the Pentagon, and public opinion. In seeking this support, the administration emphasized that the test ban constituted a victory because the United States held a clear lead in nuclear technology. Kennedy also assured the Pentagon that underground tests would continue, promises that were fulfilled after the Senate ratified the treaty in September 1963.

Although Kennedy expressed interest in improving relations with the Soviet Union and approved the sale of surplus U.S. wheat to Russia, he worried about a weakening of the Western Alliance. During the summer of 1963 the president journeyed to Europe and reaffirmed the impossibility of compromising with communism. "Today, in the world of freedom," he told a cheering throng in West Berlin, "the proudest boast is 'Ich bin ein Berliner.'" ("I am a Berliner.") Kennedy never wavered from his Cold War stance. In his last, undelivered speech, the president defined his sense of his historic mission: "We in this country, in this generation, are, by destiny rather than choice, the watchmen on the walls of world freedom."

MARCHING INTO VIETNAM

In pursuing a flexible response in the Cold War, Kennedy argued in 1961 that "the great battlefield for the defense and expansion of freedom today is the whole southern half of the globe—Asia, Latin America, Africa, and the Middle

Exhibit 11-3. Indochina

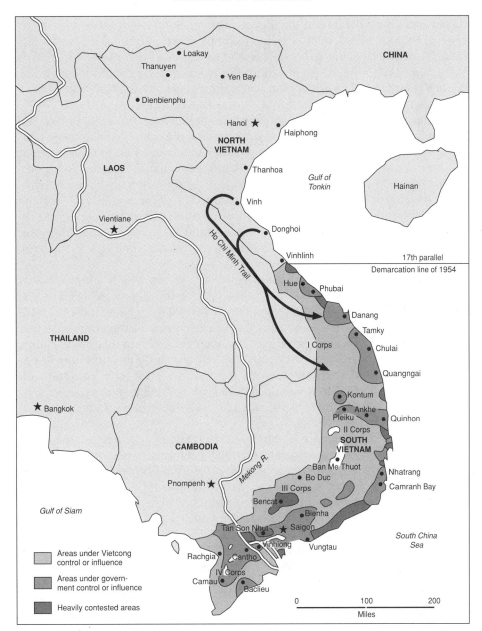

East—the lands of the rising peoples." Here the president saw communism "nibbling away" at the forces of freedom. Having been humiliated at the Bay of Pigs and having agreed in Vienna to a neutral Laos, Kennedy resolved to act decisively in Indochina's Vietnam.

By 1961 the U.S.-backed regime of Ngo Dinh Diem, a U.S.-educated Catholic, was rapidly losing support to the newly established communist Vietcong as well as to noncommunist dissidents such as Buddhist priests. Responding to Vietcong pressure, Kennedy increased the number of military advisors and dispatched Green Berets and intelligence agents to engage in covert warfare in 1961. Although presidential advisors recommended additional military assistance, Kennedy hesitated to commit conventional forces and risk a repetition of the Korean War. Instead, the president viewed Vietnam as an opportunity for counterinsurgency. The White House also urged Diem to offer political reforms to broaden support among Buddhists, but without success.

As U.S. aid poured into Vietnam, the level of violence increased. In 1962 the Vietcong National Liberation Front indicated a willingness to negotiate a neutralization of South Vietnam, but the White House remained optimistic about military victory and rebuffed the approach. Meanwhile, the United States persuaded Diem to experiment with counterinsurgency based on "strategic hamlets." Assuming that guerrilla armies required a popular base, the scheme proposed the encampment of the peasant population behind barbed wire. Lacking contact with the people, the guerrillas would lose support and disappear. However, the hamlets could not provide safety from Vietcong attack, and Vietnamese peasants resented being forcibly uprooted.

"Every quantitative measurement we have," declared McNamara with his faith in numbers, "shows we're winning this war." The State Department confirmed this optimism, announcing that 30,000 Vietcong were killed in 1962. Yet that figure was twice as large as the estimated size of the entire Vietcong organization at the beginning of the year. Exaggerated administration claims stemmed not only from poor calculations but also a deliberate effort to deceive Congress and the nation about the nature of the U.S. commitment. When *The New York Times*'s Saigon reporter David Halberstam reported failures of U.S. policy, Kennedy personally asked the newspaper to reassign him elsewhere.

By 1963 the Vietcong was stepping up terrorist attacks against the Diem regime. Yet Diem refused to institute political reforms. Tensions exploded in 1963 when South Vietnamese troops fired on a crowd of protesters and Buddhist priests set themselves on fire to protest abuses of power. Such reactions embarrassed the administration, but the president took refuge in the domino theory. "For us to withdraw from that effort," he said, "would mean a collapse not only of South Vietnam, but Southeast Asia. So we are going to stay there." But the administration began to plan a military coup to remove Diem from power. On 2 November 1963 South Vietnamese army officers, encouraged by the CIA, killed their president.

The murder shocked Kennedy but did not clearly alter his Vietnam policy. By November 1963 the administration had stationed 16,000 troops in South Vietnam. The previous month Kennedy had announced the withdrawal of 1,000 men by the end of the year and said the U.S. commitment would end in 1965. His words probably reflected the same misplaced optimism that characterized U.S. policy toward Vietnam throughout the decade. Yet Kennedy never rescinded the troop withdrawal order. Perhaps, with Diem dead, the president was considering a political solution to the war. The remaining evidence provides no perfect answer. In the absence of clear evidence, innumerable theories abound. Some, like those espoused in the 1991 movie *JFK*, link a so-called "plan" to end the war to Kennedy's sudden death.

ASSASSINATION, THE YOUTH MOVEMENT, AND CULTURAL REBELLION

Kennedy did not live to fulfill his plan. On a political junket to Texas designed to strengthen the Democrats in the 1964 elections, the president was shot and killed by sniper fire in Dallas on 22 November 1963. The alleged assailant, Lee Harvey Oswald, denied his guilt but was killed in police custody by mobster Jack Ruby before he could testify. The mystery surrounding Kennedy's death contributed to the political turmoil of the decade. Although a special presidential commission headed by Chief Justice Earl Warren reported in 1964 that Oswald was a "loner" and had acted alone, the public widely believed the murder was part of a conspiracy. A 1966 Gallup poll found that a majority doubted the validity of the Warren report and yet a majority also opposed reopening the case.

The assassination shocked the nation—not only because of the sudden death of the president but also because of the disruption of the normal continuity of public life. To most citizens the events surrounding the assassination emerged as a shared emotional experience. Surveys found that 92 percent of the public

Wide World Photos

John and Jacqueline Kennedy greeted the crowds from an open car as they rode toward Dealy Plaza in Dallas, Texas, shortly before the president's assassination on 22 November 1963.

learned of the assassination within two hours and that more than half of the entire population watched the same television coverage of the story. (For three days, the networks canceled all advertising!) Millions watched Jack Ruby shoot Oswald. The mass public mourning greatly magnified the slain president's stature. Local governments named and renamed public buildings in his honor; Kennedy's grave at Arlington National Cemetery became a national shrine; Kennedy memorabilia—picture books, coins, paintings, and jewelry—proliferated. Ironically, Kennedy created in death what had eluded him in life—a broad affirmation of consensus that transcended the differences of traditional politics.

The emotional intensity of the Kennedy assassination coincided with the coming of age of the first baby boomers—the cohort born just after World War II. Twice as numerous as their parents, teenagers formed a distinctive, self-conscious culture whose sheer numbers exerted tremendous economic and political power. Having grown up in the prosperous 1950s, the rising generation accepted affluence and consumption as expressions of its uniqueness. As children, baby boomers created an enormous market for diaper services, toys, and toddlers' shoes; as teenagers, the same generation consumed vast quantities of records, costume jewelry, and apparel. Purchasing power set the stage for the youth rebellion of the 1960s.

Nothing better expressed the teenagers' quest for personal independence than the sounds of rock and roll. Just months after the Kennedy assassination, the British "Beatles" launched their first U.S. tour in 1964 and instantly became

The long hair of the Beatles revolutionized personal fashion and social attitudes, and their use of electric rock helped to pioneer new forms of white popular music.

icons of antiestablishment feelings. During the 1960s teenagers and college students crowded dance floors that reverberated to the rhythms of "the Motown Sound," a hard-driving "soul" music named for the black Detroit record company that produced it. Black performers such as Ray Charles, James Brown, Otis Redding, Aretha Franklin, the Supremes, and the Temptations offered middle-class followers an alternative to sexually repressed music. By 1965 rock songs such as the Rolling Stones's "Let's Spend the Night Together" directly described sexual longing. Meanwhile, the arrival of British fashions such as long hair, "miniskirts," and working-class jeans encouraged liberation of the body and a new confidence in defying social decorum.

The idea of choosing one's "life-style" reflected a changing morality associated with the "sexual revolution." Even before the introduction of the birth control pill in 1960, couples were engaging more frequently in nonmarital intercourse. The trend accelerated and received more attention during the 1960s. "Life was free and so was sex," novelist Sara Davidson wrote of Berkeley at mid-decade. Surveys showed that the age of first sexual experience continued to decline and that the frequency of sexual intercourse within all social classes increased. Easier attitudes toward sexuality also caused a rise in unwanted pregnancies and an average of half a million illegal abortions each year.

The sexual revolution undermined traditional definitions of obscenity and pornography. In a series of landmark cases in the late 1950s, the Supreme Court outlawed censorship of such literary classics as *Fanny Hill*, D.H. Lawrence's *Lady Chatterly's Lover*, and Henry Miller's *Tropic of Cancer*. By the mid-1960s Hollywood had replaced its 1930s production code with a rating system that permitted nudity and obscene language as well as "mature" themes. Traditional morality and censorship persisted on television, but during the late 1960s, shows like "The Smothers Brothers" and "Laugh-In" broke precedent by joking about nonmarital sex, divorce, and "up-tight" behavior. Even more invasive television commercials introduced explicit references to sexuality. Images of women, for example, shifted from housewives to sexually seductive singles.

For many of the 20 million Americans who turned eighteen years of age between 1964 and 1970, the sexual revolution precipitated a larger assault on adult institutions. As a result of economic prosperity and the service industry's demands for extended education, college enrollment doubled to 10 million in the 1960s. Increasingly independent college youth no longer accepted control of their private lives by student deans, who customarily used curfews, sexual segregation, and threats of expulsion to dictate social behavior. During the 1960s most campuses abolished the doctrine of *in loco parentis* ("in place of parents"), which treated students as children rather than young adults. Students won the right to live in coeducational dormitories, to have opposite-sex visitors, and to stay out at night. The freedom of personal expression extended to campus political rights, including the publication of uncensored newspapers and magazines, the recruitment of political support, and public demonstrations.

Drugs became one of the most controversial routes to youth independence. Although earlier generations had consumed alcohol to defy adult morality and discipline, teenagers and college students turned to smoking marijuana, which often became a rite of initiation into youth culture. Harvard University psychologists Timothy Leary and Richard Alpert experimented with the government-provided hallucinogen LSD ("acid") and discovered states of "expanded" consciousness that approached religious ecstasy. When the university fired them for unprofessional conduct in 1963, Leary assumed the role of LSD "guru," advising a generation of students to "turn on, tune in, and drop out." A psychedelic counterculture blossomed from "beat" roots in San Francisco's Haight-Ashbury district. By 1967 the mass media had discovered the "hippie."

"I never hold back, man. I'm always on the outer limits of possibility," Haight rock vocalist Janis Joplin declared. Hippies wore their hair defiantly long and dressed in a "free-form" fashion that included bells, feathers, bandanas, beads, and earrings. Many survived in "crash pads" or in shared housing by panhandling, making crafts, selling "underground" newspapers, and "dealing" drugs. Some, like the communal Diggers, started free kitchens and health clinics. The most important facet of hippie culture involved its rejection of the mainstream's competitive individualism, materialism, and middle-class pretensions. The alternative culture sought honesty, physical pleasure, affection, sharing, cooperation, experimentation, and absolute inner freedom.

Few college students actually traveled to San Francisco during 1967's "Summer of Love" or identified themselves as hippies. Yet many sensed the counterculture's possibilities for radical change and refashioned their private lives to emulate it. Thousands of middle-class rebels left the cities to form rural communes. Others published underground comics and newspapers, produced "guerrilla" theater and alternative film documentaries, created color-crazed "pop art" posters, or sought free-form expression in traditional disciplines such as musical composition, dance, poetry, and prose. Many more adopted antiestablishment attitudes, spoke in "hip" language, wore blue jeans, and experimented with sexual freedom, marijuana, and rock music.

"Psychedelic" or "acid" rock bands such as the Jefferson Airplane, the Grateful Dead, and Joplin's Big Brother and the Holding Company integrated electric guitars with elaborate light shows, developing the piercing "San Francisco" sound. "People now sang songs they wrote themselves," observed one music critic, "not songs written for them by hacks in grimy Tin Pan Alley offices." The introspective and "spaced-out" musical style soon spread to the Beatles and Rolling Stones as well as Bob Dylan, the Byrds, Jim Morrison, and Jimi Hendrix. Tom Wolfe captured the irreverent mood of the underground culture in *The Electric Kool-Aid Acid Test* (1968), which described the exploits of writer Ken Kesey, whose Merry Pranksters traveled around the country in a psychedelically painted bus while promoting liberation through drugs, sex, and rock music.

Countercultural explorations such as Herbert Marcuse's *Eros and Civilization* (1955, 1962) and Carlos Castaneda's *The Teachings of Don Juan: A Yaqui Way of Knowledge* (1968) sought to portray alternative values that cherished the spiritual life and transcended competitive ego. Yet expressive radicalism did not stop the rise of countercultural entrepreneurs. Underworld drug marketing not only wrecked minds and bodies but helped to destroy the fabric of the emerging culture. Rock music, moreover, quickly became a corporate industry capitalized at more than $1 billion. As baby boomers took consumerism outside the traditional home-centered family, an expanded market embraced love beads, incense, transistor radios, stereos, granola, cosmetics, and hair accessories. Hollywood also earned handsome receipts by portraying youthful rebellion in *Bonnie and Clyde* (1967), *The Graduate* (1967), and *Easy Rider* (1969).

The cultural rebellion of middle-class youth paralleled an emerging political consciousness among a smaller segment of college students known as the "New

BOB DYLAN
1941–

Bob Dylan's confrontational style and provocative music made him a major catalyst and symbol of the cultural crisis of the 1960s. Dylan first captured national attention by merging blues and country music with the left-wing political content of the urban folk music scene. Then in 1965 he dramatically adopted the raucous sounds and electrified twang of rock and roll, which he combined with surreal images and poetic phrasing to attack prevailing middle-class values and U.S. institutions.

AP/Wide World Photos

Born Robert Zimmerman and raised in a small town on Minnesota's Iron Range in the 1950s, the young musician had identified with the alienation expressed by actor James Dean and, like the Beat writers, concocted fantasies of escape. In 1960 he changed his name to Dylan and took off for New York in search of his hero, folksinger Woody Guthrie, troubadour for radical causes since the 1930s.

Singing in folk clubs in New York's Greenwich Village, Dylan evoked the liberal optimism of the Kennedy era. His 1962 song, "Blowin' in the Wind," denounced the complaisance of middle-class society and quickly became an anthem of liberal dissent. Dylan wrote many songs in support of the civil rights movement ("Oxford Town," "Who Killed Davey Moore?") and performed at the March on Washington in 1963. The Cuban missile crisis inspired "A Hard Rain's Gonna Fall." "Every line of it is actually the start of a whole song," he said, "but when I wrote it, I thought I wouldn't have enough time alive to write all those songs so I put all I could into this one."

Dylan's political optimism eroded further after the Kennedy assassination. When given the Tom Paine Award in December 1963 by the Emergency Civil Liberties Committee at a swank New York hotel, he saw only the "mink and jewels." "It took me a long time to get young," he told the liberal audience, "... and I'm proud of it." For Dylan, the immense success of the Beatles's U.S. tour in 1964 suggested way to reach the mass audience he had always sought. He began to experiment with rock musicians and electrified his guitar to add a pulsating beat to his lyrical style. The result was 1965's "Like a Rolling Stone," Dylan's first major hit. With this success, he had liberated political music from the enclaves of folk and brought his lyrical protest into the cultural mainstream.

During the 1960s Dylan's gravelly voice resonated with the discontent of the youth movement and went beyond social reform to demand a transformation of consciousness. His lyrics became more metaphoric and symbolic; their juxtaposition of familiar Americana and surreal imagery suggested the absurdity and harsh hypocrisy of contemporary life.

At the peak of his success in 1966 Dylan nearly died in a motorcycle crash, and he retreated from public view. When he returned two years later, his music expressed a remarkable disavowal of hard rock. Such albums as *Nashville Skyline* (1969) and *New Morning* (1970) reflected the more mellow and personal mood of the early 1970s, and the later records *Blood on the Tracks* (1974) and *Slow Train Coming* (1979) illuminated Dylan's growing interest in spiritual values and even "born-again" Christianity. He also made movies, experimented with videos, and continued to write songs, although he seemed forever typecast by his younger audiences, who considered him a pioneer of the rock form. His occasional concert tours remained commercially successful even in the 1990s. ■

Exhibit 11-4. Arrests of Persons Under Age 18, 1960–1969
(in rounded figures)

1960	527,000
1963	789,000
1966	1,149,000
1969	1,500,000

Source: *Historical Statistics of the United States, Colonial Times to 1970* (1975).

Left." During the Cold War era, political repression and mass defections from the Communist Party had drastically weakened support for both Marxist theory and social activism, but the political challenges of the 1960s stimulated a revival of radicalism. Student-led civil rights activity in the South ignited dissent across the country. After the sit-ins of 1960, veteran activist Ella Baker helped young African Americans organize the Student Nonviolent Coordinating Committee (SNCC), which combined a Christian social ethic with a commitment to participatory democracy. The courageous attacks on segregation by SNCC leaders such as John Lewis, Diana Nash, and Robert Moses inspired many liberal white students to engage in political struggle. Equally important was the young generation's despair at the continuing Cold War. Campus radicals organized Students for a Democratic Society (SDS) in 1962, issuing a manifesto called the Port Huron Statement, drafted by University of Michigan activist Tom Hayden. "We may be the last generation in the experiment with living," SDS announced. Attacking a complacent acceptance of poverty, racism, and militarism, the student New Left called for participatory democracy to overcome the alienation caused by bureaucratic decision making.

The first massive student protest erupted at the University of California at Berkeley in 1964 when administrators banned political recruiting on campus. Borrowing tactics from the civil rights struggle, the ensuing Free Speech Movement (FSM) organized a sit-in at which 800 students submitted to arrest. "There's a time when the operation of the machine becomes so odious," declared FSM leader Mario Savio, "that you can't take part . . . and you've got to put your bodies upon the gears . . . and you've got to make it stop." Otherwise, FSM warned, education merely prepared students to take their places in an oppressive corporate order. "You can't trust anybody over thirty," FSM activist Jack Weinberg taunted. A generation once courted by President Kennedy had now set its own agenda.

BUILDING THE GREAT SOCIETY

Five days after Kennedy was killed, President Johnson stood before a joint session of Congress and pleaded earnestly, "Let us continue." Determined to preserve the liberal agenda, the new president now called for a "Great Society" to end poverty and racial injustice. Taking advantage of the public grief, he pushed legislation that Kennedy had initiated but failed to pass through Congress. By early 1964 Johnson had signed major laws involving economic development, social welfare, and civil rights. Ironically, even this success diminished Johnson's appeal. Whereas Kennedy appeared quick, witty, and inspired,

AP/Wide World Photos

Activist Mario Savio addresses Berkeley's Free Speech Movement in the fall of 1964, demanding political rights for college students.

Johnson emerged as a consummate politician, immensely experienced and skilled in political affairs but never quite reliable or sincere. The tall Texan was notorious for bullying subordinates and ignoring political criticism. Failing to charm the public, Johnson eventually personified the duplicity of government and widened the "credibility gap" between the presidency and the people.

In his first legislative triumph, Johnson saved Kennedy's tax reform program. The Revenue Act of 1964 affirmed the principle of deficit spending and stimulated a 7 percent boost in the gross national product during its first year. To all appearances, government management had created unique economic expansion. The new tax laws encouraged productivity while reducing unemployment and inflation and brought booming prosperity for U.S. corporations. Profits jumped 57 percent between 1960 and 1964 as innovative technology, including pneumatic conveyors, copying machines, piggyback freight, and containerized shipping, increased efficiency and profits. Military and space contracts, particularly in the "Sunbelt" states of the South and Southwest, stimulated prosperity and corporate consolidation. By the end of the decade 71 percent of manufacturing profits went to the nation's 400 largest firms.

In the reformist climate of the 1960s, however, the scope of corporate enterprise became an issue of public policy. Critics charged that the interaction between private business and government did not always benefit the public.

Personnel shifted easily between corporate management and federal regulatory boards that set industry standards. Although few government officials attempted to protect consumer interests, a private lawyer named Ralph Nader emerged as a consumer advocate. After his book *Unsafe at Any Speed* (1965) exposed the hazards of General Motors' Corvair, Senate hearings revealed that the world's largest corporation had investigated Nader's personal life in an effort to discredit his findings. Nader used his resulting jury award to establish research centers to monitor the quality of consumer products as well as to investigate mine safety, radiation hazards, pollution, and tax inequities.

Prosperity both reflected and encouraged U.S. enterprise abroad. During the 1960s investment in western Europe doubled, and the total value of U.S.-owned overseas plants and equipment surpassed $100 billion. While U.S. firms exported $35 billion in goods each year, foreign subsidiaries of multinational businesses sold another $45 billion in goods. By the end of the decade the United States controlled nearly three-quarters of the world's oil and produced most of its machinery, electronics, and chemicals.

Amid prosperity, however, income distribution remained lopsided. The wealthiest fifth of U.S. families received more than 45 percent of the nation's personal income in 1966, whereas the poorest fifth earned 3.7 percent. Tax loopholes accentuated the problem. Tax-exempt bonds, a refuge for wealthy investors, amounted to nearly $86 billion in 1963. More than 150 persons with incomes exceeding $200,000 paid no taxes in 1968. Corporations benefitted from similar loopholes. The percentage of federal revenues derived from corporate income taxes decreased from 20 percent in 1955 to 12 percent in 1970. Yet nearly one-quarter of all U.S. citizens still lived in poverty.

Concerned about such inequities, Johnson vowed to wage an "unconditional war on poverty." Raised in the tradition of southern populism and himself a congressional New Dealer, Johnson believed that medical care, education, job training, and racial equality could complete the New Deal. The Economic Opportunity Act of 1964 created the Office of Economic Opportunity (OEO), launched training programs for the young, and offered loans and grants for self-help projects initiated by local communities. Seeking to bypass traditional leadership, the bill's Community Action Program called for a "participatory democracy" of the poor in shaping government-funded projects. The law mandated a Job Corps for youth and VISTA (Volunteers in Service to America), which assigned volunteers to assist needy communities. The OEO also introduced the Head Start program to provide preschool aid to children of the poor.

Johnson's political genius assured passage of new civil rights laws. Although Kennedy had lined up support for his proposal in 1963, southern senators expected to weaken its provisions. Kennedy's death abruptly changed the political climate. "No memorial or eulogy," Johnson told a stunned joint session of Congress five days after Kennedy's death, "could more eloquently honor Kennedy's memory than the earliest possible passage of the Civil Rights Bill for which he fought so long." Linking the new measure to the martyred president, Johnson refused to compromise on its major provisions.

With the support of northern Republicans, two-thirds of the Senate voted to end a southern filibuster—the first time the Senate halted discussion of a civil rights measure. The Civil Rights Act of 1964 gave the federal government the power to sue to desegregate public accommodations and schools. The law also prohibited denial of equal job opportunities in all but the smallest businesses and unions and created the Equal Employment Opportunity Commission

(EEOC) to sue for compliance. To be illegal, however, racial imbalances in employment had to be the result of deliberate intent, and the law prohibited the use of quotas or preferential treatment to accomplish racial balance. African Americans and liberals nonetheless celebrated this landmark step toward equal opportunity. Yet conservatives such as Arizona Senator Barry Goldwater attacked the law's extension of federal power. Die-hard southern segregationists such as Alabama's George Wallace detected a communist conspiracy at work.

Passage of the Civil Rights Act also opened an unexpected area for social change. During the debate in Congress, the National Woman's Party protested that prohibition of discrimination because of "race, color, religion, or national origin" had omitted the word "sex." Virginia Democrat Howard Smith, an opponent of the entire bill, then introduced an amendment adding the missing category. Although some suggested he was merely making a mockery of the measure, Smith probably sought to extend to white women the same rights now offered to blacks. Whatever his motives, nearly all the women in Congress endorsed the change, which carried both houses. However, subsequent failure of the EEOC to push for compliance with the anti-sex-discrimination law frustrated women reformers. Encouraged by the popularity of Betty Friedan's book, *The Feminine Mystique* (1963), activists formed the National Organization for Women (NOW) in 1966 to exert pressure outside government. Pledged to "take the actions needed to bring women into the mainstream of American society," NOW pushed for legal abortions, maternity leave, tax-deductible child care, and an equal rights amendment to end sex discrimination. Simultaneously, a younger generation of women working within the civil rights movement developed a commitment to equality for all groups and demanded equal treatment for themselves. The two strands of feminist reform later converged in the women's liberation movement.

By the end of 1964 Congress had enacted most of Johnson's social welfare program, including $1 billion in housing legislation, federal grants for mass transportation, loans for college students, and aid for college construction. The president also expanded a Kennedy pilot project into a food stamp program for the working poor. The rapid passage of these measures dazzled the country, and the media compared Johnson's success favorably with the legislative productivity of the first one hundred days of Roosevelt's New Deal. The Kennedy administration had initiated many of these concepts, but Johnson's legislative skill translated liberal intentions into government programs.

THE ELECTION OF 1964

"I think we just delivered the South to the Republican Party," Johnson told an aide as he signed the Civil Rights Act of 1964. Angered at government interference in the private sector, Republican conservatives rallied behind Senator Goldwater, author of the best-selling book, *The Conscience of a Conservative* (1960). "Extremism in the defense of liberty is no vice," declared Goldwater in his acceptance speech to the stormy Republican National Convention, ". . . moderation in the pursuit of justice is no virtue." In his campaign speeches the Republican nominee lamented crime in the streets, political corruption, aimlessness among youth, anxiety among the elderly, and the loss of spiritual meaning. His was the first candidacy to embrace the "social issue," the discomfort

The mix of signs was Goldwater's usual view during the 1964 presidential campaign.

experienced by many voters over personally frightening aspects of social change in the 1960s. "I will give you back your freedom," said Goldwater. The Republican's saber-rattling foreign policy speeches made Johnson look like a dove.

Echoing Goldwater's agenda, George Wallace captured national attention by winning one-third of the Democratic primary vote in Wisconsin, Indiana, and Maryland. Political commentators described Wallace's support as a "backlash" against civil rights agitation and integration, but the conservative Democrat aimed his criticism at liberal paternalism and big government. "The American people," he said, "are fed up with the continuing trend toward a socialist state which subjects the individual to the dictates of an all-powerful central government." Wallace's surprising success revealed deep dissatisfactions among lower-middle-class whites about liberal support of African Americans instead of solutions to their own economic and social problems. Recognizing that Wallace threatened his support in the South, Goldwater persuaded the Alabaman to withdraw.

Johnson, himself a southerner, worried more about black activism. To gain greater support in the North, the Student Nonviolent Coordinating Committee (SNCC) had invited hundreds of white volunteers to participate in a voter registration campaign in Mississippi during the summer of 1964. The integrated Mississippi Summer project encountered violent repression from vigilantes and local officials, which resulted in mass arrests, bombings, burnings, beatings, and the murder of civil rights workers. Although only 1,200 blacks dared to register to vote during the summer's bloody events, a contingent of SNCC workers and

Frank Watte/Lyndon B. Johnson Library

Lyndon Johnson used the politics of consensus to win a 61 percent plurality in the 1964 election. Having signed civil rights legislation that year, he captured more than 90 percent of the black vote.

new black voters went to the Democratic National Convention in Atlantic City to demand political representation.

Calling themselves the Mississippi Freedom Democratic Party, they argued that the all-white Mississippi delegation should be unseated because African Americans could not participate in their selection. Johnson feared such reforms would cost white support and offered the delegates two at-large seats. In the end, no compromise was acceptable. The regular Mississippi Democrats, most of whom backed Goldwater, left the convention, and the unseated blacks remained embittered by liberal hypocrisy. As a gesture of reconciliation, Johnson chose the liberal Hubert Humphrey as his running mate, but African Americans lost confidence in and respect for their white allies.

Johnson and Humphrey sought a politics of consensus in 1964 by defending civil rights legislation and promising moderation in Vietnam. "We seek no wider war," said the president, denouncing those who would "supply American boys to do the job that Asian boys should do." In the election, the Johnson-Humphrey liberal agenda received a record 61 percent plurality and amassed 43 million votes. The Democrats won more than 90 percent of the black vote but lost five states in the Deep South. The landslide gave the president greater than two-to-one majorities in both houses of Congress. Even without the white South, the president could now attempt to fulfill the promises of the liberal agenda.

Pressing ahead with Great Society programs, Johnson signed an education bill in 1965 that based federal aid on the number of low-income families in each school district. The law enabled the federal government to influence local political decisions. For example, the Commissioner of Education ruled in 1965 that school districts had to show a "good faith substantial start" toward desegregation or lose federal funds. The next year the Office of Education issued tighter guidelines and declared an end to "paper compliance with desegregation orders." As appropriations for education reached $10 billion by the end of the decade, conservatives objected that federal aid was threatening local control over schools.

As Johnson continued to push for health care for the elderly, congressional leaders reached a compromise that incorporated Republican demands for voluntary medical insurance to cover doctors' fees and drugs. However, the heart of the Medicare package provided for hospital and nursing home care for elderly citizens through payroll taxes administered by Social Security. The law also provided Medicaid grants to states that enacted health programs for poor people of all ages. By 1970 the cost of state health care nearly equaled that of Medicare, but the law did not allow the government to control service fees. Hospital costs, which increased 7 percent in the year before Medicare, averaged 14 percent more each year for the next decade.

The Great Society peaked in 1965. Johnson signed a $1 billion Appalachia Assistance program, most of which went for road building in the economically depressed region. A portion of the $7.8 billion housing bill included rent supplements for low-income families. Johnson made the Department of Housing and Urban Development a cabinet-level office and followed that with approval of the Demonstration Cities and Metropolitan Development Act, which appropriated nearly $1 billion to attack urban blight. Congress also abolished the national-origins quota system for immigration, underscoring a shift in racial policy. The Immigration Act of 1965 limited admission to 300,000 immigrants a year but favored relatives of U.S. citizens and those with special skills rather than particular nationalities and encouraged a considerable increase in immigration from Asia and Latin America.

The Triumph of Civil Rights

The Twenty-third Amendment to the Constitution, ratified in 1964, outlawed the poll tax, long a barrier to black voting in the South. Yet when African Americans initiated a voter registration drive, including nonviolent street demonstrations in Selma, Alabama, in 1965, local officials conspired with white mobs to prevent political change. The violence climaxed on "Bloody Sunday"—7 March 1965—when state troopers attacked a peaceful march. Broadcast on national television, the atrocity forced the White House to intervene. Johnson summoned a joint session of Congress to request federal protection for black voter registrants. Borrowing the language of the civil rights movement, the first southern president since Woodrow Wilson declared, "All of us . . . must overcome the crippling legacy of bigotry and injustice—and we *shall* overcome."

The Voting Rights Act of 1965 abolished voter literacy tests and empowered the attorney general to assign federal examiners to register voters in states practicing discrimination. Applied to federal, state, and local elections, the law produced a revolution in southern life. The next year, federal examiners registered

UPI/Corbis-Bettmann

On "Bloody Sunday," Alabama state troopers used tear gas and clubs to crush a planned protest march from Selma to Montgomery to demand black suffrage. The spectacle outraged public opinion and spurred passage of the Voting Rights Act of 1965.

more than 400,000 new African American voters. By 1968 1 million southern blacks had qualified to vote. As blacks enlisted on the Democratic rolls, whites increasingly voted Republican, reviving two-party politics in the South.

The Great Society brought other dramatic gains for African Americans. Robert Weaver, appointed head of the Department of Housing and Urban Development, became the first African American cabinet member in history. Thurgood Marshall, former counsel for the NAACP, became the first African American to serve on the Supreme Court. In 1966 Massachusetts elected Edward Brooke the first African American senator since Reconstruction. Besides these token advances, many blacks made major economic strides in this era of prosperity. Black median family income increased from less than $6,000 in 1964 to more than $8,000 in 1969. At the same time, the ratio between black and white family income narrowed from 54 percent to 61 percent, and the proportion of black families living in poverty decreased from 48 percent in 1959 to 28 percent ten years later.

Despite these tangible gains, moderate black leadership could not contain the mixture of impatience, rage, and black consciousness that accompanied heightened aspirations and unchanging realities for most African Americans. After 1965 national attention shifted to the 53 percent of the African American population that resided outside the South. Northern blacks lived primarily in decaying ghettos in the older industrial cities, where the exodus of manufacturing plants to the suburbs and Sunbelt states and the transition to a suburban service economy proved disastrous for African American workers. In 1968 the

Department of Labor reported that the black unemployment rate was three times as high as the white rate. Housing, jobs, and welfare proved inadequate to meet the basic needs of black families. In Chicago, for example, Aid to Families with Dependent Children, the fastest growing welfare program of the decade, gave mothers only twenty-one cents per meal. Despite federal poverty programs, ghetto life remained depressingly unchanged during the decade.

RACIAL TURMOIL AND CULTURAL IDENTITY

In 1964 the powder keg exploded. During the next three years more than one hundred riots and rebellions occurred as angry blacks from Harlem in New York City to Watts in Los Angeles attacked business property in their communities to protest economic exploitation and police harassment. As young blacks chanted "burn, baby, burn," armed National Guardsmen patrolled city streets. Property damage approached $750 million, and dozens were killed, thousands injured. In Chicago Martin Luther King's "open-city" campaign to alleviate ghetto problems provoked rioting in 1966, and his open-housing marches into white ethnic neighborhoods brought violent retaliation. In 1967 central Detroit went up in smoke as African Americans went on a week-long rampage that

A black demonstrator turned thumbs down at the presence of National Guardsmen sent to suppress racial violence in Newark, New Jersey, in 1967. Official reports later blamed police authorities for intensifying the crisis.

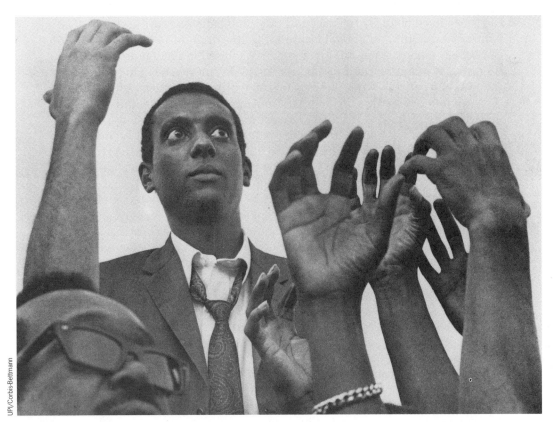

The Student Nonviolent Coordinating Committee's Stokely Carmichael, the first black leader to proclaim "Black Power" in 1966, fused black pride with militant and confrontational politics.

provoked vicious suppression by the National Guard. A six-day riot in Newark, New Jersey, left twenty-seven dead. A special report to the governor later blamed police and National Guardsmen for "excessive and unjustified force." SNCC leader H. "Rap" Brown expressed the bitter mood of 1967, urging demonstrators in Cambridge, Maryland, to "burn this town down if this town don't turn around and grant the demand of Negroes."

Reacting to the violence, Johnson appointed a National Advisory Commission on Civil Disorders chaired by Illinois Governor Otto Kerner. The nation was "moving toward two societies, one black, one white, separate and unequal," concluded the Kerner Report of 1968. Blaming the riots on white racism and white institutional power, the commission urged a massive commitment to housing, education, jobs, and welfare as well as better law enforcement techniques. However, by then the White House was preoccupied with foreign policy and remained silent on the Kerner findings.

The explosion of black anger after 1965 effectively killed the biracial, nonviolent, civil rights movement. The limited gains from liberal reform, the persistence of black poverty in the North, and the vocal white backlash encouraged African Americans to see all whites as part of a rigid "establishment." African American organizers like Stokely Carmichael increasingly identified with other colonized peoples of the third world, including the peasants fighting the United States in Vietnam. In early 1966 SNCC became the first civil rights group to oppose the war. Aware that African Americans suffered disproportionate casualties in combat, Carmichael and other militants coined the slogan "Hell No, We Won't Go!" and urged blacks to resist the draft. In 1967 African American heavyweight champion Muhammad Ali refused induction on the basis of his status as a Muslim minister and remained defiant when boxing authorities stripped him of his crown. "No Viet Cong ever called me nigger," Ali explained.

When James Meredith, the first African American to enroll at the University of Mississippi, launched a solitary protest march through Mississippi in 1966 only to be shot by a sniper, civil rights leaders rushed forward to continue the protest. Here Carmichael brushed aside talk of nonviolence and proclaimed "Black Power!" The words electrified the media and terrified whites. Martin Luther King, Jr., urged Carmichael to adopt a more moderate slogan, but black pride and cultural identity could no longer be contained by nonviolent rhetoric. SNCC soon purged whites from leadership positions. "Integration," said Carmichael, was "a subterfuge for the maintenance of white supremacy."

The magnetism of Black Power revealed widespread frustration within African American communities. "To be a Negro in this country," explained novelist James Baldwin, "is to be in a rage all the time." Eldridge Cleaver, a former convict and emerging leader of the Black Panther Party, expressed similar fury in his best-selling *Soul on Ice* (1968). For many young blacks, failure to gain equal rights, economic advancement, and cultural respect produced a powerful identity crisis, forcing a conversion from "Negro" values of assimilation and integration to "black" affirmations of ethnicity. Many blacks followed the lead of Malcolm X and changed their "slave" names to African or Muslim names. In Los Angeles Maulana Ron Karenga formed the US Organization to promote "back to black" cultural traditions and popularized "kwanza" as an African American alternative holiday to Christmas.

Through his posthumously published autobiography, Malcolm X emerged as an important cultural force. Born Malcolm Little, he had converted to the Black Muslim religion while in prison and changed his name to symbolize independence from white domination. A persuasive, charismatic speaker, he initially opposed interracial cooperation and warned that any association with "evil whites" would thwart social justice. However, after breaking with the Black Muslims in 1964, Malcolm argued that capitalism functioned as an oppressive force and that people of all colors must cooperate to achieve a socialist alternative. Assassinated in Harlem in 1965, Malcolm remained a prophet for black and white radicals seeking interracial cooperation.

The cultural aspects of Black Power—Afro hair styles, soul food, ethnic identity—paralleled efforts to organize a black political movement. In 1967 Oakland, California's Bobby Seale and Huey Newton founded the Black Panther Party to overcome economic problems in the ghetto. Viewing urban riots as self-destructive, the Panthers formed a community defense league to monitor the local police. To dramatize the right to bear arms against "occupation" of their communities by white authorities, Panthers marched into the California legislature with loaded rifles. By 1968 the Black Panther Party had devised a ten-point program embracing Marxist concepts of self-determination and opposition to "welfare colonialism." The Panthers also distributed a national weekly newspaper, established local health clinics, and provided free breakfasts and schools for black children. In 1968 the Panthers won white radical support for the Peace and Freedom Party, which ran Eldridge Cleaver for president, but the movement exerted minimal influence on the election.

Exhibit 11-5. Unemployment Rates for Whites and Blacks, 1960–1968
(percentage of each group specified of persons
16 years and older in civilian labor force)

	1960	1964	1968
White	4.9	4.6	3.2
Black	10.2	9.6	6.7
Total	5.5	5.2	3.6

Source: *Historical Statistics of the United States, Colonial Times to 1970 (1975).*

Panther militancy aroused the wrath of FBI Director J. Edgar Hoover. Fearing the rise of a "black messiah" who might harness African American anger, Hoover expanded counterintelligence activities in 1967 to "expose, disrupt, misdirect, discredit, or otherwise neutralize the activities of black nationalists." During the next two years police worked with state and federal officials to raid thirty-one Panther offices, arrest hundreds of leaders on spurious charges, and disrupt party operations through "disinformation" programs. In one grisly episode in December 1969, Chicago police and state officers raided the apartment of Panther leaders Fred Hampton and Mark Clark and shot them to death. By then, both Cleaver and Seale had fled the country, Newton remained in jail, and some forty Panther leaders had been killed in police raids.

While Black Panthers, SNCC, and Martin Luther King, Jr., contested for African American leadership, the cry of Black Power intensified the white backlash but also emboldened other ethnic groups. By the late 1960s Mexican Americans in the Southwest and California proclaimed a new "Chicano" pride. While the media focused on the militant Brown Berets, who carried guns to demonstrate their independence from Anglo authorities, Mexican American college students used confrontational tactics to obtain Chicano studies programs. The new cultural awakening produced scholarly journals such as *Aztlan*, the popular magazines *El Grito* and *La Raza*, and moving explorations of Chicano roots by novelists Raymond Barrio and Rudolfo Anaya as well as Luis Valdez's militant *Teatro Campesino*, which dramatized problems of Mexican American identity. Rudolfo "Corky" Gonzales's epic poem, "I Am Joaquin," depicted the dilemma of being "caught up in the whirl of gringo society."

Chicano consciousness, however, could not hide the bleak facts of Mexican American economic existence. Mexican Americans, the fastest-growing ethnic group in the nation, received only 70 percent of the median white income. Fully one-fifth of Mexican Americans lived below government-defined poverty levels. Such problems were exaggerated by a poverty and population explosion in Mexico that pushed hundreds of thousands of immigrants, legal and illegal, into the United States each year. Seeking better opportunities, these aliens accepted low-paying jobs, mainly in the Southwest, as field hands or service workers without benefit of union contracts or government regulation. In California the predominantly Mexican migrant workers comprised 10 percent of the state's labor force.

Seeking to improve conditions for field workers, California's Cesar Chavez used Christian nonviolence and product boycotts to win collective bargaining rights for the small but militant United Farm Workers. Organizers Corky

Cesar Chavez and the United Farm Workers (UFW), a movement of Mexican American field workers, began to demonstrate the possibilities of Chicano power in the late 1960s.

Gonzales and Jose Angel Gutierrez also formed civil rights groups in Denver and Texas to mobilize Chicano political power. Mexican Americans sent delegates to the National Council of La Raza, a consortium of twenty-six organizations that acted as a Washington lobby for all Hispanics. Constituting one-fourth of the Democratic vote in Texas and playing a major role in the Los Angeles area, where they numbered 2 million, Mexican Americans used political power to fight discrimination, liberalize immigration, and campaign for bilingual education.

Native Americans also moved from liberal reformism to militant assertions of cultural identity. When the state of Washington attempted to abridge native treaty rights to salmon fishing in the interests of conservation, local tribes invited the National Indian Youth Council to stage "fish-in" demonstrations in 1964. After years of litigation, the U.S. Supreme Court upheld the native position in 1968. Meanwhile, the Taos Pueblo in New Mexico rejected a federal offer of $10 million in compensation for seizing the sacred Blue Lake and initiated protests that led to a reversal of federal policies. In 1966 native leaders adopted the phrase "self-determination" to oppose federal termination programs. Two years later President Johnson embraced that language to demand "equality and dignity" for native peoples. In 1968 Congress passed the Indian Civil Rights Act, requiring tribal consent to state jurisdiction over civil or criminal matters. That year young activists formed the American Indian Movement, raised the cry "Red Power," and vowed to continue the struggle for tribal autonomy.

MR. JOHNSON'S WAR

The cultural conflict of the 1960s reflected not only domestic problems but the simultaneous war in Vietnam, which drained national resources and distracted public attention from problems at home. That a disproportionate number of U.S. soldiers came from minority groups accented the parallel struggles. Indeed, ethnic leaders often identified with citizens of third-world countries who confronted the power of U.S. corporations and the federal government.

Like President Kennedy, Johnson recognized the importance of undeveloped countries in the Cold War and opposed political or economic changes that might destabilize U.S. interests. In 1965, for example, Johnson ordered U.S. troops into the Dominican Republic when he suspected that communists controlled a constitutional movement to seize power from the army. Johnson also followed Kennedy's precedents in authorizing the CIA to promote pro-U.S. governments abroad. Subsequent investigations found that CIA techniques included blackmail, bribery, forgery, bombing, sabotage, espionage, propaganda, disinformation (the spreading of false information), psychological warfare, military training, and paramilitary activities. The CIA also provided financial support

The Granger Collection

Marines involved in a search-and-destroy mission in South Vietnam, 1966.

to selected individuals, political parties, private organizations, unions, and businesses. Such covert operations were concealed within the enormous military and intelligence bureaucracy.

Overt U.S. military power appeared awesome and continued to grow. By the end of the 1960s the armed forces operated 429 major and 2,972 minor military bases in thirty countries and had 1 million military personnel overseas. The nation's arsenal included 1,000 nuclear-armed intercontinental missiles and 70 nuclear-armed and -powered submarines. The nuclear storehouse amounted to the equivalent of fifteen tons of TNT for every person in the world. Total navy tonnage exceeded that of all other nations combined. The cost of the military establishment exceeded $216 million a day. Between 1945 and 1970 American taxpayers spent $1 trillion for military purposes. Yet the late 1960s brought the United States the worst military and political disaster in its history.

Just hours after the assassination of President Kennedy, Johnson conferred with the U.S. ambassador to South Vietnam, Henry Cabot Lodge, to assess the status of the war. When Lodge reported that the Vietcong had escalated military activity, Johnson replied that he was "not going to be the President who saw Southeast Asia go the way China went." Instead, he cancelled Kennedy's order to withdraw troops from South Vietnam and approved a program to accelerate attacks against North Vietnam. U.S. destroyers patrolled the Gulf of Tonkin, and PT boats occasionally attacked North Vietnamese coastal installations. As military clashes increased, the State Department secretly drafted a congressional resolution for a declaration of war in May 1964. Two months later, South Vietnamese ships, accompanied by U.S. intelligence vessels, began bombarding North Vietnamese territory in the Gulf of Tonkin. When North Vietnamese patrol boats fired on one of the destroyers, U.S. fighter planes strafed the attackers. On 4 August the navy reported a second attack on U.S. ships, although subsequent analysis blamed "freak weather effects, and an overeager sonar man" for that claim.

Johnson now ordered air reprisals on North Vietnamese bases. Insisting that the United States sought "no wider war," the president presented Congress with a reworded version of the secretly prepared May declaration of war, which stated that "Congress approves and supports the determination of the President as commander-in-chief to take all necessary measures to repel any attack against the forces of the United States and to prevent further aggression." The Tonkin Gulf Resolution passed in the House unanimously and in the Senate with only two dissenters, Wayne Morse of Oregon and Ernest Gruening of Alaska. A Harris poll showed 85 percent approval of air strikes against North Vietnam. Stopping short of a full declaration of war that might have drawn China and the Soviet Union into the conflict, Johnson had won a free hand to conduct the war as he chose.

The conflict escalated again when the Vietcong attacked a U.S. base at Pleiku in February 1965. Vowing not to be scared out of Vietnam, Johnson ordered air strikes, known as Operation Rolling Thunder, against North Vietnam. Claiming the bombings were merely retaliatory, the White House concealed the deepening commitment of air power from the U.S. public. Antiaircraft fire and poor accuracy produced a high loss of planes and indiscriminate bombing of civilian targets. The air war also required more ground troops to protect U.S. bases, and Johnson ordered 100,000 additional soldiers to Vietnam. A Gallup poll found that 61 percent of the public approved increased troop allotments. Johnson

Exhibit 11-6. Vietnam

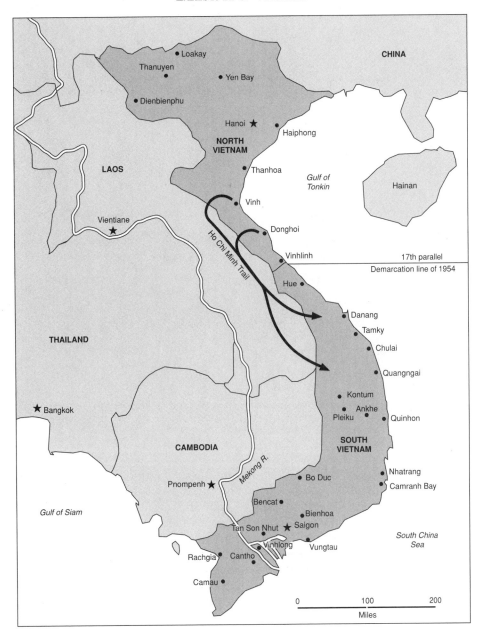

hoped to maintain enough force to prevent the communists from winning but not enough to precipitate Chinese intervention.

By the summer of 1965 the White House decided to Americanize the war because Johnson no longer believed the South Vietnamese could win on their own. U.S. ground troops began large-scale combat operations, engaging in "search-and-destroy" missions while B-52s flew 3,000 miles from Guam to bomb suspected Vietcong targets in South Vietnam. By the end of the year, the number of air attacks surpassed 70,000. In December the air force targeted industrial areas in the North. However, at Christmas, Johnson ordered a bombing

A B-52 bomber drops a 38,000-pound bomb load over Vietnam. The original AP caption for this 1966 picture expressed the military's optimism about superior U.S. firepower: "...the B-52s have sharply reduced the Communist will to fight, officials in Saigon have concluded..."

moratorium and sent diplomats across the globe to explore possibilities for peace. The main stumbling block remained White House refusal to recognize the Vietcong National Liberation Front as a political force independent of North Vietnam. Contending that North Vietnam had invaded South Vietnam, Johnson denied that the United States had become involved in a civil war.

As troop commitments rose to 385,000, antiwar sentiment surfaced at home. J. William Fulbright, chair of the Senate Foreign Relations Committee, held open hearings that criticized White House policy. Nonetheless, in June 1966 Johnson ordered the bombing of Hanoi. "We must continue to raise the price of aggression," he explained. The goal of the bombing had changed from breaking the enemy's will to cutting supply lines. However, intelligence reports showed that such bombing was militarily ineffective. Johnson promised to end the attacks if North Vietnam pledged to send no more troops south, but Hanoi responded that peace depended on withdrawal of all U.S. forces. Because the president insisted that South Vietnam's independence must be preserved, he rejected Hanoi's demand.

Despite tremendous firepower, the president's limited war could not defeat the enemy. Military advisors repeatedly made the error of assuming that a reduction of Vietcong operations indicated diminished military capability rather than changes in strategy. In late 1966 Defense Secretary McNamara commissioned a study, later known in published form as the Pentagon Papers, to evaluate the entire war policy, but the bombing continued, and reliable journalists in Vietnam denounced administration claims about the minimal number of civilian casualties.

By 1968 Johnson had ordered 500,000 soldiers to Vietnam. As ground forces confronted North Vietnamese regulars, casualty figures soared. Meanwhile, the Vietcong controlled the timing and terms of 80 percent of all military confrontations. To destroy enemy bases, U.S. planes dropped napalm, defoliants, and herbicides throughout the country. U.S. fragmentation bombs left victims riddled with millions of tiny particles that could not be detected by x-rays. The CIA also launched Operation Phoenix, an assassination program against alleged Vietcong leaders that claimed at least 20,000 victims.

The Vietcong's surprise Tet Offensive in February 1968 showed the futility of U.S. military strategy. While Johnson directed immense firepower to defend a marine outpost at Khe Sanh, communist forces launched a coordinated attack on every major city in South Vietnam. In Saigon commandos penetrated the U.S. embassy grounds. In Hue communist forces executed police officials and political enemies while the South Vietnamese retaliated against Buddhists, students, and teachers who appeared to be "VC collaborators." An estimated 32,000 insurgents were killed during the Tet Offensive, while U.S. forces suffered 4,000 killed and nearly 20,000 wounded. Yet, although the offensive greatly depleted Vietcong strength, the battles demonstrated that the enemy only had to survive to prevent the United States from "winning" the war. The Tet Offensive also revealed the inability of South Vietnamese armies to defend positions without U.S. assistance. Thus, the Tet Offensive, a military defeat for the communists, undermined public support for the war.

THE ANTIWAR MOVEMENT

Less than a month after President Johnson ordered the full-scale bombing of North Vietnam in 1965, 20,000 protesters participated in an SDS-sponsored demonstration in Washington. College students, vulnerable to the draft and increasingly concerned about issues of social justice and personal freedom, denounced the war. "Teach-in" protests spread to the major universities. At Berkeley 12,000 students and faculty participated in Vietnam Day in 1965. As draft calls reached 40,000 a month in 1966, rallies, marches, and draft-card burnings multiplied. Young men refused induction orders, thousands deserted the armed forces, and even more fled to Canada and Europe to avoid conscription. Protesters occupied military induction centers and harassed on-campus job recruiters for the military and the CIA.

To war opponents, the use of technological violence against an economically undeveloped people was equivalent to genocide. Defense contractors such as Dow Chemical, which manufactured napalm used to kill civilians in Vietnam, and Honeywell, which made antipersonnel fragmentation bombs, faced militant public protest. SDS's Carl Oglesby considered the conflict a laboratory for developing techniques to halt social revolution in the third world. Yet most protesters identified with the spirit of Joseph Heller's cult novel, *Catch-22* (1960), an absurdist view of World War II that suggested that escape was the

Exhibit 11-7. Tet Offensive

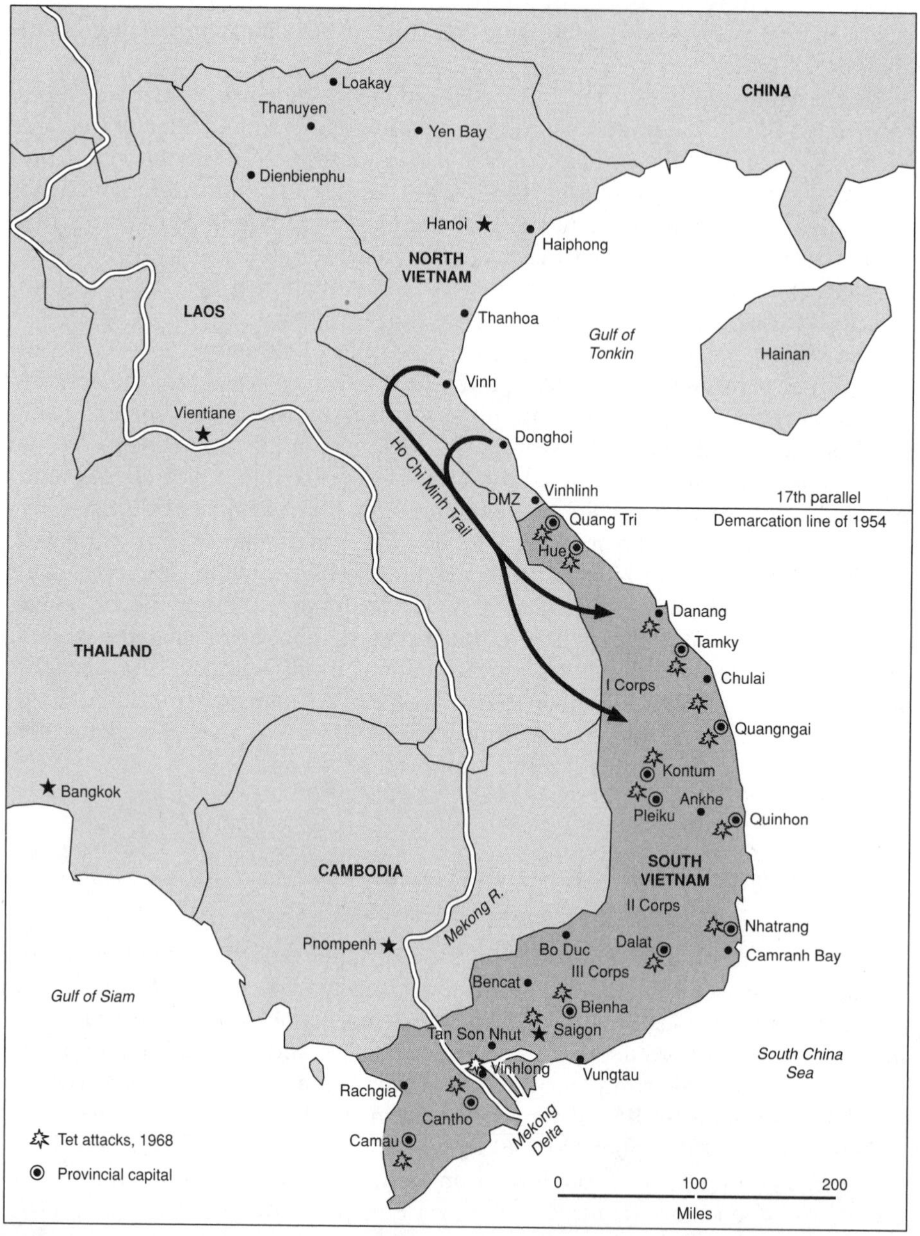

only sane response to war. Bolstered by celebrity activists such as folk singers Joan Baez and Phil Ochs, antiwar assemblies became instant communities in which outrage merged with political action.

By the fall of 1967 protest had evolved into massive resistance. A "stop-the-draft" week at the Oakland, California, Induction Center resulted in street battles between police and 20,000 activists. At a demonstration called by the National Mobilization Against the War (MOBE), more than 100,000 marchers surrounded the Pentagon. Norman Mailer's prize-winning *Armies of the Night* (1968) described the arrest of prominent protesters, including pediatrician

— WILLIAM CHILDS WESTMORELAND —
1914–

The commander of U.S. military forces in Vietnam from 1964 to 1968, General William Childs Westmoreland embodied the strengths and weaknesses of the U.S. presence in Southeast Asia. A picture-book soldier, he was ramrod straight, six feet tall, jut-jawed, brave, meticulous, and self-disciplined. In Vietnam he determined to prove that superior technology and organization skills could defeat a guerrilla army, but like civilian leaders, he underestimated the passion and power of the enemy, and he failed to appreciate the political dimensions of the war.

U.S. Army

Born in Spartanburg, South Carolina, Westmoreland devoted his entire life to the military. He attended West Point, became an expert in field artillery, and showed considerable ingenuity in tactical planning (He wrote one term paper titled "The Use of Mother's Milk as a Food for Troops in the Field"). During World War II he fought in North Africa, Sicily, France, and Germany.

During the Korean War, Westmoreland commanded a parachute troop and jumped with his men. He then went to the Pentagon's manpower office and enrolled in an advanced management program at the Harvard School of Business. Indistinguishable from the other corporate executives in the seminars, the young general became a proficient administrator and later used his association with former classmates at such companies as General Electric and Union Carbide to increase worker performance and productivity in military procurement and manpower allocation. In 1960 President Eisenhower appointed him superintendent of West Point.

Chosen to lead U.S. troops in Vietnam in January 1964, Westmoreland drew upon his vast administrative skill. Even to West-moreland's critics, his logistic achievements seemed astounding. Under his command, the military constructed six deep-water ports, five jet airfields, eighty-four tactical airstrips, and hundreds of helicopter pads; built 11 million square feet of covered storage, 5 million square yards of open storage, and 2.5 million cubic feet of cold storage; laid miles of telephone cable and radio grids; and erected bridges, roads, canals, and seaways. Westmoreland's demand for troops also appeared voracious and increased from 16,000 in 1964 to 185,000 in 1965 to 385,000 in 1966 to 470,000 in 1967 to 520,000 in 1968.

Such power inflicted immense damage but could not defeat the elusive enemy. Nor could the seemingly unending war justify the tremendous drain on U.S. resources. When political leaders recognized that victory could not be achieved, President Johnson appointed Westmoreland Chief of Staff of the Army in 1968 and ordered him back to Washington. "We have curtailed the tide of Communist aggression," Westmoreland stated in his final report on the war; ". . . the enemy has not won a single major victory."

Westmoreland retired in 1972, but his name returned to the headlines ten years later when he sued CBS, Inc., for libel. A documentary program had accused the former general of deceiving the administration about the strength of the enemy. Despite forthright denials, however, Westmoreland dropped the lawsuit without proving his case. "However desirable the American system of civilian control of the military," he argued in his memoirs, "it was a mistake to permit appointive civilian officials lacking military experience and knowledge . . . to wield undue influence in the decision-making process." ■

A confrontation takes place between military police and anti–Vietnam War protesters at the March on the Pentagon, October 1967.

Dr. Benjamin Spock and Mailer himself. The same day, 300,000 demonstrators gathered in New York City. Still another phase of the antiwar movement commenced when Catholic activists, including Father Philip Berrigan, poured blood on draft files in Baltimore. As efforts to destroy draft records spread across the country, conscientious objectors in the military refused assignment to Vietnam. Convinced that campuses served as seedbeds for antiwar activity, Johnson ordered Army Intelligence to join the FBI in putting thousands of students and faculty under surveillance. Yet by 1968 SDS boasted nearly 300 chapters and a membership of 100,000. For many of the nation's increasingly politicized students and peace activists, the Vietnam War had become a symbol of society's exploitation of the poor and powerless.

THE WAR AT HOME

As dissent against the war increased, the White House fought to curtail public criticism. Since the early 1960s, FBI Director J. Edgar Hoover had directed "counterintelligence" efforts against both the Ku Klux Klan and the civil rights movement, including wiretaps and bugs of Martin Luther King, Jr., to discredit the black leader. By 1967, however, King had followed SNCC's lead and began criticizing the war in Vietnam. The following year the FBI extended counterintelligence activities "to expose, disrupt, and otherwise neutralize . . . the New Left." Other government agencies initiated similar operations. By 1968 the army had compiled 100,000 dossiers on antiwar activists. Johnson also authorized the CIA's Operation Chaos to conduct domestic surveillance, in violation of the agency's charter, against dissidents, demonstrators, and even "suspicious" members of Congress. However, when the CIA notified Johnson that domestic dissent appeared to be independent of foreign funding, the president rejected the finding.

Johnson had hoped to finance the war without cutting Great Society funding, but as war costs rose to $2 billion a month in 1966, Johnson admitted the impossibility of spending large sums for both "guns and butter." In a year of record federal expenditures, Congress abolished the school milk program and cut appropriations for education. Although Democrats managed to preserve OEO, the antipoverty agency limped along on half its projected budget. Grass-roots protests in the cities and on college campuses offended conservatives and further weakened the liberal position. When Johnson followed King's "open-city" campaign in Chicago with the submission of an equal housing bill in 1966, two attempts to end a Senate filibuster failed, and the administration settled for a modest rat-control appropriation.

Congressional uneasiness with domestic programs also reflected the soaring inflation caused by war spending. By 1968 the military budget had reached $70 billion. Johnson had persuaded Congress to suspend Kennedy's investment tax credit and accelerated depreciation allowances in 1966, but these minor tax increases provided insufficient funds to finance the war. The president suffered a severe legislative setback when Congress refused to accept a war tax surcharge and preferred spending cuts or tax reform. Although Johnson gained a small tax surcharge in 1968, the delay in increasing taxation encouraged inflation. Rising prices and war spending produced a phenomenal rise in the federal deficit, which leaped from $3.8 billion in 1966 to $8.7 billion in 1967 to $25.2 billion in 1968. The consumer price index rose 5 percent in 1968 alone.

"The bombs in Vietnam explode at home," protested Martin Luther King, Jr. "They destroy the hopes and possibilities of a decent America." Angered by both civil rights protests and antiwar demonstrations, voters supported a conservative backlash in the 1966 congressional elections. Stressing increasing crime and the need for "law and order," Republicans made large gains in both houses of Congress. Democrats warned that education, jobs, housing reforms, and an end to discrimination were necessary to end domestic strife but acknowledged that spending huge sums for both guns and butter was no longer possible.

The conservative backlash enabled Alabama's George Wallace to attract a national following. "A bearded professor . . . thinks he knows how to settle the Vietnam War," Wallace told one audience, but he "hasn't got enough sense to park his bicycle straight." Articulating deeply held resentments against liberal government programs, ghetto rioting, and student rebellions, Wallace appealed to working people concerned about the rising crime rate and fearful of the loss of traditional values. In 1968 Wallace launched a presidential campaign through

Exhibit 11-8. Gross National Product, 1960–1968
(in rounded billions of dollars)

1960	515
1962	575
1964	650
1966	772
1968	893

Source: *Economic Report of the President* (1988).

Exhibit 11-9. Consumer Price Index, 1960–1968
(in rounded percentages)
(1967 = 100)

1960	89
1961	90
1962	91
1963	92
1964	93
1965	94
1966	97
1967	100
1968	104

Source: *Historical Statistics of the United States, Colonial Times to 1970* (1975).

Exhibit 11-10. U.S. National Defense and Veterans Outlays, 1960–1968
(in billions of dollars)

1960	47.4
1962	57.9
1964	60.5
1966	64.0
1968	88.8

Source: *Statistical Abstract of the United States* (1987).

the American Independent Party, calling for repeal of civil rights laws and for a military victory in Vietnam.

Despite Wallace's popularity among northern workers, blue-collar support of the war in 1966 appeared to be only 1 percent higher than that for the rest of the nation. The next year a national poll found 68 percent disapproval of Johnson's handling of Vietnam. At the same time, however, a majority believed that peace demonstrations constituted "acts of disloyalty against the boys fighting in Vietnam." To "hawk" and "dove" alike, the war had become a volatile political issue. Organized labor, led by AFL-CIO President George Meany, remained loyal to the Democratic Party and backed the war. In 1967 a New York City march "supporting our men in Vietnam" attracted 70,000 people. Johnson's Democratic consensus seemed to be tearing apart.

THE CHAOS OF 1968

The Vietcong's Tet Offensive of February 1968 drastically undermined support for Johnson's war policy and provoked one of the most tumultuous years in U.S. political history. As General William Westmoreland requested another 200,000 troops and mobilization of the reserves—proposals that would have added $12 billion to war costs already reaching $30 billion a year—opposition to the conflict increased. Clark Clifford, who had replaced McNamara as defense secretary, found extensive "dove" sentiment within the administration. In March 1968 antiwar Senator Eugene McCarthy of Minnesota astounded the nation by taking 42 percent of the vote in the New Hampshire Democratic primary, a serious political defeat for the president. Four days later, Senator Robert Kennedy announced his candidacy for the presidential nomination. Within a week, Johnson relieved Westmoreland of the Vietnam command and summoned a meeting of senior advisors to reassess the war effort.

The White House conference included twelve of the most prestigious members of the nation's foreign policy, business, and legal establishment. Nearly all had supported the escalation of bombing in 1967. Yet now they concluded that the present policy could not achieve its objectives without full citizen support and major budgetary sacrifices, and they warned that the war threatened the position of the U.S. dollar abroad. Johnson agonized about his response. Then, on the evening of 31 March 1968, he presented a dramatic televised speech announcing a suspension of the bombing of North Vietnam and a willingness

President Johnson listened somberly to the advice of the administration's "wise men" at a meeting in the Oval Office on 26 March 1968. Five days later, Johnson withdrew from the presidential contest.

Yoichi R. Okamoto/Lyndon B. Johnson Library

ROBERT FRANCIS KENNEDY
1925–1968

UPI/Corbis-Bettmann

Robert Kennedy's assassination signaled the end of hope in a turbulent era desperately in need of conciliation. Kennedy had served as the New Frontier's principal power broker. He was presidential campaign manager in 1960, attorney general during the stormy civil rights movement, and personal advisor on foreign policy during John F. Kennedy's presidency.

As a tough Irish American, Kennedy helped to shape counterinsurgency in Vietnam, personally supervised the CIA's covert campaigns in Cuba, and had a reputation as a cool-handed operator with a ruthless streak.

Dallas changed all that. The heir-apparent to the presidency, Bobby Kennedy began a new career in 1964 as junior senator from New York. Deeply affected by his loss, he used his prestige to push for greater commitments for those without privilege or power. He visited Cesar Chavez's striking farm workers in California, heard testimony on malnutrition in Mississippi, and held hearings on the squalor of reservation life in New Mexico. Kennedy warned in 1967 that "We cannot measure national spirit by the Dow-Jones Average, nor national achievement by the gross national product."

The senator was not among the first to question the Vietnam War. However, early in 1966 he issued a cautious call for a coalition government in Saigon. A year later he took the floor to condemn the Johnson administration's bombing: "We are all participants.... We must also feel as men the anguish of what it is we are doing." In November 1967 Kennedy delivered a spontaneous tirade on national television against U.S. slaughter of the Vietnamese. Commentators began to speculate on his availability as a presidential candidate, but Kennedy was too much of a professional to risk splitting the Democratic Party in a personal vendetta against an incumbent president. Johnson's political fall in 1968 moved the senator to action.

The eighty-five-day presidential campaign of Robert Kennedy stirred an emotional groundswell seldom seen in election politics. Kennedy's proposals for a draft lottery, corporate development of the ghettoes, and Vietnam negotiations were modest, but "Bobby" symbolized the lost idealism of the New Frontier, the flickering hope that all classes and races could share in the American Dream. He campaigned on the streets with his jacket off, tie loose, and sleeves rolled up. Excited crowds swarmed the primary trail just to touch his hand.

When Martin Luther King, Jr., was assassinated in April 1968, Kennedy went directly to a ghetto street gathering in Indianapolis and shared his own feelings of loss by quoting the Greek poet Aeschylus. A nearby graffito explained his remarkable following among African Americans: "Kennedy white but alright./ The one before, he opened the door." Yet the secret to the Kennedy campaign was the compassion he expressed toward all the nation's working people and dispossessed. Despite his stance against the war, the strict Catholic and father of ten scored heavy primary pluralities in white districts that had previously supported George Wallace.

Robert Kennedy was the only leader of his era who might have united white working people, antiwar students, and racial minorities in a coalition for change. His assassination by a Palestinian Arab incensed at the candidate's support for Israel was a harsh blow to the nation. At the Democratic Convention in Chicago delegates wept and sang the "Battle Hymn of the Republic" in his memory. ■

to negotiate with the Vietcong National Liberation Front. In a surprising post-script, he also announced his withdrawal from the presidential election.

Four days later, on the day North Vietnam agreed to peace talks, a self-proclaimed racist named James Earl Ray assassinated Martin Luther King, Jr., in Memphis, Tennessee. The murder provoked a spasm of racial violence and riots around the country. King had hoped to draw attention to the need for jobs and housing with a Poor People's March on Washington that spring, but without his presence the demonstration lost focus. Goaded by his murder, Congress at last passed the long-delayed open-housing bill, which banned discrimination in the sale and rental of about four-fifths of the nation's housing and provided more than $5 billion in mortgage and rent subsidies. Johnson's withdrawal also emboldened antiwar Democratic candidates and sparked heated campaigns by Senators McCarthy and Kennedy. The president's choice, Vice President Hubert Humphrey, remained on the sidelines, but in June Kennedy won the California primary, only to be killed minutes after his victory by Sirhan Sirhan, a Palestinian opposed to Kennedy's support for Israel. The Democratic Party foundered for want of leadership.

The assassinations of King and Kennedy underscored the political and cultural crisis. At New York's Columbia University, cooperation between black activists and SDS briefly surfaced in the spring of 1968 when the two groups separately occupied university buildings to protest campus ties to the war as

Police rioting in Chicago during the 1968 Democratic National Convention.

Exhibit 11-11. Election of 1968

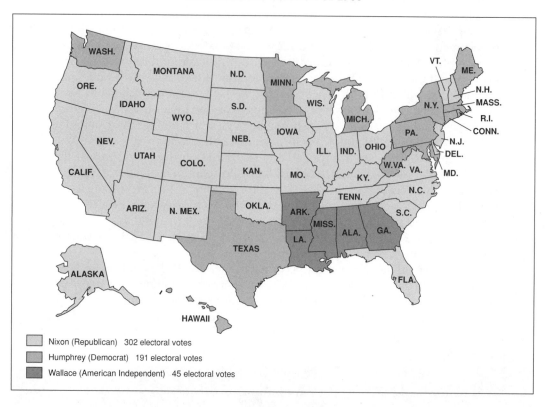

Nixon (Republican)   302 electoral votes

Humphrey (Democrat)   191 electoral votes

Wallace (American Independent)   45 electoral votes

well as planned expansion into a Harlem community park. Yet blacks called off their action just before New York City police viciously smashed the SDS occupation. The confrontation, which brought nearly 700 arrests, set the tone for clashes at every major university; more than 3,000 campus protests occurred during 1968. Public opinion polls found that most respondents blamed the demonstrators for the violence.

As the Democratic Party prepared to nominate Vice President Humphrey, several thousand peace activists and young radicals went to Chicago to demonstrate at the national convention. Refusing to allow peaceful protests, Mayor Richard Daley met the dissidents with force, permitting what a presidential commission later called a "police riot." While demonstrators chanted "the whole world is watching!" police attacked protesters and passers-by with clubs and mace. Inside the convention, party leaders defeated a dovish platform and proceeded to nominate Johnson's choice.

With the party split, Humphrey's chances seemed slim. Richard Nixon, cultivating a new image of political moderation, won the Republican nomination. Offering no concrete proposals, Nixon promised to "end the war and win the peace in the Pacific." In the face of massive civil protest and ghetto violence, the candidate vowed to "bring the American people together." His vice presidential running mate, Governor Spiro Agnew of Maryland, had achieved national prominence by attacking civil rights and antiwar demonstrators.

"Our objective in the next four years should not be to get more people on welfare rolls—we want to get more people on payrolls," said Nixon. "We're going to build this country up so that no one will dare use the U.S. flag for a doormat again." Such positions enabled the "new" Nixon to penetrate the traditional Democratic constituency of white southerners, northern Catholics and lower-middle-class Jews, and blue-collar workers—the so-called "middle Americans" who resented liberal preoccupation with racial minorities. "The working Americans have become forgotten Americans," said Nixon. In October Johnson announced a cessation of the bombing in Vietnam and narrowed Nixon's lead in the polls. Yet Humphrey could never overcome the burden of Johnson's incumbency.

Nixon won the election by less than 1 percentage point. Wallace's Independent Party, which hoped to force the election into the House of Representatives, amassed nearly 14 percent of the vote and claimed forty-five electoral votes in the Deep South. In the North Humphrey managed to preserve the New Deal coalition of labor, blacks, Jews, and Catholics. Yet Nixon and Wallace carried 57 percent of the national electorate.

The turbulence of 1968 shook the public's faith in the political system. The credibility gap and violent dissent brought widespread alienation from conventional politics. As 1968 ended, the U.S. death toll in Vietnam passed 30,000; more than 500,000 soldiers remained in that distant outpost of national aspirations. A weary nation looked to Richard Nixon to restore tranquility at home and a dignified peace abroad.

SUGGESTED READINGS

Although numerous authors have addressed the "sixties," most confuse protest movements with the larger historical context. Two good overviews are David Steigerwald, *The Sixties and the End of Modern America* (1995), and David Farber, *The Age of Great Dreams: America in the 1960s* (1994). More speculative is Edward P. Morgan, *The Sixties Experience: Hard Lessons about Modern America* (1991). One political history critical of the liberal consensus is Allen J. Matusow, *The Unraveling of America: A History of Liberalism in the 1960s* (1984).

A balanced discussion of the Kennedy administration appears in James N. Giglio, *The Presidency of John F. Kennedy* (1991), which may be supplemented with the second volume of Herbert S. Parmet's biography, *JFK: The Presidency of John F. Kennedy* (1983). More critical is Bruce Miroff, *Pragmatic Illusions: The Presidential Politics of John F. Kennedy* (1976). A briefer book is David Burner, *John F. Kennedy and a New Generation* (1988). For an insightful study of the impact of personality, see Garry Wills, *The Kennedy Imprisonment* (1982). A fine study of U.S. leadership is David Halberstam, *The Best and the Brightest* (1972). Historians' views of Kennedy are studied in Thomas Brown, *JFK: History of an Image* (1988).

Kennedy's problems with Congress are explored in Tom Wicker, *JFK and LBJ: The Influence of Personality upon Politics* (1968). The space program is well treated in Walter A. McDougall, *The Heavens and the Earth: A Political History of the Space Age* (1985); in Clayton R. Koppes, *JPL and the American Space Program: A History of the Jet Propulsion Lab* (1982); and in Tom Wolfe's journalistic *The Right Stuff*

(1979). For astronaut John Glenn, see the relevant chapters in Peter N. Carroll, *Famous In America* (1985). Problems of economic policy are described in Jim F. Heath, *John F. Kennedy and the Business Community* (1969). For the Peace Corps, see Gerard T. Rice, *The Bold Experiment: John F. Kennedy's Peace Corps* (1985). Women's politics are covered in Cynthia Harrison, *On Account of Sex: The Politics of Women's Issues, 1945–1968* (1988). For the experience of younger women, see Sara Evans, *Personal Politics: The Root of Women's Liberation in the Civil Rights Movement and the New Left* (1979). A brief survey appears in Rochelle Gatlin, *American Women Since 1945* (1987).

A thorough discussion of Kennedy's foreign policy is Michael R. Beschloss, *The Crisis Years: Kennedy and Khrushchev, 1960–1963* (1991). More critical is Richard J. Walton, *Cold War and Counterrevolution* (1972). For the Bay of Pigs, see Trumbull Higgins, *The Perfect Failure: Kennedy, Eisenhower, and the CIA at the Bay of Pigs* (1988). The Cuban missile crisis is discussed in David Detzer, *The Brink* (1979). A detailed study of the German question is Curtis Cate, *The Ides of August: The Berlin Wall Crisis, 1961* (1978). Another aspect of Kennedy policy emerges in Richard D. Mahoney, *JFK: Ordeal in Africa* (1983).

The Kennedy assassination has created a vast literature. A good starting point is Gerald L. Posner, *Case Closed: Lee Harvey Oswald and the Assassination of JFK* (1993).

For Lyndon Johnson, a good starting point is Vaughn D. Bornet, *The Presidency of Lyndon B. Johnson* (1983), and Paul Conkin, *Big Daddy From the Pedernales* (1986). A good brief biography is Bruce J. Schulman, *Lyndon B. Johnson and American Liberalism: A Brief Biography with Documents* (1995). Also insightful is Doris Kearns, *Lyndon Johnson and the American Dream* (1976). The internal workings of the administration are covered in Emmette S. Redford and Richard T. McCulley, *White House Operations: The Johnson Presidency* (1986). See also Carl Solberg's biography of the Vice President, *Hubert Humphrey* (1984).

The Republican opposition is described in Mary C. Brennan, *Turning Right in the Sixties: The Conservative Capture of the GOP* (1995), and Robert Alan Goldberg, *Barry Goldwater* (1995). The Democratic opposition is covered in William H. Chafe, *Never Stop Running: Allard Lowenstein and the Struggle to Save American Liberalism* (1993); in David Halberstam, *The Unfinished Odyssey of Robert Kennedy* (1968); in William C. Berman, *William Fulbright and the Vietnam War: The Dissent of a Political Realist* (1988); and in Lewis Chester, Geoffrey Hodgson, and Bruce Page, *An American Melodrama: The Presidential Campaign of 1968* (1969). See also Stephan Lesher, *George Wallace: American Populist* (1994), and Jody Carlson, *George C. Wallace and the Politics of Powerlessness: The Wallace Campaigns for the Presidency* (1981).

An excellent survey of the civil rights movement is Robert Weisbrot, *Freedom Bound: A History of America's Civil Rights Movement* (1990), which may be supplemented with the titles listed after the previous chapter. Kennedy's relationship to civil rights is analyzed critically in Victor S. Navasky, *Kennedy Justice* (1971), and more favorably in Carl M. Brauer, *John F. Kennedy and the Second Reconstruction* (1977). For Martin Luther King, Jr., see Stephen B. Oates, *Let the Trumpet Sound: The Life of Martin Luther King, Jr.* (1982), and David J. Garrow, *Bearing the Cross: Martin Luther King, Jr. and the Southern Christian Leadership Conference* (1986). King's organized leadership is studied in Adam Fairclough, *To Redeem the Soul of America: The Southern Christian Leadership Conference and*

Martin Luther King, Jr. (1987). The legal framework is explained in Michal R. Belknap, *Federal Law and Southern Order: Racial Violence and Constitutional Conflict in the Post-Brown South* (1987). See also Hugh Davis Graham, *The Civil Rights Era: Origins and Development of National Policy* (1990). Another facet of government policy emerges in David J. Garrow, *The FBI and Martin Luther King, Jr.* (1981). The role of student activists is presented in Clayborne Carson, *In Struggle: SNCC and the Black Awakening of the 1960s* (1981). For a biography of Malcolm X, see Bruce Perry, *Malcolm: The Life of a Man Who Changed Black America* (1991). The cultural legacy is explored in William L. Van Deburg, *New Day in Babylon: The Black Power Movement and American Culture, 1965–1975* (1992). A fine oral history is Howell Raines, *My Soul Is Rested: The Story of the Civil Rights Movement in the Deep South* (1983).

For Mexican American activism, see Carlos Munoz, Jr., *Youth, Identity, Power: The Chicano Movement* (1989), and Alfredo Mirande, *The Chicano Experience* (1985). Native American issues are summarized in James J. Rawls, *Chief Red Fox Is Dead: A History of Native Americans Since 1945* (1996), but see Vine Deloria, Jr.'s insightful *Custer Died for Your Sins: An Indian Manifesto* (1969). For immigration issues, see Reed Ueda, *Postwar Immigrant America: A Social History* (1994).

Thorough overviews of the Vietnam War include Marilyn B. Young, *The Vietnam Wars, 1945–1990* (1991), and George L. Herring, *America's Longest War: The United States and Vietnam, 1950–1975* (1986). Another excellent introduction is Neil Sheehan, *A Bright and Shining Lie: John Paul Vann and America in Vietnam* (1988). Also useful are Stanley Karnow, *Vietnam: A History* (1983), and William S. Turley, *The Second Indochina War: A Short Political and Military History* (1986). The limits of leadership are covered in Lloyd C. Gardner, *Pay Any Price: Lyndon Johnson and the Wars for Vietnam* (1995), and in Larry Berman, *Lyndon Johnson's War: The Road to Stalemate in Vietnam* (1989). A critical perspective on U.S. policy appears in George McT. Kahin, *Intervention: How America Became Involved in Vietnam* (1986). More sympathetic is R.B. Smith, *An International History of the Vietnam War: The Kennedy Strategy* (1986). Policy toward North Vietnam is described in Wallace J. Thies, *When Governments Collide: Coercion and Diplomacy in the Vietnam Conflict, 1964–1968* (1980).

The political implications of Vietnam are well treated in Herbert G. Schandler, *The Unmaking of a President: Lyndon Johnson and Vietnam* (1977); Loren Baritz, *Backfire: A History of How American Culture Led Us into Vietnam and Made Us Fight the Way We Did* (1985); and Thomas Powers, *Vietnam: The War at Home* (1984). A detailed study of the antiwar movement is Tom Wells, *The War Within: America's Battle over Vietnam* (1994). See also Charles DeBenedetti, *An American Ordeal: The Antiwar Movement of the Vietnam Era* (1990), and Todd Gitlin, *The Sixties: Years of Hope, Days of Rage* (1987). For the 1968 Democratic convention, see David Farber, *Chicago '68* (1988).

Nixon's campaign strategy is explained in Joe McGinniss, *The Selling of the President 1968* (1969). The mass media is well studied in Daniel C. Hallin, *The "Uncensored War": The Media and Vietnam* (1986); in Clarence R. Wyatt, *Paper Soldiers: The American Press and the Vietnam War* (1995); in Melvin Small, *Covering Dissent: The Media and the Anti-Vietnam War Movement* (1994); and Todd Gitlin, *The Whole World Is Watching: Mass Media in the Making & Unmaking of the New Left* (1980). The alternative media are treated in Abe Peck, *Uncovering the Sixties: The Life and Times of the Underground Press* (1985).

The youth and student movements are explored in numerous studies; particularly useful are the following: Landon Y. Jones, *Great Expectations: America and the Baby Boom Generation* (1980); Lawrence M. Baskir and William A. Strauss, *Chance and Circumstance: The Draft, the War, and the Vietnam Generation* (1978); James Miller, *"Democracy Is in the Streets": From Port Huron to the Siege of Chicago* (1987); Sherry Gershon Gottlieb, *Hell No, We Won't Go: Resisting the Draft During the Vietnam War* (1991); and Ron Kovic, *Born on the Fourth of July* (1976). A good study of cultural dissent is Jonah Raskin, *For the Hell of It: The Life and Times of Abbie Hoffman* (1997). For popular culture see David Pichaske, *A Generation in Motion: Popular Music and Culture in the Sixties* (1989), and Jon Weiner, *Come Together: John Lennon in His Time* (1991). For the roots of the counterculture, see Theodore Roszak, *The Making of the Counter Culture* (1969). Hollywood films are analyzed in Michael Ryan and Douglas Kellner, *Camera Politica: The Politics and Ideology of Contemporary Hollywood Film* (1990).

NIXON, FORD, AND CARTER: THE EMBATTLED PRESIDENCY, 1968–1980

R ichard Nixon's election revealed widespread impatience with liberal social values. Yet, while defending individual responsibility and demanding a reduction of federal power, Nixon expanded the welfare state and broadened the scope of regulatory reform. Overseas, the administration sought respect for U.S. power and military strength while it ended the nation's commitment to Vietnam and established detente with communist rivals. Despite successful foreign relations, however, Nixon's leadership unraveled because of abuse of power at home associated with the Watergate scandal. The Watergate legacy and post–Vietnam War disillusionment threatened public trust in government. As successors Gerald Ford and Jimmy Carter continued to face global instability, severe economic dislocation, and energy shortages, esteem for the presidency sank to new lows. By 1980 voters sought fresh leadership to reverse a perceived erosion of national power and declining material prospects.

NIXONIAN SOCIAL REGULATION

Addressing the racial anxieties of white southerners and northern blue-collar workers, Nixon stressed law and order, opposed school integration through busing, and cautioned against government antipoverty and antidiscrimination programs. Such rhetoric brought sharp protest from civil rights and social activists. Yet a new set of executive agencies—including the Office of Management and Budget (OMB), the Domestic Council, and the Urban Affairs Council—worked with a Democratic Congress to expand Great Society reform.

Under the leadership of Nixon advisors John Ehrlichman and Harvard sociologist Daniel Patrick Moynihan, the government indexed Social Security payments to the cost of living. Maintaining the Johnson administration's Model Cities project and the War on Poverty, the Nixon White House nearly tripled the caseload of Aid to Dependent Children (ADC), the nation's largest welfare program. Congress also quadrupled food stamp coverage when midwestern agricultural interests lobbied to extend the program to the able-bodied and to the nonelderly poor. As government spending approached one-third of the gross national product in Nixon's first term, federal income maintenance costs surpassed defense outlays for the first time in history.

The administration substantially broadened federal regulatory power. In 1970 the Occupational Safety and Health Administration (OSHA) established mandatory standards to protect employees from workplace hazards. Nixon also made environmental protection a matter of national priority. After signing the Endangered Species Act in 1969, the president endorsed the National Environmental Policy Act, which required the government to issue ecological impact statements about pending legislation or programs. The Clean Air Act of 1970 set emission standards for new cars and reorganized antipollution agencies into the Environmental Protection Agency (EPA). The new bureau outlawed the use of the pesticide DDT and implemented a congressional ban on the production and stockpiling of biological and chemical weapons.

As Nixonian regulatory agencies enforced mandates through rule-making instead of mere cease-and-desist orders, the length of the *Federal Register*'s guide

Nixon Presidential Materials Project

President Richard M. Nixon in the Oval Office with his executive staff Daniel Moynihan (left) and John Ehrlichman.

to regulations multiplied sixfold. Concerned about the cumbersome welfare bureaucracy, the White House introduced a $6 billion Family Assistance Plan in 1969 to channel money directly to the poor. The president proposed to triple the number of welfare recipients and to provide a minimum of $1,600 a year to needy families. Although Nixon labeled his plan "workfare," congressional Republicans objected to the program's loose employment requirements, whereas liberals complained of inadequate support levels. A coalition of both groups defeated the president's plan and ignored a White House request for a comprehensive health plan based on employer mandates.

Angered by noncooperation from the Democratic Congress, Nixon made major cuts in Head Start, the Job Corps, and the War on Poverty. He also introduced a "revenue sharing" plan to reduce government spending and to give the states primary responsibility for social welfare. Annual federal aid to state and local governments had tripled to $23 billion between 1960 and 1970. Despite Nixon's "new federalism," however, Washington absorbed only 5 percent of local expenditures by 1971, and federal budget deficits continued to mount.

By using social spending to sustain stability, Nixon intensified structural problems in the U.S. economy. Since the 1950s, military spending, foreign aid, and overseas investment had diverted capital from the domestic market. As the Organization of Petroleum Exporting Countries (OPEC) increased oil prices during the first half of 1971, the U.S. balance of trade deficit tripled to more than $9 billion, the most negative trade figure since the 1890s. The "dollar drain" also reduced U.S. gold reserves and further lowered currency values. When

Gas station traffic jams such as this one in Chicago were a common sight in 1974. An oil embargo by the Organization of Petroleum Exporting Countries (OPEC) and a subsequent price hike caused many service station operators to impose quotas or to close early to conserve their dwindling fuel supplies.

corporate debt and government budget deficits heightened the competition for credit, interest rates rose, and inflation set in. As a result, consumers suffered a substantial reduction in spending power and loss of savings. Moreover, the deterioration of "real" wages encouraged labor unrest and led to a wildcat strike by the Teamsters Union, to an extended walkout by automakers, and to the disruption of mail delivery by postal workers during the first strike by federal employees in U.S. history.

Nixon attempted to reduce inflation by cutting government spending and by encouraging higher interest rates, but these measures brought "stagflation"—a combination of rising prices and high unemployment rates. Consequently, the president suspended gold payments for dollars in 1971 by taking the United States off the gold standard and by ending participation in the Bretton Woods system of stabilized exchange rates that had been in effect since 1944. Establishing the first peacetime economic controls since 1947, Nixon enacted a ninety-day freeze on wages, prices, and rents and also placed a 10 percent surtax on

Exhibit 12-1. Consumer Price Index, 1968–1976
(1967 = 100)

1968	104.2
1970	116.3
1972	125.3
1974	147.4
1976	170.5

Source: *Economic Report of the President* (1988).

imports. After the president created a Cost of Living Council to monitor rising costs, however, continuing stagflation compelled him to devalue the dollar and to end the import surtax in late 1971. Such unprecedented administrative measures ironically came from a Republican chief executive who claimed to support smaller government.

AFFIRMATIVE ACTION
AND THE BURGER COURT

As federal courts integrated public schools in the South and reduced the proportion of African Americans in segregated educational facilities from 68 percent to 8 percent, Nixon professed to endorse racial equality and due process. Yet the president tailored civil rights enforcement to meet the preferences of George Wallace supporters and Republican conservatives in northern suburbs. When the Supreme Court unanimously sanctioned busing to promote school integration in 1973, the White House rejected use of "arbitrary" guidelines and proposed a congressional moratorium on the forced transfer of pupils. Federal judges responded to such pressure by slowing racial integration in the North, and the Supreme Court confined busing to districts that intentionally segregated. By 1974 half of African American pupils in northern and western states remained in schools whose racial composition was at least 95 percent black.

Nixon insisted that "black capitalism" offered the surest road to equal opportunity. As presidential advisor Daniel Moynihan called for a civil rights policy of "benign neglect," the White House denounced racial quotas as "a dangerous detour away from the traditional value of measuring a person on the basis of ability." Yet the Nixon administration quietly extended the implementation of affirmative action—the principle of compensatory racial justice—to include employment and union membership practices and thereby drove a wedge between Democratic constituencies in organized labor and in the civil rights movement. Lyndon Johnson's Department of Labor had responded to historic patterns of racial prejudice by requiring government construction contractors to end job discrimination. In 1969 the Nixon Secretary of Labor George P. Shultz introduced the "Philadelphia Plan," a program that applied a proportional system of minority hiring in federally funded construction and that required contractors to file affirmative action policies with the Labor Department's Office of Federal Contract Compliance (OFCC).

Although Labor Department officials announced that "proportional representation" was a goal, not a requirement, for contract compliance, the OFCC applied affirmative action standards to one-third of the work force. The Supreme Court upheld preferential hiring in *Griggs* v. *Duke Power Co.* (1971) by ruling that job applicants could not be subjected to aptitude tests or arbitrary job qualifications if such policies sustained discriminatory patterns. The decision paved the way for antibias suits against fire and police departments and against building contractors. Congress advanced affirmative action by expanding the enforcement powers of the Equal Employment Opportunity Commission (EEOC). By 1974 the Washington bureaucracy provided more than $240 million a year in "set-asides" for minority contractors. By then, racial and ethnic minorities constituted one-fifth of the federal government's civilian labor force.

The OFCC had not originally targeted women workers, but in 1970 Nixon approved an agency directive that ordered equal treatment of both sexes in recruitment, job opportunities, pay, and the granting of seniority rights. Congress supplemented such coverage in 1972 by prohibiting sex discrimination in all federally funded educational programs and thereby legislating equal support for men and women in collegiate athletics. The administration also continued Great Society civil rights reform by asking Congress to renew the Voting Rights Act in 1970. The new law retained federal registrars in southern states and suspended literacy tests for another five years. It also triggered the deployment of registrars anywhere in the country where more than half the minority population of voting age had failed to register.

Nixon's support for minority voting rights played a key role in the president's "southern strategy." Anticipating that newly enfranchised African Americans would vote Democratic, the president hoped to attract white southerners to the Republican fold and to end Democratic domination of the region. The White House courted white votes in the South through a series of controversial nominations to the Supreme Court. As a presidential candidate, Nixon had denounced the court for "permissiveness" for abolishing compulsory prayer in public schools and for requiring procedural protections for criminal suspects. When Chief Justice Earl Warren retired in 1969, the president chose Minnesota moderate Warren E. Burger to replace him. When a second vacancy occurred that year, the White House nominated South Carolina Judge Clement F. Haynsworth. After the Democratic Senate questioned Haynsworth about a judicial conflict of interest, however, he became the first Supreme Court nominee to be rejected in forty years.

Nixon responded to the defeat by nominating another southerner, G. Harold Carswell, a Florida appeals court judge with mediocre ratings as a jurist. Carswell failed to win Senate confirmation after revelations concerning white supremacist statements made earlier in his career. Infuriated, the president denounced "regional discrimination" and claimed that the power of appointment had been abrogated by liberals hostile to a strict interpretation of the Constitution. Yet the White House eased tensions by selecting Harry A. Blackmun, a second, well-qualified Minnesota moderate, whom the Senate easily confirmed. When two more vacancies occurred in 1971, the appointments of Lewis F. Powell, Jr., and William Rehnquist provided Nixon with the ideological consistency he desired.

Despite White House efforts to mold a conservative majority, the Burger Court had a mixed record. The high tribunal outlawed domestic national security wiretaps without judicial permission in 1972 and ruled the death penalty unconstitutional because of its cruelty and inconsistent application. In *Roe* v. *Wade* (1973), its most controversial decision, the Burger panel struck down state abortion laws as a violation of a woman's right to privacy and an intrusion into the physician-client relationship (but the justices upheld the validity of a ban on abortion during the last three months of pregnancy). In contrast, the court limited the immunity of witnesses from prosecution, permitted nonunanimous jury verdicts in state criminal cases, and compelled journalists to testify before grand juries. Moreover, in 1975 the panel reversed earlier rulings by providing a "local option" for obscenity and pornography censorship. The following year the court approved death penalty statutes if they were carefully constructed and applied without discrimination.

THE INDOCHINA STALEMATE
AND DOMESTIC TURMOIL: 1969

"Precipitate withdrawal" from Vietnam would be a "popular and easy course," Nixon told the nation in 1969, but defeat and humiliation would bring the "collapse of confidence in American leadership." The president spent his first term searching for a way to extricate the United States from Indochina without admitting defeat. Aware that massive commitments of military manpower had destroyed the Johnson presidency and had induced disaffection among soldiers and the public, the White House announced a plan to withdraw U.S. combat troops from Vietnam. Under the Nixon Doctrine of 1969 the reduction in ground forces would be offset by an escalation of the air war and by increased aid to South Vietnam. The strategy, called "Vietnamization," included a secret campaign to bomb alleged communist sanctuaries in neutral Cambodia, Vietnam's western neighbor.

By the fall of 1969, however, public frustration about Nixon's delay in ending the war was affecting the majority of U.S. citizens. Most assumed that President Johnson's decision to resort to negotiation was a major reversal of Vietnam War policy. Polls now showed that 57 percent of respondents favored a specific deadline for complete disengagement. Seizing on such disenchantment, the antiwar movement staged nationwide rallies and attracted many participants who had never before demonstrated. On 15 October 1969, Vietnam Moratorium Day, more than 200,000 protesters marched in Boston, New York, and Washington, D.C. One month later, 250,000 paraded to the Washington Monument. When 10,000 demonstrators were tear-gassed after breaking away from the rally to storm the Justice Department, Attorney General John Mitchell remarked that "it looked like the Russian Revolution."

Nixon responded to antiwar protest in a November 1969 television speech in which he declared that "we are Vietnamizing the search for peace." As the White House promised to move toward an all-volunteer army and to end the draft, the president marginalized protesters as a "vocal minority" opposed to the compliant "silent majority." With help from speech writer William Safire, Vice President Spiro Agnew dismissed demonstrators and news commentators as an "effete corps of impudent snobs who characterized themselves as intellectuals." Agnew complained that the media legitimized the antiwar message by concentrating on bad news instead of good news. He took particular aim at the "tiny enclosed fraternity of privileged men" in TV journalism who offered "instant analysis" of presidential speeches. Administration officials threatened government intervention if the "liberal" media continued to slant the news.

The difficulty of managing wartime information surfaced when newspapers published the first photographs of the recently uncovered My Lai massacre. After the Tet Offensive of 1968, 347 unarmed South Vietnamese peasants, mostly women, children, and the elderly, had been massacred by U.S. troops under the command of Lieutenant William Calley. The case epitomized the

Vice President Spiro T. Agnew executed the Nixon administration's rhetorical campaign against anti–Vietnam War dissenters and other critics.

bitter divisions caused by the Vietnam War. Whereas critics described the act as racially motivated genocide, defenders argued that villages like My Lai often were the staging grounds for vicious Vietcong attacks on U.S. troops. Others contended that the beleaguered company had cracked under the strains of a war in which commanders were expected to produce high enemy body counts. Although Nixon expressed sympathy for Calley, a military court convicted the lieutenant of murder in 1971. After the president reduced Calley's sentence, the lieutenant was paroled and received an honorable discharge in 1974.

Convinced that domestic disunity would undermine the secret talks that National Security Advisor Henry Kissinger was conducting with the Vietnamese in Paris, Nixon turned to coercive measures to maintain wartime consensus. When the liberal *New York Times* reported in 1969 that the president had ordered a highly secret bombing of Vietnam's neighbor, Cambodia, the White House ordered "national security" wiretaps of the telephone lines of four journalists and thirteen administration aides. To ascertain the source of future "leaks," Nixon officials used surplus campaign funds to hire private investigators to tap the telephone line of columnist Joseph Kraft illegally. The administration also escalated the war against dissent. Earlier, Johnson officials had failed to win the conviction of pediatrician Benjamin Spock and of Yale Chaplain William Sloane Coffin in a highly publicized case that accused the defendants of aiding draft evasion. Nixon prosecutors suffered a similar defeat when they were unable to convict Father Philip Berrigan and other Catholic radicals for participating in an alleged plot to kidnap Henry Kissinger. By using the grand jury system to collect derogatory information about antiwar radicals, however, the Justice Department hoped to discredit the dissident movement.

The most spectacular prosecution of the Vietnam War era followed the indictment of eight antiwar leaders for conspiracy to violate the antiriot provisions of the Civil Rights Act of 1968. Held responsible for the demonstrations surrounding Chicago's 1968 Democratic Convention, the defendants used the trial to showcase the revolutionary culture of the protest movement. Long-haired Yippies Jerry Rubin and Abbie Hoffman mocked government prosecutors and Judge Julius Hoffman, introduced folk songs as evidence, and provided absurdist accounts of their movement experiences. When defendant Bobby Seale objected to proceeding with the trial without his bedridden attorney, the hapless judge ordered the Black Panther gagged and chained. After five months of contentious testimony, the jury rejected nearly all of the government's arguments. Nevertheless, Judge Hoffman cited defendants and their lawyers for 175 acts of contempt. Charges against Seale, who won a separate trial, were dropped.

GLOBAL POWER: DETENTE AND THE CHILEAN COUP

Seeking to press the North Vietnamese to accept a workable settlement of the Indochinese war, Nixon turned for help to the People's Republic of China and the Soviet Union. The president's establishment of peaceful relations with the two communist powers was the most dramatic diplomatic triumph of the entire Cold War era. Washington had refused to recognize China since the Communist revolution of 1949. Cold warriors like Nixon had continually warned that recognition would lead to the abandonment of the Nationalist government on Taiwan (Formosa) and would legitimize communist subversion of established regimes. However, when the Chinese made diplomatic overtures in 1969, Nixon reasoned that he could win concessions from both Beijing and Moscow and could stabilize global tensions if he took advantage of the deepening rift between the two rivals.

Nixon and National Security Advisor Kissinger initiated the new balance of power by easing restrictions on U.S. travel to mainland China. The United States announced the end of a twenty-one-year embargo on Chinese trade in 1971. Washington also accepted the People's Republic of China's admission to the United Nations, even though China claimed the seat of the Republic of China located on Nationalist Taiwan. In 1972 Nixon formalized detente when he visited China and signed a joint communique with Chinese Premier Zhou Enlai in which the two nations pledged "peaceful mutuality." The most important part of the negotiations involved a U.S. promise to withdraw military forces from Taiwan.

President Nixon at the Great Wall of China, 1972. A dramatic reversal of policy for Nixon, detente with China remained a prime achievement of his presidency.

Nixon followed the agreement with China by traveling to Moscow for disarmament negotiations. The resulting Strategic Arms Limitation Treaty (SALT) of 1972 limited the construction of antiballistic missile sites and nuclear delivery systems. Although the accord did not rule out the development of new weapons, it represented the Cold War's first advance toward regulating existing arsenals and was the biggest step toward nuclear disarmament since the atmospheric test ban treaty of 1963. The Nixon-Brezhnev talks also produced consensus on the status quo in divided Berlin and a trade pact providing for the sale of $750 million in grain, about one-fourth of the U.S. crop, to the Soviets. When Brezhnev visited Washington in 1973, the two leaders signed additional agreements covering nuclear arms, cultural exchange, and the peaceful use of atomic energy.

Recognizing the limits of U.S. strength, Nixon and Kissinger acknowledged the Soviet Union as a superpower with virtual nuclear parity. Despite this acceptance, detente reaffirmed the president's conviction that communist negotiating partners only respected military strength and that Washington should never appear weak. The White House saw U.S. hegemony in the Western Hemisphere as a symbol of national credibility and power. Thus, the administration reacted harshly to the election of Marxist Salvador Allende as president of Chile in 1970. Although Nixon shared Kennedy's and Johnson's distrust of the CIA's intelligence capability, the president and Kissinger ordered the agency to destabilize the Allende regime. While the CIA provided $8 million to opposing poli-

Exhibit 12-2. U.S. National Defense and Veterans Outlays, 1968–1976 (in billions of dollars)

1968	88.8
1970	90.4
1972	89.9
1974	92.7
1976	108.0

Source: *Statistical Abstract of the United States* (1987).

Exhibit 12-3. U.S. National Defense as a Percentage of Total Federal Outlays, 1968–1976

1968	46.0
1970	41.8
1972	34.3
1974	29.5
1976	24.1

Source: *Statistical Abstract of the United States* (1987).

ticians, friendly media, and anticommunist unions, the U.S. government and private lending agencies refused to provide credit to Chile, thereby creating severe economic shortages and political chaos. Allende was assassinated in a bloody 1973 coup by Chilean military leaders, who executed thousands of dissidents and abolished democracy.

THE CAMBODIAN INCURSION AND KENT STATE

By the spring of 1970 Nixon had withdrawn 110,000 troops from Southeast Asia and had announced that "Vietnamization" would allow the South Vietnamese to assume the burden of fighting. To protect withdrawing U.S. forces, to defend Saigon, and to enhance his bargaining position with the North Vietnamese, however, the president decided to expand the war to include Cambodia. On 30 April 1970 Nixon went on television to tell a stunned nation that 25,000 U.S. and South Vietnamese troops had entered Cambodia in an "incursion" designed to "shorten the war." He described the operation's purpose as "cleaning out major North Vietnamese and Vietcong occupied territories" and destroying the "main headquarters for the entire Communist military operation in South Vietnam." The president also hoped to bolster the anticommunist military regime that recently had taken control of the Cambodian capital. Proclaiming that the United States could not act "like a pitiful, helpless giant," Nixon protested that he would rather be a one-term president than allow the nation to become a "second-rate power."

The Cambodian invasion brought new life to the antiwar movement. As student protests spread, Nixon dismissed activists as "bums," while Governor

Exhibit 12-4. The Thrust into Cambodia, 1970

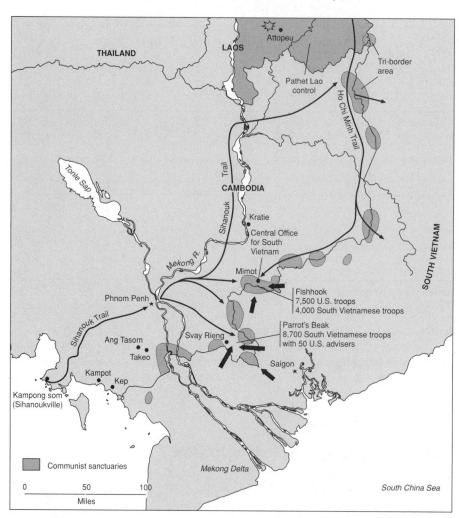

James Rhodes ordered the National Guard to police several Ohio campuses. At Kent State, rioting dissidents trashed the town business district and burned the university's Reserve Officers' Training Corps (ROTC) building. The next day, 4 May 1970, campus demonstrators failed to respond to an order to disperse during a noon rally and threw rocks and bottles at guardsmen deploying tear gas. Finding themselves surrounded, several of the tense troops wheeled around and fired into the crowd. Their actions wounded nine and killed four, including two students leaving class. The Kent State deaths electrified a nation already shocked by news of the Cambodian invasion. University presidents had warned Nixon that peace could not be restored on campuses without ending the war, but Vice President Agnew attributed the violence to "elitist" permissiveness toward "psychotic and criminal elements . . . traitors and thieves and perverts . . . in our midst."

In the most extensive student unrest in U.S. history, post–Kent State strikes closed 350 universities and colleges and mobilized millions of demonstrators,

A victim lies in the road after being shot by the National Guard during an anti–Vietnam War protest at Kent State University, Ohio.

many first-time protesters. At Mississippi's Jackson State, two more students were killed when state police responded to antiwar activism at the predominantly African American college by firing on a dormitory. Shortly thereafter, New York City construction workers assaulted several college students participating in a nonviolent antiwar demonstration on Wall Street. After receiving praise from the White House, construction and longshore unions mobilized thousands of supporters in a "Victory in Vietnam" parade down New York City's Broadway. Later that summer, the National Chicano Moratorium organized a peaceful march of 20,000 protesters in Los Angeles to emphasize that Mexican Americans accounted for nearly one-fifth of the Vietnam War casualties from the Southwest. At an ensuing street festival, county deputies made mass arrests that resulted in the killing of Chicano journalist Ruben Salazar.

Conflict over the war revealed society's profound class divisions. Until the inauguration of the draft lottery system in 1969, predominantly middle-class college students benefited from military deferments. In contrast, limited educational and job opportunities pushed poor and working-class men into military service: only 20 percent of the 3 million who served in Vietnam came from middle- or upper-class families. Polls of white northern workers revealed that nearly half supported the immediate withdrawal of troops by 1970. Yet fully half of those favoring disengagement were hostile to antiwar activism. The peace movement depicted ordinary soldiers as pawns of higher-ups. Moreover, the most effective draft evaders often were inner-city blacks who ignored Selective Service requirements. Nevertheless, many citizens viewed attacks on the armed services and on the war as extensions of class privilege legitimizing escape from military duty.

Nixon's bond with workers reflected a clever understanding of class resentment. Yet the president withdrew U.S. troops from Cambodia two months after their arrival. Aware of the military's failure to uncover communist installations and sensitive to growing antiwar sentiment, Congress set a summer deadline on the Cambodian deployment, the first such limit imposed on the commander-in-chief during the Indochinese conflict. As the administration mounted "protective-reaction" air strikes to increase the pressure on North Vietnam in the fall of 1970, the Pentagon continued to withdraw ground forces. As draft quotas and U.S. casualties declined, the press curtailed coverage of the war. Yet Nixon purposely drew attention to antiwar demonstrators as he campaigned for Republicans in the 1970 congressional elections.

RADICAL ACTIVISM AND THE WAR ON DISSENT

Most antiwar demonstrators remained committed to the countercultural values of the Johnson years. In the summer of 1969 400,000 people gathered at "Woodstock," a Bethel, New York, rock festival celebrating love, community, and peace. As the most heralded rock musicians of the era performed, crowds shared marijuana and enjoyed nudity. Woodstock's citizens proclaimed the rise of a "new generation" and the coming of a spiritually advanced "Age of Aquarius." Yet such idealism could not obscure creeping commercialism. As rock music developed into a $1 billion industry, the youth market embraced blue jeans, waterbeds, granola, "hip" cosmetics and hair accessories, and Hollywood movies like *Easy Rider* (1969) and *Woodstock* (1970). A growing illegal trade in drugs ranging from organic substances like marijuana and peyote extract to synthetic tranquilizers, amphetamines, LSD, and heroin threatened minds and bodies and tore at the fabric of the counterculture. Three rock superstars—Jimi Hendrix, Janis Joplin, and Jim Morrison—died from heavy drug abuse in 1969.

Drugs stimulated the spread of violence. Just months after Woodstock, four people died at a free Rolling Stones concert at the Altamont Speedway near Oakland, California. One African American man was stabbed to death at the event by members of the Hell's Angels motorcycle gang assigned to provide security. The counterculture's image suffered further when a self-styled "family" of hippie revolutionaries led by ex-convict Charles Manson ritualistically murdered seven wealthy Hollywood Hills residents, including pregnant movie star Sharon Tate, in 1969. The grisly details of the atrocity, which mixed sex, drugs, and political violence, brought massive media coverage and long prison sentences for Manson and his followers.

Violence also penetrated an antiwar movement frustrated about the persistence of the Vietnam conflict and government repression. After the Columbia University takeover in 1968, Students for a Democratic Society organizers formed the "Weathermen" and went underground to escape the police. Fashioning themselves as a revolutionary vanguard allied with anticolonial third-world Marxists, the New Left attacked the United States as racist and imperialist. "American radicals are perhaps the first radicals anywhere who have sought to make a revolution in a country which they hate," African American playwright Julius Lester observed in 1970. Intent on "bringing the war home" through symbolic assaults on power and privilege, secret affinity groups bombed at least fourteen government and military installations between 1969 and 1974. Three members of the Weathermen lost their lives in a 1970 explosion in a Greenwich Village townhouse used to assemble bombs. Later that year a bomb planted at a mathematics research facility at the University of Wisconsin killed a graduate student.

While young radicals romanticized the Vietcong and mocked traditional morality, activists and police engaged in violent confrontations. In Santa Barbara, California, street people reacted to police monitoring of drug traffic by rioting and burning down a branch of the Bank of America. When campus officials at the University of California at Berkeley directed police to erect barbed wire to stop use of university property for a "people's park," thousands of local residents engaged in angry protests that resulted in the killing of one demonstrator and in one hundred civilian injuries. The conflict climaxed when police helicopters tear-gassed most of the city of Berkeley. Similar tensions accompanied strikes and building seizures at San Francisco State and Cornell University, where African American students demanded black studies programs and more black faculty. Native American activists occupied San Francisco Bay's Alcatraz Island, the site of a former federal prison, for eighteen months and insisted that the government permit them to establish a cultural center there.

As the FBI continued to organize raids against the Black Panthers, African American women like Elaine Brown and Erika Huggins assumed control of the beleaguered party, and organizing spread to the nation's prisons. Several bloody confrontations in California led to the shooting death in 1970 of prisoner George Jackson, an author and Panther. The following year, New York Governor Nelson Rockefeller ordered state troopers to storm Attica prison, where 1,000 white, Puerto Rican, and black inmates had rebelled against degrading conditions by taking over the facility. The confrontation resulted in the killing of thirty-three prisoners and ten guards held as hostages. Meanwhile, juries in unrelated cases in New York and New Haven failed to convict Panther defendants of conspiracy and murder charges.

Pointing to increased militancy among dissidents, Nixon officials pressed for a more formal program of domestic intelligence. After the Kent State killings, presidential aide Tom Huston proposed an interagency intelligence unit composed of the FBI, CIA, National Security Agency, and Pentagon intelligence groups that would conduct illegal burglaries, wiretappings, mail openings, solicitation of campus informants, and interceptions of international communications. After the Huston plan had been approved by the president and had been implemented for five days, however, J. Edgar Hoover squelched the plan because it threatened FBI control of domestic security and might be disclosed publicly. Yet government agencies continued to use secret and illegal methods to monitor and disrupt domestic dissenters. For example, the Internal Revenue Service used tax audits to harass individuals and organizations with "extremist views and philosophies." Moreover, in late 1970 the White House created an Intelligence Evaluations Committee to coordinate the surveillance of radicals.

THE TORTURED ROAD
OUT OF VIETNAM

As Nixon sought a position of strength from which to negotiate with North Vietnam, he announced in early 1971 that U.S. and South Vietnamese troops

DANIEL ELLSBERG
1931–

When Daniel Ellsberg was arrested in 1985 for blockading a CIA office to protest U.S. policy in Nicaragua, he added one more chapter to a public career immersed in the contradictions of the Cold War. Born in Chicago during the Depression and raised in Detroit, Ellsberg attended an exclusive preparatory school on full scholarship before getting an economics degree from Harvard. Yet he abandoned the academic life in 1954 by volunteering for the Marines and by becoming an infantry sharpshooter. Two years later Ellsberg resumed his studies at Harvard and Cambridge. His Ph.D. thesis in economics focused on strategic military planning.

A tall, lean man with a sharp-featured, narrow face, Ellsberg embraced the Cold War as an advisor to Senator John Kennedy on foreign policy. In 1959 he signed on with the Rand Corporation, a California consultant to the Defense Department, as a strategic analyst whose speciality was nuclear warfare.

UPI/Corbis-Bettmann

By 1964 the effusive Ellsberg had become convinced that the future of democracy hinged on the war in Vietnam. First he served as special international security aide to the assistant secretary of defense. Still not satisfied, Ellsberg volunteered to become State Department liaison with the counterinsurgency effort in the Vietnamese countryside. By 1967 he was special assistant to the deputy ambassador.

With a Boy Scout's enthusiasm for containing communist aggression and preventing World War III, Ellsberg often donned military gear to accompany counterinsurgency teams on "clearing operations" in Vietnam. Yet by 1966 he began to note the failure of pacification campaigns, the rising number of civilian casualties, widespread corruption in the South Vietnamese government and military, and repeated reports of the torture of Vietcong prisoners. Ellsberg informed Defense Secretary McNamara that, although the war

had invaded Laos, where the CIA had organized covert bombing campaigns against communist insurgents since the 1960s. The new escalation inspired spring marches of hundreds of thousands of protesters, including 2,000 members of Vietnam Veterans Against the War (VVAW), who threw their military decorations on the capitol steps. In May 1971 30,000 activists reacted to the Laos deployment by blocking Washington traffic. Monitored by a unit jointly commanded by the CIA and local police, 12,000 dissidents were swept off the streets in the largest mass arrest in U.S. history. Such police activity involved widespread suspension of legal procedures, however, and federal courts later awarded the victims modest damages.

The Nixon administration faced another public relations challenge in June 1971 when *The New York Times* began to publish the secret Pentagon Papers. A history of the Vietnam War commissioned by former Defense Secretary Robert McNamara, the papers illustrated the continuity of government duplicity during the Kennedy and Johnson administrations. Fearing that future leaks might threaten Soviet and Chinese confidence in U.S. ability to conduct secret negotiations, the administration sought a court order to stop publication of the papers,

was stalemated, its level of violence continued to increase and that official reporting was not telling decision makers what they needed to know. On leaving Saigon in 1967 he proposed a high-level study of U.S. policy in Vietnam. When McNamara later ordered such an assessment, Ellsberg had returned to Rand and became one of thirty-six researchers to work on the project.

The Pentagon study convinced Ellsberg that the war stemmed from a sordid history of U.S. aggression perpetuated by several presidents. Each had chosen stalemate as a substitute for failure. Seeing no justification for U.S. policy and feeling guilty about his complicity in the pacification program, in 1969 Ellsberg made copies of the secret study report, soon to be known as the Pentagon Papers, and resigned from Rand the next year. Once he became convinced that the Nixon administration was about to repeat the mistakes and deceptions of its predecessors, he released portions of the Pentagon Papers to *The New York Times* in 1971.

The first installment of the classified study revealed that, while moving toward war, the Johnson administration had misled Americans by publicly stating that peace was its goal. After a temporary injunction halted further publication of the Pentagon Papers in the *Times*, the Supreme Court overruled any prior restraint on publication. Meanwhile, Ellsberg was indicted for conspiracy, theft, and violation of espionage laws. He responded by pointing to the "Vietnamization" of the United States. To discredit the disaffected strategist, the White House assigned his case to a newly formed Special Investigations Unit. Memorandums concerning its covert operations were later destroyed by Nixon counsel John Dean during the early Watergate coverup. In September 1971 the "plumbers" broke into the Los Angeles office of Ellsberg's psychiatrist. The resulting government misconduct resulted in dismissal of all charges against the man who had leaked the Pentagon Papers.

Once Ellsberg had undermined the presidential mystique, he threw himself into the 1970s antiwar movement with the brilliant intensity that marked his military research. He attended peace conferences, testified before congressional committees, and appeared at the trials of draft resisters. A leading advocate of nuclear disarmament, Daniel Ellsberg questioned why a rational foreign policy could not be just and humane and still serve the national interest. ■

but the Supreme Court ruled that the government had no grounds for preemptive censorship.

Dissatisfied with the court's finding, the White House ordered a Special Investigations Unit (the "plumbers") to investigate Daniel Ellsberg, a former Defense Department planner who had confessed to releasing the Pentagon Papers to expose government lying and to help end the Vietnam War. After the Justice Department indicted Ellsberg and cohort Anthony Russo for espionage and conspiracy, the plumbers burglarized the office of Ellsberg's psychiatrist to gain medical information on the defendant. When the government refused to produce wiretap logs containing conversations involving Ellsberg and Russo, prosecutors were compelled to drop all charges against them.

As South Vietnamese troops retreated from the northern provinces in 1972, North Vietnamese regulars entered the central highlands. Faced with the failure of Vietnamization, Nixon announced the mining of North Vietnam's ports. Three months after his triumphant visit to China, the president described government leaders in Hanoi as "international outlaws" and ordered the bombing of railroad lines leading to the People's Republic of China. He also instructed

U.S. Secretary of State Henry Kissinger conducts negotiations with the North Vietnamese shortly before the two sides signed a peace treaty early in 1973.

the U.S. Air Force to hit industrial targets in the North and sent B-52 bombers to attack the Vietnamese dike system. As the U.S. presidential election approached, however, Henry Kissinger and North Vietnamese negotiators secretly agreed to a military cease-fire. Under Soviet influence, Hanoi decided to postpone its political ambitions in the South while keeping its military units in the region. In turn, the Nixon administration agreed to stop bombing the North. Yet the White House allowed the South Vietnamese to veto the truce, and Kissinger abruptly announced the suspension of negotiations and the resumption of the air war.

REELECTION LANDSLIDE AND THE VIETNAM ACCORDS

As the Democratic Party became a vehicle for antiwar criticism, demands for social justice by racial minorities, and countercultural aspirations, South Dakota Senator George McGovern won the right to challenge Richard Nixon for the presidency. Under the "McGovern rules," instituted after 1968, Democratic convention delegates and nominees were chosen in open primaries, not by party bosses. The new procedures required proportional representation of women and racial minorities: The percentage of female delegates jumped from 10 to

Nicholas Sapieha/Stock, Boston

George McGovern on the campaign trail in 1972.

40 percent between 1968 and 1972. Because upper-middle-class citizens more frequently participated in primaries than working-class voters did, the McGovern system favored consideration of the cultural issues endorsed by the more affluent. As a result, delegates openly debated abortion rights, the legalization of marijuana, and gay liberation. More than one hundred convention participants publicly acknowledged their homosexuality in 1972.

A World War II bomber pilot and Great Plains populist, McGovern called for a "politics of conscience" embracing tax reform and a shift from defense spending to an investment in meeting social needs. Citing Nixon's ties to big business, he castigated the Nixon administration as "the most corrupt in history." Yet the Democratic candidate stumbled when a carelessly presented plan for a guaranteed national income conveyed confusion about economics. A second blow came when newspaper reports indicated that vice presidential nominee Thomas Eagleton had been hospitalized several times for depression. McGovern first gave Senator Eagleton a "1,000 percent" public endorsement, then asked for his resignation, and thereby conveyed indecisiveness and hypocrisy.

McGovern hoped to take advantage of the Twenty-sixth Amendment, which in 1971 awarded the vote to eighteen-year-olds. Despite these hopes, George Wallace attracted the greatest support from young voters and won Democratic primary victories in Florida, Michigan, and Maryland before being paralyzed by an assassin's bullet in May 1972. Campaigning against busing and the "suffocating bureaucracy in Washington," Wallace complained that too much attention was being paid to "the noisemakers, to the exotic." Indeed, many Democrats associated the McGovern campaign with draft card burning, campus confrontations, street riots, and disrespect for national values. Acknowledging such disaffection, Nixon penned a White House memorandum describing the "gut" issues of the campaign: crime, busing, drugs, welfare, and inflation. Deriding the capture of the Democratic Party by a radical clique, the president rejected "the policies of those who whine and whimper about our frustrations and call on us to turn inward."

Nixon's campaign followed the strategies of Kevin Phillips's *The Emerging Republican Majority* (1969), which sought to refashion the New Deal electoral coalition by recruiting Wallace voters, white southerners, urban supporters in the Southwest, working-class Catholics, suburbanites, and rural people. These voters had not benefited from the costly welfare programs established in the 1960s and clung to traditional moral and social values. The president also pointed to Kissinger's negotiations to end the Vietnam War. The results produced a Republican landslide: Nixon received 61 percent of the popular vote. Nearly equaling Johnson's rout of 1964, the president carried the entire Electoral College except for Massachusetts and the District of Columbia. Whereas McGovern received only 29 percent of the vote in the South, Nixon became the first Republican in the twentieth century to win most of the ballots of white Catholic and working-class voters. Significantly, the president took nearly 80 percent of the Wallace vote and thereby signaled an end to Franklin Roosevelt's Democratic coalition of the 1930s.

After his enthusiastic reelection, Nixon continued to press the North Vietnamese. In the "Christmas Bombing" of 1972, one of the most intensive air attacks in military history, B-52s targeted populated areas and destroyed a children's hospital at Bach Mai. Despite complaints from congressional critics that Nixon and Kissinger were conducting war "by temper tantrum," the attack supported the administration's repeated contention that brute force would push Hanoi toward peace. The president also hoped to create fears of U.S. retaliation should North Vietnam overwhelm the South. By the end of the year Nixon had dropped nearly 4 million tons of bombs on Indochina. This amount was twice the tonnage ordered by Johnson and was 1.5 times the total tonnage deployed by all armies in World War II.

Having demonstrated U.S. military firepower, Nixon announced in January 1973 that Kissinger had brokered an agreement that would "end the war and bring peace with honor." The Paris Peace Accord provided for the withdrawal from the south of 25,000 remaining U.S. troops in exchange for North Vietnam's repatriation of 587 U.S. prisoners of war. Under the terms of the treaty, Washington recognized the Vietnamese National Liberation Front (Vietcong) and resolved the nineteen-year controversy over the two Vietnams by declaring that the seventeenth parallel was a provisional boundary instead of a political or territorial line. U.S. military involvement in Vietnam ended in March 1973 with the withdrawal of the last combat troops and a televised homecoming by U.S. prisoners of war. Although Kissinger and his Vietnamese counterpart shared the 1973 Nobel Peace Prize, the terms of the accord hardly varied from those of the November 1972 agreement and virtually were identical to the ones Nixon had opposed in 1968.

WATERGATE

Nixon's second term was dominated by Watergate, a series of scandals arising from the president's obsession with winning a reelection landslide. As early as 1969 White House officials had ordered "national security" investigators to conduct surveillance of Senator Edward M. Kennedy, a potential Democratic candidate for the presidency. Kennedy had delayed reporting a late-night accident in which he had driven his car off a coastal bridge and had drowned Mary Jo Kopechne, a former campaign aide. Nixon officials organized the Committee to Re-Elect the President (CREEP) in 1971. The panel created 400 "dummy" corporations to channel secret contributions and collected $55 million from corporate donors seeking preferential treatment. CREEP also used "dirty tricks" such as signing the names of Democratic candidates to false and misleading literature to defeat strong contenders like Maine Senator Edmund Muskie.

Seeking information on Democratic National Chairman Lawrence O'Brien, CREEP Director John Mitchell approved covert entry into Democratic headquarters at Washington's Watergate complex in June 1972. When an electronic listening device malfunctioned, five CREEP operatives returned for a second entry and were arrested. Although Nixon press secretary Ron Ziegler dismissed the crime as a "third-rate burglary," money and an address book notation linked the team to White House "plumbers" (covert operatives) G. Gordon Liddy and E. Howard Hunt. CREEP and White House aides began an immediate cover-up, destroyed revealing campaign records, lied to the FBI and to the grand jury, removed incriminating evidence from a White House safe, and pressured law enforcement agencies for "cooperation." Although the disclosure would not be made for two years, Nixon initiated the Watergate cover-up by personally ordering aides to request that the CIA stop the FBI from tracing the source of Watergate funds.

By the time the trial of the Watergate burglars opened in early 1973, two of the men had received promises of executive clemency in return for continued silence. In March White House counselor John Dean brought new demands to Nixon at an Oval Office meeting in which he warned of a "cancer on the presidency" and estimated that eventual hush money payments could reach $1 million. The next day Nixon ordered Mitchell to continue the cover-up. Despite these precautions, news reports soon linked top White House and campaign aides to the Watergate affair. Attempting to place responsibility on Dean, Nixon fired the White House counsel and asked for the resignation of his key assistants, John Ehrlichman and H.R. Haldeman. The president also acceded to the appointment of a special Watergate prosecutor.

As a Senate Select Committee chaired by Democrat Sam Ervin began dramatic televised hearings on the scandal in May 1973, Dean testified about the president's knowledge of the cover-up. He also produced evidence of the plumbers unit, the illegal Huston plan, and an administration "enemies list" submitted to the Internal Revenue Service (IRS) for possible audits. Even more astounding, White House aide Alexander Butterfield revealed that Nixon had installed secret tape-recording devices in the Oval Office. Although Nixon's attorneys claimed that executive privilege and the separation of powers gave him the right to preserve the confidentiality of conversations with ad-

Former White House Counsel John Dean offered detailed testimony about presidential conversations before the Senate Select Committee on Watergate, 1973.

visors, in October 1973 a federal court ordered him to turn over nine tapes to the courts.

When Special Prosecutor Archibald Cox refused White House demands to stop subpoenas and cited the president's "noncompliance" with court orders, Nixon stunned the nation by ordering Attorney General Elliot Richardson to fire Cox and to abolish the special prosecutor's office. Richardson refused and resigned in protest. When Deputy Attorney General William Ruckelshaus objected to the presidential order, Nixon fired him and secured the compliance of Solicitor General Robert F. Bork. After a "fire storm" of protest over the "Saturday Night Massacre," however, the president relinquished the tapes and appointed a new special prosecutor, Leon Jaworski, a prominent Houston attorney. Yet three of the subpoenaed tapes were missing, and evidence revealed that extensive blank spots on the others had been caused by manual erasures.

By the fall of 1973 both the president and Vice President Agnew faced income tax problems. Agnew had been under investigation for participation in a kickback scheme with Maryland contractors. In October the vice president pleaded "no contest" to tax evasion and resigned. Adhering to the succession provisions of the Twenty-fifth Amendment, ratified in 1967, Nixon nominated House Republican leader Gerald R. Ford for the vice presidency, and Congress quickly confirmed his nomination. When the IRS announced that it was reexamining Nixon's tax deductions for the donation of his vice presidential papers, he assured a televised meeting of newspaper editors that "I'm not a crook." The agency subsequently reported that the president owed $450,000 in back taxes and penalties.

President Nixon (right) chose House Minority Leader Gerald Ford to succeed Vice President Agnew in 1973. Less than one year later, Nixon himself resigned.

THE EMBATTLED PRESIDENCY

Settlement of the Vietnam War dramatically reduced social protest. Yet in the fall of 1972 the American Indian Movement (AIM) mounted a "Trail of Broken Treaties" march to Washington and took over the Bureau of Indian Affairs (BIA). Although the native population had doubled to nearly 1 million since 1945, native average income remained less than that of African Americans. Seeking to revive historical traditions of worship, dance, poetry, and healing, activists created urban cultural centers and pressed for university Native American studies programs. In the spring of 1973 AIM focused attention on the Pine Ridge reservation in South Dakota, where Sioux dissidents had asked for help in protesting tribal corruption and federal collusion. Seizing the village of Wounded Knee and taking hostages, hundreds of AIM activists confronted federal marshals in a series of fierce clashes. U.S. officials ended the siege after seventy-one days, but they refused to reopen disputed treaty talks. A federal court dismissed charges against AIM leaders Russell Means and Dennis Banks in 1974.

Weakened by Watergate, Nixon found the implementation of his foreign policy constrained. As draft legislation expired in mid-1973, the army adopted voluntary recruitment for the first time since 1948. Moreover, the president was forced to submit to a congressionally imposed deadline of August 1973 for funding remaining combat activities in Indochina. The compromise finally

JOHN SIRICA
1904–

AP/Wide World Photos

Beneath the dark judicial robes of John Sirica sat the oldest son of a poor Italian immigrant barber. Although in 1973 he was chief judge of the federal district court in Washington, D.C., John Sirica never forgot his humble beginnings. "I came up rough-and-tough," he liked to say. "If it had not been for the Republican Party, I might never have done much better than my father." Standing before him were four members of the Spanish-speaking Cuban exile community of Miami who were on trial for their participation in the Watergate break-in. They triggered an instinctive sympathy. If it had not been for the Republican Party, the judge suspected, they might not be in his courtroom either.

Sirica had barely worked his way through law school. Poorly educated and unsuccessful as a lawyer, he managed to get a job as an assistant government attorney in the Hoover administration. With the arrival of the New Deal, he returned to an unprofitable private practice but served as chief counsel for a congressional committee investigating corruption in the Federal Communications Commission in 1944. To his annoyance, Democratic politicians squashed the case.

After the war, Sirica strengthened his position in Republican circles by campaigning actively for Eisenhower. He was also a close friend of Senator Joseph McCarthy. In recognition of Sirica's political loyalty, Eisenhower appointed Sirica to the federal court in 1957. The judge soon gained a reputation for brusqueness and impatience with abstruse legal argument. The severity of his sentences earned him the nickname "Maximum John," but many of his decisions were overturned on appeal.

ended the bombing of Cambodia, one of Nixon's most fiercely protected projects. Congress also overrode a presidential veto to pass the War Powers Act of 1973. The landmark legislation required the chief executive to inform Congress within forty-eight hours of the deployment of overseas military forces and established a sixty-day limit on the commitment of troops without congressional consent. Although no president has ever acknowledged the constitutionality of the statute, the War Powers Act provided the most important limitation on executive military initiative since 1951.

Nixon's ability to assert U.S. power also was challenged in a new Middle East war. Just as Watergate revelations climaxed in the fall of 1973, Egyptian and Syrian troops crossed into the Sinai peninsula and Golan Heights, territories Israel had seized in the 1967 war. As the Soviet Union airlifted supplies to Egypt, the United States responded by providing military equipment for the Israelis. In response, Arab oil producers ended the sale of petroleum products to nations friendly to Israel. After the United Nations brokered a cease-fire, the Soviets threatened to move troops to the Middle East to supervise the truce. Nixon immediately placed U.S. forces on worldwide alert, and Moscow agreed to the creation of a U.N. peacekeeping force. Kissinger then resumed diplomatic relations that had been broken off with Egypt since 1967 and used "shuttle diplomacy" to arrange for U.N. buffer units to monitor the fragile cease-fire.

By 1973 Sirica's seniority made him chief judge of the Washington, D.C., district court. As a loyal Republican, he felt a special obligation to ensure a fair trial for the seven men accused of breaking into Democratic Party headquarters at the Watergate complex in June 1972. For Sirica, the defendants could be divided into two social classes: E. Howard Hunt, James McCord, and G. Gordon Liddy— all privileged associates of the Nixon administration; and four Cuban exiles who apparently did their dirty work. When, to establish a conspiracy of silence, they all pleaded guilty, Sirica replied: "I don't think we should sit up here like nincompoops." Exercising his authority as a federal judge, he interrupted the courtroom examinations to ask specific questions about payments and uncovered additional incriminating evidence. After a jury convicted the burglars, Sirica delayed sentencing to pressure the defendants to talk. To his delight, McCord broke his silence under pressure, and Sirica eventually presided over the trials of many high-level coconspirators.

Meanwhile, congressional investigators had issued a subpoena for tape-recorded evidence to President Richard Nixon, but the White House had rejected the request on grounds of "executive privilege." The constitutional dispute came to Sirica's docket. "Beyond all the legal debate, one question kept nagging at me," he recalled. "If Nixon himself were not involved why would he stand on such an abstract principle . . . when by voluntarily turning over the tapes he could prove himself innocent and put the Watergate case behind him?" Sirica ordered the release of the subpoenaed material.

Nixon's compliance merely intensified the judge's outrage because, while listening to presidential tapes, he discovered that the man he had supported in 1972 was vulgar, devious, and dishonest. On the day before his seventieth birthday, in his last act as chief judge, Sirica ordered the release of grand jury files to the House of Representatives, which was debating Nixon's impeachment. This material contained explosive and incriminating evidence that forced Nixon to resign the presidency in August 1974. "I was often described as an 'obscure federal judge' and that was true," Sirica observed, "but I was not a damn fool." ■

Despite Kissinger's triumphs, the Arab oil embargo dramatized U.S. dependence on foreign energy sources and intensified chronic inflation. Fearing recession, Nixon had relaxed wage and price guidelines in 1973. When the sale of 8.5 million tons of grain to the Soviet Union led to a 20 percent increase in retail food prices, however, the president imposed a second freeze and raised the dollar price of gold another 10 percent. After failing to lower inflation and to reduce the trade deficit, Nixon conceded defeat in 1974 and allowed price controls to expire. However, the OPEC boycott quadrupled the price of crude oil and dramatically inflated the cost of petroleum products like gasoline, diesel fuel, heating oil, plastics, fertilizers, and synthetic fibers. The Agricultural and Consumer Protection Act of 1973 had sought to protect farmers by replacing New Deal acreage restrictions and price supports with government payments when market prices fell below established levels. Yet such provisions failed to protect growers when annual inflation rates soared to a twenty-five-year high of 12 percent in 1974.

Although it contained only 6 percent of the world's population, the United States consumed 30 percent of global energy production—more than 16 million barrels of oil a day. Nearly 40 percent of this amount came from overseas. Congress reacted to the oil embargo in late 1973 by authorizing construction of a controversial pipeline across Alaska. As dwindling supplies doubled gas

Activists associated with the American Indian Movement (AIM) patrolled the road to Wounded Knee, South Dakota. The village was seized in 1973 in protest against government collusion with corrupt tribal leaders.

prices, produced endless lines at gas pumps, and generated public criticism of energy hoarding by industry in 1974, the White House rejected plans to ration oil or tax oil company profits. Instead, Nixon replaced the Energy Policy Office created in 1973 with a Federal Energy Administration mandated to develop nuclear reactors and coal-burning facilities. After launching what he termed "Project Independence," the president also ordered government thermostats to be lowered to sixty-eight degrees Fahrenheit, cut official air travel by 10 percent, requested the relaxation of environmental regulations affecting energy consumption, and reduced the speed limit on interstate freeways to fifty-five miles per hour.

NIXON'S FALL AND THE FORD YEARS

Richard Nixon's presidency never survived the energy crisis. In March 1974 a grand jury indicted former White House aides Haldeman, Ehrlichman, Mitchell, and four others for perjury and hush-money payments and named the president himself as an unindicted coconspirator. Four months later, Ehrlichman and former aide Charles Colson were convicted of ordering the burglary of Ellsberg's medical records. This verdict was supported by a federal court ruling that a president has no constitutional right to authorize a break-in, even if he were targeting foreign intelligence operatives or threats to national secu-

Chief Justice Warren Burger administered the oath of office to Gerald Ford, thirty-eighth president of the United States, 9 August 1974.

rity. The House of Representatives voted 406–4 to investigate whether sufficient grounds existed for Nixon's impeachment, and the Burger Court unanimously ruled that the president had to surrender all subpoenaed tapes. "When the claim of privilege is based only on a generalized interest in confidentiality," ruled the court, "it cannot prevail over the fundamental demands of due process." The House Judiciary Committee now voted three bills of impeachment against Nixon and charged him with obstruction of justice, abuse of power, and unconstitutional defiance of its subpoenas.

The "smoking gun" of Watergate emerged when subpoenaed tapes revealed that the president had played a key role in the early cover-up. As a result, on 9 August 1974 Richard Nixon became the first chief executive in U.S. history to resign from office. "Our long national nightmare is over," newly inaugurated President Ford told the nation. "Our constitution works. Our great republic is a government of laws and not of men." The first White House occupant not elected as either president or vice president, Ford faced a nation whose faith in leaders had been shaken by Vietnam and Watergate. Public opinion was stunned, therefore, by the announcement that the president was pardoning Nixon "for all offenses against the United States." In personal testimony before Congress, Ford insisted there had been "no deal," that he had granted the pardon to remove the disruptive Watergate issue from the national spotlight. The president also offered "clemency" to Vietnam-era draft law violators and deserters, but only 6 percent of the 350,000 eligible applied.

Ford chose former New York Governor Nelson D. Rockefeller as his vice president, although the Empire State billionaire faced hostile questions about loans and gifts to state officials and his financing of a vicious biography of a former opponent. Sensitivity to political ethics also resulted in passage of the Campaign Finance Law of 1974. Although the Supreme Court later invalidated the act's spending limits, the law established check-offs on federal income tax returns to finance elections and created strict disclosure requirements for campaign contributions. Two years later, Congress restricted the proliferation of political action committees. Meanwhile, lawmakers updated the Freedom of Information Act of 1966 by setting deadlines for government response to citizen requests for documents.

After Henry Kissinger assumed the dual role of national security advisor and secretary of state, Ford pursued Nixonian detente. Late in 1974 the president went to Vladivostok to discuss arms limitations with the Soviet Union and agreed to an accord setting negotiating guidelines. At Helsinki in 1975 Ford and Soviet leader Leonid I. Brezhnev joined European leaders in signing a declaration that sought permanent peace in Europe by recognizing the territorial boundaries that emerged after World War II. The agreement also called for regional cooperation and respect for human rights such as freedom of travel. As Cold War tensions eased, Kissinger sought stability in the strategically important Middle East by pushing Israel and Egypt to accept an interim peace pact. Despite the achievement, however, U.S. diplomacy suffered when Israel was targeted by a 1975 U.N. General Assembly resolution that defined Zionism "as a form of racism."

The Ford administration faced a Congress that sought to regain the initiative in formulating foreign policy. Criticizing the Helsinki Accords for implicitly recognizing communist annexations and satellite regimes in eastern Europe, congressional leaders denied the Soviets most-favored-nation trade status until Moscow relaxed emigration restrictions on Jews and other dissenters. The legislators also sought to control the CIA in 1974 by passing the Hughes-Ryan Amendment, which required the president to report covert actions to Congress "in a timely fashion" and to certify that they served the national interest. The administration soon faced a test case in East Africa's Angola, where it opposed a nationalist movement supported by the Soviets and Cubans. Ford authorized $53 million for a covert operation in the Angolan civil war, but Iowa Democrat Dick Clark waged a successful crusade to cut off this aid in 1976. Congressional distrust of the CIA intensified when a select committee led by Senator Frank Church exposed agency involvement in foreign assassination plots and other covert actions.

Congress also defeated administration pleas for increased South Vietnamese military aid. Without such support, the Saigon government could not stop communist advances. On 30 April 1975, one day after military helicopters evacuated 1,000 citizens from the U.S. embassy, North Vietnamese troops marched into Saigon and renamed it Ho Chi Minh City. A symbol of the limits of U.S. power in an age of emerging nationalism and bipolar parity, the war in Southeast Asia brought the deaths of 1.5 million Vietnamese and left 10 million homeless. More than 56,000 members of the U.S. armed forces died in Vietnam, more than 300,000 were wounded, and the conflict's financial cost surpassed $150 billion. Although the United States rescued 120,000 Vietnamese refugees as hostilities ended, the humiliating defeat was an incalculable blow to U.S. national cohesion and pride.

Exhibit 12-5. U.S. Government Spending as a Percentage of Gross National Product, 1969–1976

1969	30.5
1976	33.9

Source: *Historical Statistics of the United States, Colonial Times to 1970* (1975).
   Economic Report of the President (1977).

Two weeks before the fall of Saigon, Khmer Rouge rebels had taken control of the Cambodian capital while the U.S.-supported government fled. In May 1975 a patrol boat under orders from the revolutionary regime seized the U.S. merchant ship *Mayaguez* and its crew of thirty-nine. Just as the vessel was being released, Ford ordered aerial bombing and a coastal island assault. Fifteen marines were killed in the ensuing combat, and twenty-three others died in a helicopter crash. Yet the Ford administration used the confrontation to suggest that the United States had resumed world leadership after the Vietnam War.

At home, inflation and unemployment continued to plague an economy suffering from international competition, sagging growth and profits, and high social welfare costs. As the era of post–World War II prosperity drew to a close in 1974, Congress passed the first housing bill since 1968, appropriated nearly $4 billion for public schools, revived the war on poverty, raised the minimum wage, and provided $12 billion for a six-year mass transit project. Seeking to close the gap between government spending and income, Ford introduced a Whip Inflation Now (WIN) program that included a 5 percent surcharge on earnings by corporations and middle-income families. Congress rejected the tax and overrode the president's veto of a bill to extend educational benefits to Vietnam veterans. Exasperated, Ford incorporated the antiinflation campaign in the 1974 congressional race. Watergate, the Nixon pardon, and 7 percent unemployment worked against the Republicans and provided the Democrats with a two-thirds majority in the House and with added strength in the Senate.

After the election, Ford agreed to the Comprehensive Employment and Training Act (CETA), a program that provided temporary jobs in state and local governments. Targeting skilled whites instead of low-skilled, unemployed nonwhites, CETA became the administration's most important antirecession weapon. The Democrats sought to stimulate recovery in 1975 by raising Social Security stipends and by extending unemployment benefits in nine states. Congress also agreed to an $18 billion individual tax cut and to lower business taxes, although it ended oil depletion allowance write-offs for large energy corporations and curbed investment-related tax shelters. In another compromise, the president signed an energy bill that maintained oil price controls but provided for gradual price increases. In addition, President Ford and Congress agreed to a $2.3 billion loan to a welfare-burdened and financially hard-pressed New York City.

JIMMY CARTER: THE ENERGY CRISIS AND "MALAISE"

Ford escaped injury when two female assailants, Lynette ("Squeaky") Fromme and Sara Jane Moore, botched separate assassination attempts in September

Promising to restore public trust in government after the Vietnam War and Watergate, newcomer Jimmy Carter refashioned the Democratic Party's electoral coalition in 1976.

1975. Despite a positive relationship with the public, however, the president faced conservative opposition from former California Governor Ronald Reagan, who came close to winning the 1976 Republican nomination. Ford and running mate Senator Robert Dole of Kansas campaigned against excessive federal spending. Yet they faced a formidable Democratic opponent in former Georgia Governor James ("Jimmy") Earl Carter, Jr., a virtual unknown. As chair of the Democratic campaign committee, Carter had helped the party to dominate the congressional elections of 1974. Yet, except for his service in the navy, the Georgia politician had never worked for the federal government.

Carter played up his outsider status by attacking a "confused and overlapping and wasteful federal bureaucracy" and called for tax reform, a national health program, and a comprehensive energy policy. Although supported by African American leaders such as Atlanta's Andrew Young, the candidate sought to capture the votes of white southerners who had deserted the Democrats in the previous two presidential elections. Indeed, the Georgian's credentials as a "born-again" Christian helped to defeat George Wallace in the southern primaries. Yet Carter also took pride in his experience as a nuclear

Exhibit 12-6. Election of 1976

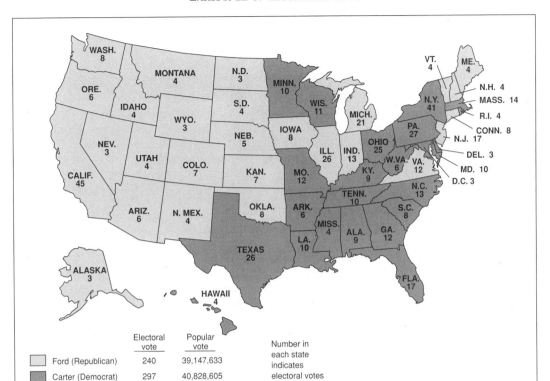

		Electoral vote	Popular vote	
	Ford (Republican)	240	39,147,633	Number in each state indicates electoral votes
	Carter (Democrat)	297	40,828,605	

engineer and member of the Trilateral Commission, an international symposium of corporate-minded leaders who engaged in long-run economic and social planning. Defeating a wide range of candidates in the early primaries, Carter easily won the Democratic nomination. To bring geographic and ideological unity to the ticket, the nominee chose Senator Walter F. Mondale, a Minnesota liberal, as his running mate.

Proclaiming "a time of healing," Carter addressed public bitterness over Vietnam and Watergate by making personal trust a key campaign issue. "We want to have faith again. We want to be proud again," he declared. The candidate also expressed populist anger toward elites. "It's time for the people to run the government," he stated softly, "and not the other way around." When Carter accused Ford of trying to "hide in the Rose Garden" of the White House, the president agreed to hold three televised debates, the first such exercise since 1960. The exposure quickly transformed the challenger into a viable candidate.

By receiving a majority of the white male vote, Ford swept the West and carried three key midwestern states. Democrats rebuilt the New Deal coalition by winning overwhelmingly among northeastern union workers, African Americans, and middle-class liberals. Because of strong support from black and white evangelicals, Carter captured all southern states except Virginia: 90 percent of the candidate's national plurality came from the South. Winning by a margin of 2 percent of the popular vote, Carter edged past Ford in a 297–240 victory in the Electoral College, and the election resulted in the closest finish

REV. ANDREW YOUNG
1932–

Stock, Boston

Andrew Young often recalled an old slavery proverb: "The Lord can make a way out of no way." The son of an African American dentist who raised his family in a racially integrated neighborhood of New Orleans, Young graduated from Howard University and received a divinity degree from the Hartford Theological Seminary in 1955. He presided over small Congregational churches in Georgia and Alabama in the late 1950s and led early voter registration drives. Appointed assistant director of the National Council of Churches in 1959, Young channeled funds into the burgeoning civil rights movement.

Joining the Southern Christian Leadership Conference (SCLC) in Atlanta in the early 1960s, Young pursued voter registration, became a trusted aide to Martin Luther King, Jr., and rose in the organizational hierarchy to become a reliable and pragmatic leader. In 1972 he became the first Georgia African American to be elected to the House of Representatives in more than one hundred years. Four years later Young supported Jimmy Carter for president because the former Georgia governor had compiled an excellent civil rights record and had a positive working relationship with black leaders.

Carter and Young believed that the nonwhite poor of the third world shared the universal human rights aspirations of the Judeo-Christian faith. Seeking to fashion a foreign policy that fused U.S. ideals and interests, the president chose civil rights activist and former minister Young as his U.N. spokesperson. Young enhanced Washington's global

since 1916. Despite the tightness of the race and the candidates' sole reliance on public campaign financing for the first time in U.S. history, voter participation remained less than 55 percent.

As Carter assumed the presidency, he faced continuing economic stagnation worsened by inflation, federal budget deficits, and increased national debt. Pressed by organized labor to respond to the recession, Congress passed a $4 billion emergency public works program in 1977. Carter also signed the Humphrey-Hawkins Act of 1978, which set a ceiling on inflation but sought to reduce unemployment by making the federal government the employer of last resort. The president also approved a generous price-support system for farmers suffering from commodity surpluses. Yet Republicans embraced proposals advanced by Senator William Roth and Representative Jack Kemp that called for a 30 percent reduction in federal income taxes and for government spending cuts. Responding to demands for fiscal restraint in 1979, Carter encouraged the Federal Reserve Board to raise interest rates, established voluntary guidelines for wage and price increases, and promised future tax relief.

Despite the Carter administration's attempts to control spending, spiraling energy costs continued to fuel inflation. Soon after taking office, Carter went on television to depict the emergency as the "moral equivalent of war." Pleading for the conservation of electricity and fuel, the president called for limits on oil imports and for subsidies to develop alternative energy. He also proposed a tax

image by denouncing white minority rule in South Africa and Rhodesia. Yet the administration soon discovered the difficulty of applying evangelical principles to foreign policy.

As Carter brokered peace talks between Israel and Egypt at Camp David, Jewish leaders criticized the president for inadequate support of Israeli and Jewish interests. Relations with the Jewish community deteriorated in 1979 when the president's brother hosted a Libyan business delegation and blamed criticism of the meeting on the "Jewish media." Slow to distance himself from such remarks, Carter courted further trouble by comparing the zeal of the guerrilla Palestine Liberation Organization (PLO) to that of the nonviolent U.S. civil rights movement. Two weeks later, in his role as U.N. Security Council president, Ambassador Young discussed the timing of a PLO resolution with the organization's U.N. representative, a Columbia University professor.

Young believed he had taken a "risk for peace" by encouraging the PLO to recognize the state of Israel. In spite of this effort, he was forced to resign because he misled Secretary of State Cyrus Vance about engaging in a meeting that violated U.S. policy. Portrayed as a conservative by civil rights activists and as a moderate by Congress, he now attracted criticism as a radical.

Rebounding from the setback, Young won Atlanta mayoralty elections in 1982 and 1986. A visionary who saw himself as a realistic innovator, he responded to the city's shrinking tax base and rising unemployment rate by soliciting business investment. Yet Young suffered another disappointment in 1990 when he lost the primary for the Democratic nomination for governor of Georgia. He later reentered public life as the prime mover in the campaign to attract the Summer Olympics of 1996 to Atlanta.

In the dedication address opening the games, the minister, social activist, peacemaker, politician, and business leader reaffirmed the themes of spiritual renewal that permeated his entire public career. Few actors on the national stage have matched the persistence, versatility, and spiritual depth of Rev. Andrew Young. ■

on excessive energy consumption and a contingency plan for gas rationing. In 1979 the crisis deepened when the Organization of Petroleum Exporting Countries (OPEC) hiked oil prices by 50 percent. After convening a domestic summit, Carter returned to television to depict the nation's inability to deal with its problems as a national "crisis of confidence" and "malaise." Outlining a ten-year, $140 billion energy program, the president faced congressional opposition from those who wanted to cut consumption by deregulating prices. The stalemate was resolved in 1980 when Carter accepted gradual deregulation of domestic energy prices and fewer rationing powers. Yet Congress agreed to impose a windfall profits tax and to fund a Department of Energy and a synthetic fuels program. Per capita energy use declined 20 percent between 1978 and 1981.

Exhibit 12-7. U.S. Gross National Product, 1976–1980
(in current dollars in billions)

1976	1782.8
1978	2243.7
1980	2732.0

Source: *Economic Report of the President* (1988).

Exhibit 12-8. U.S. Unemployment Rate, 1976–1980
(as a percentage of total labor force)

1976	7.5
1977	9.0
1978	6.0
1979	5.8
1980	7.0

Source: *Economic Report of the President* (1988).

Exhibit 12-9. U.S. Consumer Credit Outstanding, 1970–1980
(in rounded billions of dollars)

1970	141
1974	211
1977	279
1980	369

Source: *Economic Report of the President* (1988).

Exhibit 12-10. U.S. Federal Social Welfare Expenditures, 1976–1980
(in rounded billions of dollars)

1976	197.0
1978	239.7
1980	302.6

Source: *Statistical Abstract of the United States* (1987).

Carter had hoped to establish a consumer protection agency and a hospital cost-control plan. Although Congress defeated these proposals, the president signed laws that created the Department of Education (and thereby eliminated the Department of Health, Education, and Welfare), controlled strip mining, established a chemical contamination cleanup fund, and restricted the development of federal lands in Alaska. The White House also implemented an extensive program of government deregulation affecting the airline, railroad, trucking, communications, and banking industries. Yet the president approved a $1.5 billion loan to Chrysler, the nation's tenth-largest corporation, when the automaker faced bankruptcy in 1980. Pressed by advocates of tax relief, Carter agreed to a $28 billion cut in taxation, although he postponed its implementation until 1981.

Unable to protect Democratic constituencies from rising oil prices and the structural problems of the 1970s economy, the Carter administration watched helplessly as "stagflation" worsened. Annual inflation reached 13.5 percent for 1980 (the highest level since 1947), and the prime lending rate exceeded 22 percent. As loan rates surpassed the limits of potential home and car purchasers, economic stagnation pushed unemployment to more than 7 percent. Meanwhile, budget deficits approached $60 billion and forced government to borrow. When foreign investors sold off depreciated dollars, the crisis worsened.

Carter's unfamiliarity with Washington compounded the political difficulties of his presidency. Billing himself as an outsider, the Georgian chose advisors who lacked experience in congressional dealings and who could not win confidence on Capitol Hill. Carter attributed his legislative failures to narrow economic interests and single-issue lobbyists. Yet he often failed to follow up on visionary televised appeals by engaging in the detailed political negotiations expected by leaders of Congress. As the president's approval ratings fell from a high of 75 percent upon taking office to less than 25 percent, the public increasingly viewed their leader as hesitant, evasive, and removed from their problems.

SUPERPOWER LIMITS AND THE HOSTAGE CRISIS

Having promised to cut defense spending and to take a fresh approach to foreign policy, Carter canceled production of the B-1 bomber, which air force leaders wanted as a replacement for the aging B-52. The president proclaimed that the United States was at last free "of the inordinate fear of communism . . . the fear that led to the moral poverty of Vietnam." Carter also deferred development of the neutron bomb and proposed to withdraw ground troops from South Korea. Building on the foundations laid by Nixon and Ford, the president stabilized relations with the Soviet Union by signing a second Strategic Arms Limitation Treaty (SALT II) in 1979. The new accord set limits on the number of long-range missiles, bombers, and nuclear warheads that could be held by the superpowers. Such cooperation reflected an easing of Cold War tensions in Europe, where West Germany had opened diplomatic and trade relations with the Soviet bloc. Washington also exchanged ambassadors with China and agreed to sever diplomatic ties with Taiwan.

The search for political stability in the oil-rich Middle East and the chance to exert global leadership led the White House to promote a peace agreement between Egypt and Israel. After a dramatic visit to Jerusalem by Egypt's Anwar Sadat in 1977, Carter brought the Egyptian leader and Israeli Prime Minister Menachem Begin to Maryland's Camp David for a summit meeting. When further negotiations stalled two years later, the president flew to the Middle East to continue low-key diplomacy. Egypt and Israel finally signed a historic peace treaty in Washington in 1979. Yet Palestinian Arabs living in Israeli-occupied territories were not part of the accord and remained the most important stumbling block to regional peace. Carter had greater success in linking foreign policy to the aspirations of third-world people. Stressing the importance of human rights in his global strategy, he became the first president to visit black Africa. Andrew Young, the administration's African American ambassador to the United Nations, denounced apartheid in South Africa and defended the president's refusal to recognize the white minority government of Rhodesia (now Zimbabwe) until blacks were given political rights.

Carter also continued Nixon's and Ford's negotiations to return the Panama Canal to Panama by 2000. Despite strong opposition by Republican conservatives

Exhibit 12-11. The Middle East

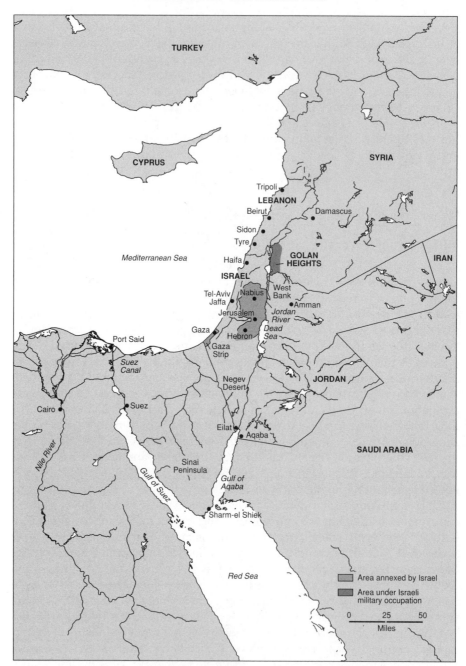

and a lengthy Senate debate, the president signed the Panama Canal treaty in 1978, although the United States reserved the right to intervene to preserve the Canal Zone's neutrality. By awarding Panama $1 billion and by negotiating the canal's sovereignty, the Carter administration removed the most obvious symbol of U.S. military aggression in the hemisphere. Congress also approved $75 million in emergency aid for Nicaragua when a 1979 revolution by Sandi-

Courtesy Jimmy Carter Library

In a substantial triumph for Carter, Israeli Prime Minister Begin and Egyptian President Sadat prepare to exchange "land for peace" at Camp David, Maryland, September 1978.

nista nationalists overthrew a brutal military dictatorship once supported by the United States.

Despite such advances, Carter was devastated when the Soviet Union sought to contain Islamic nationalism by invading neighboring Afghanistan in 1979. Placing the action in a Cold War context, the president raised alarms about "the most severe threat to world peace since the second World War." Carter promptly suspended grain sales to the Soviets and ordered a boycott of the 1980 Olympic Games in Moscow. The president also asked the Senate to shelve ratification of SALT II. Defense-minded senators from both parties had denounced the treaty for restricting development of cruise missiles while permitting the Soviets to improve "Backfire" bombers and other weapons. Yet the main objection to the accord centered on difficulties in verifying compliance, a persistent point of contention between the two superpowers. Another area of disagreement involved charges that the Soviets habitually violated the human rights of domestic dissidents.

Fearing that the Afghan operation signaled a Soviet move into Africa and the oil-rich Persian Gulf, the White House issued the Carter Doctrine of 1980. "An attempt by any outside force to gain control of the Gulf region," it proclaimed, would be regarded as an assault on U.S. "vital interests" and would be repelled "by any means necessary." To demonstrate national resolve, Carter prevailed upon Congress to resume registration for the draft. He also proposed a 25 percent growth in defense spending in the next five years. The administration already had responded to claims that the U.S. military had deteriorated after the Vietnam War by increasing annual outlays from $108 billion to $155 billion. Carter provided additional support for the military by endorsing Pentagon plans for the deployment of Trident submarines armed with nuclear missiles.

Exhibit 12-12. U.S. National Defense and Veterans Outlays, 1976–1980 (in billions of dollars)

1976	108.0
1978	123.5
1980	155.2

Source: *Statistical Abstract of the United States* (1987).

Exhibit 12-13. U.S. Research and Development, 1968–1980 (in current dollars in billions)

Year	Total	Defense and Space-related
1968	24.6	11.8
1972	28.5	11.7
1976	39.0	13.3
1980	62.6	18.2

Source: *Statistical Abstract of the United States* (1987).

U.S. citizens in Tehran are held hostage by Iranian students after the U.S. embassy was captured by Islamic revolutionary students and clergy.

Ironically, the Soviet Union did not present Carter with his most daunting foreign policy challenge. Instead, the administration floundered as a result of a crisis arising from the 1979 overthrow of Iran's pro-Western Shah Mohammed

Exhibit 12-14. Location of U.S. Hostage Rescue Effort in Iran

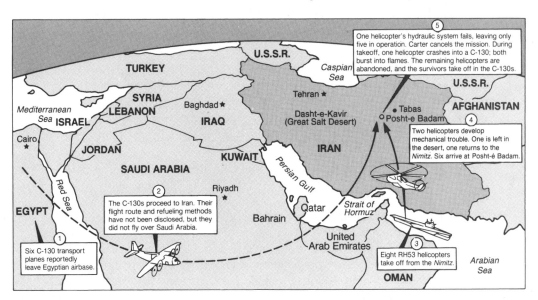

Reza Pahlavi. Led by Moslem cleric Ayatollah Ruhollah Khomeini, Shiite fundamentalists demanded a religious state that would end ties with the United States and that would purge Western secularism and materialism from their nation. The Iranians remained embittered by the CIA coup that had restored the shah in 1953. Like Nixon and Kissinger, Carter recognized Iran's importance as an oil-rich nation that bordered the Soviet Union, purchased U.S. arms, and functioned as a reliable client state. The president first supported the shah but then watched helplessly as the dictator's repressive regime crumbled. Forced into exile, the deposed leader sought medical treatment in the United States. When Kissinger and the Rockefeller family convinced Carter to grant the shah's request for U.S. entry on humanitarian grounds, outraged Iranian militants seized the U.S. embassy in Tehran, took embassy personnel hostage, and demanded repatriation of the shah and his fortune.

After the United States refused to negotiate with the militants in Tehran, the Iranian government assumed control of the hostages. Carter then froze Iranian assets in the United States, severed diplomatic relations, and ordered trade sanctions. By portraying the president as singularly committed to the release of U.S. citizens, the White House dramatized their plight. Months later, under pressure to break the deadlock, Carter ordered a military rescue, but two helicopters malfunctioned in a desert sandstorm, eight commandos were killed, and the mission was terminated. Protesting the decision to resolve the crisis through military means, Cyrus R. Vance became the first secretary of state to resign because of a disagreement about policy since William Jennings Bryan did so in 1915.

After engaging in complex negotiations with intermediaries regarding Iranian assets held in U.S. banks, Tehran agreed to release the fifty-two remaining hostages—but only after Jimmy Carter left office. Hours after the inauguration of a new president on 20 January 1981, the captives ended 444 days of incarceration. The Iranian stand-off remained a bitter symbol of the diminished global power of the United States in the post–Vietnam War era and helped to produce a major power shift in Washington.

SUGGESTED READINGS

The Nixon presidency is analyzed from a critical perspective in Stephen E. Ambrose, *Nixon: The Triumph of a Politician, 1962–1972* (1989). A more sympathetic view appears in Herbert Parmet, *Richard Nixon and His America* (1990). Other accounts include James Reichley, *Conservatives in an Age of Change: The Nixon and Ford Administrations* (1981), and John Robert Greene, *The Limits of Power: The Nixon and Ford Administrations* (1992). See also the lively Jonathan Schell, *The Time of Illusion: An Historical and Reflective Account of the Nixon Era* (1975). Provocative biographies include Garry Wills, *Nixon Agonistes: The Crisis of the Self-Made Man* (1971), and Fawn Brodie, *Richard Nixon: The Shaping of His Character* (1981). For the context of Nixon's electoral successes, see Kirkpatrick Sale, *Power Shift: The Rise of the Southern Rim and Its Challenge to the Eastern Establishment* (1975), and Kevin Phillips, *The Emerging Republican Majority* (1969). See also the early sections of William C. Berman, *America's Right Turn: From Nixon to Bush* (1994).

Civil rights advances in the Nixon years are described in Hugh Davis Graham, *The Civil Rights Era: Origins and Development of National Policy* (1990). An analysis of the president's social policies appears in the last chapter of Otis L. Graham, Jr., *Toward a Planned Society: From Roosevelt to Nixon* (1976). Nixonian economic programs are analyzed in Richard Barnet, *The Lean Years: Politics in the Age of Scarcity* (1980). For global diplomacy, see Robert S. Litwak, *Detente and the Nixon Doctrine: American Foreign Policy and the Pursuit of Stability* (1984), and Robert Hargreaves, *Superpower: A Portrait of America in the 1970s* (1973). See also Robert D. Schulzinger, *Henry Kissinger: Doctor of Diplomacy* (1989). More critical assessments appear in Mel Gurtov, *The Roots of Failure: United States Policy in the Third World* (1984), and in John Stockwell, *In Search of Enemies: A CIA Story* (1979).

Nixon's involvement in the Indochinese War can be followed in the sources listed in the relevant bibliographic segments of Chapter 11. Other important works include Harry G. Summers, Jr., *On Strategy: The Vietnam War in Context* (1981); Allan E. Goodman, *The Lost Peace: America's Search for a Negotiated Settlement of the Vietnam War* (1978); and Michael P. Sullivan, *The Vietnam War: A Study in the Making of American Policy* (1985). Norman Podhoretz, *Why We Were in Vietnam* (1982), provides a conservative defense of the Vietnam effort, and Leslie H. Gelb and Richard K. Betts, *The Irony of Vietnam: The System Worked* (1979), defends the role of national security advisors. These assessments can be compared with the highly critical Gabriel Kolko, *Anatomy of a War: Vietnam, the United States, and the Modern Historical Experience* (1986), and William Shawcross, *Sideshow: Kissinger, Nixon, and the Destruction of Cambodia* (1979). Kissinger is unflatteringly portrayed in Tad Szulc, *The Illusion of Peace: Foreign Policy in the Nixon Years* (1978), and in Seymour M. Hersh, *The Price of Power: Kissinger in the Nixon White House* (1983).

For the antiwar movement, see Christian G. Appy, *Working-Class War: American Combat Soldiers and Vietnam* (1993), and Tom Wells, *The War Within: America's*

Battle Over Vietnam (1994). A complete description of the Kent State riot appears in President's Commission on Campus Unrest, *The Kent State Tragedy: Special Report, Including Pictures* (1989). Antiwar politics and the counterculture of the 1970s are the subjects of Peter N. Carroll, *It Seemed Like Nothing Happened: The Tragedy and Promise of America in the 1970s* (1982), and of Jim Hougan, *Decadence, Radical Nostalgia, Narcissism, and Decline in the Seventies* (1975). See also Michael X. Delli Carpini, *Stability and Change in American Politics: The Coming of Age of the Generation of the 1960s* (1986). Sexual mores are described in the relevant portions of John D'Emilio and Estelle Freedman, *Intimate Matters: A History of Sexuality in America* (1988), and in Daniel Yankelovich, *The New Morality: A Profile of American Youth in the 70s* (1974).

For black power in the early 1970s, see the relevant segments of William L. Van Deburg, *New Day in Babylon: The Black Power Movement and American Culture, 1965–1975* (1992), and of Harvard Sitkoff, *The Struggle for Black Equality, 1954–1980* (1981). The civil rights struggle is surveyed in Manning Marable, *Race, Reform, and Rebellion: The Second Reconstruction in Black America, 1945–1983* (1984), and in *Black American Politics: From the Washington Marches to Jesse Jackson* (1988). For the Black Panthers, see Clayborn Carson et al., *The Black Panther Party: A Brief History with Documents* (1996). Native Americans are the focus of Philip Reno, *Mother Earth, Father Sky, and Economic Development* (1981), and of the later segments of Francis Paul Prucha, *The Great Father: The United States Government and the American Indians, Volume II* (1984). Mexican American activism is portrayed in Alfredo Mirande, *The Chicano Experience* (1985). See also the relevant portions of Ronald Takaki, *A Different Mirror: A History of Multicultural America* (1993). For feminism after 1969, see the listings in Chapter 13.

Reassessments of the New Left, counterculture, and racial justice movements appear in Todd Gitlin, *The Twilight of Common Dreams: Why America Is Wracked by Culture Wars* (1995); in E.J. Dionne, Jr., *Why Americans Hate Politics* (1991); and in sections of Michael Kazin, *The Populist Persuasion, an American History* (1995). Far more critical is Peter Collier and David J. Horowitz, *Destructive Generation: Second Thoughts About the '60s* (1989). The political consequences of radical activism and liberal social policy are graphically portrayed in Thomas Byrne Edsall with Mary D. Edsall, *Chain Reaction: The Impact of Race, Rights, and Taxes on American Politics* (1991).

Watergate is summarized in Stanley I. Kutler, *The Wars of Watergate* (1990), and in Anthony Lukas, *Nightmare: The Underside of the Nixon Years* (1976). For a view of the scandal sympathetic to Nixon, see Len Colodny and Robert Gettlin, *Silent Coup* (1992). See also Michael Schudson, *Watergate in American Memory: How We Remember, Forget, and Reconstruct the Past* (1992). For FBI abuses, see Richard Gid Powers, *Secrecy and Power: The Life of J. Edgar Hoover* (1987), and Athan G. Theoharis and John Stuart Cox, *The Boss: J. Edgar Hoover and the Great American Inquisition* (1988). The close of Nixon's public life is treated in Ambrose, *Nixon: Ruin and Recovery, 1973–1990* (1991). For Ford's presidency, see Greene, *The Limits of Power and the Presidency of Gerald R. Ford* (1995). See also James L. Sundquist, *The Decline and Resurgence of Congress* (1981), and Robert T. Hartmann, *Palace Politics: An Inside Account of the Ford Years* (1980).

Carter's rise to the Oval Office is portrayed in Patrick Anderson, *Electing Jimmy Carter: The Campaign of 1976* (1994). The Carter White House is the focus of Erwin C. Hargrove, *Jimmy Carter as President: Leadership and the Politics of the Public Good* (1988), and of Charles O. Jones, *The Trusteeship Presidency: Jimmy*

Carter and the United States Congress (1988). Assessments of Carter's presidency appear in Burton I. Kaufman, *The Presidency of James Earl Carter* (1993); in John Dumbrell, *The Carter Presidency: A Re-Evaluation* (1993); and in the last chapter of Leo P. Ribuffo, *Right Center Left: Essays in American History* (1992).

For Carter's domestic policy, see Anthony S. Campagna, *Economic Policy in the Carter Administration* (1995); Laurence E. Lynn, *The Presidency as Policymaker: Jimmy Carter and Welfare Reform* (1981); and Laurence H. Shoup, *The Carter Presidency and Beyond: Power and Politics in the 1980s* (1980). See also Haynes Johnson, *In the Absence of Power: Governing America* (1980). Pressure group politics are discussed in William F. Grover, *The President as Prisoner: A Structural Critique of the Carter and Reagan Years* (1989). Carter's 1980 defeat is analyzed by journalist Theodore H. White in the concluding segment of *America in Search of Itself: The Making of the President, 1956–1980* (1982).

Foreign relations under Carter come under scrutiny in David Skidmore, *Reversing Course: Carter's Foreign Policy, Domestic Politics, and the Failure of Reform* (1996); in Gaddis Smith, *Morality, Reason, and Power: American Diplomacy in the Carter Years* (1986); and in Timothy P. Maga, *The World of Jimmy Carter: U.S. Foreign Policy, 1977–1981* (1994). Oil diplomacy figures in portions of Daniel Yergin, *The Prize: The Epic Quest for Oil, Money, and Power* (1992), and in Michael A. Palmer, *Guardians of the Gulf: A History of America's Expanding Role in the Persian Gulf, 1933–1992* (1992).

The Apple Macintosh computer, 1984.

THE GLOBAL ECONOMY AND DOMESTIC CULTURE WARS

S haped by the global marketplace, technological innovation, and the information frontier, the late twentieth century witnessed profound developments in finance, marketing, medicine, education, and communications. Yet changes in the market and in social relations brought new dilemmas concerning the environment and social ethics. The disproportionate benefits of the new economy also heightened class and racial strife. As international trade broke down old barriers to the mobility of capital and labor, issues of ethnic and cultural diversity continued to dominate public discourse. Moreover, innovations in gender relations, sexual identities, and spiritual affinities ignited a culture war between adherents of New Age philosophy and defenders of social, religious, and nationalist traditions.

THE INTERNATIONAL MARKET AND THE INFORMATION AGE

U.S. success in the world economy stemmed from the open trading system introduced in 1947 by the General Agreement on Tariffs and Trade (GATT). After an unprecedented wave of corporate mergers in the 1960s, multinational industrial, communications, and investment corporations took advantage of reduced tariffs and fewer investment barriers to enter the global market. Participation in the world economy was promoted by bankers such as David Rockefeller, who in 1973 created the Trilateral Commission, a "think tank" of business people, planners, and politicians from western Europe, Japan, and the United States. Between 1960 and 1974 the foreign assets of U.S. banks leaped from $3 billion to $155 billion. By the 1980s U.S. investors held $1.7 trillion in overseas acquisitions, and foreign investors nearly matched that total with their U.S. investments. Free trade, integrated financial markets, and superior electronic communications enabled the United States to play a key producing and marketing role in the expanding global economy. By 1995 forty-one of the world's one hundred largest corporations were U.S.-based.

**Exhibit 13-1. U.S. Overseas Investment, 1960–1987
(in rounded dollars)**

1960	12 billion
1987	1.7 trillion

Source: *Statistical Abstract of the United States* (1996).

**Exhibit 13-2. Foreign Investment in United States, 1950–1987
(in rounded dollars)**

1950	8 billion
1987	1.5 trillion

Source: *Statistical Abstract of the United States* (1996).

Exhibit 13-3. Home Base of the One Hundred Largest Global Corporations, 1995

United States	41
Japan	37
Europe / British Commonwealth	21
Singapore	1

Source: Henry C. Dethloff, *The United States and the Global Economy Since 1945* (1997).

Although automotive and petrochemical companies benefited substantially from world trade, the global economy rested on the innovations of the information revolution after World War II. By 1980 more than two-fifths of the work force was employed in the information or "knowledge" sector, which accounted for more than one-third of the gross national product. During the 1980s, electronics firms introduced desktop computers with silicon chips to digitally process, store, and display information. Innovations such as electronic mail and the Internet communications web accelerated the pace of data transmission. As computer technology revolutionized business, government, publishing, education, retailing, and recreation, software suppliers like Microsoft offered operating systems that simplified functions such as word processing or served as guides to web sites. By 1995 the United States manufactured 60 million personal computers annually and sold more than 62 percent of these PCs abroad.

Technology also revolutionized telecommunications. During the 1960s the National Aeronautics and Space Administration (NASA) established a global communications system by deploying satellite relay stations in space. When the development of fiber-optic cables and photonic amplifiers stimulated the

Multimedia notebook computer by Digital Equipment Corporation, 1995.

— WILLIAM ("BILL") HENRY GATES III —
1955–

As a recording of the Rolling Stones blasted "Start Me Up," Microsoft chair Bill Gates unveiled Windows '95 before an audience of 2,500 journalists and computer software marketers during a 1995 event relayed by satellite from the company's Redmond, Washington, headquarters. The world's largest information provider had invested $200 million, the efforts of 500 full-time employees, and 2,000 hours of testing in a program that permits computer users to access and browse the Internet's World Wide Web. As Gates traded jokes on stage with television personality Jay Leno, business analysts anticipated that Windows '95 would earn $8 billion in the next two years.

Having set software standards for 90 percent of the world's personal computers in a $100 billion industry, Bill Gates prepared to expand Microsoft's presence in computerized banking, retailing, and telecommunications. His autobiography, *The Road Ahead* (1995), an instant best-seller, presented the blueprint for innovation on the twenty-first century's "information highway." After accumulating a personal fortune of $20 billion by 1996, Gates was the richest individual in the world and was heralded by the press as the icon of the information age. When he traveled to China, *The New York Times* estimated his influence to be greater than that of the U.S. government.

"I wrote my first software program when I was thirteen," recalled the entrepreneur. "It was for playing tic-tac-toe." When the Mother's Club of Gates's Seattle private school installed a computer terminal, the shy teenager became enamored of the "expensive, grown-up machine" that kids could control. He and childhood friend Paul Allen took entry-level software programming jobs to pay for computer play time. While attending Harvard in 1977, Gates read about a personal computer (PC) kit that featured a powerful microprocessor—a transistor chip that performed basic calculations. Gates and Allen realized that personal computers needed "software" programs to instruct them to perform complex tasks such as word processing and data retrieval. After dropping out of college, Gates joined Allen in forming Microsoft, the company that would personalize the computer revolution and become the information age's most successful enterprise.

growth of cable television in the 1980s, space satellites began transmitting TV signals worldwide. By the 1990s cable and satellite TV networks offered twenty-four-hour news, sports, music, movie, and shopping channels to more than 60 percent of U.S. households. National newspapers such as *USA Today* and *The New York Times* relied on simultaneous satellite-dispersed printing in every major city. Other applications of electronic technology included photocopying machines, mobile telephones, facsimile (fax) machines, telephone answering devices, digital time pieces, video cassette recorders, and compact disc players.

High-tech products reached consumers through new retail facilities and manufacturers' outlets in suburban shopping malls. In 1989 the largest shopping complex in the nation opened in Bloomington, Minnesota, and had more than 440 stores and restaurants. Urban strip malls, discount stores, mail-order sales, TV shopping channels, amusement "theme" parks, and credit card ser-

Microsoft's task was facilitated by corporate giant International Business Machines (IBM), which licensed Microsoft's MS-DOS software for its 1981 personal computers instead of purchasing it outright. This arrangement allowed Gates and Allen to offer software to other manufacturers, who marketed their PCs as "IBM-compatible." Yet as Microsoft sought to capture the consumer market in the 1980s, it had difficulty replacing words with pictures to signal programming commands. The company did not develop a user-friendly format until 1990, when Windows 3.0 adopted the graphic commands of Apple Computer's Macintosh. Microsoft did not achieve the full potential of Apple's "point and click" system until Windows '95 was produced.

"We're about making great software, that's our deal," explained Gates in 1996. Yet critics contended that Microsoft's market dominance resulted from monopolistic practices similar to those of nineteenth-century industrial robber barons. In 1994 the company settled a four-year government antitrust suit by agreeing to stop providing discounts to computer makers that preinstalled Microsoft software in their units. The following year Microsoft dropped a $2 billion plan to purchase a leading manufacturer of personal finance software when the Justice Department expressed concerns about maintaining competition in electronic banking and commerce. After Microsoft included software for its own Internet service in Windows '95, federal prosecutors raised additional questions. Gates

shrugged off such controversies by noting that "technological innovation by its very nature is very competitive . . . technology doesn't give anyone a lock."

Immune to external criticism, Microsoft established a distinctive, informal work climate for its 17,000 employees, who were hired on the basis of intellectual curiosity and teamwork skills instead of previous expertise. A similar disdain for traditional methods framed Gates's view of the business's future. Addressing a Las Vegas computer trade show as keynote speaker in 1994, Gates predicted that the Internet would do away with "middlemen" and "distributors" and create an "ultimate market" of "friction-free capitalism." This "world's central department store," he insisted, would include "digital wallets," videoconferencing, and global library browsing and would be a place to do business or just "hang out."

Gates announced in 1995 that every Microsoft division would refocus on products to access the Internet. In 1996 he negotiated a partnership with NBC to create a cable television news channel and web site. The following year Microsoft revealed plans to develop "Web TV"—a product that would allow consumers to receive on-line services through home television monitors and thus would erase the need for expensive computer hardware. For Gates, a multibillionaire who still used the word "cool," postindustrial capitalism offered limitless opportunity for creativity and profits. ■

vices helped to push consumer debt to more than $744 billion by 1991. Fast-food outlets provided another key to economic growth. Begun in 1954 by Ray Kroc, who at the time sold paper cups and milkshake machines, McDonald's

Exhibit 13-4. Factory Sales of U.S. Consumer Electronics and Computers, 1985–1995 (in rounded billions of dollars)

1985	22.9
1990	43.0
1995	61.7

Source: *Statistical Abstract of the United States* (1996).

Exhibit 13-5. Value of Shipments of U.S. Computers and Industrial Electronics, 1985–1994 (in rounded billions of dollars)

1985	43.9
1990	50.8
1994	63.5

Source: *Statistical Abstract of the United States* (1996).

grew into a hamburger franchising operation with nearly 10,000 worldwide outlets. The diversified fast-food industry soon filled suburban shopping strips and overseas cities with formula-produced soft drinks, pizza, fried chicken, and ice cream products.

The high-tech, global service economy dispersed population clusters and even decentralized market power and influence. As U.S. trade with Asia surpassed that of Europe in the 1980s, San Francisco became a major center of international business and global investment planning. The growth in the service sector, which accounted for nearly three-quarters of all employment by the 1990s, attracted professional and white-collar workers to the capital cities of the Midwest and to affluent western communities such as Aspen, Colorado; Jackson Hole, Wyoming; and Bellingham, Washington. Meanwhile, tourism and the retirement industry served as development magnets in the Sunbelt states of Arizona, California, Florida, and Texas, where half the nation's population growth occurred in the 1980s.

Spurred by investment from Japan and from the Middle East, U.S. financial managers prospered in the 1980s. Yet profits were sustained partially through questionable techniques such as the sale of high-risk "junk" bonds, an innovation of Wall Street broker Michael R. Milken that permitted small companies to borrow huge sums to absorb larger firms. Stocks also benefitted from leveraged buyouts, with which executives staged hostile corporate takeovers by purchasing the equity of other shareholders. Mergers and acquisitions consolidated the airlines, communications, and banking industries. Yet the resulting volatility contributed to the greatest one-day loss in stock market history in 1987 when the Dow Jones average lost nearly 23 percent of its value. The market regained its footing when the Federal Reserve poured capital into the banking system. Nevertheless, federal authorities sought to discourage further abuse by prosecuting junk bond dealer Milken for securities fraud. After Milken received a ten-year prison sentence and paid $600 million in fines in 1990, the government convicted several Wall Street brokers of insider trading and stock fraud.

Exhibit 13-6. U.S. Corporate After-Tax Profits, 1980–1994* (in rounded billions of dollars with inventory valuation and capital consumption adjustments)

1980	82.3
1985	185.7
1990	229.0
1994	331.2

Source: *Economic Report of the President* (1996).

**Exhibit 13-7. Percentage Distribution of U.S. Household
Aggregate Income, 1993**

Top 1 percent of household income receivers	20.3
Top 5 percent of household income receivers	47.0

Source: *Statistical Abstract of the United States* (1996).

The banking boom also generated economic instability. Beginning in 1980, federal deregulation phased out interest rate ceilings on savings accounts and increased federal deposit insurance to $100,000. (See Chapters 12 and 14 for more on deregulation.) Commercial banks took advantage of such freedoms by extending high-interest loans to developing nations and by engaging in risky real estate development at home. Stung by defaults and bankruptcies in both markets, 221 lending institutions failed in 1988. Meanwhile, Congress permitted savings and loans (S&Ls) to invest in the money market and to pump funds into risky commercial real estate. Compelled to offer substantial interest rates to attract capital, S&Ls accepted $370 billion in uninsured deposits between 1982 and 1987. Mismanagement and fraud led to the bankruptcy of more than 500 thrift institutions by the end of the decade.

Congress responded to the S&L crisis in 1989 with a bailout of $166 billion to cover depositor losses and with a $50 billion fund for buying and selling off failed institutions. Yet the S&L debacle eroded confidence in the government's ability to monitor financial greed and to punish those who abused investor trust. Popular Hollywood films such as *Rollover* (1981) and *Wall Street* (1987) reflected such insecurity. Federal prosecutors sought to restore public faith by bringing fraud indictments against Charles Keating, the president of a California S&L whose failure had cost taxpayers $2 billion. Yet Keating successfully appealed his conviction after a short stay in prison. Public cynicism also intensified when a 1990 U.S. Senate investigation resulted in a mere reprimand of five senators charged with exerting improper influence on Keating's behalf.

The S&L and Wall Street scandals demonstrated the relative immunity of the rich and powerful from legal and moral accountability. Public concern about economic inequity was justified by the distribution of wealth and income. Between 1979 and 1993 the median wages for the richest 5 percent of U.S. families increased 29 percent. By the early 1990s the wealthiest 1 percent of U.S. households owned 39 percent of total family wealth and nearly half of all family financial assets. Meanwhile, the wealthiest 5 percent of household incomes earned 20 percent of national income (and the richest 20 percent of households netted nearly half the nation's earnings). Chief executive officers of large corporations in the 1990s made nearly 150 times the pay of the average factory employee.

YOUNG URBAN PROFESSIONALS

The global economy and information age provided expanded opportunities for the skilled college graduates of the "baby boom" era. Clustered around Boston,

Atlanta, Washington, D.C., Minneapolis-St. Paul, San Francisco, Seattle, and other "high-tech" service centers, young, urban professionals, or "yuppies," specialized in law, marketing, computer trades, the media, health services, and government. Their intensity and informality revitalized U.S. business with team play, networking skills, and a strong entrepreneurial spirit. Urban professionals like Apple Computer cofounder Stephen Jobs saw the workplace as an arena for translating personal growth goals into practical life strategies. Attorneys in "public interest" law, for example, organized class action lawsuits against corporate polluters, cigarette companies, and employers charged with discriminatory labor policies.

By emphasizing countercultural values such as self-fulfillment and openness to change, the new professionals helped to reshape consumption patterns. "Postmodern" townhouses, condominiums, theaters, and specialty shops contributed to the "gentrification" of urban neighborhoods. Although the high rents that accompanied renovation of historical districts often displaced less affluent tenants and shopkeepers, the new middle class played an active role in neighborhood associations and campaigns to make cities safer and more livable. Improvement also took on a personal character. Instructional "workout" videos and manuals produced by actress and social activist Jane Fonda led millions in daily exercise and aerobics routines in the body-conscious 1970s and 1980s. Jogging, bicycling, body building, indoor sports, and hot tubs provided convenient outlets for professionals with limited recreational time and considerable disposable income. Such activities were supplanted in the 1990s by more "extreme" pursuits that included rollerblading, snowboarding, hang gliding, windsurfing, and bungee jumping.

Eating habits also changed. Urban professionals opted for tasty, lower-calorie, nutritional meals that did not require extensive preparation. Carry-home specialties—often reheated in microwave ovens—frequently replaced home-cooked meals. The new diet also featured natural and organic foods, frozen yogurt desserts, fresh-ground coffees, domestic wines, "light" beers, and mineral waters. A proliferation of gourmet restaurants included specialists in "California cuisine"—an aesthetically presented cookery that replaced salty and fatty foods with fresh fish, poultry, and vegetables prepared with subtle seasoning. Genetic engineering of vegetables and plants promised to enhance future food quality. Meanwhile, espresso bars, juice counters, and microbreweries served as gathering places for the young professionals of the 1990s.

New computer technologies also changed the form of visual media. Sophisticated animated films such as *Who Framed Roger Rabbit?* (1988), Disney's *The Little Mermaid* (1989), and Steven Spielberg's dinosaur saga, *Jurassic Park* (1993), appealed both to young and adult audiences. The creation of pseudodocumentaries such as *Forrest Gump* (1994), which included the faked appearance of President Kennedy, effectively blurred distinctions between fantasy and reality. Such visual techniques—which required no foreign language translations— helped Hollywood build an international market as U.S. films dominated ticket sales in countries as diverse as Japan, Brazil, and South Africa. TV commercials, instead of using real footage, manipulated graphic designs to immerse consumers in impossible but captivating situations. Meanwhile, hand-held cameras created "amateur professionalism" in pornographic and other films and helped to entice middle-class viewers into video rental stores.

Trends in popular music reflected the fragmentation of cultural identity after the early 1970s. Although country and western, gospel, soul, and rock music continued to attract loyal fans, the disco rhythms of big-city gay and black dance clubs found their way to the airwaves and recording studios. In turn, disco and mainstream rock were supplanted in the late 1970s by the more confrontive sounds of "heavy metal" and "punk" rock. After the launching in 1981 of Warner Communications's MTV (Music Television), a twenty-four-hour cable outlet originally devoted to rock videos, young consumers could sample musical styles ranging from "techno-pop," "reggae," "rap," and "hip-hop" to "grunge," "alternative rock," and "new folk." MTV even created a second channel for fans in the their thirties and forties.

Facing competition from specialized cable programming, network television struggled to attract new audiences by using fresh approaches. Widely viewed 1980s TV series—"Hill Street Blues," "Miami Vice," "St. Elsewhere," and "L.A. Law"—explored the work life of urban professionals. The trend continued in the 1990s with such popular series as "Law and Order," "NYPD Blue," "New York Undercover," and "ER." To attract the offspring of baby boomers, or "Generation X," the networks introduced blatant sexuality and "trash-talk" into daytime serials and evening shows like "Melrose Place." Tailoring comedies such as "Seinfeld," "Friends," "Politically Incorrect," and "The David Letterman Show" to the irreverent tastes of "twenty-somethings," producers presented parodies of family life like "Married with Children," "Roseanne," and the animated "The Simpsons." Commercial TV also offered confrontive "tabloid" news shows that featured sensational scandal and gossip. Yet many young consumers preferred the diversions of CD-ROMS and "virtual reality" or "surfed" the "chat rooms" and web sites of the Internet.

THE NEW AGE

Although college graduates of the 1970s and 1980s placed a higher value on career goals than their immediate predecessors did, countercultural life-styles proved to have staying power. Throughout the late 1970s, a period of increased tolerance of pornography, birth control, and abortion, public opinion polls continued to show substantial acceptance of premarital sex. Many baby boomers remained skeptical about marriage; the number of couples "living together" quintupled between 1970 and 1987, and the divorce rate leaped by 50 percent

Exhibit 13-8. U.S. Divorce Rate, 1970–1990
(per 1,000 population)

1970	3.5
1975	4.6
1980	5.2
1985	5.0
1990	4.7

Source: *Statistical Abstract of the United States* (1996).

MADONNA LOUISE VERONICA CICCONE
1958–

Agence France Presse/Corbis-Bettmann

"I was born and raised in Detroit," an unknown Madonna Ciccone scribbled in an audition statement for a New York movie producer, "where I began my career in petulance and preciousness. By the time I was in fifth grade, I knew I either wanted to be a nun or a movie star. During high school I became slightly schizophrenic as I couldn't choose between class virgin or the other kind."

Known simply as Madonna, Ciccone emerged as a cultural icon, the most financially successful female entertainer in history. One of eight children in a middle-class Catholic family, she was devastated when she was six years old by the death of her mother. In 1978 she dropped out of the University of Michigan and flew to New York with $37 in her pocket. After enrolling for classes with the third-string troupe of Martha Graham's prestigious American Dance Center, she rented a fourth-floor "walk-up" in Manhattan's East Village, worked at Dunkin' Donuts, posed in the nude for art classes, and sifted through garbage for food. After a one-year stint as a back-up vocalist and dancer for a Parisian disco act, Madonna returned to the United States and began singing with "alternative" music bands and lip-synching on the Lower Manhattan disco and "hip-hop" club circuit.

Adopting a trampy, punk look that featured rags, safety pins, and the use of underwear as outer garments, the aspiring performer set her mind on a pop music singing career. Building on personal contacts with club musicians and disk jockeys, Madonna garnered a Warner Bros. recording commitment in 1983. Her first album, the disco-oriented *Madonna*, attracted little attention until the vocalist took it upon herself to promote club exposure and air play. The collection eventually sold 9 million copies, and three of its cuts rose to the Top Ten. Madonna also benefited from the immense popularity of MTV, whose twenty-four-hour cable television programming placed her videos on "heavy" rotation. An appearance as a charming street-waif in the film *Desperately Seeking Susan* (1984) contributed to the performer's mystique.

Abandoning bracelets and crucifixes for a white silk wedding dress and for a belt buckle reading "Boy Toy," Madonna cut a new song titled "Like a Virgin" (1984), from the album of the same name. The collection, which sold 11 million copies, also featured "Material Girl," a simultaneous tribute to and parody of Marilyn Monroe. Another album, *True Blue* (1988), reached sales of 17 million and in-

**Exhibit 13-9. Annual U.S. Birth Rate, 1975–1993
(per 1,000 population)**

1975	14.6
1978	15.0
1981	15.8
1984	15.6
1987	15.7
1990	16.7
1993	15.5

Source: *Statistical Abstract of the United States* (1996).

cluded the controversial "Papa Don't Preach," a portrait of a pregnant single woman who chooses to keep her baby.

Aware of Madonna's loyal following among young women, including many African American and Hispanic fans, the Pepsi corporation agreed to sponsor a 1989 concert tour and to pay the performer $5 million for three commercials. When the video for "Like a Prayer," the title song of Madonna's new album, included footage of the singer kissing a black saint and dancing provocatively before burning crosses, the company pulled the commercial and severed its relationship with the star, although it paid her full fee. "Express Yourself," the album's second hit, told listeners never to settle for "second best"—anything less than truth and self-respect.

After an appearance in the Disney film, *Dick Tracy* (1990), Madonna embarked on "Blond Ambition," a twenty-five-city world concert tour that promoted her new album of the same name. Sold out in every venue, the tour produced a Home Box Office (HBO) television special watched by more viewers than any nonsports, pay TV event in history. Madonna used the show to highlight a production number called "Vogue," a postmodern pastiche of past movie and fashion styles that tied the performer to a historical legacy of stardom.

By 1990 Madonna's eighteen consecutive Top Five hits had earned her record companies a half-billion dollars and netted the disciplined entertainer $125 million. Yet a "horrible fear of being mediocre" continually pushed her to take risks. One result was "Justify My Love," a sexually explicit song and video banned from MTV in 1991. Another was *Truth or Dare: On the Road, Behind the Scenes, and in Bed with Madonna* (1991), a film documentary of the Blond Ambition tour produced with $4 million of the star's own funds. The following year Madonna completed an album called *Erotica*. Meanwhile, she released a $50 edition of *Sex*, a coffee-table collection of photographs and quotations depicting Madonna's sexual fantasies.

"I think I've been terribly misunderstood because sex is the subject matter I so often deal with," Madonna countered in response to widespread criticism. After becoming sole owner of her own record company in 1992, she constantly sought recognition as an artist instead of as a marketer. She took a small role in *A League of Their Own* (1992), an engaging film about women's professional baseball during World War II. However, she did not receive positive notice until she starred in *Evita* (1997), another story of female empowerment.

A strong woman who liked to taunt concert audiences with "I'm the boss around here," Madonna delivered a baby girl out of wedlock in 1996. The fulfillment from having and raising a child, she once said, would "always dwarf people recognizing you on the street." Madonna's mixture of toughness and vulnerability spoke to many women. Sampling a diversity of postures and styles, she brilliantly embodied the postmodern synthesis of high and mass culture. ■

in the 1970s and peaked at 5.2 per 1,000 by decade's end. The trend continued in the 1980s when the annual number of divorces amounted to half the annual number of marriages. As a result, second marriages and stepparenting became common, and two-income couples often divided child care and household chores. In contrast, birth rates declined to record lows and bottomed out at 1.8 children per family in 1976.

Innovations in family structure influenced the precepts and practices of organized religion. As Protestant and Jewish denominations accepted women in official capacities, some congregations addressed social concerns like racism, child abuse, and homelessness. While urban professionals encouraged the

Jewish community to debate divisive issues such as affirmative action, the religious role of homosexuals, and Israel's response to the Palestinians, activists forced Roman Catholics to address controversies involving divorce, birth control, interfaith marriage, clerical celibacy, and homosexuality.

The professional middle class also supported the growth of alternative religions. Young cultural dissidents of the 1960s and 1970s had experimented with Asian spiritual traditions such as Zen Buddhism, Tibetan Buddhism, yoga, the *I Ching*, and the martial arts. These interests led some to join sects like the Church of Scientology, the Hari Krishnas, and the Unification Church of Korea's Reverend Sun Myung Moon. Fearing a loss of personal autonomy by their children, some parents hired "deprogrammers" to reverse what they perceived as the brainwashing of members of these groups. The worst apprehensions of anticultists were confirmed in 1978 when more than 900 followers of the California-based People's Temple committed suicide in Guyana under orders from their spiritual leader, the Reverend Jim Jones. Cult experts predicted a wave of similar mass suicides as the world approached the next millennium.

Less demanding spiritual philosophies and movements also proliferated. Scientists of the 1970s and 1980s such as Fritjof Capra and David Bohm argued that the relativism of quantum physics had destroyed distinctions between spirit and matter. They received support from psychologists like Robert Ornstein and Karl Pribram, who pointed to the mind's ability to influence bodily states such as the pulse and the respiratory rate. The fusion of these ideas produced a "holistic" synthesis that united spiritual and material realities and signaled what enthusiasts considered to be the dawning of a "New Age." This synthesis facilitated the acceptance of holistic approaches involving preventive and natural medicine, balanced nutrition, acupuncture, meditation, biofeedback, hydrotherapy, and Rolfing.

Like the counterculture, the New Age appealed to the consumption habits of urban professionals. Practitioners led paid self-improvement and inspirational seminars and conducted sessions on the use of the body's "auras" and "energy fields." Others instructed clients in the more controversial techniques of "channeling," accessing past lives, healing disease by using rock crystals, and communicating with various spirits and "galactic" messengers. Actress Shirley MacLaine popularized the movement by writing several best-selling books. In the arts, harpists, flutists, pianists, and acoustic guitarists produced simple, meditative, light music for New Age record companies.

Despite frequent commercialism, the diverse New Age movement represented an attempt to overcome the rootlessness and isolation of the modern city and suburb. Like the counterculture from which it took its roots, the New Age, in its emphasis on psychic powers, illustrated a frank impatience with the rationalism of middle-class life. Moreover, the new spirituality conflicted with church doctrine because it erased distinctions between "good" and "evil" and considered all things and people divine. Although its adherents found organized religion either bland or irrelevant, they nevertheless sought answers to the problems of life. By 1987 the movement toward alternative spirituality helped explain why 20 percent of Americans between eighteen and twenty-four years of age (31 percent on the West Coast) claimed a religious belief other than Protestant, Catholic, or Jewish.

SPACE, PLANET EARTH, AND THE NATURAL ENVIRONMENT

Interest in spirituality combined with the legacy of Vietnam War–era dissent to stimulate new concern about ecological issues. The focus on planet Earth initially surfaced as a result of the U.S. space program. In 1969 the landing of astronauts Neil A. Armstrong and Col. Edwin E. Aldrin, Jr., on the Moon in the *Apollo 11* spacecraft was televised worldwide. "That's one small step for a man," said Armstrong, "one giant leap for mankind." A series of manned spaceflights resulted in linkage with a Soviet satellite in 1975. NASA used its *Skylab* space station to launch vehicles to explore the solar system and beyond. The project enabled *Pioneer 10* to become the first human-made object to leave the solar system; *Voyager 2* to fly past the planets Uranus and Neptune; and *Magellan* to map the topography of Venus, where it discovered a global warming pattern similar to Earth's. In 1990 NASA deployed the Hubble Space Telescope, which photographed portions of the Milky Way galaxy 10 million light-years away.

NASA also inaugurated a series of manned space flights. In 1986, however, an explosion killed seven *Challenger* space shuttle astronauts, including the project's first civilian, a New England schoolteacher. Despite the tragedy, shuttles continued to perform space missions such as synthesizing chemicals in a vacuum. Meanwhile, space technology fascinated moviegoers and video game players. Films such as *Star Wars* (1977) and its sequels, the *Star Trek* film series (of which the first was released in 1978), and *E.T., The Extra-Terrestrial* (1982)

NASA employees monitor a space mission at Houston's Mission Control headquarters.

Planet Earth as viewed from space. Environmental scientists of the 1970s and 1980s continually warned of the vulnerability of global life forms to ecological disaster and insisted upon the interconnectedness of all living things.

thrilled audiences with exotic creatures, cyborgs, and rapid galactic travel simulated through computer imagery.

"We all inhabit this planet. We all breathe the same air," President Kennedy had told college students in 1963. Space photographs confirmed that Earth was a small and frail island of life in an immense universe. Beginning in the 1960s, biologists such as Rachel Carson emphasized that human existence depended upon the health of the physical environment. Carson's *Silent Spring* (1962) graphically illustrated the poisonous effect of pesticides on living things, including people. "The question is whether any civilization can wage relentless war on life without destroying it," she warned. Environmentalists like Barry Commoner explained that humans live within Earth's atmosphere and must limit air pollution from manufacturing and auto exhausts. In *The Closing Circle* (1971), Commoner declared that the industrial system interferes with nature's attempts to regenerate Earth's air, water, and soil. An international study, *The Limits to Growth* (1972), concluded that economic growth threatened to exhaust the planet's resources by the end of the twentieth century.

By April 1970, when environmentalists organized university teach-ins to celebrate the first Earth Day, a national ecological movement had begun. Activists directed attention toward toxic residues from fossil fuels and petrochemical fertilizers, nonbiodegradable waste from plastics and detergents, industrial pollutants that turned rivers into fire hazards, and damage to the atmosphere's ozone layer from aerosol sprays and other chemicals. Corporate polluters and government officials responded to the environmental pressure because protesters addressed consumer values such as quality of life, personal well-being, and the creative use of leisure. Activists in the 1970s and 1980s also campaigned for lower energy rates, inexpensive and safe alternatives to electric power, and programs for recycling waste.

The central environmental debate of the 1970s and 1980s focused on nuclear power. Responding to energy needs dramatized by the Arab oil boycott of 1973–1974 (see Chapter 12), federal officials pushed nuclear energy as a stimulant to industrial development. "We can't live in a Garden of Eden and still have a technological society," Atomic Energy Commissioner Dixie Lee Ray explained in 1974. In contrast, environmentalists like E.F. Schumacher, author of *Small Is Beautiful* (1973), insisted that human survival depended on a harmonious relationship with nature and required a livable technology that uses solar, geothermal, and wind power. Other activists concentrated on the inability of the nuclear industry to manage radioactive storage facilities safely.

Antinuclear protesters at sites such as Seabrook, New Hampshire, revived civil disobedience tactics in the mid-1970s to call attention to the health, safety, and financial problems of atomic fission. A near "meltdown" of the reactor core at a nuclear facility at Three Mile Island, Pennsylvania, shifted attention in 1979 to the credibility of industry management and government regulators. "The history of the nuclear power industry," consumer advocate Ralph Nader told more than 100,000 demonstrators gathered in Washington, "is replete with cover-ups, deceptions, outright lies, error, negligence, arrogance, greed...." Public confidence slipped further when the graphite core of a reactor in the Ukraine burned for several days in 1986 and spread radioactivity across eastern Europe and Scandinavia. As evidence of the lethal effects of nuclear waste mounted, experts estimated that the cleanup costs for three U.S. government nuclear waste disposal sites would be $100 billion. The sites included eastern Washington's Hanford Nuclear Reservation, the plutonium source for the Cold War nuclear arsenal.

Threats to the environment crossed national boundaries. Scientists warned that depletion of Amazon rainforests by developers and fast-food cattle interests was dangerously lowering global atmospheric oxygen levels. In addition, sulfuric emissions from the burning of cheap coal by U.S. factories and power plants resulted in "acid rain" that was defoliating trees and contaminating lakes in Canada and the northern Midwest. Although the federal government moderated regulations to accommodate industrial interests, 1988 figures revealed that Earth's atmosphere had lost 2.3 percent of its ozone layer, an essential shield from the ultraviolet rays that cause skin cancer and a barrier to excessive heating by the sun. Under the Montreal Protocol of 1989, Washington joined seventy-nine nations in banning dangerous carbon-based chemicals and in agreeing to halve the production of ozone-depleting substances. The United States also signed a treaty limiting carbon dioxide emissions, cited by scientists as a cause of the "greenhouse effect," which may produce global warming.

Despite such efforts, the nation suffered the worst environmental disaster in its history in 1989 when the *Valdez*, an Exxon-owned oil tanker, ran aground in Prince William Sound in Alaska and spilled 11 million gallons of crude petroleum into the pristine, fish-laden waterway. After the corporation absorbed

$2.5 billion in cleanup and rehabilitation costs, Congress passed legislation requiring spillers to rectify the damages of such accidents and dedicated special oil taxes to a federal cleanup fund. The Energy Policy Act of 1992 sought to decrease U.S. dependence on petroleum by encouraging natural gas development and by promoting the use of nongasoline fuels for motor vehicles.

Environmental regulations also protected endangered species such as the northern spotted owl and the Pacific Northwest salmon. Such programs sought to preserve ecological systems such as old-growth forests while providing suitable recreation areas for hikers, campers, fishers, hunters, and outdoor enthusiasts. Despite protests from local logging communities and "wise use" advocates, nationwide conservationist sentiment enabled the federal government to limit the harvesting of timber in the national forests of the Pacific Northwest. Voter support for the environment was strong enough to produce a 1994 law by which Congress protected 8 million acres of federal wilderness and created three national parks in California.

The most terrifying aspect of the environmental crisis centered on the dangers of nuclear war. Three chilling cult movie classics, *Mad Max* (1980), *Road Warrior* (1981), and *Blade Runner* (1982), portrayed the bleak human and physical landscapes resulting from nuclear apocalypse. In 1983 astronomer Carl Sagan gave credence to such fears by warning that radioactive dust clouds from atomic war might block the sun's rays and produce a "nuclear winter" that would destroy all plant life and would condemn the human species to imminent death. That year's television special, "The Day After," graphically illustrated the potential effects of a nuclear explosion on the typical U.S. town of Lawrence, Kansas. As strategic thinkers such as Daniel Ellsberg and Robert McNamara (see Chapters 12 and 14) led campaigns for nuclear disarmament, hard rock music videos explored postapocalyptic fantasies, and computerized video games simulated the latest advances in laser weaponry and missile technology.

FEMINISM AND GENDER IDENTITY

Sexual identity emerged as a defining force in an information age that blurred traditional gender roles. The feminist revolution grew out of the 1960s notion that the "personal" was "political." Struggling against exploitation, competition, "sexism," and female passivity, 200 supporters of the Women's International Terrorist Conspiracy from Hell (WITCH) had drawn attention to radical feminism in 1968 by protesting outside the Miss America Pageant. The activists tossed "instruments of torture" such as brassieres and high-heeled shoes into a "freedom trash can." Feminists soon organized liberatory "rap groups" and "consciousness-raising" sessions to build women's collective self-esteem. Inspired by the politics of identity, Gloria Steinem launched *Ms.* magazine in 1971. Calls for the restructuring of patriarchy and capitalism appeared in provocative books such as Kate Millett's *Sexual Politics* (1969), Shulamith Firestone's *Dialectic of Sex: The Case for Feminist Revolution* (1970), and Robin Morgan's *Sisterhood Is Powerful* (1970). These works inspired scholarly research and the spread of women's studies classes and programs.

Opponents of economic discrimination against women constituted another segment of the feminist movement. Demanding that the market treat women

An abortion rights march in New York City. Such efforts became less frequent after the 1973 Supreme Court decision legalizing abortion.

equally as individuals, these activists organized groups such as the National Organization for Women (NOW), the academic Women's Equity Action League (WEAL), and the Professional Women's Caucus (PWC). Demands for economic inclusion had led to passage of the Equal Pay Act of 1963, which compensated more than 173,000 women for past discrimination. Reformers also promoted "equal pay for equal work" by lobbying cities and states to enact "comparative worth" programs. Meanwhile, groups like the National Women's Political Caucus helped to break down gender barriers to holding office. As congresswomen such as Shirley Chisholm and Bella Abzug assumed prominence in the 1970s, the number of women in state legislatures tripled, and 14,000 women won elected office. The federally funded National Women's Conference, held in Houston in 1977, wove together the various strands of the movement by endorsing government-financed day care for children, shelters for battered women, and legal protections for lesbians.

Radical and reformist feminists joined forces to endorse the equal rights amendment, which Congress approved and sent to the states for ratification in 1972. The following year, women's rights activists welcomed *Roe* v. *Wade*, the Supreme Court's landmark decision on abortion. "Pro-choice" leaders in the National Abortion Rights Action League (NARAL) insisted on women's freedom to control their bodies and to determine their destinies and social roles. Skirting such issues, the court ruled that state antiabortion laws were unconstitutional intrusions into the client-physician relationship when applied during the first three months of pregnancy. After 1973 abortion clinics and hospitals performed more than 1.5 million legal abortion procedures each year. While women's groups mobilized to defend the right of "free choice," a growing feminist health movement explored alternative methods of birthing, healing, and treatment of women's diseases such as breast cancer. In turn, "ecofeminists" combined nurturance and cooperation with holistic approaches to environmental care.

During the 1980s and 1990s women activists attacked the last legal bastions of segregation by sex. As several corporations settled class-action bias suits filed by female employees, the Supreme Court outlawed sex discrimination in private clubs and organizations. Meanwhile, federal courts ordered publicly supported schools and military academies to open their doors to women. On the religious front, women successfully pressed Protestant and Jewish denominations to ordain them as ministers and rabbis, and sexist language and imagery began to disappear from religious ritual. National politics experienced similar changes when forty-seven female candidates won election to the House of Representatives in 1992.

By 1980 women constituted the majority of university students and received ten times as many professional degrees as they had a decade earlier. Education improved women's occupational prospects. By the 1990s 58 percent of women more than sixteen years old participated in the labor force, and females held 45 percent of all jobs. Although women filled less than 7 percent of top executive positions, they constituted nearly half of all managerial and professional employees and began to build lucrative careers as entrepreneurs. As wages for skilled female labor caught up to prevailing wage rates for men, the median salary of women employees rose between 1979 and 1990, while the male median salary fell. Yet women in clerical, office, retail sales, and other low-status jobs earned only three-quarters of the male wage rate, and women continued to be overrepresented in these jobs. Detecting a "feminization" of poverty, social critics noted that households headed by women were five times more likely to be destitute than households with male breadwinners.

As women made important strides in the marketplace and public affairs, feminists continued to attack the objectification of female bodies and gender stereotyping in the mass media. After the Anita Hill controversy in 1993 (see Chapter 14), national attention focused on sexual harassment in business, government, and the military. College campuses increased awareness concerning "date rape" and other improprieties against women. As women's activists opened crisis centers, shelters, and self-defense clinics to assist victims of rape, family violence, and child abuse, feminist attorney Catherine McKinnon blamed the $4-billion-a-year pornography industry for men's crimes against women. Although McKinnon proposed legislation to treat the publication of obscene material as an attack on women's civil rights, feminist veterans like Betty Friedan opposed such solutions on First Amendment grounds.

GAY POWER AND MULTICULTURALISM

Homosexuals embraced identity politics in the gay and lesbian liberation struggle. This political movement dated to 1969, when New York City police raided the Stonewall Inn, a gay men's bar in Greenwich Village, and angry patrons fought back for the first time. Gay men and lesbian women soon announced a national gay power and civil rights movement that portrayed homosexuality as a chosen life-style instead of as a disease or criminal pastime. By 1975 the American Psychiatric Society dropped its classification of homosexuality as a mental disorder. Each year the anniversary of the Stonewall riot prompted a celebration of gay pride. Forming groups like the National Gay Task Force, homosexual activists fought for local civil rights ordinances, mounted court cases against discrimination, and organized for inclusion of gays in the military and other institutions (see Chapter 14). In 1987 more than 200,000 people marched in a gay pride demonstration in Washington, D.C.

Despite growing solidarity, the gay male population was decimated by the acquired immunodeficiency syndrome (AIDS) epidemic, first detected in 1981. Transmitted by infected blood or semen, the AIDS virus destroys the body's immune system. Initially spread through anal intercourse, the sharing of intravenous needles, or transfusions of contaminated blood, the disease took an early toll among homosexual men, drug abusers, and hemophiliacs. Within the homosexual community, gays initiated campaigns to close bathhouses, the scene of unprotected promiscuous sex, to limit sexual partners, and to promote the use of condoms, but activists accused the federal government of delaying AIDS research and condemned the media for failing to issue explicit warnings against dangerous sexual practices. By the mid-1990s more than 100,000 U.S. victims of AIDS had died, 160,000 were symptomatic, and more than a million people had tested positive for the virus that causes AIDS. Although researchers found that multiple drug therapy prolonged patient life expectancy, such treatment was extremely expensive and often not covered by medical insurance.

Gay and lesbian power provided one example of the struggle to open educational and employment opportunities and political participation to people of all backgrounds. Congress embraced this principle by passing the Americans with Disabilities Act of 1990, which forbade job discrimination against the handicapped, for whom its also provided access to public accommodations. Affirmative action was another form of inclusion. Federal law required that publicly supported agencies and institutions address sex and race discrimination by establishing minority "set-asides" in hiring or admissions. Among the leading supporters of affirmative action, colleges and universities went beyond the letter of the law to incorporate multicultural studies into curricula. Intent on creating a social climate of diversity and tolerance, some institutions enacted controversial speech codes that banned derogatory comments about race, gender, or sexual orientation.

Exhibit 13-10. Annual U.S. Deaths from AIDS

Before 1986	12,494
1989	26,355
1992	38,813
1995	31,256

Source: *Statistical Abstract of the United States* (1996).

An AIDS-awareness advertisement distributed in the late 1980s by the New York City Department of Public Health.

NATIVE PEOPLES AND
ECONOMIC REVITALIZATION

American Indians fused identity politics with new plans for economic development and control of natural resources. After 1971 the Alaska Native Land Claims Act distributed nearly $1 billion and 40 million acres to that state's indigenous people. Beginning in 1977 more than a dozen U.S. tribes filed federal lawsuits and land claims based on a 1790 statute limiting the sale of Native American holdings. In 1980 the Supreme Court upheld a $107 million award compensating the South Dakota Sioux for U.S. seizure of the Black Hills a century earlier. Three tribes in northern Maine won an $81.5 million settlement in a similar action. The U.S. Civil Rights Commission also asked the federal government to negotiate eastern Indian land disputes. Accordingly, Washington settled the long-standing claims of the Wampanoag of Massachusetts to the island of Martha's Vineyard and awarded $50 million in damages to the Catawba of South Carolina for nineteenth-century land expropriations.

During the 1980s Indian tribes obtained the right to receive federal funding on the same basis as states. Although state governments sought to subject native peoples to environmental restrictions, federal courts upheld Indian rights to fishing and other resources. Civil suits resulted in financial awards to tribes in Wisconsin and Washington state in the 1990s, and the government ceded hundreds of thousands of acres to resolve a land dispute between Arizona's Navajo and Hopi. Native economic prospects were further enhanced in 1988 by a Supreme Court decision and the Indian Gaming Reservation Act, which enabled tribes in twenty-three states to build reservation gambling casinos, the source of more than $6 billion in annual profits.

Economic vitality stimulated renewed interest in tribal traditions of spirituality, dance, drumming, and storytelling. Powwows, cleansing sweats, and vision quests counteracted historical legacies of racism by enhancing self-esteem and ethnic pride. Indian leaders also succeeded in compelling archeologists and anthropologists to turn over Native American remains for respectful treatment and reburial. The cultural renaissance found expression in the literary works of Leslie Marmon, Gerald Vizenor, and Louise Erdric. Five hundred years after Columbus first explored the New World, the U.S. Native American population surpassed 2 million. Yet poverty, unemployment, alcoholism, and suicide continued to plague young natives whose reservations and urban communities were untouched by capital investment or tourist development.

AFRICAN AMERICAN
IDENTITY POLITICS

As black Americans pursued identity politics in the civil rights and black power movements of the 1960s and 1970s, white scholars and administrators gradually incorporated African American perspectives and black studies programs into university curricula. Alex Haley's *Roots* (1976), a personal story of black genealogy, popularized African American history for a mass audience. More than 130 million viewers, or at least half the nation, watched at least one segment of the televised version of the book in 1977. African American artists considered their work an assertion of cultural independence. Race-conscious poetry emerged from literary figures such as Nikki Giovanni and Maya Angelou. Critically acclaimed black novelists included Nobel Prize winner Toni Morrison, whose *Beloved* (1987) explored psychological themes within a historical context. Alice Walker's *The Color Purple* (1982), made into a popular film four years later, portrayed a direct connection to the African legacy. Terry McMillan's *Waiting to Exhale* (1992), a humorous portrait of urban black women, also appeared in a screen version. Other significant African American novelists included Ishmael Reed, Al Young, and John Edgar Wideman.

Black creative energies had an enormous impact on the performing arts. Pulitzer Prize winning playwright August Wilson used African techniques of storytelling and ensemble performance in *Ma Rainey's Black Bottom* (1984) and *Fences* (1987). Filmmaker Spike Lee brought black themes to mainstream audiences with provocative features such as *Do the Right Thing* (1989), *Malcolm X* (1992), and *Get on the Bus* (1996). New directors like John Singleton incorporated inner-city gang life into movies such as *Boyz in the Hood* (1991). Rap music, a product of black street subculture, carved out a significant corner of the recording industry and spawned a new generation of African American producers and pop cultural icons. As black spending power reached nearly $500 billion a year, mainstream African American entertainment and sports figures such as Bill Cosby, Eddie Murphy, Michael Jackson, Whitney Houston, Michael Jordan, and Oprah Winfrey became mainstays of international television, movies, and the celebrity press. Black family life also received unprecedented attention in comedy series produced by upstart television networks like Fox.

African American consumer power was buttressed by an increasingly prosperous black middle class. By 1986 more than one-fifth of black families earned more than $35,000 a year. Government statistics revealed that 70 percent of the African American population lived above the poverty level (compared with 90 percent for whites). The annual income of black men leaped by half in the 1980s, while wage rates for African American women rose to equal those of white females. More than a million blacks were attending college by the 1980s, and African Americans constituted 18 percent of the nation's social workers and 14 percent of its educational and vocational counselors. Economic well-being translated into political power. Between 1964 and 1980 the number of elected black officials had jumped from 103 to more than 4000. In the 1980s major cities like Chicago, Philadelphia, Los Angeles, and New York chose African American mayors, and Virginia's L. Douglas Wilder became the first black governor. After the 1992 elections, thirty-eight African American members sat in the House of Representatives.

Despite such success, more than 30 percent of African Americans continued to live in poverty and to earn fewer than $10,000 a year. Teenage unemployment among blacks in decaying northern cities had skyrocketed from 10 percent in the 1950s to 40 percent in the 1960s. By 1985 jobless rates among adult black men averaged 60 percent. Although economic opportunities for affluent African Americans broadened in the 1980s, black poverty increased by 10 percent. By 1990 an African American citizen was nearly three times as likely to be without a job as was a white citizen. The inability of black men to support families led large numbers of African American women to have babies without getting married. By the mid-1980s 60 percent of black infants were born out of wedlock, and more than half of all African American children less than six years old lived

Black poverty persisted throughout the 1980s. One-third of all blacks and 45 percent of black children remained poor during this decade.

in poverty. Although blacks constituted less than 13 percent of the U.S. population, African American families constituted more than half of Aid to Families with Dependent Children recipients.

As the inner city became the warehouse for society's unwanted, poverty and hopelessness produced an urban "underclass"—a population of unemployed and untrained people who relied on hustling and crime to survive. By the early 1990s violent street gangs contracted with powerful drug syndicates to sell "crack," an inexpensive but highly addictive cocaine derivative. As gang members sought prestige and territorial sovereignty, communities across the nation were terrorized and helpless to protect themselves. Government crime statistics for the 1980s showed that 30 percent of violent assaults and 60 percent of robberies were committed by blacks. By the mid-1990s 7 percent of the nation's

Exhibit 13-11. Number of Inmates in State and Federal Prisons in the United States, 1970–1994 (in rounded figures)

1970	196,000
1975	241,000
1980	316,000
1985	481,000
1990	740,000
1994	1,000,000

Source: *Statistical Abstract of the United States* (1996).

A participant in the Los Angeles riot of 1992 voices his outrage at the acquittal of police officers who had been videotaped while brutally beating black motorist Rodney King.

African American population was behind bars, and blacks constituted more than half the U.S. prison population.

Racially motivated police abuse and oppressive social conditions produced periodic outbursts of black rioting after the mid-1970s. The most lethal race rebellion in U.S. history occurred in Los Angeles in 1992 after a white suburban jury acquitted four L.A. policemen of assault after a videotaped beating of black motorist Rodney King. Four days of violence resulted in the death of fifty people and $1 billion in property damage. Although two of the officers subsequently were convicted of violating King's federal civil rights, the Los Angeles uprising underscored the persistence of racial and ethnic tension in a city shared by whites, Latinos, Asians, and blacks. Racial antagonism resurfaced in 1995 when former athlete and media star O.J. Simpson, an African American, was acquitted of a brutal double murder when a predominantly black Los Angeles jury questioned police procedures and disbelieved the testimony of a white officer who lied about using racial slurs. Disturbed by negative images of African American men and seeking to renew black family cohesion, Nation of Islam minister Louis Farrakhan convened a "Million Man March" in Washington, D.C., in 1995.

New Immigrants and Ethnic Communities

The global economy stimulated the mobility of labor as well as the transfer of capital and goods. Between 1950 and 1990 nearly 20 million legal immigrants came to the United States. More than 8.3 million newcomers arrived in the 1980s, and these immigrants accounted for one-third of U.S. population growth during the decade. By 1990 foreign-born residents constituted 8 percent of the federal census count. The most numerous of the new arrivals were Hispanics, whose numbers increased by more than 60 percent in the 1970s and by 50 percent in the 1980s. By 1995 more than 27 million U.S. residents were Hispanics—more than 9 percent of the total population.

Two-thirds of Hispanics came from Mexico. During the 1970s Mexican population growth and endemic poverty encouraged between 3.5 and 6 million Mexicans to immigrate north of the border illegally. These "undocumented aliens" willingly accepted low-paying jobs, mainly in the Southwest, and constituted 10 percent of California's labor pool. Although Chicanos continued to work as migrant field hands, a larger number of them found employment in the service sector or worked for nonunion subcontractors in the garment trade. Unionization of Mexican American women became a national issue in the early 1970s when the Amalgamated Clothing Workers organized a consumer boycott to support a strike against the manufacturer of Farah pants. After the workers gained a union contract, the company gradually moved its operations to Mexico. As a contingent labor force, Mexican Americans received only 70 percent of median white income. By 1980 one-fifth of the Chicano community lived in poverty, and median educational levels for Chicanos remained less than tenth-grade.

Building on the success of Cesar Chavez, Mexican American activists such as Corky Gonzales and Jose Angel Gutierrez organized civil rights protests in Denver and South Texas in the late 1960s and early 1970s. In Los Angeles and Denver, young Chicanos asserted independence from Anglo authorities by wielding weapons as Brown Berets. The rural New Mexican activist Reies Lopez Tijerina also armed followers to protest the loss of historic land claims. Asserting ethnic pride, Mexican American students at southwestern universities adopted confrontational tactics to establish Chicano studies programs. The cultural awakening produced scholarly journals such as *Aztlan*, the popular magazines *El Grito* and *La Raza*, and moving explorations of Chicano roots by novelists and poets such as Raymond Barrio, Rudolfo Anaya, Lorna Dee

Exhibit 13-12. Number of Immigrants to the United States, 1980–1994 (in rounded figures)

1980	531,000
1985	570,000
1990	1,500,000
1994	804,000

Source: *Statistical Abstract of the United States* (1996).

**Exhibit 13-13. The Twelve Largest Sources of Legal Immigration to
United States, 1980–1993
(in rounded figures)**

Mexico	2,939,800
Philippines	683,400
Vietnam	594,000
China / Taiwan	526,300
Korea	402,700
India	383,800
Dominican Republic	380,600
El Salvador	315,000
Jamaica	273,800
Former Soviet Union	243,200
Haiti	208,800
Cuba	195,000

Source: *Statistical Abstract of the United States* (1996).

Cervantes, and Angela de Hoyos. Film director Luis Valdez introduced Chicano themes in *Boulevard Nights* (1979), *Zoot Suit* (1981), and *La Bamba* (1987), and movies like *Mi Vida Loca* (1994) and *Selena* (1997) dramatized barrio life and Mexican American popular culture.

As Mexican Americans gained an economic foothold, middle-class and professional organizations substituted political lobbying for protest. By the 1970s the Congress of Mexican American Unity served as an umbrella for 200 civic groups, and Mexican Americans played a major role in the National Council of La Raza, a consortium of twenty-six Hispanic organizations. In Texas, where Hispanics constituted one-fourth of the Democratic vote, Mexican Americans launched the career of San Antonio Mayor Henry G. Cisneros, later appointed Secretary of Housing and Urban Development. Numbering 2 million in the Los Angeles area, Mexican Americans elected public officials, used political clout to fight discrimination, and campaigned for bilingual education. Such efforts often met challenges from whites. Although the Supreme Court ruled in *Lau* v. *Nichols* (1974) that public schools were required to teach children in a language they understood, California voters overrode Hispanic objections to declare English the official state language in 1986. Moreover, intensive lobbying failed to defeat a controversial 1996 ballot measure denying state schooling and social services to illegal immigrants, although local courts delayed its implementation.

The appeal of economic opportunity also reached the Caribbean. Immigrants from impoverished Puerto Rico, the Dominican Republic, Haiti, and Jamaica flocked to the United States in the 1980s and 1990s. Moreover, civil strife and military repression prompted hundreds of thousands of Salvadorans and Guatemalans to leave their homes and to enter the United States illegally. Many of these immigrants sought sanctuary in churches and synagogues. Political refugees from Nicaragua and Colombia added to the influx. Yet none of these exiles had the impact on U.S. society of those abandoning Fidel Castro's Cuba. Between 1959 and 1970 an average of 20,000 Cubans migrated to the United States each year, most of them skilled professionals or white-collar workers. After an additional 275,000 emigres arrived in the 1970s, Castro permitted a

Exhibit 13-14. The Eight Largest Sources of Legal Immigration to the United States in Fiscal Year 1994 (in rounded figures)

Mexico	111,000
Former Soviet Union	63,000
China / Taiwan	54,000
Philippines	54,000
Dominican Republic	51,000
Vietnam	41,000
India	35,000
Poland	28,000

Source: *Statistical Abstract of the United States* (1996).

maritime exodus of 125,000 people, including criminals and drug addicts, in 1980. Further migration of working-class people boosted the Cuban American population to more than 1 million.

Forming a community of 750,000 people in Miami, Cuban Americans used capital investments and entrepreneurial skills to help make the city the financial and cultural center of Latin America. Strictly Catholic, economically ambitious, and fiercely anticommunist, the Cuban Americans thrived in Florida politics and repeatedly won local offices, molded Republican conservatism, and influenced the anti-Castro policies of the U.S. government. Although Miami's mansions and estates were home to prominent sports and entertainment figures, the poverty of the city's underclass and its proximity to Latin America attracted the international narcotics trade. In the 1980s the multibillion-dollar industry brought rising cocaine addiction, rampant police corruption, soaring crime and homicide rates, and schemes for laundering proceeds from drug sales.

As Los Angeles replaced New York as the leading port of entry in the 1970s, Asian immigrants accounted for more than 40 percent of newcomers to the United States. By 1990 Asians and Pacific Islanders constituted 3 percent of the national population. Taking advantage of the liberal provisions of the Immigration Act of 1965, more than 6 million newcomers from China, Taiwan, Hong Kong, and Korea initiated a new wave of migration between 1970 and 1995. Many of these immigrants used start-up capital and U.S. family ties to establish small businesses, particularly retail food stores and restaurants. Between 1975 and 1978 the United States welcomed 176,000 refugees from the Indochinese War, some of whom were aided by relocation funds appropriated by Congress. An additional 663,000 refugees arrived in the 1980s from Vietnam, Cambodia, and Laos, many of them "boat people" with few assets. Nearly a half-million Filipinos made homes in the United States in the same decade.

Asian immigrants flocked to Hawaii and to the Chinatowns of New York, San Francisco, and Los Angeles. In New York more than 70 percent of Chinese residents worked in low-wage service and garment trades. Unregulated clothing subcontractors in New York and Los Angeles recruited recent female immigrants as "sweatshop" seamstresses who received minimal pay and no benefits. Despite low per capita income, Asian Americans won a reputation for hard work, strong kinship bonds, and educational achievement. The children of Asian immigrants, particularly Japanese and Chinese Americans, sought college training in large numbers and excelled at mathematics and the physical sciences. The richness of Chinese ethnic culture and family life was conveyed in Amy Tan's popular novel, *The Joy Luck Club* (1989). Japanese Americans also received recognition in 1988 and 1992 when Congress created a $1.6 billion fund to compensate citizens interned in U.S. concentration camps during World War II.

Although immigrants from Asia and Latin America provided cheap labor for the booming economy of the Southwest and the West, state officials complained that the newcomers created excessive social welfare burdens. Accordingly, Congress passed the Immigration Act of 1986, which fined employers who knowingly hired illegal aliens or undocumented laborers. The law also provided amnesty to illegal workers who had arrived before 1982 and encouraged 2 million of an estimated 6 million to register with the federal government. Yet about 300,000 illegal immigrants continued to arrive each year during the 1990s. While Asians and Hispanics constituted a majority of such illegals, undocumented workers included 120,000 immigrants from Ireland, many of whom came to the United States through Canada.

Refugee laws passed in 1977 and 1980 swelled the number of Soviet Jews and anticommunist exiles from eastern Europe. Nearly 350,000 residents of the former Soviet Union came between 1971 and 1994. Another quarter of a million, mainly business and professional workers, fled Iran's Islamic revolution of 1979. In addition, more than 100,000 migrants from the Middle East arrived in the 1980s and boosted the total Arab American population to 2 million. Settling mainly in the Detroit area, the transplanted Middle Easterners organized the Arab American Antidiscrimination Committee to oppose negative stereotypes and to promote shared interests in U.S. foreign policy.

Although poor immigrants served as a labor force for low-wage service and manufacturing industries, professionally trained foreigners were actively pursued by U.S. corporations, research facilities, and medical institutions. Seeking to exploit the "brain drain" from former communist nations, Congress passed the Immigration Act of 1990, which increased the legal immigration quota and made allowances for skilled newcomers, particularly engineers, scientists, and professionals. An additional 40,000 "green cards" admitting foreign workers were distributed each year by lottery. To encourage aliens to become citizens, naturalization procedures were moved from the courts to the Justice Department. By the mid-1990s legal immigration to the United States had increased to 900,000 annually.

THE POSTINDUSTRIAL WORKING CLASS

The global economy and information age produced economic losers as well as winners. Although industrialists captured a healthy share of the world market after World War II, they were slow to modernize manufacturing facilities, and this delay led to a sharp decline in worker productivity by the 1970s. Foreign competition particularly hurt the automobile industry, whose managers were slow to recognize consumer demand for smaller, energy-efficient cars in an era of rising gas prices. By the early 1980s Japan was producing more autos and

**Exhibit 13-15. U.S. Factory Sales of Cars, Trucks, and Buses, 1980–1994
(in millions of units)**

1980	8.1
1985	11.5
1990	9.7
1994	12.1

Source: *Statistical Abstract of the United States* (1996).

trucks than the United States for the first time in history and ranked as the world's largest steel manufacturer.

Plant closings devastated midwestern "rust belt" cities like Detroit, Gary, and Youngstown and contributed to declining property values and the failure of other regional businesses. In the western mountain states, metal-mining operations never recovered from the slump of the 1970s. Falling energy prices generated similar havoc in the South and Southwest, where prosperity depended upon the health of the oil and natural gas industries. Northern Great Plains agriculture suffered from international competition as well. As falling land values and commodity prices produced a wave of bankruptcies and foreclosures, farm income fell from $27 billion in 1979 to less than $13 billion in 1983.

Although the automakers rebounded in the mid-1980s by marketing compact cars, minivans, jeeps, and pickup trucks, global competition, corporate mergers, and investor profit demands often forced manufacturing and white-collar firms to cut costs through "downsizing," which usually meant contraction of the labor force. Some companies used bankruptcy proceedings to fire workers, discard union contracts, and cancel pension obligations. Employees suffered when corporations relocated to countries with lower labor costs or tax rates. As automation, plant consolidations, bankruptcies, and runaway factories reduced the number of skilled manufacturing jobs, eroded wage scales, and decimated pension funds, one-third of the work force experienced a loss of real income after 1973. Between 1979 and 1995 the median earnings of all employees decreased nearly 5 percent. Narrowing employment opportunities decreased labor militancy. After mounting 424 major strikes in 1974, workers participated in only forty walkouts in 1990. Union membership plummeted from 35 percent of the labor force in the 1970s to 11 percent in the 1990s.

Education offered the key to better jobs in the new information economy. Yet three-quarters of the working-age population lacked a college degree. As private college expenses leaped from $3,000 a year in 1970 to more than $15,000 by 1990 and as the tuition costs at public universities quadrupled, higher education remained outside the financial reach of most people. By 1994 a student from the wealthiest 25 percent of families had nineteen times the chance of earning a bachelor of arts degree by age twenty-four than a student from the poorest 25 percent did. Critics worried that working people could no longer enjoy the consumer life-style that had long supported national cohesion. As housing prices jumped by a third between 1975 and 1995, young couples were priced out of the market. Although nearly one-third of families with children less than eighteen years old were supported by two working parents, housing, utility, and health care costs left little room for discretionary spending or substantial savings.

The demands of the high-tech economy had a devastating effect on high school dropouts, whose wages fell nearly 23 percent between 1979 and 1995. Relegated to unskilled and semiskilled menial and service positions, untrained workers constituted a contingent labor force subject to piecework assignments or easy replacement. By the mid-1990s the temporary jobs provider Manpower had become the largest employer in the nation. The segmented U.S. economy led to increased poverty rates. By the 1980s nearly one in seven people and 20 percent of children were impoverished, and children constituted 38 percent of the nation's poor. Ten percent of the population still paid for groceries with food stamps in 1994.

WHITE ETHNICS AND THE CHRISTIAN RIGHT

The civil rights and social protest movements of the 1960s stimulated a counter-movement of social conservatives who questioned the welfare state, the counterculture, and identity politics. White ethnics—the descendants of early-twentieth-century immigrants from southern, central, and eastern Europe—were a key constituency of the new conservatism. As Michael Novak suggested in the influential *The Unmeltable Ethnics* (1971), millions of Italian, Greek, and Slavic Americans rejected the homogeneity of media culture and continued to uphold traditional practices in religion, dance, food, music, and humor. Responding to assertions of ethnic identity, major universities introduced programs to study unassimilated groups. Hollywood films such as *The Godfather, Parts I* and *II* (1971, 1974), *Rocky* (1976), *The Deer Hunter* (1978), and *Crossing Delancey* (1988) depicted vital religious and social traditions among white ethnics.

George Wallace tapped the electoral potential of blue-collar and middle-class ethnics by espousing traditional virtues of patriotism, religion, the work ethic, and family solidarity. Working-class whites blamed "permissive" schools, "liberal" media, misguided judges, and amoral officials for rising welfare costs, higher taxes, increased drug use, and the doubling of crime rates between 1960 and 1980. In the 1970s such concerns led urban voters to elect "law and order" mayors like Philadelphia Police Commissioner Frank Rizzo. Neighborhood anticrime groups such as the Guardian Angels and the Jewish Defense League (JDL) established foot patrols to protect city residents, although such efforts sometimes raised racial tensions. The most controversial expression of white ethnic power centered around the 1970s campaign against court-ordered busing. Designed to achieve racial integration in the public schools, busing raised fears that crime, drug use, and poverty would undermine stable neighborhoods. Antibusing activists such as Boston's Louise Day Hicks led demonstrations and boycotts to protest the imposition of school integration by court orders.

The conservative backlash found its most dramatic expression in Reverend Jerry Falwell's Moral Majority, founded in 1979. Earlier, radio crusaders such as Reverend Carl McIntyre and Reverend Billy James Hargis had combined evangelical enthusiasm with harsh assaults on liberal social programs and world communism. As Sunbelt cities exploded in the 1960s and '70s (the Southwest boasted five of the nation's ten largest cities by 1980), evangelical churches expanded their influence. Between 1965 and 1974 the Southern Baptist Convention gained almost 2 million followers, and its total membership reached 12.5 million. Meanwhile, mainstream liberal Protestant denominations lost members to charismatic sects whose followers believed themselves to possess divinely inspired powers of healing and prophecy.

Through his televised pulpit, Falwell mobilized conservative Protestants who sought a Christian republic. By revitalizing political involvement and social activism among fundamentalists of the Southwest and the West, the evangelical leader fused anticommunism with a condemnation of "modernist" teachings such as evolution. The movement complained that a liberal "eastern Establishment" had destroyed traditional religion and education by imposing "value-free" standards on churches and schools. Condemning "secular humanism" as a misguided philosophy that placed man above God, fundamentalists preached against "sin" and "moral decadence" and attacked abortion, the equal rights amendment (ERA), gay rights, and "satanic" rock music. They also struggled to replace evolutionist teachings with creationist doctrines that conformed to Biblical teaching. Christian activists sought election to local school boards and monitored school libraries and curricula. Others controlled education through home schooling.

Using computer lists, direct mail, telephone marketing, and audio cassettes, the Christian Right organized 50 million "born-again" Protestants. The new religious conservatism fostered a variety of popular television evangelists such as Pat Robertson, who created cable TV's Christian Broadcasting Network (CBN). Robertson used his national television audience to campaign for the Republican presidential nomination in 1988, although he finished poorly. Other television preachers such as Jim Bakker, Jimmy Swaggart, Robert Schuler, and Oral Roberts corporatized their ministries and mobilized followers to support charities, seminaries, colleges, and foreign missions. Even though Swaggart was defrocked for sexual misconduct and Bakker received a forty-five-year prison sentence for bilking contributors of more than $150 million, televangelism and Christian popular media remained influential forces. Robertson's Christian Coalition, an issue-oriented political lobby, assumed a major role in the Republican Party and conservative circles in the 1990s.

By adhering to the notion that divine law determined ethical norms, traditionalists within Protestant, Catholic, and Jewish denominations forged a conservative civil religion. Insisting that social commitments and responsibilities were more important than individual rights, they attacked the dominance of secular values among the "new class" of professionals and academics. *Commentary*, a conservative Jewish journal, complained of a departure from the discipline and moral foundations of Western civilization. Social critic Allan Bloom used these precepts to assail higher education in *The Closing of the American Mind* (1987). Noting that one-fifth of U.S. adults were functionally illiterate in the mid-1980s, Secretary of Education William J. Bennett, a Catholic intellectual, called for more educational emphasis on academic standards, on traditional morality and ethics, and on the humanities. Catholic critics Phyllis Schlafly and William F. Buckley, Jr., castigated a self-indulgent youth culture that immersed itself in sex and drugs and discarded family and religious obligations.

REV. JERRY FALWELL
1933–

When Rev. Jerry Falwell resigned from his leadership of the Moral Majority in 1987, he was the most influential conservative voice in American life. His Sunday evening cable TV program reached into 34 million homes. His enterprises and holdings included television's National Christian Network, Liberty Baptist College, an Israeli-made private jet, and the 18,000-member Thomas Road Baptist Church of Lynchburg, Virginia. Falwell traveled 200,000 air miles each year to raise the annual $100 million needed to sustain these interests. Once described as the "sleeping giant" of American politics, the Virginia preacher was credited with controlling the votes of an estimated 21 million evangelicals.

Falwell came from a successful but disreputable Lynchburg family that included bootlegging and a dance hall among its enterprises. A bright student and an accomplished athlete with a flair for rowdiness, he studied mechanical engineering at a local college. One night Falwell attended a Baptist service, fell in love with (and subsequently married) the church pianist, and instantly became a "born again" Christian. Two months later he decided to enter the ministry and transferred to a Baptist Bible college in Missouri.

Upon graduation in 1956 Falwell returned to Lynchburg to found an independent fundamentalist church in an abandoned bottling facility. He started the Thomas Road Baptist Church with $1,000 and seventy-five families. Falwell immediately arranged to broadcast services by radio. Six months later his "Old Time Gospel Hour," which merely recorded the service as it occurred, made it to television.

A six-footer with a large waistline and a deep, booming voice, Falwell wore dark suits and always carried a Bible. His upbeat theol-

CULTURE WAR

As birth rates rose from 14.6 per 1,000 to 16.7 per 1,000 between 1975 and 1990, cultural traditionalists reasserted 1950s "family values." In country music, popular among white southerners and westerners, recordings emphasized how adultery, divorce, drinking, and alienating work undermined meaningful family life. Defenders of family discipline assailed the mass media for subjecting children to sex, violence, and antisocial messages. Concerned about the loss of parental control, Mary "Tipper" Gore, wife of Tennessee Senator Al Gore, led a successful campaign in the late 1980s to place warning labels on recordings containing sexually explicit lyrics. Another parents' group, Mothers Against Drunk Driving (MADD), sponsored national advertising, pressed for tougher sentences for drinking offenders, and helped to pass legislation in 1984 denying federal highway funds to states that did not raise the drinking age to twenty-one. Sensitivity to victims' rights led the Supreme Court to restrict repeated death penalty appeals in 1991 and to allow juries to consider presentencing testimony about murder victims from victim's families.

ogy conveyed images of success and messages of hope and redemption. At the same time, Falwell never strayed from the fundamentalist belief in the accuracy of the Bible or from resistance to anything that conflicted with spiritual command. But in 1977 the Lynchburg preacher reversed a long-standing fundamentalist isolation from social action and politics by affirming a religious leader's right to disseminate views on abortion, pornography, and homosexuality. During that year, Falwell helped singer Anita Bryant to repeal a Florida county ordinance granting equal rights to homosexuals, whom the minister accused of "perversion and immorality." In 1978 and 1979 he fashioned two "Clean Up America" campaigns to counteract "a tide of permissiveness and moral decay." These efforts climaxed in the founding of the Moral Majority in 1979.

Falwell described the independent Moral Majority as a united front for God and country. He professed to speak for the vast majority of citizens who subscribed to traditional values in opposition to the "godless minority" that ruled the country. In *Listen America!* (1980) Falwell explained that this "coalition of God-fearing moral Americans" would "reverse the politicalization of immorality" by

seeking influence, not control. The enemy was "secular humanism" in government—the attempt to solve problems apart from God. "I believe in the separation of church and state but not in the separation of God and government," Falwell remarked.

The Moral Majority registered 4 million new voters for the 1980 elections and urged another 10 million to vote. After signing up more than 2 million Moral Majority members, Falwell had created a massive political action movement. Yet he rejected party affiliations and simply chose to identify himself as "a noisy Baptist" who had a "divine mandate" to fight for laws to save America. Politicizing the struggle between "good and evil," Falwell warned that a weakened national defense reflected moral impotence. "Jesus was not a pacifist. He was not a sissy," he once proclaimed.

Although Falwell eventually retreated from the national spotlight, his mobilization of evangelical social conservatives dramatically realigned national politics and set the stage for the powerful media and lobbying presence of Pat Robertson's and Ralph Reed's Christian Coalition. ■

Drug use stimulated another battle in the effort to sustain traditional values. As cocaine addiction spread to the middle class and victimized top entertainment and sports figures in the 1980s, some corporations began mandatory testing of job applicants and employees. After the Supreme Court upheld the right of public school officials to search students without warrants, the federal government ordered drug tests for more than 1 million civilian employees. Under the Omnibus Drug Act of 1986, Congress spent $1.7 billion in a "war on drugs"

Exhibit 13-16. Percentage of Eighteen- to Twenty-five-year-olds Admitting to Previous Drug Use, 1979–1995

Year	Marijuana	Cocaine	Hallucinogens
1979	68.1	27.3	24.9
1988	56.4	19.7	13.8
1994	43.4	9.6	11.7

Source: *Statistical Abstract of the United States* (1996).

that included enforcement, education, and treatment. The United States even sent troops to Bolivia to wipe out cocaine-processing laboratories. Yet when Colombian drug cartels began to smuggle less refined cocaine across U.S. borders, domestic dealers began producing "crack." Distributed at cut-rate prices to white and black consumers by inner-city youth gangs, the narcotic led to rampant drug addiction and violent turf wars. As heroin replaced crack as the hard drug of choice in the mid-1990s, big-city crimes of violence declined, but casual use of marijuana increased among high school students.

As the number of one-parent families jumped by 79 percent in the 1970s, moral traditionalists agonized about a perceived deterioration of sexual mores. During the next decade, the proportion of children born out of wedlock increased from 18 percent to 28 percent, and the number of unwed teenage mothers leaped by 38 percent. By 1993 12.4 million families were headed by women and did not include men. Half of such families in the African American and Hispanic communities lived in poverty. Harsh evaluations of illegitimacy in the 1990s fostered a concerted political effort to break the cycle of "dependence" among "welfare mothers" by terminating government subsidies and by encouraging participation in the work force (see Chapter 14).

"Family values" advocates also criticized homosexuality as an immoral, sacrilegious, and decadent life-style. In *Bowers* v. *Hardwick* (1986), the Supreme Court upheld a Georgia law that made sodomy a criminal offense and thereby refused to extend constitutional rights of privacy to consensual relations between homosexuals. Fears concerning the spread of homosexuality discouraged the government from using graphic advertising to promote the use of "safe sex" to contain the AIDS epidemic. This dispute was resolved in 1988 when Surgeon General C. Everett Koop, a conservative Christian, called for a national AIDS education program that stressed both abstinence and precautionary measures. Yet the issue of government support of homosexuality resurfaced the next year when the National Endowment for the Arts (NEA) funded a Cincinnati arts show featuring homoerotic and religiously provocative photography by Robert Mapplethorp. Although Congress reauthorized NEA financing in 1990, it limited grants to work "sensitive to the general standard of decency."

The most intense debate over family values centered on abortion. Insisting that the fetus was a sacred form of human life, the Roman Catholic Church and groups such as National Right to Life denounced legalized abortion as murder of the unborn. Social conservatives like Phyllis Schlafly argued that abortion placed the individual needs of the potential mother above those of family and society. Viewing sex as a procreative ritual and childbearing as a God-given privilege, abortion opponents objected to "family planning." A broad movement of conservative Catholics, Protestants, and Jews picketed abortion clinics and mounted massive demonstrations in the 1980s. As tactics escalated in the next decade, the radical Operation Rescue blocked entry to abortion facilities to disrupt their procedures. After a series of clinic bombings and fatal shootings, however, Congress passed a 1994 law prohibiting the use of force or intimidation against women entering abortion centers. In 1997 the Supreme Court upheld the right of local authorities to regulate access to clinics by antiabortion protesters.

Although the court refused to reverse *Roe* v. *Wade* or grant states the power to outlaw abortion, pro-lifers succeeded in limiting taxpayer support of the procedure. In 1976 Congress passed an amendment introduced by Illinois's Henry

Mass protests in Washington and across the country reflected the growing strength of the antiabortion movement and the Christian right in the 1970s and 1980s.

J. Hyde barring Medicaid funds for abortions for women on welfare. The court upheld this provision in 1980. Nine years later, the justices concluded that unborn children had protectable rights and prohibited the use of tax-supported facilities for abortions not essential to save the mother's life. In 1991 the tribunal upheld a congressional ban on federal funding for abortion counseling. The next year, the court permitted states to erect abortion restrictions that did not interfere with the privileges granted in *Roe*.

When federal regulators began to test a French drug capable of terminating pregnancy in the 1990s, the ensuing controversy illustrated how advances in medical technology could threaten moral beliefs. Such concerns had surfaced earlier when critics argued that prenatal diagnosis of inherited disorders could lead to abortion on the basis of gender. Traditionalists also were concerned about sperm donation for artificial insemination and in vitro fertilization, in

**Exhibit 13-17. Legal Abortions Performed in the United States, 1980–1992
(in rounded millions)**

1980	1.6
1985	1.6
1990	1.6
1992	1.5

Source: *Statistical Abstract of the United States* (1996).

which an egg is fertilized before placement in the womb. When a New Jersey woman agreed to act as a paid "surrogate" mother but sued to keep the baby in 1987, a state court ruled that she had contractual obligations to surrender custody to the natural father and his infertile wife. The resulting furor inspired several state laws that prohibited compensation of surrogate mothers. Meanwhile, advances in the creation and alteration of human genes led to federal guidelines on DNA experiments. When researchers used cell replication to "clone" a sheep in 1997, the government suspended support of laboratory research on human reproduction.

Advances in artificial life support affected the end of life and the emotional legal issues surrounding it. After the parents of a comatose patient, Karen Ann Quinlan, sued to disconnect an artificial respirator in 1975, eighteen states followed with laws declaring that legal death was defined by the cessation of brain activity, not of heartbeat. In 1976 California became the first state to allow patients to authorize withdrawal of life-sustaining procedures. The Supreme Court acknowledged an individual's right to refuse medical treatment in 1990 but upheld legislation requiring "clear and convincing evidence" of a patient's wishes. The following year, Congress ordered health care organizations to inform clients about the right to complete "living wills" to register these requests in case of medical contingencies. Dramatizing the need for "right-to-die" legislation for terminally ill people in pain, Michigan's Dr. Jack Kevorkian helped more than forty people commit suicide in the 1990s. Publicity over Kevorkian's efforts led Oregon voters to pass a 1994 ballot measure legalizing suicide under medical supervision. Yet court appeals and bans in other states prolonged the ethical controversy about euthanasia.

RIGHTS, RACE, AND TAXES

After the introduction of the equal rights amendment (ERA) in 1972, feminism became a focal point of the cultural war. Stop-ERA organizer Phyllis Schlafly lobbied furiously against the measure by claiming it would "neuterize" society and would relieve men of the obligation to support their families. Fearing that ERA would force women into the male-dominated labor market and require placement of children in day care, opponents linked the amendment to an attack on the family and to a radical transformation of gender roles. As the debate shifted from issues of equality to a conflict over traditional values, anti-ERA activists raised the specter of a military draft that would place women in combat. By arguing that women should not take advantage of traditional roles or protections, feminists cut themselves off from less privileged cohorts. Not surprisingly, ERA fell three states short of ratification in 1982 and six votes shy of reconsideration the following year. Nine states in the traditional South were among those that rejected the measure.

The ERA controversy illustrated the conflict between individual rights and traditional obligations. Similar polarization marked the confrontation over affirmative action (see Chapter 12). As the courts and regulatory agencies penalized nonminorities for the past policies of employers, the costs of civil rights reform became more broadly distributed, and whites complained of "reverse discrimination." The controversy was particularly bitter in higher education, where institutions set aside admissions slots for minority students even if their grades and test scores were lower than those of rejected white applicants. In the *Bakke* case of 1978 the Supreme Court ruled that affirmative action numeric quotas in medical school admissions violated civil rights law but that race could be considered to secure a more diverse student body. The court tightened restrictions on minority set-aside programs in 1989 and limited the use of statistics in job discrimination suits. Not satisfied with these modifications, California voters passed a 1996 ballot initiative ending the state's affirmative action programs in hiring, contracting, and university admissions.

Dissatisfaction with affirmative action reflected a widespread belief that the "liberal establishment" sought to impose a racial and cultural agenda by extending preferential treatment to minorities. The Supreme Court responded to such fears in 1993 by ruling that congressional districts could not be drawn solely on the basis of race. Social conservatives also complained that the federal government did not link welfare payments to reciprocal obligations such as work or public service. Arguing that poverty stemmed from lax moral discipline and poor family life, critics like Ralph Reed of the Christian Coalition blamed crime and drug addiction on "elite" permissiveness. Antigovernment sentiment was buttressed by resentment about rising tax burdens. As the

Addison Geary/Stock, Boston

The fastest growing age segment of the American population of the 1980s, the elderly sought alternatives to institutionalized care and demoralizing nursing homes.

PHYLLIS SCHLAFLY

1924–

"Politics is too important to be left to politicians," declared conservative Republican Phyllis Schlafly in 1969. "More women should strive for the elected positions now held by men, and more women should support those who do." Women's leadership, she added, "can raise the moral tone of politics. They keep their ideals while playing the game."

Spoken in the language of feminism, Schlafly's appeal certainly did not reflect a feminist agenda. Just the opposite was the case. During the 1970s she would emerge as the nation's most vocal opponent of the proposed equal rights amendment (ERA).

Long involved in Republican politics, Schlafly preferred to identify herself as an Alton, Illinois, "housewife" and mother of six. Born into a pious Roman Catholic family in St. Louis, she had watched her mother enter the work force when her father lost his job during the Depression. "We had less money than anybody I knew," she recalled. After achieving academic success at Radcliffe and obtaining a government job in Washington, she married a wealthy corporate lawyer— "who rescued me from the life of a working girl," she later said— and moved to southern Illinois.

Busy as a homemaker, Schlafly found time to participate in community organizations and Republican politics. As a supporter of the conservative Robert Taft, she ran as the "powder-puff" candidate for Congress in 1952 and lost to the Democratic incumbent. "Sex had nothing to do with it," she insisted. Endorsing the fervent anticommunist crusade of the 1950s, she cultivated an expertise on national defense issues as a leader of the Daughters of the American Revolution. In 1963 Schlafly was the only woman to testify to the Senate in opposition of ratification of the nuclear test ban treaty by denouncing the value of "communist promises."

Schlafly achieved celebrity status in Republican circles the next year when her campaign biography of Barry Goldwater, *A Choice,*

median earnings of male employees fell 11.5 percent between 1979 and 1995, middle-class families viewed taxation as an extortion of money from those who worked to support those who did not. Influenced by conservative think tanks such as the American Enterprise Institute and the Heritage Foundation, public opinion identified liberalism with the reallocation of scarce resources instead of the creation of new ones.

Exhibit 13-18. U.S. Life Expectancy in Years at Birth, 1970–1995

1970	70.8
1975	72.6
1980	73.7
1985	74.7
1990	75.4
1995	76.3 (estimate)

Source: *Statistical Abstract of the United States* (1996).

Not an Echo, sold 3 million copies. Goldwater's loss failed to dampen her spirits. Pursuing her enthusiastic opposition to detente, she proceeded to coauthor a series of small books exposing Soviet perfidy and the failure of liberals to stand up to the communist menace. When her ardent conservatism cost her the leadership of the National Federation of Republican Women, she organized an independent network of her supporters and began publishing a newsletter called "The Phyllis Schlafly Report." Working outside the Republican establishment, Schlafly earned no rewards from Nixon's victory in 1968. When the president opened diplomatic relations with China and signed the SALT disarmament treaty, she broke with the administration.

Congressional passage of the ERA in 1972 rejuvenated her career. "Their motive is totally radical," she said of the new feminists. "They hate men, marriage, and children. They are out to destroy morality and the family. They look upon husbands as exploiters, children as an evil to be avoided (by abortion if necessary), and the family as an institution which keeps women in 'second-class citizenship.'" Announcing a new lobbying group called Stop-ERA, Schlafly led her conservative army into battle on multiple fronts. Arguing that feminists were selfish and socially irresponsible, she wrote articles, gave lectures, organized public demonstrations, and sought private meetings with key legislators in the states. Her 1977 book, *The Power of the Positive Woman*, warned that the ERA would "mandate the gender-free, rigid, absolute equality of treatment of men and women" and would create "a constitutional mandate that the husband no longer has the primary duty to support his wife and child." She also protested that the ERA would permit women to serve equally with men in the armed forces.

Widely recognized as the voice of conservative women, Schlafly made numerous appearances before Congress during the 1980s to defend Social Security rights for homemakers, to lobby against abortion and against sex education for children, to protest the inclusion of women in the military, and to oppose laws against sexual harassment in the workplace. Her moment of greatest triumph, however, occurred when the ERA failed to gain ratification by the necessary three-fourths of the states in 1982.

"A woman should spend the first twenty years of her life growing up," she explained, "the next twenty raising the next generation, and the third saving the world." With the defeat of the ERA she claimed to have met all three goals. ■

As medical technology prolonged life but increased health care costs, care of the elderly raised profound contradictions concerning the role of government. Modern medicine used expensive diagnostic tools such as radioactive isotopes, ultrasound and magnetic resonance imaging (MRI), angiograms (x-rays of blood vessels), and computed tomography (CT) scans. New approaches to coronary disease included "pacemakers" to regulate heartbeat, heart transplants, artificial hearts, and coronary artery bypass surgery. Laser procedures, chemo-

Exhibit 13-19. Percentage of the U.S. Population Over Age Sixty-four, 1960–2020

1960	9.2
1980	11.3
2000	13.0 (estimate)
2020	17.7 (estimate)

Source: *Department of Commerce and Bureau of the Census.*

Exhibit 13-20. Percentage of Respondents Indicating Trust in the U.S. Government, 1964–1994

	1964	1984	1994
Trust government to do what's right "always"	76	44	19
Trust government to do what's right "only sometimes"	22	53	72

Source: *Time*/CNN poll, *Time,* September 26, 1994.

therapy, radiation treatment, and pharmaceuticals revolutionized the treatment of disease. Such techniques contributed to a five-year increase in average life expectancy between 1960 and 1990. During that period the proportion of the U.S. population greater than sixty-five years old grew from 9.2 to 12.6 percent. Yet health care spending rose from 5.3 percent of the gross national product to 11.6 percent. By 1990 annual government medical expenditures had surpassed a staggering $253 billion. As yearly nursing care costs exceeded $72 billion in 1994, cherished government programs like Social Security, Medicare, and Medicaid came under scrutiny because of fear of future insolvency (see Chapter 14).

Unable to resolve many of the nation's problems, Washington came under intense criticism. In 1964 more than three-quarters of respondents had expressed faith that government would "always" do what was right; by 1994 the proportion had dropped to 19 percent. Media events such as the 1976 Bicentennial, the 1982 dedication of the Vietnam Memorial, the 1984 and 1996 Olympics, and the gala 1986 Statue of Liberty celebration sought to unite a fragmented society. Yet wounds like those produced by the Vietnam War continued to fester. Indeed, in Hollywood movies such as *Rambo* (1982), the Vietnam War veteran emerged as a symbol of the latent anger the conflict had generated. Frank portraits of the war appeared in films like *Platoon* (1986), *Full Metal Jacket* (1987), and *Hamburger Hill* (1987), as well as in popular novels by veteran Timothy O'Brien. Yet even as the United States extended full diplomatic relations to Hanoi in 1997, bitterness over the Vietnam War and the plight of military personnel as yet unaccounted for prevented full healing of war-related malaise.

As racial and ethnic minorities began to constitute nearly one-fourth of the U.S. population, the nation witnessed an outpouring of white supremacy and charismatic nationalism. In Texas a resurgent Ku Klux Klan accused Vietnamese immigrants of using family labor to take over the Gulf shrimping industry and vowed to stop illegal immigration from Mexico. Members of another Klan wing lynched a young African American man in Alabama, although a suit by the Southern Poverty Law Center forced the splinter organization to sell off its assets and to cease operations. David Duke, a former Louisiana Klansman, won election as a state legislator and drew headlines in close races for public office. Meanwhile, activists like Tom Metzger of White Aryan Resistance (WAR) organized gangs of young racist "skinheads" in major cities, particularly on the West Coast.

Racist groups such as the Order, the Aryan Nation, and Christian Identity complained of the dilution of national character and armed themselves for race war. Weapons violations led to several confrontations between these groups and government authorities. At Ruby Ridge, the Idaho home of white suprem-acist leader Randy Weaver, a controversial shoot-out in 1992 killed Weaver's wife and son and a federal marshal. Another confrontation led to the death of seventy-five adults and children near Waco, Texas, in 1993, when govern-ment agents ended a fifty-one-day siege by setting fire to the compound of the armed, racially mixed Branch Davidian sect. White supremacist and antigov-ernment views also dominated the independent militia movement, active in the Midwest and the western interior. Federal prosecutors tied such radicalism to two men charged with the murder of 165 people in the 1995 bombing of the federal building in Oklahoma City—the worst act of domestic terrorism in U.S. history.

The continuing presence of extremist groups and a series of African Ameri-can church burnings in the mid-1990s pointed to the obstacles to achiev-ing national consensus amid diversity. Global technology, information age communication, immigration, and identity politics all underscored the multi-cultural basis of U.S. society. Yet the same forces generated xenophobic fears of other cultures and deep suspicions concerning the media, government bureau-cracy, and institutions like universities and the judiciary. Ultimately, the con-flicts such social and cultural issues raised required resolution in the political arena.

SUGGESTED READINGS

A brief introduction to the growth of the world market can be found in Henry C. Dethloff, *The United States and the Global Economy Since 1945* (1997). See also Robert Schaeffer, *Understanding Globalization: The Social Consequences of Political and Economic Change* (1997), and Bennett Harrison, *Lean and Mean: The Changing Landscape of Corporate Power in the Age of Flexibility*. For the impact of internation-alization on one region, see William G. Robbins, *Colony and Empire: The Capitalist Transformation of the American West* (1994). Documents related to modern U.S. economic history are collected in Harold G. Vatter and John F. Walker, eds., *History of the U.S. Economy since World War II* (1996). For the computer revolu-tion, see portions of George Basalla, *The Evolution of Technology* (1988); of Kenneth Flamm, *Creating the Computer: Government, Industry, and High Technol-ogy* (1988); and of David F. Noble, *Forces of Production: A Social History of Indus-trial Automation* (1984). Technology's impact on medicine is discussed in Loren R. Graham, *Between Science and Values* (1981), and in Basile S. Yanovsky, *Medi-cine, Science, and Life* (1978).

The rise of upwardly mobile professionals is treated in Michael X. Carpini, *Stability and Change in American Politics: The Coming of Age of the Generation of the 1960s* (1986). See also Landon Y. Jones, *Great Expectations: America and the Baby Boom Generation* (1980). Suburban life after the 1960s is the focus of the relevant segments of Kenneth T. Jackson, *Crabgrass Frontier: The Suburbanization of the United States* (1985). Ties between "yuppie" life-styles and earlier protest culture are addressed in Lauren Kessler, *After All These Years: Sixties Ideals in a Different World* (1991), and in Annie Gottlieb, *Do You Believe in Magic? The Second Coming of the Sixties Generation* (1987). See also Jack Whalen and Richard Flacks, *Beyond the Barricades: The Sixties Generation Grows Up* (1989). The resurgence of community activism is depicted in Harry C. Boyte, *The Backyard Revolution: Understanding the New Citizen Movement* (1980).

Persistent countercultural mores are explored in the later segments of John D'Emilio and Estelle B. Freedman, *Intimate Matters: A History of Sexuality in America* (1988), and in Jay Stevens, *Storming Heaven: LSD and the American Dream* (1987). For differing perspectives on 1980s consumerism, see Debora Silverman, *Selling Culture: Bloomingdale's Diana Vreeland and the New Aristocracy of Taste in Reagan's America* (1986), and Warren J. Belasco, *Appetite for Change: How the Counterculture Took on the Food Industry, 1966–1988* (1990). Also useful are sections of Samuel Hays and Barbara D. Hays, *Beauty, Health, and Permanence: Environmental Politics in the United States, 1955–1985* (1987). The social ethics of professionals are explored in Robert N. Bellah et al., *Habits of the Heart: Individualism and Commitment in American Life* (1985). More critical accounts appear in Christopher Lasch, *The Culture of Narcissism: American Life in an Age of Diminishing Expectations* (1979), and in portions of *The True and Only Heaven: Progress and Its Critics* (1991).

For holistic science and New Age spirituality, see John P. Briggs and F. David Peat, *Looking Glass Universe: The Emerging Science of Wholeness* (1984). Space technology and its implications are explored in the relevant segments of Walter A. McDougall, . . . *The Heavens and the Earth: A Political History of the Space Age* (1985). The best overview of the environmental movement is Hays and Hays, *Beauty, Health, and Permanence*. See also earlier works such as Frank Graham, *Since Silent Spring* (1970), and Jonathan Schell, *The Fate of the Earth* (1982). For the environmental controversies of the resource-rich western states, see Richard White, *It's Your Misfortune and None of My Own: A History of the American West* (1991). The nuclear debate is addressed in Jerome Brian Price, *The Antinuclear Movement* (1982).

The roots of 1970s feminism are vividly portrayed in Alice Echols, *Daring to Be Bad: Radical Feminism in America, 1967–1975* (1989). More general overviews appear in Rochelle Gatlin, *American Women Since 1945* (1987), and William Chafe, *Women and Equality: Changing Patterns in American Culture* (1977). The ERA is the focus of Donald G. Mathews and Jane Sherron De Hart, *Sex, Gender, and the Politics of ERA* (1990), and of the provocative Mary Frances Berry, *Why ERA Failed: Politics, Women's Rights and the Amending Process of the Constitution* (1986). See also Myra Marx Ferree and Beth Hess, *Controversy and Coalition: The New Feminist Movement* (1985), and Ethel Klein, *Gender Politics: From Consciousness to Mass Politics* (1984). The abortion rights controversy is discussed in David Garrow, *Liberty and Sexuality: The Right to Privacy and the Making of* Roe v. Wade (1994), and Kristin Luker, *Abortion and the Politics of Womanhood* (1984). Struggles for homosexual rights are described in Barry D. Adam, *The Rise of a Gay and Lesbian Movement* (1987), and in the relevant sections of D'Emilio and Freedman, *Intimate Matters*.

The "postmodern" roots of multiculturalism can be traced in Andreas Huyssen, *After the Great Divide: Modernism, Mass Culture, Postmodernism* (1986), and in Frederic Jameson, *Postmodernism, or the Cultural Logic of Late Capitalism* (1991). For an appeal for multicultural scholarship, see Melefi Kete Asante, *The Afrocentric Idea* (1987). The politicization of cultural studies is the subject of Benjamin Barber, *An Aristocracy of Everyone: The Politics of Education and the Future of America* (1992). Harsh critiques of multiculturalism and "political correctness" include Allan Bloom, *The Closing of the American Mind* (1987), and

Roger Kimball, *Tenured Radicals: How Politics Has Corrupted Our Higher Education* (1990). For a reassertion of ideas about pluralist democracy, see Arthur M. Schlesinger, Jr., *The Disuniting of America: Reflections on a Multicultural Society* (1993). Identity politics is criticized by radical activist Todd Gitlin in *The Twilight of Common Dreams: Why America Is Wracked by Culture Wars* (1995). Historian David A. Hollinger seeks to resolve the conflict in *Postethnic America: Beyond Multiculturalism* (1995).

For native peoples after 1973, see Philip Reno, *Mother Earth, Father Sky, and Economic Development* (1981), and the later segments of Francis Paul Prucha, *The Great Father: The United States Government and the American Indians, Vol. II* (1984). An overview of recent African American history is presented in Manning Marable, *Black American Politics: From the Washington Marches to Jesse Jackson* (1988). See also the useful Katherine Tate, *From Protest to Politics: The New Black Voters in American Elections* (1993). One of the most important African American leaders is portrayed in Adolph L. Reed, Jr., *The Jesse Jackson Phenomenon* (1986), and in the relevant segments of Allen D. Hertzke, *Echoes of Discontent: Jesse Jackson, Pat Robertson, and the Resurgence of Populism* (1993).

Treatments of the new wave of immigration include Gil Loescher and John A. Scanlan, *Calculated Kindness: Refugees and America's Half Open Door, 1945 to the Present* (1986), and David Reimers, *Still the Golden Door: The Third World Comes to America* (1985). See also the later segments of John Bodnar, *The Transplanted: A History of Immigrants in Urban America* (1985), and of Roger Daniels, *Coming to America: A History of Immigration and Ethnicity in American Life* (1991).

Asian ethnicity is the focus of Daniels, *Asian America: Chinese and Japanese in the United States since 1850* (1988); Ronald Takaki, *Strangers from a Different Shore: A History of Asian Americans* (1989); and Stephen S. Fugita and David J. O'Brien, *Japanese American Ethnicity: The Persistence of Community* (1991). For Hispanics, see Alejandro Portes and Robert L. Bach, *Latin Journey: Cuban and Mexican Immigrants in the United States* (1985). Mexican Americans are the subject of Rodolfo Acuna, *Occupied America: A History of Chicanos* (1988); of Juan Gomez Quinones, *Chicano Politics: Reality and Promise, 1940–1990* (1990); and of Alfredo Mirande, *The Chicano Experience* (1985). See also Takaki, *A Different Mirror: A History of Multicultural America* (1993). White ethnicity is the focus of Richard D. Alba, *Italian Americans: The Twilight of Ethnicity* (1985), and of Richard Krickus, *Pursuing the American Dream: White Ethnics and the New Populism* (1976). See also Peter Schrag, *The Decline of the WASP* (1976).

A growing literature on the postindustrial workplace includes Harrison, *Lean and Mean*; Jon C. Teaford, *Cities of the Heartland: The Rise and Fall of the Industrial Midwest* (1993); and Kathryn Marie Dudley, *The End of the Line: Lost Jobs, New Lives in Post-industrial America* (1994). Working-class experience is treated in David M. Gordon et al., *Segmented Work, Divided Workers: The Historical Transformation of Labor in the United States* (1982), and in Eileen Boris, *Home to Work: Motherhood and the Politics of Industrial Homework* (1994). For nonelite social perspectives, see David Halle, *America's Working Man: Work, Home, and Politics Among Blue-Collar Property Owners* (1984); Craig Reeinarman, *American States of Mind: Political Beliefs and Behavior Among Private and Public Workers* (1987); and Clarence Y.H. Lo, *Small Property versus Big Government: Social Origins of the Property Tax Revolt* (1990). See also Barbara Ehrenreich, *Fear of Falling: The Inner Life of the Middle Class* (1991) and Robert Zussman, *Mechanics of the Middle Class: Work and Politics Among American Engineers* (1985).

The revitalization of evangelical Christianity is placed in historical context in George M. Marsden, *Religion and American Culture* (1990), and in Robert Wuthnow, *The Restructuring of American Religion: Society and Faith Since World War II* (1988). The social and cultural influence of religious conservatives is addressed in Steve Bruce, *The Rise and Fall of the Christian Right: Conservative Protestant Politics in America, 1978–1988* (1988); in Michael Lienesch, *Redeeming America: Piety and Politics in the New Christian Right* (1993); and in Sara Diamond, *Spiritual Warfare: The Politics of the Christian Right* (1989). For Pat Robertson's activities, see Hertzke, *Echoes of Discontent*, and Dinesh D'Souza, *Falwell Before the Millennium: A Critical Biography* (1986). See also Duane M. Oldfield, *The Right and the Righteous: The Christian Right Confronts the Republican Party* (1996). Catholic conservatives are the focus of Patrick Allitt, *Catholic Intellectuals and Conservative Politics in America: 1950–1985* (1993).

The evolution of post-1945 conservative political and social thought is summarized in Mark Gerson, *The Neoconservative Vision: From the Cold War to the Culture Wars* (1995); in Melvin J. Thorne, *American Conservative Thought Since World War II: The Core Ideas* (1990); and in Jerome L. Himmelstein, *To the Right: The Transformation of American Conservatism* (1990). These works supplement standard treatments such as George Nash, *The Conservative Intellectual Movement in America Since 1945* (1976); Peter Steinfels, *The Neo-Conservatives: The Men Who Are Changing America's Politics* (1979); and William Harbour, *The Foundations of Conservative Thought: An Anglo-American Tradition in Perspective* (1982). See also Paul Gottfried and Thomas Fleming, *The Conservative Movement* (1988). For the influence of secular conservatives, see J. David Hoeveler, Jr., *Watch on the Right: Conservative Intellectuals in the Reagan Era* (1991); James Allen Smith, *The Idea Brokers: Think Tanks and the Rise of the New Policy Elite* (1991); and Sidney Blumenthal, *The Rise of the Counter-Establishment: From Conservative Ideology to Political Power* (1986).

The cultural confrontations of the post-Vietnam era are the focus of James Davison Hunter, *Culture Wars: The Struggle to Define America* (1991); of John Kenneth White, *The New Politics of Old Values* (1988); and of Ira Shor, *Culture Wars: School and Society in the Conservative Restoration, 1969–1984* (1986). See also Jeffrey Goldfarb, *The Cynical Society: The Culture of Politics and the Politics of Culture in American Life* (1991). Racial conflict is analyzed in Lawrence H. Fuchs, *The American Kaleidoscope: Race, Ethnicity, and the Civic Culture* (1990), and in Edward G. Carmines and James A. Stimson, *Issue Evolution: Race and the Transformation of American Politics* (1989). See also David Theo Goldberg, ed., *Anatomy of Racism* (1990). Two excellent case studies are Ronald P. Formisano, *Boston Against Busing: Race, Class, and Ethnicity in the 1960s and 1970s* (1991), and Jonathan Rieder, *Canarsie: The Jews and Italians of Brooklyn Against Liberalism* (1985).

An extensive literature on conservative populism includes Thomas Byrne Edsall with Mary D. Edsall, *Chain Reaction: The Impact of Race, Rights, and Taxes on American Politics* (1991), and E.J. Dionne, Jr., *Why Americans Hate Politics* (1991). See also the later segments of Michael Kazin, *The Populist Persuasion, An American History* (1995), and of David A. Horowitz, *Beyond Left and Right: Insurgency and the Establishment* (1997). For the roots of neopopulism, consult Dan T. Carter, *The Politics of Rage: George Wallace, the Origins of the New Conservatism, and the Transformation of Politics* (1995), and Stephen Lesher, *George Wallace: American Populist* (1994). Populist skepticism toward elites is addressed in

Stephen B. Greenberg, *Middle Class Dreams: The Politics and Power of the New American Majority* (1995), and in William Greider, *Who Will Tell the People: The Betrayal of American Democracy* (1992). See also Kevin J. Phillips, *Arrogant Capital: Washington, Wall Street, and the Frustration of American Politics* (1994), and *Boiling Point: Republicans, Democrats, and the Decline of Middle-Class Prosperity* (1993).

Critical approaches to conservatism include Thomas Ferguson and Joel Rogers, *Right Turn: The Decline of the Democrats and the Future of American Politics* (1986); Herbert I. Schiller, *Culture, Inc.: The Corporate Takeover of Public Expression* (1989); and Michael Parenti, *Democracy for the Few* (1995). See Donald L. Bartlett and James B. Steele, *America: What Went Wrong?* (1992). For agrarian discontent in the age of the global market, consult Catherine McNicol Stock, *Rural Radicals: Righteous Rage in the American Grain* (1996). The extreme right is portrayed in Michael Barkun, *Religion and the Racist Right: The Origins of the Christian Identity Movement* (1994). Questions concerning the elderly and government responsibility are explored in Jill Quadagno, *The Transformation of Old Age Society: Class and Politics in the American Welfare State* (1988).

14

Former President Gerald Ford, Ronald Reagan, and George Bush campaigning for the 1980 election.

Former President Gerald Ford, Ronald Reagan, and George Bush campaigning for the 1980 election.

AP/Wide World Photos

REAGAN, BUSH, AND CLINTON: POLITICAL REALIGNMENT, 1980–1996

R onald Reagan effected the most dramatic change of government since the New Deal. Reacting to economic stagnation at home and declining influence abroad, the California Republican sought to restore the national sense of mission. The former movie actor and governor mobilized a new coalition of social conservatives, free-market advocates, and foreign policy hawks behind an ambitious program of government deregulation, welfare cuts, tax relief, and increased military spending. "Reaganomics" generated an economic boom in the 1980s, but trade imbalances and federal budget deficits threatened market stability. As the Cold War with the Soviet Union drew to a close, Presidents George Bush and Bill Clinton struggled to strengthen prosperity and define the U.S. role in a "new world order." Meanwhile, the electorate followed Reagan's lead in seeking reduced federal spending and increased government accountability but rejected ideological extremes and moved to the political center.

THE 1980 ELECTION AND REAGANOMICS

Having responded to inflation with reduced federal spending and tight monetary policies, Jimmy Carter faced an uprising of traditional Democratic constituencies in the labor and civil rights movements. The president used the powers of incumbency to turn back a presidential primary challenge from Senator Edward Kennedy. Yet Carter faced a more effective opponent when Ronald Reagan defeated George Bush in the race for the Republican nomination. A minor star in 1940s movies, Reagan had forged anticommunist credentials as president of the Screen Actors Guild during the Hollywood Red Scare. As his movie career declined in the early 1950s, the actor became national spokesperson for defense contractor General Electric. Moving into politics, Reagan espoused fiscal and social conservatism and Cold War interventionism. After winning the governorship of California in 1966, he attracted attention as a militant opponent of student activism and as a supporter of the Vietnam War.

By 1980 Reagan had become the leading voice of the nation's conservatives by questioning detente with the Soviets, by demanding a strong defense, and by attacking government bureaucracy and inflationary social spending. The Republican candidate promised to "take the government off the backs of the people" by cutting government "waste, extravagance, abuse, and outright fraud." He also identified with the social values advanced by the Christian Right, particularly by the Moral Majority followers of Baptist minister Jerry Falwell. By promoting family cohesion, religious worship, and traditional education, the nominee expressed the desire of Protestant evangelicals and conservative Catholics to redeem the nation from moral permissiveness and collectivist values. Accepting the presidential nomination, the Californian asked Republican convention delegates to join his "crusade" to "recapture our destiny." "God bless America!" he concluded.

Asking voters if they were "better off" than they had been four years earlier, Reagan assured a frustrated electorate that it did "not have to go on sharing scarcity." Instead, the candidate proclaimed "morning in America" and promised to restore U.S. global power and respect. Democratic allusions to Reagan

Exhibit 14-1. Election of 1980

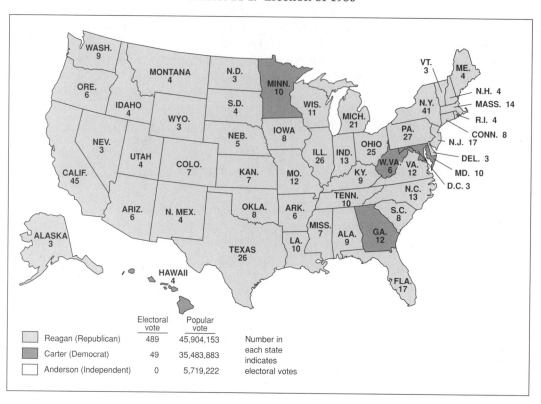

	Electoral vote	Popular vote	
Reagan (Republican)	489	45,904,153	Number in each state indicates electoral votes
Carter (Democrat)	49	35,483,883	
Anderson (Independent)	0	5,719,222	

as a right-wing threat to peace backfired when the challenger appeared relaxed and amiable in a nationally televised debate. Although Reagan won support from corporate leaders seeking to reduce social costs and to regain a competitive edge in the world economy, his rejection of Carter's notion of "limits" attracted a broad coalition of upscale professionals, young entrepreneurs, and blue-collar workers anxious about economic opportunity. As the White House waited in vain for settlement of the Iran hostage crisis, Reagan and vice presidential candidate George Bush captured 51 percent of the popular vote, compared with 41 percent for Carter and Mondale. Running as an independent, Representative John B. Anderson, a liberal Illinois Republican, received nearly 7 percent of the presidential ballots.

The one-sided nature of the 1980 contest surfaced in the Electoral College vote, where the Republican prevailed by an overwhelming 489–49. Having supported a constitutional amendment to ban abortion, Reagan carried 61 percent of "born-again" white Protestants, who helped him capture seven southern states that Carter had carried in 1976. Meanwhile, Republicans won control of the Senate for the first time since 1952. As low Democratic turnout, particularly in the East, contributed to less than 53 percent participation among eligible voters, Jimmy Carter became the second consecutive presidential incumbent to suffer defeat.

George Bush had accused Reagan of espousing "voodoo economics" during the Republican primaries. Yet the former governor insisted that he could reduce

David Stockman, director of the federal Office of Management and Budget during the Reagan administration.

government spending while increasing outlays for defense, could lower taxes while balancing the federal budget, and could simultaneously restore economic prosperity. Such reasoning originated with "supply-side" economists like Arthur Laffer of the University of Southern California and consultants associated with conservative "think tanks" such as the Heritage Foundation and the American Enterprise Institute. These advisors insisted that government regulations and high taxes held back production and inflated prices. Supply-side policy called for generous tax cuts and government deregulation. Reagan argued that investors would anticipate improvements from his economic program and would spur market recovery. Accepting the logic of the Kemp-Roth supply-side tax proposal, the president called for the largest tax cut in U.S. history.

As Democrats lashed out against "Reaganomics," Office of Management and Budget director David Stockman appeared before Congress to demonstrate that tax relief would not interfere with a balanced budget, even if accompanied by added military spending. Although Stockman acknowledged that tax cuts served the interests of the administration's wealthy supporters, the budget plan reflected the widespread belief that the economy could sustain growth without inflation. Accordingly, Democrats cooperated in passing the Economic Recovery Act of 1981, which enacted a three-year individual income tax reduction of 25 percent. The law offered incentives for individual retirement accounts (IRAs), reduced capital gains taxes and maximum tax rates, increased amounts exempted from estate and gift taxes, and indexed returns to inflation. Congress also lowered corporate tax rates, accelerated depreciation allowances, and reduced the windfall profits tax on oil. Although House Democrats subsequently

Exhibit 14-2. U.S. Gross National Product, 1981–1987
(in current dollars in billions)

1981	3,052.6
1983	3,405.7
1985	4,010.3
1987	4,486.2

Source: *Economic Report of the President* (1988).

tightened loopholes and restored some cuts, Reagan tax relief pumped billions of dollars into the economy.

REAGAN DEREGULATION

Committed to free-market reform, the Reagan administration accelerated Carter's steps toward deregulation. A 1982 court order divested American Telephone and Telegraph (AT&T) of its local telephone service business and permitted its subsidiaries to enter computer processing and information fields. The Banking Act of 1982 enabled lenders to increase new services such as interest-bearing checking and money market accounts. Continued dismantling of federal airline regulation introduced lower fares and more flexible schedules. Yet the administration provoked the ire of environmentalists when it cut Carter's energy windfall profits tax and eliminated federal funding of alternative fuels research. Further conflict emerged when Secretary of the Interior James G. Watt, a Wyoming attorney, leased off-shore drilling rights to oil and gas interests and proposed the harvesting of timber from national parks. After activists won Watt's resignation in 1983, Environmental Protection Agency (EPA) head Anne M. Burford was forced to resign, and cleanup "Superfund" administrator Rita M. Lavelle was convicted of perjury in a scandal involving EPA collusion with industrial polluters.

Deregulation also led to administration conflict with organized labor. When Reagan reduced the authority of the Occupational Safety and Health Administration (OSHA) in 1981, union leaders complained that the government had abandoned workers to suffer from excessive noise levels and lethal chemical exposures. After airline controls were lifted, air traffic controllers protested that the Federal Aviation Administration (FAA) had not allocated sufficient resources to deal with increased domestic flights. When 12,000 controllers went on strike, Reagan dissolved their union and ordered the FAA to use military personnel in their place. The harsh strategy mirrored the private sector's desire to cut labor costs in an age of global competition.

Reagan's Justice Department also abandoned affirmative action and school desegregation suits. Moreover, the president sought to lessen Washington's commitment to the welfare system. Viewing discretionary social spending as counterproductive and inflationary, the White House hoped to restore post–World War II prosperity by returning to a budget in which safety net functions were confined to Social Security. Accordingly, Reagan and Congress made $35 billion worth of domestic program cuts in 1981 through a drastic reduction

Exhibit 14-3. U.S. Unemployment Rates, 1981–1987
(as a percentage of the total labor force)

Year	Total	Black
1981	7.5	14.3
1983	9.5	15.6
1985	7.1	13.1
1987	6.1	13.0

Source: *Economic Report of the President* (1988).

of welfare. Confining the provision of benefits to the "truly needy," the government removed 400,000 families from Aid to Families with Dependent Children (AFDC) and took nearly 1 million people off the food stamp rolls. Discretionary social expenditure as a share of gross national product declined by more than a third during Reagan's tenure.

Despite the severity of such measures, the Democratic House moderated some administration policies. As unemployment averaged 10.8 percent in 1982, the president signed gas tax and highway jobs measures that appropriated $71 billion to fund transportation projects for the next four years. Reagan also created a 1983 bipartisan commission on the impending bankruptcy of the Social Security program, and the commission's recommendations for increased payroll taxes were signed into law. Yet Congress refused to implement the White House's "new federalism," a proposal to shift welfare programs to the poorly funded states. Congress also ignored the president's plan to provide tuition tax credits for private school education because the plan was perceived as a threat to public schooling and racial integration. Nor did Congress approve requests to abolish the Departments of Education and Energy. Constitutional amendments concerning balanced budgets, abortion, and public school prayer also met defeat.

REELECTION AND THE
REAGAN DOCTRINE

Reagan's tax cuts coincided with a sharp drop in global oil prices and a return of prosperity. "We Brought America Back," the White House proclaimed. The economic boom strengthened voter faith in the Republican Party as the promoter of opportunity. Burdened by the legacy of Carter's tight money policies, the Democrats disagreed on how to regain the electorate's confidence. African American minister and civil rights advocate Jesse Jackson pieced together a "rainbow coalition" of racial minorities, feminists, peace activists, and the poor. Senator Gary Hart of Colorado cultivated urban professionals involved in the "high-tech" service economy. Despite these initiatives, former Vice President Walter Mondale emerged as the 1984 Democratic presidential nominee by deferring to party power bases in labor, education, and the big cities. At the urging of feminists, Mondale chose Representative Geraldine A. Ferraro of New York

Exhibit 14-4. U.S. Voter Participation, 1980–1984
(as a percentage of all eligible voters)

1980	52.8
1984	53.3

Source: *Statistical Abstract of the United States* (1996).

as his running mate—the first woman nominated for national executive office by a major party.

The Democrats tried to preserve the alliance of unions, big government, and urban developers that had financed the party's presidential races since World War II. Yet global competition reduced tolerance of government regulation and social spending among business interests once friendly to the Democratic Party. Meanwhile, the diminished role of manufacturing eroded union membership and bargaining power. Since the 1970s both parties had competed for financial backing by relying on election specialists, media advisors, and legal consultants. Democrats increasingly leaned on their upper-middle-class base by combining calls for fiscal integrity with a focus on education, the environment, and civil rights. Although the Democratic candidate won the AFL-CIO's first-ever presidential endorsement in 1984, when Mondale told television debate viewers that he would raise taxes to ease federal deficits, he failed to assure labor voters that he would embrace reforms to shift the tax burden to the affluent.

The Democrats emerged from the 1984 election with 90 percent of the African American ballots, nearly two-thirds of the Hispanic vote, and a 53 percent majority among those earning less than $12,500 a year. Yet Reagan's communications skills fused with expert polling and advertising to produce a stunning Republican victory. Winning 59 percent of the popular vote, the president captured majorities in every state but Mondale's Minnesota and the District of Columbia. Republicans won the votes of 80 percent of evangelical Christians, 72 percent of southern whites, 67 percent of white males, and 68 percent of those earning more than $50,000 a year. Even more disturbing to Democrats was Reagan's 55 percent victory among eighteen- to twenty-nine-year-olds, a group who preferred Republican promises of economic growth to the "status quo" politics of the losers. The election also dramatized the conversion of "Reagan Democrats"—Republican voters from working-class families once loyal to the New Deal—who were more comfortable with the president's pro-market policies than with the Democrats's social liberalism.

Reagan contrasted the "evil empire" of the Soviet Union with the moral superiority of the United States—the "blessed land" of a "chosen people." Jimmy Carter had translated this moral imperative into a demand that allies like Chile and El Salvador adhere to higher standards in guaranteeing human rights. In contrast, U.N. Ambassador Jeane J. Kirkpatrick, a Georgetown University foreign affairs specialist, rejected this policy as naive and insisted that right-wing "authoritarian" dictatorships were capable of democratic change, whereas left-wing "totalitarian" regimes were not. Blaming "world terrorism" and most global conflict on Soviet adventurism in developing nations, national security planners fashioned an unofficial "Reagan Doctrine" to rebuild the CIA's covert action capability. In 1983 the president persuaded Congress to lift the Carter-era restrictions in Angola and personally designated the anticommunist UNITA to be the recipient of $11 million in military aid. The United States also supplied anticommunist rebels in Afghanistan, Cambodia, Ethiopia, and Nicaragua.

Although the administration insisted that communism contributed to the worst human rights abuses, the White House faced intense congressional pressure when the white minority government of South Africa violently suppressed black demonstrations in 1984. As U.S. civil rights leaders led daily antiapartheid protests at Washington's South African embassy, conservative Republicans embraced the campaign to demonstrate opposition to racism. Reagan responded with a policy of "constructive engagement" that called for peaceful persuasion of an anticommunist ally rich in strategic resources. Not satisfied, Congress handed the president his most dramatic foreign policy reversal by overriding his veto of South African trade sanctions in 1986. After the defeat, Reagan recognized the government of reformer Corazon Aquino when Philippine dictator Ferdinand E. Marcos was ousted by a democratic movement. U.S. officials also escorted dictator Jean-Claude Duvalier out of Haiti. As relations cooled with military governments in Chile and Paraguay, Reagan announced that the United States encouraged democratic movements among right-wing allies.

THE MIDDLE EAST QUAGMIRE

U.S. policy faced its most daunting challenges in the Middle East, where it sought to protect regional oil fields and shipping lanes and to support Israel and "moderate" Arab leaders. When Reagan sent 1,200 Marines to act as a peacekeeping force during the Lebanese civil war in 1982, the troops clashed with Syrian forces and with Moslem militias allied with Iran. Seeking to oust Washington from Lebanon, Islamic revolutionaries exploded massive truck bombs to destroy the U.S. embassy and Marine headquarters and killed 241 U.S. servicemen. For the first time in history, Congress invoked the War Powers Act. Although Reagan did not recognize the statute's constitutionality, he agreed to withdraw all troops within eighteen months. With the consensus on Middle East policy shattered, the president removed the last forces in 1984. Like its predecessors, the Reagan administration underestimated the region's pervasive nationalism and fundamentalism and failed to convene peace talks between Israel and the Palestine Liberation Organization (PLO).

Perceived as a supporter of Israeli expansion and as an imperial power in the region, the United States continued to be the target of violent attacks, kidnappings, and hijackings. After declaring a trade embargo against radical Libya, which the White House accused of supporting terror campaigns, the president unleashed an air and naval attack in 1986. Once Washington linked the Libyans to the bombing of a West German discotheque frequented by U.S. soldiers, the administration orchestrated a second military attack against Libya that killed forty people and destroyed the family quarters of Libyan leader Muammar al-Qaddafi. To further traumatize Qaddafi, Reagan officials coordinated a "disinformation" campaign that suggested that further attacks were imminent.

The administration also sought to contain revolutionary Iran, which it tied to Shiite Moslems holding U.S. hostages in Lebanon. Embargoing military

Exhibit 14-5. Lebanon, 1983

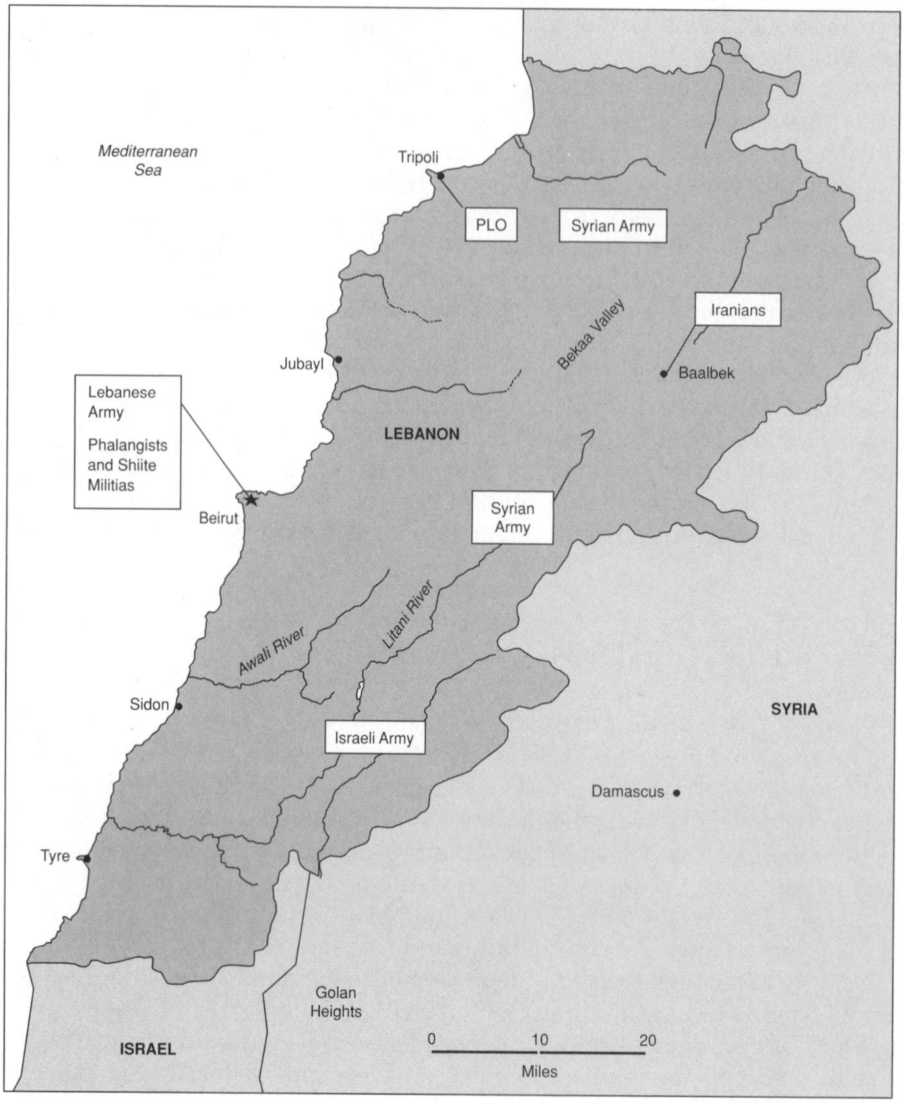

shipments to Tehran, Reagan pledged never to negotiate with terrorists. Never-theless, in 1985 the president permitted National Security Council officials to use Israeli intermediaries and private arms dealers to arrange a secret exchange of U.S. weapons for hostages. The deal sent 2,000 antitank missiles to Iran for use in its war with Iraq. In return, Tehran agreed to arrange the release of U.S. captives in Lebanon, although a key hostage—William Buckley, the CIA's Beirut station chief and counterterror expert—already had died as a result of torture. When a Beirut newspaper leaked details of the arms-for-hostage accord in 1986, the administration abruptly ended the relationship with Iran. Nevertheless, the covert arrangement would haunt the president for the remainder of his term.

Military personnel sift through the wreckage of the U.S. Marine barracks in Beirut after a devastating bombing by Moslem fighters allied with Iran in 1982.

After the break in relations with Iran, the United States insisted that Tehran obey a U.N. Security Council resolution for a cease-fire in the war with Iraq. Concerned in 1987 about the mining of Persian Gulf oil traffic lanes and wary of increased Soviet influence, Reagan invoked the Carter Doctrine, which outlined Washington's interest in a stable Persian Gulf. During the next two years, the president deployed a navy task force of minesweepers, warships, and helicopters to clear shipping lanes and to escort oil tankers through the dangerous

Exhibit 14-6. Libya and the Gulf of Sidra

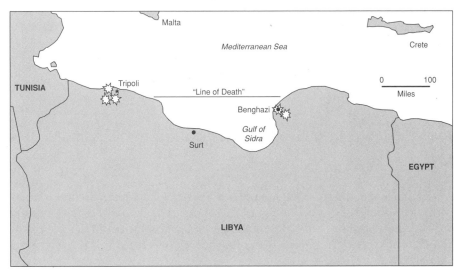

Exhibit 14-7. Persian Gulf Shipping Lanes

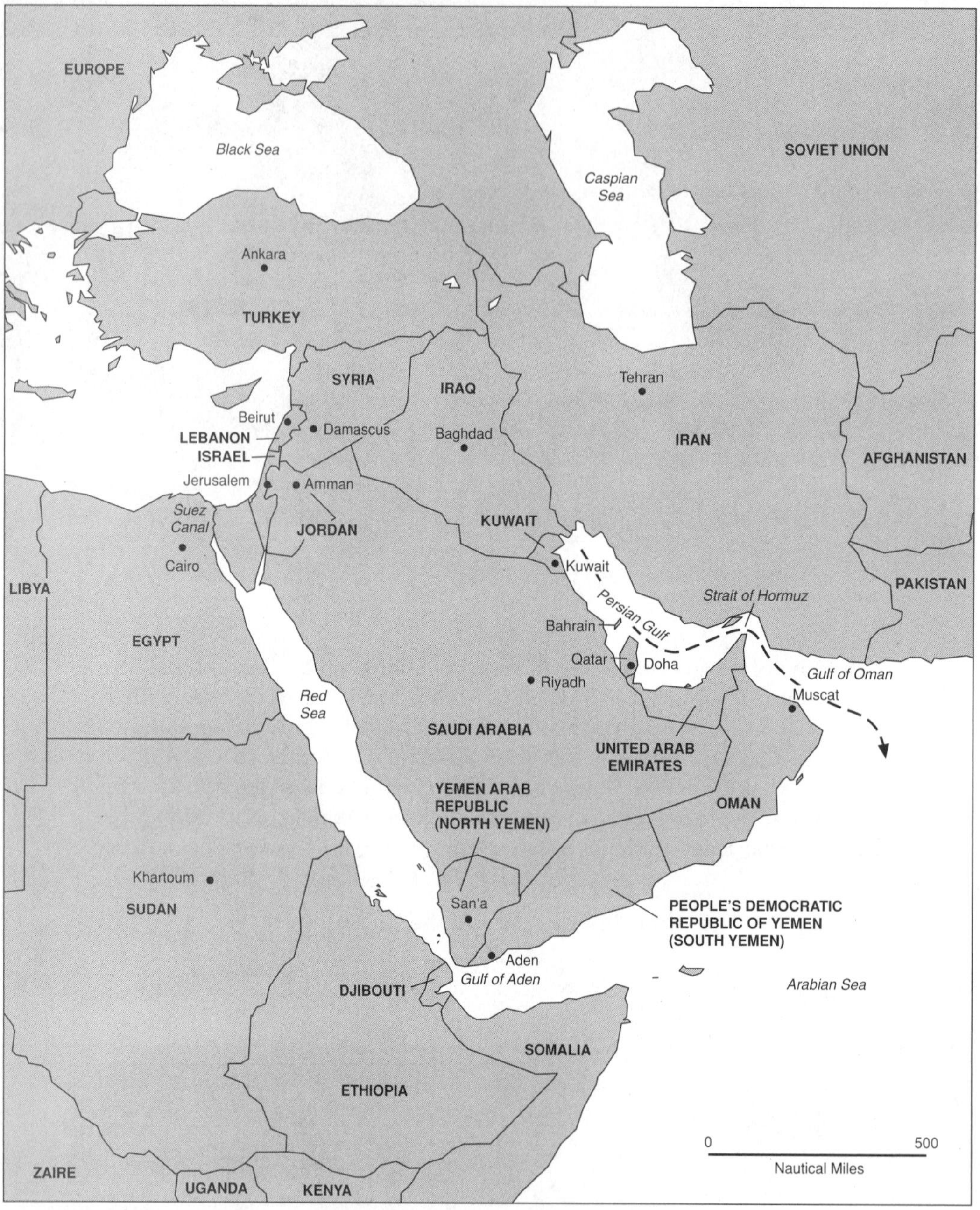

waters. Yet intervention in the area proved costly when an accidental Iraqi air attack took the lives of twenty-eight U.S. sailors and when a U.S. missile strike destroyed an Iranian airliner that had been mistaken for a military plane and killed 290 civilians. Despite increased tensions, however, Iran agreed to peace talks with Iraq in 1988.

CRUSADE IN CENTRAL AMERICA

Reagan officials pursued a vigilant anticommunist policy in the Caribbean and Central America. Cuba's Fidel Castro had permitted 125,000 exiles to flee to Florida in 1980, but the United States charged that many were criminals, mental patients, or social undesirables. As relations between Havana and Washington deteriorated, Castro opened ties with the Marxist government of the tiny Caribbean island of Grenada. When dissident communists murdered Grenada's prime minister and other leaders in 1983, Reagan used the pretext of civil strife to mount an invasion against the Cuban client state. Labeling the operation a "rescue mission" to protect 1,000 U.S. medical students, the president dispatched 4,600 marines, rangers, and paratroopers to take control of the island. Polls revealed public endorsement of the nation's first military victory in the post–Vietnam War era.

In Central America's impoverished El Salvador, the Reagan administration pursued a more controversial policy by arming a right-wing military government whose security forces and "death squads" killed 30,000 civilians in a bloody civil war between 1980 and 1983. When a centrist leader won internationally supervised elections in 1984, Congress approved another $200 million to defeat the left-wing guerrillas and to assist the government. Yet efforts to incorporate the socialist rebels into the political structure were threatened in 1988 when right-wingers regained control of El Salvador's legislature. In neighboring Nicaragua, Reagan authorized the CIA to support a rebel army of "contras" to overthrow the Sandinista government, which the White House saw as a front for Cuban and Soviet expansion. Administration policy in Central

Exhibit 14-8. Central America and the Caribbean

JEANE J. KIRKPATRICK
1926–

Leonard Freed/Magnum Photos

Like her boss, Ronald Reagan, Jeane Kirkpatrick became a prominent Republican after years of loyalty to the Democratic Party. Born into a staunchly Democratic family, Kirkpatrick went to Barnard and Columbia but delayed her career to meet family responsibilities. She returned to academic life in the early 1960s, joined the faculty of Georgetown University in 1967, and completed her Ph.D. in political science at Columbia University the following year. Quickly establishing herself as a prolific and respected scholar, Kirkpatrick did important work on U.S. politics and foreign policy.

Kirkpatrick played an active role in the Democratic Party in the 1960s and early 1970s but grew steadily estranged from liberal politics after 1968. Controversies over the Vietnam War seemed to change the party in ways she found extremely disturbing. Kirkpatrick particularly objected to the influx of Democratic dissidents she described as "antiwar, antigrowth, antibusiness, antilabor . . . ." Moreover, she found that Democrats now expressed a reluctance to wield military power to defend U.S. interests. Kirkpatrick preferred an older version of liberalism best articulated in the 1970s by Senators Henry Jackson of Washington and Hubert Humphrey of Minnesota. Characterizing herself as a "welfare conservative," she defended the "noble tradition of caring in domestic affairs, of . . . providing minimum standards of well-being" while simultaneously "being deeply persuaded of the legitimacy and success of American society and the failure and tyranny of Communist societies."

In 1972 Kirkpatrick helped to organize the Coalition for a Democratic Majority to limit the influence of George McGovern's wing of the Democratic Party. These neoconservatives opposed the values of the counterculture and explicitly rejected the view that the United States was a sick society dominated

America was strongly opposed by many religious leaders, particularly in the Catholic community. After learning of CIA assassination manuals and the secret mining of Nicaraguan ports, Congress passed the Boland Amendments of 1982 and 1984, both designed to prohibit the use of military or intelligence funds for covert action against Nicaragua's government.

Frustrated by congressional interference with Nicaraguan "freedom fighters," Reagan officials violated Boland Amendment restrictions by secretly raising $36,700,000 from wealthy U.S. donors and conservative allies such as Saudi Arabia and Taiwan. Meanwhile, CIA Director William Casey, National Security Advisor Rear Admiral John M. Poindexter, and National Security Council aide Lieutenant Colonel Oliver North coordinated an illegal scheme to help the contras by diverting unlawful profits from the illegal Iranian arms sales. The top-secret campaign also depended on illegal CIA operations and pressure on the governments of Honduras and Costa Rica to permit Nicaraguan contra rebels to operate from their territory.

Disclosure of the Iran-Contra fund diversion in 1986 created the greatest crisis of Reagan's tenure. Having weathered an assassin's bullet in 1981, the

by materialism and technology. They saw the McGovern campaign as dangerously radical and predicated on unrealistic, utopian reform impulses. In particular, coalition members believed that the Democratic nominee lacked sensitivity to the threat that communism and the Soviet Union posed to U.S. interests.

The issue of foreign policy finally prompted Kirkpatrick's break with the party during the Carter administration. She insisted that the Democratic president reflected the guilt-ridden and irresolute approach to world affairs that pervaded the leadership of his party. Kirkpatrick voiced these concerns in a biting article for the conservative journal *Commentary*. Titled "Dictatorships and Double Standards," her polemic attacked the failure of Carter's foreign policy as "clear to everyone except its architects." Kirkpatrick particularly scored the administration for opposing pro-U.S., right-wing authoritarians while tolerating leftist or revolutionary regimes unfriendly to the United States. She found the source of this double standard in liberal guilt about the alleged U.S. role as a defender of an exploitive status quo in the third world. Kirkpatrick further argued that for all their faults, right-wing authoritarians more easily accepted democratic reforms than left-wing

totalitarians did. Consequently, support of rightist dictatorships served both U.S. interests and national political ideals. "Liberal idealism," she concluded, "need not be identical with masochism, and need not be incompatible with the defense of freedom and the national interest."

Deeply impressed by the *Commentary* piece, Ronald Reagan appointed Kirkpatrick ambassador to the United Nations shortly after his election in 1980. During her five years at the United Nations, she acquired a reputation as a combative and forthright advocate of U.S. policy, but her role as U.N. ambassador increasingly frustrated her. Kirkpatrick called the body a "dismal show" where conflicts never were resolved. When Reagan did not appoint her to a high-level policy-making position, she resigned in 1985 and returned to Georgetown. Almost simultaneously, she joined the Republican Party. One of the few prominent women to serve in the Reagan administration, Kirkpatrick often received press consideration as a possible candidate for elective office or for a future political appointment. Adored by conservatives and vilified by liberals, Jeane Kirkpatrick remained an outspoken beacon of plain talk and provocative viewpoints. ■

president had forged a reputation as a "teflon" leader who survived both misfortune and criticism with ease. However, after denying the arms sale to Iran had ever occurred and after insisting that missiles were not traded for hostages, Reagan faced questions about his involvement in the violations of the Boland Amendments. A commission led by former Senator John Tower concluded in 1987 that the commander-in-chief had mismanaged his staff but had no knowledge of the funding of the contras. Reagan fired North, accepted Poindexter's resignation, and agreed to the appointment of a special prosecutor. After televised hearings in which North presented a passionate defense of his actions, a joint panel of the House and Senate cited the administration for violating congressional restrictions on covert activity and for "pervasive dishonesty and inordinate secrecy." When the Nicaraguan government agreed to peace talks with its domestic rivals in 1988, Congress ended military aid to the contras.

Despite such reverses, the Reagan administration managed to survive the scandal. After Special Prosecutor Lawrence Walsh successfully prosecuted North and Poindexter for obstructing Congress, an appeals court reversed the verdicts because the Iran-Contra committee had granted the defendants lim-

AP/Wide World Photos

CIA Director William Casey, named by National Security Council aide Oliver North as the mastermind of the scheme to divert funds from the sale of arms to Iran to the Nicaraguan contras.

ited immunity. After the perjury indictment of Defense Secretary Caspar W. Weinberger, public consideration of the matter was closed when Weinberger and five other officials received presidential pardons from Reagan's successor in 1992. Although Reagan had been compelled to testify as a witness in court proceedings, he never accepted legal or moral responsibility for the actions committed in his name, nor acknowledged how Iran-Contra had diminished his political effectiveness.

COLD WAR CATHARSIS

Having won the White House with promises to revitalize the national defense, Reagan initiated the largest peacetime military buildup in U.S. history. Congress approved an $18 billion increase in defense spending in a 1981 budget that embraced construction of neutron bombs, production of the B-1 bomber canceled by Carter, and creation of a rapid deployment force. Insisting that the United States could win the Cold War by forcing the Soviets to spend beyond their means, Reagan prevailed on Congress to raise annual defense outlays from $157 billion in 1981 to $233 billion in 1986. The most important feature of the president's plan was the Strategic Defense Initiative (SDI), introduced in a 1983 television address. Dubbed "Star Wars," the $26 billion research and develop-

Lt. Colonel North's televised testimony before the Joint Select Committee on Iran-Contra revealed the deep divisions among U.S. citizens regarding the fundamentals of foreign policy.

ment project sought to explore the use of space satellites and laser weapons to fend off nuclear missiles. Although Congress only appropriated a fraction of the proposed funding, many scientists joined the Soviets in expressing concerns about the potential militarization of space.

Viewing arms control as an inadequate response to an aggressive Soviet military machine, Reagan offhandedly acknowledged the possibility of a "limited" nuclear war in which damage might be confined to Europe. By 1982, however, grass-roots activists on both sides of the Atlantic had mounted a "nuclear freeze" movement that called upon the superpowers to declare a mutual and verifiable moratorium on the testing, deployment, and production of atomic weapons. In the largest demonstration to that point in U.S. history,

Exhibit 14-9. National Defense Spending, 1980–1988
(in rounded billions of dollars)

1980	134.0
1982	185.3
1984	227.4
1986	273.4
1988	290.4

Source: *Statistical Abstract of the United States* (1996).

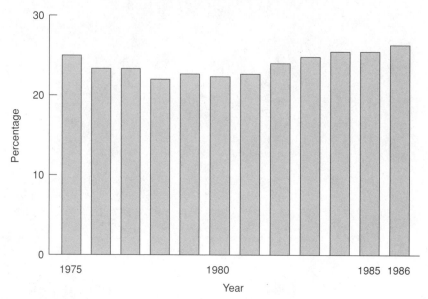

**Exhibit 14-10. U.S. National Defense as a Percentage
of Total Federal Outlays, 1975–1986**

Source: *Statistical Abstract of the United States* (1987).

600,000 protesters rallied in New York City's Central Park to end the nuclear arms race. As the nuclear freeze resolution came before the House, the president argued that passage would weaken the U.S. bargaining position in the SALT negotiations, and the proposal met a narrow 204–202 defeat. Nevertheless, in 1983 the White House declared that nuclear war should be deterred at all costs and committed the nation to SALT II. Congress also moderated the arms race in 1985 by eliminating funding for fifty of the one hundred MX missiles the administration requested.

Despite militant anticommunism, Reagan found himself drawn to accommodation with the Soviet Union. In 1981 the president responded to the agricultural lobby by ending the Carter embargo on grain sales to Moscow. Two years later Reagan negotiated a new five-year wheat sales pact. The White House made another concession by permitting the export of construction equipment for a Siberian-European pipeline after Western allies objected to earlier sanctions protesting martial law in communist Poland. Moreover, as the

**Exhibit 14-11. U.S. Research and Development, 1980–1988
(in billions of dollars)**

Year	Total	Defense and Space-related
1980	62.6	18.2
1984	101.2	31.8
1988	132.9	43.7

Source: *Statistical Abstract of the United States* (1996).

Soviet Secretary Gorbachev and President Reagan at the Geneva summit of 1985, the first of four such meetings between the two superpower leaders.

Soviets initiated democratic political reforms, liberalized censorship policies, and extended travel freedoms, European leaders and members of Congress pushed the United States toward negotiations with Soviet Communist Party leader Mikhail Gorbachev. At the Geneva conference of 1985, the first summit in six years, Gorbachev expressed a desire for *glasnost* ("openness") at home and abroad. Seeking to modernize his economy through western investment, lower defense costs, and the provision of consumer commodities, the Russian leader persuaded Reagan to work toward a 50 percent cut in nuclear weapons.

When Reagan and Gorbachev met again in Iceland in 1986, they nearly reached consensus on major arms reduction, but the Soviets insisted that the United States first confine development of Star Wars to laboratory research. Nevertheless, the summit resulted in an intermediate nuclear force (INF) treaty in 1987 that provided for the mutual dismantling of 2,611 medium- and short-range missiles in Europe. The pact included the most extensive system of weapons surveillance ever negotiated by the two superpowers. It was followed by Moscow's 1988 announcement of its intention to withdraw troops from Afghanistan. The United States signed on as a coguarantor of the resulting Geneva accords but struck an agreement that allowed it to arm Afghan Moslem rebels if the Soviets continued to supply the Marxist government in Kabul. The following month, the Senate took a major step toward ending the Cold War by ratifying the INF treaty.

THE LIMITS OF REAGANISM

Despite espousal of conservative rhetoric concerning free-market economics, Reagan's pragmatism carried over into domestic affairs. Although the administration promoted welfare spending cuts, Social Security outlays continued to expand from $138 billion in 1981 to $200 billion in 1986, while Medicare expenditures jumped from $41 billion to $74 billion. The president also maintained agricultural price supports, even authorizing government purchases of $2 billion in surplus dairy products. Facing protests by farmers suffering from mortgage foreclosures and bankruptcies in 1985, Reagan signed a five-year bill that appropriated nearly $170 billion in agricultural income subsidies, price supports, and food stamps. The White House made similar concessions after the EPA scandals when it approved legislation for stricter handling of hazardous wastes and agreed to a new $8.5 billion Superfund to clean up toxic dumps, although Congress overrode a veto to spend another $18 billion to combat water pollution. The president also accepted a $10.8 billion government bailout of bankrupt savings and loans.

Subsidies to special interests, hefty defense increases, continued social welfare spending, and reluctance to raise taxes thwarted the administration's plan to control the federal budget deficit. Facing a $220 billion shortfall in 1985, Congress passed the Gramm-Rudman-Hollings Act. The legislation established deficit-reduction targets and required the president to make across-the-board cuts if they were not met. Yet Congress failed to agree on budget reductions, and the Supreme Court ruled the automatic cuts unconstitutional in 1986. By the next fiscal year, spending had surpassed income by $576 billion. As the national debt grew beyond $3 trillion in the late 1980s, the United States became the world's largest borrower.

Exhibit 14-12. U.S. Federal Spending and Budget Deficits, 1980–1988 (in rounded billions of dollars)

Year	Outlays	Deficit
1980	590.9	73.8
1982	745.7	127.9
1984	851.8	185.3
1986	990.3	221.2
1988	1,064.1	155.2

Source: *Statistical Abstract of the United States* (1996).

Exhibit 14-13. U.S. Federal Spending on Human Resources, 1980–1988 (in rounded billions of dollars)

1980	313
1984	432
1988	533

Source: *Statistical Abstract of the United States* (1996).

**Exhibit 14-14. U.S. Government Spending as a Percentage
of Gross National Product, 1976–1986**

1976	33.9
1986	22.8

Source: *Economic Report of the President* (1977).
   Economic Report of the President (1988).

**Exhibit 14-15. U.S. Federal Debt, 1980–1988
(in rounded billions of dollars)**

1980	909
1984	1,565
1988	2,601

Source: *Economic Report of the President* (1996).

**Exhibit 14-16. U.S. Merchandise Trade Deficits, 1980–1988
(in rounded billions of dollars)**

1980	24.2
1982	31.8
1984	107.9
1986	152.7
1988	118.6

Source: *Statistical Abstract of the United States* (1996).

After failing to reverse the deficit, Congress enacted comprehensive tax reform in 1986. Corporations had received $150 billion in tax breaks during the first five years of the Reagan era. By reducing the number of income brackets, new legislation lowered tax rates on wealthy individuals and companies. Yet the law also eliminated or curtailed many business deductions and raised capital gains rates, measures that resulted in a return of $120 billion in tax obligations to businesses in the next five years. New regulations also eliminated millions of low-income taxpayers from the tax rolls.

Despite its commitment to economic growth, the administration failed to arrest foreign trade deficits. Because budget shortfalls prompted government borrowing on international exchanges, foreign consumers had fewer dollars with which to buy U.S. exports. Overseas manufacturing by U.S. multinationals also cost thousands of jobs at home. Congress sought to relieve textile, shoe, and copper producers by curbing imports in 1985, but Reagan vetoed the measure as protectionist. Yet as the trade deficit with Japan surpassed $50 billion in 1987 and Tokyo "dumped" below-cost computer chips on the U.S. market, the president overcame free-market sentiments to approve tariffs on Japanese electronic exports. He also signed a 1988 measure permitting retaliation against unfair trade practices and providing more than $3 billion to aid industries and workers facing overseas competition. When Congress passed another bill

Exhibit 14-17. U.S. Consumer Price Index, 1981–1987
(1967 = 100)

1981	272.4
1983	298.4
1985	322.2
1987	340.4

Source: *Economic Report of the President* (1988).

requiring manufacturers to provide sixty days' notice of plant closings and major layoffs, Reagan let it become law without his signature.

The president's record in placing conservatives on the Supreme Court was similarly mixed. Reagan appointed Arizona Judge Sandra Day O'Connor as the first woman Supreme Court justice in history in 1981, although O'Connor's record demonstrated moderate support for abortion rights. When Chief Justice Warren Burger retired in 1986, the White House chose Antonin Scalia, a conservative academic, to fill the vacancy and elevated William Rehnquist, the panel's most conservative member, to the presiding chair. Reagan anticipated exerting further judicial influence when he selected appeals court judge and constitutional scholar Robert H. Bork to fill a third vacancy in 1987. However, after regaining control of the Senate in the previous year's elections, the Democrats

Sandra Day O'Connor became the first woman to serve on the Supreme Court in 1981. Reagan's three appointments moved the political ideology of the court to the right.

rejected Bork's strict interpretation of constitutional rights protections as "extremist." Forced to abandon the nominee after a campaign by feminists and civil rights activists, the president settled on the less abrasive Anthony M. Kennedy, a California judge.

GEORGE BUSH AND THE END OF THE COLD WAR

After Ronald Reagan received the highest public opinion rating ever awarded to a departing president, Democratic candidates scrambled to win their party's 1988 nomination. Despite Reagan's popularity, workers and middle-class citizens had experienced no notable increase in income under his administration. In contrast, 1980s tax cuts boosted the earnings of the richest 1 percent of families by 87 percent—the greatest upward redistribution of income in U.S. history. Moreover, tax breaks and reduced federal regulation encouraged financial speculation and corporate mergers and led cost-conscious companies to downsize and phase out skilled manufacturing positions.

Once Democrat front-runner Gary Hart was forced out of the race by accusations of marital infidelity, Jesse Jackson responded to the economic inequities of the 1980s by refashioning a second presidential campaign around populist issues. Appealing to white workers and farmers as well as people of color, Jackson campaigned for higher taxes on corporations and the regulation of plant closings and relocations overseas. Although Jackson received nearly a third of the Democratic primary vote, Massachusetts Governor Michael Dukakis, a political centrist, emerged as the party nominee. A Greek American with extensive public administration experience, Dukakis took pride in his use

Exhibit 14-18. U.S. Corporate Profits and Dividends After Taxes, 1981–1987 (in billions of dollars, including inventory valuation and capital consumption adjustments)

1981	106.8
1983	136.5
1985	180.9
1987	167.8

Source: *Economic Report of the President* (1988).

Exhibit 14-19. U.S. Consumer Credit Outstanding, 1980–1987 (in rounded billions of dollars as of December of each year)

1980	369
1981	390
1983	468
1985	657
1987	756

Source: *Economic Report of the President* (1988).

REV. JESSE L. JACKSON
1941–

"God hasn't finished with me yet," Baptist minister Jesse L. Jackson told the 1984 Democratic National Convention after finishing third in the party's presidential sweepstakes. Four years later Jackson swept across the country in a fiery presidential campaign that brought him nearly a third of all Democratic primary votes. By the 1990s, Jackson's biracial reform agenda had earned him a reputation as the conscience of the Democratic Party and as a spokesperson for the nation's people of color.

Jackson was the illegitimate son of a teenage domestic from the cotton mill town of Greenville, South Carolina. He won an athletic scholarship to the University of Illinois but transferred to predominately black North Carolina Agricultural and Technical College in Greensboro after Illinois placed him on academic probation in his first year. Arriving in Greensboro months after students initiated the 1960 lunch-counter sit-ins, he became the star quarterback, student body president, and leader of the nonviolent demonstrations that ultimately integrated downtown businesses.

Chosen for a Rockefeller Foundation grant, Jackson attended the Chicago Theological Seminary but left one semester short of graduation to work with Martin Luther King, Jr.'s

AP/Wide World Photos

Southern Christian Leadership Conference (SCLC). King made the young activist head of Operation Breadbasket—an SCLC campaign that used boycotts and mass picketing to win jobs and contracts for black workers and businesses. However, the ambitious and individualistic Jackson received criticism for using heavy-handed tactics to intimidate businesses and came into frequent conflict with King and his associates. In 1971, citing Jackson's lack of organizational loyalty and discipline, the SCLC suspended the young minister, who wore his hair in a "natural," or Afro, style and liked to appear in African dashiki robes. Jackson seized the opportunity to create his own group, Operation PUSH (People United to Save Humanity).

Chicago-based PUSH sought to build a national campaign to restore African American pride. "I am somebody," Jackson chanted with the black youngsters he addressed. "I may be poor, but I am somebody." Jackson brought his self-help motivational programs into the public schools, where he crusaded against drug abuse, teenage pregnancy, truancy, and high drop-out rates. Between 1971 and 1983 PUSH attracted $17 million in government grants and private donations, al-

of tax incentives, an educated labor force, and a balanced budget to fashion an economic "miracle" in his home state. Combining proposals for national health insurance and investment in education with fiscal moderation, the governor chose Senator Lloyd Bentsen, a Texas conservative with expertise in finance, as his vice presidential partner.

Aware of the uneven distribution of Reagan-era prosperity, Republican campaign strategist Lee Atwater prepared the party for the 1988 election by concentrating on social issues. Seeking a coalition of nonaffluent white southerners and middle-class voters in northern suburbs, Atwater positioned the Republicans as opponents of crime, supporters of "family values," and defenders of patriotism. After defeating Senate Minority Leader Robert Dole in early primar-

though critics pointed to the organization's chaotic financial administration and poor management. "I'm a tree-shaker, not a jelly-maker," Jackson later explained.

An influential supporter of Jimmy Carter in 1976 and 1980, Jackson left PUSH to mount voter registration drives in 1983. After that year's election of Chicago African American reform mayor Harold Washington, Jackson announced his candidacy for the presidency. Party leaders, he proclaimed, were "too silent" and "too passive" about Ronald Reagan's policies. Jackson promised to represent "the poor and dispossessed of this nation" and to forge a "rainbow coalition" for those who were "rejected and . . . despised." Yet his campaign faltered when a black reporter revealed that the candidate had privately referred to Jews as "hymies" and to New York City as "Hymietown." Jackson apologized but never managed to repair the break with the Jewish community. Relations worsened when he was slow to disavow the support of Louis Farrakan, a Nation of Islam leader given to anti-Semitic pronouncements.

Addressing a broad constituency of peace activists, organized labor, environmentalists, farmers, liberals, and racial minorities, Jackson launched the National Rainbow Coalition and announced his second presidential candidacy in 1987. This time he combined an emphasis on the traditional values of self-respect and hard work with a populist program of economic justice. Jackson proposed to tax corporate mergers and to enact protections against plant closings and farm foreclosures. He spoke of "economic violence" against those "locked out of the system" and castigated multinational companies for exploiting cheap overseas labor at the expense of jobs at home.

Jackson sought to revitalize the U.S. economy by investing 10 percent of all public employee pension funds in housing, mass transit, and infrastructure. He promised to fund education and health care by cutting defense spending and by taxing corporate and individual wealth. "If I can win, you can win. We the people can win!" Jackson told voters in the 1988 Democratic presidential primaries. Astounding political professionals, the candidate finished a strong second.

By tying liberal programs to structural changes in the global economy, Jackson moved beyond the politics of race. Yet he continued to raise racial issues as a leading media commentator in the 1990s. Jackson played a key role in popularizing the term *African American* and in convincing Congress to make the birthday of Martin Luther King, Jr., a national holiday. He campaigned against South African apartheid, supported a U.S. role in restoring democracy in Haiti, and pushed for statehood for the District of Columbia. Recognized as a prime authority on racial discrimination, he participated in negotiations to end bias in corporations, the media, and professional athletics. Ever the caretaker of souls, Jackson denounced drugs and gang violence with customary fervor. Yet he also attacked welfare reform as a heartless abdication of national responsibility and pressed political leaders to address issues of social justice. ■

ies, Vice President George Bush won the party nomination. A Yale graduate, a World War II pilot, and the son of a former Republican senator from Connecticut, Bush had a successful early career in the Texas oil business. After two terms in the House, he served the Nixon White House as U.N. ambassador, chair of the Republican National Committee, and liaison to China. Bush spent the final year of the Ford presidency as CIA director. A social moderate and an internationalist, he chose James Danforth ("Dan") Quayle III, a conservative Indiana senator, as his running mate.

Following Atwater's strategy, Bush attacked Dukakis as an "ice man," a Harvard elitist whose membership in the rights-oriented American Civil Liberties Union (ACLU) betrayed liberal social values. Republicans focused on the

Exhibit 14-20. Election of 1988

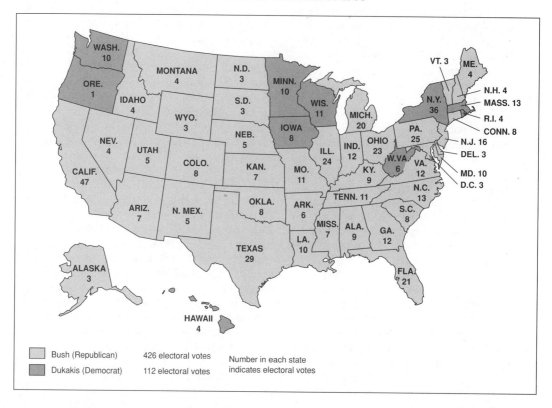

Bush (Republican) — 426 electoral votes
Dukakis (Democrat) — 112 electoral votes

Number in each state indicates electoral votes

Democratic governor's opposition to the death penalty and his vetoes of legislation requiring public school students to recite the Pledge of Allegiance and of a bill banning prison furloughs for first-degree murderers. Television ads dramatized the case of Willie Horton, a black convict serving a life sentence for murder who had raped a white woman while on furlough from a Massachusetts prison. The Republican candidates also celebrated Ronald Reagan's restoration of national dignity and the taming of the Soviet Union. Promising to sustain Reagan's legacy of domestic prosperity and deregulation, Bush issued an emphatic promise: "Read my lips—no new taxes!" To soften his image, the vice president spoke of a "kinder" and "gentler" nation whose volunteer charities formed "a thousand points of light."

Failing to respond to the Republican cultural assault and having no broad-based appeal, Dukakis suffered a humiliating defeat. In November the Bush-Quayle ticket captured 54 percent of the popular vote and a 426–112 victory in the Electoral College and swept the Republican Party to its fifth victory in the last six presidential elections. By taking 63 percent of the white male vote as well as most of that of southerners and suburbanites, Republicans tightened their grip on the key "Reagan Democrats." Once again, voter apathy and cynicism about politics lowered participation rates to barely more than 50 percent.

As Bush assumed the presidency in 1989, he responded slowly to East Germany's dismantling of the Berlin Wall and to the replacement of eastern Eu-

UPI/Corbis-Bettmann

George Bush, forty-first president of the United States.

rope's communist governments with democratic movements. Counseling caution, the president met with Mikhail Gorbachev after the Soviet Union's withdrawal from Afghanistan and its first free elections. Once Gorbachev was selected as the Soviet president in 1990, the two leaders accepted a mutual framework for nuclear disarmament and agreed to stop producing chemical weapons. The Cold War effectively ended later that year when the Conference on Security and Cooperation in Europe (comprising thirty European nations plus the United States and Canada) sponsored a treaty drastically limiting U.S. and Soviet forces and arms on the continent. After the signing of the Strategic Arms Reduction Treaty (START) in 1991, both nuclear superpowers eliminated most short-range nuclear weapons. When Gorbachev resigned as president, the Soviet Union dissolved, breaking up into its constituent republics, the most powerful of which was Russia.

Although Bush waited for signs of reform before providing aid to the former Soviet republics, he welcomed Russian president Boris Yeltsin as a negotiating

Exhibit 14-21. U.S. Voter Participation, 1984–1988
(as a percentage of eligible voters)

1984	53.3
1988	50.3

Source: *Statistical Abstract of the United States* (1996).

Exhibit 14-22. Bosnia, 1995

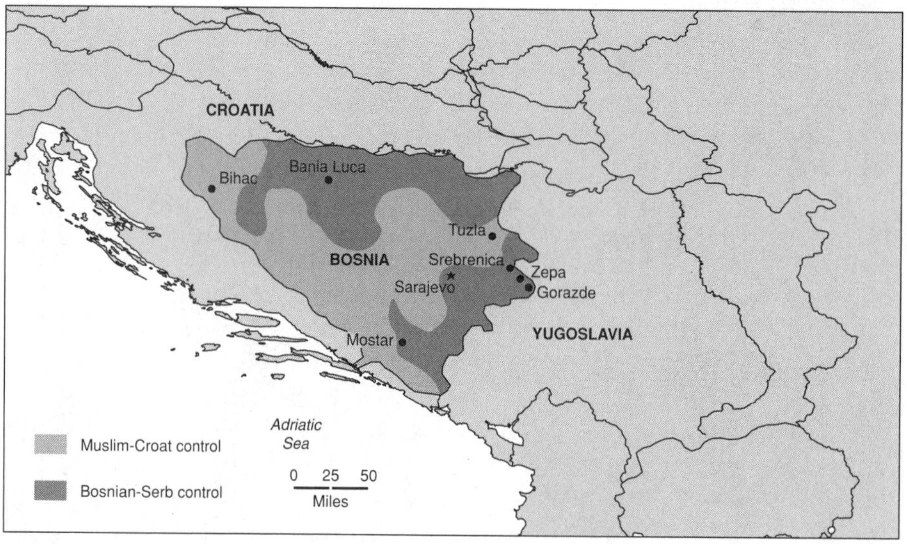

partner. Meeting in Moscow in early 1993, the two leaders signed START II, which reduced world tensions by providing for the gradual elimination of all land-based nuclear missiles. Yet the end of the Cold War destabilized world politics instead of bringing peace. When the communist federation in Yugoslavia dissolved in 1992, Croatian and Serbian military forces mounted armed attacks on the Muslim-dominated breakaway state of Bosnia-Herzegovina. Although the Croats soon recognized Bosnian independence, the Serbian army and nationalist militias initiated a genocidal campaign of "ethnic cleansing" to rid Bosnia of Muslims. The Bush administration joined European allies in imposing sanctions on Serbia. When the Bosnian Serbs cut off supply lines to the capital city of Sarajevo, Congress authorized the use of U.S. military force to assist in the delivery of food and medical supplies.

THE GULF WAR AND THE NEW WORLD ORDER

Although the slaughter of Bosnian civilians rekindled bitter memories of World War II, the United States had no vital interests in southeastern Europe. This contrasted with the situation in the Persian Gulf, the oil lifeline for Western Europe and Japan—Washington's partners in the global economy. In the summer of 1990 Iraqi President Saddam Hussein invaded his oil-rich neighbor Kuwait, annexed it, and placed troops on the Saudi Arabian border. The U.N. Security Council unanimously condemned Iraq as an aggressor and demanded unconditional withdrawal. The council then ordered an economic embargo against Baghdad and authorized U.N. members to use all necessary means to

Iraqi prisoners captured on the first day of the ground attack during the Persian Gulf War of 1991. By the end of the war more than 70,000 Iraqis would be in Allied custody.

liberate Kuwait. In cooperation with the Soviets and twenty-six other countries, including Saudi Arabia, Egypt, and Syria, Bush organized Operation Desert Storm. Under the leadership of General Colin Powell, whom the president had appointed as the first African American Chair of the Joint Chiefs of Staff, and of General H. Norman Schwarzkopf, 540,000 U.S. and 160,000 Allied troops participated in the largest military mobilization since World War II.

After spirited debate and a 52–47 vote in the Senate early in 1991, Congress authorized the Bush administration to use force to back the U.N. mandate. The Gulf War began with a six-week air and missile campaign that included 70,000 bombing sorties in its first month. Once Iraq's air force, radar, communications, and chemical weapons plants had been destroyed, Bush set a deadline for Baghdad's withdrawal from Kuwait. As Hussein predicted victory in "the mother of all battles," the United States orchestrated an attack from the west on Iraqi ground forces along a front that was 300 miles wide. Expecting an assault from the Persian Gulf, Hussein's troops retreated or were left isolated while his infantry fled Kuwait. Yet Bush was anxious to avoid the extensive casualties and controversy of a prolonged war and feared the rise of nationalistic sentiment in Baghdad. Accordingly, the White House terminated the one-sided rout within hours and celebrated the most decisive U.S. military victory since World War II.

Bush also depicted the triumph of the U.S., European, and Arab alliance as the fruit of the post–Cold War "new world order." Proclaiming that the time had come "to put an end to Arab-Israeli conflict," the president sought to stabilize the volatile Middle East by arranging peace talks between Israel, neigh-

Exhibit 14-23. Persian Gulf War

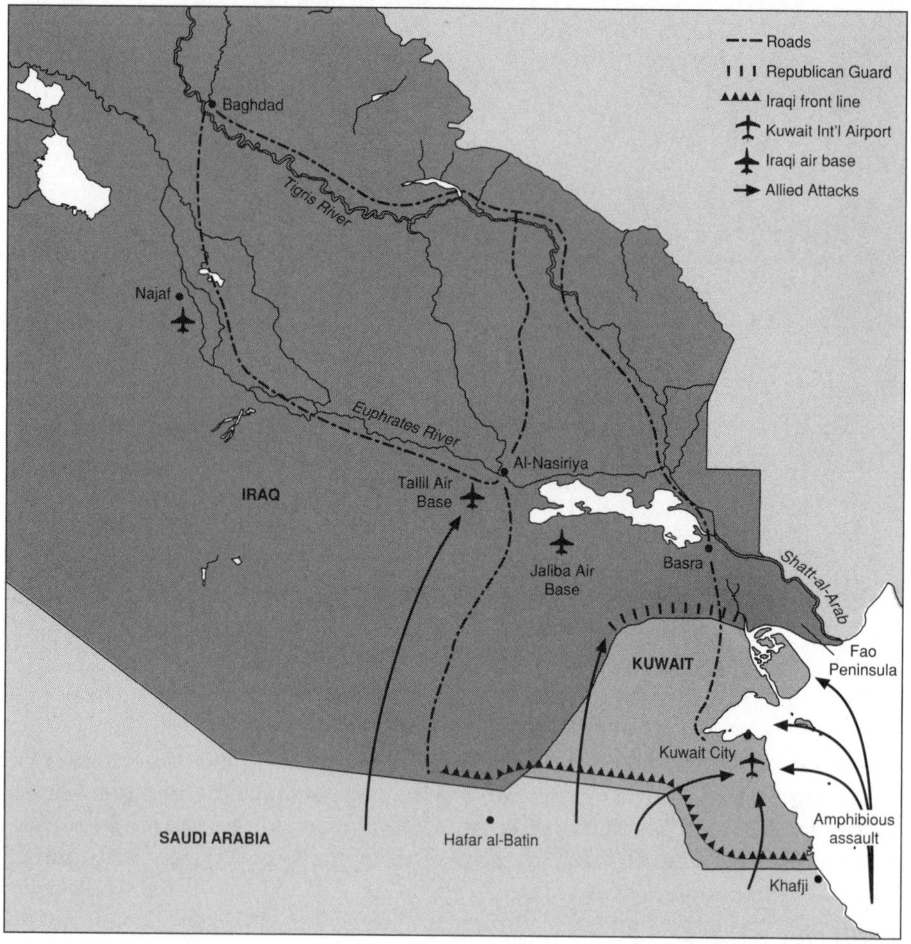

boring Arab states, and the Palestinians. Under U.S. and Soviet auspices, the Madrid Conference of 1991 addressed Bush's call for a "comprehensive" accord grounded on the "principle of territory for peace." When the conservative Israeli government expanded Jewish settlements in the West Bank and Gaza, however, Secretary of State James A. Baker III prevailed on the president to postpone $10 billion in Israeli housing loan guarantees. Washington's displeasure with Israel contributed to a 1992 victory by the opposition Israeli Labor Party, which promised to restrain the growth of settlements and accepted restrictions on the use of the loan guarantees. Bush also honored international commitments by sending 28,000 troops to Somalia in 1992 after famine and factional warfare prompted the U.N. Security Council to request military protection for food relief efforts.

The Bush White House closely monitored events in Central America, where Panamanian leader General Manuel Noriega Morena had been indicted by the Reagan administration for drug trafficking and money laundering. When Noriega halted free elections and incited violence against U.S. citizens and military officers in 1989, Bush mobilized 24,000 troops to capture and arrest the dictator. After inflicting 700 Panamanian casualties and detaining 4,000 people, the army forced Noriega to seek refuge in Panama's Vatican embassy, where he surrendered, and from which he was returned to the United States to stand trial. After military authorities installed Panama's duly elected leader as president, the Bush administration granted the new government $462 million in emergency aid. For Nicaragua, where a conservative defeated Sandinista President Daniel Ortega in internationally supervised elections in 1990, Congress approved $300 million in economic assistance. Tensions also eased in El Salvador when Washington brokered a 1992 peace treaty ending the twelve-year civil war.

ECONOMIC STAGNATION AND THE ELECTION OF 1992

Most comfortable with foreign policy and trapped in "gridlock" with a Democratic Congress, Bush compiled a mixed record in domestic affairs. The president fulfilled campaign promises by awarding grants to establish volunteer service projects and by providing $22 billion in tax credits and aid for child care programs. Bush also signed the Clean Air Act of 1990, which reduced the emission of industrial pollutants that cause acid rain, which placed new pollution controls on autos, and which phased out the use of chemicals that threaten the ozone layer. A six-year transportation bill passed in 1991 provided more than $150 billion for mass transit and other projects. Yet Bush vetoed legislation to permit workers to leave jobs for family emergencies, to allow voters to register at state motor vehicle bureaus, to provide urban aid, and to cap campaign spending on congressional elections.

Concerned about declining support among social conservatives, the White House endorsed a constitutional amendment in 1989 to protect the flag. Yet Congress would go no further than to pass a law prohibiting flag desecration, and the measure was overturned by the Supreme Court on First Amendment grounds. Anxious to move the tribunal to the right, Bush appointed conservative New Hampshire federal judge David H. Souter to the court. Yet the president ran into objections from liberals and civil rights advocates when he sought to replace retiring African American Justice Thurgood Marshall in 1991 with federal appeals court judge Clarence Thomas. A black conservative, Thomas had administered cuts as Reagan's chair of the Equal Employment Opportunities Commission (EEOC). The nomination became more controversial when African American law professor Anita Hill, a former EEOC employee, charged Thomas with sexual harassment. Despite rancorous televised hearings and criticism from women's groups, the appointment was confirmed by a close 52–48 vote.

Bush faced bitter opposition from his own political party as a result of a 1990 budget stalemate. The controversy emerged when House Democrats forced the White House to accept a tax hike in exchange for lower federal spending.

Exhibit 14-24. U.S. Federal Budget Deficits, 1988–1992
(in rounded billions of dollars)

1988	155
1990	221
1992	290

Source: *Statistical Abstract of the United States* (1996).

Apprehensive about the $3.2 trillion national debt and about annual federal budget deficits of more than $220 billion, Bush consented to higher taxes of $146 billion if Congress would promise to cut the deficit by $500 billion in five years. Nearly half the projected savings were to come from increasing tax rates on top incomes, one-fourth from entitlement cuts, and one-fourth from defense reductions. Yet Republicans argued that federal taxation already amounted to nearly one-fifth of the gross domestic product and condemned the president for betraying his campaign promise of "no new taxes."

The reversal of the administration's position on tax policy added to the perception that Bush was not focusing on the nation's economic difficulties. Shortly after the president took office in 1989, he had encountered a recession characterized by poor rates of investment and stagnating income, a result in part of excessive speculation during the 1980s. Bankruptcy rates were particularly severe in the deregulated savings and loan industry. Faced with the insolvency of 250 lending institutions in 1989, Congress provided the Federal Deposit Insurance Corporation with $20 billion and added another $73 billion in the next four years to reimburse investors and to rehabilitate delinquent banks. In another move to revitalize the economy, the president supplemented unemployment benefits with nearly $6 billion in 1991. Nevertheless, when Bush sought reelection in 1992, joblessness had risen to 7.5 percent, the annual trade deficit had ballooned to $150 billion, and the yearly budget deficit was nearing $300 billion. Since 1977, moreover, the poorest two-fifths of families had experienced an absolute decline in earnings.

Ironically, the president's success in defeating Saddam Hussein removed foreign policy from consideration and opened the door for Democratic criticism of White House economic policy. As the 1992 presidential campaign approached, former California Governor Edmund (Jerry) Brown campaigned for a flat (single-rate) income tax, denounced plant closings, and used a free telephone number to recruit volunteers to challenge money-driven politics. Senator Paul Simon of Illinois and former Senator Paul E. Tsongas of Massachusetts focused on targeted spending cuts to balance the federal budget. Tennessee Senator Albert (Al) Gore, Jr., combined fiscal moderation with attention to the environment, to education, and to computer literacy. Yet the Democratic front-runner turned out to be the virtually unknown governor of Arkansas—William (Bill) Jefferson Clinton.

Raised by a widowed mother who worked outside the home, Clinton had aspired to political life since boyhood. During the height of the Vietnam controversy in the mid-1960s, he attended Georgetown University and worked for antiwar Senator J.W. Fulbright of Arkansas. Opposed to the U.S. presence in Vietnam, Clinton accepted a prestigious Rhodes scholarship to attend Oxford University and managed to avoid the draft. A graduate of Yale Law School,

Baby boomers in the White House—President Bill Clinton and First Lady Hillary Rodham Clinton.

Clinton won election as the nation's youngest governor in 1978 and served five terms. In 1990, after cofounding the Democratic Leadership Council, which he also chaired, he pushed the party to adopt moderate positions on the budget and on social issues such as abortion, crime, and welfare. Despite questions about his personal life, Clinton used his centrist political base to sweep six southern primaries and to capture the 1992 Democratic presidential nomination. Defying political wisdom, he chose fellow southerner Al Gore as his running mate.

By opposing "tax and spend" liberalism and by promising to "reinvent government" and to reform welfare, Clinton took his place as a "New Democrat." However, he also criticized the "trickle-down economics" of the Republicans. Rallying to the cry, "it's the economy, stupid," Clinton aides promoted their candidate as an agent of change who would rescue the beleaguered middle

Exhibit 14-25. U.S. Gross Federal Debt, 1988–1992
(in rounded trillions of dollars)

1988	2.6
1990	3.2
1992	4.0

Source: *Statistical Abstract of the United States* (1996).

**Exhibit 14-26. U.S. Merchandise Trade Deficits, 1988–1992
(in rounded billions of dollars)**

1988	119
1990	102
1992	84

Source: *Statistical Abstract of the United States* (1996).

**Exhibit 14-27. U.S. Federal Social Welfare Spending, 1980–1990
(in rounded billions and as a percentage of gross national product)**

Year	Amount	Percentage
1980	303	11.4
1985	451	11.3
1990	617	11.1

Source: *Statistical Abstract of the United States* (1996).

class by "Putting People First." Bush survived a spirited primary challenge from former Nixon speech writer Patrick Buchanan, who fused conservative social values and economic nationalism. Yet Buchanan's strident references to "culture wars" during his convention address alienated party moderates and independents, particularly among the half of the electorate now living in suburbs. Bush was also hurt by the third-party candidacy of H. Ross Perot, a self-made billionaire who promised to break Washington gridlock by taking government away from the "politicians." Launching his campaign on a cable TV talk show, Perot called for federal spending cuts and a balanced budget, tighter trade regulations, and a national industrial policy.

Although Perot performed well in three televised debates, Clinton outdid his rivals as a master of modern media. Through televised "town meetings" (including an effective pitch for the youth vote on MTV), the Arkansas governor established personal rapport with voters. By positioning himself as a centrist, Clinton captured a plurality of independent votes, equaled Bush's total among whites, and made strong inroads among Republican suburbanites. Taking seven of the ten largest states and several southern states, the 1992 Democratic ticket received 370 votes in the Electoral College compared with 168 for the Republicans. In the popular ballot, Clinton scored 43 percent in contrast to 37 percent for Bush and to 19 percent for Perot—certainly not a Clinton mandate. In winning only their second presidential contest since 1964, however, the Democrats benefitted from a voter turnout of 55 percent of eligible voters, the highest participation rate in twenty years.

BILL CLINTON AND
POST–COLD WAR DIPLOMACY

Clinton's inaugural address focused on economic revitalization and citizen assumption of personal responsibility. However, amid the instabilities of the post–

Exhibit 14-28. The Election of 1992

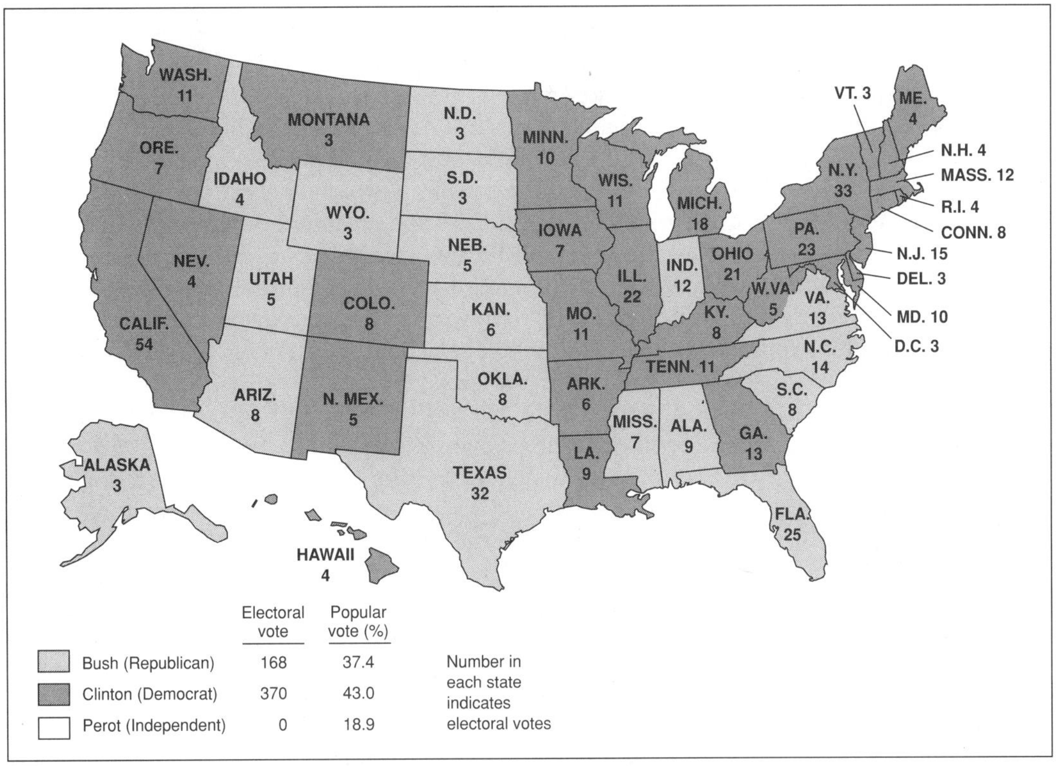

	Electoral vote	Popular vote (%)
Bush (Republican)	168	37.4
Clinton (Democrat)	370	43.0
Perot (Independent)	0	18.9

Number in each state indicates electoral votes

Exhibit 14-29. U.S. Voter Participation, 1988–1992
(as a percentage of eligible voters)

1988	50.3
1992	55.1

Source: *Statistical Abstract of the United States* (1996).

Cold War period, global politics assumed a more important role than the leader of the world's sole superpower anticipated. Weeks after taking office, Clinton met with Russian President Yeltsin. As the two nations extended a mutual moratorium on nuclear testing, the White House promised to provide $1.6 billion in emergency aid to the struggling Russians. Having suppressed a 1992 rebellion led by nationalist and communist members of Parliament, Yeltsin's hold on power was tenuous. When the Russian leader sent the army to the province of Chechnya in 1994 to subdue a separatist revolt, poorly equipped troops suffered major losses and inflicted huge civilian casualties. Yet after continued support from Clinton, Yeltsin prevailed in Russia's first democratic elections, withdrew the military from Chechnya, and survived a dangerous coronary bypass operation in 1996.

The Clinton administration continued Bush's enforcement of economic sanctions against Iraq until international inspectors certified the dismantling of

Baghdad's chemical, biological, and nuclear weapons. U.S. fighter planes also led Allied patrols of "no-fly" zones to prevent Iraqi attacks on rebellious ethnic enclaves. Days before leaving office in 1993, Bush had bombed air defense sites in southern Iraq used to disrupt Allied monitors. After receiving information that Saddam Hussein had sponsored a plan to assassinate former president Bush, Clinton unleashed cruise missile attacks on Baghdad intelligence head-quarters in 1993. The White House orchestrated a second series of strikes after Hussein attacked Kurdish enclaves in northern Iraq. When Baghdad mobilized a large military force at Kuwait's border in 1994, the president deployed 36,000 troops to the region before the Iraqis withdrew. Hardened by these provoca-tions, the United States insisted on enforcing sanctions despite their huge toll on Iraq's civilians and children. In 1996, however, Iraq agreed to permit the United Nations to administer its foreign oil sales and to channel oil revenues back to Iraq to provide food and medical relief.

The complexities of post–Cold War policy also emerged in Somalia, where the U.S. military turned food relief efforts over to the United Nations in 1993. Finding themselves in the middle of factional strife, commanders initiated a campaign to capture General Mohammed Farah Aidid, a powerful warlord who refused to engage in peace talks. When fighting erupted, Aidid's followers killed eighteen U.S. soldiers and paraded their bodies before jubilant crowds. Under intense congressional pressure, Clinton ordered 15,000 more troops to Somalia, but only to assure an orderly military withdrawal by April 1994. Con-demned for allowing the Somalia operation to drift from humanitarian aid to involvement in a civil war, the White House promised to seek purely political solutions to the conflict.

Although peacemaking failed in Somalia, the Clinton administration as-sumed an important role as an international power broker. After a military coup overthrew Haiti's freely elected Jean-Bertrand Aristide in 1991, President Bush had supported a U.N. oil and arms embargo against the regime but returned thousands of refugees who had entered the United States after fleeing the Carib-

Exhibit 14-30. Deployment of U.S. Troops to Somalia, 1993

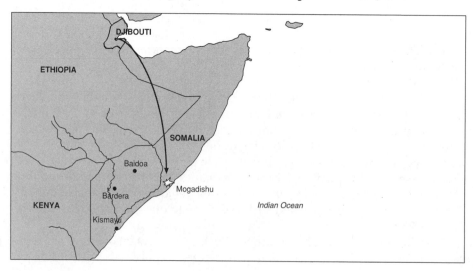

bean island. Clinton upheld the refugee policy in 1993 but supervised an agreement to restore democracy. When Haitian ships blocked a U.S. attempt to implement the accord, the president backed reimposition of the U.N. embargo and threatened an invasion. In a final attempt to win a peaceful transition of leadership, Clinton sent Senator Sam Nunn, retired General Colin Powell, and former President Jimmy Carter to Haiti in 1994. Once the Haitian military accepted Washington's offers of relocation and financial assistance, the president dispatched 15,000 troops to the island to maintain order while Aristide completed his term of office. Opposed by many in Congress, the deployment restored democracy.

Anxious to please the large population of Cuban Americans in southern Florida without encouraging a mass influx of refugees, Clinton mixed conciliatory and hard-line stances toward the communist government of Cuba's Fidel Castro. Once Cuba's subsidies from the Soviet Union disappeared, the Bush administration sought to expedite the overthrow of Cuban communism by tightening trade sanctions. Clinton followed a different course by relaxing travel restrictions and by permitting humanitarian relief and cultural exchanges with the island. Yet when Havana shot down two planes belonging to a Cuban exile group in 1996, the president signed the Helms-Burton bill, which permitted citizens to sue foreign companies that had acquired or conducted commerce with properties confiscated by the Cuban government. Clinton avoided a confrontation with European and Canadian allies, who protested the measure as a violation of their sovereignty, by invoking a clause of the law that allowed him to postpone enactment of its provisions.

Communism continued to figure in post–Cold War diplomacy when intelligence indicated that North Korea was assembling materials to develop nuclear weapons. Clinton dispatched Jimmy Carter to forge a 1994 agreement by which Japan and South Korea financed construction of atomic reactors incapable of producing weapons-grade plutonium. In another effort at alleviating tensions with a communist power, the administration prevailed on Vietnam to assist efforts to locate the remains of more than 2,000 U.S. servicemen missing in action during the Vietnam War. While extending formal diplomatic recognition to the former adversary in 1995, Clinton celebrated "the opportunity to bind up our wounds." In yet another effort directed at international healing, the White House appointed former Senator George Mitchell to coordinate 1996 peace talks on British-held Northern Ireland. When the nationalist Irish Republican Army (IRA) refused to agree to a cease-fire, the negotiations sputtered and sporadic terrorism continued.

The struggle to realize a peaceful "new world order" received its greatest challenge in Bosnia. As Serbian militias continued "ethnic cleansing" and shelled Sarajevo, Clinton called for North Atlantic Treaty Organization (NATO) air strikes against Serbian positions. Such a policy endangered European peacekeepers already on the ground, and the United States agreed to confine its efforts to the enforcement of U.N. "no-fly" zones. Under pressure from Senate Republican leader Robert Dole, the administration stopped using military force to enforce the arms embargo against the besieged Bosnian Muslims, although Clinton deferred to European allies by vetoing a bill to unilaterally lift the arms embargo. In 1995 the president took the initiative in Bosnia by convening a peace conference outside Dayton, Ohio. The ensuing accords established a cease-fire between the warring parties and organized internationally supervised elections. The agreement also called for the deployment of 20,000 U.S. troops to the region as part of a NATO peacekeeping force, a provision that Congress acceded to but did not endorse.

Clinton exerted his strongest efforts at personal diplomacy in the Middle East. After the Labor government of Yitzhak Rabin conducted secret talks in Norway with Yasir Arafat's Palestine Liberation Organization, the president invited both leaders to Washington in 1993 to sign a Declaration of Principles. Marked by a historic handshake between the former adversaries, the pact included mutual recognition and a renunciation of armed conflict and terrorism. It also provided for an interim period of Palestinian self-rule in Gaza and in much of the West Bank, to be followed by Israeli troop withdrawals and negotiations for a permanent settlement. One year later, Israel and Jordan signed another treaty. Although renewed conflict seriously undermined these agreements, the Clinton administration pressed both sides to preserve the peace process.

Despite Clinton's focus on peacekeeping, the administration sought a credible response to foreign-based terrorism. In 1988 a bomb had destroyed a U.S. civilian airliner over Scotland and had killed all 259 people on board. After federal prosecutors indicted two Libyan intelligence officers and Tripoli denied requests for their extradition, Congress banned all aid to Libya, and the United Nations imposed economic sanctions. Meanwhile, Washington linked Iran to Islamic fundamentalists convicted of the 1993 bombing of the New York World Trade Center and of plots to blow up the U.N. complex and other buildings. In 1996 Clinton signed legislation placing sanctions on foreign companies investing in the oil industries of Libya or Iran. Although European petroleum importers objected to interference with their economic sovereignty, suspicion of Iran heightened in 1996 when Saudi investigators linked Tehran to a terrorist bomb that killed nineteen soldiers at a U.S. military facility in Saudi Arabia.

CLINTON AND THE DOMESTIC AGENDA

After taking office as economic recovery began in 1993, Clinton produced a five-year budget that proposed to cut the federal deficit by nearly $500 billion. The president had hoped to enact a $70 billion energy tax to fund a massive jobs programs. Instead, he responded to frustration with big government by agreeing to provide half the deficit reduction by cutting defense spending, Medicare payments to doctors and hospitals, and discretionary appropriations.

Exhibit 14-31. U.S. Federal Budget Deficits, 1992–1996 (in rounded billions of dollars)

1992	290
1994	203
1996	146 (estimate)

Source: *Statistical Abstract of the United States* (1996).

**Exhibit 14-32. U.S. Gross Federal Debt, 1992–1996
(in rounded trillions of dollars)**

1992	4.0
1994	4.6
1996	5.2 (estimate)

Source: *Statistical Abstract of the United States* (1996).

The second half of the deficit reduction would come from increased gas taxes, higher tax rates on wealthy individuals, and additional taxes on affluent Social Security recipients. When not one Republican supported the budget, the House passed the measure by a single vote, and Vice President Gore was forced to break a tie in the Senate. Gambling that deficit reduction would lower interest rates and would extend the recovery, the president assigned Gore to chair a committee to trim the federal bureaucracy.

Clinton found eliciting congressional cooperation for moderate social programs easier. Congress passed the Family Leave Act, which permits workers in large companies to take twelve weeks of unpaid leave for family or medical purposes. The president also signed the Motor Voter registration bill, which Bush had vetoed. The Brady bill, another piece of unfinished legislation from the Bush era, established a five-day waiting period for handgun purchases, although the measure was to be replaced in five years by the computer checking system favored by the National Rifle Association. Clinton also won approval for his National Service Plan, which provided selected students with $10,000 each in earnings from community service work to help pay for higher education. A rider in the budget bill eased the financial burden of college students by permitting the government to extend the terms of tuition loans without using private lenders. Seeking to position himself in the political center, the president appointed moderates Ruth Bader Ginsburg and Stephen G. Breyer to the Supreme Court.

The most important achievement of the Clinton administration's first year was ratification of the North American Free Trade Agreement (NAFTA), which Bush had signed in late 1992. The controversial treaty eliminated taxes or rules impeding the flow of trade between the United States, Mexico, and Canada. Seeking to overcome the objections of union activists and environmentalists, Clinton had completed supplemental agreements establishing labor and pollution standards. Nevertheless, the AFL-CIO argued that lower trade barriers would encourage multinational corporations to desert the United States for cheaper labor in Mexico. Similar protectionist fears dominated Ross Perot's opposition to the pact, which emerged in a widely viewed television debate with Vice President Gore. Ironically, Republican free-trade supporters like House Minority Leader Newt Gingrich provided the administration with the votes needed to overcome the resistance of Democratic protectionists. After the enactment of NAFTA, ten nations at the Pacific Summit joined the United States in calling for extended trade liberalization.

Despite moderate legislative successes, the Clinton administration suffered stunning political reverses in its first year. Inadequate background checks and poor groundwork resulted in the president's early withdrawal of his nominations for several political offices. Clinton also made a tactical error when he

FEDERICO F. PEÑA
1947–

Reuters/Corbis-Bettmann

The rapid rise of Energy Secretary Federico Peña illustrated the ethnic dimension of the "New Democrat" political movement. A member of a prominent South Texas Hispanic family, Peña grew up in Brownsville. The son of a cotton broker who stressed discipline, he served as an altar boy before attending the University of Texas at Austin. Peña joined protests against the Vietnam War before earning his law degree in 1972. He then moved to Denver, where he became a staff lawyer for the Mexican American Legal Defense and Educational Fund. Peña concentrated on police brutality and voting rights cases before signing on as legal advisor to the Chicano Education Project, which involved him in efforts to promote bilingual education.

At thirty-one, Peña began his political career with election to the Colorado legislature, where he was chosen as Democratic minority speaker within three years. He built on these successes in 1983 by running for mayor of Denver against a fourteen-year incumbent. Although only 18 percent of the city was Hispanic, Peña won the support of voters with the slogan, "Denver: Imagine a Great City." Yet in the mid-1980s an economic slump in the oil, mining, and high-technology industries produced high vacancy rates in downtown Denver offices and prompted the defeat of Peña's proposal to build a new convention center. When he stood for reelection in 1987, Peña faced a twenty-two-point deficit in the polls. Resorting to negative advertising, he portrayed his Republican opponent as a tool of big business and scored another close victory.

Peña continued to face difficulties in 1988 when voters nearly recalled him after a blizzard fell and many neighborhood streets remained uncleared. However, the mayor promoted Denver as a major trade and commercial center and won approval of a $330 million bond issue to repair and build roads, bridges, and public buildings. He also gained public support for the convention center, a multibillion-dollar airport, and a major-league baseball franchise.

Seeking to implement a campaign promise that executive appointments would reflect diversity, President Clinton opened his first cabinet to an unprecedented number of women, African Americans, and Hispanics. Named as secretary of transportation, a position in which he supervised more than 100,000 employees, Peña enforced stricter fuel economy standards and encouraged the establishment of new airlines to compete with the major carriers. He also developed plans for environmentally protective high-speed trains and directed the investment of pension funds in the modernization of transportation systems.

When a vacancy occurred in the Department of Energy in 1997, Clinton appointed Peña to the high-profile post. The secretary's experience as transportation and infrastructure czar made him a logical choice for the nomination. The 1996 campaign's large Democratic Hispanic vote also impressed White House advisors. A jogger fond of cooking Mexican cuisine, Federico Peña perfectly combined the virtues of urban professionalism with long-standing traditions of ethnic identity and politics. ■

addressed the emotional issue of homosexuality at the beginning of his term. After making campaign promises to gay activists, and viewing bias as an obstacle to the optimal use of human resources, the president prepared an executive

Exhibit 14-33. U.S. Merchandise Trade Deficits, 1992–1995
(in rounded billions of dollars)

1992	84
1995	160

Source: *Statistical Abstract of the United States* (1996).

order ending discrimination against homosexuals in the armed forces. After a firestorm of opposition within the military and Congress, he amended the order to permit homosexuals to serve only if they did not publicly acknowledge their sexual orientation or engage in homosexual acts ("don't ask, don't tell"). Because the president had shifted positions in midstream, critics accused him of "waffling," an accusation the White House had difficulty in countering.

A more telling disappointment came when Congress refused to act on a national health insurance plan advanced by a panel led by the president's wife, Hillary Rodham Clinton. The administration sought to elevate health care to a civil right and to divide the responsibility to provide medical services between government and the market. It also proposed to enroll consumers in health care alliances that would contract for medical coverage with private insurers. Government regulation of premiums, costs, and quality were to assure "managed competition" in a system in which employers would absorb most of the costs. Clinton hoped to provide health care insurance for 40 million uncovered citizens, to reduce welfare costs, to increase the quality of the labor force, and to enhance family security. However, small businesses and some employers opposed the 1,342-page proposal, and an intensive television campaign by private insurers helped to kill the legislation when it aroused public anxieties about government bureaucracy.

Immobilized by the health care disaster, the administration returned to more modest proposals in 1994. Congress passed Clinton's Goals 2000 legislation, a $400 million "human investment" designed to establish the first national educational standards. Congress also approved $575 million for projects encouraging defense contractors to diversify into production for civilian markets. The session's most important legislation was the Omnibus Crime Bill, which created a six-year, $30 billion trust fund to provide grants to the states to hire 100,000 more police, to build prisons, and to create crime prevention programs. A centrist combination of punishment and prevention, the measure banned nineteen assault weapons, expanded the federal death penalty, and mandated life imprisonment for three-time violent federal offenders ("three strikes, you're out"). The bill also appropriated more than $1.6 billion to fight violence against women and $1 billion for special courts to rehabilitate nonviolent drug abusers.

Despite administration success on the crime issue, Republican leaders believed the Democrat-led Congress was vulnerable in 1994. Five years earlier, House Speaker James Wright had resigned his seat amid charges of ethical misconduct. In 1992 a government investigation revealed rampant abuses at the House bank and post office. The inquiry resulted in the indictment of Dan Rostenkowski, the Democratic chair of the House Ways and Means Committee. Public outrage regarding congressional corruption became so intense that Congress outlawed midterm raises in the Twenty-seventh Amendment, ratified by the states in 1992. Charging the Democratic leadership with a forty-year record of cronyism and greed, Minority Leader Newt Gingrich prepared to take control of the House by drafting a "Contract with America." Signed as a manifesto and 1994 campaign tool by 350 Republican House incumbents and candidates, the document promised votes on mandatory term limits, a balanced budget amendment, welfare reform, tougher law enforcement, deregulation, "profamily" legislation, and a strong national defense.

REINVENTING REFORM

The Contract with America helped Republicans take 230 seats in the House, compared with 204 for the Democrats, and produced a 52–48 Republican majority in the Senate. In a reversal of gains made in 1992, the Democrats lost 54 percent of the male vote and 62 percent of the white male vote, although 54 percent of women voted Democratic. Ideologically opposed to big government, first-year Republicans influenced the most independent Congress since 1946. Starting with internal business, the House opened the 1995 session by eliminating many committees and subcommittees, by cutting committee staffs by one-third, by agreeing to abide by workplace rules imposed elsewhere by federal law, and by placing term limits on House and committee officers.

Gingrich's House fulfilled the Contract with America by passing a bill to curb unfunded federal government mandates, a measure that Clinton signed. A proposal to provide the president with line-item veto power was sent to the Senate, although Clinton did not sign it until 1996. In another bold move, the House passed a constitutional amendment requiring a balanced budget by the year 2002, but this measure fell one vote short of the necessary two-thirds majority in the Senate and was again three votes shy of such a majority in 1996. To round out its agenda, the House legislated welfare reform, capital gains tax relief, and a $500 tax credit for children, although none of these bills made it to the Senate in 1995. Meanwhile, Gingrich honored the Contract with America by introducing a constitutional amendment to limit congressional terms to twelve years, although the proposal fell short of the necessary two-thirds majority.

Stunned by the health care disaster and his party's loss of Congress, Clinton sought to repair the damage by delivering a 1995 State of the Union address proclaiming that the era of big government was over. Yet as the White House moved to reestablish its centrist credentials, congressional Republicans overestimated the president's weakness. Promising a budget that would lead to elimination of the federal deficit in seven years, Gingrich and Senate Majority Leader Bob Dole combined substantial tax cuts with reductions in the growth of Medicare and Medicaid and decreased aid to education and the environment. After the Democrats ran television commercials that accused the Republican leadership of attacking health care for the elderly, Clinton vetoed the appropriations bill. Without a budget, the government shut down twice in November and December 1995, which disrupted Social Security and Medicare payments as well as the operation of national parks and museums. As congressional approval ratings plunged to less than 30 percent, Clinton's popularity soared beyond the fifty-fifth percentile, providing a signal to the White House that the public approved of the president's tough stance.

Riding high in the polls, Clinton waited until the spring of 1996 to accept a budget. Although the president embraced moderate reductions in domestic spending, the Republicans dropped restrictions on environmental regulation and restored cuts affecting education, job training, and the environment. As both parties began looking ahead to the coming election, congressional leaders and the White House moved toward the political center. Republicans accepted a minimum wage increase formerly opposed by Dole, now a presidential candidate. In another gesture of conciliation, Clinton and Congress agreed to a telecommunications bill that replaced government regulation with guarantees of open competition among telephone, information, and cable TV companies. The president also approved a seven-year farm bill that abolished New Deal planting restrictions and provided for gradual reductions of crop subsidies.

Health care and welfare reform proved to be the most dramatic examples of the new bipartisanship. The Kassenbaum-Kennedy bill sought to correct weaknesses in the medical system by allowing workers to carry insurance from job to job, by establishing medical savings accounts, by increasing health insurance tax deductions for the self-employed, and by providing tax breaks for long-term health care insurance. Initiated by the Reagan administration, welfare reform had been a target of both Clinton's presidential campaign and the Republican Contract with America. The White House now sought to avoid Republican criticism by agreeing to the most far-reaching changes in the federal public assistance program since its inception in the 1930s. The Welfare Reform Act of 1996 returned aid programs to the states through federal block grants, compelled nearly a half-million adult recipients to find work in two years, placed a five-year limit on help to the needy, and restricted aid to legal immigrants who were not citizens.

Declaring that government assistance provided a second chance, not a way of life, Clinton promoted welfare reform as a means to bring the poor into the economic mainstream. Yet congressional liberals, federal welfare officials, and activists like Jesse Jackson questioned what they perceived as the abandonment of poor women and children. The president promised to use his next term to add tax incentives for businesses that hired former welfare recipients, to provide extra funds for job training, and to protect legal immigrants from the bill's restrictions. The White House balanced this appeal to its Democratic base by assuring Republicans that the $2 billion deficit in the Medicare hospital trust fund required the attention of a bipartisan commission.

Aware of the political advantage of centrist policies, Clinton argued that smaller government could be fine-tuned to serve the needs of middle-class families. The White House insisted that the 1996 telecommunications bill include provisions protecting children from dissemination of indecent material on the Internet and requiring TV manufacturers to equip large-screen models with "V-chips" allowing parents to block offensive programming. Clinton asked the television networks to adopt a ratings system to insulate young viewers from depictions of sex and violence. After attacking cigarette smoking as "the most significant public health hazard facing our people," the president authorized the Food and Drug Administration to regulate nicotine as an addictive drug and to limit the marketing of tobacco to minors. Clinton also signed the Sanctity of Marriage Act, a Republican measure that prohibited federal recognition of same-sex unions. Meanwhile, the White House vetoed a ban on "partial-birth"

PATRICK ("PAT") BUCHANAN
1938–

"I'm entitled to be a heretic," Pat Buchanan once declared. Combining radical conservatism and populist social values, the scrappy media commentator and Republican campaigner embodied some of the most jarring contradictions of 1990s political life.

The third of nine children, Buchanan grew up in a large house in the suburbs of Washington, D.C. His father was an accountant whose heroes were Francisco Franco, Douglas MacArthur, and Joseph McCarthy. A product of Catholic schooling from the primary grades to Georgetown, where he received a scholarship to attend college, Buchanan absorbed the Cold War notion that communism was the ideological enemy of Christianity.

After graduating from the Columbia University School of Journalism on scholarship, the ambitious writer found work as a reporter and editorialist for the conservative Republican *St. Louis Globe-Democrat*. An avid reader of William F. Buckley's *National Review*, Buchanan supported Barry Goldwater in 1964. Viewing Richard Nixon as the conservative hope for the next presidential race, he joined the former vice president's staff, brought Maryland Governor Spiro Agnew to his boss's attention, and served as press secretary and speech writer in the 1968 campaign.

Once Nixon won, Buchanan became a special assistant who briefed the president on media coverage. The first in the administration to grasp the significance of George Wallace's populism, Buchanan drew up press releases that contrasted the traditional values of Nixon's "new majority" of "middle Americans" with the "liberal elitism" of the media and intelligentsia. After returning to journal-

abortions because the measure failed to protect the mother's health and ability to have more children.

THE 1996 ELECTION AND THE TWENTY-FIRST CENTURY

Seeking to take advantage of Clinton's midterm slip in the polls, several candidates competed for the 1996 Republican presidential nomination. Former Tennessee Governor Lamar Alexander, secretary of education under Bush, pursued the support of Republican moderates and southerners. Publishing magnate Steve Forbes used his family fortune to promote the flat tax and a balanced budget. In contrast, Pat Buchanan mounted a populist crusade against NAFTA-induced plant closings and mobilized antiabortion social conservatives. Yet Bob Dole emerged as the Republican nominee when he won key southern primaries. An experienced legislator, Dole called for economic growth through a 15 percent tax cut, for reduced government regulation, and for the delegation of welfare and anticrime programs to the states. After resigning his Senate seat to

ism to produce a widely syndicated newspaper column, Buchanan cofounded *Crossfire*, a television commentary series on the Cable News Network (CNN). During Ronald Reagan's second term, he resurfaced in public life as director of communications and supplied the media with White House rhetoric on the Nicaraguan "freedom fighters."

Dissenting from George Bush's globalism, Buchanan campaigned furiously against U.S. involvement in the Gulf War. "There are only two groups that are beating the drums for war in the Middle East," he declared on television, "the Israeli Defense Ministry and its amen corner in the United States." If the United States went to war, he warned, fighting would be done by "kids with names like McAllister, Murphy, Gonzales, and Leroy Brown." Buchanan expanded upon such populism when he challenged Bush for the Republican presidential nomination in 1992. Portraying the incumbent as rich, indifferent, and out of touch, Buchanan tapped voter frustration about economic stagnation by taking 40 percent of the New Hampshire primary vote. At the Republican Convention, he expanded his perspective to warn of an emerging "cultural war . . . for the soul of America."

Mobilizing against Republican front-runner Bob Dole in 1996, Buchanan forged a coalition of Reagan Democrats, protectionists, social conservatives, and supporters of the far right. A bitter opponent of the North American Free Trade Agreement (NAFTA), he agreed with labor leaders and progressive activists like Ralph Nader in condemning corporate plant closings and overseas relocations. Buchanan shocked Republican officials by denouncing "blood-sucking multinational banks" and "the money lenders of the Fortune 500." Yet he also blamed unemployment on illegal immigration, a problem he sought to rectify with a security fence across the entire border with Mexico. After a narrow victory over Dole in New Hampshire, Buchanan sought to rally the Christian right by stressing opposition to abortion, but he finished a distant second in South Carolina and never recovered.

Although Buchanan delegates managed to keep strong antiabortion language in the Republican platform, consensus-oriented politicians minimized the candidate's exposure at the 1996 convention. A dissident among Republican supporters of the global economy, Pat Buchanan had become a politician with no institutional base. ∎

devote himself to the contest full-time, Dole chose former football star Jack Kemp, the secretary of housing and urban development during the Reagan administration, as his running mate. Although Ross Perot of the Reform Party got a late start in the race, he vigorously promoted campaign finance reform.

Clinton focused on winning the votes of suburban women ("soccer moms") by demonstrating his administration's interest in families and children. The president also offset Dole's concerns about immigration and affirmative action by addressing the positive features of cultural diversity. Clinton and Gore promoted education, job training, and computer literacy as a "bridge to the twenty-first-century" information age while Democratic "attack ads" relentlessly lambasted the Republicans for trying to cut Medicare. Unable to reap the full impact of his message of economic growth because of a booming Clinton-era economy, Dole raised the specter of Whitewater, a scandal involving financial abuses by Clinton associates during his Arkansas governorship, and condemned improper fund raising by the Democratic National Committee. Yet the poorly focused Dole campaign never cut the lead the president had forged in early 1996.

Becoming only the third twentieth-century Democrat to win two presidential contests, Clinton breezed to an easy victory by accumulating 49 percent of the

Republican presidential candidate Robert Dole, the senior senator from Kansas, confronts his opponent, incumbent Democratic President Bill Clinton, during the Clinton-Dole debate of 1996.

Exhibit 14-34. Election of 1996

		Electoral vote	Popular vote (%)	
	Clinton (Democrat)	379	49	Number in each state represents electoral votes
	Dole (Republican)	159	41	
	Perot (Independent)	0	8	

popular vote compared with 41 percent for Dole and with 8 percent for Perot. In the Electoral College, the Democratic ticket prevailed by 379–159 and took seven of the eight largest states. Although Dole carried most of the mountain West and the Southeast, Clinton equaled the Republican total among men, outpaced his opponents among independents, prevailed among suburbanites, and took 54 percent of the women's tally. As in 1992, the electorate ranked the economy and jobs as its most pressing concerns. Despite tightening the Republican lead in the House, voters once again ensured divided government by assigning control of Congress and the White House to different parties.

By tailoring a modest agenda to middle-class voters and suburbanites, Bill Clinton rescued the Democratic Party from political oblivion. As 1996 presidential and congressional election costs surpassed $1.3 billion, financial influence assumed an unprecedented influence in national politics and led critics to wonder whether the system could address large social and economic problems. Although the White House preached the virtues of the global market and the information frontier, business analysts fretted about inadequate rates of savings, investment, and job creation. Reformers like Ralph Nader contended that globalization exported high-wage jobs and contributed to polarization of the rich and the poor. Progressives like Jesse Jackson and former New York Governor Mario Cuomo wondered how centrist politics could incorporate the urban underclass into the economic mainstream. Increasingly cynical about politics, middle-class citizens despaired that leaders could muster the courage and the vision to make the difficult decisions that the next century would certainly present.

On the edge of a new millennium in a world of continuing promise and peril, the nation's people looked to the future with the same mixture of hope and anxiety that had inaugurated the twentieth century.

SUGGESTED READINGS

Ronald Reagan's political success is the subject of Hedrick Smith, *Reagan: The Man, the President* (1981). See also the relevant segments of William E. Leuchtenburg, *In the Shadow of FDR: From Harry Truman to Ronald Reagan* (1985), and of Alonzo L. Hamby, *Liberalism and its Challengers: From F.D.R. to Bush* (rev. ed., 1992). Critical assessments include Robert Dallek, *Ronald Reagan: The Politics of Symbolism* (1984); Paul D. Erickson, *Reagan Speaks: The Making of an American Myth* (1985); and Lou Cannon, *President Reagan: The Role of a Lifetime* (1991). For an insightful psychological analysis, see Garry Wills, *Reagan's America: Innocents at Home* (1987). A useful but critical overview can be found in Haynes Johnson, *Sleepwalking Through History: America in the Reagan Years* (1991). See also Michael P. Rogin, *Ronald Reagan the Movie, and Other Episodes in Political Demonology* (1987).

Reagan's mastery of political discourse is explored in William K. Muir, *The Bully Pulpit: The Presidential Leadership of Ronald Reagan* (1992), and in the final chapter of David Green, *Shaping Political Consciousness: The Language of Politics in America from McKinley to Reagan* (1987). See also Jeffrey Bell, *Populism and Elitism: Politics in the Age of Equality* (1992), and portions of William C. Berman, *America's Right Turn: From Nixon to Bush* (1994). For Reagan's views on economics, see Amos Kiewe, *A Shining City on a Hill: Ronald Reagan's Economic Rhetoric, 1951–1989* (1991). A portrait of the president's most innovative appointment appears in Nancy Maveety, *Justice Sandra Day O'Connor: Strategist on the Supreme Court* (1996). For Reagan and the New Right, see the listings in Chapter 13.

The Reagan administration's cuts in domestic spending are analyzed in the final segments of Michael B. Katz, *The Undeserving Poor: From the War on Poverty to the War on Welfare* (1989). See also Thomas Byrne Edsall, *The New Politics of Equality: How Political Power Shapes Economic Policy* (1984), and Greg J. Duncan, *Years of Poverty, Years of Plenty: The Changing Economic Fortunes of American Workers and Families* (1984). For Reagan labor policy, see the relevant segments of James A. Gross, *Broken Promise: The Subversion of U.S. Labor Relations Policy, 1947–1994* (1995). Reagan's environmental policy is assessed in the last portions of Richard H.K. Vietor, *Energy Policy in America Since 1945: A Study in Business-Government Relations* (1984), and the administration's approach to race is surveyed in Robert Detlefsen, *Civil Rights Under Reagan* (1990). For balanced evaluations of the domestic impact of the Reagan presidency, see Sidney Blumenthal and Thomas Byrne Edsall, eds., *The Reagan Legacy* (1988).

Cold War policy in the Reagan years is explored in the later segments of Raymond L. Garthoff, *Detente and Confrontation: American-Soviet Relations from Nixon to Reagan* (1985), and in Strobe Talbott, *Deadly Gambits: The Reagan Administration and the Stalemate in Nuclear Arms Control* (1984). See also Keith L. Shimko, *Images and Arms Control: Perceptions of the Soviet Union in the Reagan Administration* (1991). Star Wars is the focus of Rebecca S. Bjork, *The Strategic Defense Initiative: Symbolic Containment of the Nuclear Threat* (1992). For overviews, see the later sections of John Lewis Gaddis, *The Long Peace: Inquiries Into the History of the Cold War* (1987), and of Thomas J. McCormick, *America's Half-Century: United States Foreign Policy in the Cold War* (1989). For Reagan's involvement in policy, see the relevant portions of John Prados, *Keeper of the Keys: A History of the National Security Council from Truman to Bush* (1991), and of Francis P. Wormuth and Edwin P. Firmage, *To Chain the Dog of War: The Powers of Congress in History and Law* (1986). A useful analysis appears in Coral Bell, *The Reagan Paradox: American Foreign Policy in the 1980s* (1989).

Reagan's Persian Gulf policies are discussed in sections of Michael A. Palmer, *Guardians of the Gulf: A History of America's Expanding Role in the Persian Gulf, 1933–1992* (1992). For Iran-Contra, see Theodore Draper, *A Very Thin Cone: The Iran-Contra Affair* (1991). Central American policy is assessed in the appropriate portions of Robert Kagan, *A Twilight Struggle: American Power and Nicaragua, 1977–1990* (1995); of Raymond Bonner, *Weakness and Deceit: United States Policy and El Salvador* (1984); and of Walter LaFeber, *Inevitable Revolutions: The United States in Central America* (1983). See also Mark P. Lagon, *The Reagan Doctrine: Sources of American Conduct in the Cold War's Last Chapter* (1994), and Jay Peterzell, *Reagan's Secret Wars* (1984).

For the Bush presidency, see Blumenthal, *Pledging Allegiance: The Last Campaign of the Cold War* (1990); Michael Duffy, *Marching in Place: The Status-Quo Presidency of George Bush* (1992); and Charles Kolb, *White House Daze: The Unmaking of Domestic Policy in the Bush Years* (1994). Environmental issues are the focus of the relevant segments of Robert A. Stanley, *Presidential Influence and Environmental Policy* (1992). Bush economic and social policies are placed in historical context in the appropriate chapters of Berman, *America's Right Turn*, and of Hamby, *Liberalism and its Challengers*.

The background to the Gulf War is provided in Palmer, *Guardians of the Gulf*. Specific studies include Alex Roberto Hybel, *Power Over Rationality: The Bush Administration and the Gulf Crisis* (1993); Richard J. Barnet, *The Rockets' Red Glare: War, Politics, and the American Presidency* (1991); and Bob Woodward, *The Commanders* (1991). On foreign policy decision making, see the relevant portions of Harold Koh, *The National Security Constitution: Sharing Power After the Iran-Contra Affair* (1992), and of Louis Fisher, *Presidential War Powers* (1995).

The end of the Cold War stimulated an outpouring of scholarship. For the involvement of peace groups, see John Lofland, *Polite Protesters: The American Peace Movement of the 1980s* (1993), and David Cortright, *Peace Works: The Citizen's Role in Ending the Cold War* (1993). Overviews of the Cold War include H.W. Brands, *The Devil We Knew: Americans and the Cold War* (1993); Warren I. Cohen, *America in the Age of Soviet Power, 1945–1991* (1993); Michael J. Hogan, ed., *The End of the Cold War: Its Meaning and Implications* (1992); and Richard Ned Lebow and Janice Gross Stein, *We All Lost the Cold War* (1994). See also the previously listed works of Gaddis and McCormick.

The first years of the Clinton era are assessed in Stanley Allen Renshon, *High Hopes: The Clinton Presidency and the Politics of Ambition* (1996). See also Elizabeth Drew, *On the Edge: The Clinton Presidency* (1994). For policy making and politics, see Bob Woodward, *Inside the Clinton White House* (1994) and *The Choice* (1996). Another view can be found in James B. Stewart, *Blood Sport: The President and His Adversaries* (1996). For the president and first lady, see Roger Morris, *Partners in Power: The Clintons and Their America* (1996). Future prospects are evaluated in Michael F. Spath, *Dangerous Delusions: America on the Brink* (1995).

INDEX